Hu

Cla

Suf

0 6

University Campus Barnsley

Telephone: 01226 216 885

Catalogue: https://webopac.barnsley.ac.uk

Class No: ....3.2.a...a...Phils.A.X.F.

This book is to be returned on or before the last date stamped below. Thank you!

POLITICS: AN INTRODUCTION

'An immensely useful text. It should do well with undergraduates at home and abroad.'

Bill Jones, editor and co-author of *Politics UK*

'An excellent introductory text, bringing together key theoretical perspectives with up-to-date empirical information.'

Sonia Mazey, *Hertford College, Oxford University*

'The most useful, wide-ranging and accessible introductory politics text I have come across.'

Erika Cudworth, *East London University*

The second edition of this user-friendly text for students taking introductory courses in politics builds on the success of the first edition. It provides a completely updated and stimulating coverage of topics essential to the understanding of contemporary politics including:

The individual and social dimension of politics • Political socialisation • Political culture • Political participation • Democracy and democratisation • Concepts and issues • Political thought • Political ideologies • Local governance • The machinery of government • Parties, interest groups and public opinion • Political communication and the media • The policy process • Politics and governance above the territorial state • The processes of globalisation

Ideal for students taking combined degree courses at introductory level in politics and the social sciences, it emphasises the individual and social dimension of politics rather than the institutional and covers theories and concepts in an accessible way.

New features of the second edition include:

- a new chapter on 'Democracy and democratisation'
- a much expanded chapter on 'Political communication and the media'
- updated examples drawn from Western democracies and other political systems, bringing fresh perspectives to recent political events and issues
- expanded sections on nationalism, religion, alternative politics, globalisation and ethnic conflict
- a support website structured by chapter with links to other resources

User-friendly textbook features include:

- marginal notes and comments, key words and definitions, cross-referencing
- extracts from key political manifestos, documents, articles
- illustrated biographies of key thinkers and political figures
- annotated key texts for further reading and a comprehensive bibliography

Barrie Axford and **Gary K. Browning** are Professors of Politics at Oxford Brookes University. **Richard Huggins** is Senior Lecturer in Politics at Oxford Brookes University. **Ben Rosamond** is Reader in Politics and International Studies at the University of Warwick.

POLITICS: AN INTRODUCTION

Second Edition

- Barrie Axford
- Gary K. Browning
- Richard Huggins
- Ben Rosamond
- with Alan Grant and John Turner

Routledge
Taylor & Francis Group

LONDON AND NEW YORK

First published 1997
by Routledge
2 Park Square, Milton Park, Abingdon, Oxon OX14 4RN

Simultaneously published in the USA and Canada
by Routledge
270 Madison Ave, New York, NY 10016

Second Edition 2002
Reprinted 2005, 2006 (twice)

Routledge is an imprint of the Taylor & Francis Group, an informa business

© 1997, 2002 Barrie Axford, Gary K. Browning, Richard Huggins,
Ben Rosamond with Alan Grant and John Turner

Typeset in Garamond by Keystroke, Jacaranda Lodge, Wolverhampton
Printed and bound by Bell & Bain Ltd., Glasgow

British Library Cataloguing in Publication Data
A catalogue record for this book is available from the British Library

Library of Congress Cataloging in Publication Data
A catalog record for this book has been requested

ISBN 10: 0-415-25181-8 (hbk)
ISBN 10: 0-415-22642-2 (pbk)
ISBN 13: 978-0-415-215181-5 (hbk)
ISBN 13: 978-0-415-22642-4 (pbk)

CONTENTS

FIGURES AND TABLES

Figures

Tables

BIOGRAPHIES

Biographies of key thinkers and political figures in order of appearance include:

AUTHORS

Barrie Axford is Professor of Politics at Oxford Brookes University and Director of Research in the School of Social Sciences and Law. His publications include *The Global System* (1995), *Unity and Diversity in the New Europe*, joint editor with Peter Lang (2000), *The New Media and Politics*, joint editor (2000). He is currently working on books on democracy and democratisation, Britain and globalisation, and practical citizenship. His research interests include: theories and practice of globalisation, networks and borders in the global system, European governance and the information society, processes of democratisation, political communications, new media and politics.

Gary K. Browning is Professor of Politics at Oxford Brookes University. He has written many articles and books on political theory and the history of political thought, including *Understanding Contemporary Society* (ed.) (2000), *Lyotard and the End of Grand Narratives* (2000), *Hegel and the History of Political Philosophy* (1999), *Hegel's Phenomenology of Spirit: A Reappraisal* (ed.) (1997) and *Plato and Hegel: Two Modes of Philosophising about Politics* (1991). He has been joint editor of the PSA journal *Politics* and is currently general editor of *Contemporary Political Theory*. He is currently working on monographs on *Critical Political Economy*, *Democracy* and *Collingwood*.

Alan Grant is Principal Lecturer and Head of the Department of Politics at Oxford Brookes University. He has research interests in a number of areas in American politics. These include the electoral process, with particular reference to the financing of elections and proposals for reform; the role of political action committees; the territorial distribution of power with the US federal system and recent movements to devolve power to the states. He is the author of *The American Political Process*, the seventh edition of which is due to be published by Routledge in 2003. He is also the co-author and editor of *Contemporary American Politics* (1995) and *American Politics: 2000 and Beyond* (2000) and co-author of *The 'Politics Today' Companion to American Government* (2002).

Richard Huggins is Senior Lecturer in Politics and Deputy Head of the School of Social Sciences and Law – Academic Affairs at Oxford Brookes University. His research interests currently include the European Information Society Project, the impact of 'New Media' on the conduct and form of politics and the transformation of democracy under the impact of new media. He is also engaged in research into crime, social order and governance. Recent publications include a co-edited volume, *New Media – New Politics* (2001), 'In Search of a European Audio-Visual Identity' in B. Axford *et al.* (2000) *Unity and Diversity in the New Europe*. He is currently editing a special edition of the journal *Telematics and Infomatics* on *Local Democracy and ICTs* (forthcoming 2002).

Ben Rosamond is Reader in Politics and International Studies at the University of Warwick. He has published many articles on the subject of globalisation and Europeanisation. His books include *Globalisation and the European Union* (forthcoming), *Theories of European Integration* (2000) and (as co-editor) *New Regionalisms in the Global Political Economy: Theories and Cases* (2002). His research interests include theoretical approaches to regional integration; globalisation and European integration; British political economy in European and global contexts; the sociology of knowledge and disciplinary pathologies in political science.

John Turner is the Director of the Centre for Democracy Studies at Oxford Brookes University and is course manager for the MA in Politics of Democracy. Recent publications include *The Tories and Europe* (2000), 'The Permanent Campaign in Political Marketing' *European Journal of Marketing* (2001) and 'New Labour's Negative Campaign in the London Mayoral Election' *Public Affairs* (2001). He has regularly carried out focus group research for a number of organisations including the *Guardian*, the *Observer*, Channel 4 News, the Conservative Party, Business for Sterling and the Countryside Alliance.

PREFACE

When we wrote the first edition of this book some five years ago, we were concerned that there were few texts which were usable for our first-year undergraduate programme. Our more pressing concern was that the market lacked a lively introduction to political science that covered the spectrum of political studies as widely as possible. There were good texts on institutions, some fine books using systematic comparison and others introducing students to the study of political ideologies. Nothing really got to grips with our preferred approach to the foundation-level teaching of politics at university level. The responses to the first edition of the book reassured us that we have tapped into a more general concern about the ways to teach politics to new students, and it will be useful to reiterate them here.

The approach we outlined in the first edition remains the same now, and can be summed up as follows. First, we aim to demonstrate why politics matters, and therefore why the subject should be studied. It is our belief that those new to the subject should be encouraged to think about themselves as political actors in a political world. Students come to the study of politics for a variety of reasons, and many treat 'the political' as a separate, and peripheral, sphere of human existence. But such a view is sustainable only by adopting a very restricted definition of politics. Our position is that politics is much more than a realm of human activity populated by legislators, cabinets, parties, activists and *apparatchiks*, and we say more about this in the introductory chapter. More important to stress here is our belief that the successful student of politics (or political science, government, or any other label for the subject) is not someone who has just accumulated a cache of facts about various political systems, or who has learned by rote the main principles of Thomas Hobbes' theory of government. Rather, studying politics involves acquiring concepts, analytical frameworks and ideas which make it easier to understand, interpret and (perhaps) to explain the complexities of political life. It is about being able to understand argument and counter-argument over normative and analytical questions.

Our strategy as teachers – and now as writers of this textbook – is to introduce the study of politics by asking students to confront their own experience of the political world and by asking them to think seriously about the boundaries of the political. While this may strike some as an approach slanted towards what is still generally, if a little unhelpfully, called political behaviour, it is not intended to endorse a behavioural view of politics. Our intention is to persuade students to see themselves as part of political life and as actors in it. This is why the earlier chapters in the book are concerned with the individual in politics. Later chapters concentrate upon corporate political actors and wider political processes to give a fuller picture of the complexities of government and politics, both within and beyond the territorial state and bounded societies.

Another method we use to demonstrate the wide-ranging scope and relevance of politics is to draw upon less conventional sources, as these are appropriate to the subject matter of different chapters. The point is to offer readers a more catholic range of illustrative and reading materials, which will help them to appreciate how politics both infuses all sorts of human activity and how the study of politics is illuminated by reference to, for example, literary genres like the novel, as well as film or theatre. So, at times, in the sections headed 'Further reading' at the end of each chapter, we have interspersed standard academic references with somewhat more exotic fare.

It is also worth pointing out that the book is not an explicitly comparative textbook. This does not mean that it is dilatory in its use of illustrative materials of a comparative nature, or that it is Anglocentric. Rather, the book does not adopt any systematic framework of comparison, least of all one which trades on the detailed comparison of a few political systems. Of course we are all aware of the advantages of comparison and of the extent to which much good social science is by definition comparative. But we want to avoid focusing on Britain, the USA and France, or on any other permutation of countries, because the main purpose of the text is the study of politics. To complement our general approach we offer a broad range of illustrative case study and comparative materials throughout the text.

In the first edition of the book, we were anxious to make connections between personal experience and wider structures and processes that impinge on individual consciousness and action. This remains a key aim of the book. In addition, we have extended and strengthened our focus on international and global matters. Since 1997 the world has become more interconnected and interdependent, if contentiously so, and any textbook on politics must acknowledge these new arenas in which politics and political discourse take place. We have also made some changes to the content and organisation of the book, which, allow new and important subjects such as democracy and the role of the media in politics to be examined more fully.

Finally, we wanted to continue a style of writing and presentation that students would find user-friendly but not patronising. The use of think points and exercises throughout the text is not an attempt to spoon-feed the reader. They should be taken as opportunities to think more deeply about the material introduced in the text and may be used either by the individual reader or by the seminar group. As far as possible, we have tried to highlight the most important terms found in the text. These appear as key words and reappear in a consolidated glossary at the end of the book.

In this edition, as in the last, the composition and production of the book owed much to the commitment shown by Routledge and in particular by Moira Taylor. Her advice has been invaluable in seeing the project to fruition and we are very grateful for the forbearance of editorial staff at Routledge at points throughout the process. Thanks are also due to a battalion of referees whose comments on draft chapters were thoughtful and constructive. The alacrity of their collective response was a great help to us. Once again, we are grateful to Alan Grant for contributing the chapter on subnational government and politics. The critical responses to the first edition in various reviews were overwhelmingly favourable and we have been able to incorporate some of the suggestions for changes made in these reviews and in more informal feedback from colleagues in other institutions. A number of our students have made useful and sometimes salutary comments on different parts of the second edition in its draft stages, and we are very grateful for their views and for the anonymous (and mostly very favourable) feedback elicited through student evaluations.

Barrie Axford, Gary K. Browning,
Richard Huggins, Ben Rosamond

ACKNOWLEDGEMENTS

While every effort has been made to trace copyright holders and obtain permission for use of photographs, in some cases this has not been possible. Any omissions brought to our attention will be remedied in future editions.

Benazir Bhutto, courtesy of www.PPUK.com; Anthony Giddens, courtesy of the London School of Economics Photography Department; Francis Fukuyama, courtesy of Francis Fukuyama; Jeremy Bentham, 1829, by Henry William Pickersgill, courtesy of the National Portrait Gallery, London; Adam Smith, 1787, by James Tassie, courtesy of the National Portrait Gallery, London; Alexander Solzhenitsyn, 1999, courtesy of Popperfoto/Reuter; Robert Putnam by Martha Stewart, courtesy of Robert Putnam; James M. Buchanan, courtesy of James M. Buchanan; International protesters at the Prague WTO meeting in 2000, courtesy of Jorge Ordonez; Stop Esso poster, courtesy of Stop Esso Campaign; Robert Nozick, courtesy of his wife; Jean-François Lyotard, courtesy of Sijmen Hendriks; Sir Isaiah Berlin, courtesy of Clive Barda/Performing Arts Library, London; Quentin Skinner by Nigel Luckhurst, courtesy of Quentin Skinner; Thomas Hobbes by John Michael Wright, courtesy of the National Portrait Gallery; Jean-Jacques Rousseau engraving by Robert Hare after Latour, courtesy of the Mary Evans Picture Library; John Stuart Mill by John and Charles Watkins, courtesy of the National Portrait Gallery; Karl Marx, courtesy of the Hulton Getty Archive Picture Collection; Carole Pateman by Scott Quintard, courtesy of Carole Pateman; John Maynard Keynes, courtesy of the Mary Evans Picture Library; Edmund Burke, courtesy of the Mary Evans Picture Library; V. I. Lenin, 1920, courtesy of AKG, London; Adolf Hitler, courtesy of AKG, London; Benito Mussolini, courtesy of AKG, London; Mary Wollstonecraft, courtesy of AKG/British Library, London; Betty Friedan, courtesy of Associated Press, London; Ken Livingstone, courtesy of the Greater London Authority; Megawati Sukarnoputri, courtesy of Associated Press, London; Joseph Bové by Alain Rauchvarger, courtesy of the French Farmers' Union; World Trade Organisation protesters in Seattle, November 1999, courtesy of Popperfoto/ Reuter; Naomi Klein by Gordon Terris, courtesy of SMG Newspapers Limited; Manuel Castells by Jane Scherr, courtesy of Jane Scherr; Winners and Losers cartoon, courtesy of Cartoonists and Writers Syndicate; Tony Blair at the Davos World Economic Forum, 2000, courtesy of Lookat Photos, Zurich, Switzerland.

Thanks also to Guardian Newspapers Limited for permission to use the Suzanne Goldenberg extract from 'Few women on the road to democracy' (*Guardian*, 26 January 2002) and The Financial Times Limited for permission to use the extract from 'Survey of South Korea' by Bethan Hutton (*Financial Times*, 26 June 1995).

Introduction

Barrie Axford and Gary K. Browning

Politics is important. Although this judgement is, in part, a matter of intuition, we would be left in no doubt after a day spent watching television news programmes and reading most newspapers. Life and death issues such as war and peace are shaped by political ideologies and decisions, and by the exigencies of political fortune. The state is ever present in our everyday lives and decisions that affect us all are being taken by organisations that are inter-state, such as the North Atlantic Treaty Organisation (NATO) and trans-state, such as the European Central Bank (ECB). Law and order, economic trans-actions, the values of a society and the myriad ways in which people of different nations interact with one another all involve political influences. Contested ideas of what is right and wrong and cultural identifications which give shape to people's notions of who they are reflect political allegiances. For all this, it is sometimes difficult to be entirely clear about what constitutes 'the political' and resolute about where politics takes place.

THINK POINT

Are the following political acts? If so, why are they political?

▤ A conversation in a bar about the crime rate.

▤ Taking part in a demonstration against the transport of live animals.

▤ Taking or not taking drugs.

▤ Watching news on television.

These acts may strike you as curious illustrations to use in a book about politics; but many people, including some new to the study of politics, have a rather narrow conception of 'the political'. The political sphere is seen as an arena populated largely by politicians, political parties, elections and the various institutions of government. Beyond these core actors and institutions lies a more shadowy world of pressure groups, the media and the ubiquitous 'social context' of politics, a pot-pourri of economic, cultural and social institutions and processes which provide the backdrop to political activity. This rough and ready conception of politics is confined, by and large, to what goes on inside territorial units of governance called nation-states, although sometimes it takes on board what goes on between them. Let us be quite clear here: we are not suggesting that this is wrong – no serious attempt to cover key aspects of political activity could dispense with these topics – rather that it is but one way to define politics and to delimit the field of study.

At this point, having thought about the four cases above, you might like to offer a definition of politics yourself. The sort of questions you should ask yourself are these:

▨ Is there an essence to political behaviour?

▨ If so, how does it differ from other sorts of behaviour?

For example, if having a conversation about crime rates in a bar is a political act, what makes it political? Is it something intrinsic to the act itself or is it made political by the context in which it is taking place? Context does not mean just the physical setting, in this case the bar, but factors such as the prevailing climate of opinion, the country in which the conversation is taking place, perhaps even the frame of mind of the people involved. The same might be asked about writing a poem or song. On the face of it a private act of creativity does not look like a political act, but if we were to locate that activity in a certain context, perhaps under a system of government in which any form of uncensored creativity is considered to be dangerous dissent, potentially regime threatening, then it becomes a political act almost by default. Boris Pasternak's *Dr. Zhivago* expresses how the practice of poetry and the continued cultivation of a personal standpoint was taken to be a dangerous counter-revolutionary activity in Soviet Russia. The urban revolutionary group The Weathermen took their name and inspiration from Bob Dylan's song 'Subterranean Homesick Blues' (1965). The song itself is enigmatic but the turbulent context of 1960s America provided a climate in which it could inspire such an extreme reaction. For the student of politics these are important considerations because they either expand or limit the scope of what is studied and also influence how it is studied.

If, as one recent textbook on the subject says, politics is the process by which groups make collective decisions (Hague and Harrop 2001), then it becomes a matter of both professional convention and judgement to decide how that process works and how best to study it. Suppose we were to examine how different interests try to affect a government's decision to build a new runway at an international airport. One way to proceed would be to look at the issue as a battle between interests with different kinds of resources – money, membership and so on – and to see how effectively these resources were deployed to influence public authorities and established ways of making policy decisions. This would be perfectly legitimate and would undoubtedly fall within the rubric of the definition supplied above. We might also use the issue to investigate the planning process and its effectiveness in involving citizens in decision-making. If, however, we were more concerned with the motivations of those involved, perhaps in why they became activists, we would be better employed in looking at the relationships between their behaviour and factors which may have influenced it. At this point, the student of politics often has to draw upon seemingly non-political factors to aid explanation. For example, studying the leadership style of American presidents or British prime ministers may require attention to their family background and psychological make-up as well as to the ways in which they are constrained by powerful sectional interests or foreign policy commitments. Students of voting behaviour have always recognised the need to relate that core political activity to the social and personal factors which affect it, including the television-viewing habits of different sections of an electorate. In recent years feminists, among others, have also been responsible for pushing out the boundaries of political debate and language and therefore of the study of politics, by insisting that personal and particularly sexual relationships are inherently political. In doing so, they have challenged the status of the concept of 'state' as the key unit for political analysis and the locus for political activity, arguing that interpersonal relations are also political because they involve power and authority.

But while politics is in a sense everywhere and of undoubted significance to the quality of people's lives, it remains a very elusive activity to pin down. No single focus, no entire approach can provide all the answers to political questions. The purpose of this book is to provide a comprehensive introduction to the study of politics, one that is both sensitive to conventional definitions of political thought and action and aware of the need to address newer and more contested accounts of the nature of politics. We have no illusions about the scale of this task, and in this new edition we have tried to combine accessibility with a robust examination of the main concepts, fields and issues in politics and a full appreciation of the various approaches to its study.

Some features of the book

There are a number of features which make the book accessible to the reader and useful as an interactive text between instructors and students:

- It covers a wide range of political activities in a wide variety of settings.

- It examines the various features of the political landscape by interspersing the narrative with a range of *extracts* reflecting aspects of political life and thinking, and *exercises* and *think points* designed to allow the reader to develop these topics more fully through discussion.

▓ It provides useful biographies of key thinkers and activists.

▓ The book is designed as an interactive text in class between instructors and students through the use of the exercises, think points and readings.

▓ Each chapter stands as an introduction to a topic in its own right, but there is extensive and systematic cross-referencing to the treatment of concepts and issues in other chapters, where this is appropriate, to demonstrate the connections between topics and chapters. For example, the reader is encouraged to recognise that a concept like individualism can be usefully dealt with under a number of headings.

▓ Thus the book may be read by people interested in particular themes, but also by those who are looking for a general treatment of the study of politics.

▓ Key words in the vocabulary of politics are highlighted in the text and short definitions are provided in the margins the first time they are used.

▓ A glossary of all the key words used is provided at the end of the book.

▓ In order to support readers who wish to find out more about the topics covered, in addition to the references made in the text itself, which includes the labelling of key works, a short annotated bibliography is set out at the end of each chapter.

▓ To provide further support for readers a website has been created at <http://www.routledge.com/textbooks/0415251818> or <http://www.routledge.com/textbooks/0415226422>. This page will contain updates on reading matter, links to other useful sites and updates on some of the current events referred to in the text.

▓ The book is designed to show that the study of politics is about making connections between its manifestations at a number of levels. For this reason, we have strengthened our references to the links between the personal, the local and the global, indicating connections between them, as well as with processes and institutions at the national and societal levels of analysis. This seems a matter of growing importance, even more crucial than when the first edition was published in 1997, even if it is not susceptible to a simple form of explanation whereby the different sites of politics are seen as forming an uncomplicated system.

▓ Not all students see themselves as part of a political world, let alone as political animals, so it is part of the remit of a book of this sort to introduce readers to the study of politics in ways that are intelligible and user-friendly. We have been at pains to explore the place of individuals in political life, both from the standpoint of certain strains of political philosophy and ideology which have a strong **normative** component and through the insights of **empirical** research into individual motivations and behaviour. There are two main reasons for doing this: (1) to show to readers that they too occupy a political space and possess some form of political identity, and (2) to introduce a properly human dimension to the study of politics. This

Normative The prescription of what should or ought to be the case as opposed to what, descriptively, is the case.

Empirical A term meaning sense or understanding derived from experience.

does not mean that we advocate an approach to the study of politics in which the individual is at the centre of inquiry and social and political structures are marginal (arguments which are taken up in different ways in Chapters 1 to 4), but that we want to demonstrate the ways in which individuals relate to and both affect and are affected by these larger structures, up to and including what many people now call the global level.

As for the last concept, while the issues of inter- and trans-nationality are addressed in detail in Chapters 14 and 15, we have introduced a global dimension into other chapters where this seemed appropriate. For example, the discussion of democracy in Chapter 5 makes explicit reference both to the impact of global communications technologies on the quality of democratic life and to the prospects for global institutions of democracy. The overall approach of the book is multi-dimensional in that it explores the relationships between political activity and economic and social factors and, where relevant, cuts across conventional divides – the individual, the societal and the global – the better to understand complex relationships between actors and institutions. The gathering pace of globalising pressures means that it is the world which is now becoming an appropriate '**unit for analysis**', as well as national and subnational political systems that interact with one another in supra-national and global contexts. In doing all this we take full note of the methodological issues involved, and debates about these are reported in full.

Unit for analysis The concrete object of inquiry: the individual, the primary group, e.g. the family, voluntary associations, formal organisations like political parties, whole societies, nation-states, even the world as a whole.

Explanation in politics

The study of politics is fraught with issues for the would-be observer. Not only is there the distinction between what are called normative and empirical approaches to study, but there is also the question of whether to pitch inquiry at the individual level of analysis or at the societal or even the global. Since the end of the Second World War the extent to which political study lends itself to 'scientific' methods has been hotly disputed, especially with regard to aspects of political behaviour like voting and other areas of political participation. Whether or not an approach may be called scientific is still very much open to question. If the term means something as broad as gaining systematic knowledge of the world around us, both natural and human, then most students of politics would have little trouble with saying that the discipline is scientific, or potentially so. Of course some normative theorists would argue that systematic knowledge is not enough and that the purpose of studying politics is to uncover information relevant to the achievement of a better or even the best society or the good life. Others, who may or may not be wedded to normative theorising, still doubt that politics can ever be studied scientifically if by that is meant any of the following.

Theories of politics that can be disproved by empirical evidence

For example, it might be asked how you could 'disprove' that democracy is a better form of government than dictatorship. The point here is that some fundamental political questions do not lend themselves to claims of truth or falsity. On a more mundane basis, critics also argue that proof is also hard to come by given the difficulty of agreeing on the definition of key concepts, collecting data, controlling for all the different factors which may affect something like voting or deciding what impels people to fly planes into the World Trade Center in New York.

The ability to replicate methods and results through laboratory experimentation and/or statistical methods

For both ethical and logistical reasons, social and political researchers are rarely able to conduct the kinds of controlled experiments common in the natural and technological sciences. Where they are able to generate and manipulate large bodies of statistical data, issues about the representativeness of the samples used and the integrity of data sources over time present major constraints on the use of rigorous scientific method. When comparative research is being conducted these problems are exacerbated due to the relatively small number of cases (for example, countries) which can be studied, the problem with establishing functional equivalence across different systems (would ritual beheading of a ruler be the equivalent of a presidential election in terms of securing the peaceful succession of elites?) and, as we shall see below, because of the need both to generalise about political phenomena and to remain sensitive to local context and local meanings.

The ability to rely on the visible and the measurable to explain political phenomena

False consciousness A term associated with Marxist thought which maintains that individuals and the class to which they belong may well demonstrate a sense of social understanding that is predominantly 'false', in that it hides from them or prevents them from recognising the 'real' nature of their position within the social order and the extent to which they are exploited.

It may be possible to examine the relationships between, say, the social characteristics of Congressional Districts in the USA and their voting patterns over a long period of time. Collectable documentary evidence exists for such activities, as do reliable databases and easy-to-use statistical packages for computer analysis. But the same may not be true of the 'proof' needed to explain some critical but less observable relationships in political life. Take, for example, the thesis that in capitalist societies working classes are always in a state of '**false consciousness**', meaning that they either do not recognise their subordination to a dominant class, or else they are persuaded to applaud or to rationalise it in some way. In both cases they are held to be 'falsely conscious' because they fail to recognise their own real interests. Now, if the concept of false consciousness were part of a research project, just how would you set about proving (1) that people are suffering from it, and (2) that as a result they do not act in their own best interests?

The ability to distinguish between and maintain the separation of fact and value

The idea that a scientific study of politics would be value-free – that is, not based only on things being a matter of opinion – strikes many people as at best mistaken and at worst morally repugnant. Clearly there are important considerations here, not least for comparative research across nations. If we study something like legislatures across quite different political systems, it is often hard to abstain from making judgements on the basis of criteria which have little to do with the hard and 'neutral' evidence available to us. Thus we might observe that in democratic systems, legislatures are institutions for helping to keep governments accountable, while in authoritarian systems they are a convenient means of making the passage of laws appear legitimate. Classifying legislatures on the basis of the functions they perform is a proper task for political scientists; making statements about the propriety of the tasks performed by particular legislatures may be thought at best unprofessional and at worst unscientific. As with the normative–empirical distinction, there are different views on this issue.

The ability to make clear-cut statements about the causal relationships between variables

Study of the relationships between variables (for example, voting and age and voting and social class) would seem to require causal analysis; that is, accounts which tell us what makes something change over time, but this has always been a very contentious issue in the social sciences. Modern social scientists are very wary about making statements of the order 'x causes y' because of the deterministic feel of such pronouncements and also because any patterns of social causation (if such things exist) are likely to be very complex and probably not easily measurable. There is also the problem of deciding:

1 whether (or when) causation refers to a direct causal relationship between one thing and another (I tripped him, he fell down);
2 whether a more indirect link is implied, wherein causal factors are either contributory, or something which does not involve a direct relationship between discrete events (cause and effect);
3 whether there is a situation in which outcomes occur necessarily because of the properties of the objects involved (a bomb going off due to its combustible nature, a plane flying because of its aerodynamic qualities) but contingently due to the circumstances in which they are found (was the bomb in a building or outside, did it explode in good or bad weather?).

Thus social scientists are often more inclined to caution when making statements about relationships between variables, preferring to talk about 'tendencies' or 'probabilities', or 'degrees of association', especially where the nature of the relationship is to be shown using statistical analysis.

The ability to make lawlike assertions or specify invariant relationships, or else establish clear limits to the explanatory power of a theory

There are no laws in the social sciences, or, to be properly and scientifically cautious, there are no laws yet. For the most part students of politics have to be content with more humble achievements: cataloguing the incidence of phenomena, setting up schemes of classification (participatory democracy, liberal democracy, democratic–elitist and so on) and fitting cases into them. The widespread use of statistical methods has led to an empirical political science which uses the language of variables, which talks about degrees of association between them and which looks for probabilistic and not causal relationships. As we shall see in Chapters 2, 3 and 4, the development of a political science made in this image is closely linked with the rise of what Heinz Eulau (1963) called 'the behavioural persuasion in politics', which revolutionised (some critics say trivialised) the study of individual political behaviour, and entrenched the collection and analysis of numerical data at the heart of political research. Thus students of politics need to be wary about making generalisations. A generalisation is a measure (often an approximate measure) of the number of objects or cases which belong to some category, or a statement about the common properties of things. Thus we might say that x per cent of people in Britain support the principle of capital punishment, or, more loosely, that 'most' young people under 18 prefer MTV to Mozart. Generalisations do not, of themselves, give any clue to causation, they simply identify and record what things have in common and how many of them share certain characteristics. The difficulty with what might otherwise appear as a useful, indeed necessary, attempt to establish whether there are regularities in social life is that when it is applied to the allegedly common properties found in different societies over long periods of time, we run the risk of ignoring that which is particular, local and culturally unique. The idea that certain phenomena are invariant (unchanging) across time and space, which some theories of long-term, large-scale change (e.g. Marxism) require may understate the differences between objects.

If a scientific study of politics entails that its explanatory procedures are to ape the natural sciences, then it runs into the difficulties that arise from the fact that human political actors, unlike the processes explained by natural science, impart meaning to the world. The meanings attaching to political terms and conceptions change over time and space, so explanations in politics tend to lack the invariant objects of analysis that allow for powerful laws or even plausible generalisations. In the light of the changing conceptions and institutions of politics across time and space, the historical study of politics may be seen as valuable. The historical study of politics tracks changing aspects of political thought and practice without adding general theories which supply explanations of why these changes took place. In this book the analysis of institutions and processes tries to reflect an historical and descriptive approach to the study of politics, as well as explicating various theoretical positions. Even in the absence of theorising, description is often supplemented by the use of **models**, which, while not supplying explanations or predictions of future behaviour, set out clear ways in which the logic of political action and institutional change may be understood. Of course, there are grand theories of the human condition, and some of them are rehearsed in the chapters which follow, notably Chapter 7.

Model A representation of events and processes which focuses on key aspects of what is going on in them.

The language of politics

A focus upon the allegedly scientific nature of political study necessarily draws attention to the very language of politics. Symbolic representation of the world around us is the key element in the construction of any language system. We use language not only to express and exchange common understandings, but also to tell others who we are. When journalists talk about politics as being 'a battleground' or use some theatrical metaphor for political conflict, they are not just describing a state of affairs, but locating it in a system of meaning where politics is understood as an adversarial pursuit, perhaps red in tooth and claw.

The point is that language is not a neutral medium of communication, even if it is a rich one. Many words carry messages which are very context-specific in their meaning, and, as was highlighted above, the meaning of terms and concepts change across time and space. To describe someone as 'homely' in the USA is taken as a form of insult because of its associations with plainness, whereas in Britain the word carries overtones of warmth, cosiness and so on. Feminists believe that apparently neutral language, or terms which have been accepted as generic descriptions of things – 'mankind', or 'His will be done' to refer to the power of the Christian God – are symbolic devices in the subjugation of women. We can see something of the same thing when talking about political terms or words used in the study of politics. 'Terrorist' is not a neutral or unambiguous term that lends itself readily to simple classification. If we were to classify a 'terrorist' as someone who challenges the power of the government of an independent state through violent means, have we abrogated our duty to distinguish not only between types of terrorism, but also whether a regime is deemed legitimate or not? When does terrorism commute to legitimate opposition, or the terrorist become the liberator? Should a captured terrorist be treated as a prisoner of war, an ordinary criminal or someone who forfeits all claims to civilised treatment? The use of descriptive political concepts for purposes of classification, model-building and analysis is also shot through with ambiguity and contested meanings. This is not, or not only, because commentators cannot agree on how to describe visible phenomena, but because they cannot agree on the various manifestations of the phenomena, or even on criteria by which they would be able to recognise them. The classic case of this is the key concept of 'power'. Some of the debates involving the term 'power' are set down in Chapters 3, 11 and 13. For now it is enough to note that as a concept (and concepts are the building blocks of any body of knowledge) power is essentially contested, because there are different definitions of what power 'is' and therefore how it appears or is exercised.

Essentially contested concepts like 'power' or 'freedom' are sometimes difficult because they have normative aspects; that is, they express values. Thinking about values in politics lends itself to distinct types of theorising, and these are discussed in the chapters on political ideas and practice (Chapters 6, 7 and 8). Values cannot be settled by pointing to actual features of the political worlds in which we live. Values are supported by reasons which may be questioned or challenged, regardless of science. Philosophical analysis may clarify the nature of the values being discussed, but it cannot demonstrate in a knockdown fashion what is to be done. Values are, however, of considerable importance in political life, for they are what animate people, and political theorists and ideologists have offered a variety of justifications for selected political values as constituting important signposts for the direction of political practice.

The organisation and contents of the book

This book is aimed at providing a general introduction to politics. In pursuit of this goal it does not deploy any single approach as offering the high road to complete explanation. Neither does it privilege any one area of politics over another. We have not tried to undertake any systematic form of comparative analysis, although comparison is an integral part of all forms of knowledge generation. Comparisons are made, mainly across national societies, and we have sought to take illustrative materials from a wide range of countries as they are appropriate to the topic under discussion. As the main purpose of comparison in this book is to ground the discussion of concepts and theories in actual politics, rather than to compare features of different political systems, we have not attempted any systematic use of the many forms of the comparative method to describe variations in political phenomena, test hypotheses about them, establish classifications of political types or make predictions on the basis of our observations. Rather, we have reported on the application of the comparative method by different sorts of theorists and investigators, and we have reported summaries of comparative data to support discussions of topics as various as human rights and political participation.

A great deal of illustrative material is used because we believe that politics comes alive for the student when it can be seen how decisions and actions affect particular people at specific times. Theories are of interest in that they abstract from the particular, but it may be argued that they are only relevant and interesting insofar as they actually relate to specific cases. Throughout the book, we have tried to introduce 'real-world' illustrations and brief case studies to make the connections between theory and practice. The book as a whole aims to make the complex nature of politics accessible and to relate it to everyday experience. Overall, we have sought to engage readers, so that they will reflect on or argue with what has been written. One obvious way we have tried to do this is by introducing think points to encourage reflection and argument about what has been written. In other words, they are meant to foster the reader's active and critical engagement with the book. As in the first edition, think points are not answered directly in the text itself, partly because they do not admit of simple and obvious responses and need to be thought through and discussed. Politics is a diverse set of activities; learning about politics is a process of thinking through arguments that are often difficult and seldom uncontested. The main aim of the use of think points is to facilitate this process. The book covers four broad areas of politics:

Part 1: People and politics, Chapters 1–5

In Chapter 1, without assuming answers to the disputed question about the nature and worth of politics, the concept of the individual is explored, along with the issue of how far it is possible to study politics without having to theorise about entities larger than the individual. The idea of the individual as this appears (or does not appear) in different types of society and different sorts of social theory is examined and the impact of the individual upon different forms of the collective is explored. The conclusion of the chapter points to a larger theme of the book, namely that politics is a multi-dimensional project in which institutions such as laws, moral rules, and corporate and collective bodies all matter, just as individuals matter.

In Chapter 2 the area of political socialisation, or how people learn about politics and acquire political identities, is discussed. The various attempts by political scientists to understand these complex processes are reviewed. The conclusion of this chapter is that the individual who is socialised (by the family, the school and other key institutions and processes) does not get lost in a thicket of social roles. Individuals are presented as active subjects involved in rather than conditioned by the processes of socialisation. Readers are invited to reflect upon their own experiences of socialisation.

Chapter 3 moves from the individual experience of social learning to examine political cultures and collective identities. The analysis recognises that the relationships between individual behaviour and attitudes and social and political norms are interactive. It explores the constructed nature of political cultures and the fact that they change over time. It offers a critique of the the idea of political cultures as monolithic, and emphasises the political importance of subcultures and hybrid identities. At the same time it acknow-ledges that relatively common frameworks of assumptions and values serve to anchor individual behaviour and give meaning to institutional forms like electoral systems. Other themes, such as the putative link between political culture and political stability and the ideological functions of cultural norms as elements in different forms of social control, are also rehearsed.

Chapter 4 continues the discussion of the interaction between individual behaviour and political and social contexts by looking at the area of political participation. A variety of ongoing practices are observed, from the conventional to the exotic. Different theories of participation are advanced, drawing upon explanations used by economists to explain consumer behaviour, psychological theories of motivation and the more cautious attempts to associate different forms of political participation with various individual and social characteristics. The relationship between political trust and civic engagement is covered in some detail and this provides a link to Chapter 5.

In Chapter 5, which is new to this edition, we tackle the important and contested issues of democracy and democratisation. The chapter examines different and sometimes competing concepts and theories of democracy, posing questions about the ways in which recent social, political and cultural changes – including globalisation – have altered the meanings found in classical theories of democracy and received wisdom about the processes of democratisation.

Part 2: Politics and ideas, Chapters 6–8

These chapters switch the focus of attention from the institutional and cultural settings of political behaviour to more general and evaluative forms of political thinking, which draw upon philosophical styles of thought, and explore their relevance to current issues in politics.

Chapter 6 takes various concepts and issues and looks at recent attempts to theorise about them. Justice, rights, equality and freedom are examined, and leading normative theorists of politics such as Rawls, Nozick and Berlin are analysed. Distinct ways of interpreting these concepts are highlighted and the relevance of theoretical analysis to practical action is shown by relating the abstract discussion of political concepts to practical concrete issues taken from contemporary events.

In Chapter 7 the variety of thinking and theorising which goes under the heading of political thought is discussed. The distinctiveness of Islamic political thought and the special questions thrown up by the treatment of women in political thought are examined. The rest of the chapter is devoted to looking at a number of classical political philosophers whose works have stood the test of time in opening up theoretical and evaluative perspectives on the meaning and purpose of political life. The nature and methodology of the history of political thought are examined as part of the process of reviewing the contributions of past political philosophers. At the same time, some of the most engaging and thoughtful scholarship of recent years in this area is also reviewed.

Chapter 8, on political ideology, concludes this part of the book. Political ideology is a style of thought of great importance, but a tricky subject to get to grips with. Ideologies are explained as mapping out large-scale visions of society and politics and as helping to orient individuals within a political culture. They are also seen as linking individuals to the structures of social and political life. Political ideologies are taken as being poised between theory and practice. A number of ideologies are reviewed and exemplified in the form of extracts.

Part 3: Politics in action, Chapters 9–13

This segment of the book continues the theme of making connections between the individual and the larger structures of state and sub-state governance, and, where appropriate, between these and international and global structures. It also examines those structures and processes that link civil society and the state through aggregating and articulating the demands of citizens. The chapters explore the relations between citizens and the machinery of government at national and subnational levels, and the manner in which various kinds of social and political groupings – parties and interest groups – try to exert influence over decision-makers. The changing character of political communications is explored and the roles of print media, broadcast media and information and communications technologies (ICTs) in politics are also examined. The final chapter in Part 3 looks at policy processes and at the ways in which resources are allocated and distributed.

In Chapter 9 the focus of analysis is on subnational politics and government, looking at the territorial distribution of power across different forms of state. Issues of subnational rule in various sorts of unitary and federal system are explored, including the vexed question of the constitutional relationships between federating units, and between these and central governments. The legal and democratic status of local government in an era of big government is also considered.

Chapter 10 examines different aspects of national government. In this chapter the formal institutions of national government are discussed in established and emerging democracies, authoritarian regimes and different types of developing nations. The increasing significance of political executives of different types of regime is explored, along with the issue of executive–legislative relations, including that of accountability. The theme of the state is central to this analysis, but light is also cast on the transformation of the state which is taking place 'from within'. In subsequent chapters (Chapters 14 and 15) we consider changes wrought from outside the territorial boundaries of the state.

Chapter 11 takes up what might be called the more informal aspects of politics and government, by examining important features of the politics of influence and the processes of demand articulation and aggregation. The main areas discussed are: the role and significance of political parties in democratic and other sorts of politics; the role of interest groups in articulating demands from sections of the population. Changing patterns of group mediation and influence are explored, along with the growing phenomenon of extra-territorial interest articulation. Finally, we examine the ways in which public opinion is expressed and managed in different political systems, and ask whether the mediation of public opinion is vital to the health of democracy.

Chapter 12 looks at the nature and changing character of political communications and the role of different media of communication in democratic and non-democratic politics. The chapter takes electoral communication as a paradigm case of political communication, but also stresses the importance of political communication in thoroughly mediatised cultures in many parts of the world.

Chapter 13, the last in Part 3, uses the policy process as a way of highlighting important aspects of the working of different kinds of political systems. The examination of the highly topical policy networks debate not only casts light on the formal processes of resource allocation, but also illuminates more general discussions of the nature and distribution of power in societies. The nature of public policy is discussed, and models and theories of the process examined. Some of these are very abstract, but the emphasis of the chapter is on exemplifying these debates through case study materials.

Part 4: Politics beyond the nation-state, Chapters 14 and 15

In these last two chapters of the book we look at politics beyond the nation-state. Throughout the text we have referred to the global dimension of an increasing amount of political, economic and cultural activity, and these two chapters set out to examine what the idea of politics beyond the state really means. In both chapters the nation-state is the conceptual point of departure.

In Chapter 14 some conventional thinking about the nature of national and international politics and governance is explored. Key concepts in the analysis of international relations, such as sovereignty, are outlined and various ways of theorising international politics are analysed, especially as these bear on the formation of international organisations and multilateral institutions. The European Union and aspects of international governance are discussed in greater detail to illustrate the particular nature of politics beyond the nation-state and to exemplify the features of nation-less forms of governance.

Chapter 15 develops the analysis of territorial forms of politics and government as a way into the discussion of globalising processes which are affecting the conduct of national politics and the autonomy of the territorial state, and which may be redrawing the boundaries of political community and the nature of political identities. The vexed question of what is meant by globalisation is examined. Globalisation is presented as a contested phenomenon in terms of its impact upon individual, local, organisational and national identities, and one which is contributing to a redefinition of social and political life.

At the end of this substantial book, which has been thoroughly updated and revised to ensure topicality, we hope that the reader will feel that he or she has been offered a digestible and thorough introduction to the diverse areas of political life and to the ways in which these are studied. We have tried to present politics and the study of politics as being not just about institutions or processes or ideas but about all of these, and as being more than just a study of discrete topics. There is no doubt that whatever the merits of this book, students of politics will still feel somewhat at sea given the scope and complexity of the subject being studied, but then uncertainty is a useful intellectual state and an endemic political one.

PART 1
PEOPLE AND POLITICS

INDIVIDUALS: IS POLITICS REALLY ABOUT PEOPLE?

POLITICAL SOCIALISATION

POLITICAL CULTURE

POLITICAL PARTICIPATION

DEMOCRACY AND DEMOCRATISATION

CHAPTER 1

Individuals

Is Politics Really About People?

Barrie Axford

▌ Introduction

In the Introduction to this volume we learned that the concepts and ideas which are at the heart of political study are themselves intellectual battle-grounds. Key terms like 'power' and 'freedom' are linguistic and often moral minefields over which the student of politics has to pass with great care, and it is easy to confuse or else conflate the normative with the empirical, or to transgress seeming rules about the basis of scientific inquiry. So in the study of politics very little can be taken for granted, and this caveat extends to what we study and how we study it.

In this chapter we will begin our examination of the nature of political inquiry and the scope and content of politics by looking at the place of the individual in political life. The term 'individual' is in common use, so much so that we tend to take its meaning for granted. We are all individuals in the sense that we are single human animals, but while this is a necessary starting point for analysis, it is not sufficient to explain the importance of the concept in much political and social science. The idea of the individual and the quality of individuality suggest uniqueness and originality. Each of us is unique in certain definable ways but, perhaps more significantly, in undefinable ways too. What makes each of us different is very hard to explain, despite a great deal of research into what contributes to the making of an individual's 'personality'. A good deal of scientific (and not so scientific) debate has centred on whether personality is innate (genetic) or made through social intercourse and social learning. The important point for our purposes lies not so much in expla-nations of individuality, but in the status ascribed to the individual in political and social theory, as well as in everyday life. For example, a society or any social unit which sees itself as made up of individuals is likely to be one where the virtues of independence are strongly embedded in custom and law. In such societies expressions of individuality are applauded, and attempts to constrain the free choices of individuals in lawful pursuit of their interests would require careful justification. In influential strands of Western political philosophy, the status of the individual has been enshrined in belief systems that assert both the *centrality* of the individual in explanations of social life, and the *primacy* of the individual relative to any or all collective forms – the group, the political party, the nation, the state and so on. Needless to say such doctrines have been hotly contested on the basis of their theoretical premises and because of their political implications. As such we will not only look at expressions of individualism but also consider the status of the individual as the appropriate unit for analysis in the study of politics, as well as discussing the pros and cons of pitching inquiry at the individual **level of analysis**.

Level of analysis The difference between studying individuals and collectives of different sorts. Choosing one level of analysis as opposed to another determines the sort of inferences which can be made from data.

Of course, in a discipline where little can be taken for granted, choosing the individual as a starting point for analysis is contentious, despite the common-sense assumption that in politics, as in life, people are at the centre of things. But we should not be misled by the appeal of common-sense assumptions and explanations. While the study of politics is necessarily a blend of sophisticated common sense, normative judgement and scientific knowledge or professional technique, it is also, in Thomas Kuhn's (1970) expression 'pre-paradigmatic', or lacking in agreement on the fundamental questions for inquiry and on the rules under which knowledge can be generated. In this chapter we start with the concept of the individual, and with what motivates and influences political behaviour, and then consider individuals as members of groups, political parties, legislatures, nation-states and beyond. This is a valuable approach to the study of politics, but by no means the only one. Given the complexity of political life, how could it be otherwise?

Three questions for analysis

There are three main issues about the individual and politics that will be addressed in this chapter. Some of the points discussed here will be re-examined in later chapters from different perspectives. The issues are:

First, the key question of the relationships between the individual (sometimes termed the agent or the subject) and wider social processes and institutions (often called structures). Individualistic or agent-centred accounts of social and political life argue that 'social wholes', that is institutions like social classes or nations, are reducible to or explained by the motives and actions of individuals. Put simply, such an argument holds that the whole is no more than the sum of its parts. At the other extreme, structure-centred positions believe that individual identities and behaviour are formed and take place within social relations which are governed by rules, or by 'history encoded into rules' as the sociologists March and Simon say (1958). Because of this, to edit Karl Marx slightly, while people may make their own history, they do so in circumstances over which they have had little or no control. Between these poles lies a range of possible explanations which try to reconcile individualistic and holistic theories.

Second, the extent to which the concept and status of the individual, along with related ideas about notions like individual rights, are rooted in a particular intellectual tradition known generally as **Enlightenment** philosophy and associated with a particular historical pattern of social and political development, usually called **modernity**.

The spread of ideas and institutions associated with the Enlightenment around the world has been a feature of the ways in which many societies became modern, but not all have embraced its precepts fully. For example, societies and political systems influenced by Marxism-Leninism, like those of the former Soviet Union and the People's Republic of China, have preferred to subsume individuality in wider collective identities and purposes – those of 'the State', 'the Party' or the idea of 'the People' as a whole. In fact, cultures that have emphasised the collective good over the good of individuals have often been very hostile to the concept of individual rights or to the idea that, in the last resort, the individual is arbiter of her own fate. Even within those mainly Western countries where individualism has flourished there are significant variations in how the individual is perceived, and in how far individualism is incorporated into customary practice, constitutional rights and notions like consumer sovereignty. It may be that the dominant ideology of Enlightenment individualism is giving way in the West to a **postmodern** version of individuality and new forms of politics to accompany it. This shift is sometimes discussed in terms of the transformation of modernity into postmodernity (the idea of the 'postmodern individual' is examined later in the chapter on pages 51–2).

Third, the extent to which the individual retains the capacity for effective political action. This is not just a matter of noting that under certain types of government, or in some political cultures, people are freer to express dissent or influence political decisions than in others. Clearly this is important, but even within open and democratic systems the capacity of individual citizens to influence policy turns on access to the kinds of resources that may be useful coin in the political realm – money of course, but also information, weight of numbers, expertise and so on. In what is often called the global age the individual's ability to intervene effectively as a political actor may be affected by the relocation of decision-making from national governments to supra-territorial bodies like the European Union. At such a pass the possibility of face-to-face interaction or of any kind of intimate connection between governors and governed is remote, and individuals have to rely more upon forms of mediated interaction – pressure groups, political parties, newspapers, faxes, WAP-phones or the Internet – to exercise their power as individuals.

Let us examine each of these issues in some detail.

Enlightenment The eighteenth-century Enlightenment 'project' was based upon a belief in the universality of reason and the power of scientific explanation. The individual was at the centre of the philosophical and political project, with human emancipation seen as following from the spread of rational inquiry and decision-making.

Modernity The distinct way of life found in 'modern' societies. A process beginning in Western Europe in about the fifteenth century, the idea of modernity achieved its full intellectual flowering during the Enlightenment. It is usual to tie modernity, or becoming modern, to the emergence of the nation-state, industrialism and the institution of private property. Modernity is also linked to the growth of bureaucratic organisations, secular beliefs and the value of individuality.

Postmodern Literally, beyond the modern, and suggesting a fragmentation of modernist beliefs, identities and certainties.

See Chapter 15 for an extended discussion of globalisation and the relationships between individual actors and global processes.

Parts or wholes: should we study individuals or structures?

This is one of the fundamental questions of political and social analysis, and one which appears in different ways throughout this book. The agency–structure divide referred to above highlights apparently fundamental differences in assumptions about and approaches to the study of political and social life. Because of this it is quite common to find radically different positions in the literature about the value of one approach relative to another. We can identify three main positions on this issue.

▨ The first, which we will call '*mutual exclusivity*', requires that one studies either individuals or structures, but not both, and insists that studying one precludes making inferences about the other. Attempts to do so merely end up in fallacious inferences being made about complex and possibly causal relationships. In this view, it is crucial to avoid discussing collectives – for example, political parties, parliaments or social classes – in terms of the characteristics of the individuals who populate them. This '*individualistic fallacy*' treats institutions (structures) as no more than individuals writ large. On the other hand, it is equally important not to discuss individuals as if they simply take on the characteristics of the organisations of which they are members. This would constitute an '*ecological or systemic fallacy*' found, for example, in some discussions of the ways in which institutions such as political parties, armed forces and workplace organisations determine the views and behaviour of members. Attention to the appropriate level of analysis makes for good social science, or so it is often argued. However, the rigid separation of individual and structural levels of analysis is subject to increasing criticism, and we shall take this up below under the third approach to agency–structure relations.

▨ The second strand, which we will call *reductionist*, holds that one set of variables may be explained wholly or in part by reference to another set. Thus inquiry couched at the individual level of analysis might take collective or structural concepts, such as the state or the **political system** or the middle class, to be no more than expressions of the aggregate behaviour and attitudes of individuals at a particular time and in a particular place. Structural accounts of political life reduce individual motivation to an effect of pre-existing social, economic, cultural and political forms, or else remove individuals (agency) from any constitutive part in the making of social life, save as the players of predetermined historical roles. As we shall see below there are many variations on these stark positions.

▨ The third, which we will label *structurationist*, following the example of the sociologist Anthony Giddens, attempts to bridge the divide by arguing that what others call structures are in fact the product of the day-to-day interaction of individuals with each other and with the institutions of daily living with which they are in contact. For example, from a structurationist perspective, the institutions of democracy are reproduced through both

Political system A concept sometimes used as a synonym for 'country', but which technically refers to the relationships, processes and institutions which make up a distinct political universe. Thus the Italian political system is made up of 'inputs' from society to the formal institutions of government, in the form of public opinion, pressure group activity and so on, while the institutions of government process these inputs to produce 'outputs' in the form of laws, policies, and even norms and values. For a critical discussion of this concept as applied to the policy process, see Chapter 13.

Key text: A. Giddens (1993) *New Rules of Sociological Method* (2nd edn), Cambridge: Polity Press.

routine and dramatic actions by individuals when they vote, stand as candidates, follow courses in current affairs, or take to the streets in protest against a government policy or the World Trade Organisation (WTO). To take a different example, the reproduction of capitalism as a worldwide system of production and exchange is reliant upon mundane actions like shoppers buying goods in a supermarket. These shoppers are not consciously reproducing capitalism when they buy a tin of dog meat or an avocado pear, but the effect is the same as if they were. In both cases the point is that structure of any sort is not external to individuals, but is given form and has meaning through routine social practices by individuals or by individuals in concert. In other words, structures are *socially constructed* by people who engage in various forms of social practice. At the same time, structures are not just reducible to individual motivations and actions, since they often pre-exist and outlast individual actors and thus achieve a sort of permanence or, as Giddens says, 'objectivity' for many people because of this. So actors make (or reproduce) structures, but they are also informed or constrained, and their lives are given a context by them.

Anthony Giddens

Anthony Giddens is Director of the London School of Economics and Political Science. He is one of the foremost sociologists in the world and author of many books. His range of interests covers the philosophy of the social sciences to globalisation, and it is work on the latter that has made him Tony Blair's 'favourite guru', notably for books on social democracy in the twenty-first century, such as *The Third Way* (1998).

THINK POINT

Do you think that individuals really do 'construct' reality in the ways that Giddens suggests?

Are there any examples from your own life that might lend themselves to this sort of interpretation?

Forms of individualist analysis

Using individuals as the unit for analysis is strongly associated with certain types of political and social inquiry. These cluster under the broad heading of **methodological individualism**, but show some important differences of emphasis as well as deriving from different intellectual traditions. Voluntarist approaches regard social life as mutable, no more than the outcome of the

Methodological individualism
A philosophical and empirical focus upon the individual and individual behaviour.

Behaviourism A movement in postwar political science, notably in the USA, concerned with establishing law-like generalisations about the political world and with shifting the emphasis of political studies away from its traditional legal-institutional forms. With a focus upon individual behaviour, the 'behaviouralist approach' is linked with quantitative research techniques designed to generate testable hypotheses about measurable attitudes and observable behaviour, thus rendering the study of politics more scientific.

These ideas are discussed extensively in Chapters 2 and 3.

unconstrained choices and actions of individuals. Some strands of economic theorising applied to political life offer a particularly stark theory of human motivation which takes as axiomatic the self-interested behaviour of individuals, and this is explored more fully below in the section on 'The modern individual'.

Behaviouralist assumptions about individuals as units for analysis seldom go this far. Behaviouralists are concerned with personal needs and motivations, and concentrate upon attitude formation, perceptions and social learning processes which involve the internalisation by individuals of cultural values and norms. Much of this sort of work involves studying what people actually do – as voters, members of voluntary associations or family members – by employing a range of research techniques including sample surveys, oral interviews and detailed observation of individuals and small groups.

Other variants of the individualist approach to politics and social life, sometimes clustered under the title 'Subjectivist or interpretative sociology', reject the behaviouralist claim that studying what people do or how they acquire identities and learn roles is a very fruitful way to understand both the complexities of individual psychology and the patterns of social life. Instead, they argue that researchers should look for the meanings which underlie action, so that each individual's experience and perceptions become the appropriate subject matter for the study of politics (Berger and Luckmann, 1966). Unlike the behaviouralists who sought to make the study of politics systematic, even scientific, by looking for regularities across the sum of individual behaviours, and who also tried to identify the laws which might follow from such observations, subjectivists believe that it is impossible to generalise from individual experience.

Forms of functional and structural analysis

Functionalism A term used to describe a range of theories that stress the extent to which norms and values underlie social and political stability. Stable societies are seen as being able to carry out the basic 'functional' imperatives – socialisation, integration, reproduction and so on – necessary for their survival.

Key text: T. Parsons (1967) *Sociological Theory and Modern Society*, New York: Free Press.

Marxism After Karl Marx. Emphasis is usually placed on the way in which economic processes and constraints shape social relations and relations of power.

Like their individualist counterparts, accounts which privilege structures as the right units of and level for analysis also differ about what phenomena they study and in the kind of questions they ask about them. By and large, structure-centred arguments concentrate upon whole societies, nations, government institutions, organisations or social groupings like class, but also take in social institutions like that of private property or marriage. Most, though by no means all, structural accounts believe that social phenomena can be explained without reference to the motivations and expectations of individuals. For example, **functionalism** attempts to uncover the requisites necessary for the maintenance, modernisation and stability of social and political systems. Basically these involve the ways in which individuals are socialised into roles and how they adapt to changing circumstances in their pursuit of socially sanctioned goals.

Marxism as a body of doctrine appears mainly structuralist, in that it too is exercised by the large-scale and long-term forces which shape societies – class conflict, technological developments and property conventions – and not with the personal histories of individuals (Althusser 1969). Yet some debates over the canonical status of Marx's thought depict him as a humanist, very aware of the role of individuals in making history. But even in this guise he is never a fully paid-up voluntarist, more a theorist attuned to the idea that social life can be explained by charting the strong currents in world history, but also by taking note of the scurryings of human actors who are not entirely preconditioned by social forces.

Marxism is taken up in greater detail in Chapter 8.

Structurationist arguments start from the point that structures have to be made (and reproduced) by agents. This, says the philosopher Roy Bhaskar (1976), is not always (or often for that matter) a case of people consciously deciding to reproduce something – the institutions of democracy, capitalism or marriage – although it can be. More often reproduction results from people simply doing routine things – witness our supermarket shopper – and having unintended or perhaps unthought of consequences following from their actions. At the same time, actions can only have meaning for individuals when they are set in meaningful contexts; indeed some actions, perhaps voting or obtaining a passport, are only possible within very particular and recognisable structures, like elections and laws on nationality.

THINK POINT

These are rather abstract ideas. Look through them again, perhaps making more detailed reference to some of the authors cited. Think about how these ideas can be translated into more concrete matters relating to the study and conduct of politics and perhaps in relation to your own experience.

The modern individual

The concept of modernity, which we defined above, is a complex one, referring to an historical period, a cluster of institutions which are usually understood as being typically modern and a body of philosophical thought. The institutional forms are industrialism, market capitalism, the nation-state and the international system of nation-states. The political sociologist Goran Therborn (1995, p. 4) talks about modernity being an 'epoch turned to the future', while Anthony Giddens (1990) says that modernity refers to 'modes of social life and organisation which emerged in Europe from about the sixteenth century onwards and which subsequently became more or less world-wide in their influence'. Of most direct concern to this chapter is the whole body of cultural and philosophical knowledge which is the heritage of the European Enlightenment.

The Enlightenment took place during the period when the various structures of modern societies were being laid down in Europe, and so its impact upon the ways in which people perceived these processes, how they explained them and how they came to understand their own place in the wider scheme of things is seminal. Enlightenment thought emphasised the possibility of individual and social progress through scientific knowledge applied rationally. In this scheme of things the individual is central, because the individual is the rational agent of change and thus the main engine of social progress. Above all, the individual subject is said to be 'indivisible', and to possess certain innate characteristics which are unique and unchanging. Chief among these is the capacity for reason or rational thought. The political ideology known as liberalism also places great stress on the capacities of the rational individual as both a key political and economic actor.

Liberalism as an ideology is examined in Chapter 8.

The modern age established a new and radical form of individualism, which came to a full flowering with the Enlightenment of the eighteenth century. In pre-modern times and in traditional societies, the individual was seen as a figure subject to the overwhelming forces of history and circumstance, a being hedged about by all manner of constraints – including those of birth, status and rank – as well as by superstition and custom. **Renaissance** thought and Enlightenment rationality freed the individual from this great weight of history and tradition, at least in principle. No longer simply a small part of the medieval *Great Chain of Being*, the individual or human subject was reborn as sovereign or autonomous, ready and equipped to play a full part in the making of the world, but this time as a lead player. Raymond Williams, the philosopher and literary critic, has this to say on the making of the modern individual:

The Renaissance A sixteenth-century movement in Europe which brought a more questioning and secular approach to art and literature and thus to the place of humans in the order of things.

> The emergence of notions of individuality in the modern sense can be related to the break-up of the medieval social, economic and religious order. In the general movement against feudalism there was a new stress on a man's personal existence over and above his place or function in a rigid hierarchical society. There was a related stress, in Protestantism, on a man's direct and individual relation to God, as opposed to this relation mediated by the Church. But it was not until the late seventeenth and eighteenth centuries that a new mode of analysis, in logic and mathematics, postulated the individual as the substantial category . . . from which other categories, and especially collective categories were derived. The political thought of the Enlightenment mainly followed this model. Argument began from individuals, who had an initial and primary existence, and laws and forms of society derived from them: by submission, as in Hobbes, by contract or consent, or by the new version of natural law in liberal thought. In classical economics, trade was described in a model which postulated separate individuals who . . . decided at some starting point to enter into economic or commercial relations. In utilitarian ethics, separate individuals calculated the consequences of this or that action which they might undertake.
>
> (Williams 1976: 135–6)

The Enlightenment creed outlined by Williams is very far from dead, but the history of modern societies has been anything but a linear progress towards the good society where rationality, self-development and individual autonomy hold sway. Liberal theories of government, based on individual rights and the consent of the governed, have had to come to terms with the phenomenon of mass politics, brokered by organised political parties and regulated by the bureaucratic structures of the nation-state. Modernism's claim to relegate the brutish and irrational side of human nature to the historical dustbin and to lead humankind to sunlit uplands peopled by rational beings who exercise a complete, though benign, mastery over nature also looks somewhat threadbare in the light of much recent history. Any catalogue of this more drear account of the unfolding of modernity would have to include the random, but, tellingly, the more systematic plundering of the idea that individuals possess universal qualities and enjoy 'inalienable' rights as a consequence of their very humanity. All lists are selective, but the following all point to a dark side of modernity in which the systematic exclusion (and worse) of people is justified on the basis of their imputed collective attributes, and through the use of stereotypes:

- the 'Terror' which followed the definitive modern event of the French Revolution in 1789.

- the near-genocide of the Native American peoples carried out by those claiming to act in the name of freedom and a 'Manifest Destiny' to tame a savage frontier.

- the horror of the extermination of Jews, homosexuals and gypsies by the Nazis during the 1930s and the Second World War.

- the 'ethnic cleansing' or forced expulsion of ethnic Albanians in Kosovo in 1999.

- the persecution of East Timoreans by the Indonesian government and armed forces for some twenty-five years up to 1999.

THINK POINT

Of course, not all societies have developed out of the liberal or Enlightenment traditions. Should these be judged harshly for not adhering to liberal principles?

Document

Erasing History: Ethnic Cleansing in Kosovo

Report released by the U.S. Department of State,
Washington, DC,
May 1999

EXECUTIVE SUMMARY

This report is part of a larger international effort to lay out the contours of the ethnic cleansing in Kosovo, which dramatically accelerated in mid-March, 1999. In preparing this, the United States Government has drawn on its own resources, as well as reports received from international organizations and non-governmental organizations (NGOs) to date. We encourage others to make their own contributions to record these events, get the facts out, and ultimately, hold the perpetrators of these crimes accountable.

This document provides a chronology of events after the departure of the OSCE's Kosovo Verification Mission on March 19, 1999, which prior to its departure had been regularly issuing human rights reporting. It is compiled from hundreds, if not thousands, of reported violations of human rights and humanitarian law since late March 1999. Due to lack of outside access to Kosovo, this report represents only a partial account of the ethnic cleansing.

The term 'ethnic cleansing' generally entails the systematic and forced removal of members of an ethnic group from their communities to change the ethnic composition of a region. Although we are still gaining information on all aspects of Serbian efforts to ethnically cleanse Kosovo, reports of human rights and humanitarian law violations we have received fall under seven broad categories:

1. Forced expulsions: The regime of Slobodan Milosevic is conducting a campaign of forced migration on a scale not seen in Europe since the Second World War. More than 90 percent of all ethnic Albanians have been expelled from their homes in Kosovo. In contrast to last fall, when attacks on civilians by Serb security forces generally occurred in small villages, this spring Yugoslav Army and Special Police units have joined with recently-armed Serb civilians to expel their neighbors from almost all towns and villages in Kosovo:

> An estimated 600,000 internally displaced persons are now struggling to survive in Kosovo. They are scattered throughout the province, often taking shelter in isolated forests and mountain valleys. Approximately 700,000 Kosovars have taken refuge in Albania, Bosnia-Herzegovina, the Former Yugoslav Republic of Macedonia, and the Republic of Montenegro since hostilities commenced in March 1998. Over three-fourths of these people have arrived since late March.

2. Looting and Burning: Some 500 residential areas have been at least partially burned since late March, including over 300 villages burned since April 4, according to overhead imagery. Besides houses and apartments, mosques, churches, schools, and medical facilities have also been targeted and destroyed. Many settlements have been totally destroyed in an attempt to ensure that the ethnic Albanian residents do not return.

3. Detentions: There are consistent refugee reports that Serbian forces are separating military-aged men from their families in a systematic pattern. At the time of writing, the total number of missing men and their fate is unknown.

4. Summary Execution: Refugees have provided accounts of summary executions in at least 70 towns and villages throughout Kosovo. In addition to random executions, Serbian authorities are targeting intellectuals, professionals, and community leaders.

5. Rape: Ethnic Albanian women are reportedly being raped in increasing numbers. Refugee accounts indicate systematic and organized mass rapes in Djakovica and Pec. We believe that many crimes of gender violence have not been reported due to the cultural stigma attached to these offenses in Kosovar society.

6. Violations of Medical Neutrality: NGOs report that since late March, violations of medical neutrality in Kosovo have accelerated dramatically. Serb authorities have looted and destroyed dozens of medical facilities, murdered Kosovar Albanian physicians, expelled ethnic Albanian patients and care providers from hospitals, and have used large numbers of health facilities as protective cover for military activities. The apparent goal is to effectively deny health care to ethnic Albanians and extinguish the community base that Kosovo's health professionals provide.

7. Identity Cleansing: Refugees report that Serbian authorities have confiscated passports and other identity papers, systematically destroyed voter registers and other aspects of Kosovo's civil registry, and even removed license plates from departing vehicles as part of a policy to prevent returns to Kosovo. Reports of identity cleansing are prevalent in refugee camps in Macedonia and Albania.

Can you think of any other examples of the gap between liberal principles and intentions and political realities?

Now it might be argued that all these examples are really aberrations, disfiguring the larger historical canvas of modernity, but hardly destroying it. Clearly this is a difficult argument to address in any detail here, but the idea that in the making of the modern world darker forces are released as well as those expressing rationality and humanity is an important modification to Enlightenment thinking on the nature and status of the individual. The struggle of reason against more elemental forces like instinct, repression or neuroses of various sorts reveals a self which is more ambivalent, fragmented and uncertain than the confident, whole subject of the Enlightenment. Some sense of the variety of intellectual and practical objections to the rational individual capable of making free moral choices is conveyed in the following extract:

> The entire thrust of modern natural science and philosophy since the time of (Immanuel) Kant and (Friedrich) Hegel has been to deny the possibility of autonomous moral choice, and to understand human behaviour entirely in terms of sub-human and sub-rational impulses. What once appeared to Kant as free and rational choice was seen by Marx as the product of economic forces, or by Freud as deeply hidden sexual urges. According to Darwin, man literally evolved from the sub-human, more and more of what he was understandable in terms of biology and bio-chemistry. The social sciences this century have told us that man is the product of his social and environmental conditioning, and that human behaviour, like animal behaviour operates according to certain deterministic laws . . . Modern man now sees that there is a continuum from the 'living slime', as Nietzsche puts it, all the way up to himself . . . Autonomous man, rationally able to follow laws he created for himself, was reduced to a self-congratulatory myth.
>
> (Fukuyama 1992: 297)

Key text: F. Fukuyama (1992) *The End of History and the Last Man*, London: Hamish Hamilton.

Fukuyama's argument here is in some measure critical of the tendency which he discerns in both the social and the natural sciences, to equate humankind with all animal life. But the debate about the allegedly unique nature of humans and the notional 'rights' of non-human animals, which is the subject of a fully fledged politics in some parts of the world (an issue which is taken up in Chapter 8), still leaves us to address the matter of how far the model of the rational individual explains certain social and political phenomena, and to what extent we need to look to other explanations, where individual action is embedded in the customs, morals and habits of the communities and societies in which it occurs. We will examine these issues by looking at the application of the model of the rational individual to economic life (and by extrapolation to political life as well) and by seeing how unfettered individualism is tempered by cultural factors.

Francis Fukuyama

Francis Fukuyama is the Omer L. and Nancy Hirst Professor of Public Policy at the Institute of Public Policy at George Mason University and Director of the Institute's International Transactions Program. He is also a consultant to the RAND Corporation in Washington, DC. Dr Fukuyama's book *The End of History and the Last Man* was published in 1992 and has appeared in over twenty foreign editions. It made the bestseller lists in the United States, France, Japan and Chile, and was a subject of intense debate in both academic and policy-making circles.

Individuals as utility maximisers: the myth of 'economic' man

Much of the reasoning behind the concept of the rational individual derives from the classical ideas of liberalism, and from modifications to liberal dogmas in the form of mathematical public choice theory, with its theoretical emphasis on the self-interested behaviour of individuals, who make choices in market situations based on their own preferences. In addition, it has been influenced by some variants of economic thinking devoted to economic liberalism as the justification for free-market principles. In both strands of thinking (see Dunleavy and O'Leary 1987) individual decisions are responsible for societal outcomes. Only individuals have goals, wants and needs, not collective entities like 'society' or 'the state'. In its most pristine form, seen particularly in public choice theory, proponents of this view claim to have uncovered fundamental and universal truths about human nature and individual behaviour, whether in economics, politics or any other area of human existence.

The intellectual basis for much of this reasoning is the claim that human beings are rational utility-maximising individuals. In other words, humans behave selfishly by trying to get as much of the things they want, thus maximising the benefit to themselves, at the same time as they minimise the costs incurred in actually getting those things. Such 'rational' calculation narrows motivation to what course of action or inaction is most likely to serve one's own preferences. Social life thus becomes a series of marketplaces in which individuals exercise what economists call 'effective demand' by demonstrating their willingness or reluctance to pay for goods or services. From the point of view of political behaviour, the decision to vote or not to vote, or to join a voluntary organisation, would be taken on the basis of whether it maximised our utility, or as the nineteenth-century philosopher Jeremy Bentham put it rather more eloquently, whether or not it contributes to the achievement of pleasure and the avoidance of pain.

Jeremy Bentham

The philosopher and jurist Jeremy Bentham (1748–1832) was born in Spitalfields, London, on 15 February 1748. He spent his life criticising the existing law and suggesting ways for its improvement. His father's death in 1792 left him financially independent, and for nearly forty years he lived quietly in Westminster, producing between ten and twenty sheets of manuscript a day, even when he was in his eighties. He will always be associated with the doctrine of utilitarianism and the principle of 'the greatest happiness of the greatest number'. This, however, was only his starting point for a radical critique of society, which aimed to test the usefulness of existing institutions, practices and beliefs against an objective evaluative standard. He was an outspoken advocate of law reform, a pugnacious critic of established political doctrines like natural law and contractarianism, and the first to produce a utilitarian justification for democracy. He also had much to say of note on subjects as diverse as prison reform, religion, poor relief, international law and animal welfare. A visionary far ahead of his time, he advocated universal suffrage and the decriminalisation of homosexuality.

One of the consequences of this line of reasoning, at least in its pure form, is that what we normally call 'society' – the outcome of various interactions between individuals, involving degrees of both love and hate – largely disappears, to be glimpsed only fleetingly as the product of the negotiations between self-interested individuals in various kinds of market, to create a sort of society effect.

As a justification for limited governmental intervention in the rational, market-driven behaviour of individuals these precepts have been used in a variety of ways by political **elites** in quite different systems. The economic and social policies of Margaret Thatcher in the UK or Ronald Reagan in the USA during the 1980s are 'strong' versions of the thesis, because they applauded the virtues of economic individualism. Elsewhere, for example, on the self-styled 'intelligent island' of Singapore and in other Asian economies which developed

Elite The best or the most noble; in contemporary usage it is generally applied to those who have high status or a high formal position in politics, culture and society.

very fast in the early and mid-1990s, the unfettered working of the free market has been compromised by the willingness of governments to intervene by protecting domestic industries from foreign competition, restricting foreign investment, funding local research and development, and subsidising local industries.

These are important insights into the purity of liberal economic theory applied to real-world situations, but let us consider in more detail the whole question of utility as the cornerstone of the model of economic man. The best-known definition of utility is Bentham's pleasure over pain principle referred to above, which has the considerable merit of being intelligible and, apparently, sensible. The following extract contains what you might call a Benthamite theory of voting and the behaviour of political parties, courtesy of work based on the theory of economic democracy formulated by the economist Anthony Downs (1956):

Key text: A. Downs (1956) *An Economic Theory of Democracy*, New York: Harper and Row.

> Political parties are assumed to be homogeneous groups of of politicians, which function as single, unitary actors. They formulate ideologies, or packages of policies, to reduce the cost to voters of collecting and evaluating the vast amount of imformation necessary to make an optimal voting decision. . . . Parties' policies can be arranged upon a single ideological dimension, which more-or-less corresponds to the familiar left–right dimension. . . . Voters vote for the party which occupies the position closest to their own most preferred position. . . . If the voters are rational and if voting involves some cost (in the form of information gathering, decision-taking, shoe leather and general mental distress during election campaigns) then a real benefit must accrue from the act of voting. . . . Despite this the influence that a particular voter wields . . . is likely to be extremely small. In all but the smallest electorates the voter is likely to have an almost infinitesimal effect. . . . The difference between the various (party political) packages on offer may be quite large, but it is likely that each voter, considering the tiny chance of actually bringing about a change, will not expect a worthwhile return on his investment . . . the consequences of voting are so unlikely to offset the costs that it would not seem rational to vote at all.
>
> (Laver 1981: 102)

In similar vein, the theory of the calculating individual would suggest that it is not rational to join organisations which are striving to produce benefits that would be available to people whether or not they are members of the organisation. These benefits, called 'public goods' to distinguish them from benefits only available to those who are members, or who pay for them, would include things like clean air or universal welfare benefits, from which individuals could not be excluded even though they had incurred no costs, or paid no dues to acquire them. In Mancur Olson's well-known book *The Logic of Collective Action* (1965) this problem is referred to as the phenomenon of the 'free-rider', a concept which has figured widely in discussions of the difficulty of mobilising and sustaining certain types of interest groups and action by citizens.

THINK POINT

Consider your own motives for voting or not voting.

Would you fit the model of the rational voter?

Would you join a group devoted to pursuing the public interest?

If not, why not?

Well and good, there is a neatness about rational explanations of individual action or inaction. But there are still the obvious facts that many people do vote, and that some people seem to pursue goals that have nothing to do with personal utility. The evidence, seemingly, is all around us. People join organisations like Friends of the Earth and Jubilee 2000, or donate money to charity without the expectation of personal material reward. Others intervene to prevent old ladies from being mugged, while some, in places like Tiananmen Square in Beijing, or Belgrade, are prepared to stand in the way of armoured vehicles and tanks, or risk violence, and when they do, their reasons are couched in terms of honour, religion, justice, freedom and love, not self-interest. In competitive elections in systems dominated by major political parties, independents and minor party candidates still stand for office time and again in the sure and certain knowledge that they will not be elected. Are these people acting irrationally, at least according to the lights of utilitarian reasoning, and if they are, does it matter? Here is an example of a chronic political activist whose 'rewards' lay in the act of campaigning, rather than in the prospect of winning.

Document

Obituary: Screaming Lord Sutch

Anarchic, irreverent performer on by-election platforms
and horror-filled rock music sets
Guardian, Saturday 19 June 1999

Screaming Lord Sutch, who has committed suicide aged 58, was an outsider, shaped by postwar poverty, who achieved celebrity in the early 1960s, and fame in the Thatcher era as founder and frontman of the Official Monster Raving Loony party. When his mother was asked about her son and his exploits, she explained that it was, after all, just an act, indeed that his whole life was just an act.

Sutch ran for parliament 39 times, first as the National Teenage party candidate in the 1963 Stratford-on-Avon by-election that followed the Profumo scandal. The narrowly victorious Conservative, Angus Maude, treated him, Sutch recalled, like 'vermin from another planet'. In the 1966 general election he fought Prime Minister Harold Wilson in Huyton and picked up 585 votes. Four years later, he ran in Westminster as the Young Ideas party candidate, and in 1974 for the Go To Blazes party in Stafford and Stone.

But it was in the next decade, with the flowering of Thatcherism, that Sutch first ran as an OMRLP candidate. The contest was Bermondsey, the Labour candidate Peter Tatchell, and the victor the Liberal Simon Hughes. Sutch advocated a statue to Tommy Steele – 'the Bermondsey bombshell and the only decent thing to come out of the place' – and attracted 97 votes.

Soon after, at the Darlington by-election, the local paper reported that more people were in the toilets at Sutch's (pre-election) victory party than attended the Social Democratic party's rally. Sutch won 374 votes. In the 1983 election 11 candidates ran for the OMRLP, with Sutch 'against Margaret Thatcher – a nasty experience, as Denis can testify'. The following year it was Chesterfield and Tony Benn.

Thus did a decade unfold where, whatever the national crisis, whatever the earnest fatuities of the victorious by-election candidate, there on the edge of the screen would be Sutch, or a sidekick, a Shakespearean antick for the TV age. It was a great joke, but the viewer could never be absolutely certain that Sutch was in on it.

Anthony Downs offers a mitigating circumstance in which the strict definition of rationality might be stretched to cover such eventualities. He suggests that if no one voted, democracy would collapse because there would be no challenges to incumbents in office, and thus no approximation of the market competition necessary to keep politicians and parties on their toes, and thus ensure an adequate supply of public goods. So every (rational) citizen is still prepared to shoulder some costs in order to insure themselves against the even higher costs which would accrue should societal breakdown occur. Other theorists, like Riker and Ordeshook (1968), offer a different slant on the calculus of voting. They argue that voters derive *positive satisfaction* from complying with the ethical imperative implied in the status of citizen, which status is consummated by the act of voting. The actual act then becomes a symbolic reaffirmation of a voter's allegiance to the political system, to a particular party or to the very idea of democracy, as well as an expression of a citizen's **political competence**. Writing about public sanitation in the United States, Matthew Crenson (1987) has suggested that individuals may well be persuaded to join public interest groups where it can be made clear that their failure to participate will result in group failure and the deleterious effects of a 'public bad'. He has also argued that people are more likely to contribute to the prevention of a collective 'bad' – dirty air or poor sanitation – than to the securing of a collective good – a better environment and so on. People, it seems, are more easily mobilised in response to threats than in response to promises (see also Jordan and Maloney 1996).

All this is a considerable relaxation of the rationality principle, allowing that the concept of self-interest may not be as narrow as writers like Downs and Olson believe, and that people can derive pleasure from things like 'doing one's duty as a citizen', or get satisfaction – psychic pleasure if you like – from helping others. The strong concept of 'utility' now becomes another way of describing whatever preferences people have, or of saying that people do what they want to do. Without too much effort this less rigorous definition of utility might be extended to the 'satisfactions' experienced by a suicide bomber in a busy

Political competence Both a formal status, in the sense that as a citizen one has the right to vote, and a practical skill, for example in terms of organising a demonstration or writing to a member of Congress or Parliament.

street in Tel Aviv or the West Bank, seeking a 'marriage' with death. There is also the sense that not all behaviour or choices need be considered as rational where that means making a calculation based on having access to all relevant information and then seeking to maximise utility. There must be occasions when the costs of acquiring perfect information would have to be considered too expensive, and thus irrational. In such circumstances the individual, faced with the need to choose, falls back on habit, or appeals to tradition or even expediency.

Key text: B. Barry (1970) *Sociologists, Economists and Democracy*, London: Collier-Macmillan.

All of this suggests a more complex and messy model of the nature of individuality than can be contained in the economic version. People are embedded in a variety of social and cultural groups, and what they think, feel and do is often intimately related to how deeply they are embedded in these identities. As Francis Fukuyama says (1995: 21), 'social and therefore moral behaviour coexists with self-interested, utility-maximising behaviour . . . human beings act for non-utilitarian ends in a-rational, group-oriented ways'. These aspects of sociability modify the force of simple cost–benefit calculations and the desire to fulfil our own interests is mediated by the variable intensity of our social relationships and moral obligations as parents, workers, members of a softball club or activists in a single-issue pressure group dedicated to combating the introduction of genetically modified foods. The rational actor of economic theory is only a pale shadow of her flesh-and-blood counterpart, who is making decisions in situations which are encumbered with history, cultural values and imperfect information.

THINK POINT

Review the argument. How convincing do you find the concept of the rational actor?

EXERCISE

Below is a well-known exercise in rational choice and the problems of collective action. It is called the 'prisoner's dilemma'.

The scenario: Bill and Ted are prime suspects in a bank robbery. Police have circumstantial evidence that both were involved, including possession of safe-breaking equipment, baseball clubs which could be used as weapons, and so on, but no actual witnesses. What they need is a confession from either or both of the suspects. At the police station, the prisoners are separated and each is presented with the same deal, which is that if they make a full confession which implicates their partner, they will be granted immunity from prosecution while their accomplice will carry all the blame and go to gaol for a long time. If they refuse, they may well end up taking all the blame themselves. Having no knowledge of how their partner is reacting, each has to make up his mind how to respond.

continued

continued

Here are their options, set out in the form of a game-play matrix:

The entries in each cell of the matrix show how many years each prisoner will receive as their sentence. Bill's sentence is shown in words, Ted's using numbers.

BILL'S OPTIONS

		stay silent	confess
TED'S OPTIONS			
stay silent		one, 1	none, 5
confess		five, 0	three, 3

Figure 1.1 Game-play matrix

Both Bill and Ted are old hands at this sort of thing. They can see the options quite clearly. Critically, they do not know what the other may be doing. Given the same scenario, how would you read the options, and what would you decide to do?

Individualism in action

The difficulty with economic reasoning applied to the motivations of individuals is that while it may explain a good deal of human behaviour, it runs into difficulties explaining those acts which are non-utilitarian, at least without a great deal of conceptual stretching. As a theory of individual motivation, therefore, it is like the curate's egg – only good in parts. Even Adam Smith, the eighteenth-century father of what is often called neo-classical economics, believed that economic life is firmly embedded in social life, and that individual motivations and behaviour have to be understood in relation to the customs, morals and habits of the society in which they take place.

This argument raises an important point about the very idea of individualism and about the status of the individual in modernity. Because human action is embedded in social and cultural life, it follows that the concept of the individual, and the intellectual and moral qualities attached to that status, are themselves socially constructed and culturally sanctioned. In other words, they are not the innate characteristics of human beings (despite what utilitarian economics says) but are made and reproduced by people in the context of particular cultural rules and expectations. Where rules and expectations about the status of the individual exist, one might expect to find widespread evidence

Adam Smith

Adam Smith, 1723–90. By publishing in 1776 *An Inquiry into the Nature and Causes of the Wealth of Nations*, Adam Smith founded the science of political economy. So significant were the effects of this book for the modern world that it has been described as one of the most important ever written. It is referred to in every history of the subject. The basic doctrine of *The Wealth of Nations* was that labour is the only source of a nation's wealth. Smith advocated division of labour in the productive process, stressed the importance of individual enterprise and argued the benefits of free trade. The true wealth of a nation, he held, lay not in gold but in the achievement of an abundance of the necessities of life. He warned against unnecessary intervention by the state in this process.

of individualism in both political theory and constitutional forms, as well as in the self-perceptions of ordinary people. For example, the Constitution of the United States and the Declaration of Independence which preceded it are documents redolent with the spirit of individualism and individual rights.

Although the American revolutionaries of 1776 sought to enhance the public good, it is the political theory of liberalism, with its insistence on the independence of people from each other and from 'primitive' attachments, that is most readily associated with 'American-ness' or the American creed. Political authority, particularly governmental authority, had to be fitted into a society of individuals. Curiously, or so one might think, dedication to an individualistic value system, and to the liberal creed, has itself been a feature of the cohesion and stability of American society, at least until recently, legitimating the competitive instinct, entrepreneurship, thrift and the other qualities of 'rugged individualism' as *cultural* norms. So it comes as no surprise that the typical American hero is a combination of individualism without eccentricity, charm without sophistication, and of course, wholehearted patriotism. John Wayne springs to mind as the embodiment of these virtues, but so does the archetypal loner in the guise of practically all Clint Eastwood's 'Western' characters, along with the maverick Randle McMurphy in Ken Kesey's novel *One Flew Over the Cuckoo's Nest*.

In fact, the pantheon is very large and contains some unexpected figures who lack the physical presence and glamour of Hollywood film stars. The appeal of the rank outsider Ross Perot as a candidate in the 1992 presidential election

From the American Declaration of Independence, 1776: 'We hold these truths to be self-evident, that all men are created equal, that they are endowed by their Creator with certain inalienable rights, that among these are Life, Liberty and the Pursuit of Happiness.'

The concept of culture and the importance of cultural norms are examined in Chapter 3.

was based on his opposition to 'big government' in Washington, and the fact that he exemplified many of the qualities of American individualism, being a self-made billionaire and an advocate of self-help. Perot's much quoted aphorism 'Eagles don't flock; you have to find them one at a time' could be taken as a convenient summary of American individualism. The 'Unabomber' too, who for nearly two decades waged a one-man war in the USA against what he saw as the evils of the mass-consumption society, evoked an ambivalent response among a public shocked at his disregard for human life apparent in his bombing campaign, and romanced by his lone crusade. In the contest for the Republican Party's choice for presidential candidate in 2000, John McCain generated a good deal of support across the political spectrum largely because of his military record and his courage in the face of extreme adversity while a prisoner of war in North Vietnam in the late 1960s to early 1970s.

French individualism also displays some of the features of the American strain, but unlike its 'New World' counterpart it has an almost anarchistic character. In France, cultural and political values associated with the French Revolution of 1789 have produced a highly fragmented society where the individual citizen is suspicious of both the government and many types of collective action. As a consequence the French seem far less inclined to participate in social organisation than say the British or Americans, except where it involves spontaneous and direct action against the French state, for example by students or farmers anxious to protect their livelihoods.

Thus robust individualism abounds in France and the United States, but there are also individualists in countries like Russia, Japan or Italy, if by that we mean that it would not be hard to find people who have a strong sense of their own identity, or who are imbued with an independence of spirit and a critical cast of mind when it comes to evaluating the role of government in the affairs of citizens. In Alexander Solzhenitsyn's account of life in the prison camps of the Soviet 'Gulag', *One Day in the Life of Ivan Denisovitch*, the hero shows exactly the same wiles of stubbornness and inventiveness used by Randle McMurphy in his guerrilla war with authority inside the mental hospital where he is a voluntary patient. The difference is that in the United States, as in many other countries in the West, the status of the individual at the centre of social life has been institutionalised in thought and custom, as well as in law. Because of this there is a culturally sanctioned expectation that individuals will behave as social critics as well as utility maximisers.

THINK POINT

Do you think of yourself in this way? What does being or acting as an 'individual' mean to you?

Alexander Solzhenitsyn is a Russian novelist and historian who was awarded the Nobel Prize for Literature for 1970 and was exiled from the Soviet Union in 1974. Among his celebrated works are *One Day in the Life of Ivan Denisovich* (1962), *The Gulag Archipelago* (1974), *Cancer Ward* (1968), *The First Circle* (1968) and *August 1914* (1971). Despite exile in the USA, Solzhenitsyn remained committed to Russian culture and traditions. He was reinvested with Soviet citizenship in 1994 during the period of glasnost (openness). and now lives in Russia.

Alexander Solzhenitsyn

Individuals and rights

The protection of individuals in many societies has often taken the form of translating rights-based political theory into laws and public policy, or else of appropriating the language of rights as political slogans – the right to work, or the right to control over one's body – which are sometimes translated into an organised politics. In practice, the articulation and codifying of rights takes different forms across the globe. More often than not, these forms have been expressed as rights associated with **citizenship** of particular countries and have not been extended to non-nationals. But after the Second World War in Western Europe, attempts were made to establish a system of rights which transcends national boundaries. These efforts were part of the broader processes of European unification and were particularly evident in the setting up of the Council of Europe in 1949, and in the adoption in 1950 of a United Nations inspired European Convention for the Protection of Human Rights and Fundamental Freedoms. The latter was given some judicial teeth through the European Court of Human Rights (1959), which hears appeals from individuals and from collective bodies. The Council of Europe system of supranational rights includes rights to life, liberty and both the individual and collective pursuit of happiness. Freedom of conscience and of religion are guaranteed, along with freedom of expression and association.

By prohibiting torture and use of the death penalty in peacetime, the Council of Europe has tried to exclude authoritarian regimes in Western Europe and, until after the fall of communism, those in Eastern Europe too. As a sign of the changed or changing times, Russia was formally admitted to

Citizen A member of a particular territorial state and the rights attaching to that status. Modern conceptions of citizenship stress universal rights and obligations, and there is now a transnational doctrine of human rights, but the legal status and the rights and obligations that follow from it remain attached to particular countries.

Supranational means literally 'above the national', but see Chapters 14 and 15 for an extended discussion.

the Council of Europe in 1996, although the issue of human rights continues to be one of the crucial barriers to the membership of some other former communist states.

Document

The 41 Member States of
the Council of Europe (*circa* 1999)

Albania: member since 13.7.1995
Andorra: member since 10.10.1994
Austria: member since 16.4.1956
Belgium: member since 5.5.1949
Bulgaria: member since 7.5.1992
Croatia: member since 6.11.1996
Cyprus: member since 24.5.1961
Czech Republic: member since 30.6.1993
Denmark: member since 5.5.1949
Estonia: member since 14.5.1993
Finland: member since 5.5.1989
France: member since 5.5.1949
Georgia: member since 27.4.1999
Germany: member since 13.7.1950
Greece: member since 9.8.1949
Hungary: member since 6.11.1990
Iceland: member since 9.3.1950
Ireland: member since 5.5.1949
Italy: member since 5.5.1949
Latvia: member since 10.2.1995
Liechtenstein: member since 23.11.1978
Lithuania: member since 14.5.1993
Luxembourg: member since 5.5.1949
the 'former Yugoslav Republic of Macedonia': member since 9.11.1995
Malta: member since 29.4.1965
Moldova: member since 13.7.1995
Netherlands: member since 5.5.1949
Norway: member since 5.5.1949
Poland: member since 29.11.1991
Portugal: member since 22.9.1976
Romania: member since 7.10.1993
Russian Federation: member since 28.2.1996
San Marino: member since 16.11.1988
Slovakia: member since 30.6.1993
Slovenia: member since 14.5.1993
Spain: member since 24.11.1977
Sweden: member since 5.5.1949
Switzerland: member since 6.5.1963
Turkey: member since 13.4.1950
Ukraine: member since 9.11.1995
United Kingdom: member since 5.5.1949

THINK POINT

Can you observe any patterns in this list?

The language of rights also finds its way into the Social Chapter of the Maastricht Treaty on European Union, signed in 1991 and ratified by the member states over the next three years, and into the Amsterdam Treaty of 1997, which was specifically designed to give a 'popular' dimension to European integration. In the following extract some of the 'rights' contained in the treaties are set out, though many of them are little more than generalised statements of intent. Maastricht also laid down the skeleton of a European citizenship, among other things extending to all citizens of member states of the European Union the right to stand as candidates for election to the European Parliament in any Euro-constituency in the Union.

Document

Citizenship Rights in the European Union

The Amsterdam Treaty builds on the foundations created by successive Treaties since the Treaty of Rome in 1957.

Citizen's Rights

The notion of citizenship was not mentioned specifically in the Treaty of Rome. The Tindemans Report in 1975 devoted a chapter to the idea of a 'Citizen's Europe', which proposed that the Community guarantee fundamental human rights. The first direct elections to the European Parliament in 1979 were an expression by the people of Europe of their rights as citizens of Europe, which gave greater legitimacy to the Community. Today, this is the only direct democratic link that the citizen has with the European Union, hence the significance of the granting of further powers to the European Parliament. In 1984, the Parliament adopted the Draft Treaty on European Union, which specifically dealt with citizenship and the rights that this implies. The common passport, driving licence, flag, and anthem serve as identifiable symbols of European citizenship and encourage a 'we' feeling among citizens. In more concrete terms, the Single European Act (1986) made way for the free circulation of capital, goods, people and services by 1992. It is important to note that European citizenship is additional to national citizenship.

The Maastricht Treaty

The Treaty on European Union (TEU) set out to involve the citizens even further. Signed in 1992, the Maastricht Treaty had as one of its objectives . . . to strengthen the protection of the rights and interests of the nationals of its Member States through the introduction of a citizenship of the Union. [Title 1, Article B]

It also stated that the EU will have respect for human rights as guaranteed by the 1950 European Convention for the Protection of Human Rights and Fundamental Freedoms. Citizenship of the European Union was defined and established in the Treaty on European Union so that every citizen of a Member State is automatically a citizen of the Union. This implies, and it is so stated, that each citizen of the Union will have the same rights under the Treaty as any other citizen. [Art. 8(1)]

Articles 8a to 8d of the Maastricht Treaty list the specific rights of citizens of the Union which include:

- The right to move freely and reside within the territory of the Member States.
- The right to vote in the municipal and European Parliament elections in the Member State in which one resides.
- The right to the protection, when outside the Union, of the diplomatic authorities of any Member State (if one's own state has no embassy or consulate).

- The right to petition the European Parliament on any matter which comes within the Community's field of activity and which directly affects the petitioner(s).
- The right to apply to the Ombudsman (appointed by the European Parliament) concerning any maladministration by any of the Community Institutions (with the exception of the Court of Justice).

The Amsterdam Treaty

The Amsterdam Treaty has placed the interests of the citizens at its heart. Article 8a establishes citizenship of the Union and stresses that this European citizenship is complementary to national citizenship, not a replacement. Citizens may write to any of the Institutions of the Union in their own language and will be answered in the same language as per new Article 8d of the Treaty. Furthermore, steps have been taken for the protection of individuals regarding the processing of personal data. Respect for the status of churches and religious associations are included under the heading of fundamental rights and non-discrimination.

Fundamental Rights and non-discrimination are key principles which this Treaty seeks to enshrine.

Within the chapter on fundamental rights, social rights as defined in the European Social Charter (1961) and the Community Charter of the Fundamental Social Rights of Workers (1989) are confirmed as fundamental.

The new Article 6a has a significant anti-discrimination clause which aims at promoting equality of the sexes, and prohibiting discrimination on grounds of disability, ethnic origin, religion or belief, age or sexual orientation. The Treaty also includes a declaration on persons with a disability which states that . . . when drawing up measures under Article 100a, the institutions of the Community shall take account of the needs of persons with a disability.

Apart from its obvious merits, the emphasis on fundamental rights and non-discrimination in the Amsterdam Treaty will strengthen the laws and rules of the European Union which aspiring Member States from Central and Eastern Europe (CEEC) will have to adopt in full to fulfil the criteria for membership. The EU will commence accession negotiations with Cyprus, Hungary, Poland, Estonia, the Czech Republic, and Slovenia in Spring 1998, while the preparation of talks with other applicant countries will also be speeded up at this time. It is part of the political criteria for membership that the applicant country has respect for democracy, the rule of law, human rights, and respect for minorities.

The Treaty sets out measures to ensure the application of the principles of non-discrimination and the upholding of fundamental human rights. In the event of a breach of these principles by a Member State, sanctions can be imposed by the Council of Ministers, acting by qualified majority on a proposal from the Commission, or of one third of the Member States and after consulting the European Parliament. The form taken by these sanctions may be economic or political penalties, such as the suspension of voting rights. These measures are largely precautionary and were inserted in the Treaty in advance of the future accession of countries from Central and Eastern Europe which may have only recently developed democratic structures.

The European Court of Justice will have the right to interpret conventions at the request of national courts. Furthermore, every individual still has the right, under Treaty articles, to bring proceedings before the European Court of Justice if he or she feels that an Institution has breached his/her fundamental rights. The right of recourse to the European Ombudsman under the Maastricht Treaty still applies.

The provisions in the Treaty should make it easier for action to be taken to combat racism and discrimination. The establishment of a European Monitoring Centre on Racism and Xenophobia, which has its seat in Vienna, is in addition to the Treaty changes. This will provide a forum for the exchange of information and expertise in this area and complement action in the legislative field.

The Amsterdam Treaty is more clearly based on the interests of citizens than any other previous Treaty revision. Overall, the changes are positive and wide-ranging, giving citizens increased rights, and providing States with greater means of enforcing the principles of non-discrimination. Although the Treaties have encouraged equality through the prohibition of discrimination on grounds of nationality, gender or religious views, this Treaty has enforced this through the active promotion of equality between men and women (Arts. 2 and 3). Furthermore, Article 213b on data protection, the declaration against religious discrimination, which respects the status of churches, and the other changes and declarations, demonstrate the Union's determination to develop a Europe of 'Freedom, Security and Justice'.

(The European Movement: *Guide to the Amsterdam Treaty*, 1997)

These 'rights' strike some commentators as very insubstantial. At the same time, the formal incorporation of the language of rights into public law and policy can have great symbolic and perhaps great substantive importance. In 1999, the UK government incorporated the European Convention on Human Rights into domestic law and in the following year enacted the Human Rights Act. Both these measures are radical in that they enshrine the principle of human rights *per se* into a system of law highly suspicious of such abstract notions.

Rights are also part of the language of international relations, but quite often as part of the rhetoric by which regimes offer praise and blame, rather than as a firm commitment to those whose rights have been violated. The Gulf War of 1991 was fought in part over the issue of Saddam Hussein's violation of the independent status of Kuwait, and the NATO intervention in Kosovo in 1999 was justified in terms of the legitimate aim to protect ethnic Albanians in that part of greater Serbia. Despite evidence of the international desire to protect the rights of relatively powerless groups of people, humanitarian concerns and attention to the rights of individuals and groups often suffer out of respect for the *rights* of nation-states in international law and convention. Looking at the Gulf War, it is the failure to intervene on behalf of the Marsh Arabs in the south of Iraq, who were also the recipients of Saddam's displeasure, which points up the limits of intervention in pursuit of human rights. Subsequent discussions of the merits of imposing sanctions on the Iraqi regime to force Saddam out of office have stressed the ways in which these measures have deprived ordinary Iraqi people of the basic material resources necessary to sustain all sorts of social rights – to livelihood, to good health and to happiness. In other cases, international outcry is rarely matched by firm action on the part of governments and international bodies. Early in 1996, the Nigerian military government executed the poet Ken Saro-Wiwa following a suspect trial, but no sanctions followed; while the disastrous floods in Mozambique early in 2000 produced a tardy and patchy response from donors of aid and relief.

Goran Therborn (1995) identifies two areas of basic rights associated with the protection and enhancement of the status of the individual. These are rights which are *claims* upon the state and its resources, and rights to *act* in relation to other members of society as well as *vis-à-vis* the state. The first set includes rights to membership – the grounds on which people are allowed into a country as visitors, migrants, asylum seekers and settlers, and the rules which govern their treatment as sojourners. It also includes rights to welfare, pensions and other social entitlements. Such rights were introduced at different points during the often protracted transition to modernity, and there is wide variation in their application across different social and political systems. There follows an extract from Therborn's book (1995) which deals with the variations in rights to membership:

The importance of state membership was reinforced . . . with the new turn of migration into Europe.

The legal tradition contains two major criteria for state membership, for citizenship, namely 'soil' or 'blood'. . . . The former means that you acquire your citizenship by the place where you were born, and the latter that it depends on who your parents (or ancestors) were. By and large, settlement countries – the New Worlds – and empires, like the British and the French, have tended to opt for soil, the other European countries for blood. . . .

In fact the blood or soil distinction does not adequately capture post-World War II varieties in Europe and the trajectories of their general tendency towards restrictiveness. The UK has, since 1971 increasingly narrowed the gate for entrants from the non-white Commonwealth, while keeping, in spite of IRA terrorism, an open door on Irish immigration. Irish residents in the UK have the same rights as British citizens. . . . Germany has been in many ways more restrictive. Labour imports were conceived as 'Gastarbeiter' [guest-workers] and denied any rights to permanent residence. Until 1990 people who were unable to claim German descent had no right to citizenship, however long they had been in Germany. . . . Since that date, fifteen years of residence, or in the case of youngsters aged between 16 to 23, eight years of residence and six years of school, entitles a claim to citizenship.

On the other hand, blood-rights have allowed a large number of Eastern Europeans to enter (West) Germany claiming German descent.

Political rights are most accessible in Britain, and since 1984, in Ireland. . . . Sweden gave foreign residents the right to vote in local elections in 1976, followed by Denmark and Norway, and by Iceland and Finland, but only with regard to other Nordic citizens. . . .

In Eastern Europe postwar citizenship lost one of its otherwise most important accessories, the passport. . . . With the exception of the Yugoslavs since the mid-1950s, the Hungarians since the mid-1980s and, to a more limited extent, the Poles since the mid-1970s, a passport to Eastern Europeans was not a right but a special privilege, earned by loyal service or by post-retirement age. On the other hand, Eastern European regimes such as that of the USSR and the GDR, used their power to deprive citizens of their citizenship rights. Alexander Solzhenitsyn and Wolf Biermann were the most famous, or notorious cases.

After the war, the individual right to vote was an issue only by exception. . . . Greek women joined their Balkan sisters in 1952. . . . But Swiss women had to wait for recognition of their political maturity till 1971 and most Iberian women till the end of the dictatorships in the mid-1970s. . . .

> The political distance between Finland and the Iberian peninsula, in terms of female enfranchisement, turned out to be about seventy years, between France (1946) and Norway (1913), somewhat above thirty years
>
> (Therborn 1995: 86–8; reproduced with the permission of Sage Publications Ltd)

THINK POINT

What inferences can you draw from these comparative data?

Therborn's data are drawn from the continent of Europe, but similar, if not greater, variations in rights as entitlements can be seen in other parts of the world. In the United States, civil rights extended to erstwhile black slaves after the Civil War of 1861 to 1865 remained entirely notional for large sections of black America until well into the 1960s due to entrenched local sentiments and the contested power of individual states to pass and impose discriminatory legislation. Australia and New Zealand enfranchised women long before most European countries, but paid scant attention to the rights of indigenous minorities, while military regimes in Argentina and Chile between the 1960s and 1980s systematically degraded the rights of individual citizens in their quest to stamp out political opposition. In Burma (Myanmar) today, most forms of political opposition are treated as occasions for repression, from the house arrest of leaders of the Pro-Democracy Movement to those deemed 'guilty' of open discussion of domestic politics on the Internet. Before the fall of the apartheid system in 1994, South Africa was an unhappy blend of respect for individual rights and the rule of law, extended to the white population, and both legal and customary discrimination against black people and other people of colour. It is clear that contrary to the tenets of individualism and sometimes regardless of legal requirements, in some regimes certain rights have been advanced or withheld on the basis of the possession of collective attributes like sex or race, regardless of the singular qualities of individuals. But in a curious inversion of this offensive practice, the stereotyping of individuals recently has achieved a certain political correctness when applied in 'appropriate' contexts, although this sometimes smacks of an Orwellian regard for the subtleties of 'Newspeak'. Thus in movies like *Pocahontas* and *The Patriot* the English are subject to 'acceptable stereotyping' as arch colonialists.

In George Orwell's book 1984, *the authorities systematically rewrote the language, giving new meanings to words, outlawing the use of others and establishing usage as either correct or incorrect, depending on the context and the climate of official opinion.*

THINK POINT

How does this idea strike you? Is it ever 'acceptable' to stereotype?

The second category of rights mentioned by Therborn is that of *rights to act*. Rights to act define the legitimate scope of actions, and include freedom of association, freedom of expression and voting rights. Some sense of the considerable variation in introducing measures which require at least a mathematical equality in the form of rights may be seen in Table 1.1.

Table 1.1 The introduction of universal franchise – selected countries

Country	Universal male suffrage	Universal adult suffrage
Belgium	1894	1948
Netherlands	1918	1922
France	1848	1946
Germany	1871	1919
Ireland	1918	1923
UK	1918	1928
Denmark	1849	1918
Norway	1900	1915
Switzerland	1848	1971

Source: Pierson (1991)

Other areas which fall under the rubric of rights to act are those dealing with discrimination and harassment, and the rights of workers to dispose of their labour freely and to enjoy rights relating to safety at work or job security. In the industrial economies of Western capitalism, these sort of rights have often conflicted with the rights of property-holders in the form of owners of industrial or financial capital to deploy their assets in ways likely to maximise profits. Where such conflicts have arisen, the state, in either judicial or bureaucratic guise, has usually intervened to mediate disputes between capital and labour, or with respect to the extension or limitation of the welfare state. The system of welfare states established in many parts of the world after 1945 was premised on the idea that it was the duty of the state to guard against and ameliorate market failures. In recent years it has become an article of faith for many governments that they must be sensitive to the constraints of global markets, even where this means limiting some forms of welfare provision and thus curtailing the rights of citizens.

The relationship between states and global markets is taken up in Chapter 15.

Individualism and collectivism

In his great study *Democracy in America* (1954) Alexis de Tocqueville noted that never had there been a country so committed to individual wants as opposed to collective needs as the United States. As we have noted, individual liberty is a highly esteemed American value, the stock-in-trade of election speeches by presidential hopefuls and those politicians with less lofty ambitions. For all this, over the years the emphasis upon individual rights has been qualified to accommodate the interests of certain collective groups such as ethnic minorities and women. The civil rights legislation enacted during the 1960s was interpreted first by federal government officials and then by the courts as endorsing the use of affirmative action and sometimes positive discrimination (special preferences or quotas in education and employment) for members of specifically defined disadvantaged groups – women, blacks, Hispanics and Native Americans. For the first time, and contrary to Tocqueville's dictum, American federal policy was defined in terms of rights and privileges for groups rather than individuals. This redefinition remains a source of important constitutional and political dispute in the USA and finds echoes in the politics of countries with quite different legal and cultural traditions.

Other forms of collectivism, particularly those associated with the expansion of the welfare states in Western Europe after the Second World War, sought to harness the use of public power to further social and economic freedoms, especially of those categories of people who are relatively powerless. Examples of this may be seen in Scandinavian legislation passed in the early 1980s, whereby parents are forbidden to smack their children, schools having been barred from administering corporal punishment in the years following the Second World War. State action to protect or enhance the rights of individuals (particularly children and wives) in societal groupings like the family also flowered under aggressively interventionist communist regimes in the Soviet Union and the German Democratic Republic (which today is part of a reunified Germany). It is of course a paradox that these same regimes systematically restricted the rights of citizens in other important respects, for example with regard to freedom of speech, movement and freedom of association.

THINK POINT

On what sort of grounds do you think the state/public authorities could intervene legitimately to protect individual interests?

Even in countries with a considerable distrust of government, and a public philosophy that societies ought to be judged on the basis of how well they do in making individuals happy – the United States is again the obvious example – individual freedoms, like the freedom to smoke in public spaces, to drive an automobile without a seat-belt, or to own some kinds of firearm, are proscribed in the name of the public interest, or of claiming to know what is in the best interests of individuals. Much intervention of this sort is justified on the grounds that the duty of government is not just to uphold the rights of the individual to *do* something, but to ensure that people in general are protected *from* unfettered individualism, where those freedoms may create passive smokers, victims of the playing of loud music in apartment blocks, abused children and citizens threatened by the 'right' of individuals to bear arms. The philosophical debates which underlie such practical and political questions are taken up again in Chapters 6 to 8.

For some libertarians and all anarchists, there are great dangers in governments assuming a moral responsibility for the physical and mental well-being of their citizens, to the point where explicit guidance (counselling) may be given on what to eat and drink, or how and with whom to make love. These

Anarchy is often used rather loosely as a synonym for disorder, but in fact it refers to the doctrine which counsels the absence of formal government.

sorts of objections turn on what should constitute the legitimate scope of government intervention and on the notion that a civil society made up of sovereign individuals, or of individuals who have entered freely into associations with each other, should be free from restrictions imposed by the state. The difficulties, both morally and with respect to the use of legal enforcement, lie in the interpretation of what is meant by undue constraint, and on where the balance between freedom *to* and freedom *from* should rest. In the UK in the case of *Brown versus Regina* in 1994, the House of Lords, acting in its capacity as a court of appeal, ruled that forms of sexual preference involving degrees of physical violence (sado-masochism) between consenting adults are illegal on the grounds that their actions infringed the Offences Against the Person Act of 1861. When the federal authorities in the United States laid siege to the compound of the religious sect the Branch Davidians in Waco, Texas in 1993, they justified their actions as necessary (1) to control the stockpiling of weapons said to be taking place there, and (2) to protect those members allegedly menaced by the actions of the cult's leader David Koresh and his apocalyptic visions. Opponents of intervention, however, saw the actions as a further example of the expansion of federal power and the willingness of government to intervene in the affairs of private individuals and organisations.

Follow this hyperlink to a speech made by Charlton Heston, well-known actor and President of the National Rifle Association of the USA, to the Yale University Union on 16 April 1999: <http://www.nrahq.org/ transcripts/yale.shtml>. His speech is both an attack on government action in the affairs of private citizens and on government's inaction in what he would see as a legitimate area of intervention.

From these observations we can see that the competing claims of individualism and different forms of collectivism (ranging from voluntary associations, informal organisations like families, larger social and cultural categories like social classes or ethnic groups, to the state itself) can lead to substantively different prescriptions about the nature and extent of government action. At the same time it is necessary to recognise that in many countries, strains of individualism and collectivism do coexist. This is not to deny that some societies are more individualistic or more collectivist than others, but just to note that we should beware of simple categories and stereotypes. Furthermore, when considering forms of collectivism, it is important to distinguish between those societies which place a great deal of stress upon communal identities and activities, or on the important social functions of voluntary associations of private individuals, and those which privilege the state as the regulator of all social activity and the arbiter of individual morality. Let us look at some of these distinctions more closely.

While Americans may take pride in being individualists, a belief in the virtues of collective action is also an established part of their culutural and political tradition. Some 60 per cent of Americans belong to one or more voluntary associations, though there is some evidence that the intensity of civic engagement is declining (Putnam 2001; and see Chapter 4 for an extended discussion of the relationships between social capital and political participation). Membership in voluntary associations covers a wide spectrum of American life and includes social clubs, fraternal and charitable bodies like the Shriners, the Buffalos and the Rotarians; organisations representing the professions like the American Bar Association; educational associations, for example parent–teacher associations (PTAs) and college fraternities and sororities. 'Economic' groups representing business, labour and agriculture, as well as 'cause' groups devoted to the promotion of a whole range of public interest issues, vie for the ear of decision-makers. In fact, one of the Founding Fathers of the American Republic, James Madison, wrote that groups of various sorts can be the product of 'the most frivolous and fanciful distinctions'.

In Chapter 4, the question of civic association is taken up again in relation to the argument that in the USA and in some other countries, there has been a marked decline in the numbers of individuals joining voluntary associations. For some observers, this trend, if real, is damaging to the quality of political participation and the health of democracy.

THINK POINT

- What about your own experience?
- How many groups are you a member of?
- What about your parents and friends?

By contrast, Japan is often spoken of as a society which is not very individualistic and in which there is a high degree of respect for the state. While it is true that the Japanese state plays a larger role in the life of its citizens than does the state in the USA, as the following extract makes clear, the Japanese are also joiners of private associations which make up that broad area of civil society between the family on the one hand and the state on the other.

> Like the United States, Japanese society supports a dense network of voluntary organisations. Many of these are what the Japanese call 'iemoto' groups, centred around a traditional art or craft like Kabuki theatre, flower arranging, or classical tea ceremony. These groups are hierarchical, like families, with strong vertical ties between masters and disciples, but they are not based on kinship and are entered into on a voluntary basis. Iemoto organisations . . . pervade Japanese society, extending far beyond the traditonal arts to encompass religious, political and professional organisations. . . .
>
> It is more accurate to say that the Japanese have a group-oriented rather than a state-oriented culture. While most Japanese respect the state, their primary emotional attachments – the loyalties that make them stay in the office until ten at night or miss weekends with their families – are to the private corporations, businesses or universities which employ them.
>
> (Fukuyama 1995: 54–5)

The robustness of civil societies populated by self-regarding individuals and by voluntary associations, and which are separate from and formally

See Chapter 11, where the role and power of special interest and other kinds of groups is examined.

ungoverned by the state, is often taken as a sign of the health of democratic systems. Although it is quite common to find the influence of (some kinds of) voluntary associations criticised as being too great, even undemocratic, support for thriving, pluralistic civil societies usually stresses the value of intermediate associations in constraining both the harsher side of individualism and the power of the state. For example, the famous German sociologist Max Weber wrote favourably that it was a 'characteristic . . . of the specifically American democracy that it did not constitute a formless sand heap of individuals, but rather a buzzing complex of strictly exclusive, yet voluntary associations'. One of the main effects of state socialism in countries modelled on the Soviet system was to damage the institutions and associations of civil society, from churches to newspapers and down to the family itself. The following extract, from a family history of three generations of Chinese women, and told by the youngest, gives some indication of the almost pathological fears or paranoia felt by leaders of the Chinese Communist Party during the period known as the 'Cultural Revolution' under Chairman Mao Zedong, which made them try to root out opposition and see potential threats to their security throughout the fabric of Chinese society:

Mao's Red Guards

Mao wanted the Red Guards (mostly young people, intensely loyal to Mao alone) to be his shock troops. He could see that most people were not responding to his repeated calls to attack the capitalist-roaders. . . . If he was to get the population to act, Mao would have to remove authority from the Party and establish absolute loyalty and obedience to himself alone. To achieve this he needed terror – an intense terror that would block all other considerations and crush all other fears. He saw boys and girls in their teens and early twenties as his ideal agents. They had been brought up in the fanatical personality cult of Mao and the militant doctrine of 'class struggle'. They were endowed with the qualities of youth – they were rebellious, fearless, eager to fight for a 'just' cause, thirsty for adventure and action. They were also irresponsible, ignorant and easy to manipulate – and prone to violence. Only they could give Mao the immense force that he needed to terrorize the whole society. . . . One slogan summed up the Red Guard's mission: 'We vow to launch a bloody war against anyone who dares to resist the Cultural Revolution, who dares to oppose Chairman Mao'. . . .

To arouse the young to mob violence, victims were necessary. The most conspicuous targets in my school were the teachers, some of whom had been victimised by work teams and school authorities in the last few months. Now the rebellious children set upon them. . . . In practically every school in China, teachers were abused and beaten, sometimes fatally. Some school children set up prisons in which teachers were tortured.

(Chan 1993: 375–6)

Of course this is a highly personal account of much wider social and political events and processes, but it does draw attention to some of the salient features of a political system and society that tried to eradicate social and cultural pluralism in the name of revolution. But it is not only in such determinedly singular or monistic regimes that there is a dearth of voluntary associations.

In southern Italy, Spain and many of the nations of Latin America the gap between the individual or the family unit of loyalty and the state was not, and to some extent is still not, bridged by a rich seam of private associations. The drive towards sociability which so marks countries like the USA, Britain and Japan is much less apparent, and has led some observers to suggest that such countries are less stable, perhaps less democratic, than those with many intermediate associations.

This is clearly a contentious argument and turns on the idea that individuals are either forced to confront the state more directly in the relative absence of organisations which mediate their demands, or else that they are not shielded from the full force of state power by a pluralistic civil society. Francis Fukuyama goes further, suggesting that in those societies with strong familial traditions – Latin Catholic societies, or the Chinese, where the family-oriented tenets of Confucian philosophy run deep – trust in people outside the family or in extended social relationships is low.

THINK POINT

Does this argument look rather like stereotyping?

Of course in all societies the reasons why individuals join voluntary associations are likely to be very complex. We have seen already that elegant but over-simplified rational choice arguments do not capture this complexity. Neither does the assumption which is usually attributed to **pluralist** accounts of group formation, that groups will form almost spontaneously because individuals share goals or values and wish to see these enhanced or protected. The question of why individuals engage in different forms of political participation is taken up in Chapter 4. Here we should just note that different individual needs are met through membership or other forms of support for such bodies, and that these embrace both self-interested and non-material or, as they are sometimes called, *expressive* desires, perhaps contributing to the emotional needs of individuals as well as to their material well-being.

Highly pluralistic political systems often reflect the richness of civil society and are also a means of defending it against what Harold Laski, the English socialist writer, called the power of the state – 'the one compulsory association'. But for some, pluralism is a defence not only against monism or **total-itarianism**, but also against the threats to sociability posed by unbridled individualism. Thus, much of the concern of early pluralist thought was to reject individualism since it encouraged the 'free-riding' syndrome of which we spoke earlier. The rejection of aggressive individualism is apparent too in recently fashionable ways of thinking about the organisation of societies and the place of individuals in them.

Pluralism The belief that there is, or else there should be, diversity. Political pluralism recognises and encourages variety in social, cultural and ideological forms and processes. Pluralist theories examine the influence of social groups in the making of public policy, where there may be competition among groups with different resources.

Totalitarianism The ideology that there is only one fundamental principle of social and political organisation to which everything else must be subordinated. In totalitarian systems control is exerted over all aspects of life.

COMMUNITARIANISM

See Chapter 4 for a fuller treatment of political trust in the context of changes in political participation.

Communitarian thought, which has become very fashionable since the late 1980s, due in part to the writing of sociologists like Amitai Etzioni in the United States and to its take-up by politicians seeking to offset the growing disenchantment with conventional politics and the alleged decay of social and political trust, falls somewhere between the poles of liberal individualism and statist collectivism.

For Communitarians like Richard Rorty (1992), the individual is firmly embedded in the cultural and social institutions of a society. The individual is socially situated and so is neither isolated nor selfish, and certainly not alienated from others. On the contrary, people are connected through patterns of friendship, communities of trust and reciprocity and networks of power. Just what Communitarians mean by the term 'community' is not always clear, but what seems to be implied is the primacy (both theoretical and practical) of group or associative identities, with their complex mix of rights and duties. After the unfettered free-market liberalism of the 1980s in both Britain and the United States, some leading politicians, notably Tony Blair, prime minister and leader of the Labour Party in Britain, have flirted with Communitarian thinking to signal a break with ideologies from the radical right and the older, 'unmodernised' left. In Italy, Silvio Berlusconi, leader of the political movement *Forza Italia*, has also expressed sympathy with the principles of Communitarian thinking. The downsides of this sometimes romanticised version of associative identities and local governance are the accompanying dangers of sectarianism, group-think, and the sort of 'we-feeling' which tips over into a strong distrust of outsiders. At this point euphemisms like 'ethnic cleansing' begin to look like acceptable items for a political agenda concerned to defend or promote group or local identities. A more benign form of communitarianism is found in the following example.

Document

The Kibbutz Philosophy of Communal Living

Kibbutz Shomrat is located in the North of Israel in the coastal area. There are 248 kibbutz members and candidates and about 100 children.

The kibbutz was the first kibbutz founded after the Declaration of Independence in 1948. Most of the founding members are Ha Shomer HaTzair members and Holocaust survivors from Hungary, Czecho Slovakia and Romania.

They made their way here through illegal immigration (Hapalah) and camps on Cyprus. The Vatikim – the founding members – were joined by the 'Mordechai Anelevitz' group from Argentina and Uruguay in the 1950s and Ha Shomer HaTzair groups from Argentina, the USA and Canada in the 1960s, as well as by some Israeli youth groups. Kibbutz is a unique way of life, ever changing, with the most democratic system that we know. Every decision about changes in our community is ultimately decided by the kibbutz in a one man/woman vote.

The kibbutzim are organized in kibbutz organizations and Shomrat belongs to the Kibbutz Ha'Artzi, politically affiliated with Meretz.

Nowadays the kibbutzim are going through many changes. One of the fundamental principles of the kibbutz ideology – one for all and all for one – seems to be outdated. More and more voices are heard in favor of differential wages, the children sleep in the parents' homes and we 'pay' for our food and other services that were 'free' before.

So how are decisions made in a situation of change?

There are many committees made up of voted-in kibbutz members, that prepare issues for decision making in their field before they come to a general vote, for example: education, health, and general management.

Many kibbutz members work as professionals in the city and their salary is paid to the kibbutz. Less attractive work in the kibbutz is done by hired workers from 'the outside'.

Shomrat celebrated its 50 year existence. There is still much work to be done to promise a good future for its inhabitants.

Beyond individualism and collectivism: the postmodern condition

For all that Communitarianism offers us a way of understanding the place of the cultural and the social in making the individual, it could be argued that it is just another side of the modernist tradition, albeit one that attempts to combine respect for the individual with older sentiments praising the value of collective identities. Set against both are a range of positions which have become known as postmodernism, to distinguish them from the tenets and claims of modernist (Enlightenment) thinking. Postmodernist ideas arose out of a great disenchantment with both the rationalist and collectivist arguments about the nature of the individual and of social life in general. Instead of assuming that identities are fixed, because human nature is like that – as in economic reasoning – or because social forces or cultural values impose rigid and unchanging identities on people – as members of a social class, as an ethnic group or the denizens of a local community – postmodernists like Lyotard (1984) argue that identity can be formed or reformed more or less at will, and around any sort of focus or stimulus. The point is that in a post-modern world there are no absolutes, and so identity formation becomes a matter of choice and circumstance. In a more radical version of pluralism, cultural and political differences are applauded.

THINK POINT

- Does this make sense to you?

- How easy would it be for you to take on new identities at will?

- Is changing your allegiance to a particular brand or style of dress of the same order as changing your political allegiance, or your sexual preference?

If this suggests a pluralism run riot, from a political standpoint its implications are enormous, although a fully fledged postmodern politics is hardly in evidence in any part of the world, least of all those parts just emerging from authoritarian rule. Postmodernist claims about the nature of the individual and the fluidity of social life do legitimate a blossoming of all sorts of political demands and positions which were previously suppressed in some countries, or less than central to the political and policy agenda in others. Areas like gender politics or the specific demands of people of colour are good examples, but more exotic forms of what some people call the politics of identity are prepared to make fatness a political issue, or offer levitation and tantric sex as a means of getting in touch with who you are.

In fact, some forms of ethnic identity or ultra-nationalism, in Bosnia, Kosovo, East Timor and Rwanda, seem to intimate a return to pre-modern conflicts and identities, rather than the opposite. It is also something of an irony that those who wish to undo modernist politics often couch their demands and justifications for them in the language of rights which is the legacy of liberalism and of the Enlightenment they so despise. Strands of feminist thinking have been particularly critical of the moral and intellectual bankruptcy of modernist thought, preferring to see notions of individualism, and even community, as part of a male-centred realm of discourse, only masquerading as universal traits and which left women marginalised, or unequal in terms of status and of power.

THINK POINT

What would you see as the advantages and disadvantages of a postmodern politics of difference?

There is now a great profusion of organisations claiming to represent or act on behalf of all sorts of interests and identities. Some of them, perhaps those advocating gender equality, have actually moved from the margins of political debate closer to the centre in some countries of the West. On the other hand, the greater public awareness of racial and gender inequalities may have served only to glamorise or entrench their status as victims, rather than providing them with a firm basis and the necessary resources to affect mainstream politics.

Individuals and the capacity for meaningful political action

As individuals and as social beings we live in an increasingly complex and interconnected world. This is not just because government is big, or because of vast business corporations, it is also because we have to come to terms with flows of information, knowledge and power which are global rather than local. People have to confront not just local or national rules about the appropriate way to organise their life, but those originating in institutions like the European Union, the World Trade Organisation and various transnational business corporations, such as Time-Warner and America On Line (AOL).

When individual citizens express their grievances about litter on the streets, noise from a local factory, or basing national defence on nuclear weapons, we

For more on the processes of globalisation, see Chapter 15.

might say that their chances of success or just of making a decent fist of it vary with the following sorts of factors:

- The extent to which expressions of dissent or difference are allowed or encouraged, both culturally and in law. In some regimes dissent of any kind to the claim that the party, the Führer or the absolute monarch fully represents or embodies the will and interests of the people would be circumscribed or prevented. But even the most draconian action on the part of rulers seldom eradicates opposition completely, although quite often it is driven underground, to surface through dissident magazines and songs, or in forms of dress. Sometimes it comes into the open only through the activities of transnational protest groups and social movements which keep the cause alive through the world's media and via the Internet.

- The extent to which apparently 'open' systems are really accessible to ordinary citizens. It is one thing to believe that strategically endowed actors like cabinet ministers or four-star generals, or even members of an internationally famous rock band, can influence the course of events, and quite another to extend this reasoning to John and Jane Doe. All political systems and decision-making processes include some kinds of demands and issues and exclude others. The key questions are: On what basis does inclusion and exclusion take place? Are some people or groups systematically favoured or disadvantaged? We take up these questions more fully in Chapters 4, 11 and 13, where both political participation and the policy processes are examined.

- The sorts of resources available to the individual. It is likely that the relevance or use of a resource – money, status, expertise, communication skills and access to the media of communication – will vary from system to system and probably from issue to issue (although this is a point hotly contested in discussions about the distribution and exercise of power). There is also the question of whether the possession of some resources, for example mastery of a technical skill, might be offset by the fact that an individual is evaluated solely on the basis of membership of a collectivity like an ethnic group or being female. The ease and effectiveness with which particular resources can be brought to bear may be affected by the weight of cultural norms and institutionalised practices which either facilitate or hinder individual action.

For a detailed examination of the variety of barriers to the participation of women in parliaments, follow up this hyperlink: <http://www.idea.int/women/parl/toc.htm>.

The matter of resources is a very complex one. In trying to understand whether an individual or a group has been, or can be, an effective actor, we should not assume that all outcomes are dependent on the mobilisation of effective resources, any more than we should believe that all decisions made by individuals are rational. An apparent lack of resources may not leave an individual without influence and certainly not without value. Where there is a generalised expectation that individuals – ordinary people – will or ought to behave as social critics, even their most limited and infrequent intervention – say through the act of voting – will have symbolic worth, both for each individual and for the political universe of which he or she is a part. But the chances of individuals affecting outcomes has to be very limited, unless we are talking about matters which involve mainly private and local exchanges, and negotiations bearing on their own lives as mothers, fathers, students or members of the local volley-ball team. When intervention has to be made with respect to issues that are not local but international or transnational, the opportunities for effective action may be more limited. However, this does not mean that individuals are simply moulded by bigger forces or unable to act except in parochial matters. For one thing, they may join groups which are not only better endowed with resources, but may be dedicated to the piece-meal or wholesale transformation of society. Amidst all the evidence to the contrary, affirmations of individuality are not hard to find. Occasionally politicians resign on matters of principle, conscientious objectors refuse to enlist in the armed forces of a country and workers flout the 'dress codes' now much in evidence as part of the expression of corporate cultures. 'Whistle-blowers' risk jobs, status and sometimes much worse to bring information about the conduct of businesses, charities and government departments and agencies to the attention of the wider public. These examples and others you may think of are not without moral overtones, but for the purposes of this chapter they are best understood as demonstrations of the symbolic and substantive aspects of individuality. In the rest of this book some of these issues and themes will be revisited to inform topics as various as feminism and globalisation.

Conclusion

The message to take from this opening chapter is that the study of politics cannot dispense with the concept of the individual, but that we often need to see her acting in the context of wider social, political and cultural structures, which both enable and constrain action. In other words, the study of political life requires a multidimensional approach which is sensitive to the place of the individual in political life and aware of the importance of larger social, cultural and political structures. Different theoretical traditions privilege different units and levels of analysis, in the same way that different political and cultural traditions emphasise either individuality or collectivism of one sort or another. In Chapter 2 we examine the ways in which individuals learn about politics and acquire political identities.

Chapter summary

☐ The individual is at the centre of political and social life, but methodological individualism is only one of the ways to approach the study of politics.

☐ There are also a variety of intellectual traditions on how to conceptualise and theorise the individual and individualism.

☐ In real-life politics, the importance of the individual varies across different types of political systems.

☐ This variation is observable in the rights accorded to individuals and in the scope they have for action in pursuit of personal goals or preferences.

☐ In some political systems the status of the individual is downplayed or sacrificed to the good of the whole, whether this is the nation, the state or some concept such as 'the people'.

☐ Sometimes these restrictions are imposed and draconian, but some are the product of political philosophies that seek to marry individualism and collectivism.

☐ Even in systems that applaud individualism, freedom of action is usually tempered in the interests of fairness, equality of opportunity or social harmony.

☐ The result is that the power of individuals and their capacity for political action show great variation across political systems.

Key texts

Barry, B. (1970) *Sociologists, Economists and Democracy*, London: Collier-Macmillan.

Downs, A. (1956) *An Economic Theory of Democracy*, New York: Harper and Row.

Fukuyama, F. (1992) *The End of History and the Last Man*, London: Hamish Hamilton.

Giddens, A. (1993) *New Rules of Sociological Method* (2nd edn), Cambridge: Polity Press.

Parsons, T. (1967) *Sociological Theory and Modern Society*, New York: Free Press.

Further reading

Bellah, R. M. *et al.* (1985) *Habits of the Heart*, Berkeley, CA: University of California Press. Elegaic account of the values of community and smallness applied to American society.

Hirschman, A. O. (1970) *Exit, Voice and Loyalty*, Cambridge, MA: Harvard University Press. The application of rational choice theory to a variety of social situations. It is quite fun to use the concepts to examine your own choices and what affects them.

Peake, M. (1972) *Titus Groan*, Harmondsworth: Penguin. This, the first volume of Peake's gothic masterpiece, tells the story of the boyhood of Titus Groan, heir to Gormenghast and to its ageless, stifling traditions which inhibit initiative and change.

Pirsig, R. M. (1974) *Zen and the Art of Motorcycle Maintenance*, New York: Bodley Head. Pirsig's cult classic of the 1970s is a marvellous compression of some of the main debates in Western philosophy, including the place of the individual, as well as a sort of intellectual 'Easy Rider.'

Wolfe, T. (1970) *The Electric Kool-Aid Acid Test*, London: Fontana. Examines the tensions between rampant individualism and the Communitarian impulses of the early hippy drug culture in California in the 1960s.

You can access the relevant Internet sites given in this chapter by entering the URLs (Unique Resource Locators) listed into the 'open location' box in your computer. To do this you will need access to the Internet through an Internet service provider or through your university, college or school. Once entered you can store the addresses as 'bookmarks' for quick access.

Political Socialisation

Ben Rosamond

▌ Introduction

How do people learn about politics? What are the origins of their political views? At first sight these questions might seem quite banal. In response one might say that we learn about the political world from a fairly predictable range of sources; the media (newspapers, television, radio) spring to mind. Then there are those (the readers of this book perhaps) who learn about politics in a relatively formal way. Others learn about politics through being participants in the political process. Presumably a certain amount of political knowledge is the initial stimulus for political action, but active participation in pressure groups and political parties provides opportunities for the deepening of political knowledge. The same may be true for individuals whose careers take them into public office, as representatives or bureaucrats perhaps. Such people develop an understanding of how politics operates that the ordinary citizen cannot hope to match.

However, like most issues in political science, the question of how people learn about politics is far from simple. After all, what is political knowledge? Is it simply a matter of knowing about the main institutions of government in a country, along with having an idea of the platforms of the principal political parties and a sense of what the main political issues of the day might be? Or does it concern a more subtle set of cognitions about authority and human relations which do not apply exclusively to the world of formal political activity? Might it be that 'what we know' about politics is intimately related to 'what we know' about our families or our working lives and so on? In other words, the nature of what people learn about politics and what constitutes knowledge about politics is a matter of debate.

So to return to our original question: to ask how people learn about politics presupposes that we agree about the matter of politics. Anyone who has read the Introduction to this volume will realise that this is a far from easy question. In addition, the mechanisms through which political knowledge is acquired are also much disputed. There are those who see families as the main seedbed of political views; others point to education, while others still would argue that the process of learning about politics is influenced decisively by the various experiences that life may bring. Going deeper still, there is the question of the psychology of political learning: the mental processes which are involved in conveying and receiving political information.

Finally, there is the question of *when* people learn about politics. The preceding discussion should give a clue to the main lines of the debate. In essence, there is an argument about the importance of pre-adult experiences in fixing political views versus the impact wrought by changes in circumstance throughout life.

This chapter seeks to unpack these questions by reflecting upon the ways in which political scientists have sought to come to terms with the question of the acquisition of political knowledge and political views. Beginning the substantive content of the book with a chapter on political learning is a deliberate decision. After all, we could have started with a discussion of political institutions or with an analysis of the main strands in political thought over the centuries. To start with the issue of learning about politics, or **political socialisation**, gives you a chance to reflect upon your own socialisation, your own political views and your own experience of politics. Moreover, it may also help to reinforce the points made in the Introduction about how political phenomena do not necessarily confine themselves to the world of governments, parliaments and political parties.

Political socialisation The process, or the set of processes, through which people learn about politics and acquire political values. There is much dispute about which processes are significant and about when in the life cycle the most important socialisation takes place.

Political socialisation

Political socialisation is the term applied by political scientists to embrace the debates outlined in the opening paragraphs of this chapter. Political socialisation is an important concept because people are not born with an innate knowledge of politics. We do not begin our lives with an in-built sense of political tradition. Neither our role in the political life of our society nor our particular political views are genetically pre-programmed. Thus, as Michael Rush puts it:

> Political socialisation may be defined as the process by which individuals in a given society become acquainted with the political system and which to a certain degree determines their perceptions and their reactions to political phenomena.
>
> (Rush 1992: 92)

Three questions emerge from this basic definition:

1 What is the purpose of political socialisation?
2 What can be said about the processes by which individuals become acquainted with politics?
3 What can be said about the implied connection between socialisation, on the one hand, and the formulation of political views and types of political behaviour, on the other?

These three questions form the guiding thread of this chapter and, to some extent, of the two chapters that follow.

THINK POINT

What about you?

▨ A very good place to start is with your own experience of political socialisation.

▨ Pause for a few moments to consider your political views, your level of political activism and your general level of knowledge about the political process of your country. We will call this your 'political profile'.

▨ Now consider the acquisition of that political profile. Why is it that you think about politics in the way that you do? What do you think motivates you to act politically? ('Acting politically' may mean that you are an aloof or apathetic bystander as well as a fully fledged activist.)

▨ How and why did you come to know so much (or so little) about the political process?

What is political socialisation for?

This question cuts to the heart of political science. It might be rephrased as: 'Why do people have to be political?' Aristotle (384–322 BC) argued in *The Politics* that 'man is by nature a political animal' (Aristotle 1985: 3). By this, Aristotle meant that people, by virtue of their natural propensity to congregate, need to be part of a political community in order to flourish as human beings. It follows that since humans are political in the most basic sense of that term, they need to acquire political skills to take part in the most complete expression of human community – the state. Projecting from Aristotle's insight, the first argument would be that political socialisation is required because it is an essential component of being a person. The thinking of Aristotle is echoed in those influential strands of recent democratic thought which argue that a fully functioning democratic polity requires a politically literate citizenry. Individual self-development is then best served by the active pursuit of and engagement with political knowledge.

Such reasoning tends to work outwards from the citizen. Alternatively, we might turn the argument on its head and suggest that any regime requires mass political socialisation into certain regime-friendly norms if it is to survive. From this vantage point, socialisation becomes (arguably) a more sinister process

Aristotle (384–322 BC) is often thought of as the first political scientist. Even by the philosophical standards of ancient Greece, Aristotle was a remarkable polymath. Twenty-two of his works survive covering subjects as apparently diverse as physics, astronomy, literary criticism, ethics and biology. Aristotle's work has been a major influence on subsequent Western (and Islamic) thinking. His *Politics* is typical of this influence in that it reflects Aristotle's concern for classification, his belief in the power of rationality, his preference for pragmatism and his reluctance to prescribe universal truths. No constitution could be universally ideal. Rather, constitutions should be tailored to fit the society in question. *Politics* contains significant reflection on the conditions for political stability and the comparative analysis of constitutions.

Aristotle

where individuals are moulded into particular roles whose primary function is to serve the system. Of course, the degree to which this process is sinister or oppressive will be related largely to the nature of the regime. Put another way, if we opt to understand political socialisation as serving the functional needs of the regime, then our perception of the regime becomes all-important. Let us take the example of the regime that characterises much of the industrialised and post-industrial Western world. We will call it capitalist liberal democracy. The extracts below give two alternative accounts of the nature of the regime in such systems. These are followed by respective deductions about the purpose of political socialisation.

VERSION 1

The system

Liberal democracy is a system that maximises the freedom of individuals in society. The state is receptive to the demands made upon it by the diversity of groups within society and public policy is largely a synthesis of those demands. In a system of democratic governance, ultimate authority rests with individuals. Moreover, the state does not intervene excessively in civil society, and thus enables individuals to go about their business as they please within the rule of law.

Political socialisation

This is the mechanism by which people acquire the values, norms and habits that enable them to maximise their individual liberty within a system of pluralist liberal democracy. Socialisation is about (1) learning to be an individual, and (2) acquiring the political knowledge and habits which might optimise that individuality through participation in the liberal democratic polity.

VERSION 2

The system

Liberal democracy is the political system that underpins exploitative capitalist relations of production. This supports the concentration of power and wealth in the hands of a privileged ruling group or elite and results in the economic exploitation of the vast majority of the population. Liberal notions of freedom are an ideological mask for these deep, systemic inequalities.

Political socialisation

This is a mechanism of control which largely indoctrinates the vast majority of the population into belief systems and acceptable forms of behaviour which support (or at least do not threaten) the interest of the ruling groups. This involves the legitimation of inequality and the dispersion throughout society of the view that the current regime is somehow natural or irreplaceable. Socialisation diverts oppressed groups from their real interests by teaching human beings that they are atomised individuals and by masking the inequalities of the system as a whole.

These are two polar positions that deliberately caricature rather complex arguments, but the crucial point for our analysis is that perspective is everything. If we think of political socialisation in terms of Version 1, it is quite easy to reconcile the 'individual-up' view with the idea that regimes require socialisation to function properly. Version 2, on the other hand, provides a strong basis for the view that political socialisation usually works against the 'real' interests of people. Here socialisation is about the reinforcement of power rather than the empowerment of the individual. Either way, it would appear to be true that socialisation is necessary because it provides the social glue that binds the citizen to her or his political system. Regimes of any kind do not last for long without political support. Political support relies upon people recognising the validity of their political arrangements. As one writer puts it, '[p]residents are not respected, laws are not obeyed, taxes are not paid, political stability does not prevail – unless people believe' (Jaros 1973: 7).

So far we have been thinking of the relationship between socialisation and ongoing or long-standing regimes. However, we also need to pay attention to the role political socialisation may play in the transformation of political systems. In such situations incoming political elites are confronted with the difficulty of 'educating' their population about the ways of the new regime. The problem, of course, is that socialisation into a new political system requires the 'unlearning' of old political values, traditions and habits. Sometimes this process of re-education is enforced through brutal indoctrination, as in the case of the Khmer Rouge regime of Pol Pot in Cambodia in the 1970s.

Pol Pot

Pol Pot (1925–98) was notorious as leader of the genocidal Khmer Rouge regime that ruled Cambodia between 1975 and 1979. Pol Pot expounded a particularly reactionary and xenophobic variant of Maoism that rejected modern urban living while championing the virtues of agrarian communism. Progress towards this end was brutal, with an estimated two million Cambodians losing their lives as forced evacuations from Cambodia's cities were accompanied by the violent suppression of dissent. Indoctrination was central to Pol Pot's project. The Khmer Rouge planned to achieve their utopia through a four-year plan, with the first year dubbed 'year zero'. Religion was disallowed. Citizens were forced to dress identically. Intellectuals, professionals and officials were tortured and killed. Prisoners of the regime – often destined for violent death – were subjected to rudimentary brainwashing techniques. The Khmer Rouge government fell in 1979 following a Vietnamese invasion. Pol Pot was never prosecuted for his crimes and died in obscure exile in Thailand, still the leading figure of a hardline Khmer Rouge faction.

More often than not, new habits, practices and values emerge in the wake of major ruptures to political life such as wars or revolutions. The following extract offers a particularly newsworthy example: the development of a new constitutional order for post-Taliban Afghanistan. Notice, in particular, the emerging debate over the issue of women's rights:

Document

Few Women on the Road to Democracy

Suzanne Goldenberg in Heart
Guardian, 26 January 2002

The highly delicate project of installing a broad-based and representative government in Afghanistan moved a step forward yesterday with the naming of a commission to select the country's decision makers. The 21 people announced by the interim leader, Hamid Karzai, are charged with summoning a loya jirga, or grand council of tribal elders, who in turn will decide on the transitional government to rule Afghanistan for 18 months from next June.

Their choices will be intensely scrutinised as the commission seeks to balance competing ethnic, clan and regional interests against an unfamiliar imperative for Afghanistan: representation for women. However, only two of the commission's representatives are women – a statistic that will cause dismay among activists and western observers, but is already more than some traditional Afghan leaders can stomach. For weeks, United Nations officials had sifted the list, seeking to balance rival factions, and to ensure the appearance of independence for the commission.

They completed their monumental task of whittling down a list of nearly 400 potential candidates to 21 a week ago, but UN officials said the announcement was timed to coincide with the visit to Kabul yesterday of the UN secretary general, Kofi Annan. 'I know not everybody will be entirely happy with the list, but it is a good list,' Mr Annan said. 'Let's support them and work with them.'

The work of the commission is crucial in ensuring that the loya jirga is seen by ordinary Afghans, as well as by warlords and tribal leaders, as legitimate. Its announcement is also expected to sharpen the rivalries between various Afghan groups, who have so far held back from directly challenging Mr Karzai, as they see his six-month administration as a passing phase. However, the 18-month transitional government offers far greater takings, and different Afghan factions have begun to compete for a place on the loya jirga. Mr Karzai – who is expected to seek a seat in the new government – seemed acutely aware of this as he read out the list of 21 names. He emphasised that the list was drawn up by the UN, and said he knew only four of the appointees.

'This shows this is a really nice commission, a real impartial commission and I hope that they, together with the UN, will be successful in their work and give Afghanistan a good, representative, fair loya jirga,' he said.

The commission is headed by Ismael Qasimyar, an Afghan expert on law and the constitution. One of his two deputies is a woman: Mahboba Hoqoqmal, a lecturer in political science.

Their mission is fraught as various Afghan factions vie for power.

A number of warlords have transformed themselves into politicians, and in Pakistan former Taliban leaders have formed a political party in the hope of taking part in the political process.

Afghanistan's women's rights activists have camped out in Kabul for weeks pressing their demand that the next government provide constitutional safeguards for equal rights.

UN officials admit that Mr Karzai's government is heavily weighted in favour of ethnic Tajiks from the Panjshir valley, followers of the assassinated warrior, Ahmed Shah Massoud, who control the foreign, defence and interior ministries.

The transitional government, in sharp contrast, must give greater power to Pashtuns, who are the largest ethnic group in Afghanistan.

Clearly, the installation of a new government in Afghanistan is predicated on the view that various voices need to be represented. But as soon as the interim government was established by the Bonn Agreement of 5 December 2001, it was clear that old patterns of politics would not simply fade away. For example, it was reported that conservative forces were still contemplating the retention of stoning and amputation as punishments for certain categories of crime, in spite of expectations that international human rights standards would be incorporated into the new Afghan legal system (*ABC News Online*, Australia, 30 December 2001, <http://abc.net.au/news/newsitems/s449313.htm>).

We may not be born with a ready-made set of orientations towards things political, but any shift in patterns of socialisation is likely to encounter the legacy of old patterns.

This dilemma has been particularly prevalent in post-communist Central and Eastern Europe. Communism (or state socialism) provided a distinctive mode of political organisation in which a single party (the Communist Party) ruled without any permissible opposition. Most political activity and virtually all significant career paths were directed through the party hierarchy. Social, political and economic life tended to be directed centrally by the state. It is also worth remembering that communism was a model of politics that had been more or less imposed upon the countries of Central and Eastern Europe after 1945. As many writers on the left were eager to point out, the communism which dominated the eastern half of the European continent for forty years was a Soviet-style communism that on the whole bore little resemblance to indigenous varieties of socialism and social democracy in those countries.

The dramatic events of 1989 and after resulted in the astonishingly rapid collapse of communist regimes. In the euphoria which followed there was much talk of a transition to both liberal democratic polities and market-based capitalist economies. This was even dubbed by one writer, the American foreign policy analyst Francis Fukuyama (1992), as the 'end of history' because of what he saw as the inevitability of the spread of Western liberal democratic market values. But if a transition was to take place, communism would have to be 'unlearned' and replaced by the values, norms, information and skills that might be necessary in the post-communist environment. This fact was not lost on policy-makers within the ex-communist countries, and there was no shortage of outside agencies willing to provide assistance and aid to facilitate the so-called transition. To take one of many examples, the European Commission's aid package PHARE (Poland and Hungary Assistance for Restructuring the Economy, later expanded to several other countries in the region), which began in 1989, was devised with the explicit aim of transferring knowledge and skills. As the Commission's literature put it, the package was designed to bring about 'fundamental changes in attitudes, values and behaviour, as well as the means to acquire specific occupational and management skills' (cited in Axford and Booth 1995: 120). Another example is supplied by the Polish Center for Citizenship Education, itself part of an international network of organisations concerned with 'civic education'.

Center for Citizenship Education

Democracy in Poland, as elsewhere, will not succeed without responsible and active citizens, citizens who recognize their rights and freedoms, trust democratic institutions and participate in the life of their communities. Unfortunately, the process of creating a civil society faces several obstacles. For instance: disenchantment with the imperfect institutions and procedures of a young democracy, nostalgia for the control and social welfare of the former state, pauperization and the exclusion of entire groups of people, including many of the younger generation. We believe that active citizenry forms the foundation for democracy and that education plays a critical role in this process.

The Center for Citizenship Education (CCE) aims to support schools and local governments in promoting civic attitudes and democratic values among Polish youth. We focus our attention on teaching the practical skills necessary in a democratic state and civil society. We provide practical knowledge that is closely connected with real life in the school and local community.

(<http://www.ceo.org.pl/english.htm>)

So can individuals, be they managers, workers, civil servants or whatever, be educated in the ways of the West? Can they be taught not only how to restructure their economies along market-capitalist lines and how to build the institutions of liberal democratic political systems, but also how to acquire the value sets which underpin them? There are, of course, plenty of debates about the propriety or otherwise of Western organisations offering a model of modernisation to post-communist countries. Our task, however, is to focus on the idea of knowledge- and value-transfer.

Some of the research that has been conducted by scholars from a variety of disciplines does seem to suggest that the modernising perspective of aid, assistance and training packages from the West to Eastern Europe is fundamentally naive. Most obviously, the legacy of the communist period is evident. The communist experience had generated certain patterns of behaviour and expectations among mass populations which, it is argued, have been involved in the transformation process in quite complex ways. Poland provides a good example. The sociologist Zygmunt Bauman has cautioned against the assumption that the breakdown of communism arose simply because of a mass disillusionment with the system combined with a widespread desire for its replacement by capitalist liberal democracy. Bauman notes:

at the height of popular disaffection in Poland, during the heyday of Solidarity [an independent trade union movement] and the years of its legal suppression, research after research found that a large (and growing!) majority of the population wanted the state to deliver more of its, specifically communist, promise.

(Bauman 1994: 20)

In other words, opinion surveys were showing that Poles had not straightforwardly exchanged their preference for a centralised state-administered regime for an alternative Western-style model founded upon notions of individual responsibility. Thus, if we accept that communist regimes did not necessarily fall because of a desire to replace them with something 'better', it follows that communist attitudinal patterns were not automatically purged by the 'revolutions' of 1989 and after. Other surveys of opinion show that Poles tend to display apparently inconsistent beliefs about economic restructuring. So, for instance, declining support for the privatisation of state-owned enterprises combines with the view that privatisation is proceeding at too slow a pace (Kolarska-Bobinska 1994). The point is that what we might call incoming sets of ideas (things like private enterprise, private property, individualism and democracy) are not straightforwardly absorbed. Their interaction with previously learned sets of values will transform them and displace their meanings. Indeed, as Eva Hoffman points out, it is important to understand not only the legacy of communism:

> Eastern Europe today is haunted by its various pasts, pursued equally by its memories, its amnesias, and its wilful deletions. There is the immensely complex legacy of the communist era, of course, but also the palpable presence of earlier periods, whose ghosts were supposedly slain by communism.
>
> (Hoffman 1994: xv)

We might even speculate that the experience of being socialised into new patterns of behaviour and alternative values is not new to the people of countries like Poland. The historical experience of having external models recurrently imposed from outside is likely to generate a sense of cynicism about the re-socialisation process itself.

This brief discussion about post-communist Eastern Europe ought to act as a warning against jumping to premature conclusions in political science. Broad generalisations about the place of socialisation and value-transfer in this context cannot hope to do justice to the complexity and nuance of the situation. What is evident is the dissonance between intention and outcomes. It is true that there are those who would seek to re-socialise populations and key groups in such countries with the intention of producing market economies and liberal democratic polities, but in such situations *prior* patterns of socialisation would appear to intervene in unpredictable ways.

The processes of political socialisation

So far, we have established that socialisation is likely to be an important component of regime stability and that it is something which cannot be administered with the expectation of predictable consequences. The task now is to begin to address the 'when' and 'how' questions raised in the introduction to this chapter.

When?

Key text: D. Kavanagh (1983) *Political Science and Political Behaviour*, London: Unwin Hyman.

The 'when' question has been a matter of lively debate in the literature on political socialisation. Dennis Kavanagh labels the two sides of the debate the *primacy* and *recency* schools. The titles are suggestive of the emphasis given to the crucial period of political socialisation. Adherents of the primacy school emphasise the importance of childhood (and early childhood in particular), whereas analysts from the recency perspective point to the importance of the ongoing socialisation and re-socialisation processes that occur throughout life. However, it is important to remember that this is more than simply a debate about when political learning takes place. It is sometimes forgotten that the primacy and recency schools are based upon very different assumptions and thus represent thoroughly different ways of thinking about the world in general and human learning in particular.

Primacy theory draws upon a branch of psychology that places emphasis upon the centrality of the early years to individual development. The key concept of the 'critical period' becomes useful here. The best-known example of the critical period emerged from studies of species of duck. These revealed that the birds would not develop 'normally' unless certain sorts of information were acquired within a few hours of hatching. In human terms, the argument would be that the brain is best equipped for the receipt of certain sorts of information at certain critical (or 'sensitive') periods in early childhood. Studies of language acquisition reveal that it is extremely difficult for a person to learn basic linguistic skills in the period beyond childhood. This is believed to be because children are physiologically and psychologically ready to respond to external stimuli in ways that lead them to obtain the knowledge and skills associated with language. So individuals are likely to be socialised to certain sorts of key political information in a critical period in early childhood, probably in the environment provided by immediate family and guardians. Obviously infants and young children will not have the mental equipment to develop fully formulated opinions on the pressing political issues of the day; neither will they arrive at sophisticated notions of voting preference. The argument of primacy theorists is that the sorts of values which are embedded in the early stages of childhood 'kick in' during later life as the individual becomes acquainted with the public world of politics.

In contrast, *recency* approaches to political socialisation are built around the view that political learning is an ongoing process related to changing experiences throughout the life cycle. This position draws on psychological studies of identity formation which suggest that self-definition and self-understanding are subject to change. In particular, there is a sense in which the development of a 'mature' identity involves the rejection of earlier influences. In terms of political learning, the argument appears to be that the results of socialisation are never fully embedded, that changing circumstances can produce crises of political identity and re-socialisation into new habits, norms and beliefs.

THINK POINT

Think about your own experience of politics.

■ Which of the two frameworks outlined above, 'primacy' or 'recency', seems best placed to explain your political socialisation?

Key texts: H. Hyman (1959) *Political Socialization: A Study in the Psychology of Political Behaviour*, New York: Free Press. D. Easton and J. Dennis (1969) *Children and the Political System: Origins of Political Legitimacy*, New York: McGraw-Hill.

Both positions have been supported by empirical research. The first classic study in this area was Herbert Hyman's *Political Socialization* (Hyman 1959). Hyman's data appeared to support the claim that children in the United States tended to acquire the political preferences of their parents. This could be taken as evidence of the transmission of political values in childhood. In their research reported in *Children and the Political System* David Easton and Jack Dennis (1969) studied the acquisition of political values in childhood. They concluded that childhood political socialisation occurred as a four-stage process in which children learned about authority. In the first stage children would recognise that certain individuals were somehow endowed with authority. So, a parent would be able to stipulate bedtime or a police officer would be able to arrest miscreants. Second, children would realise that authority has both public and private faces. At this stage it would become apparent that the type of authority exercised by the parent is qualitatively different from that of the police officer. In the third stage children would recognise that authority can be embedded in institutions such as governments, parliaments and courts. The final and most sophisticated stage would occur at the point when children understood that institutions have an existence that is separate from the individuals who work within them.

The third and fourth stages in the Easton and Dennis model constitute recognition of what is commonly understood to be the political world: the domain of authoritative institutions. What is interesting is that Easton and Dennis understand the process of learning about politics as beginning prior to a formal understanding of politicians, parties, parliaments and so on. From this viewpoint it is not necessary to be able to understand oneself in relation to 'political' objects in order to be socialised politically. Moreover, what is learned early matters:

> What enters the mind first remains there to provide lenses and categories for perceiving and sorting later perceptions. Furthermore, early learning occurs during the period of plasticity and openness: the assumptions acquired in childhood frequently appear to be absorbed in an un-questioned fashion. Such assumptions can become inarticulate major premises which then exercise a background effect on thought and overt behaviour precisely because they are not made sufficiently conscious to become open to challenge.
>
> (Greenstein *et al.* 1970, cited in Kavanagh 1983: 45)

Support for the recency school is frequently found in accounts of the ways in which individuals adapt to new (political) environments. For example, in the UK politicians elected to Parliament frequently speak of the club-like atmosphere of the House of Commons, which imposes particular and peculiar rules and practices upon new members. Effective political behaviour in such an environment is unlikely to be accomplished without a thorough learning of these quirks of procedure. The following extract gives an idea of some of these customs:

Where Members sit and speak; the form and style of debate

By convention, Ministers sit on the front bench on the right-hand of the Speaker: the Chief Whip usually sits in this row immediately next to the gangway. Elder statesman and former Prime Ministers have often sat on the first front bench seat beyond the gangway. Parliamentary Private Secretaries usually sit in the row behind their minister. Official Opposition spokesmen use the front bench to the Speaker's left. Minority parties sit on the benches (often the front two) below the gangway on the left, though a minority party that identifies with the Government may sit on the right-hand side. There is nothing sacrosanct about these places, and on sundry occasions, when a Member has deliberately chosen to occupy a place on the front bench or on the opposite side of the House from normal, there is no redress for such action. Indeed, the latter may happen when a large Government majority means there are too few places for its supporters on its own side. 'Crossing the floor', which has come to mean permanently changing party, is possible but naturally very uncommon. If a Member leaves one opposition party to join another, he or she may well not *literally* cross the floor, but would sit with their new party when they next entered the Chamber. A few Members (for instance John Horam, Reg Prentice and Alan Howarth) have served as ministers in governments of both major parties.

Members may speak only from where they were called, which must be *within the House*: that is, in front of the Chair, and not beyond the Bar (the white line across the width of the Chamber). They may not speak from the floor of the House between the red lines (traditionally supposed to be two sword-lengths apart). They may speak from the side-galleries, but due to the lack of microphones there is a strong disincentive from doing so. Also, the Speaker will not call a Member in the Gallery if there is room downstairs. They must stand whilst speaking, but a disabled or incapacitated Member is naturally allowed to address the House seated.

The style of debate in the House has traditionally been one of cut-and-thrust; listening to other Members' speeches and intervening in them in spontaneous reaction to opponents' views. It is thus very different from the debating style in use in some overseas legislatures, where reading of set-piece speeches from a podium or from individual desks is much more often the norm. This style of debate can make the Commons Chamber a live, rather noisy place, with robustly expressed opinion, many interventions, expressions of approval or disapproval, and sometimes of repartee and banter.

There is, of course, a fine line to be drawn between vigorous debate and forthright expression of views, and the deliberate attempt to intimidate an opponent. Members have the right, when speaking, to be heard without unendurable background noise (deliberate or accidental), and the Chair will call for order if it appears there is an attempt to drown out a Member or, for instance, when a number of Members are leaving the Chamber, or conversing

continued

continued

loudly. The Speaker also has the right to inform a Member who has failed to observe the courtesies of debate that he or she need not expect to get priority in being called to speak. But successive Speakers have taken care not to bridle the traditional vigour and forthrightness of the expression of opinion in the House, for the style of the House of Commons has never thrived on excessive politeness and restraint. The profound deference towards Ministers and Prime Ministers apparent in some overseas parliaments is generally lacking in the Commons.

To maintain the spontaneity of debate, reading a prepared speech is not allowed. Not every Member, however, is a good extempore speaker, so copious notes are allowed. Notes are not permitted at all in putting Supplementary Questions, although the absolute ban on direct quotations has recently been lifted. Ministers, however, have notes on possible supplementary questions, drawn up by their Civil Servants.

(Extract from *Some Traditions and Customs of the House of Commons* <http://www.parliament.uk/commons/lib/fs52.pdf>)

Bear in mind that some of these procedures have undergone recent processes of modernisation. Things were even more complex a century ago. The same source quotes the MP Alfred Kinnear's attempt to explain one particular aspect of parliamentary protocol as it stood in 1900:

At all times remove your hat on entering the House, and put it on upon taking your seat; and remove it again on rising for whatever purpose. If the MP asks a question he will stand, and with his hat off; and he may receive the answer of the Minister seated and with his hat on. If on a division he should have to challenge the ruling of the chair, he will sit and put his hat on. If he wishes to address the Speaker on a point of order not connected with a division, he will do so standing with his hat off. When he leaves the House to participate in a division he will take his hat off, but will vote with it on. If the Queen sends a message to be read from the chair, the Member will uncover. In short, how to take his seat, how to behave at prayers, and what to do with his hat, form between them the ABC of the parliamentary scholar.

(<http://www.parliament.uk/commons/lib/fs52.pdf>)

Learning the 'rules of the game' has clearly always been a crucial aspect of how to become an effective parliamentarian. But becoming accustomed to these norms is not simply a matter of learning to live with a series of apparently quirky rules of procedure or customs. MPs have to get to grips with how the House of Commons really works – the culture of Parliament – if they are to have influence and if they seek personal career advancement. The following reflections come from the former Conservative MP Nigel Forman in his book on British politics:

Another interesting aspect of parliamentary culture in the House of Commons is the extent to which the institutionalised party conflict is organised, even ritualised, by the party Whips working through what are known as 'the usual channels'. This phrase is a euphemism for the sometimes heated and vigorous discussions which take place every day that the House is sitting behind the scenes and off the record between the Leader of the House and the Chief Whip for the Government and the Leader of the Opposition and the Opposition Chief Whip for the official Opposition. Without the benefit of these discussions, which often include Ministers, Whips and their opposite numbers on the opposition front bench, the whole place would probably grind to a halt. As it is, the essential deal between the two sides is based upon two assumptions: that the government must get its business done . . . and that the Opposition must have its full opportunities to oppose.

. . . Indeed the co-operative principle is reflected in the attitudes and behaviour of individual MPs who all strive very hard, as soon as they get to Westminster, to secure 'a pair' – that is a member on the other side who will agree on specific occasions to stay away from the division lobbies when the votes are called, so that the overall result of the vote is not affected. . . . A final aspect of parliamentary culture which is worth mentioning is the fondness of MPs in all parties, but especially on the Conservative side, for dining clubs and informal political gatherings of all kinds. . . . In the Labour Party, the various factions usually like to meet, talk and perhaps plot in the Tea Room. In the Conservative Party they prefer the Members' Dining Room or private rooms on the terrace level or even their own London homes.

. . . The views of such groups, as and when they are clarified, are then propounded and taken forward by the MPs concerned, who lose little time in passing on the essence of their discussions either to the party whips or sometimes, in suitably veiled form, to lobby journalists. It is in these ways and in these symposia (in the Greek sense of the word) that much political opinion at Westminster is moulded and developed.

(Forman 1991: 154–5)

From Forman's account, we may draw the conclusion that the political values of an individual are subject to heavy mediation, especially in situations where that individual enters a new environment. This mediation has several aspects. The norms embedded in institutions such as the British House of Commons provide 'rules of the game'. This means that the pursuit of one's political values has to be accommodated within these norms; to 'get on' in Parliament, an MP has to play by the rules of a very long-established political game. However, the process of learning these new rules may also involve the transfer of new values, be they the values residing in Parliament or those of the relevant parliamentary party. Some varieties of institutionalist political science warn the student against the assumption that actors bring ready-made sets of values and interests into institutional settings. Participation within institutions is seen as a generator of values and understandings. Such views have much in common with recency approaches to political socialisation.

How?

From the discussions above, it should be clear that learning about politics is more than the conscious and deliberate induction into the world of institutions, parties and issues. If some of the evidence unveiled by empirical research is correct, it would be fair to argue that the boundaries set by parents for their children may be as important, if not more important, to political learning than reading a textbook or attending formal lectures about the functions of government. In short, we are not always going to be conscious of political socialisation.

This is not to say that political socialisation is never deliberate. Recent history is littered with authoritarian regimes that have sought to teach appropriate values and norms to their populations from an early age. Communist political systems again provide some useful exhibits. In such regimes, centralised syllabuses in schools and higher education were seen as a vital component in the creation of citizens equipped for the task of building communism. In the USSR public authorities laid down firm guidelines for the moral education of the young. One report from 1964 described how schoolchildren in the Soviet Union were taught about

> the inevitability of the end of capitalism and the victory of socialism and communism and the leading and organising role of the Communist Party of the Soviet Union in the building of communism in our country. History and society study are important means of bringing the pupils up in a spirit of selfless love for, and devotion to, their socialist motherland, in a spirit of peace and friendship among the nations in a spirit of proletarian internationalism.
>
> (cited in Lane 1978: 497)

The authorities in the USSR clearly saw a linkage between the development of a certain moral code among the young and long-term regime stability. It is also interesting to note the way in which children's literature and school workbooks were laced with ideological messages. Take the examples of mathematics problems used in Soviet education quoted by Michael Rush:

> The first cosmonaut was a citizen of the Soviet Union, Comrade Yuri Gagarin. He made a flight around the earth in 108 minutes. How many hours and how many minutes did the first flight around the earth last?
>
> A brigade of oil workers must drill 6 kilometres 650 metres per year. In the first half of the year it drilled 4 kilometres 900 metres, and in the second 1 kilometre 50 metres less. Did the brigade fulfil its annual plan? If it over-fulfilled it, by how much?
>
> (Rush 1992: 94)

In the German Democratic Republic a system of 'polytechnic' secondary schooling was introduced in 1958. Pupils in this system were to be trained for the practicalities of manual labour in a society striving for the achievement of communism. According to the official justification, the curriculum took the following form:

> In handicraft classes, which are taken from the first to the sixth grade, the children learn to handle simple tools, work with various materials and produce useful objects. . . . From the seventh grade onwards, children go once a week to a factory for what is known as polytechnical instruction. This consists of a theoretical part, comprising the two subjects 'Introduction to socialist production' and 'Technical drawing', and in practical participation in the production process of the factory, under the heading of 'Production work'. . . . They learn to work steadily and painstakingly, to be orderly and disciplined and they realize the value of working together. It is not so much their performance that is important, but the development of skills and character traits.
>
> (cited in Childs 1983: 174–5)

THINK POINT

- What do you think of political socialisation through education as practised in the communist period in such countries?
- Is there something in the nature of communist regimes that required such overt educational political socialisation?
- Do you see any parallel processes occurring in your own country's educational system?

An immediate response from the vantage point of Western countries would be that such socialisation is a crass and abhorrent attribute of authoritarian governments with nothing in the way of democratic credentials. Having said that, the United States and most Western European countries have developed programmes of 'civic' education in schools. Programmes of this sort vary from country to country, but in general they tend to form a compulsory part of secondary education in which pupils are taught about basic constitutional principles and the functioning of political and legal processes.

Moreover, it is quite plausible to argue that the function of school curricula in Western countries is identical to that of the old communist countries: the induction of young people into regime-friendly values. The key difference would reside in the argument that control of the curriculum in the West is generally subject to forms of democratic control and popular input.

So far we have looked largely at the alleged socialising effects of families and schools. In the literature on socialisation these are labelled **agents of social-isation**. The family and education are by no means the only agents of socialisation. We might look at the socialising impact of the workplace, social class, peer groups, leisure activities or membership of religious groups. One

Agents of socialisation Those individuals, groups or institutions which are responsible for the transmission of the information through which people acquire their socialisation.

agency worthy of deeper investigation here is the mass media. The mass media may be divided into print media (such as newspapers) and electronic media (such as film, radio, television and information technology). For the purposes of this discussion, we will attend briefly to the socialising role played by electronic media, particularly film.

Do we find values transmitted, or at least embedded, in films designed for children? An obvious test case would be the films made by the Walt Disney Corporation. Disney acquired a reputation for the production of exquisitely animated feature-length productions, usually in the form of clearly plotted stories. From our point of view, it is interesting to look at these films in terms of the values being conveyed. The critically acclaimed *Fantasia* (James Algar *et al.* 1940) consists of a series of animated interpretations of pieces of classical music. In one of these sequences, a collection of flying horses, nymphs and various other mythological characters are animated to the music of Beethoven. To some eyes, this particular section of the film is most notable for its presentation (and thus reinforcement) of quite stark gender stereotypes – perhaps typical of the time. *Bambi* (David Hand, 1942) tells the story of a young male deer brought up by his mother in a deeply idyllic woodland environment, who is taught the crucial lessons about life, responsibility and being a man by his (largely absent) father. More recently, *Pocahontas* (Mike Gabriel and Eric Goldberg, 1995), the tale of a love affair between a native American Princess and an English colonial sea captain, juxtaposes the harmonious values of indigenous cultures with the barbarian tendencies of supposedly 'civilising' cultures. Yet the brief relationship between Pocahontas and John Smith is a testimony to the possibilities of congruous intercultural understanding.

Such media become important if we accept the view that core values are imprinted at an early age. A recency-based explanation could point to the role of movies and other media in shaping adult political sensibilities. After all, some films are the transmitters of overtly political messages. Take *Salvador* (1986), Oliver Stone's scathing critique of US foreign policy in Central America, or *Bob Roberts* (1992), Tim Robbins' cutting satire on fundamentalist neo-conservatism in the USA. Some movies might not be directly 'political', but may seek to convey particular sorts of values. Examples would include the compelling drama *12 Angry Men* (Sidney Lumet, 1957), in which a liberal juror played by Henry Fonda seeks to overturn the prejudiced rush to convict a young murder suspect by the other eleven; or the feminist road movie *Thelma and Louise* (Ridley Scott, 1991).

At this point it is worth injecting a note of caution. To what extent do stimuli provided by the media alter perceptions or reinforce pre-existing cognitions? Unfortunately, there is no clear answer to this question, in spite of much research. As Hans Kleinsteuber puts it:

> [I]f we ask people whether media have any effect, we get an ambiguous answer: they accept an effect for people in general, but deny it in respect of themselves . . . [W]ith political proselytising what is important is the

previous attitude of the recipient: even the technically best advertising spot will not change a voter's mind if the party says nothing to him, the programme does not meet his expectations or the leading candidate seems untrustworthy.

(Kleinsteuber 1995: 129)

Of course, it is very difficult to measure the impact of the media upon the cognitions of an individual, and herein lies one of the main problems of research into political socialisation. It is quite easy to establish the values which agents might be transmitting, but altogether more demanding to establish whether exposure to the agent actually has an effect. As Kleinsteuber's comment illustrates, asking someone whether or not they have been influenced is not likely to yield particularly reliable responses.

The importance of political socialisation

The study of political learning or political socialisation is not an insulated discrete topic. That much should already be clear. To conclude this chapter it is worth addressing three particular questions about the wider implications of political socialisation for, respectively, political science, politics and the political system.

What does political socialisation tell us about political science?

Why did political scientists become interested in socialisation? This is worthy of some extended discussion. Anyone who has seriously thought about politics would have contemplated either the relationship between political learning and political action or the way in which types of regime might be underpinned by certain sorts of formal or informal socialisation. We have seen that these ways of thinking go back at least as far as ancient Greece. But political socialisation as a *concept* emerged very much in the environment of political science in the United States during the 1950s.

As most commentators acknowledge, the appearance of political socialisation as a serious subject of empirical enquiry was bound up with the so-called behavioural revolution in political science. In this viewpoint of **behaviouralism** the main purpose of political, and for that matter social, science is the explanation of individual and collective behaviour. As David Sanders puts it, '[t]he central question that behaviouralists ask is: "Why do individuals, institutional actors and nation states behave in the way that they do?"' (Sanders 1995: 74). Framing the problematic of enquiry in this way suggests that behaviouralists are interested in establishing patterns of causation. The basic pattern of behavioural reasoning is illustrated in Figure 2.1. This raises a number of subsidiary questions that guide behaviourally oriented research. These might include:

Behaviouralism A movement in postwar political science, notably in the USA, concerned with establishing law-like generalisations about the political world and with shifting the emphasis of political studies away from its traditional legal-institutional manifestation. With a focus on individual behaviour, the 'behavioural approach' means literally a focus upon individual behaviour. The 'behavioural approach' is linked with quantitative research techniques designed to generate testable hypotheses about measurable attitudes and observable behaviour, thus rendering the study of politics more scientific.

1 Why does stimulus *x* produce response *y* and not an alternative response?
2 How do the political systemic consequences *z* of behaviour *y* influence future political behaviour?

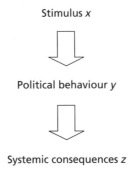

Stimulus *x*

Political behaviour *y*

Systemic consequences *z*

Figure 2.1 Basic reasoning of behavioural political science

Key text: H. Eulau (1963) *The Behavioural Persuasion in Politics*, New York: Random House.

Furthermore, behaviouralists insist that we must be able to observe behaviour and test hypotheses empirically. The resulting body of empirical political theory will be open to verification or falsification. In other words, the behavioural movement was entangled with the quest to make the study of social phenomena more *scientific*. We have already addressed the question of whether or not the study of politics can be scientific in the Introduction to this book, and it might be worth thinking about that issue again. For behaviouralists, the accumulation of empirical data from observable political phenomena in pursuit of particular hypotheses could lead to the tantalising prospect of law-like generalisations about the political world. But it was not just that the results of research would be scientifically valid. Behaviouralists – like others of a positivist persuasion – also believed that the ways in which they devised and conducted research projects should aspire to operate in the manner of the natural sciences.

The importance of political socialisation should be clear. If we are able to derive empirical generalisations about how, when and from whom people learn about politics, then we have a potentially powerful set of tools for explaining how people behave politically. In addition, because of the behaviouralist concentration upon what is readily observable, enquiries into political socialisation have tended to concentrate on measurable sources of political information such as school curricula or the mass media or research into the patterns of learning among children across time.

THINK POINT

■ What do you make of behaviouralist approaches to the study of politics?

■ Do they have any obvious weaknesses?

For its advocates, behaviouralism had a number of advantages over other forms of political study. Perhaps the least controversial claim made on the approach's behalf was that it widened the scope of political science. Behaviouralism, argue its champions, focused attention away from the traditionally legalistic study of political institutions and constitutions towards the political actions of real people in all levels of the political system. More contentiously, behaviour is treated as the single most important unit of analysis in the study of politics; more important than, for example, institutional rules or norms. Doing political science in this way was made possible by advances in research methods that employed large-scale surveys amenable to sophisticated statistical analysis. Developments in computer hardware and software have made such techniques less burdensome on the researcher and enabled the collection and processing of enormous quantities of data.

For its opponents, behaviouralism was a deeply flawed approach to the study of politics for two reasons. The first line of criticism is that behaviouralism is likely to produce work that is overtly empiricist. In other words, the tenets of behaviouralism are said to encourage the asinine accumulation of facts. Generalisations emerge once regularities begin to form within a mass of accumulated empirical data. For many social scientists this approach is wrong-headed because it neglects the importance of devising theoretical and conceptual categories prior to the accumulation and manipulation of data (Sartori 1970). What we get is a political science based on phenomena that are amenable to easy measurement rather than those that are of theoretical importance. Theories, runs the argument, are the only things we have to help us sort through the disordered mess of the social world so that we may ask meaningful questions and choose relevant data. Indeed, there are elements of the political world that cannot be counted or meaningfully quantified, suggesting that behaviouralists run the risk of missing out important elements of their explanations.

In his discussion of behaviouralism, Sanders (1995) argues that this tendency is likely to neglect potentially important explanations on the grounds that they may be difficult or impossible to organise. He points to studies of voting behaviour which have managed to achieve quite sophisticated analyses of individual motivations for voting based upon the interplay of various factors such as social background, ideological and party identification and economic perceptions. But there is no incorporation into voting studies of, for example, the ways in which individuals conceptualise themselves. As Sanders puts it, 'it is very hard to envisage how the responses to such questions – given the difficulty of measuring those responses systematically – could ever be incorporated into formal analysis. As a result they are largely excluded from the analytic frame' (Sanders 1995: 66).

The second and related point is that behaviouralist political science elevates the quantifiable and relegates the theoretical. Behaviouralist-influenced political scientists have a predisposition for measuring things. Data are valid if they can be measured. The other side of the coin is that data are not valid if they are not quantifiable. This betrays a rather contentious set of assumptions about the political world and how that world might be studied. For instance, many critics note that the pseudo-scientific bent of behaviouralism leads many researchers to neglect the fact that they themselves are actors in the social and political world that they seek to explain. Objectivity is not easily achieved. Of particular importance is the behavioural assumption that theory and observation can be separated. The researcher is portrayed as an objective onlooker who then builds empirical theory based upon what he or she has observed. But we can argue quite strongly that all observation is influenced by a pre-existing theoretical position. Thus how the researcher observes is likely to be subject to some sort of theoretical preconception. Indeed, the selection of what is to be observed is equally likely to be conditioned in the same way. This scientism is also accused of neglecting the normative element of political enquiry. So-called value freedom is taken to be a good thing among behaviouralists, but the marginalisation of values also potentially sidelines the great questions of political philosophy – questions about rights, freedom, justice and so on.

The use of powerful arguments of this sort by critics has led to the abandonment of much of the most zealous and positivistic behaviouralism. Having said that, behaviouralism is still one of the most influential components of contemporary political science. A behavioural emphasis is central to the study of elections and voting, perhaps the best-known and most publicised manifestation of the study of politics.

In the context of this volume, behaviouralism is important, not only because it provides a good case study of a particular way of 'doing' political science, but also because of the content of this chapter and of Chapters 3 and 4. As we will see, it is not necessary to be a behaviouralist to study political behaviour. But it very difficult to understand the work that has been done on socialisation, political culture and political participation without a basic sense of what behaviouralist political science was all about.

What does political socialisation tell us about politics?

This can be stated with more brevity. As indicated above, the work done on political socialisation rather suggests that politics is a very broad-based activity, by no means confined to the world of formal political institutions. The study of political socialisation opens up the study of politics to both the analysis of political behaviour (how individuals and groups operate within the bounds set by institutions) and research into the factors lying behind political action. Moreover, one of the basic assumptions of much work on political socialisation is the idea that orientations to political objects are the product of the mobilisation of other sorts of values which we may learn in other arenas, whether as a child watching a Disney film or as an adult confronting problems in the workplace. So politics is not necessarily a separate sphere of human existence somehow apart from all other aspects of life. In many ways it is our life.

What does political socialisation tell us about the political system?

The study of political socialisation raises some intrinsically interesting questions about the ways in which individuals acquire their political views and their orientations towards political objects. However, it is also worth drawing out some rather bigger issues that will be developed and argued through in the course of the next few chapters. Most prominently, there is the matter of the relationship between what we learn about politics and the stability or otherwise of the political system within which we live. Is what we learn about politics, in terms of particular chunks of knowledge as well as deeper values, somehow supportive of the regime? On the other hand, might it be possible to learn and mobilise around dysfunctional or anti-regime values? Also, what is it that we learn when we are socialised? This is very much the concern of Chapter 3. Finally, does the way in which we are socialised influence the way in which we engage in political action (Chapter 4)?

Unfortunately, we will have to leave these questions hanging for now. In addition, you should not expect to have any clear-cut answers to this issue even by the time you have finished reading this book. Unfortunately, political science is never that simple, but eventually you should be able to address these questions with greater conceptual sophistication.

Conclusion

We all learn about politics, but not in ways that may be immediately obvious. How often do we think that a 6-year-old child sitting in a classroom, completing a writing exercise set by the teacher, is being socialised politically? When we sit down to watch a film, do we imagine that it may propagate certain sets of values that reinforce or clash with our own? Of course, there is considerable dispute about whether either of these examples should be understood as an instance of the acquisition of political values and norms. Much depends upon what we think politics is all about and what we regard as politically relevant knowledge. The great advantage of studying socialisation is that it raises these difficult questions. With any luck, in so doing it makes us less complacent about the subject we study.

Chapter summary

> ☐ Learning about politics is not just about acquiring formal knowledge about the workings of a political system. Rather, it is a matter of developing core values and attitudes as well as perceptions of authority that together influence political views and shape political behaviour.

continued

continued

■ Political scientists use the phrase 'political socialisation' to capture this process.

■ It is difficult to see how a regime could remain legitimate or stable without its subjects being socialised into sets of relevant norms. This may be viewed as a process of malign indoctrination or as a desirable functional necessity.

■ Debate rages as to whether the key processes of political socialisation occur within the early stages of a person's life, or whether changing life experiences produce significant moments of re-socialisation. These two views may be usefully labelled the 'primacy' and 'recency' views.

■ Political socialisation takes place through agents of socialisation, such as families, schools, peer groups and the media.

■ The study of political socialisation directs us towards some of the less formal aspects of the political process. Moreover, it is studied because some political scientists believe that patterns of socialisation into core societal values explain the ways in which different political systems work.

Key texts

Easton, D. and Dennis, J. (1969) *Children and the Political System: Origins of Political Legitimacy*, New York: McGraw-Hill. The most famous study of pre-adult political socialisation.

Eulau, H. (1963) *The Behavioural Persuasion in Politics*, New York: Random House. A helpful discussion from a leading practitioner of behaviouralism.

Hyman, H. (1959) *Political Socialization: A Study in the Psychology of Political Behaviour*, New York: Free Press. Still worth a read. Usually regarded as the first systematic study of political socialisation.

Kavanagh, D. (1983) *Political Science and Political Behaviour*, London: Unwin Hyman. A clear, critical discussion of the main themes of behavioural political science.

Further reading

Kundera, M. (1987) *Life is Elsewhere*, London: Faber and Faber. First published in 1973, Milan Kundera's black comic novel explores the artistic growth of a poet and his exposure and absorption of Stalinist ideas.

Milgram, S. (1974) *Obedience to Authority: An Experimental View*, New York:

Harper and Row. Just how far are people prepared to go when required to obey authority? Milgram's experiments remain controversial and his conclusions are often troubling.

Mill, J. S. (1964) *Autobiography of John Stuart Mill*, New York: New American Library. First published in 1873, this is the life story of one of the nineteenth-century's most notable liberal political thinkers. Of particular interest is Mill's detailed account of his strict experimental education at the hands of his father James Mill, himself a close associate of the utilitarian philosopher Jeremy Bentham.

Young, H. (1990) *One of Us*, London: Pan. A biography of the former British Prime Minister Margaret Thatcher, notable for the attention that it pays to the formative impact of her early years upon her political ideas.

EXERCISE

Write a short statement of between 500 and 1000 words reflecting on your own political socialisation experiences. Putting these thoughts down on paper should be a valuable exercise; it will help you to see the connections between personal experience and the study of politics. Remember you will not be writing about your views on particular political issues. Rather, you should be thinking about where those views came from and the factors in your life which have had cause to influence or change your perspective on the political world.

The following guidelines may be of help:

1   What are my political views? Not just which political party do I support but how do I feel about broader issues; indeed, do I have any discernible political views?

2   Can I identify any agents of socialisation that may have acted as formative political influences? Here we are talking about parents, teachers, friends as well as the media.

3   At what points in my life do I think my key socialisation experiences occurred? Childhood, adolescence, adulthood?

4   Have my views about politics changed over time? If so, do these changes reflect new socialisation experiences brought about in new environments (such as moving to a new area, changing schools or starting a new job)?

Contents

Political Culture

Ben Rosamond

▌ Introduction

Put crudely, Chapter 2 considered how human beings learn about politics. This chapter, to put it equally crudely, asks what it is that they learn? This is not simply what people are taught about politics in a formal sense, but also what they come to feel for and regard as natural about the society in which they live. The term used by students of politics to denote such values is **political culture**. Culture is a rather elusive concept. Raymond Williams once stated that '[c]ulture is one of the two or three most complicated words in the English language' (Williams 1976: 76). It is a term used in everyday discourse to represent at least two distinct things. The first is culture as 'high culture'. To say that a person is *cultured* suggests that he or she is well read or has been exposed with beneficial effects to the virtues associated with great music, literature or art. Here 'culture' is about personal or social improvement. The second sense in which 'culture' is commonly used relates to the depiction of difference. So it is frequently the case that disparities in habit, behaviour and outlook between two or more nationalities are explained by recourse to culture. Thus Germans are frequently portrayed as methodical, Australians as casual and flippant, the French as volatile and romantic, the English as reserved and soulless.

Reflection on national cultural stereotypes infuses a lot of the very best humour. The success of British comedy series such as *Monty Python's Flying Circus*, *Fawlty Towers* and *Yes Minister* is often ascribed to the way in which these programmes construct comic reflections upon British (or, more often, English) cultural stereotypes. So in the case of *Fawlty Towers*, the writers – John

Political culture The set of values, beliefs and attitudes within which a political system operates.

Cleese and Connie Booth – created an English grotesque in the form of hotel owner Basil Fawlty, a man of deeply reactionary sentiments who is cursed with the inability to control a world populated by (invariably) 'modern', cosmopolitan characters (a perfect metaphor for Britain in the mid-1970s perhaps). While humour with a 'cultural' foundation is frequently used in a self-deprecatory manner, it is of course also the case that cultural stereotyping can infect more pernicious forms of comedy.

So what is the use of 'culture' to the political scientist? After all, it is surely unseemly for supposedly detached members of the academic community to be engaging in the use of stereotypes. The answer lies partly with the elementary observation that there are notable variations in the ways in which politics is conducted from country to country. Therefore, the point of investigating politics through the lens provided by a cultural approach lies in the ways that 'culture' can be used to give a conceptual grounding to the designation of difference. So if there is an assumption underlying the work of those who use the concept of political culture, it is that distinct norms, rules, habits, traditions and belief systems sit at the heart of each political system. These in turn shape the behaviour of the main participants in the political process.

Defining political culture is a controversial business. A paper written in the 1970s unearthed in excess of thirty meanings of the concept (Patrick 1976). Dennis Kavanagh has written widely on political culture. His preferred definition seems to be the following:

> For our purposes we may regard the political culture as a shorthand expression to denote the set of values within which a political system operates. It is something between the state of public opinion and an individual's personality characteristics.
>
> (Kavanagh 1983: 49)

Another much-used definition was that provided by the American political scientists Gabriel Almond and Sidney Verba in their major work *The Civic Culture*. They wrote of political culture as the 'pattern of orientations to political objects among the members of the nation' (Almond and Verba 1963: 15). By 'political objects', Almond and Verba meant institutions such as parliaments and political parties, as well as less tangible aspects of a nation's political life such as conventional accounts of its history. Political culture is not simply to do with what we believe, but is also bound up with the ways in which we behave politically (particularly collectively). So political culture can also be understood in terms of the political practices and rituals of a given community.

Key text: G. A. Almond and S. Verba (1963) *The Civic Culture: Political Attitudes and Democracy in Five Nations*, Princeton: Princeton University Press.

THINK POINT

- What are the components of your country's political culture?

- A useful way to engage with a new concept is to try it out for yourself. Spend a few minutes writing down what you consider to be the main elements of your country's political culture, taking into account the definition of the concept outlined above.

▨ Remember that you are not engaged in an exercise to describe the formal institutional make-up of your country. What you are briefed to do here is to think about the memories, traditions, habits, beliefs, norms and rules which inform political action by both elites and masses.

▨ You might also think about *your* place in your country's political culture. What are your orientations to 'political objects'?

▨ The uses of political culture

Dennis Kavanagh has frequently stated in his work that 'political culture' is a new term for an old idea. Indeed, a random trawl through the annals of political thought will yield many cases of thinkers who have contemplated the relationship between regimes and the value systems underpinning them.

So we can go back to the writings of Plato (427–347 BC), commonly believed to be the founder of political thought, to find explicit statements about what we now know as political culture. In *The Republic* Plato stated:

> [g]overnments vary as the dispositions of men vary, and that there must be as many of one as there are of the other. For we cannot suppose that States are made of 'oak and rock' and not out of the human natures which are in them.
>
> (Plato 1945: 32)

Plato's student Aristotle (384–322 BC) brought his organised way of thinking into the study of what we have come to know as political culture. In his *Politics* Aristotle tried to work out the most suitable form of human government. To achieve this end, he did not focus simply on institutions but also on social structures and their attendant value systems. What emerges is a celebration of the virtues of civility, consensus and partnership in politics. This is in turn associated with a mixture of oligarchic (rule by the few) and democratic characteristics and control by the 'middle classes' (in Aristotle's terms, those who are neither rich nor poor).

In modern political thought very few key writers have failed to make the connection between the dispositions of people and the sorts of political system in which they lived. Jean-Jacques Rousseau, writing in the eighteenth century, wrote much about the importance of morality and custom as the basis of political stability. From a different perspective, the most famous critic of the French Revolution, Edmund Burke, placed considerable emphasis on the vital importance of tradition and the destructive consequences of uprooting well-established political norms. His *Reflections on the Revolution in France* (1790) (Burke 1982) is a quite devastating polemic against the use – as he saw it – of abstract theorising to displace long-standing institutions that rested on appropriate cultural foundations. To engineer a rupture with the past, as the French revolutionaries had done, was seriously misplaced. Progress, argued Burke, is best achieved in the context of continuity and with reference to past precedent and tradition.

There does seem to be a common theme throughout these diverse writings. The purpose of investigating what we now know as political culture has predominantly been to establish the nature of the relationship between regime stability and the structure of beliefs, values and traditions. The claim being made is that political culture filters our perceptions, influences our attitudes and has a major say in the extent and manner of our political participation (Dogan and Pelassy 1990). To be more precise, the relationship being proposed seems to take the form shown in Figure 3.1. Of course, we have to be careful with such grand schemes. As with all frameworks for analysis, there are certain assumptions being made. For example, the approach described in Figure 3.1 assumes that there is an identifiable political culture into which individuals are socialised. Moreover, the approach assumes that the make-up of a political culture will influence patterns of behaviour within a political system and that these behavioural patterns, in turn, have a major influence on the stability of a regime.

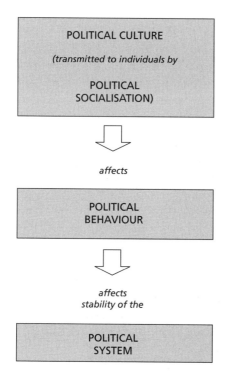

Figure 3.1 Political culture and political stability

THINK POINT

▪ Take a close look at Figure 3.1. Can you think of any objections to the causal chain being proposed?

▪ To what extent do you think that it is possible to explain stability with reference to the underpinnings provided by political culture?

The civic culture

The entry of the concept of political culture into the lexicon of political studies is most associated with the rise of the behavioural movement, discussed in Chapter 2. The attractiveness of the idea of political culture to behaviouralists should be obvious. The promise of finding firm relationships between certain sorts of cultural conditions and various levels of political stability dovetailed well with the behaviouralists' quest for scientific precision in explanation. In addition, the study of attitudes and beliefs about politics amongst citizens was testimony to the behaviouralists' emphasis on non-institutional forms of politics.

The leading example of the behavioural study of political culture remains *The Civic Culture* by the American political scientists Gabriel Almond and Sidney Verba, first published in 1963. *The Civic Culture* was a report on an extensive survey carried out in five countries – the United States, the United Kingdom, Italy, the Federal Republic of Germany and Mexico – in 1959. The methods used by Almond and Verba and their team of researchers say much about their understanding of political culture. The aim of the surveys was to acquire a mass of comparative data on public opinion from which conclusions about political culture could be drawn. Respondents – of whom there were about 1000 in each country – were asked three sorts of questions about their attitudes to political objects. *Cognitive* questions were used to test the respondents' factual knowledge and beliefs about their respective political systems. *Affective* questions dealt with the ways in which those surveyed felt

One of America's most important and prolific political scientists, Almond (b. 1911) is celebrated for his pioneering contribution to the development of comparative politics. In particular he is credited with having much to do with promoting theoretical rigour and thereby preventing the splintering of the discipline into a series of disparate and non-communicating area studies specialisms. Almond's comparative credentials mean that his work spans both developing and advanced industrial societies. Almond has authored and edited some fifteen books, including (with Sidney Verba) *The Civic Culture* (1963). He is currently Professor Emeritus of Political Science at Stanford University in California.

Gabriel A. Almond

about those political objects – their attitudes to their political system. Finally, *evaluative* questions sought to ascertain opinions and judgements about the political objects, a test of wider political values.

THINK POINT

Consider the description above of Almond and Verba's methodology.

▪ Does it seem to you to be a useful way of conducting research into political culture?

▪ Can you think of any problems with the methods used?

▪ Do you think that the methods used might pre-empt certain sorts of conclusion?

Armed with their data, Almond and Verba went on to make some influential and provocative statements about political culture. They identified three ideal types of individual and collective (national) political culture: parochial, subject and participant. A *parochial* political culture was characterised by general ignorance about political objects and a consequent lack of involvement in political activity. *Subject* political cultures were characterised by widespread knowledge about political processes, but a disinclination to participate in political activity, often because of feelings of powerlessness. *Participant* political cultures combined knowledge about politics with a willingness to participate in the political process. In such situations, people feel able to affect change; that their political activity will make a difference.

It is important to remember two points. First, Almond and Verba regarded these types of political culture as the properties of both individuals and political systems as a whole. It was thought possible to aggregate individual orientations. The assumption, therefore, is that it is possible to link the 'micro' and the 'macro' aspects of politics. Second, the three categories are **ideal types**. This means that they represent an attempt to impose a classification upon the disordered and messy reality of the human world. This is said to aid investigation and to further knowledge by providing order to our thinking (see Burger 1976). Real-world political cultures would invariably appear as some sort of mixture of these ideal types and this is very much what Almond and Verba's research showed.

In fact Almond and Verba concluded that all three ideal types would be unsatisfactory as cultural underpinnings for a stable democratic polity. Parochialism was a characteristic of 'traditional' societies and not of mature democracies, where developed institutions require a qualitatively different sort of value system. Subject political cultures were also deemed unsuitable. While citizens in such situations possessed the requisite political knowledge, they did not possess the sense that they could be effective democratic actors. On the other hand, a participant political culture carried with it the danger of a kind of democratic overload. Too many citizens trying to effect change through mass participation would be a source of instability that could seriously undermine the normative ideal of democratic stability.

Thus, in terms of their conclusions, Almond and Verba argued that the best sort of political culture for a stable democratic system would involve a mix of

Ideal type A social scientific technique that imposes an analytical order on the social world and provides clear categories to guide further investigation.

Civic culture The type of political culture thought by some to provide the best environment for stable democratic politics to occur. It combines the optimum mix of subject and participant political attitudes.

subject and participant elements. They labelled this mixture the **civic culture**. In a civic culture, citizens would possess high levels of knowledge about the political process and feel empowered as political actors. Crucially, however, they would recognise the legitimacy of elites to make decisions on their behalf. At the same time, elites would be sensitive to the preferences of the mass population. The resultant system is a balance (a conclusion which echoes that of Aristotle, a point acknowledged by Almond (1980) himself). Almond and Verba argued that the political cultures of the United States and, in particular, the United Kingdom came near to the civic culture ideal.

Criticisms of *The Civic Culture*

The work of Almond and Verba was subjected to much scrutiny. In particular, *The Civic Culture* appeared to be vulnerable to five sorts of criticism. While all of these were directed specifically at this one study, it is true that they could also be used to question various aspects of the cultural approach to politics.

The first, and perhaps most obvious, line of objection concerned the apparent Anglo-American bias of the study. In the concluding pages of *The Civic Culture* Almond and Verba argued:

> the development of a stable and effective democratic government depends upon more than the structures of government and politics: it depends upon the orientations that people have to the political process – upon the political culture. Unless a political culture is able to support a democratic system, the chances for the success of that system are slim. . . . The civic culture appears to be particularly appropriate for a democratic political system. It is not the only form of democratic political culture, but it seems to be the one most congruent with a stable, democratic system.
>
> (Almond and Verba 1963: 498)

A few pages earlier, the explicit claim is made that the political systems of Germany, Italy and Mexico lack the necessary cultural basis for democratic stability (Almond and Verba 1963: 496). The US and Britain clearly have what it takes for democratic stability to prevail in the long term.

But not all stable political systems possess the qualities associated with the civic culture. Arend Lijphart noted that certain societies with explicitly non-consensual political cultures were able to achieve democratic stability. This suggested that the structure of political institutions could intervene to overcome divisiveness and hostility in the political culture. Lijphart's argument was that consensual behaviour among political elites with appropriate institutional support could ensure the effective governance of societies that were divided on religious, ideological, linguistic, regional, cultural, racial or ethnic lines. This form of democracy was labelled **consociational democracy** (Lijphart 1977, 1991). The two key criteria for the successful operation of a consociational democracy were identified as (1) the existence of a segmented

Consociational democracy
A form of government said to characterise deeply divided, albeit stable, countries. It involves the creation of power-sharing institutions among coalescent political elites.

society, where those segments are largely autonomous, and (2) the existence of executive power-sharing among political elites. The major instances of consociational democracy identified by Lijphart are shown in Table 3.1. Apart from questioning a tendency towards the wholesale dismissal of continental European polities as unstable, Lijphart's important contribution also raises more profound questions of explanation in political science. In essence, Lijphart is saying that institutions matter and can ameliorate the impact of political culture upon the political system, whereas Almond and Verba's version is that institutions are largely derived from a cultural base. For Lijphart there is no direct connection between the shape of a political culture and the stability of its governance. Of course, Lijphart did not jettison the idea of culture altogether. Power-sharing in consociational democracies is reliant upon a coalescent elite political culture. But then we need to ask what role the institutional environment plays in the promotion of coalescent attitudes among political elites. If it does play a role, culture becomes a derivative of institutions.

Table 3.1 Cases of consociational democracy

Austria 1945–66
Belgium 1918–
Canada 1840–67; contemporary (partial)
Cyprus 1960–3
Israel 1948– (partial)
Lebanon 1943–75
Luxembourg *c.*1917–67
Malaysia 1955–
Netherlands 1917–67
Netherlands Antilles 1950–85
Surinam 1958–73
Switzerland 1943–

Source: Lijphart (1991)

This last point touches on the second strand of criticism. This concerns the deeper-lying issue of the sorts of causal relationships that were being assumed by the authors of *The Civic Culture*. Some of the most cogent criticisms of the study argued that Almond and Verba had assumed that political structures could be explained with reference to political cultures. In other words, the allegation is that the authors of *The Civic Culture* understood degrees of democratic stability as being determined or caused by political culture. Two alternative positions exist. First, the chain of causation could be turned around so that we could explain the level of civic culture in a society with reference to the level of democratic stability. So, here, democratic stability creates and sustains what is understood as the civic culture. Second, there is the more complex position developed by Carole Pateman (1971), which argues that culture and structures are interdependent and mutually reinforcing. And in any case, how is democratic stability to be measured? While students of the relationship between culture and stability have drawn up elaborate schemes for the measurement of political culture, they would appear to have been less successful in the creation of criteria for measuring levels of stability in a given political system.

The third and fourth sources of criticism derive from the survey methodology used to obtain data about political culture. The third criticism of *The Civic Culture* compares the claims made about political culture to the size of the sample interviewed. In his critique of Almond and Verba, Dennis Kavanagh makes several challenging points along these lines. Around 1000 individuals in each country were interviewed. This is a reasonably large sample, but not enough to allow the confident construction of a general theory of political culture. Kavanagh's argument is that such methods do not produce valid sample sizes of the various subgroups in each country. He dissects the British sample to prove the point:

> The British sample . . . contains only 24 respondents who had been to university . . . 58 members of the Labour Party, and only 58 from Wales and 94 from Scotland. This has always been a problem with representative British samples; over 80 percent of respondents live in England and three fifths share the characteristics of being English, white Protestant and resident in urban areas.
>
> (Kavanagh 1980: 131)

The broader point which is raised by Kavanagh's examination of the sampling deficiencies of *The Civic Culture* is the probable coexistence of a range of subgroups within any given country. Therefore countries may contain a variety of political cultures and identities (see 'Subcultures' on pp. 94–7 below). The mistake may be to assume that there is such a thing as a *national* political culture that can be revealed through scientific measurement.

The fourth objection relates to the difficulty of establishing the meaning of responses to surveys. This is a perennial problem in survey work and is by no means confined to Almond and Verba's investigations. The designer of the questionnaire has an agenda. The purpose of conducting surveys is to test hypotheses, and so the questions seek to extract information from respondents that might help in the confirmation or refutation of those hypotheses. There are three particular dangers here. First, the respondent may also have an agenda and may interpret the questions in a way that is completely at variance with the purposes of the questionnaire. This clash of interpretations may not be revealed overtly; it may be invisible. The consequence is a distortion in the results. Second, *The Civic Culture* interviews asked people a very detailed list of questions about their political orientations (see Almond and Verba 1963: 526–49). The danger here that the interview process may actually construct political orientations in individuals which may have been either not coherent or not present prior to the administration of the survey. Third, there is the possibility that the same response to the same question in different countries may not have equivalent meanings. This problem of functional equivalence is a major bugbear in comparative research. So in some countries violence is eschewed as a method in politics; in others it is used on a regular basis, but may be regarded as a perfectly acceptable way of ordering political life. Observers brought up in a country like the UK, where general elections are infrequent occurrences, have often regarded a country like Italy, where elections have tended to occur often, as a prime example of political instability. But such a view may mistake the local (Italian) function of elections, which could be described as reordering the executive in the same way as Cabinet reshuffles (comparatively frequent occurrences) are used to reorder it in the British system.

The fifth and final point does not require elaboration, and does not really amount to a criticism because Almond and Verba were well aware of the issue when they did their work. Quite simply, political cultures evolve, and any attempt, no matter how successful, to measure political culture can only be a snapshot of political culture at that particular time.

THINK POINT

Go back to thinking about your country's political culture.

▧ Do you think that it might have changed over the last ten, fifty or 100 years?

▧ If so, how and, more importantly, why?

An alternative approach: political culture and ideology

Much of the work done on political culture since the Second World War has followed from behavioural premises. However, that represents only one way of defining and using the concept of political culture from a range of alternative perspectives. By way of demonstration, we now turn to a very different way of 'doing' political science to see how notions of political culture might be employed. At first sight Marxism, with its emphasis on the economic dimensions of social life, may not be an obvious site for the discussion of things cultural. However, largely through the use of the concept of ideology, a number of Marxist and neo-Marxist thinkers have drawn up some striking and influential ideas about the operation of culture in politics.

To begin this discussion, it is worth reflecting a little on the distinctive contribution made by Marxism to the understanding of ideology (for a much fuller elaboration, see Chapter 8). Marx and Engels tended to regard the dominant ideas of any historical epoch as an expression of the interests of the most powerful social groups. In other words, dominant attitudes and systems of political and cultural thought at any given time are rooted in a power relationship. The class controlling economic life disperses throughout society its attitudinal pattern and the belief systems that support it. This reveals two important attributes of the Marxist conception of ideology. First, ideology can be partially understood as *false consciousness*, which may mask the 'real interests' of the bulk of society. Broadly speaking, in contemporary society such real interests are defined as the overthrow of capitalism and its replacement with a system of social relations that does not rely on exploitation. The dominant ideas found in a capitalist society serve to legitimate the system of exploitation and inequality upon which capitalism depends for its survival. Second, ideas are expressions of material circumstances. Attitudes, cognitions, beliefs and ideologies are rooted in the structure of production relations in any given society. So those endowed with power in relation to the means of production possess the dominant value sets, although it is also true that countervailing revolutionary ideas develop in the material conditions of the mass urbanised working class that capitalism begets.

A major contribution in the Marxist tradition to the study of ideology (and, for our purposes, to the study of political culture) was made by the Italian Antonio Gramsci. He composed his most important works while a political prisoner of the Mussolini regime in the late 1920s and 1930s (Gramsci 1970). Among the questions that most preoccupied Gramsci was why there had not been a successful communist revolutionary overthrow of a regime in an advanced Western capitalist country. After all, Marxist theory appeared to suggest that the conditions would develop in capitalist societies for a revolutionary transition to communism. For Gramsci, the explanation resided in the ability of advanced capitalist regimes to rule by consent rather than by coercion. It was intellectual and moral leadership rather than military and police repression that explained the persistence of capitalist relations of production. The key concept here is the idea of **hegemony**. In the Gramscian sense, hegemony describes the non-coercive aspects of a ruling group's power over society. It is about the diffusion of a particular way of looking at the world, which in turn affects dominant mores, values and beliefs. What we normally

Key text: A. Gramsci (1970) *Selections from the Prison Notebooks*, London: Lawrence & Wishart.

Hegemony A term used to describe the non-coercive aspects of domination, the diffusion throughout society of the value and knowledge systems of a ruling group.

Antonio Gramsci

Antonio Gramsci (1891–1937) was one Italy's foremost intellectuals of the twentieth century, and stands out as one of the most original and creative minds in the Marxist movement. After a brilliant university career, Gramsci worked as a journalist on socialist newspapers in Turin. He became a leading light in the Italian Communist Party and was sent to prison in 1926 under 'exceptional laws' enacted by the fascist-dominated Italian legislature. Although subjected to severe physical and mental strain by the experience of incarceration, Gramsci's *Prison Notebooks* (published long after his death) remain exceptional contributions to Marxist thought. Gramsci's emphasis on the ideological and consentative aspects of domination along with his understanding of the failings of and potential for socialism have provoked much debate among both intellectuals and left-leaning political activists and thinkers.

regard as 'common sense' may in fact be bound up with the exercise of hegemony.

From this perspective, political culture becomes the prevailing value system and knowledge structure that is dispersed throughout society by the dominant classes at any given time (what Gramsci (1970) termed the 'historic bloc'). It follows that those seeking to transform economy and society in advanced capitalist countries need to attend to the development of a plausible counter-hegemony which replaces the 'common sense' of capitalism with an alternative value system. Of course, this cannot be imposed coercively; people cannot be forced to be communists – they must regard it as commonsensical to be part of a communistic, egalitarian social framework.

Gramsci's ideas were taken a stage further by the French structuralist Marxist Louis Althusser (1971), writing around thirty to forty years later. Althusser was interested in theorising about the ways in which hegemony actually worked. It is here that his provocative idea of ideological state apparatuses (ISAs) is interesting. To begin with, Althusser maintained that in order to understand the persistence of capitalist relations of production we need to focus upon the power of the state. For Althusser, the state has two key apparatuses: repressive and ideological. The former, which includes the military and the police, functions via coercion in the last instance. ISAs, on the other hand, work ideologically. They are agencies for the dispersal of a particular hegemony throughout society. Althusser listed the ISAs as follows:

1 Religion.
2 Education.
3 Family.
4 Law.
5 Politics.
6 Trade unions.
7 Communications.
8 Culture.

The argument is that the ideological supports of state power, and therefore of capitalism, are deeply embedded in society in a variety of seemingly 'private' institutions. Note also that neither Gramsci nor Althusser was thinking about how particular *governments* remain in office. Rather, their concern was with the props that support much broader patterns of socio-economic organisation. Their focus is less on holders of political office than with underlying structures of power exercised through economic relations.

The most obvious criticism to be levelled at this sort of approach is that it seems to lead to the conclusion that a whole host of institutions in 'civil society' lack any meaningful autonomy. In the last instance, goes the counter-argument, it may be true that political parties, trade unions, religious institutions and prevailing literary customs might all lend support to the prevailing regime, but to paint with such a broad brush is to misunderstand the multiple conflicts which occur within and between the ISAs. Thus a lot of meaningful politics may go on within the ISA structure. Indeed, what

Althusser calls ISAs may be sites of resistance to the dominant knowledge and attitudinal patterns associated with capitalism.

Marxism has gone through something of a crisis in recent years, but one area where it remains strong is in its Gramscian manifestation. For example, some of the most influential writing on contemporary British politics (and in particular the phenomenon of Thatcherism) has been developed by the sociologist Stuart Hall (1988), who admits a clear intellectual debt to Gramsci. Hall explained the ascendancy of Conservative governments in Britain after 1979 in terms of the ability of a conservative coalition to articulate 'authoritarian populist' themes which successfully latched on to various discontents felt by a people confronted by post-imperial economic decline. An important set of ideas in international relations theory is associated with the so-called neo-Gramscian school represented by scholars such as Robert Cox (1987, 1996) and Stephen Gill (1993). Here the emphasis is on the power of knowledge and ideas in the global political economy. From this point of view, the dominant organising principles of global economics and politics have become associated with the powerful script of neo-liberalism which emphasises the sanctity of free markets, the dangers of state intervention, the freeing of capital movements and the importance of free trade to the efficient allocation of resources on a global scale.

Subcultures

One obvious objection to the idea of national political cultures is that such things do not exist. Rather, goes the argument, while recognising that culture is important, we should also acknowledge that several political cultures may co-exist within any given political system. Our attention should be focused upon the interaction of different subcultures and the impact of that interaction upon the political system as a whole. So the idea of subcultures becomes an important corollary to the ideas developed above about political culture. The term 'subculture' is frequently used as shorthand for describing societal groups who possess clear identities. Such identity is often expressed through forms of behaviour and forms of expression such as fashion. A political subculture may be defined as a group of the population that possesses a distinct and consistent set of attitudes, beliefs and orientations to political objects.

The identification of political subcultures is complicated somewhat by the variety of possible ways in which such strata might be conceived. In his book *Political Culture* (1972), Dennis Kavanagh identifies four distinct bases on which subcultures develop:

1 Elite versus mass culture.
2 Cultural divisions within elites.
3 Generational subcultures.
4 Social structure.

Each of these ways of thinking about the basis of subcultural divisions directs us towards particular forms of investigation. The elite-versus-mass idea concentrates attention upon the attitudinal differences that might obtain between the political class as a whole and the remainder of the population. The separation of elite from mass is useful because it provokes the hypothesis that exposure to particular sorts of knowledge and access to decision-making channels provides a common socialising experience for political elites. Thus, rather than seeing elites as representative of the attitudes of particular sectors of the population, this approach treats the political elite as an investigable subculture in its own right. Indeed, a number of classic studies argue that elites tend to be well versed in self-recruitment and that political systems develop ways of socialising their elites into distinct attitudinal patterns (Heath 1981; Mills 1956). The work by Prewitt (1970) on the United States suggested that American political elites tend to develop a consensus upon basic (unspoken) norms and rules of the game.

The second way of thinking about subcultures is associated with the idea that the most important venue for politics is the zone populated by elite groups. Here, degrees of stability are not likely to be related to the prevailing 'macro'-political culture in society as a whole, but to the level of cultural consensus or divergence between elite groups. For Lijphart (1977), as we have seen above (pp. 88–9), the nature of elite behaviour – particularly whether it is coalescent or adversarial – is the key to understanding the functioning of democratic polities.

The generational model of political subcultures takes us on to very different terrain. The argument here is that distinct political cultures belong to particular generations. The idea gives rise to the view that political culture possesses a dynamism. Political culture changes over time as particular generations become socialised into distinct value sets, reach political maturity in possession of those value sets and eventually die out to be replaced by a new generational political culture. The consequences for political systems should be clear. Agendas change in line with priorities that are derived from underlying values; political parties and political institutions need to adapt accordingly.

Such ideas are particularly associated with the work of Ronald Inglehart (1977, 1991), who maintained that Western societies in the 1970s were undergoing fundamental political changes thanks to generational shifts in prevailing values. The core argument revolved around what Inglehart saw as a transition from materialist to post-materialist values. Materialist values are associated with the pursuit of economic and physical security as overriding priorities, whereas post-materialist values are those that elevate self-expression, belonging and participation over basic material needs. The consequences for politics of such a transition would, of course, be quite profound. The traditional emphasis on military security and material economic welfare would be displaced by the 'new' politics of ecology, community and popular participation. Some empirical research in the 1970s appeared to confirm a definite value difference between generations. Older generations seemed to be more firmly embedded in a structure of materialist values, while younger generations were clearly more amenable to post-materialist concerns.

Key text: R. Inglehart (1977) *The Silent Revolution: Changing Values and Political Styles Among Western Publics*, Princeton: Princeton University Press.

Why does this transition take place? Inglehart makes clear the basis of his argument:

The hypothesis of an intergenerational shift from materialist towards postmaterialist values is based on two key concepts: people value most highly those things that are relatively scarce; though to a large extent, a person's basic values reflect the conditions that prevailed during his or her pre-adult years.

(Inglehart 1991: 488)

So values are rooted in material circumstances, but notice that Inglehart favours a model of political socialisation emphasising the durability of pre-adult experiences. Those raised in the aftermath of the First World War, in the Great Depression or during the Second World War are much more likely to place a premium on values that emphasise the primary importance of basic material needs. Those socialised during periods of rapid economic growth – with its attendant consumerism – and in conditions of peace do not regard basic material commodities as scarce resources. This creates a psychological space in which post-materialist ideas can flourish.

THINK POINT

- What do you think of the Inglehart hypothesis?
- Does it resonate at all with your own experiences?

Finally, there is much to be said for the approach that understands subcultures as derivatives of a nation's social structure. From this point of view, political subcultures are attitudinal expressions of the various class, religious, linguistic and ethnic divisions which characterise any country. So, for example, in most Western countries it is possible to speak of working-class culture giving rise to certain sorts of beliefs and values that historically have been channelled into political systems by social democratic, labour and communist political parties. Some states are divided along religious lines. In the Netherlands, say, we might identify distinctive Catholic and Calvinist political cultures. Countries like Belgium and Switzerland are divided along linguistic lines. The elaborate features of the Swiss federal model are certainly comprehensible in terms of the various linguistic groups forming the social structure in Switzerland.

Political scientists (or perhaps more accurately political sociologists) who focus on social structure are interested in the relationship between the operation of the political system and the composition of the society that feeds it. One powerful and influential argument associated with the work of Stein Rokkan is that the pattern of *political cleavages* (that is the main lines of political conflict) in any country may be understood with reference to the underlying foundations of the social structure.

In his work with Seymour Martin Lipset (Lipset and Rokkan 1967), Rokkan developed a model of the evolution of cleavage structures in Western political systems. Lipset and Rokkan maintained that the origins of key social cleavages could be found in two important historical processes: nation-building (the 'national revolution') and industrialisation ('the industrial revolution'). This model is depicted in Figure 3.2.

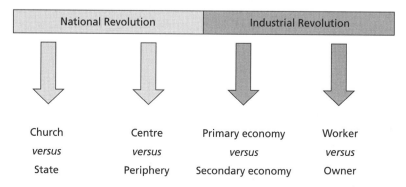

Figure 3.2 The Lipset and Rokkan model

The process of nation-building throws up two sorts of conflict that grow out of the attempts of central elites to gain control over a national territory through the production of standardised norms and a common legal framework. The first is a clash with pre-existing religious forms of authority (the Church) over matters such as education; the second involves a series of conflicts with peripheral communities that may resist the centralising tendencies of the state elite. During industrialisation, conflicts develop between those engaged in pre-industrial forms of production, particularly agriculture, and the new urban bourgeoisie. Intensive industrialisation then creates the fourth line of social cleavage between the bourgeois classes and the social by-product of capitalism, the concentrated urbanised working classes. In each case and on each side of the cleavage line there develop distinct interests, identities and value systems. Should these conflicts fail to be resolved by the time of democratisation, they will acquire institutional expressions in the form of political parties.

THINK POINT

What about gender? The argument about social subcultures is a very powerful one. It makes explicit the connection between social divisions and political cleavage patterns. Yet perhaps the most obvious and fundamental division in society is the gender divide. Now, while feminism has been an important political movement in most Western countries, gender has not become an issue around which politics in general, and party politics in particular, has revolved.

- Why do you think this is?

- What can we say about this issue in terms of political culture?

- Are there male and female political subcultures?

- If not, why not?

Culture and political identity

So, there are many different ways of thinking about political culture. If anything unites the diversity of cultural approaches to the study of politics, it is that there is a connection between the framework provided by political culture and the sense of 'who we are' politically. In other words, the claim is that the scope and limits of political identity are shaped by the prevailing cultural framework. But it is not just that having a French identity is a product of exposure to French political culture. Rather, the components of French identity may be said to include a series of common assumptions, attitudes, dispositions and beliefs. The boundaries between political identity and political culture are not easily drawn.

If this all sounds rather vague, that is because 'identity' is a very slippery concept. One writer even recommends that its use should be avoided as much as possible (Sparkes 1994: 251–2), and books have been written by the most eminent political scientists that take a couple of hundred pages to pin the term down (Mackenzie 1978). Having said that, 'identity' is everywhere in the political world. We might even say that it is endemic to the human condition. As Craig Calhoun says, 'We know of no people without names, no languages or cultures in which some manner of distinctions between self and other, we and they, are not made' (Calhoun 1994: 1). From this we can take it that identity is about the subjective concept one has of oneself ('who I am') in relation to others, since part of understanding who I am is embedded in analysis of who I am not. Political identity, if it is to be defined at all, may be said to be about collective subjective expressions or individual associations with particular collectives ('I am French', or 'I am black', or 'I am Jewish', or 'I am a woman' and so on).

What is clear is that there are many possible bases for political identity. Anthony Smith argues that each person is made up of multiple identities and that these identities bring with them certain sorts of role. He mentions bases such as gender, social class, ethnicity, religion, territorial location and family. The identities which emerge from these bases may coexist, so it is possible to identify with a whole range of collectivities simultaneously. Of course it is also possible that the possession of multiple political identities may prevent an individual from assuming the purpose and role associated with a single political identity. A hypothetical and highly stylised example may clarify this. Imagine a country divided approximately equally along class and religious lines. This means that citizens of that country have two available bases for identification. Table 3.2 presents two possible scenarios for the distribution of the population among the available social categories. In scenario A divisions of class and religion reinforce one another, whereas in scenario B religious and socio-economic categories are cross-cutting. Thus we might speculate that countries with scenario A will witness a more robust and polarised form of politics as Catholic and working-class identities work together to produce common causes against a more affluent Protestant middle class.

Table 3.2 Possible relationships between social categories and political identities

	Scenario A Catholic (%)	Protestant (%)	Scenario B Catholic (%)	Protestant (%)
Working class	50	0	25	25
Middle class	0	50	25	25

Alternatively, some identities would seem to prevail over others. The problem posed at the end of the previous section about gender offers a good entry point here. Why isn't gender – perhaps the most fundamental of all social divisions – the basis for mass political identities, which in turn structure political debate and produce political parties? The answer is much debated (Githens *et al.* 1994). Anthony Smith sums up the views of many analysts when he writes:

> [T]he very universality and all-encompassing nature of gender differ-entiation makes it a less cohesive and potent base for collective identification and mobilization. Despite the rise of feminism in specific countries, gender identity, which spans the globe, is inevitably more attenuated and taken for granted than other kinds of collective identity in the modern world. Geographically separated, divided by class and ethnically fragmented, gender cleavages must ally themselves to other more cohesive identities if they are to inspire collective consciousness and action.
>
> (Smith 1991: 4)

This may be true, but as most feminists would argue, Smith's explanation leaves out the question of power – in this the economic, social and ideological power exercised by men over women.

Thus, the emergence of a given identity may reflect or be constrained by the exercise of power. To take another example, it has often been suggested that early Marxists underestimated drastically the powerful forces of nationalist sentiment. In abstract, as Marx and Engels argued, the working men (*sic*) may have no country. In reality, however, millions of working men marched to their death while fighting for their country in the course of the twentieth century.

This brings us to the question of *where* political identities come from. Political socialisation, as discussed in Chapter 2, is clearly important. Indeed, we may be able to identify particularly powerful agents of socialisation responsible for the propagation of particular identities and the subjugation or discouragement of others. However, *why* individuals and groups coalesce around particular identities and roles is a matter of some dispute. One way of thinking about identity formation is to make a link between identity and material interests. Here, political identities become expressions of a person's social location. For example, being working class means that a person has a set of objectively defined interests that are pursued most effectively through the assumption of a socialist identity. Alternatively, being French implies allegiance to a certain set of 'national' interests. International politics, diplomacy and war may be understood as negotiations and conflicts between different national identities (see also Chapter 14).

Such 'rationalistic' perspectives may be contrasted with what some call 'constructivist' approaches to identity. Here the concern is to question the assumption that identities are objectively determined or that they exist outside of everyday political interaction. Rather, identities are always *socially constructed*; they are products of human interaction and subject to change. The historian Eric Hobsbawm has written about the 'invention of traditions', which he defines as 'a set of principles, normally governed by overtly or tacitly accepted rules and of a ritual or symbolic nature, which seek to inculcate certain values and norms of behaviour by repetition which automatically implies continuity with the past' (Hobsbawm 1992: 1). This kind of approach is useful for the deeper understanding of phenomena such as Scottish nationalism or the politics of the Jewish diaspora. Others within the constructivist perspective seek to explain the emergence of what has come to be known as 'identity politics' – the proliferation in recent years of new forms of politics around issues of ecology, lifestyle and the like. Anthony Giddens (1991) takes the view that such 'life politics' are explained by the appearance of globalisation (see Chapter 15) and greater risk which force the self to become 'reflexive'. In other words, confronted by contingency and uncertainty, individuals become more prone to construct plausible narratives of who they are and what they should do.

By studying cultural questions and surveying changes in the political culture we get a better idea of how to confront the messy thicket of identity politics. Everybody is somebody. That would seem to be an inescapable fact about the political world. How they become who they are, and what happens when they realise who they are and what they should do accordingly are really what the study of politics is all about.

Three case studies of political culture

We have seen already that the use of the term 'political culture' in the study of politics is highly contestable. To use the term and to apply it to the analysis of political situations is to accept certain sorts of assumptions about the importance of cultural phenomena. This section presents three case studies that deliberately favour a cultural approach. This does not mean that 'political culture' is the only or, for that matter, the 'best' way in which to make sense of the issues under discussion. However, the use of the cultural approach does allow the investigator to select data from the array of materials on offer and to develop and interrogate particular sets of hypotheses. Like all frameworks, the cultural approach to politics tends to condition the sorts of question we ask, governs our data collection and to some extent has an impact upon the kinds of explanation we offer.

The rise and fall of the 'Asian Tigers': a cultural phenomenon?

For many years the attention of politicians, policy-makers and the media in the West was drawn to the meteoric rise to prominence of newly industrialised economies in parts of Asia. Of particular interest were the factors that might underpin the remarkable post-war growth rates of economies such as Japan and, more recently, those of Taiwan, Singapore, South Korea and Malaysia.

Like all phenomena in the political world, the rise of these so-called 'tiger' economies in Asia was amenable to explanation from a number of alternative approaches. One of the most popular explanations – at least until the so-called Asian financial crisis that commenced in 1997 – was built around the idea that cultural factors were involved. Indeed, a number of thinkers suggested that the countries concerned possessed cultures that were highly conducive to an impressively productive variant of capitalism. In particular, it was the role played by so-called 'Confucian' values that most attracted the attention of Western commentators. The term is derived from the thought of the Chinese philosopher Kung Fu-tzu (Confucius in Latin) who is believed to have lived between 551 and 479 BC. Confucian thought is built around the advocacy of self-control and duty to others. This value structure, it is argued, remains deeply embedded in Asian societies, so that notions of 'community' and 'family' prevail over Western-style individualism.

At first sight, there would seem to be something in this analysis. For instance, in recent years the government of Singapore has been an enthusiastic sponsor of the teaching of Confucian values in schools. Lee Kuan Yew, then Singapore's Senior Minister, put it like this: 'A Confucianist view of order between subject and ruler – this helps in the rapid transformation of society . . . in other words you fit yourself into society – the exact opposite of the American rights of the individual' (*The Economist*, 21 January 1995). The idea here is that a Confucian value infrastructure provides a solid basis for rapid industrialisation without the attendant breakdown of family life and the dislocating social consequences that seem to have followed in the West. In the case of Singapore, there is an evident commitment to use the existing 'Eastern' cultural framework to avoid the mistakes of 'the West'. Such views became popular among opinion-formers and politicians across Asia. The 'Asian Way' came to be portrayed as a distinct route to modernity. Take this statement from *Voice of Malaysia* radio in May 1993:

> Datu Seri Dr Mahatir Mohamed [the Malaysian Prime Minister] has asked Malaysians not to accept western-style democracy as it could result in negative effects. The prime minister said such an extreme principle had caused moral decay, homosexual activities, single parents and economic slowdown because of poor work ethics.
>
> (*Financial Times*, 5 March 1994)

Notice how politics and economics are being connected in this statement. It is not simply that the West's underlying value structure is inadequate. What is important is the West's supposed obsession with 'liberalism'. This has the effect of causing moral decay and, in turn, is said to undermine productivity, economic growth and industrial advance.

Some 'Western' analysts concluded that there are important lessons to be learned. For example, the former British Conservative MP David Howell (1995) argued that Western countries should contemplate a degree of 'Easternisation'. His argument was that the core values of East Asian societies were central to economic success. In particular, the role of the family as the main provider of social security removed the need for an expansive, expensive and paternalistic (Western-style) welfare state. The Confucian culture provided cohesive moral standards that bound individuals into community networks. With such security embedded, individuals were able to pursue excellence in all aspects of their lives.

One of the most interesting things about the alleged correlation between Asian/Confucian values and economic success is the way in which it recalls one of the most powerful social scientific theses ever devised. The German sociologist Max Weber accounted for the rise of capitalism as a system of production in Western Europe with reference to the work ethics associated with Protestantism. In *The Protestant Ethic and the Spirit of Capitalism*, written in 1904–5, Weber (1930) maintained that the variety of reformed Christianity which emerged in Europe after the fifteenth century developed a uniquely ascetic character that in turn encouraged the accumulation strategies associated with capitalism. That is to say, values of hard work (as the main purpose of human life) and thrift (i.e. limited enjoyment of the fruits of one's labour) generated psychological and behavioural consequences resulting in the emergence of capitalism as the European method of organising the production, distribution and exchange of goods. What is even more fascinating is that Weber dismissed Confucianism, seeing it as the cause of economic 'backwardness' in China!

The issues raised by all of this are, of course, legion. Perhaps most obviously, there is the problem of cause and effect. The Confucian connection is an engaging hypothesis, but as social scientists we do not really have the where-withal to test the idea that values correlate with economic success with any degree of certainty. In some ways that problem does not matter, because the existence of the hypothesis has spilled over into an important debate which has interested key political actors both in Asia and the West. Whether or not Confucian values matter is secondary to the two facts that some Asian politicians were able to generate public support and legitimacy around the idea of a distinctive 'Asian Way' and that Western policy-makers became interested in the question of whether there were positive lessons to be leaned with a view to regaining a competitive foothold in world markets.

Powerful critical rebuttals of the Confucian thesis come from those arguing that the emergence of capitalism in Asia actually denotes the spread of core 'Western' approaches to the organisation of economic and social life. It is of course true that capitalism will acquire distinctive local characteristics wherever it emerges, but the argument here is rather that capitalism brings with it an

Along with Karl Marx and Emile Durkheim, Max Weber (1864–1920) is regarded as one of the founding pillars of modern sociology, but his colossal influence reaches into all contemporary social scientific disciplines. By the age of 32 Weber had held chairs in both economics and politics in his native Germany. For political scientists, Weber's work on power, the state, bureaucracy, class and the origins of capitalism (to name but a few) have all become required reading. Moreover, Weber's anti-empiricist studies of philosophy and methodology repay careful reading for contemporary students of politics. For example, his notion of ideal types shows us how to develop abstract concepts for analytical purposes.

Max Weber

inevitable and more or less irresistible logic. So while certain sorts of values may have helped Asian countries to 'develop' and 'modernise', these very values will be undermined by the powerful logic of industrial capitalism, thereby forcing the emergence of Western-style welfare institutions. The following newspaper article makes the point with concrete reference to South Korea.

Document

Confucius to Beveridge – The Outline of a Welfare State is Emerging

Bethan Hutton

Financial Times, 26 January 1995

Korea, perhaps more than any other east Asian nation, has prided itself on upholding the Confucian values of frugality and the importance of family ties. Traditionally, when Koreans hit hard times they relied on two things: substantial personal savings and the support of large, close-knit families. In the past, consequently, a Western-style state welfare system was considered both unwelcome and largely unnecessary. But now that Korea is becoming a fully developed country, there is a feeling that it needs a welfare system to match its advanced status. National health insurance, state pensions, unemployment insurance and other welfare measures have either already been introduced or are planned.

The state is not about to do away with the role of the family or private savings. Children are still considered to have an obligation to support their parents, and vice versa. That attitude is not going to disappear overnight.

Nonetheless, there is unease in some quarters about the innovations. Some Koreans complain that the introduction of social security is undermining the traditional family support system. But others argue that other social changes – urbanisation, lower birth rates, greater longevity, the trend towards nuclear families – were already having an impact on the traditional informal welfare system, and so a more organised approach is now necessary to fill the gaps.

Another worry sometimes heard is that a state safety net will act as a disincentive to the high savings rates, which have played such an important role in Korea's industrial development. Savings rates have indeed slipped over the past few years – from about 39 per cent in 1988 to about 34 per cent now – but as wages have risen in real terms, it could be argued that a proportionally lower savings rate could still provide just as comfortable a cushion against misfortune. And to some extent, personal savings will be replaced directly with government organised savings in the form of the national pension scheme. Whether this will have a disproportionate impact on the savings rate will not become clear for some time.

Korea is not alone in hoping to find a way to preserve the best aspects of the traditional system, while providing the kind of safety net necessary in a modern, urbanised society. Several other east Asian countries are working on the same task, but Korean bureaucrats and academics do not believe that anyone has yet found a perfect solution.

The Korean approach has been to introduce welfare at a very basic level, and gradually increase its scope and level of benefits. This is based on the belief that once a level of welfare provision has been established, it is difficult to reduce it. The ministries involved are well aware of the perils of encouraging welfare dependency.

One of the first elements of the welfare system to be introduced was a national health insurance scheme. From its start with employees of large companies in the late 1970s, the scheme now covers the entire population. However, insurance does not cover the full cost of inpatient or outpatient care, so it is still necessary to resort to personal savings for major treatment. There are special programmes providing free medical care for very low income or disadvantaged groups. As yet there is little private health insurance, but there is obviously scope for that market to expand. Welfare programmes for those on very low incomes tend to focus on encouraging self-sufficiency through work, by offering retraining, places on government projects, or subsidised loans to set up small businesses. Cash payments and benefits in kind to those unable to work are very low, supporting a minimum standard of living well below the official poverty line. Benefits are expected to increase over the next few years, while maintaining incentives to work.

Unemployment is not yet a real problem in Korea. However, the first stage of a compulsory unemployment insurance scheme will be introduced this summer. The most significant measure currently being rolled out is the national pension scheme. Occupational pension schemes for civil servants and the military have existed since the 1960s, but it was not until 1988 that a general state scheme was introduced, starting with workplaces with more than 10 workers, and gradually expanding to cover smaller employers and the self-employed. This year the scheme is due to extend to the rural self-employed, and the final phase, taking in the urban self-employed, is due by 1998. As yet, the market for private pensions is underdeveloped. The current contribution level to the national scheme is 6 per cent of income, shared equally between employee, employer, and a transfer from the retirement fund which would previously have provided a lump sum in place of a pension. Contributions are due to be increased to 9 per cent, again divided equally between the three sources. Final pension payouts are linked to the recipient's average lifetime salary, and the formula used has an equalising effect, so that lower paid workers receive perhaps 60 per cent of their pre-retirement income, while higher earners receive only 30 per cent. The national pension funds are invested in the stock market, fixed interest securities and elsewhere, such as infrastructure projects. But there is some concern about the management of the substantial amounts of money being accumulated by the scheme. Asset allocation is decided by a government committee, dominated by ministers, with a few representatives from trade unions and the private sector.

The worry expressed by some outside the government is that funds can be directed into areas of government priority – whether infrastructure projects or propping up the stock market at politically sensitive moments – rather than into those investments which will produce the best return for scheme members. As the pot of money under management grows, the government may come under pressure to distance itself from the management.

One enthusiastic government official described the current plans for social welfare as Korea's 'Beveridge plan'. The Korean version, with its step-by-step approach, is far less radical than the UK original, though it may not seem so to die-hard Confucianists.

A further argument against the thesis arose from the problem of establishing what, precisely, was 'Asian' about Asian values. As Francis Fukuyama notes:

> The idea of Asian values was … problematic from the start. As anyone knows who has spent time in that part of the world, there are huge cultural differences not only among the various countries but also among the ethnic groups that make up multicultural societies like Singapore and Malaysia. In southern China, families are both large and cohesive; in Japan, much less large and socially less significant. Whereas in Japan, South Korea, and Taiwan the state has traditionally commanded substantial respect, in many parts of Southeast Asia it has been historically weak or non-existent. Confucian societies tend to invest more resources in education than do Islamic, Malay, or Catholic ones – indeed, Lee Kuan Yew was forced to pull back from his embrace of Confucianism for the simple reason that it did not reflect the cultural heritage of the 15 percent of Singapore's population that is of Malay descent.
>
> (Fukuyama 1998:
> <http://www.findarticles.com/cf_o/m1061/n2_v105/20217503/p1/article.jhtml>)

So the empirical basis of Asian values themselves (regardless of whether they had any impact) was always very debatable. Their use, as suggested above, seemed to be part of deliberate rhetorical strategies by elites. Indeed, another way of pouring cold water on to the idea of 'Asian values' has been to suggest that they emerged as an item of political discourse to lend legitimacy to the political aims of South East Asian politicians such as Lee and Mahatir. In particular, the discourse of 'Asian values' may be regarded as a convenient prop for the continuation of authoritarian forms of government at the expense of democratisation. Fukuyama again sees rather more nuance than much of the debate seems to have allowed for:

> Aside from inculcating good work habits, Asian values have also been said to have a political dimension. Thus, Lee and Mahathir have argued that their brand of authoritarian government is well-suited to Confucian traditions of hierarchy and enables the state to focus its resources on economic development while avoiding the high degree of social disorder characteristic of Western democracies.

continued

continued

> Unfortunately, the alleged cultural fit between Asian values and authoritarian government is a matter more of convenience than of principle. In any old and complex cultural system – whether Confucianism or Christianity – it is possible to find sources legitimating totally contradictory practices. Historically, Christians reading the same Bible have both promoted and condemned slavery. Similarly, if Lee Kuan Yew can cite Confucian sources to support rule by benevolent authoritarianism, Taiwan's Lee Teng-hui has cited other sources to prove the compatibility of Confucian tradition with the kind of democratic institutions he has sought to build in his island nation. All cultural systems evolve. Given the examples of Japan, South Korea, and Taiwan, who is to say that Asian values constitute an insuperable obstacle to the establishment of Western-style democracy?
>
> (Fukuyama 1998: <http://www.findarticles.com/cf_o/m1061/n2_v105/20217503/p1/article.jhtml>)

In some ways the financial crisis that commenced in the summer of 1997 and which hit several South-East and East Asian countries might have signalled the end of the Asian values thesis. After all, the rapid downturn in economic fortunes that spread across East and South-East Asia rather dented the reputation of the so-called 'tigers' as sources of unalloyed growth and dynamism. A series of massive speculative attacks saw the value of several Asian currencies drop dramatically. Governments were forced to sell foreign exchange reserves and put up interest rates to protect their currencies. This slowed economic growth and, in addition to the massive social costs associated with resultant unemployment and financial losses, many Asian countries' banking systems seemed ill-prepared and largely incapable of dealing with the crisis.

Suddenly Confucian values were being blamed because they spawned both 'bad' economic management and a variety of shady practices that undermined efficiency and lined the pockets of privileged elites. Suddenly the erstwhile tigers of Japan and Korea were being grouped with the nepotistic government of President Suharto in Indonesia. An analysis in *Time* magazine summarised well this line of thinking while going on to show how such thinking reproduced some of the homogenising stereotypes associated with earlier, more positive accounts of Asian values.

> Commentators who favor general explanations tend to focus on the broad contours of 'Confucian' or 'crony' capitalism and the malpractices these evils breed. . . . These [explanations] are static in that they don't explain why Asia's multiple sins came together in 1997 to cause such trouble. Surely, Confucianism and crony capitalism, implicit guarantees and other institutional peculiarities are not new. One wonders why it took several decades for them to wreak havoc on the economies of a previously dynamic region.
>
> (Mushkat 1998: <http://www.time.com/time/magazine/1998/int/980309/asia.what_really_caused_8.html>)

There is much analysis of the Asian crisis and its causes and many explanations have been offered. For some, the crisis was a generic crisis of 'globalisation' (see Chapter 15) – a consequence of capital mobility and the freedom from regulation of those market actors that engage in currency speculation. For others, it was a crisis that could have been averted in Asia had there been more robust regulatory institutions capable of dealing with the consequences of mobile financial capital (for a summary and discussion see Dieter 1998; Haggard 2000). The latter diagnosis – largely supported by the International Monetary Fund (IMF) – has been summarised as 'a failure of institutional accountability, understood as the absence of transparency, moral hazards, the inadequate rule of law – in short, "crony capitalism"' (<http://www.unrisd.org/engindex/research/asia.htm>).

This argument – itself now as powerful a tool of political discourse as the 'Asian values' idea that pre-dated it – is again emphasising the determining effect of a particular kind of culture. In this case it is economic culture or, perhaps, the (alleged) weaknesses of the Asian culture of capitalism. It is about culture in the sense of embedded norms and established practices of economic management that differ markedly from a liberal Anglo-Saxon model of regulation. As a pair of American commentators put it in the *Wall Street Journal*:

> The debacle in Asia was caused by 'crony capitalism', an oxymoron describing the ways in which politicians infect markets by distorting prices and artificially creating winners and losers. Investors were encouraged to take enormous gambles in real estate, finance, and other industries – and when these gambles produced big losses, the current crisis ensued. We don't face this problem in the US, so we shouldn't fear being infected by Asia's ills.
>
> (Sacks and Thiel 1998: <http://www.independent.org/tii/content/op_ed/sacks_thiel_imf_bailout.html>)

This case shows us how political analysis can be about different sorts of things. There are 'cultural' hypotheses about both the spectacular rise of Asian economies and their recent crisis. On the face of it, these explanations seem to be at best contentious and more often than not full of dubious assumptions. But, as students of political culture, our interest should not necessarily be diverted. What is especially interesting in this case is how rather stereotypical ideas about the interplay between Asian cultural values and economic fortunes become staples of political and media discourse. Whether or not the 'Asian values' theses are 'true' perhaps matters less than the fact that a number of key people have a stake in believing them to be true. This is something that is well worthy of further investigation.

The European Union: creating a new political culture?

As we will observe in Chapter 14, the European Union (EU) consists of a remarkable set of institutions and political practices above and beyond the traditional framework of the nation-state. There is an argument to suggest that the EU has developed into a fully functioning political system. Much work on the EU, and European integration more generally, has been concerned with mapping the formal and less formal aspects of the system of EU institutions, as well as attending to their relationship with the institutions of (national) government in the component member states. The relationship between European integration and the behaviour of pressure groups is another area of academic enquiry, as is more overtly theoretical work that tries to understand the dynamics of regional integration in Europe and the wider global political economy.

But we can also ask some very important questions about culture. Most obviously, does the evolution of a system of European institutions bring with it a corresponding European political culture? In addition, to what extent are the norms, habits, attitudes and dispositions of political actors in contemporary Europe shaped by the processes of European integration?

The founders of what we now know as the European Union tended to regard political culture as a secondary phenomenon. Their project was to create a single market among member state economies. This would be presided over by a set of new institutions above the nation-state. The emphasis on the efficient, functional, technocratic management of economic life was given theoretical support by scholars of the neo-functionalist school, who argued that this elite-driven process would ultimately sell itself to pressure groups and mass publics alike. Both theorists and practitioners of European integration envisaged the transference of 'loyalties' (that is to say patterns of political behaviour) away from nation-states towards the new supranational European framework. Thus economic integration combined with the development of European-level institutions would produce a polity of sorts with its own norms (see Rosamond 2000: ch. 3).

The literature on political culture and political socialisation (introduced earlier in this chapter and in Chapter 2) suggests that political systems work best when they are underwritten by a robust set of belief values and norms. There is little evidence of a coherent EU political culture, and thus the dilemmas for proponents of European integration is how best to create such a culture. The dilemma is sharpened by the obvious observation that the EU consists (at present) of fifteen member states, each of which possesses its own distinctive political culture. Economic integration may be possible in the face of such diversity. However, pro-Europeans worry about three things. First, there is the concern that mass allegiance to (or indeed understanding of) the project of integration will not be forthcoming without a vibrant sense of cultural belonging. Second, they fear that the lack of an EU political culture disables the development of a fully functioning participatory political system. After all, authority undeniably is drifting away from national governments to the European level (Hooghe and Marks 2001; Schmitter 1996), yet public engagement with this 'Europeanisation' of governance remains primitive to say the least (Sinnott and Niedermayer 1995). Third, some economists worry that the lack of a common European identity means that the emerging European economy will continue to mean that 'European consumers do not feel "European" in a political or legal sense', so that 'the weakness of our collective European identity . . . is both a source and a symptom of deeper commercial malfunctioning' (The Henley Centre for Market Research, cited in Shore 2000: 20).

For long periods after the founding of the European Communities in the 1950s, it was assumed that economic integration would 'spill over' into the realm of politics and that citizens and key social groups would transfer their loyalties away from national political systems. In the absence of this shift and in light of the sorts of concerns outlined in the above paragraphs, concerted effort has been devoted since the early 1970s to thinking of how best to bring about the 'requisite underpinnings' (Howe 1995) of a genuine community of Europeans.

The following initiatives have been the most prominent:

▨ In 1973 the (then nine) member states signed a 'Declaration on the European Identity' (note the definite article!) (European Commission 1973). This affirmed their commonalities (for example, commitments to economic progress, the rule of law, social justice, democracy, human rights and individualism).

▨ The idea of a 'People's Europe' appeared with some frequency throughout the 1970s and 1980s. The idea of a 'cultural dimension' to European integration emerged from these discussions and European audiovisual policy became a vehicle for the creation of a cohesive European cultural space.

▨ The 1992 Treaty on European Union (the Maastricht Treaty) provided a substantial stimulus to giving EU cultural policy a legal basis. Many of the initiatives since have used Article 151 of the Treaties as their springboard (see document below)

Document

Cultural Activity

General Overview

Cultural cooperation has become a recognised aim of community action, with an appropriate legal basis. It is also at the heart of the 'ever closer union among the peoples of Europe' that the Member States have resolved to construct.

Article 151 of the Treaty on the European Union signed in Maastricht defined three major objectives for community action in the cultural field:

• to contribute to the flowering of the cultures of the Member States, while respecting their national and regional diversity and at the same time bringing the common cultural heritage to the fore;

- to encourage contemporary cultural creation;
- to foster cooperation between the Member States and with third countries and the competent international organisations.

Community action is based on cooperation and respects cultural diversity and the principle of subsidiarity. Its role is to supplement and support Member States' action in order to:

- improve the knowledge and dissemination of the culture and history of the European peoples;
- conserve and safeguard cultural heritage of European significance;
- support cultural exchanges and artistic and literary creation.

In concrete terms, these new competencies were reflected into the implementation of three cultural programmes between 1996 and 1999.

- *Kaléidoscope (1996–1999)* which aimed to encourage artistic and cultural creation and cooperation of a European dimension.
- *Ariane (1997–1999)* for support in the field of books and reading, including by means of translation.
- *Raphaël (1997–1999)* which aimed to supplement Member State policies in the field of cultural heritage of European significance.

Since the beginning of the year 2000, the *'Culture 2000' framework programme* replaces the previous actions over a period of 5 years (2000–2004). Equipped with this new programme, the Community aims to implement a new approach to cultural action.

It seeks to encourage the creation of a cultural area common to Europeans and to promote cooperation between cultural operators in order to develop intercultural dialogue, knowledge of history and culture, the transnational dissemination of culture, cultural diversity, artistic creation, the promotion of heritage and socio-economic and social integration. The Culture 2000 programme also supports the *European cultural capital cities*.

In addition to these aims and areas for action, it has been clearly stipulated that the Community must henceforth take cultural aspects into account in the definition and implementation of its policies as a whole.

<http://europa.eu.int/comm/culture/overview_en.html>

THINK POINT

Can a European culture be engineered in this way?

Key text: C. Shore (2000) *Building Europe: The Cultural Politics of European Integration,* London: Routledge.

In concrete terms, much of the product of these campaigns has been concerned to supply European citizens with information about the activities of the EU. However, as Cris Shore (2000) carefully documents in his book *Building Europe: The Cultural Politics of European Integration*, the Commission has sought to induce a European consciousness through the initiation of various educational exchange programmes, by arguing for the alignment of the EU to certain populist causes (such as lotteries and sports teams) and by creating discernible symbols of the EU. Most prominent among the latter is the European flag which was first used in 1986 (you can find out the graphical specifications for the correct reproduction of the flag at <http://europa.eu.int/abc/symbols/emblem/graphics/graphics_en.htm>).

These initiatives seem feebly insignificant in comparison to the advent of the euro, a single currency serving twelve of the EU's fifteen member states (the

exceptions are Denmark, Sweden and the UK). The countries of the 'euro-zone' are engaged in a monetary union. At one level, this is a technical exercise in which exchange rates between participating states are irrevocably fixed and monetary policy is exercised at a European level. But money is rather more than a unit of account. As Dyson (1994) points out, currencies are deeply symbolic. From 1 January 2002, the euro-zone countries began using euro notes and coins. This was followed by the relatively rapid discontinuation of the twelve national currencies. As an achievement, the single currency is a remarkable event. As a potential cultural shift, it is perhaps too early to make a judgement. But we can speculate about the possible impact of the day-to-day reality of hundreds of millions of Europeans using euro notes and coins in their daily business. As a single currency becomes normalised and taken for granted, so its potential power as a shaper of identity may become all the more potent. Theorists of national identity such as Michael Billig (1995) have written on the ways in which the 'banal' (taken-for-granted) aspects of life are rather more crucial shapers of actors' identities than grand flag-waving forms of cultural symbolism. In that respect, the advent of the euro may help to reinforce what Laura Cram (2001) has called 'banal Europeanism' – those elements of European integration that are so embedded in the lives of Europeans that they are barely noticed, yet shape political attitudes and action.

A cultural analysis of European integration may also be applied away from the obvious realms of cultural and monetary policy. There is some evidence to suggest that the EU policy process and the EU's institutions have developed their own distinctive cultures. The disparities between British political culture and that of the EU's institutions is explored by Stephen George (1994). George found that the culture of the European Parliament came as something of a shock to British Members of the European Parliament (MEPs) who had been schooled in the adversarial Westminster system:

the most difficult thing that British members had to adjust to in the European Parliament was the constant talking around issues. It was . . . as though it was more important for everybody to have their say than it was to get on with the business in hand. The constant revision of drafts and reports to account for the views of minorities remained beyond the comprehension of some British MEPs, used to a system in which ritual denunciations of the proposals of political opponents were invariably ignored.

(George 1994: 53)

The experience of European integration revealed further differences in elite political cultures. As George notes, there is a contrast between British and continental European approaches to decision-making which are rooted in different sorts of attitudes, norms and values. The British approach may be summed up as taking a step-by-step approach to problem-solving, whereas other European decision-making systems are more attuned to the setting of long-term goals prior to laying out the details of how these goals might be achieved. Consequently, disagreements, which often flare up in the inter-governmental forums of the EU, may not necessarily reflect different philosophical positions on a given issue, but may derive from alternative conceptions of how policy should be made and how issues should be negotiated.

That said, in his detailed study of British MEPs, Martin Westlake (1994) suggests that working in the environment provided by the European Parliament has tended to socialise these politicians away from the cultural norms of British party political culture. Westlake's analysis of MEPs' attitudes over time seems to endorse the view that support for an expanded role for the Parliament and for pro-integrationist attitudes more generally are the consequence of time spent working in the institution.

After 11 September 2001: a clash of civilisations?

On 11 September 2001 two commercial aircraft were hijacked and piloted into the twin towers of the World Trade Center in New York. A third hit the Pentagon, the headquarters of the US military in Washington, DC, while a fourth crashed, presumably *en route* to another target in the US capital city. Over 3000 people lost their lives.

It has since been widely accepted that the perpetrators of these atrocities were members of the *Al Qaida* terrorist organisation, a group noted for its adherence to a particular version of fundamentalist Islam, its international reach and its leadership by the exiled Saudi multi-millionaire Osama bin Laden. *Al Qaida*'s aims involve the installation of governments that adhere to its reading of Islamic law (*Sharia*). It displays particular contempt for governments in the Islamic world that it defines as corrupt or under Western influence. The organisation's prime foe is the United States, which it defines as the quintessential enemy of Islam. In 1998, bin Laden issued a *fatwah* in which he called for a *jihad* (holy war) against the United States. According to bin Laden, the American military presence in the Arabian peninsula – a constant feature since the Gulf War of the early 1990s – amounted to a violation of Islam's holiest sites. The *fatwah* went on:

We – with God's help – call on every Muslim who believes in God and wishes to be rewarded to comply with God's order to kill the Americans and plunder their money wherever and whenever they find it. We also call on Muslim *ulema*, leaders, youths, and soldiers to launch the raid on Satan's US troops and the devil's supporters allying with them, and to displace those who are behind them so that they may learn a lesson.

(<http://www.ict.org.il/articles/fatwah.htm>)

The response to the events of 11 September eventually involved a US-led attack on Afghanistan. The ruling Taliban regime was shielding bin Laden and many terrorist training camps were thought to exist throughout Afghanistan. The nature and implications of this so-called 'War Against Terrorism' are discussed further in Chapter 14. For now, it is worth reminding ourselves that George Bush's administration along with those of key allies such as the UK bent over backwards in their efforts to decouple the campaign against *Al Qaida* from any idea that the action being taken was born out of hostility to Islam as a religion or to Muslims generally.

Even so, the debate following 11 September was notable for the deployment of one of the most provocative ideas produced by a political scientist in recent memory: Samuel Huntington's 'clash of civilisations' thesis. A paper of that name first appeared in the journal *Foreign Affairs* in 1993 (Huntington 1993). It was followed three years later by a book-length treatment in an attempt to flesh out Huntington's core argument.

Huntington (b. 1927), Albert J. Weatherhead III University Professor and Director of the John M. Olin Institute for Strategic Studies at Harvard University, is perhaps best known as the author of *The Clash of Civilizations*, one of the most provocative discussions of the emerging post-Cold War world order. The book's influence may be gauged from the fact that it has been translated into over twenty languages. He has also made seminal contributions to the study of American politics, comparative politics, the politics of development and aspects of military and strategic studies. Huntington has held numerous prestigious academic and public appointments, including working for the administrations of US Presidents Lyndon Johnson and Jimmy Carter. He was founding editor of *Foreign Policy*, now a 'must read' journal for members of the academic and policy communities working on international relations.

Samuel P. Huntington

Huntington's work is motivated by a desire to think through the shape of the emerging world order after the Cold War. In essence, his argument is that cultural differences are likely to be at the heart of future global conflicts:

Key text: S. Huntington (1996) *The Clash of Civilizations and the Remaking of World Order*, New York: Simon & Schuster.

In this new world, local politics is the politics of ethnicity; global politics is the politics of civilizations. The rivalry of the superpowers is replaced by the clash of civilizations.

In this new world, the most pervasive, important, and dangerous conflicts will not be between social classes, rich and poor, or other economically defined groups, but between peoples belonging to different cultural entities. Tribal wars and ethnic conflicts will occur within civilizations. Violence between states and groups from different civilizations, however, carries with it the potential for escalation as other states and groups from these civilizations rally to the support of their 'kin countries'.

(Huntington 1996: 28)

The Cold War order aligned a world of nation-states into two rival camps, each with a leading superpower (the USA and the USSR). The end of the Cold War dispenses with this tight bipolar alignment of countries and – for Huntington – gives way to a situation where civilisational values come to form the basis of allegiances, alignments, alliances, and thus also of rivalry and enmity between competing civilisations:

The philosophical assumptions, underlying values, social relations, customs, and overall outlooks on life differ significantly among civilizations. The revitalization of religion throughout much of the world is reinforcing these cultural differences. Cultures can change, and the nature of their impact on politics and economics can vary from one period to another. Yet the major differences in political and economic development among civilizations are clearly rooted in their different cultures. East Asian economic success has its source in East Asian culture, as do the difficulties East Asian societies have had in achieving stable democratic political systems. Islamic culture explains in large part the failure of democracy to emerge in much of the Muslim world. Developments in the postcommunist societies of Eastern Europe and the former Soviet Union are shaped by their civilizational identities. Those with Western Christian heritages are making progress toward economic development and democratic politics; the prospects for economic and political development in the Orthodox countries are uncertain; the prospects in the Muslim republics are bleak.

(Huntington 1996: 28–9)

Huntington identifies 'seven or eight' major civilisations in the post-Cold War world. The 'West' is perhaps the most important. It is the most powerful and thereby exercises a pull on other civilisations either to emulate (Westernise) or to differentiate themselves further (as in the case of Islamic and Confucian societies).

THINK POINT

- Will cultures clash?

- What do you think of the Huntington hypothesis?

- Will civilisations come into conflict with one another because of cultural disparity?

Yet again, we have culture being offered as the explanation for a political phenomenon. Huntington's thesis was intended to be a set of reflections upon the emergent trends in world politics. Within hours of the attacks on the World Trade Center and the Pentagon, commentators were invoking Huntington's work as a framework for understanding the terrible events. This was a *prima facie* case of two civilisational value systems – the West and fundamentalist Islam – coming into conflict. One (Islam in a virulent form) had become intolerant of the other ('the West') to the point of committing extreme violence. Neither the attack on the USA nor the subsequent reaction was about strategic or national interests as traditionally understood. It was a conflict about values – and incommensurable civilisational values at that.

Huntington's thesis has proved to be extremely controversial, and thus it is hardly surprising that any attempt to apply a 'clash of civilisations' reading to the attack on the USA and the 'War Against Terrorism' is equally likely to provoke much debate.

Huntington has been taken to task for his slippery understanding of 'civilisation'. Two sorts of objection arise here. The first is that Huntington is never clear about what differentiates one civilisation from another. Religion seems to be important in some cases, but Catholic Latin American countries form their own civilisational bloc, while Southern European Catholic countries (such as Spain) are part of the West. On the other hand, Huntington feels able to treat most of sub-Saharan Africa as a civilisation – in spite of Africa's ethnic and religious diversity. The second objection is that civilisational factors seem to be explanations of first and last resort. Instances of conflict and crisis must, by Huntington's apparent reckoning, be about the deep value disparities that characterise different civilisations (Burma 2001).

One of Huntington's most scathing critics has been Edward Said. Said sees the clash of civilisations thesis as not only crude but excessively pernicious. He maintains that Huntington's book should be read as a 'crudely articulated manual in the art of maintaining a wartime status in the minds of Americans and others' (Said 2001: 573). Moreover, '[w]hat is described as "Islam" belongs to the discourse of Orientalism, a construction fabricated to whip up feelings of hostility and antipathy against a part of the world that happens to be of strategic importance' (Said 2001: 586). In other words, this view sees Huntington's work as a component of a much broader rhetorical strategy that actively constructs images of Islam as a different, unified, hostile entity and sells these images in support of particular American strategic interests. It is part of an act of defining new enemies – coherent others – to bolster self-image and to justify certain patterns of foreign policy and military expenditure.

Conclusion

The lessons to be learned from the analysis of political culture in its own right are clearly important for the student of politics. The centrality of attitudes, beliefs and orientations to political life in all its manifestations is difficult to deny. The connections which may be made between levels of political stability and types of political culture provide the basis for much lively debate among political scientists. But this chapter has also delved a little deeper, and in so doing has made a number of observations about the conduct of political science. The study of political culture reveals very clearly that political phenomena may be read from a variety of different perspectives. The 'cultural approach' is a clearly discernible subfield of political enquiry which chooses to investigate phenomena such as political stability, terrorism, regional integration and economic advance using culture as an independent variable (i.e. that which does the explaining). It is also true that the subject of political culture, as we have seen, may be approached from radically different viewpoints. This point is important, not simply because there is a choice of ways of 'doing' political science. It is important for 'readers' of political science to appreciate that every piece of analysis has a theoretical homeland which does much to define the hypotheses generated and the agenda for research thereafter. The case study of *The Civic Culture* tells us much about the difficulties of inference in political science and the perils of constructing chains of causation. Such matters are not confined to the study of political culture; they pervade everything that you will read about in this book and everything that you will study subsequently.

Chapter summary

- The term political culture refers to the complex of values, beliefs and attitudes that define the rules of the game in a political system.

- The study of these phenomena has a long history and has been central to the history of political science.

- The study of political culture became associated with the behavioural revolution in political science after the Second World War. Students of political culture such as Almond and Verba were interested in the relationship between political culture and regime stability. They concluded that the optimum political culture for a liberal democratic polity involved a mixture of 'subject' and 'participant' attitudes.

- Studying a book like Almond and Verba's *The Civic Culture* gives us insight into the complexities and pitfalls of undertaking political analysis.

- Behaviouralists do not have a monopoly on the study of attitudes, beliefs, norms and framing ideas in political life. Alternative accounts, such as those coming from the Marxist tradition, treat the subject in quite distinct ways. Writers like Gramsci and Althusser pay attention to the relationship between prevailing values and the exercise of power by ruling groups.

- Some analysts prefer to engage in the study of subcultures with a political system. The ways in which cultural difference is integrated into the political system may help to explain particular features of a polity, such as its party system.

- The study of political culture is also bound up with the issue of political identity. The manufacture and reinforcement of identity is an integral part of politics.

- Cultural readings may be applied to many and varied political phenomena. 'Culture' as an explanation is vulnerable to quite profound criticism, but it is notable how frequently 'cultural' accounts of politics crop up in the media and in the rhetoric of politicians themselves.

EXERCISE

- This chapter includes three case studies in which contemporary issues are addressed through the lens of political culture. Your task is to write a similar short case study that develops an analysis of any political issue in terms of culture. You can use newspapers and news magazines as your sources, but remember that you need to go beyond conventional journalistic treatments of issues. Your job is to reread the issue using the concepts and ideas developed in this chapter.

- The selection of the case study is obviously up to you and should reflect your own interests and knowledge. However, it may be useful to look for an instance of political conflict or for a situation where political actors are exposed to a new environment.

- When you have completed the case study, take some time to think about how much – or how little – the use of political culture has told you about the issues in question. Has it enhanced or given a new angle to your understanding of your chosen issue? What else is there still to explain?

Key texts

Almond, G. A. and Verba, S. (1963) *The Civic Culture: Political Attitudes and Democracy in Five Nations*, Princeton: Princeton University Press. The classic study of political culture. Rooted in particular assumptions and much criticised, this nevertheless remains the essential benchmark for all subsequent discussions of the concept.

Gramsci, A. (1970) *Selections from the Prison Notebooks*, trans. Quentin Hoare, London: Lawrence & Wishart. Astonishing set of reflections on history and politics, penned in the late 1920s and early 1930s by an Italian Marxist prisoner of the Mussolini regime. Very influential upon subsequent 'alternative' formulations of political culture.

Inglehart, R. (1977) *The Silent Revolution: Changing Values and Political Styles Among Western Publics*, Princeton: Princeton University Press. Pathbreaking and rigorous, if controversial, attempt to map the contours of generational politico-cultural change in Western societies.

Huntington, S. (1996) *The Clash of Civilizations and the Remaking of World Order*, New York: Simon & Schuster. The book-length version of Samuel Huntington's powerful and highly controversial thesis about the emerging post-Cold War order.

Shore, C. (2000) *Building Europe: The Cultural Politics of European Integration*, London: Routledge. A wonderfully rich ethnographic analysis of the culture of EU institutions combines with a brilliant critical discussion of European cultural policy to produce one of the best recent books on European integration.

Further reading

Anonymous (1996) *Primary Colors*, New York: Warner Books. A very funny (yet utterly accurate) journey through the highways and byways of United States politics. The book follows the path to the White House of a southern Democrat presidential candidate through the eyes of one of his close aides.

Barnes, J. (1998) *England, England*, London: Jonathan Cape. A tycoon re-creates England as a theme park on the Isle of Wight. Julian Barnes' novel is a highly accomplished and funny satire on Englishness and the idea of England.

James, C. L. R. (1963) *Beyond a Boundary*, London: Stanley Paul. Probably the best book ever written about cricket, but a lot more besides. James supplies a brilliant discussion of the interplay between sport, the legacies of Empire and the forging of black Caribbean identity.

Kundera, M. (1984) *The Joke*, Harmondsworth: Penguin. Originally published in Czech (as *Zert*) in 1967, this intricate satirical love story reveals Milan Kundera's affection for Czechoslovakian culture and his deep understanding of the character of that country's politics under communism.

Parks, T. (1998) *Europa*, London: Vintage. A macabre stream-of-consciousness account of a fictional coach trip from Milan to the European Parliament in Strasbourg that gradually reveals a deep distaste for the idea of European cultural unity.

Paxman, J. (1999) *The English: A Portrait of a People*, Harmondsworth: Penguin. An acerbic, funny and thoughtful analysis of the components of contemporary Englishness.

Political Participation

Barrie Axford

▮ **Introduction: what is political participation?**

Political participation A term to denote the actions by which individuals take part in the political process. Debate centres on the causes of participation and non-participation.

Social engineering refers to the process whereby an existing state of affairs, for example low self-esteem among some ethnic minorities, is altered through policies and practice designed to bring about what is seen as a more desirable state of affairs.

Individuals who are socialised into a political culture have undergone a learning process that provides with them the resources – knowledge and skills, attitudes and beliefs – to function as reasonably competent political actors within that milieu. As we have noted in previous chapters, the process of social and political learning is often diffuse and the learning curve rather shallow, unless it forms part of a deliberate programme of social engineering. Individuals who are socialised into particular cultures will have been exposed to the same beliefs and values, and will thus be able to recognise and respond to relevant cultural symbols and cues, such as popular beliefs about the role of government, although not always in the same ways.

For the student of political behaviour, of enduring interest is the extent to which individuals conform or differ in the ways they think and feel about politics and vary in the extent to which they participate in political activity. Research shows considerable variations across political systems and also within them. In this chapter we will examine the factors that introduce variations in the level and intensity of political participation, and by doing so we will learn more about the ways in which psychological, cultural, social and political factors, as well as other more immediate stimuli, influence political behaviour.

With the exception of voting, political participation is a minority sport in all modern political systems. Some individuals are highly active in politics, joining political parties and canvassing on behalf of particular candidates in elections. Others may join single-issue pressure groups with the aim of advancing causes, and a few – very few – become career politicians by successfully standing for public office. In complete contrast, some people abstain completely from political activity, refusing even to vote, while others (not necessarily part of the same category) are completely **apathetic** about the political world in all its guises.

Apathy Implies an inattention to or unconcern with and a passivity about politics.

From early November 1999, the Shorenstein Center at Harvard University conducted weekly national polls designed to measure public attention to the presidential election campaign then being conducted in the USA. During the average week over a six-month period, nearly half (46 per cent) of adults under 30 claimed to be paying no attention at all to the campaign and a quarter said they were paying 'only a little' attention. Only 4 per cent said they were paying 'a great deal' of attention and 8 per cent claimed to be giving the campaign 'quite a bit' of attention. Among adults 30 years of age and older, nearly twice as many (22 per cent) were paying 'a great deal' or 'quite a bit' of attention.

The study of political participation is the examination of both activity and non-activity and the reasons underlying both.

THINK POINT

▨ Are you politically active?

▨ What activities have you undertaken?

▨ Are you more or less politically active than your friends and acquaintances?

The definition of political participation is far from straightforward. One problem is that all definitions are more or less exclusive. For example, we might define political participation as those voluntary actions through which people seek to influence the making of public policy. The emphasis on 'voluntary' actions immediately excludes those forms of participation that are coerced. A good example of participation that is coerced or at least manipulated in some way is the mass mobilisation of support for authoritarian regimes seen at carefully staged rallies or in 'spontaneous' street protests to acclaim a military leader, or to denounce opposition parties and rival governments. But such a definition would also have to exclude voting in democratic countries where casting a ballot is obligatory under law, as occurs, for example, in Australia, Luxembourg, Brazil and Ecuador.

Exclusive definitions are also problematic because they may carry with them some normative baggage. For example, voting and standing for public office are acknowledged forms of political participation, but (at least on some definitions) protesting in the street or building a barricade against the police or tax collectors might not be. The basis for inclusion and exclusion is not always scientific. In fact it owes more to what are seen as legitimate forms of

For a discussion of normative approaches to politics, see the Introduction to this book, pp. 4–10.

G8 refers to the seven richest world economies plus Russia.

activity; and what is legitimate varies considerably with time and place. Think of the anti-G8 protests in Genoa in the summer of 2001. In democratic political systems, a great many people recognise the legitimacy of peaceful protest, but would probably baulk at the idea that violent protest is a legitimate form of political participation where there are other opportunities for citizens to articulate their demands. But applied to regimes where most forms of visible and routine opposition are proscribed – Afghanistan under the Taliban, Iraq and Myanmar come to mind – this qualification may carry less weight. Such difficult judgements are not only a matter of noting the legality of various forms of participation – in both Italy and Myanmar there are laws limiting the right of people to protest – but turn on culturally sanctioned ideas about what is acceptable political behaviour.

What we need is an inclusive definition of political participation, but one that is sensitive to context. The authors of a major study on political participation in Britain suggest that political participation consists of taking part in the process of formulation, passage and implementation of public policies. It is concerned with action by citizens which is aimed at influencing decisions taken by public representatives and officials. This may be action that tries to shape the attitudes of decision-makers on matters yet to be decided, or it may be action in protest at the outcome of a decision (Parry *et al.* 1992: 16). Inclusive definitions tend to be anodyne, but do have the considerable merit of accommodating a very wide range of actions across what we might call conventional political participation (communicating with a Member of Parliament, voting, joining a political party) and unconventional forms (such as boycotting supermarkets suspected of stocking GM foods or forming a virtual network of activists to raise consciousness and campaign about global warming).

Key text: G. Parry, G. Moyser and N. Day (1992) *Political Participation and Democracy in Britain*, Cambridge: Cambridge University Press.

Of course, the very distinction between conventional and unconventional political activity is problematic. What seemed unusual and on the fringes of legitimacy in the 1950s and 1960s – anti-Vietnam War demonstrations, trade union marches – look old hat and staid in the new millennium when thousands take to the streets to protest about global capitalism and action is planned across the Internet.

In addition, political participation is not confined to successful actions. Much (perhaps even the bulk) of the activity falling within the broad definition offered above is fruitless in relation to its avowed intent – influencing the outcomes of decisions – although it may serve to raise the political consciousness and improve the political skills of participants. There is also the question of where politics – and thus political participation – begins and ends. Although Parry and his colleagues do not examine more passive forms of behaviour, given our strictures about the flexibility of the definition relative to time and place, it is easy to imagine circumstances in which conversations about political issues with friends, reading certain kinds of books and joking with work colleagues or family about politicians would all be important types of political activity in their own right. So their definition is useful but possibly too restricted in defining the political realm. It also pushes the student of

See the Introduction to this book for a discussion of this issue.

politics to examine only those activities designed to influence governmental policy, but not those actions which seek to affect societal and cultural values as much as they seek to change public policy (for example, some forms of feminism and environmentalism). Because of this limitation, our catholic or inclusive definition of political participation must take on board those actions aimed at influencing civil society as well as government. Further, as students of politics in a globalised world we also need our inclusive definition to recognise the scope for politics and governance beyond the territorial state and the arenas for political action that are available there.

Civil society refers to that realm of social activity that is not to do with the state or the market, and that would include, for example, membership of voluntary associations like football clubs and pub quiz teams.

See Chapter 14 for governnance beyond the nation-state and Chapter 15 for a full discussion of globalisation.

1 Voting in national elections.
2 Voting in referendums.
3 Canvassing or otherwise campaigning in elections.
4 Active membership of a political party.
5 Active membership of a pressure group.
6 Taking part in political demonstrations, industrial strikes with political objectives, rent strikes in public housing, and similar activities aimed at changing public policy.
7 Various forms of civil disobedience, such as refusing to pay taxes or obey a conscription order.
8 Membership of government advisory committees.
9 Membership of consumers' councils for publicly owned industries.
10 Client involvement in the implementation of social policies.
11 Various forms of community action, such as those concerned with housing or environmental issues of the day.

Figure 4.1 The main types of political participation
Source: Birch (1993: 81)

The next step in defining the concept of political participation is to classify the different types of political activity. In his book *The Concepts and Theories of Modern Democracy* (1993), Anthony Birch lists what he understands as the main conventional types of political participation. The list is reproduced in Figure 4.1. However, as noted above, other activities may be regarded as forms of political participation. Dressing in a particular way, choosing brand x over brand y when shopping, deciding which stories to read to one's child and going fox-hunting are all actions with 'political' connotations in that they expand or limit the choices available and reflect one world view as opposed to another. Indeed, if the feminist idea of the personal as political has any meaning, then a multiplicity of supposedly 'private' actions, such as negotiations over who does the household chores, become political – it all depends on the context in which the actions are taking place.

Let us stay with the classification of the concept for the moment. In an important and influential early statement on the subject, Lester Milbrath (1965) developed an argument in which political participation was seen as a

Key text: A. H. Birch (1993) *The Concepts and Theories of Modern Democracy*, London: Routledge.

Key text: L. Milbrath (1965) *Political Participation: How and Why Do People Get Involved in Politics?*, Chicago: Rand McNally.

hierarchical activity. Milbrath arranged the American population along a one-dimensional hierarchy depicting different intensities of political participation. Individuals could be located in one of three groups: 'gladiators', 'spectators' and 'apathetics'. Approximately one-third of the American public was located in the apathetics category. These were individuals who abstained from any form of political activity, even voting. Spectators – about three-fifths of the population – involved themselves minimally in politics. Usually, these were people who did little more than vote in elections. This left as little as one-twentieth of the US public actively and widely involved in politics as gladiators.

Look back at the definition of 'apathy' above. Milbrath may have been too lax in his use of the term to cover all forms of non-participation.

THINK POINT

Does this image describe you and people like you?

While most studies have confirmed that intensive and committed political participation is a minority activity, research conducted after the first edition of Milbrath's study suggested that the hierarchical model of participation was in need of amendment. Milbrath's original hierarchy suggested that those in the upper echelons (gladiators) also engaged in the activities of spectators and less intensive gladiators. However, later studies depict more specialisation in political participation. So, rather than arranging participants in a single hierarchy of less or more intensive activity, we should acknowledge that the bulk of participation takes place in relatively specialised domains; that is, people tend not to serve apprenticeships in political activism, graduating from less intense to more intense forms and then remaining active across the range. Instead they opt in and out of activism, depending on the issue; or else graduate straight to the higher reaches of engagement. This path-breaking work also originated in the United States, but was confirmed in a growing number of comparative studies. Key work was done by Sidney Verba and Norman H. Nie in *Participation in America* (1972) and by Verba *et al.* in *The Modes of Democratic Participation* (1971) and *Participation and Political Equality* (1978). The key insight to emerge from these studies was the idea of modes (types) of political participation, which allowed a more sophisticated classification, such as that seen in Figure 4.2. There are various classifications

Key texts: S. Verba and N. H. Nie (1972) *Participation in America: Political Democracy and Social Equality*, New York: Harper & Row; S. Verba, N. H. Nie and J.-O. Kim (1971) *The Modes of Democratic Participation: A Cross-National Comparison*, Beverly Hills: Sage; (1978) *Participation and Political Equality: A Seven Nation Comparison*, Cambridge: Cambridge University Press.

available in the literature, but, to reiterate, the crucial point is that the research conducted by Verba and his colleagues indicates that participants tend, with very few exceptions, to be specialists in a particular mode. Rather than being complete activists, so-called 'gladiators' in fact specialise, for example, in writing letters to politicians and public officials, or being candidates for office. This finding is echoed more recently in the work done on participation in Britain (Parry *et al.* 1992: ch. 3).

Protestors
Community activists (local issues)
Party and campaign workers
Communicators
Contactors (of politicians/officials on specific matters)
Voters
Inactive

Figure 4.2 Modes of political participation

Who participates? Some individual and social correlates of political participation

In this section and in the one following, we will look more closely at various factors which are related to political participation. You will note that we talk about 'related to' here as opposed to the much firmer 'caused by'. This caution is important if students of politics are to avoid spurious generalisations and false inferences. We will be concerned with a variety of explanations or partial explanations for who participates in politics and why. They are not mutually exclusive, because in real life each may contribute to a decision to vote for a particular party or to stay at home watching *Big Brother*. Unfortunately there is no unified or general theory of political participation, and so what we have is a mixture of universal interpretations of behaviour, like the economic model of activism canvassed in Chapter 1 (see pp. 28–34), and less ambitious attempts to establish statistically valid relationships between variables – for example, levels of education/sorts of television programmes watched and the type and intensity of political participation – in one or more countries.

We will look at both personal and social characteristics associated with different forms of political participation across countries, asking the question 'Who participates?' In the subsequent section we will explore both motivational (psychological and cultural) and structural (social conditions, legal constraints) factors which influence why people do or do not get involved in political activity. Because of the great variety of data available we have been quite selective in choosing illustrative material. A number of general points should be made about who participates in politics and what is known about who participates:

■ Much of the early data collected came from the Anglo-American democracies, although an increasing body of material is now available from other European democracies, Japan, India, the post-communist regimes of Eastern and Central Europe and parts of Central and South America. Very little reliable statistical information is available on, for example, the People's Republic of China and North Korea. The overall point to bear in mind is that some of the apparently general findings still rely on a quite limited number of cases and types of political system.

■ Often, information about individuals has come from large-scale survey analysis and sometimes from longitudinal studies of attitudes and behaviour conducted over a period of time. Other information has been produced by looking at the relationships between what are called 'aggregate statistics', such as census data on the social make-up of parliamentary constituencies or voting districts, and notionally dependent political variables, such as the percentage of votes cast for extreme right-wing parties. Qualitative studies of political participation that look beyond degrees of statistical correlation and examine motivation at the level of individual psychology are still relatively scarce, even in the area of political leadership, although biographies of key leaders abound.

■ A great deal of the early work on 'who participates' was conducted during the 1950s and 1960s and, with some refinements, this work has been largely corroborated by studies done since then. However, it is always possible that significant social and political trends were missed or glossed over because data were collected at a specific point in time and inferences were made which were not followed through into subsequent investigations. Snapshot insights into attitudes and beliefs can be very misleading, which is why an increasing number of large studies on political participation rely upon longitudinal data.

■ Most research on political participation is conducted within territorial nation-states, or else relies upon comparisons between them. Yet the forces of globalisation are altering the arenas of governance and political action. There is a growing number of empirical studies on international **social movements**, such as anti-globalisation movements, women's movements, community movements and peace movements (Tarrow 1998), and on the global politics conducted by international non-governmental organisations, such as the International Campaign to Ban Land-mines (Boli and Thomas 2000), but these are less interested in the motivations and social correlates of participants than in the ways in which their activism is shaping the emerging world polity.

■ All findings continue to show that political participation is a highly skewed activity, regardless of country. The more intense or select the activity

Social movement A network of informal interactions between individuals, groups and/or organisations engaged in a political or cultural activity, on the basis of a shared collective identity.

(standing for office as opposed to voting), the more skewed the social profile of those engaged in it and the fewer the numbers involved. There is also some evidence to suggest that different kinds of political and associational activity are strongly linked to certain social and individual characteristics. Data collected about the membership of civic organisations such as Friends of the Earth (FoE) and Amnesty International's British Section (AIBS) in the mid-1990s reveal some interesting comparisons, some of which are reported in Table 4.1.

Table 4.1 Characteristics of membership in selected voluntary organisations – UK data

	FoE (%)	AIBS (%)
Educated to degree level	35	26
	n=238	*n*=98
Household income £20,000-plus		
£20,001–£30,000	21	20
£30,001–£40,000	11	14
over £40,000	12	20
	n=301	*n*=192
Occupational categories		
clerical worker	8	8
professional	49	53
managerial	11	15
	n=455	*n*=271
Self-perceived class		
working class	21	23
middle class	74	71
	n=644	*n*=341

Source: Adapted from Jordan and Maloney (1996)

THINK POINT

What do these data tell us about the membership of the two organisations?

It is clear from these data that the middle class are the dominant social group in both organisations, but why should this be so? One possible explanation is that middle-class people have, or are more likely to have, greater disposable income to spend on membership than do working-class people. There are some difficulties with this explanation, however, and they illustrate the problems with making inferences from data like these. There is an obvious discrepancy between the self-perceived middle-class position of some 74 per cent of members of FoE and the fact that only 35 per cent attended university and 44 per cent have incomes higher than the UK national average of some £18,000 (*circa* 1996, when the study was published). Although the figures are different for AIBS, the pattern is the same. At least a proportion of those calling themselves middle class must, on 'objective' or measurable criteria fall outside this class, being less well educated and less handsomely paid. They may of course rely on other factors to define their middle-classness, like the sort of newspaper they read, the political party they vote for, the sort of wine they drink, or the kind of social aspirations they have. Here, too, the data are not terribly helpful in establishing a profile of membership which fits some neat pattern of cause and effect. Parties and groups of the left, centre-left and ecological fringe attract the vote of the self-assigned middle-class activists of FoE and AIBS, so that they vote 'out of their class' at least where that is understood on the basis of 'hard' data on income and employment.

Membership of voluntary organisations (political parties, trade unions, churches, sports clubs, women's groups, etc.) varies considerably across countries, as Table 4.2 shows. Although it is possible to make some observations from these data, along the lines that the countries of Southern Europe fall well behind all other groupings except Japan, we would be hard put to explain these differences simply in terms of the social characteristics of the various populations, nor, it seems, on the basis of their political history. All the countries of Eastern Europe have higher levels of voluntary activity than France, one of the members of the founding club of modern democracies. Nigeria, much criticised for its record on human rights and political freedoms,

Table 4.2 The extension of civil society, 1990–91 (percentage of the population belonging to a voluntary organisation)

Germanic Western Europe	70	E. Germany	84
Austria	54	Hungary	54
Belgium	59	Latvia	68
Britain	53	Lithuania	60
Denmark	81	Russia	66
Finland	78		
Iceland	90	*North America*	63
Ireland	49	Canada	65
Netherlands	84	USA	60
Sweden	84		
W. Germany	68	*New Latin World*	41
		Brazil	43
Latin Western Europe	35	Chile	45
France	39	Mexico	36
Italy	36		
Portugal	34	*Ex-colonial Zone*	
Spain	30	Nigeria	86
Eastern Europe	67		
Bulgaria	60	Japan	36
Estonia	73		

Source: World Values Survey 1990–91 (directed by R. Inglehart), Institute for Social Research, University of Michigan (data file)

tops the league table of voluntary activity. But we cannot make too many inferences from the figures; we can only describe them. It may be that cultural factors play a greater part in explaining the propensity of a population to join different forms of collective action, but, as we saw in Chapter 3, this is a minefield for the unwary.

Selected variables and political participation: a brief inventory

GENDER

In recent years national and cross-national research into voting behaviour has identified a 'gender gap' in the political dispositions of women and men. The concept refers to a whole raft of phenomena, including differing rates of turnout, party identification, political attitudes on a range of policy issues, and even profoundly felt political values (Mueller 1988; Norris 1996). Much of the early research on voting patterns among men and women (Duverger 1955; and discussed in Randall 1987) indicated that, generally speaking, women were more inclined to vote for centre and right-wing political parties than men. The tendency for women to be politically conservative was explained by a number of factors, including their lower trade union membership, stronger religious observance and greater longevity (age, too, being associated with conservatism).

Benazir Bhutto: Not the usual profile of a political gladiator

Political activist with the Pakistan Peoples Party (PPP), Pakistan, 1977–84; repeatedly imprisoned and kept under house arrest by the Pakistani government; political exile in London, England, 1984–86; returned to Pakistan in April 1986; Pakistan Peoples Party, Karachi, Pakistan co-chair, beginning in 1986. After elections held November 1988, invited to form the government, became Prime Minister in 1988 but her government was illegally dismissed in August 1990. She again came to power after her party won a majority in elections held in October 1993. Her government was once again dismissed illegally in November 1996 and she became Leader of the Opposition, National Assembly, Islamic Republic of Pakistan.

Table 4.3, however, modifies this finding quite substantially, while still showing marked variations between different countries. The table demonstrates that the conventional wisdom about women's greater conservatism is no longer valid, although, of themselves, the data do not reveal anything about the motivations of women (or men) voters, or about the meaning that they attach to political allegiance. On 1994 figures, women are more left wing than men in Portugal, Spain, Canada, the USA, Denmark and both Germanys (although Germany was united by this time, data are split in this table). In Britain, Australia, Luxembourg, Italy, Ireland and France, women were more conservative. No significant differences can be seen in the other countries. There is also some recent evidence which indicates that there is an age factor operating, with younger women not only more left wing than their older sisters, but also more so than their male counterparts (Norris 1996).

Table 4.3 Percentage of votes cast by men and women for parties of the right and left: selected countries, 1994

| | lwp | | | rwp | | | L–R lead | |
	W	M	Gap	W	M	Gap	W	M
Britain	45	51	–6	34	24	10	11	27
Australia	46	52	–6	48	41	7	–2	11
Luxemb'rg	28	30	–2	44	34	10	–16	–4
Italy	7	8	0	71	67	5	–64	–59
Ireland	16	18	–2	75	73	3	–59	–55
France	12	13	–1	36	33	3	–24	–20
Greece	52	54	–2	41	39	2	11	15
Belgium	30	27	3	31	29	3	–1	–1
Netherlands	30	30	0	45	46	–2	–15	–17
Denmark	34	28	6	43	40	3	–9	–12
W. Germany	40	39	1	38	41	–3	2	–2
Spain	28	27	1	45	48	4	–17	–21
USA	46	41	5	37	38	–1	9	3
Portugal	80	76	4	20	24	–4	60	53
E. Germany	50	42	8	47	49	–2	2	–7
Canada	59	44	15	28	37	–9	31	7
All	38	36	2	43	41	1	–5	–4

Key: lwp = left-wing parties; rwp = right-wing parties; L–R lead = left–right lead; W = women; M = Men; Gap = gender gap. A negative gender gap indicates that women are more right wing. A positive gender gap shows that they are more left wing

Note: Figures are rounded to the nearest decimal point.

Source: Eurobarometer, 1994, using Australian and Canadian general elections of 1993; US presidential election of 1992; major parties in European elections in 1994

EDUCATION

Almond and Verba (1963) suggested that education socialises citizens into democratic political cultures, although their data showed that this process varied across systems. Generally speaking, those with higher education are more likely to participate in politics regardless of the activity than those who are less well educated. Clearly there are problems with tying down indicators of educational attainment which would enable cross-national comparisons to be made and like to be compared with like (do terms like 'higher education' or 'further education' refer to the same thing in different countries? Where would vocational and post-experience education be located in any classification?). For all this, it seems that those with educational qualifications of any sort, and university graduates in particular, are not only more likely to participate, but are also more confident in their ability to understand politics. In Table 4.4 the relationship between educational qualifications and different sorts of political activity is outlined, including more radical forms of activism like taking part in a demonstration.

Table 4.4 Education and political participation – UK

Activity	Graduates (%)	Those with intermediate qualifications (%)	Those with no qualifications (%)
Contacted MP	29	11	8
Signed petition	52	37	29
Gone on protest	17	7	2

Source: Jowell *et al.* (1987)

Of course, higher education is not always a foolproof guide to involvement in what Milbrath called 'gladiatorial' activities. Recruitment to a leadership position in a political organisation which is conscious of its ideological integrity may mean that only those judged pure or loyal ('Is he one of us?' as ex-UK prime minister Margaret Thatcher opined) are eligible for office. In addition, there is often room for the maverick to challenge and sometimes flout the usual rules governing elite recruitment, by taking advantage of circumstances, or through using other attributes to secure office – charm, communication skills and possibly money. Occasionally, individuals have office thrust upon them by force of circumstance. By and large, the stereotype of the political activist and especially the elected representative as male, middle-aged and married still holds good. Table 4.5 gives some comparative figures on this phenomenon by listing percentages of female legislators in national parliaments.

THINK POINT

What inferences can you make from the data in Table 4.5 on page 132?

Table 4.5 Women in Parliaments: regional averages

	Single House or lower House (%)	Upper House or Senate (%)	Both Houses combined (%)
Nordic countries	38.9	–	38.9
Europe – OSCE member countries including Nordic countries	16.8	14.8	16.4
Americas	15.7	17.4	16.0
Asia	14.8	13.0	14.6
Europe – OSCE member countries excluding Nordic countries	14.7	14.8	14.7
Sub-Saharan Africa	12.8	12.8	12.8
Pacific	11.3	25.9	12.8
Arab States	4.6	2.5	4.3

Note: Regions are classified by descending order of the percentage of women in the lower or single House.

Source: Inter-Parliamentary Union, Women in National Parliaments, July 2001

DISABILITY

Findings from a major survey of people with various forms of physical disability (*Disability Research Consortium, Bureau of Economic Research, Rutgers University and New Jersey Developmental Disabilities Council*, April 1999) indicate that most people with disabilities feel well qualified to participate in politics, and are as likely as similar people without disabilities to participate in several non-electoral political and civic activities. They are, however, less likely on average to vote, make contributions to campaigns or political organisations, or contact elected representatives and public officials. The participation gaps are concentrated among people with disabilities who are unemployed, older and have difficulty going outside alone – those who are employed and/or younger (18–44) are, in fact, about as likely as otherwise similar people without disabilities to engage in these activities.

LIFE CYCLE TRANSITIONS

Quite a lot of research on political participation indicates that critical points in a person's life history can affect (disrupt and reshape) past patterns and levels of political involvement (Stoker and Jennings 1995). For example, being married (or partnered) seems to produce both a marked convergence in the participation rates of partners and a falling off in these rates, at least in the higher registers of activity. Research into other life cycle influences, for example divorce or the death of a family member, have not been studied as much as the standard socio-economic variables of class, occupation, income or sex, but given the significance of the networks of social and emotional interaction which centre on the family (or some surrogate for it), changes in close family circumstances may well have a formative and transformative impact on political participation.

Age differences in rates of participation have been studied to a much greater extent. Here the finding for the USA, Britain and France and for many of the other Western European liberal democracies is that between the ages of 50 and 60 political participation rates decline, except for those deeply involved as gladiators, but there is considerable variation across countries in the effects of age. In Germany, at least with regard to voting turnout, age is not a good predictor of activism, while unconventional forms of political participation are less obviously associated with the 'normal' pattern, which sees very low participation for those under twenty, rising steeply in the mid-forties and falling off more erratically towards old age (Parry *et al.* 1992). The young are much more inclined towards different types of protest activity than any other age group. The general finding, that political participation tends to rise and fall with age, would also have to be modified in the light of developments like the emergence of the 'grey lobby' in some Western countries; that is, of interest organisations devoted to articulating the demands of older people, as the following document shows:

Document

Parties Bow to Grey power

BBC News Online, 12 February 2001

Politicians are keen to win the 11m pensioner votes. If there is one thing politicians have learned over the past year it is that they ignore pensioners at their peril. There are around 11 million votes at stake here and 'grey power' is now a real force to be reckoned with. This is partly due to demographic changes – Britain is getting older by the year – but also because pensioner groups led by people like ex-trade union leader Jack Jones are becoming increasingly active. They have for decades believed they have come near the bottom of politicians' list of priorities but are now flexing their muscles – and to pretty good effect. All the parties are falling over themselves to woo the grey vote with William Hague's latest policy announcement being just the most recent.

The discussion of standard personal and social variables goes some way towards building a profile of the factors associated with different kinds of political activism. Other explanations of activism concentrate upon the importance of 'resource variables' in predicting participation. Schlozman *et al.* (1996), drawing upon American data, write about the significance of 'civic skills' acquired as a member of a religious organisation, or some non-political body, in disposing people towards political activism. Some of these skills, notably those derived from formal education, are related to a person's social and economic status in a community, but others are not. While this may be a particularly American slant on the factors influencing participation, comparative data suggest that higher participation in voluntary associations is also linked with higher rates of political participation. While the relationships between political participation and involvement in voluntary associations has been noted for a long time, in recent years the connection has been the focus of a great deal of research and commentary triggered by an alleged decline in civic activity across many democracies and the consequences of this decline for the rate and quality of political participation and the health of democratic life.

Some of these issues are taken further in Chapter 5.

Social capital and political participation

The concept of social capital has become one of the most discussed issues in the study of politics. Although there are disagreements about how to define social capital, it is probably uncontentious to say that it consists of the networks and norms of reciprocity and trust that are built up through interpersonal connections. When people associate with one another through the host of voluntary associations that populate diverse societies, they develop better skills of social intercourse, treat co-operation as routine and desirable and come to rely on and to trust one another. Of course, such an argument runs directly counter to the claims of those students of rational activism who counsel the illogic of collective action (Olson (1965) and the discussion in Chapter 1, pp. 28–34), so it is important to remember that theories of the relationships between social capital and political participation are not based simply on an assessment of the inherent or psychological attributes of individuals but refer to wider cultural phenomena found in different social groups.

In what is now seen as a seminal contribution, the American political scientist Robert Putnam (1995a, 1995b, 2001) has emphasised the relationship between high levels of social capital and political engagement and stressed the links between both factors and the quality of democratic life. Putnam first detected the correlation between high levels of civic engagement and involvement in public affairs in his study of social capital in Italy, where he found that the clearest determinant of governmental success was civic involvement. Regions with high voter turnout, high newspaper readership, and active choral societies and other community organisations tended to flourish, while those localities bereft of community ties tended to experience poor-quality public administration.

His argument is that in the United States there has been a significant change in patterns of social interactions since the 1950s, particularly in the levels of face-to-face contact afforded through memberships of voluntary community associations. Putnam is concerned that many activities common in the 1950s have been in steady decline. These activities include many low-cost political interventions – going to political meetings, attending Parent–Teacher Associations and the like – as well as some higher cost gladiatorial activities such as canvassing at election times and working for a candidate. There is even a suggestion that the decline in social capital is responsible for a growing reluctance on the part of Americans to offer themselves as candidates for public office and all types of public service. Nor does the malaise stop there. Other communal activities, such as joining social and leisure clubs, campaigning with neighbours on local issues, even entertaining family and friends at home, have all declined.

Putnam's most well-known article on the subject is entitled 'Bowling Alone – America's Declining Social Capital', where the fall-off in the number of Americans joining bowling leagues is taken as symptomatic of the more general problem.

For Putnam, the main consequence of the decline of social capital is a diminution of social trust, which in turn affects the propensity for civic engagement and good government. Social trust refers to the belief that others will take care of our interests, or, at the very least, not seek to harm us. Obviously, trust is often a function of interpersonal relationships, but it is easy to see that the willingness of people to trust each other (and, by implication, authority figures and institutions that are able to affect the quality of life) may be a cultural phenomenon. In Chapter 1 we talked about Francis Fukuyama's argument that different cultures display varying levels of social trust (p. 47), and that the willingness of individuals to trust strangers and institutions beyond the family can have profound social and political consequences. You will also recall from Chapter 3 that in Almond and Verba's ideal civic culture, trust is an important ingredient of political stability. In fact there is an implicit assumption that social and political trust (the latter defined as feelings of trust in relation to political institutions) are closely linked. As Kenneth Newton says, 'social trust is regarded as a strong determinant of, or influence upon, political support of various kinds, including support for the political community, confidence in institutions and trust in political leaders' (1999: 170). As we shall see later in this section (pp. 142–3) the assumed correspondence between social and political trust may be misplaced. For the moment, let us return to Putnam's thesis and look at some of the issues arising from it.

To reiterate: what Putnam observes in the USA is a long-term depletion of social capital that produces growing cynicism about government and politics, which in turn is having damaging effects on conventional political participation – leading to lower electoral turnout, political activism and civic engagement Many factors have contributed to these changes, including greater affluence, consumerism, the rise of youth culture with its emphasis on self-gratification, and changing patterns of work, notably the growing partici- pation rates of women in the workforce. Also contributory is the part played by television, or more accurately, watching television.

Television and political participation: the triumph of the couch potato?

Television is a ubiquitous medium, especially in the affluent democracies of the western world. TV screens are found in practically every home and in many commercial and public spaces. Americans (admittedly a limiting case) watch, on average, 4 hours of television a day. The spread of TV since the 1950s at least

continued

continued

coincides with the decline in rates of civic engagement in the USA. Data from the US General Social Survey shows that those generational cohorts which watch TV the most as children participate in collective activities the least as adults (Campbell *et al.* 1999). A good deal of other research (e.g. Comstock and Paik 1991) suggests that television has dampened the extent to which people engage in social activities outside the home. In addition, a substantial amount of recent scholarship confirms that finding for countries other than the USA (Norris 1999; Shah 1997).

The case for the observed effects of television viewing on social capital/civic engagement is two-fold. First is the argument that time spent watching TV is time not spent doing other things – joining a club, caring for the elderly, helping with a political campaign. Second is the thesis that where people are habitual viewers and look to TV as the primary source of entertainment and leisure, the result is to privatise leisure time, deepening the trend towards an inward and self-obsessed society and culture.

All this sounds very plausible, but needs to be treated with some caution. For one thing, it could be argued that the implied causality is spurious because the argument is equally plausible that people who are least likely to be involved with community activities are those who watch a lot of TV; not that avid viewing makes people less likely to be active citizens. For another, not all TV watching can be correlated with a decline in civic participation. Watching news and current affairs programmes is linked to greater interest and activity in civic affairs, although in audience terms, this is a small percentage of viewers.

EXERCISE

Conduct this exercise among members of your class or seminar group. The results you produce may not be representative of the student body, let alone the whole population, but should provide interesting material for class discussion of the issue of the effects of television upon social capital. The questions are based on a study carried out by the Roper Foundation in the USA and repeated over a period of time between 1974 and 1996.

1 Battery of political participation items
Have you done any of these things in the past year?

- Written to your Congressman/Senator/MP/MEP/Deputy
- Attended a political rally or speech
- Attended a public meeting on town or school/college affairs
- Held or run for political office
- Served on a committee for some local organisation

Served as an officer of some club or organisation

Written a letter to the paper

Signed a petition

Worked for a political party

Made a speech

Written an article for a magazine or newspaper

Been a member of some group like Charter 88, or some other group which is interested in better government?

2 Time spent watching television

On the average weekday, about how much time do you spend . . .

reading newspapers

watching TV

reading magazines

listening to the radio

reading books?

- Less than 15 minutes
- 15–29 minutes
- 30–44 minutes
- 45–59 minutes
- 1 hour to less than 3 hours
- 3 to less than 5 hours
- 5 to less than 7 hours
- 7 hours or more?

3 Reason for watching television

People watch television for many different reasons. Here are some of them. Which two or three of the following are you most often looking for when you decide to watch television?

To be entertained

To be amused

To learn something

To keep up with what's going on

To have a little excitement

To forget about the cares of the day

To relax my mind

To improve my mind.

4 Activities that people are doing more or less than a year ago

Go down the list and note all the things you are doing more now than a year ago? Now would you go through that list again, and note all those things you are doing less now than a year ago?

Entertaining friends in your home

continued

continued

- Shopping in large shopping centres
- Going to take-out places for ready-cooked food
- Visiting friends or relatives who live nearby
- Eating out at restaurants
- Watching TV
- Going out to places of public entertainment
- Reading books
- Shopping in stores that are not located in main shopping centres
- Spending time at home
- Visiting friends or relatives who do not live nearby
- Buying food, beverages and other supplies in large quantities and shopping less often
- Phoning a store to see if they have an item in stock before going to buy it
- Buying goods on the Internet
- Surfing the Internet.

5 Ways people enjoy spending a free week night
Thinking of a week night after your evening meal, would you note all the ways you would enjoy spending a free evening?

- Going out to a movie
- Going out to watch a sporting event
- Going out to visit friends
- Having friends over to visit
- Spending time with your partner
- Spending time with your children
- Watching sports on TV
- Watching entertainment shows on TV
- Reading a book
- Reading a magazine
- Reading a newspaper
- Playing cards
- Doing needed things around the house
- Pursuing a hobby
- Going to a club
- Other (specify).

6 Words and phrases used to describe commercial television
Read the following list and note each word or phrase you would use to describe (1) terrestrial television; (2) cable TV; (3) satellite TV:

- Interesting
- Dull
- Educational
- Lots of variety

- In bad taste
- Relaxing
- Getting better
- Getting worse
- Informative
- Uninteresting
- Important
- Generally good
- All the same
- Too simple-minded
- Lots of fun
- Serious
- Imaginative
- Stimulating.

7 Habitual television watching

Some people like to have a television set on in the background, even when they are not actually watching it. Do you find you will frequently have the set on even though you are not really watching it, or are you the kind who either watches it or turns it off?

- On in the background
- Watch or turn off.

Alternatively, you could take the less demanding 'Couch Potato test' at <http://www.queendom.com/tests/fx/couch_potato.html>.

Other questions about the assumed link between social capital and civic engagement include:

1 *Complex causation.* As with many intuitively plausible and apparently clear-cut arguments, in reality there is likely to be a very complex relationship between variables, rather than a simple cause and effect. The debate about the impact of television consumption on social capital illustrates this concern quite neatly.

2 *The reliability of the evidence cited.* Robert Putnam has presented some compelling evidence for the decline in social capital in the United States over the past generation, measured by a variety of indices of participation in church-related groups, labour unions, PTAs, traditional women's clubs, fraternal organisations and mainline civic organisations. Verba *et al.*'s recent study of civic voluntarism (1995) offers some data that are consistent with these findings, but also much that supports Americans' deserved reputation for continued high levels of involvement in voluntary associations. Of particular note is their evidence that participation has modestly increased at the level of community and local problem-solving activities, and that the

decrease in voter turnout has not been accompanied by a general decrease in citizen activism, even on campaign-related activities.

In *What if Civic Life Didn't Die?*, Michael Schudson (1997) questions Putnam's methodology, and this has been a recurring theme in many of the criticisms of Putnam's work. If there has been a decline in civic involvement, Schudson writes, it is far smaller than Putnam believes. Writing in the *American Prospect* (2000), Garry Wills argues in 'Putnam's America' that Putnam has simply underestimated the emergence of new organisations and new sources of social capital, while focusing too narrowly on 'imagined good old days'. While it may be true that membership in more traditional voluntary organisations has declined, during the same period reviewed by Putnam, there occurred a massive growth in the 'social movement society' (Meyer and Tarrow 1998) comprising the Civil Rights, anti-Vietnam war, women's environmentalist and gay movements, as well as a host of other civic groups.

In addition, the tendency to make rather dire inferences about the levels of political interest and engagement among young people (for a summary of work see Huggins 2000) needs to be tempered by the knowledge that low interest in conventional social and political engagement does not necessarily mean a rejection of politics as such, as the following extract from a research report makes clear:

> Except for voting, students are unlikely to think that conventional political participation is particularly important. An overwhelming four out of five students in all countries indicated that they do not intend to participate in the conventional political activities generally associated with adult political involvement: joining a party, writing letters to newspapers about social and political concerns, and being a candidate for a local or city office. Nevertheless, students across the various countries are open to forms of civic and political engagement unrelated to electoral politics or parties. On average, 59 percent of students reported that they expect to collect money for a social cause or charity. On average, 44 percent said that they would participate in a non-violent protest march. Respondents were also very likely to endorse adults participating in environmental or community betterment organizations as a way to demonstrate good citizenship.
>
> Only a minority of students reported that they are likely to engage in protest activities that are illegal in most countries, such as spray-painting slogans on walls, blocking traffic and occupying buildings.
>
> (*Citizenship and Education in Twenty-eight Countries: Civic Knowledge and Engagement at Age Fourteen* (2001), The International Association for the Evaluation of Educational Achievement (IEA), Amsterdam, The Netherlands)

Of course, the relative dearth of social capital among some sections of a population may be explained quite simply. The finding that participation is lowest among those disabled people who have difficulty going outside the home alone – despite the fact that these forms of participation can be done inside the home – indicates the importance of accessible transportation and interaction with mainstream society. Isolation and confinement to one's home can decrease 'social capital' – the social skills, knowledge, connections and identification developed from regular interaction with many other people. The loss of social capital, through isolationism or ostracism, can cause a self-perpetuating spiral into obscurity not only for the individual but also for the political ideas, experiences and groups from which the individual is drawn.

3 *Comparability: a purely American phenomenon?* One of the criticisms of Putnam's thesis is that, even if true, it applies only to the United States. A study for the Organisation for Economic Cooperation and Development (OECD) using comparative data for fifty-six countries and published in 2001 shows that human and social capital can be of key importance in contributing to a wide range of positive outcomes, including higher income, life satisfaction and social cohesion. Of course, these data neither fully endorse nor deny Putnam's thesis, but in an interesting article on 'Social Capital in Britain', Peter Hall (1999) argues that there is no real erosion of social participation in the UK, although there is some evidence of a decline in levels of social trust. Even these findings are contested, since Hall also opines that young people generally are more self-centred and less socially engaged than their parents. As we have noted above, this finding should be treated with some caution. Moreover, Hall also argues that stocks of social capital are closely related to the policy climate fostered by government. Under the New Labour government in the UK, re-elected in 2001, the social agenda promotes voluntary activity and caring attitudes, so if Hall is to be believed, we would expect to see an upturn in civic engagement in the near future. Data from Spain (Torcal and Moreno 1998), a relatively new democracy, indicate enduringly low levels of social trust which has proved resistant to social changes and economic improvements in recent years. The authors of the study argue that this lack of trust has contributed to the low presence of social capital and that both factors impinge upon democratic politics, with rates of conventional participation being quite low.

4 *Other possible explanations.* Looking at allegedly declining social capital is only one way of trying to explain the changing dynamics and patterns of political participation. Other possible explanations include:

■ The chronic failure of governments to perform well, leading to a decline in confidence and growing cynicism about the efficacy of established policies and procedures, especially their failure to meet public expectations about improving the quality of life. Evidence for a strong and enduring correlation between economic performance and confidence in government is difficult to interpret. A twenty-four-nation analysis of the relationships between support for political institutions and objective indicators of economic performance (McAllister 1999) suggests that support seems unaffected by changes in actual performance, but may be affected by people's perception of their own economic well-being.

- Concerns with a democratic deficit: which highlight disenchantment with representative institutions and with the relative 'distance' of political elites from public opinion. Again the evidence is far from clear. Widespread decline in the membership of political parties across democracies suggests a weakening of these modern political organisations as vehicles for activism, and declining electoral turnout across many systems is often taken as a signal indicator of democratic ill-health. At the same time, more unconventional means of political engagement are flourishing and (as we shall see in Chapter 5) what is sometimes taken as a harbinger of democratic malaise may be revealed as the basis for democratic renewal as the boundaries of politics change.

- Cultural factors – from modernity to postmodernity: In some respects cultural explanations of changing values and dispositions towards political participation are closer to the social capital thesis than the positions canvassed above. The key difference is that arguments which identify major cultural shifts, for example, Ronald Inglehart's 'post-materialist'(1977, 1997) thesis outlined in Chapter 3, often point to the increased potential and demand for political participation. Post-materialists, says Inglehart, are better educated, more cosmopolitan, and generally more critical of usual politics than their materialist counterparts. They demonstrate higher levels of political competence and are more inclined to play an active role in decision-making. Postmaterialism implies a decline in support for traditional and modern institutions and values, but critically, this need not imply a challenge to democracy.

This welter of possible explanations further underlines our point about complex causation. None of the factors referred to are mutually exclusive, and all are likely to be contributory in some way.

5 *Making false inferences*: The implied relationship between social and political trust, which is at the heart of the Putnam thesis, demonstrates the dangers in making plausible inferences from contested data. As Kenneth Newton says (1999: 179), much commentary assumes that trust is seam-less and that social trust created by voluntary organisations (social capital) creates a strong civil society and reinforces political trust. The research findings are rather more ambiguous. Analysing data from *Eurobarometer* studies and from the *World Values Survey* between the mid-1970s and mid-1990s, Newton concludes that there is not a close and consistent link between 'social and political trust, between social trust and political behaviour, or between activity in voluntary associations and political attitudes of trust and confidence' (1999: 185). Rather, with minor fluctuations, figures show continuing high levels of social trust over the period. While this finding is more pronounced for Western Europe than for the USA, the data analysed

See Chapter 11 for a discussion of political parties.

provide evidence for generally higher levels of social trust in America than do Putnam's studies. These differences may owe more to what is being measured in each case than to weaknesses in the methods employed, but once again, the message is to be very cautious about taking findings for granted. Interestingly, Newton's argument is that there has been a decline in levels of political trust, but one caused by political factors and contingency rather than attributable to the erosion of social trust and the paucity of social capital.

So, the response to the question 'Is the United States – or anywhere else – becoming a "nation of spectators?", as the final report of the National Commission on Civic Renewal suggests? Or is civic life healthier than Robert Putnam and other scholars believe?' is to be agnostic. Ultimately, Putnam's position represents only the beginning of the debate.

Robert Putnam is the Peter and Isabel Malkin Professor of Public Policy at Harvard University. He has written seven books and is a contributor to the *New York Times*, the *Washington Post* and the *American Prospect*.

Robert Putnam

In the next section of the chapter we address the question of why people participate in politics by looking more closely at motivational factors, which directs us to the psychology of politics or towards economic theories of activism and towards structural and cultural factors that may dispose people to participate. The structure–agency issue, as noted in Chapter 1, is contested in the social sciences (for which see Hay 1995). However, it is possible to think productively about the explanation for levels of political participation in structure–agency terms. We begin with some agency-based observations.

Why do some people participate in politics and others abstain?

So far we have looked at some of the factors – primarily social and cultural – that are linked to different rates and intensities of political participation. We have also pointed to research findings that suggest the greater propensity of certain categories of people to be politically active and the tendency towards specialisation among those engaged in the higher registers of activism. But why do people participate in politics and how can we assess their motivations and dispositions?

As one might expect, there is considerable disagreement about how to answer this question. Ultimately, much will depend on the theoretical perspective being used. To illustrate, we will look at some forms of methodological individualism, starting with rational choice theory, and then address some structural explanations for variability in activism (which emphasise the conditioning effects of social, institutional and ideological environments upon human action).

Agency: the rational actor. Rational choice theory has become one of the most influential frameworks for the study of politics (see Ward 1995). It has been especially useful in the explanation of the engagement or non-engagement of people in the political process, although as we noted in Chapter 1, it offers a very stark, some would say bleak, view of human motivation. The basic premise of rational choice theory is that those engaged in political activity aspire to achieve their aims through the most efficient means; they are – in the broadest sense of the term – self-interested. The genesis of rational choice approaches to politics is rooted in the history of political thought, in the work of writers such as Thomas Hobbes in the seventeenth century. However, the most compelling and systematic uses of the approach began to emerge in the 1950s in the work of political economists such as James Buchanan and Anthony Downs.

For a discussion of rational choice and a definition, see Chapter 1, pp. 28–34.

James M. Buchanan

Economist James M. Buchanan was winner of the 1986 Nobel Prize in Economic Science. Among the many influential books he has written are *The Calculus of Consent: Logical Foundations of Constitutional Democracy* (1962) with Gordon Tullock; *Cost and Choice* (1969); *The Limits of Liberty* (1975); and *Liberty, Market, and State* (1985); and his autobiography, *Better than Plowing and Other Personal Essays* (1992). Most recently he published with Roger Congleton *Politics by Principle, Not Interest*.

In *An Economic Theory of Democracy* (1957), the American political scientist Anthony Downs presented a ground-breaking application of microeconomic models to the study of politics in general and voting in particular. Downs' analysis is built around the axiom that individuals base their electoral choice upon a calculation of costs and benefits. Thus the choice of whether or not to vote hinges on whether the individual feels that the act imposes costs greater than it yields benefits. Notice that the whole approach is built around the idea that the individual is always rational and able to calculate costs in relation to benefits; and that as an axiom individuals seek to minimise personal cost while maximising personal gain. A favourite metaphor is that of politics as a supermarket. As Iain McLean puts it, 'when I go to vote I am doing something similar but not identical to what I do when I go shopping. In both cases I *buy* what I *want*' (McLean 1987: 9–10).

Should an individual decide that her or his vote will make no difference to the outcome of an election, then that individual will not vote. Moreover, should the benefits associated with a particular electoral outcome accrue to the individual whether or not she or he votes, there is no incentive to vote. The individual may calculate that non-participation is rational in such situations. This is known as 'free-riding' and was explored at some length in Chapter 1, pp. 28–34.

Rational choice approaches provide a powerful script for those seeking to explore the reasons for any sort of political participation. Notice that, aside from being a particular brand of theory with its own basic assumptions, rational choice is clearly an agent-centred interpretation of participation or non-participation, but it offers a very one-dimensional view of human nature.

Key text: A. Downs (1957) *An Economic Theory of Democracy*, New York: Harper & Row.

Agency: political efficacy and trust

To answer the question of why some individuals participate in politics while others do not, we may need to offer a more complex theory of motivation than rational self-interest. Clearly, some individuals feel that by participating they will be able to make a difference to how an issue is resolved. At the other extreme is that metaphorical shrug of the shoulders which expresses resignation – 'why bother when my participation will make no difference?' In other words, feelings of **political efficacy** are important to the extent and quality of political participation. Having a sense of political efficacy is clearly related to individual psychology and to the emotional links an individual has to political institutions and practices. At the same time feelings of powerfulness and powerlessness are obviously related to cultural values and attitudes, and also to experience.

A sense of political efficacy is about the extent to which a person feels that he or she can make a difference politically as well as the degree to which that person feels politically competent. A useful way of thinking about efficacy is to map the ways in which the possession of such feelings might affect political behaviour. Table 4.6 attempts to do this by deriving hypotheses from plotting feelings of efficacy against levels of trust in the system.

Political efficacy The extent to which an individual feels that his or her participation in politics will be effective.

Table 4.6 Political efficacy and trust in the system

	High level of trust in the system	Low level of trust in the system
High political efficacy	Participation that is supportive of the regime.	Participation that is designed to reform or revolutionise the regime.
Low political efficacy	Voting and 'patriotic' support for the regime only.	Alienation and withdrawal from politics.

Consider too the following passage, which is taken from the concluding pages of the autobiography of the first black President of South Africa, Nelson Mandela. Mandela was a political prisoner of the apartheid regime in South Africa between 1964 and 1990. Here he describes the formation of his political views:

> It was only when I began to learn that my boyhood freedom was an illusion, when I discovered as a young man that my freedom had already been taken from me, that I began to hunger for it. At first, as a student, I wanted freedom for myself, the transitory freedoms of being able to stay out at night, read what I pleased, and go where I chose. Later, as a young man in Johannesburg, I yearned for the basic and honourable freedoms of achieving my potential, of earning my keep, of marrying and having a family – the freedom not to be obstructed in a lawful life.
>
> But then I slowly saw that not only was I not free, but my brothers and sisters were not free. I saw that it was not just my freedom that was curtailed, but the freedom of everyone who looked like I did. That is when I joined the African National Congress, and that is when the hunger for my own freedom became the hunger for the freedom of my people. It was this desire for the freedom of my people to live their lives with dignity and self-respect that animated my life, that transformed a frightened young man into a bold one, that drove a law-abiding attorney to become a criminal, that turned a family-loving husband into a man without a home, that forced a life-loving man to live like a monk.

At first sight this statement is the recollection of the main events of Mandela's political socialisation. But it is also the memoir of an individual sustained by feelings of political efficacy in spite of being located in a system of justice which he did not trust. In terms of Table 4.6, it would seem appropriate to place Mandela in the top right-hand quadrant (low trust in the regime plus a high sense of political efficacy). Much research emphasises the links between efficacy, trust and political stability, including the path-breaking study of *The Civic Culture* by Almond and Verba (1963), but there is no convincing explanation of any necessary connections between these things.

Nelson Mandela was born at Qunu, near Umtata, on 18 July 1918. In 1944 he helped found the ANC Youth League, whose Programme of Action was adopted by the ANC in 1949. By 1952 Mandela was both Transvaal President of the ANC and Deputy National President. When the ANC was banned after the Sharpeville massacre in 1960, he was detained until 1961 when he went underground to lead a campaign for a new national convention. Later he was arrested for leaving the country illegally and for incitement to strike, and was convicted and jailed for five years in November 1962. While serving his sentence he was also convicted of sabotage and sentenced to life imprisonment. After his release in 1990, Mandela agreed to the suspension of armed struggle. He was inaugurated as the first democratically elected State President of South Africa on 10 May 1994 and served until June 1999. He retired from public life in June 1999. He now resides in his birthplace – Qunu, Transkei.

Nelson Mandela

However, it requires no great stretch of the imagination to see that a widespread lack of trust coupled with high levels of perceived efficacy may promote a political climate in which anti-state behaviour and even forms of terrorism contribute to political uncertainty and social unease.

Structural explanations: the law, society and ideas

We turn now to some structure-based explanations for levels of political participation. One of the main determinants of political participation is the legal framework in any given state. In all countries certain kinds of political activity are proscribed by law whereas others are perfectly legitimate. Notice, though, that the proscription of forms of participation may not prevent groups of people from engaging in the banned activity. The distribution of dissident *samizdat* (underground) literature in the former communist states of Eastern Europe was technically illegal, but practised widely. Opposition to the regime in Nazi Germany was an illegal act (whereas putting people to death in gas chambers for no reason other than that they were Jewish, gypsies or homosexuals was technically lawful). Terrorist activities are, by definition, beyond the bounds of acceptable participation, but much depends upon the nature of the regime that calls a particular form of activity 'terrorism'. Other forms of political participation are deemed to be acceptable and seminal, but are still regulated. Voting in elections provides an obvious example.

Elections have a number of functions, chief among which are legitimating the transfer of power and expressing the idea of popular sovereignty. In democratic countries legislatures are composed largely on the basis of the popular vote, and different kinds of electoral system exist to translate citizen preferences into parliamentary seats. For the citizen, elections provide a particularly low-cost method of participating in the political process. Voting, not surprisingly, is the most common form of political participation.

Elections are heavily regulated and all countries place restrictions on who can vote. Non-adults, usually defined as under-18s, are normally denied the franchise, and some countries do not allow either prisoners or those in institutions and defined as mentally ill to vote. Otherwise, there is universal adult suffrage, although this is a relatively recent phenomenon in most countries. For example, the granting of the vote to women lagged behind the achievement of full-scale male suffrage. A particularly stark example is Switzerland, where full female suffrage in federal elections was not achieved until 1971. Of course, in a number of countries the denial of voting rights to women produced mass movements demanding equality at the ballot box. So the withholding of one form of political participation to women produced another (and at the time more unconventional) form of political participation. In Britain the Suffragette Movement campaigned vigorously – often through programmes of civil disobedience – for votes for women in the years leading up to the First World War. The 1918 Representation of the People Act granted the vote to women householders over 30 years of age and to those over 35 who were the wives of householders. All women over 21 were granted the vote in 1928. In the United States a great deal of the impetus behind the black civil rights movement of the 1960s came from highly iniquitous electoral arrangements (see Piven and Cloward 1977). In theory, the Thirteenth, Fourteenth and Fifteenth Amendments to the US Constitution (passed in the wake of the American Civil War between 1860 and 1865) guaranteed racial equality. In practice, various devices such as extremely difficult literacy tests and poll taxes facilitated the exclusion of black people from the electoral register.

So, electoral law can have an impact upon the types of participation practised by those who do not have the franchise. It is also true that the precise nature of the voting system can have an effect upon the quality of participation available. This is an issue which political scientists have debated for a long time. At issue is the impact and the implied merits of different sorts of electoral system and whether they enable voters to cast 'real' ballots; that is, they do not discriminate against the supporters of minority parties. While each democratic country has its own electoral system and the merits of each is subject to detailed and often technical commentary (Reeve and Ware 1992), the debate has turned on the respective consequences and merits of plurality and proportional representation systems of election. The main differences between these systems is described in Table 4.7. It is important to remember that the electoral systems described here are very much ideal types. The purpose of this discussion is not to discuss the pros and cons of electoral systems, but to understand how the structure of electoral law might influence the agency of political participation.

In his book *Political Parties*, Maurice Duverger (1964) argued that the single ballot, simple majority system (plurality) favours a two-party system (this has become known as Duverger's Law). Conversely, he hypothesised that PR (proportional representation) systems are conducive to multi-party political systems. If it is correct that the electoral system structures the party system, it

Key text: A. Reeve and A. Ware (1992) *Electoral Systems: A Comparative and Theoretical Discussion*, London: Routledge.

Key text: M. Duverger (1964) *Political Parties: Their Organization and Activity in the Modern State*, London: Methuen.

Table 4.7 Main types of electoral system

1. *Plurality*

Countries are divided into electoral districts (constituencies). Each district elects a single member to the legislature. The candidate with the highest number of votes wins the election. A majority of the votes cast is not necessary to win the election in any given district.

2. *Proportional Representation (PR)*

Seats in the legislature are usually allocated in accordance with the proportion of the vote cast for each party. The most common method for achieving this end is the use of multi-member constituencies where parties field lists of candidates. The number of representatives elected for that party will reflect the proportion of votes cast for that party in the constituency. PR systems frequently operate with the entire country as a single constituency. Thresholds sometimes operate. In such cases parties need to achieve a minimum proportion of the vote before representation is permitted.

---

follows that the range of choices available to the electorate is similarly conditioned. For example, the mechanisms of a plurality system where winner takes all is thought to favour the existence of inclusive, mass parties spanning large portions of the political spectrum. In other words, there is an incentive for cognate political forces to coalesce into single parties. Small parties with limited electoral appeal tend not to prosper (unless they command significant regional concentrations of support). Conversely, in a PR system where seats are allocated in more or less strict proportion to the votes cast, smaller political parties representing narrow sectors of political opinion should be able to secure representation. One related feature of plurality systems is the phenomenon of tactical voting. In such situations, electors cannot necessarily vote for the party they favour the most because they know that it has no chance of winning. However, they do cast their votes for the party most likely to displace their least favoured party.

These examples suggest that the structure of the electoral system may place constraints upon the range of available opportunities for participation among the electorate. Other writers have presented evidence to suggest that the nature of the electoral system may have deeper consequences. Some researchers have suggested that PR systems facilitate the entry of women and members of ethnic minority groups into national parliaments, thereby broadening the social profile of the 'gladiators'. The work of Vicky Randall (1987) appears to confirm the impression that women are better represented in the parliaments of countries using PR systems than of those using plurality systems. This finding is confirmed by Kerstin Barkman, who explains the constraints placed upon women by a plurality system such as that of the United Kingdom:

Key text: V. Randall (1987) *Women and Politics: An International Perspective*, Basingstoke: Macmillan.

Women don't appear to lose votes . . . but on the other hand, if they managed to get selected as candidates, they are often taken on for 'hopeless' seats and are rarely given safe seats. . . . Party selection panels are not openly discriminatory; on the contrary most party headquarters profess themselves in favour of more women in parliament. Selection is decentralised though, and the ideological stance of the centre is often not reflected in the decisions made by constituency selection committees . . . the 'mental maps' of the selectors ensure that the chosen candidate conforms to a typical career pattern usually comprising higher education, a professional career and extensive political experience, all normally accomplished by the age of forty. This is a male pattern and unlikely to be feasible for most women, particularly if they marry and have children.

(Barkman 1995: 141)

This commentary raises deeper structural questions about reasons for participation and non-participation. Studies of gender differences in participation generally emphasise the role of further types of structural constraint: social structure and dominant cultural norms.

Many commentators have sought to explain levels and types of participation with reference to social structure. In such approaches researchers seek to establish whether categories such as class, religion, gender or ethnicity correlate with particular modes or intensities of participation. This method is frequently deployed in studies of voting behaviour, but clearly it has wider applications. It is relatively easy to identify correlations between social groups and levels of political participation, but altogether more difficult to account for these trends. In their exhaustive study of political participation in Britain, Parry, Moyser and Day discovered that working-class people were less inclined to participate in politics than the salaried middle classes. This, they argue, may be attributable to the 'disadvantageous resource position' of the working class (Parry *et al.* 1992: 131). A very powerful hypothesis, therefore, would be that certain groups in the population are better equipped to participate, and to participate effectively, than others. Resources are a matter not simply of access to money, but also of access to political skills and political information.

Ideas-based and cultural explanations emphasise the ways in which dominant belief systems structure patterns of political preference and political behaviour across society. There are two ways in which such ideational structures may be thought to operate. First, certain patterns of belief offer disincentives to participate. Feminists would argue that patriarchal belief systems devalue the public role of women, who are treated predominantly as child-rearers and home-makers. The 'gendering' of ideas about politics dissuades women from entering (or for that matter challenging) what is understood as the conventional realm of politics. It also works on the perceptions of others, such as party selection panels, thereby producing discrimination (see Chapman (1993) for a much fuller discussion). It is often argued that a component of the oppression of particular social groups is the ideological masking of their 'real interests'. A classic literary statement of this view may be found in Robert Tressell's novel *The Ragged Trousered Philanthropists*, which was written in the early years of the twentieth century. In this extract, the book's main character, Owen, reflects on the failure of the majority of working-class people to engage in the sorts of participation necessary to overthrow the exploitative capitalist system in which they live and work:

> And the future, as far as he could see, was hopeless as the past; darker, for there would surely come a time, if he lived long enough, when he would be unable to work any more.
>
> He thought of his child. Was he to be a slave and a drudge all his life also? It would be better for the boy to die now.
>
> As Owen thought of his child's future there sprung up within him a feeling of hatred and fury against the majority of his fellow workmen.
>
> They were the enemy. Those who not only quietly submitted like so many cattle to the existing state of things, but defended it, and opposed and ridiculed any suggestion to alter it.
>
> They were the real oppressors – the men who spoke of themselves as 'The likes of us', who, having lived in poverty and degradation all their lives considered that what had been good enough for them was good enough for the children they had been the cause of bringing into existence.
>
> He hated and despised them because they calmly saw their children condemned to hard labour and poverty for life, and deliberately refused to make any effort to secure for them better conditions than those they had themselves.
>
> (Tressell 1965: 45–6)

THINK POINT

Can you think of other ways in which ideas and cultural values might structure political behaviour?

Immediate stimuli

When push comes to shove, what changes a predisposition to participate in a certain way, or with particular ends in mind rather than others, may not be the fact that one is black, or religious, married or middle class, but that one had been there, or had read about it in the newspaper, or saw it on television. Not just these stimuli, of course, but the power of some immediate stimulus to precipitate action. Pictures of famine in Sudan, or the destruction of the World Trade Center in New York, may be powerful triggers to some forms of activism. The broad coalition of opposition to GM crops and foodstuffs and to factory farming seems to be made up of professional activists, ideological purists and single-issue enthusiasts. Many of the latter had no previous record of political activism, but were constrained to act because of the intensity of feeling (joy, revulsion, concern) generated by the issue at hand. If informed journalistic commentary is to be believed, the Saudi extremist Osama Bin Laden was moved to militant and then terrorist opposition to the United States when American forces were allowed into Saudi Arabia during the Gulf War of 1991 and thus, on his reasoning, defiled the two holy places of Mecca and Medina.

Osama Bin Laden is both one of the CIA's most wanted men and a hero to many young people in the Arab world. Even before the attack on the World Trade Center, he and his associates were already being sought by the US on charges of international terrorism, including in connection with the 1998 bombing of American embassies in Africa and the attack on the USS Cole in Yemen. Born in Saudi Arabia in 1959 into a wealthy family, the young Bin Laden was politicised by the Soviet invasion of Afghanistan in 1980.

Osama Bin Laden

Of course, as cautious social scientists, we should be wary of simple causation. The impact of particular circumstances, and events are likely to be filtered through previous experience and the predispositions laid down during critical periods of socialisation. How we respond to circumstance, when we react – indeed, if we react at all – may well vary with the skills and competences we have picked up on the way, with the resources we can call upon to help us and with the expectations of those around us.

Case study: electoral turnout and political participation

By examining electoral data, we can construct a picture of mass political participation and change in a country. In turn this describes a graph of what we might call ideological stability or change, charting the successes and failures of the main contenders for office, identifying new political forces and watching them wax and wane.

Of course, looking at electoral data for some countries may not reveal anything at all about the nature of ideological change or the pattern of political participation, because there may be only one party in power over the whole period of study and a legal requirement to vote. Variations in electoral turnout can give some clue as to the legitimacy of the political system, but this too may be an unreliable indicator. For one thing, turnout varies between countries, and the level of turnout, in itself, is no guide to the stability or democratic credentials of a country, as the data in Table 4.8 show.

The United Kingdom, considered on most counts to be the most stable of the countries sampled here, had the lowest turnout in its most recent

Table 4.8 Electoral turnout: selected countries

Country	Date	Election type	Registered votes (%)
Bulgaria	2001	Parliamentary	67.03
United Kingdom	2001	Parliamentary	59.35
Cyprus	2001	Parliamentary	91.75
Italy	2001	Parliamentary	N/A
Senegal	2001	Parliamentary	67.41
Peru	2001	Legislative	81.82
		Presidential	82.78
Moldova	2001	Presidential	70.30
Uganda	2001	Presidential	67.52
Bahrain	2001	Referendum	90.20

parliamentary general election. High voter turnouts in more authoritarian or less stable states could be an indication of electoral approval and legitimacy; on the other hand, they may be a credit to the power of the state to mobilise expressions of popular support at critical junctures, through appeals to national unity, out of fear, or by using some form of coercion. By the same token the notoriously low turnouts in USA presidential elections (averaging 51 per cent) might be taken as a sign of enduring and culturally sanctioned distrust of central government or big government, but not of the overall illegitimacy of the system of government. Figures for the UK general election of 2001 show a marked downturn in voting (59 per cent rounded), a fall of 11.1 per cent from 1997 and the lowest for all general elections since 1918. This result may be read in a number of ways:

- practical considerations (*too busy to vote, too wet to go out and so on*);

- problems with election procedures and management (*inconvenient siting of polling stations, inadequacy of postal voting arrangements and so on*);

- failure of the main contenders to generate enthusiasm among the electorate (*which may be a product of an uninspiring campaign or one made into an exercise in marketing*);

- electorate unable to distinguish between the main contenders and their programmes, and thus opting for the 'devil you know' (*which may reflect the decline of the ideological differences between contending parties*);

- electorate increasingly cynical and distrustful of politicians and of political parties (*see our earlier discussion in this chapter on trust and civic engagement*);

- electorate doubtful about the efficacy of Parliament as a vehicle for making law and scrutinising government;

- electorate unhappy about an electoral system that usually discriminates against third and minor parties;

▓ the result reflects the erosion of social capital in the UK and the increasing reluctance of people to engage in even low-cost political activities like voting (*see our discussion earlier in this chapter*);

▓ electorate unhappy with the health of representative democracy in the UK (*if true, this would indicate that the legitimacy of the whole parliamentary system would be under threat*).

Now, all of these are plausible to some degree and none are mutually exclusive. In some respects they each address questions we have covered earlier in the chapter; namely, the vexed issue of declining civic engagement and its connection to levels of mass political participation. In a report published in the summer of 2001, the United Kingdom Electoral Commission drew upon survey research conducted by the polling organisation MORI to inform its evaluation of the result.

MORI's research for the Electoral Commission on voter attitudes shows that interest in politics has remained stable over the past three decades: people are no more 'turned-off' by politics than they were in the past. Voter engagement is an issue, rather than apathy. In addition, civic duty and habit are key motivators to voting, and people have positive attitudes towards voting; yet, turnout at 59 per cent was the lowest in any general election since 1918.

When asked why they did not vote in the general election, unprompted answers focused less on the parties and disinterest than on practical considerations:

▓ One-fifth of non-voters (21 per cent) said that they did not vote because 'I couldn't get to the polling station because it was too inconvenient'. Women and those not in full/part-time employment were most likely to give this reason, although there was little difference between urban and rural non-voters.

▓ One in six non-voters (16 per cent) said they did not vote because they 'Were away on election day'. Taken with the above, these percentages equate to significant proportions of the electorate.

▓ One in ten (11 per cent) said they did not vote because they 'Did not receive a polling card/postal vote'.

▓ Ten per cent said they were 'Not interested in politics'.

How does one interpret these results in light of the civic engagement debate? When asked what they thought could be done to increase turnout, respondents made a number of suggestions, including compulsory voting (17 per cent mentioned this). Support was also strong for reforming the mechanics of voting, especially voting by telephone/mobile phone, and 66 per cent of non-voters said this would have made them 'more likely' to have voted this time. Information can also play a role, and the research found a significant proportion who said they received too little information about candidates and policies during the election campaign.

All these factors may help to encourage people to vote or discourage them from voting, but equally important are likely to be the perceptions people have of the political process in the long term, what they think of election campaigns in the short term and how they view the outcomes which both deliver. Although they are couched in terms of practical considerations affecting the level of turnout, the responses may be rationalisations for not voting and may disguise deeper concerns about the procedures of democratic governance. Table 4.9 shows variations in turnout at UK general elections since 1945.

Table 4.9 UK general elections: electorates and turnout 1945 to 2001

Year	Electorate	Turnout (%) *
1945	33,240,391	72.8
1950	34,412,255	83.9
1951	34,919,331	82.6
1955	34,852,179	76.8
1959	35,397,304	78.7
1964	35,894,054	77.1
1966	35,957,245	75.8
1970	39,342,013	72.0
Feb 1974	39,753,863	78.8
Oct 1974	40,072,970	72.8
1979	41,095,649	76.0
1983	42,192,999	72.7
1987	43,180,753	75.3
1992	43,249,721	77.7
1997	43,765,391	71.5
2001	44,405,826	59.4

* total valid vote as a percentage of the electorate

Figures for many other countries show some stability over much the same period, though there is evidence of fluctuation and, in a number of cases, a fall-off in more recent elections. For example, Paraguay recorded an 85 per cent turnout in 1963 and an 81 per cent poll in 1998, with a low of 66 per cent in one of the intervening elections. Norway recorded 76 per cent in 1949 and 75 per cent in 2001, but some of the intervening polls produced turnouts of 80 per cent and more. Finally, the turnout in Barbados in 1957 was 65 per cent, with 63 per cent voting in 1999. The lowest turnout in between was 60 per cent. Overall, it is very hard to substantiate the argument that electoral turnout is in secular and long-term decline, and even harder to make inferences from data on turnout to the health or otherwise of democracy.

Conclusion: a crisis of political participation?

Without participation there would be no politics. It is not surprising, therefore, that much of the intellectual energy of political science has been taken up with trying to understand what motivates some people to become involved in politics, what motivates others to abstain from the conventional political arena and why some are totally disengaged. Our cumulative knowledge about these questions has increased considerably with the development of sophisticated survey methods and with advances in information technology which facilitate the processing of large datasets.

All well and good, but the study of political participation in isolation bars us from posing some interesting questions. In the context of this book, we would do well to reflect on the extent to which rates and types of participation in a given society may be understood in relation to that country's political-cultural framework and/or to prevailing patterns of political socialisation. Moreover, it is always proper to think about the systemic consequences of participation. It is here that we touch on the highly charged normative debate about the relationship between participation and democracy. Is too much participation the cause of overload in the political system? Do too many demands make it impossible for political elites to govern effectively? Or does political participation constitute the most effective means of expressing ourselves as human beings? Can we, should we, forgo a little political stability in the interests of maximising citizen involvement in politics? As we shall see, political participation is valued in democracies, although not too much. Some of the concerns expressed in this chapter point to a crisis of political participation and perhaps a crisis for democracy too. Our data leave this claim unproven, but still central to a discussion of the changing nature of politics. Some of these questions are taken up in Chapter 5 and, as key issues in political philosophy, others are examined in Part 2 of the book.

Chapter summary

- Political participation is a minority activity everywhere, with the signal exception of voting.

- The concept of political participation needs to be inclusive, but sensitive to context.

- Simple models of a hierarchy of political activism are misplaced and need to be revised in light of research that stresses the specialisation of activists.

- Social correlates of political participation suggest that the profile of activists is a highly skewed variable across all countries studied.

- Theories of political participation stress either individual attributes or point to structural and other constraints on the type and intensity of activism.

- A more inclusive theory must be sensitive to individual motivation and structural conditions.

- Claims made about the decline of social capital and civic engagement are hard to substantiate from comparative data and contentious even with regard to the USA.

- Electoral data reveal evidence of declining turnouts for some systems, but it is difficult to interpret the meaning of decline for the functioning of democratic governance.

- the crisis of participation thesis remains unproven, but of central concern to students of politics and practitioners.

Key texts

Birch, A. H. (1993) *The Concepts and Theories of Modern Democracy*, London: Routledge.

Downs, A. (1957) *An Economic Theory of Democracy*, New York: Harper & Row.

Duverger, M. (1964) *Political Parties: Their Organization and Activity in the Modern State*, London: Methuen.

Milbrath, L. (1965) *Political Participation: How and Why Do People Get Involved in Politics?*, Chicago: Rand McNally.

Parry, G., Moyser, G. and Day, N. (1992) *Political Participation and Democracy in Britain*, Cambridge: Cambridge University Press.

Randall, R. (1987) *Women and Politics: An International Perspective*, Basingstoke: Macmillan.

Reeve, V. and Ware, A. (1992) *Electoral Systems: A Comparative and Theoretical Discussion*, London: Routledge.

Verba, S. and Nie, N. H. (1972) *Participation in America: Political Democracy and Social Equality*, New York: Harper & Row.

Verba, S., Nie, N. H. and Kim, J.-O. (1971) *The Modes of Democratic Participation: A Cross-National Comparison*, Beverly Hills: Sage.

Verba, S., Nie, N. H. and Kim, J.-O. (1978) *Participation and Political Equality: A Seven Nation Comparison*, Cambridge: Cambridge University Press.

Further reading

Downs, A. (1957) *An Economic Theory of Democracy*, New York: Harper & Row. The classic, controversial rational choice account of why people vote (or don't vote) as they do.

Milbrath, L. (1965) *Political Participation: How and Why Do People Get Involved in Politics?*, Chicago: Rand McNally. Perhaps the first systematic attempt to think about political participation. It develops the famous gladiators–spectators–apathetics hierarchy.

Milbrath, L. and Goel, M. (1977) *Political Participation: How and Why Do People Get Involved in Politics*, Chicago: Rand McNally. Rather more than a standard second edition. Read in conjunction with the 1965 volume, this careful reappraisal gives a good account of the development of US political science over a decade.

Norris, P (ed.) (1999) *Critical Citizens*, Oxford: Oxford University Press. A book of essays that offer up-to-date empirical analyses on aspects of public opinion, civic engagement and political participation.

Parry, G., Moyser, G. and Day, N. (1992) *Political Participation and Democracy in Britain*, Cambridge: Cambridge University Press. Extensive report on a major research project. It also provides a state-of-the-art theoretical discussion.

Putnam, R. (2001) *Bowling Alone: The Collapse and Revival of American Community*, New York: Simon & Schuster: Book-length version of the Putnam thesis.

Democracy and Democratisation

Richard Huggins

Introduction

[Democracy is the] endpoint of mankind's ideological evolution and the universalization of liberal democracy as the final form of human government.

(Francis Fukuyama (1989), 'The End of History?',
The National Interest 16: 4)

This chapter explores **democracy** and **democratisation** – two of the most important and commonly used terms in politics in recent years. Indeed, in recent history it might appear that democracy has 'won' the ideological struggles with other, competing political ideologies such as communism. This is clearly what Francis Fukuyama meant when he talked about the 'end of history' and the universalisation of liberal democracy; we can certainly see increasing evidence and examples of democratic forms of government and process of governance all around us.

However, despite the apparent familiarity of these concepts, they remain strangely elusive and quite difficult concepts to define. On the one hand, everyone feels that they know, almost implicitly, what these concepts mean. On the other, their actual meanings and significance remain indistinct, ambiguous and at times thoroughly problematic.

There are also two related and, at the same time, distinct elements to this chapter. The first is the concept of *democracy*, the description of a particular type of politics, namely, rule by the people. Second is the notion of a process

Democracy From the original Greek, the term means, literally, rule by the people, or by the many. In modern political systems it is usually linked with universal suffrage, free elections and with notions like the consent of the governed.

Democratisation The processes by which states move towards more democratic forms of political systems.

Key text: F. Fukuyama (1989) 'The End of History?', *The National Interest* 16, pp. 3–18.

by which political units reach democratic political organisation, practices and forms. Again, put simply, the process through which political entities reach democracy – in other words, *democratisation*.

In this chapter we examine the concept of democracy and explore some definitions, and different models and concepts of democracy, then go on to explore the concept of democratisation. We look at some important criticisms of democracy as a concept and as political practice and finally we look at the future of democracy in relation to globalisation and technological developments in new media. However, before doing any of this we need to outline some key contextual points and difficulties that should be borne in mind when thinking about and discussing democracy and democratisation.

Democracy in the contemporary context

A few contextual points about democracy will help the process of analysing this complex concept.

First, we need to be aware of the apparently central connection between liberalism and democracy which is stressed in terms of the concept of **liberal democracy**. However, the actual relationship – as we will see throughout this chapter – may not be as close as we think. In general terms liberalism stresses individual freedom, limited government and the rule of law, while democracy stresses participation and popular sovereignty. At the heart of discussions about democracy is a tension between these two strands.

Furthermore, there is a moral and ethnocentric dimension to discussions of democracy. Who, for example, can argue against democracy? The practice of democracy, institutions of democracy and the ideas often associated with democracy – freedom of speech, assembly, protest, the right to elect political representatives and protection from arbiter power – are ideas and values that many of us simply take for granted as politically and morally right, proper and sensible ways to organise contemporary political society.

This moral, perhaps ethnocentric (and certainly system-centric) perspective extends to politicians, business leaders, social and political activists and others, and it would seem that 'We are all democrats now'. Democracy is enjoying a period of significant global popularity, and the past fifteen years or so have witnessed a significant increase in the number of democracies in the world. In many ways the history of the nineteenth and twentieth centuries has been about the struggle for and the extension of democracy culminating in the 'great victory' of democracy in 1989 to 1992 with the collapse of the Berlin Wall and the disintegration of the former Soviet Union.

But to present the history of democracy as a slow but ultimately successful struggle between arbitrary and unrepresentative power (e.g. the monarchy or state socialism) and representative and accountable government is to over-simplify both the idea and the history of democratisation. There are a number of questions and issues that remain unresolved. For example, actual levels of democratic accountability remain unclear in some cases; in others the

Liberal democracy A doctrine, and sometimes a practice, which combines freedom with the idea of popular sovereignty.

institutions of democracy appear to be in decline, and levels of participation in elections and interest in politics in general are apparently not what they should be. Some commentators have identified a significant crisis of social capital and public trust in government (Putnam 1995; Fukuyama 2001) and others lament voter apathy, media salaciousness and the re-emergence of the 'tyranny of the majority' in the populist politics of, for example, Silvio Berlusconni in Italy, George Bush in the USA or Herder in Austria. In general terms some commentators, while noting the apparent popularity of democracy as a minimal form of procedural politics, lament the actual 'poor health of democracy' and argue for a significant reappraisal of the practice of this form of politics (Crouch 2000: 1).

Other major questions remain unresolved altogether. For example, the nature of democracy and democratic accountability in the European Union remains hugely problematic especially in regard to the discreditable position of the European Commission in 1999 (George and Bache 2001). Furthermore, the transformation to democracy in some of the former Soviet Republics – for example, Russia or Belarus – and the countries of Eastern Europe, the former Yugoslavia and Albania looks less straightforward than in the early 1990s (Gill and Marwick 2000; Katsiaficas 2001; Brown 2001).

Others have identified the process of globalisation as both a threat to and opportunity for increasing levels of democracy, in forms and practice, around the world. Those against point at what they see as the collusion between big multinational corporations, transnational capital and organisations of multi-lateral co-operation, G8, IMF, WTO and the EU in privileging the needs and commercial benefits of capitalism over the rights, freedoms and livelihoods of citizens (Klein 2000; Monbiot 2000; and see the SCHNEWS website at <http://www.schnews.co.uk/>). The images of powerful political leaders behind fences and heavily protected from protesters, coupled with the violence visited on the protesters by police – for example, in Genoa in July 2001 with the killing of the activist protestor Carlo Giuliani – all add to the sense that the democratic rights of 'the people' have been fundamentally eroded by global capital.

Other commentators have pointed to the growing sense of cosmopolitan democracy afforded by globalisation and the coming together of people, across traditional boundaries, to act in democratic ways (Archibughi *et al.* 1998). Indeed, even the act of global protest hints at alternative futures for global democratic action.

Furthermore, if some have spoken of a crisis of democratic participation, others have highlighted the potential of the technologies of globalisation – for example, new media and information and communications technology – to enhance, develop and even redefine democracy in form and practice (Axford and Huggins 2001).

On a more local level civil liberties activists point to the erosion of democratic freedoms through the increased use of CCTV monitoring and the enforced testing for narcotic drugs of those arrested by police forces. On the other hand, activists point to the reinvigoration of local politics in terms

Protesters at the World Trade Organisation meeting in Prague, 2000

of popular protest against road building and environmental damage, and the positive linking of local and global issues through initiatives such as Agenda 21 (Mason 1999).

On a personal level, issues related to the body and the governance of the self in terms of sexual identity, reproductive rights, the right to life and possibly to self-determination of death become increasingly important as medical technology facilitates greater intervention in the biology of human existence. Genetic engineering and genetic modification may still be developing sciences but the implications for human beings and for traditional notions of rights and the moral and legal frameworks through which decisions and policy are formulated are clearly being stretched by advances in medical and genetic technology (Williams and Bendelow 1998; Holliday and Hassard 2001).

It is clear that there are significant challenges to the structures, processes and practice of democracy in contemporary society. Indeed, for myriad reasons, commentators argue that we are witnessing several transformations of democracy (McGrew 1997), and it is important to ask what the twenty-first century holds for both the form and practice of democracy (Beck 1999).

We can see then that the concept of democracy is one that is very much at the centre of (global) political thought and action at the beginning of the new millennium, and that the discussion extends from the very local – ultimately the individual self – to the global system.

Conceptualising democracy: the search for a definition

As we have already indicated, the concept of democracy is in some senses both clear – in a common-sense way – and somewhat less clear when we get down to actually analysing what we think constitutes democratic form and practices.

At the very least we might expect democracy to mean that some form of political power is exercised by the people over their political leaders – but for many this is a small amount of democracy. But this is – in the main – what people mean when they talk of democracy. Fukuyama's universalisation of 'liberal democracy as the final form of human government' refers to parliamentary, multi-party democracy associated with capitalist economies, individual (particularly economic) freedom and civil and legal rights based around the freedoms of expression and speech and legal limits on state intervention in an individual life. In some ways this conception of liberal democracy is strongly associated with *representative* democracy, in which the power of the people is represented by others within institutions and legal or constitutionally prescribed limits. Few of us actually participate in day-to-day democratic politics in terms of deliberation or direct action. We rely instead on a protective and accountable set of procedures and rules for the distribution and exercise of political power and economic and social resources in our communities.

In this section we will work through some of the key ideas and concepts of democracy and explore different models of democracy. However, it is important to note that these models often overlap, share many central ideas and may not be as different from each other as we at first think. Often differences between different models of democracy may be of degree rather than stark difference.

Origins of democracy

The concept and term 'democracy' originates from the Greek concept of *Demos* as *the people* and, in this sense, translated readily into the idea that democracy means rule by the people. In the Athenian city-state all citizens were involved in the democratic process through debate, deliberation and participation. It is this model of democracy that is often held up as both an ideal and an example of how democracy should function. You can see below an outline of Aristotle's main features of democracy taken from his study *Politics*, completed in 323 BC.

Key text: Aristotle (1992) *The Politics*, Harmondsworth: Penguin.

Aristotle's features of democracy

1. Elections to office by all from among all.
2. Rule of all over each and of each by turns over all.

---

continued

continued

3. Offices filled by lot, either all or at any rate those not calling for experience or skill.

4. No tenure of office dependent on the possession of a property qualification or only on the lowest possible.

5. Short terms for all offices or for as many as possible.

6. All to sit on juries chosen from all and adjudicating on all or most matters.

7. The assembly as the sovereign authority in everything, or at least the most important matters, officials having no sovereign power over any, or over as few as possible.

8. Payment for services, in the assembly, in the law-courts, and in the offices, is regular for all.

9. As birth, wealth, and education are the defining marks of oligarchy, so their opposites, low birth, low incomes, and mechanical occupations, are regarded as typical of democracy.

10. No official has perpetual tenure.

(Aristotle 1992: 363–43) [323 BC]

There are some important limits to this model of democracy which, though advocating participation and direct involvement of the citizen, is also based on a small social and economic elite who enjoy political power and privilege on the back of a slave economy. I think it immediately alerts us to certain limits of democracy and to some of its flaws, and you may want to think about why this model retains such appeal. This model and praise of Athenian or classical democracy is certainly a durable one.

Representative democracy

Representative democracy
A form of democracy in which citizens elect political representatives through periodic, popular elections who then represent the people within a system of government at national (for example, in a parliament) or local (for example, in a local authority or city council) level.

If classical democracy does represent an example of direct democracy in which citizens were directly and centrally involved it is also clear that modern democracy does not tend to work in this way. Most countries that are classified as democratic exhibit forms of representative democracy (most readily identified as liberal democracy) in which limited and indirect forms of democratic politics are practised. In representative democracies the people elect representatives who then govern, and popular participation is limited primarily to voting in local and national elections. The people exercise minimal, if in fact any, political power and 'real' political power is confined to elected political activists and elites. In representative democracies political freedom and participation tends to be measured in terms of individual freedoms, civil liberties and political rights. These include freedom of association, movement, speech, information, voting rights and freedom of conscience. There are considerable limits to the levels of political participation and direct involvement of the people in representative democracies. Many people are critical of these limits and alternatives are readily sought. One such alternative is deliberative democracy.

Deliberative democracy

Deliberative democracy in its simplest terms 'refers to a conception of democratic government that secures a central place for reasoned discussion in political life' (Cooke 2000: 947) and this way of thinking about democracy has become quite popular in recent years, with significant contributions being made to the discussion by major theorists such as John Rawls (1997) and Jurgen Habermas (1996). It has also been the case that this way of thinking about democracy has led to experiments in practical developments in local and national government (for example, the use of citizens' panels and juries, Internet discussion boards and local referenda on community issues (Axford and Huggins 2001b; Smith and Wales 2000; Woodward 2000)).

Recently, interest in deliberative democracy has heightened partly as a strategic solution to the perceived crisis of democracy and partly as interest grows in the potential of ICTs to open new spaces and channels for political discussion, debate and deliberation. As a consequence the concept is enjoying popular currency among democratic theorists, with a number arguing for the remodelling of politics along deliberative lines (Gutmann and Thompson 1996; Habermas 1996).

For Elster (1998) deliberative democracy contains two constituent elements. The first, the democratic element, is the participation in collective decision-making by those affected by the decision. The second, the deliberative element, refers to the inclusion in the decision-making process of deliberation over means and ends by participants 'committed to the values of rationality and impartiality' (Elster 1998: 8). For Fishkin (1991) there are three elements in the deliberative process: first, the exchange of political messages between individuals; second, the opportunity to reflect on these messages; and third, the enabling messages to be processed interactively and tested against rival arguments.

The idea of deliberative democracy is currently attracting considerable attention, and a number of commentators argue that deliberative techniques could be used to reinvigorate contemporary democracy. One example of how deliberative projects might be contributing to the transformation of the political process in Britain is UK Citizens Online Democracy (UKCOD), a citizen-created service designed to promote online discussion and information dissemination. This project has been running since 1996 and has involved the creation of discussion forums at local and national levels on a range of issues. These have included local taxation rates for local councils, European Monetary Union and a major project for the 1997 general election in Britain which involved discussion on constitutional reform and transport policy. Participation in the election project was high, from both public and politicians. The leaders of the three main parties and politicians from fourteen other parties competing in the elections were involved in online discussion with the public (Coleman 1997). UKCOD aims to increase information and debate among the citizenry, but to what extent such experiments represent a significant development of democracy or an increase in the quality of democracy is open to question.

Deliberative democracy A form of democracy which stresses the participation of the people in collective decision-making through a process of rational and considered deliberation.

ICTs: information and communication technologies.

Citizens' panels – emerging deliberative democracy or sophisticated political marketing. Talkback *in Oxford City, UK*

In the City of Oxford the City Council, Thames Valley Police, County Council and the Area Health Authority have established a large citizen body which is consulted through extensive postal questionnaires and telephone interviews on a regular basis about services, local information, policy and legislative proposals. This system, called *Talkback*, involves nearly 1000 participants who are representative of the City's general population and one-third of the group is rotated every year. The response rates to the surveys are high, around 65 per cent, and the authorities involved use the information gathered in a number of strategic ways. Now, such a process can be seen as simply a matter of gaining feedback on the services provided by local authorities to the local tax-payer but this may underestimate the possible reflexivity in the process. Furthermore the design of the questionnaire includes both direct questions on services and more complex questions about the power and responsibilities of bodies and organisations within the local area and the institutional and political organisation of the local authorities. One survey attempted to explore concepts of and local participation in civil society much along the lines of an exploration of social capital. The question is does such a panel constitute merely a consultation exercise or does it offer an example of a deliberative procedure in the making?

Direct democracy A form of democracy in which all members of the political community participate directly in the processes of decision-making

Direct democracy

While classical, direct democracy appears not to be a viable form of political system for mass societies, some commentators have noted recent trends in political organisation and practice which they maintain might constitute some form of direct democracy. Such trends are related to the development of media cultures and the rise of the media-adept politician. However, in general, commentators are critical of the central role of the media and media professional to the process of political communication and representation, and argue that this development has led to a corruption of the political process in favour of individual leaders and image-based, personality-led politics. Furthermore, the ability of political leaders to use the media to bypass traditional institutions of government, such as legislative assemblies, and organisations of political mobilisation – for example, political parties – has strengthened the position of the leader at the expense of democratic accountability and the integrity of the political process. The increased use of public opinion polling and other methods of gauging popular sentiment creates an even stronger link between the personalised, charismatic leader and the public. The result, some argue, is the creation of a negative form of direct democracy or an 'authoritarian pseudo-democracy based on plebiscitary opinion poll-ism and direct democracy-ism' (Poli 1998) or a 'listening dictatorship' (Donovan 1998).

Commentators frequently point to recent developments in Italian politics as an example of these trends where the fragmentation of the party system and the rise of charismatic leaders – such as Bossi and Di Pietro and the emergence of the newspaper *Forza Italia* as a vehicle for the political aspiration of Silvio Berlusconi – appear to provide evidence of this new form of direct democracy. Berlusconi and *Forza Italia*'s reliance on a slick and efficient electoral machine, television promotion, market research and a core of senior managers from Berlusconi's *Fininvest* business empire (McCarthy 1996; Seisselberg 1996) appears to be a clear example of the worst excesses of politics in media cultures which can lead to a form of 'democratic czarism' (Donovan 1998).

The central concern of critics of this form of democracy is the perceived ease with which direct and popular democracy can lead to intolerance and demagogy with the potential for political leaders to court uninformed public opinion. Interestingly such arguments echo Alexis de Tocqueville's observations about democracy in his book *Democracy in America* (1954, first published in 1835), which argued that democratic politics – by giving power and voice to the masses – can create a 'tyranny of the majority' in which minority rights can be threatened by the intolerant masses. For commentators like Barber the recent emergence of leader-dominated plebiscitary democracy, underpinned by a rabid media culture of talk-radio and 'scream' television (Barber 1995) results in democratic values being displaced by populism and demagogy.

It seems, then, that there are a number of different and competing models of democracy. As stated earlier in this chapter, the contested nature of democracy is a vital element of any analysis of the concept, and any assessment of a country's level of democratic politics and participation will be conditional upon the model of democracy operating as the context for that assessment. The more complex, developed and elaborate the model, the less the number of countries that will or can be assessed as democratic. Figure 5.1 outlines another, more detailed classification of different models of democracy.

THINK POINT

Try working through these models and rating your own country against them. When you have done this, see if you can decide what type of model describes your country's politics best.

Towards a minimal definition of democracy

As can be seen there are a number of different conceptions and models of democracy available to us. Some overlap, while others are radically different and incompatible. Like most things in politics judgement and value will depend on your world view, your political socialisation, political culture and political values. However, a minimal definition of democracy as a political system may be one which states that a political system is democratic if the entire adult population have the opportunity to participate in decision-making in that society (Dahl 1991), and to enjoy legal, political and civil protection of individual rights and freedoms.

Key text: R. A. Dahl (1961) *Who Governs? Democracy and Power in an American City*, New Haven, Conn.: Yale University Press.

Key text: K. Marx (1985) *The Communist Manifesto*, Harmondsworth: Penguin.

Key text: J. S. Mill (1972) *Utilitarianism, Liberty, Representative Government*, London: Dent.

Key text: J.-J. Rousseau (1974) *The Social Contract*, Harmondsworth: Penguin.

Model of democracy	Justification and key features	Key thinker and key text
Classical	Citizens enjoy political equality, direct participation in legislative and judicial functions, Assembly of Citizens is sovereign.	 Aristotle, 384–322 BC, *The Politics*.
Protective	Citizens require protection from those who govern and from each other. Sovereignty lies in the people but is vested in representatives, regular elections, secret ballot, party competition, centrality of constitutionalism, state and civil society separate.	James Madison, 1751–1836, *The Federalist*, 1788.
Developmental	Participation is both necessary and beneficial for the development of an informed, engaged and mature citizenry. Popular sovereignty, universal franchise, representative government, constitutional checks and balances, especially in relation to individual rights and freedoms, extensive participation in all levels of government.	 John Stuart Mill, 1806–73, *Considerations on Representative Government*, 1861.
Radical	Citizens should enjoy political and economic equality which will facilitate equal freedom and dependence in the process of collective development. Political system characterised by a division of legislative and executive functions, direct participation of citizens in the legislature through public meetings, unanimity on public issues desirable, executive positions in the hands of magistrates or administrators, executive appointed either by direct election or by lot.	 Jean-Jacques Rousseau, 1712–78, *The Social Contract*, 1762.

Model of democracy	Justification and key features	Key thinker and key text
Direct (communism)	Free development of all can only be achieved through the free development of each. All forms of government, state and politics replaced by self-regulation, all public affairs governed collectively, consensus, removal of all coercive forces and replacement with self-monitoring, distribution of all administrative tasks by rotation or election.	 Karl Marx, 1818–83, *The Communist Manifesto*, 1847.
Pluralism	Secures government by minorities, which in turn underpins political liberty. Focus on citizen and political rights, systematic checks and balances between the different elements of the state, competitive party system, diverse range of interest groups, government mediates between different groups and demands, constitutional rules supported by political culture.	 R. A. Dahl, 1961, *Who Governs? Democracy and Power in an American City*, New Haven, Conn, Yale University Press.
Competitive elitism	Focus on the selection of and competition between skilled and competent political elite. Competition within this elite acts as a check on political leaders. Parliamentary government with a strong executive, party competition, dominant parties, political leadership, central, independent and professional bureaucracy, constitutional and practical limits on the range of political decisions.	 Max Weber, 1864–1920, *Politics as a Vocation*.

Figure 5.1 Models of democracy

This 'minimal definition' leads us back to the notions of representative and liberal democracy and the limitations of this model. However, it does afford us some opportunity to make comparisons between different countries and political systems, and this minimal definition is pretty much on offer as a global model for democratisation and the future global democracy. We will explore the concept, process and practice of democratisation in the next section.

Conceptualising democratisation: process and practice

If, in the old days, the USSR had dumped its stock of gold on the world market, that market would have been completely destabilized. If the Eastern bloc countries were to put back into circulation the vast stock of freedom they have been keeping on ice, they would similarly destabilize the very fragile metabolism of Western Values, which requires that freedom no longer manifest itself as action but as a virtual and consensual form of interaction, not as drama, but as the universal pyschodrama of liberalism. A sudden injection of freedom as a lived relationship – as violent and active transcendence, as Idea – would be catastrophic in every way for our air-conditioned redistribution of values.

(Jean Baudrillard (1994) *The Illusion of the End*, Cambridge, Polity Press: 30)

Taking even the minimal definition above of full adult suffrage and free elections then, democracy as an actual lived and experienced mode of organising and practising politics is not actually very long lived. Even 'old' democracies such as the United Kingdom have had full adult suffrage for only the past seventy years or so and many established democracies have excluded particular groups from political rights until very recently, for example African Americans in the USA or women in Switzerland. Furthermore, if we consider more radical or extensive models of democracy, then it might be more accurate to talk of an ongoing process of democratisation rather than as if some places have achieved a perfect state of democracy and others have not.

This section is about this process of democratisation which appears to be one of the most important processes currently observable in the contemporary world. Since the collapse of communism in Eastern Europe and the former Soviet Union there has been a considerable acceleration of democratic form and practices in terms of representative, liberal democracy, and this has generated considerable interest among politicians, scholars and others. But it is important not to take too narrow a focus on democratisation. I think it may be reasonably argued that the process of democratisation extends well beyond the former communist states of Eastern Europe and the Soviet Union. It includes many countries that do not fall so readily into the post-communist group. This includes South America, which has seen substantial democratic developments in the past decade, and Africa, with the particularly dramatic democratisation of the Republic of South Africa after apartheid and many other parts of the world. In Western Europe, countries such as Spain, Portugal and Greece have moved towards fully functioning democracies in the past thirty years and – perhaps more controversially in terms of democratic, civil and political rights – the process of democratisation is one that Northern Ireland is currently struggling to complete. (You may notice that the Freedom House Survey on p. 174 excludes Northern Ireland from the calculation of political freedom for the United Kingdom.) Furthermore, the process appears to be continually accelerating as Pakistan's current military leader, General Perver Musharraf, announced on 14 August 2001 that Pakistan would look to re-establish democracy with the holding of provincial and federal elections starting on 1 October 2002.

From these examples democratisation may be seen as a global process which is affecting a number of countries and appears to be a global trend. As you can see from Table 5.1, some measures of democratisation suggest that the world is experiencing a significant and general trend of democratisation.

Table 5.1 The global trend in democratisation

Period	Free	Partly free	Not free
1990–1991	65	50	50
1995–1996	76	62	53
2000–2001	86	58	48

Source: Freedom House, 2000, *Freedom in the World* survey, available at <www.freedomhouse.org>

Democratisation refers to the process by which states move towards more democratic forms of political system. Now, assessment of democratisation will obviously be conditional on the type of definition of democracy that is employed, and it is fair to say that most measures of democratisation rely on a conception of democracy that is a liberal, representative one. Using such criteria commentators are able to identify a significant twentieth-century trend of democratisation across the globe. Thus Potter (1997) highlights that in 1975 at least 68 per cent of countries throughout the world were authoritarian, but by 1995 this figure had dropped to 26 per cent (Potter 1997: 1). This process of democratisation began in the 1970s in Southern Europe, spread to South America and parts of Asia in the 1980s and into parts of Africa, Eastern Europe and the former Soviet Union in the 1990s. Huntington (1991) locates these recent trends in more long-term general waves of democratisation which are outlined below.

Key text: S. Huntington (1991) *The Third Wave: Democratization in the Late Twentieth Century*, Norman, Okla, and London: University of Oklahoma Press.

Samuel Huntington's waves of democratisation

First, long wave 1828–1926

Including: USA, Britain, France, Italy, Argentina and British overseas dominions

First, reverse wave 1922–42

Including: Italy, Germany and Argentina

Second, short wave 1943–62

Including: Italy, West Germany, India, Japan and Israel

Second, reverse wave 1958–1975

Including: Argentina, Chile and Brazil

Third wave 1974 to present

Including: Spain, Portugal, Chile, Argentina, Asia, Africa and Eastern Europe
(Adapted from Huntington 1991)

For Huntington waves of democratisation are defined as 'a group of transitions from non-democratic to democratic regimes that occur within a specified period of time and that significantly outnumber transitions in the opposite direction during that period' (Huntington 1991: 15). Interestingly, Huntington's waves of democratisation are accompanied by reverse waves in which countries that had democratised cease to be democratic and adopt different forms of authoritarian rule such as Fascism (Italy), Nazism (Germany) and military dictatorship (Chile). This tendency alerts us to the need for democracies to reach a stable and consolidated state in which the long-term stability of democratic forms of government and politics are secure, stable and legitimate. This distinction, between consolidated and non-consolidated democracies, adds a further dimension to comparative studies of democracy and has particular relevance when considering the transformation being experienced in the former communist states in Europe and the former USSR. A brief look at Table 5.2, which offers a comparative summary of levels of freedom in different countries, indicates that, on these measures, the process of democratisation in Poland or Slovenia has been very different to that in Russia or Belarus.

Explaining democratisation

If we accept that by certain definitions democratisation has increased at the level of systemic politics, it seems reasonable to ask why has this has been the case. In this section we will look briefly at some of the main explanations of the process of democratisation.

Potter (1997) identifies three theoretical approaches that can be used to explain patterns of democratisation. The first is the *modernisation* approach which emphasises a number of social and economic factors that are seen as either necessary for explaining the existence of consolidated democracies or as necessary for democratisation to succeed. Put simply, this approach suggests that levels of democracy are directly related to a country's level of socio-economic development or modernisation. Thus stable democratic government in France or Britain or the USA is a direct outcome of the economic 'success' and stability of these countries. The second is the *transition* approach which places greater emphasis on the role of political elites and political processes to explain the process of democratisation. Here, it is argued, the actions of political elites, the political choices and strategies they adopt and their commitment to democratisation explain the success (or otherwise) of transitions to democracy. The third approach is the *structural* approach which emphasises changes in the structures of power that are favourable to the process of democratisation. Here the emphasis is on how democratisation is related to long-term historical processes of changing social structures of class, state and transnational power, and therefore the path to liberal democracy is an outcome of changes in these structures rather than other factors (Potter 1997).

All these explanations give significant emphasis to the relationship between economic development and democratic politics. Given this, it is perhaps not surprising that some commentators argue that what democratisation really means is commercialisation and capitalism and not freedom or genuine democracy. It is arguable that this approach also explains some of the apparent dissatisfaction and disenchantment that now accompanies the post-1989 experience of democracy (see e.g. Lagos 2001; Rose 2001). For Smith, the meaning of democratisation has been 'diluted, such that it often signifies nothing more than consumerism, free market policies and the most superficial liberal-democratic electoral reforms' (Smith 1998: 5). And data from some countries indicates that new democracies have a long way to go to reach consolidation and legitimacy in the eyes of the people. In part this reflects the significant social costs of transformation and democratisation, and it is also easy to overlook the considerable human costs of the processes discussed in this chapter.

While considerable commentary is extended to the process of democratisation at the level of the nation-state (and, as we shall see, at the level of the global political order), it is also important to consider democratisation as a process that is going on throughout other organisations and reinvigorating democratic form and practice in established or consolidated democracies. In the next section we discuss the possible emergence of deliberative models of democratic participation as an outcome of the local responses to Agenda 21 which is an example of the ongoing process of democratisation in the United Kingdom. Another example might be Anthony Giddens' work on *The Third Way* (1998) and the growing interest in notions of stakeholders that can be identified in a number of political programmes around the world.

For Giddens the politics of the 'old left' (classical social democracy) and neoliberalism present stark and ultimately unsustainable political programmes. In *The Third Way* Giddens argues that given the current state of the world a

Table 5.2 Comparative measures of freedom

Trend	Country	Political rights	Civil liberties	Freedom rating
	Afghanistan	7	7	Not free
▲	Albania	4	5	Partly free
	Argentina	1	2	Free
	Belarus	6	6	Not free
	Belgium	1	2	Free
	Benin	2	2	Free
	China (PRC)	7	6	Not free
	Czech Republic	1	2	Free
	Dominican Republic	2	2	Free
	East Timor	6	3	Free
	Fiji	6	3	Partly free
	Finland	1	1	Free
▼	Guatemala	3	4	Partly free
	India	2	3	Free
▼	Iran	6	6	Not free
▼	Jamaica	2	2	Free
	Japan	1	2	Free
▼	Kenya	6	5	Not free
	Kuwait	4	5	Partly free
	Libya	7	7	Not free
	Macedonia	4	3	Partly free
	Mongolia	2	3	Free
▼	Mozambique	3	4	Partly free
▼	Namibia	2	3	Free
	New Zealand	1	1	Free
	Pakistan	6	5	Not free
▲	Paraguay	4	3	Partly free
	Poland	1	2	Free
	Romania	2	2	Free
	Russia	5	5	Partly free
	San Marino	1	1	Free
	Saudi Arabia	7	7	Not free
	Singapore	5	5	Partly free
	Slovenia	1	2	Free
	Suriname	1	2	Free
	Sweden	1	1	Free
	Taiwan (Republic of China)	1	2	Free
	Tajikstan	6	6	Not free
	Turkey	4	5	Partly free
	Turkmenistan	7	7	Free
	Tuvalu	1	1	Free
▲	United Kingdom	1	2	Free
	United States	1	1	Free
	Uzbekistan	7	6	Not free
	Venezuela	3	5	Partly free

Note:

Freedom in the World is an evaluation of political rights and civil liberties in the world that Freedom House has carried out since 1973. *Political rights* are the formation of political parties that represent a significant range of voter choice, compete in open competition and can be elected to positions of power. *Civil liberties* include respect and protection for religious, ethnic, economic, linguistic, gender and family rights, personal freedoms and freedoms of the press, belief and association. The survey rates each country on a seven-point scale for both political rights and civil liberties with 1 being the most free and 7 the least. The world is divided into three broad categories: Free = 1–3, Partly free = 3.5–5 and Not free = 5.5–7. See Piano and Puddington 2001.

Source: See *Freedom in the World* – Freedom House: <www.freedomhouse.org>

renewal of social democracy is required, one that offers a third way between neoliberalism and classical social democracy. For Giddens old-style social democracy allowed free market capitalism to create many of the problems Marx identified as characteristic of this form of socio-economic organisation while also encouraging extensive state intervention in the economy, social organisation and individual life. On the other hand, neoliberals favoured unrestricted market forces, a minimal state, contraction of the welfare state and traditional social values in relation to the family and other aspects of social behaviour (Giddens 1998).

Giddens identifies five dilemmas which all political thinking has to account for and deal with. These are:

1 Globalisation – what is it and what are its effects?
2 Individualism – to what extent are societies experiencing more individualism?
3 Left and Right – the disintegration of significant distinctions in politics.
4 Political agency – to what extent are traditional mechanisms of democracy in decline?
5 Ecological problems – how can these be integrated into political programmes?

For Giddens the answer is to build a third way on the values of equality, protection of the vulnerable, freedom as autonomy, no rights without responsibilities, no authority without democracy, cosmopolitan pluralism and philosophic conservatism. These values underpin a politics of the third way:

Key text: A. Giddens (1998) *The Third Way*, Cambridge: Polity Press.

The Third Way Programme

The radical centre
The new democratic state – the state without enemies
Active civil society
The democratic family
The new mixed economy
Equality as inclusion
Positive welfare
The social investment state
The cosmopolitan nation
Cosmopolitan democracy

(Giddens 1998)

Giddens' model has received a lot of attention, and the term 'third way' is used by politicians, social commentators, policy-makers and academics around the world. However, it remains to be seen what a third-way politics would actually look like and how effective, in terms of reinvigorating democracy, it would actually be.

The criticisms and limits of democracy and democratisation

Democracy – as a political practice of decision-making that requires the participation of all those affected by the outcome of the decision – is not being practised on the Left because the voices of women, gays/lesbians/bisexuals/transgenders, and people of colour are not being heeded.

(Greta Gaard, Green Party of Minnesota, 'Toward a Radical Democracy on the Left', *Synthesis/Regeneration*, 13 (Spring, 1997): 1)

My theme is the poor health of democracy. Many will regard this as a strange pre-occupation at a time when democracy could be said to be enjoying a world-historical peak. But this peak relates to the minimal though admittedly absolutely vital criterion of democracy as the choice of government in free elections based on universal adult suffrage. I want to go beyond such minimalism and appraise our current democratic practices in the light of an admittedly ambitious maximal model.

(Colin Crouch (2000) *Post-Democracy*, London, Fabian Society: 1)

The fundamental critique of democracy lies with the expression of democracy as liberal democratic ideas and institutions and the apparently fundamental association of these ideas with (unrestrained) capitalism, particularly since that capitalism has become more multinational, corporate and global. In this section we will consider four main critics of liberal democracy: feminism, republicanism, radicalism, environmentalism.

Feminist critiques of liberal democracy

As can be seen from the Greta Gaard quotation above, feminism offers a strong critique of democracy, especially liberal democracy as practised and advocated in many states. As we can see from Gaard's comments, feminists are critical of the way in which liberal democracy fails to recognise the voices or political and social claims for participation of (among others) women.

One of the most important contributions to this debate has been by the political theorist Carole Pateman who has argued against narrow, liberal, representative democratic form and practice for the past three decades and has encouraged a useful discussion among political theorists and writers on democracy about the crucial limitations of democracy in relation to the participation of women in political society (Carter and Stokes 1998).

Pateman's work outlines a significant concern with the effective social and political marginalisation and subordination of women in liberal democracy. Pateman's key contribution to this debate may be found in her book *The Sexual Contract* (1988) in which she argues that women are effectively consigned to the private sphere of social activity (principally the 'home') and that they tend to be dominated by men in both private and public spheres. For Pateman inequalities in the distribution of political power along gender lines are critically left unchallenged by many forms of democracy and democratic participation needs to be extended into the private sphere of life and especially into the organisation of the family. Pateman conceptualises liberal society as

Key text: C. Pateman (1988) *The Sexual Contract*, Cambridge: Polity Press.

> a series of male clubs – usually, as Virginia Woolf points out in *Three Guineas*, distinguished by their own costumes and uniforms – that embrace parliament, the courts, political parties, the military and police, universities, workplaces, trade unions, public (private) schools, exclusive clubs and popular leisure clubs, from all of which women are excluded or to which they are mere auxiliaries.
>
> (Pateman 1988: 210)

This critique extends to the study of politics where Pateman notes that it is 'frequently overlooked how recently democratic or universal suffrage was established. Political scientists have remained remarkably silent about the struggle for womanhood suffrage . . . and the political meaning and consequences of enfranchisement' (Pateman 1988: 211).

While Pateman's work has been criticised for stressing a universal and essentialist conception of women and sexual relations (Sullivan 1998), her work marks an important contribution to the debate about democracy and remains highly relevant. A recent special edition of the *Journal of Democracy* on *Women and Democracy* notes the continued centrality of cultural obstacles to equal representation for women in politics. Norris and Ingelhart argue that a

> fundamental problem facing the worldwide process of democratization is the continued lack of gender equality in political leadership. The basic facts are not in dispute: Today women represent only one in seven parliamentarians, one in ten cabinet ministers, and, at the apex of power, one in 20 heads of state or government.
>
> (Norris and Ingelhart 2001: 126)

THINK POINT

- What do you make of this feminist critique of liberal democracy? Do you think that there are structural or cultural barriers to the participation of women in politics?

■ If you do not, how do you account for the statistics to which Norris and Ingelhart draw attention in the above quotation?

Republican critiques of liberal democracy

Republican critiques of liberal democracy stress the value and importance of the wider community and some notion of pubic good over the supremacy of the individual in terms of political goals and outcomes. Like the concept of democracy, republicanism has a long history and can also be traced back to classical times; for example, Cicero's (106–43) *The Republic* offers a defence of republican government. In the 1960s civic republicanism was particularly fashionable, and one thinker who is associated with this mode of thinking about democracy and the politics of social organisation is Hannah Arendt. For Arendt modern liberal, representative democracy denied the importance of public happiness and public freedom, and conceptualised politics as a kind of burden best pursued by the few and not the rest of us. In her book *On Revolution*, Arendt likens representative government to oligarchy and argues

> That representative government has in fact become oligarchic government is true enough, though not in the classical sense of rule by the few in the interests of the few; what we today call democracy is a form of government where the few rule, at least supposedly, in the interest of the many. This government is democratic in that popular welfare and private happiness are its chief goals; but it can be called oligarchic in the sense that public happiness and public freedom become the privilege of the few.
>
> (Arendt 1990: 269)

Arendt's answer was to increase the levels of and opportunities for participation in democratic politics through the creation of council democracy inspired by the type of political organisations that emerged during revolutionary periods in French (French Revolution or the Paris Commune) and Russian history (the revolutions of 1917) and in Hungary in 1956. For Arendt such models offered an alternative to parliamentary, party-based political systems that, she felt, systematically limited the degree to which citizens could actively or usefully participate in the political process.

THINK POINT

How workable do you think this model of democracy is? Do you think that participation, in its own right, is valuable for democracy?

Radical critiques of liberal democracy

One of the most radical critiques of liberal democracy may be found in Marxist thought which argues that liberal, parliamentary democracy is simply a part of the systematic exploitation of the workers. For Marxists like Ralph Miliband, parliamentary democracy is a sham by which the workers are pacified by the image of participation and democracy while actual power relations – inequalities between rich and poor, between the politically weak and politically strong – are left unchallenged. However, Marxism as a way of thinking about and analysing politics has not had an easy time since the early 1990s, and such analysis has been subject to considerable revision and amendment. The 'Left' has had to reconsider a number of central ideas, beliefs and theories in the past few decades and, consequently, radical critiques of liberal democracy from the 'Left' have become sophisticated.

Chantal Mouffe and Ernesto Laclau provide an interesting example of what Smith has called a 'radical democratic imaginary' (1998) and we will consider their approach to democracy briefly here. Commenting on the rise of social movements and shifts in the political landscape, Laclau and Mouffe note,

> The new forms of social conflict have . . . thrown into crisis theoretical and political frameworks . . . [that] correspond to the classical discourses of the Left, and the characteristic modes in which it has conceived the agents of social change, the structuring of social spaces, and the privileged points for the unleashing of historical transformations.
>
> (Laclau and Mouffe, quoted in Smith 1998: 2)

As a consequence Laclau and Mouffe note that socialism is in crisis and that the systematic and universal narrative of socialism fails to account for the politicisation of new and different areas of social life and new forms of political conflict. Laclau and Mouffe draw from a wide range of traditions of political thought which includes Gramsci, liberal democracy itself, post-structualism, phenomenology, psycholoanalysis and Foucault (Carter and Stokes 1998; Smith 1998), to argue for a conception of democracy that stresses radical, pluralist practice and political activism.

> Pluralism is *radical* only to the extent that each term of this plurality finds within itself the principle of its own validity, without this having to be sought in a transcendent or underlying positive ground for the hierarchy of meaning of them all and the source and guarantee of their legitimacy. And this radical pluralism is *democratic* to the extent that the auto-constitutivity of each one of its terms is the result of displacements of the egalitarian imaginary.
>
> (Laclau and Mouffe, quoted in Smith 1998: 167)

For Laclau and Mouffe pluralism, difference and autonomy are the keys to radical democratic politics and are reflected in the proliferation of social movements which occupy the contemporary political landscape. These social movements are accommodated by neither the political theory of traditional socialist thought nor the institutionalised politics of liberal democracy. Rather, they offer a radical alternative in their own right.

Environmental critiques of liberal democracy

Environmentalism, like democracy, is a term that possesses a range of meanings and can be contested. Also, like democracy, it is a concept that possesses a clear ethical as well as political dimension. Despite (or perhaps because of) its diversity, environmentalism has presented a number of challenges to existing models of democratic politics and, like some of the other critiques mentioned above, one of the key developments has been the emphasis on diversity of values, interests and non-institutional forms of protest and political action that have contributed to the re-evaluation of the usefulness of existing models of democracy. In particular, environmentalism has drawn attention to both the future interests and environmental well-being of future generations and the significance of non-human species of life (Mason 1999). The range of potential and actual threats to the environment are considerable (for a survey see Brown 2001), and environmentalism offers a range of responses and critiques of liberal democracy.

At the more radical end of the environmental spectrum ecocentrics are deeply ambivalent about liberal democracy. They are frustrated by the slowness of majoritarian electoral politics and what they see as the populist or pro-business stance of many leaders, such as George Bush manifested in his recurrent refusals to support environmental protection measures such as the Kyoto Climate Change Conference agreement of 1997.

Ecocentrics advocate a more participatory democratic politics in which small-scale communities are the focus of political action and in which ecocentric values are employed to put protection of the environment at the centre of the political process. But there are potential contradictions here between the expression of human free will and the moral requirement of protecting the planet and non-human life forms that, taken to extreme, could themselves be profoundly illiberal and anti-democratic.

Ecocentric conceptions are only one of many environmental approaches and critiques of liberal democracy and to focus on these does not do justice to the range and sophistication of green political thought. The relationship between environmental concerns and democracy is clearly an area of growing significance, and students of politics need to examine these developments closely. There are, for example, interesting developments around the globalisation of environmental rights through the growth of international laws and agreements which focus on the protection of the environment. These include the Rio Earth Summit (1992), the Kyoto Summit (1997) and UN initiatives such as the *Ksentini Report* which outline key environmental dimensions to political rights, including the right to information about the environment, the right to receive and disseminate information about the environment, the right to participation in environmental planning and decision-making processes, the right to freedom of association for the purpose of protecting the environment and the right to effective remedies for environmental harm in administrative or judicial proceedings (Boyle 1996).

The connections between the global and local in terms of democracy and environmentalism are clearly demonstrated by Michael Mason's recent study

The **Stop Esso Campaign** highlights key environmental concerns about the ineffectiveness of liberal democracy to protect the environment.

of the impact of Agenda 21 in the London Borough of Islington (Mason 1999). This study offers an example of how environmental democracy is moving forward and, at the same time, how new forms of deliberative and participatory politics may develop. Agenda 21 initiatives are an outcome of the 1992 Rio Earth Summit (United Nations 1993), and these initiatives encourage the consultation of the public over social and environmental issues. Local government in the United Kingdom has, in general, been relatively keen to embrace these initiatives, and one consequence of this has been the growth of local experiments in consultation and participation in local politics.

In the case of Islington a charter for sustainable development was agreed in 1995 which was founded on four principles (Mason 1999):

1 The encouragement of individual and collective responsibility for the environment
2 The creation of a viable system for protecting the environment
3 Equal access for all to a good-quality environment
4 The promotion of a healthy and safe environment.

This charter and the Local Agenda 21 planning process has been led by a borough-wide Agenda 21 forum which includes a range of community representatives, neighbourhood forums, local businesses, public sector organisations and voluntary groups. The process has been characterised by wide-ranging consultation, procedural openness and community involvement. However, while noting these developments as favourable, Mason also draws attention to the systemic limits that remain in place within a political system founded upon representative notions of political governance.

THINK POINT

How do you think the environment should be managed? How would you get your voice and opinions heard about environmental issues in your local neighbourhood?

We can see then that there are considerable limits to the notion of democracy as conceptualised within liberal democratic forms and practices. It is, however, this form of democracy that is very much the one on offer as a model of democracy for those states undergoing the process of democratisation, or indeed as a model for global democracy through transnational organisations such as the United Nations or the European Union. In the next section of this chapter we will consider some of the futures for democracy in relation to two significant developments of recent years: globalisation and technological innovation.

Futures of democracy and democratisation

Today, the forces of democracy face a new source of corruption all the more sinister because it appears so innocuous, often even identifying itself with the liberty it undermines. Having survived the nation-state and in time subordinated it to its own liberal purposes, can democracy now survive globalization?

(Barber 2001: 275)

If the definition, roots and meaning of democracy are problematic then the same is also true for the future of democracy. Indeed, some would argue that the future is far from bright for democracy. A range of factors are identified as limiting the workings of democracy in both theory and practice. These include environmental crisis, globalisation and the collapse of the Left. In this section we will focus on two significant developments for democracy and democratisation. First, the fierce arguments ranging over the relationship between globalisation and democracy, and second, issues related to the emergence of 'digital democracy'.

Globalisation and democracy

In a recent essay Benjamin Barber (2001), an advocate of strong and vital democracy, has made a stirring argument highlighting what he sees as the threat that globalisation poses to democracy. Referring to what he sees as an 'ironic and radical asymmetry' he argues that whilst globalisation has taken place in the markets of goods, labour, currencies and information, no such developments have been experienced in civic and democratic institutions that, hitherto, have comprised the context of the free market (Barber 2001: 275). For Barber, capitalism has escaped from the institutional box of democracy and is running dangerously and destructively out of control.

Barber argues that democracy has served the free market well and that the benefits of a free market economy have followed the development of democracy rather than the other way round. However, in the late twentieth century the extensive and pervasive manifestations of global capitalism ('McWorld' as Barber (1996) calls it), including rampant privatisation, commercialisation and consumer culture, have resulted in a more efficient and complete domination of social and economic life. The ultimate result has been that this 'concert of forces has been damaging to the pluralism of our society and the democracy of our political and civic life' (Barber 2001: 276).

Interestingly at the centre of Barber's arguments is the notion that globalisation is accompanied and facilitated by privatisation, radical commercialisation and colonising commercialisation that has 'demanded a quite astonishing and perfectly overt infantalizing of consumers' (Barber 2001: 293).

Elite nostalgia aside, Barber's possibly overly pessimistic reading is a clear reiteration of classic liberal notions of democracy and his method of breaking the 'vicious circle' is to reimagine the institutions of nation-state liberal democracy as reinvigorated and written large across the global system. Whether or not this can be done leaves more radical and certainly more nuanced readings of globalisation off the agenda.

Examples of more nuanced readings of the relationship between and the future for democracy and globalisation may be found in the work of those writers pursuing the theme of cosmopolitan democracy (Archibughi and Held 1995; Held 1996; Archibughi *et al.* 1998). For David Held globalisation offers both an opportunity and a necessity for the creation of a cosmopolitan democracy that will encourage the creation of democratic mechanisms of accountability and legitimacy at the global level. Held argues that

> The theory of cosmopolitan democracy is one of the few political theories which examines systematically the democratic implications of the fact that nation-states are enmeshed today in complex interconnected relations. Our world is a world of *overlapping communities of fate*, where the fate of one country and that of another are more entwined than ever before. In this world, there are many issues which stretch beyond the borders of countries and challenge the relevance of those borders in key respects.
>
> (Held 1998: 26)

Such challenges include the continued development of regional, international and global flows of resources and networks of interaction, increasing interconnectedness of political communities across social, cultural, environmental and economic lines and more specific issues that include pollution and environmental threats, use and distribution of natural resources, and regulation of global networks of finance, trade and commerce which pose specific problems for democracy.

For Held **cosmopolitan democracy** offers an opportunity to create a global, democratic response to these developments. In the short term Held argues for a reform of UN governing institutions such as the Security Council, creation of a UN second chamber, enhanced political regionalisation – for example, in the EU – the use of transnational referenda, the creation of a new international Human Rights Court and the establishment of an effective and accountable international military force. Beyond issues related to governance Held advocates more democratic organisational forms in the economy and the provision of resources to those in the most vulnerable social positions (Held 1998).

In the longer term Held argues for the creation of a New Charter of Rights and Obligations locked into different domains of political, social and economic power, a global parliament, the separation of political and economic interests, the public funding of deliberative assemblies and electoral processes, an interconnected global legal system and a permanent shift of a nation-state's coercive capability to regional and global institutions. In the long term, economic reorganisation would result in a multisectoral economy characterised by a plurality of ownership and a social framework of investment priorities which would be set through public deliberation and government decision, while an extensive market regulation of goods and labour would remain (Held 1998).

Although Held can point to general evidence and trends to support his arguments, this model seems a little utopian to say the least and would not impress more radical critics. Another model of cosmopolitan democracy and governance is as follows.

Cosmopolitan democracy
A globalised form of democracy that is perceived as transnational, multi-levelled and cosmopolitan. Some people argue that such political organisation is emerging in response to the economic and cultural globalisation.

Boutros Boutros-Ghali: An Agenda for Democratisation. A Model for Global Democracy?

United Nations

Centre of the model for global democracy through the promotion of democratisation and reform of its own institutions and the strengthening of intergovernmental machinery.

Member states

All member states should take a full role in the global agenda with an increased attention to and engagement with international affairs by all member states. States should engage in dialogue, avoid isolationism, oppose unilateralism, accept democratic decision-making, oppose aggression, respect the rule of law.

New actors

Integration of non-state actors into existing international structures and mechanisms – this includes the key actors in the process of globalisation, the transnational entities of business and finance.

Regional organisations

Growing importance of regional groupings which can contribute political, diplomatic, financial, material and military resources to the global project of democratisation.

NGOs

Massive increase in number and range of NGOs. Such organisations are self-governing organisations increasingly taking on important roles in world affairs by carrying the voices and needs of a variety of communities into international arenas. To deepen further the democratising potential of these organisations further NGOs should be invited to participate in member state delegations.

Parliamentarians

Essential link between international organisations and public opinion. To consolidate the contribution of parliamentarians to international democratisation member states should encourage and facilitate greater involvement of parliamentarians in United Nations efforts to provide support for democratisation within states.

Local authorities

To strengthen local frameworks for global problem-solving and to deepen the involvement of local authorities in the UN system UN resident coordinators should maintain regular dialogue with local authorities and member states should involve local authorities more directly in the processes of consultation and facilitate local authority involvement in UN bodies.

(This model also contains a role for *academia*, *business* and the *media*, all of whom are charged with delivering their roles in a more global, responsible and cooperative way.)

(Boutros-Ghali 2000: 105–24)

THINK POINT

What do you think of the Held and Boutros-Ghali models? What might be the advantages and disadvantages of organising global politics in these ways? How achievable do you think these aims are?

Neither of these models is likely to appeal to anti-globalisation protesters, who are likely to see both models as examples of the global carve-up of humanity and resources that favours only the developed capitalist societies and 'big' business within them.

Have a look at the extract below taken from *Justice?*, a publication of the Brighton Direct Action collective. Think about the model of global governance and democracy implied in this piece and about the responses of such activists to the Held or Boutros-Ghali plans for the global, collective future.

Document

Published in Brighton by *Justice?* – Brighton's Direct Action collective, issue 316, Friday 3 August 2001

GENOA SOCIAL FORUM

Anti-capitalist demonstrations and protest were coordinated in Genoa by the Genoa Social Forum which acted as an umbrella organisation for activists in the run up to and during the G8 summit in July 2001.

BLAIR-FACED LIAR

A week after the massive protests in Genoa, the free-trade-is-good-for-you brigade are on the offensive. In the New Labour corner Prime Minister Blair and Chancellor Gordon Brown went on a tour of Brazil and Argentina with an official government spokesman saying, 'The Prime Minister believes people at the sharp end of the globalisation debate have a much more realistic view of the benefits of globalisation.'

Maybe the 12,000 people attending the World Social Forum in Porto Alegre, Brazil earlier this year just weren't listening. The Forum was set up to counter Davos – another one of those corporate shingdigs where the ruling elite decide how to carve up the planet – and to declare that 'another world is possible.' Francois Houtart from the World Forum of Alternatives certainly hasn't got Blair's message. In Porto Alegre he described globalisation as 'a fragmenting and destructive process; destroying communities, cultures, economies and the environment.'

Meanwhile in Argentina this week, thousands of jobless people and state employees set up roadblocks in more than 40 cities, protesting at the government's austerity plan and demanding jobs. Argentina has been in recession for the past four years and the government's answer to this economic hiccup is the usual one of slashing wages, pensions, deep spending cuts and increasing privatisation. This is in order to save about a billion quid, and to assure creditors that it won't default on its debt, which currently stands at a staggering £91.5 billion. Blair reckons the spending cuts were 'a very significant step forward' but for who? The banks maybe, but certainly not for ordinary Argentinians. In a ruling last year a federal judge concluded 'Since 1976 our country has been put under the rule of foreign creditors and under the supervision of the International Monetary Fund by means of a vulgar and offensive economic policy that forced Argentina to go down on its knees in order to benefit national and foreign private firms.'

MOORE OF THE SAME

Over in the World Trade Organisation corner, Director General Mike Moore has been seriously getting his neo-liberal knickers in a twist. At a two-day meeting in Geneva this week he told negotiators to pull their fingers out or there won't be a new global trade round in Qatar in November. Moore is scared that the WTO will become irrelevant if a new trade round isn't launched after the kicking it got in Seattle (see SchNEWS 240). Along with his pals in the European Commission and some of the world's richest countries, he's been threatening developing countries by telling them that 'a[nother] round would help the poor and weak countries more than anyone else. The big guys can fend for themselves. But without multilateral rules, the poor are subject to the law of the jungle.'

Like Blair, Moore doesn't take too kindly to the 'stuff-capitalism posse', telling anyone that will listen 'If you oppose the WTO, you are opposing lifting the poor out of poverty.' But it's not only protestors who oppose a new round. India's Ambassador to the WTO, Srinivasan Narayanan, said just a few weeks ago, 'We're not ready for it [a new round]. We'll lose more than we'll gain.' While one delegate from Lesotho added 'What has the WTO and market liberalisation brought for Lesotho? Up till now, I haven't seen anything. The only thing I have seen is the opposite. The agreement on agriculture has almost wiped out our domestic industry.' Federico Cuello Camilo the Dominican Republic's Trade Ambassador added 'The WTO was supposed to have been an impartial referee of common rules, where countries could learn to play the game . . . It hasn't turned out like that. The rules are biased against the weak, and nothing has changed since Seattle.'

As Aileen Kwa from Focus on the Global South points out, 'Negotiations at the WTO institutionalise the law of the jungle. Arm-twisting is commonplace and weak countries are constantly threatened that their food aid would be cut off, or their loan suspended, if they do not tow-the-line.' She adds, 'While the majority of developing countries are refusing to back down, their positions could easily collapse without massive civil society backing.'

The real problem for Blair, Moore and cronies is the growing movement opposed to the way the world is being run. At its most spectacular you've see it on the streets and TV screens when the global elite meet up to plan further carving up of the planet. But every day across the world people are fighting for a better, fairer world.

Digital democracy An umbrella term that refers to the application of advanced ICTs and new media to the political process. This can take many forms, from politicians having websites and e-mail, to more elaborate and structured use of ICTs in, for example, electoral systems or participatory processes involving citizens and politicians.

Digital democracy

Relatively recent developments in information technology, particularly in terms of the increased opportunities for interactivity between political actors and the public, have excited and alarmed many commentators. The notion that new technologies and new media can facilitate both qualitative and quantitative changes in the nature and extent of public communication and politics is being explored by commentators, policy-makers, politicians and activists alike (Hague and Loader 1999; Tambini 1999; Hacker and van Dijk 2000; Axford and Huggins 2001).

Some have noted how the formal and conventional debating and dialogical interactions taking place within institutions of government and state and between members of these institutions and the citizen are or may be affected by the deployment of new technologies (Coleman *et al.* 1999). In such approaches it is the introduction of communication and information technology directly into formal institutions of politics and the encouraging of the public to communicate and interact with members of such organisations that forms the focus of study (Coleman 1999). The focus of such studies is on the nature and extent of technology use – for example, e-mail and discussion lists with politicians – at local, national and transnational levels, and the embeddedness of technology within the infrastructure and organisational practices of political organisations, for example, in the new Scottish Parliament

(Smith and Gray 1999). At the local level attention has been focused on the increasing use of electronic communication in civic networking projects (Tsagarousianou *et al.* 1998) and deliberative practice involving policy initiatives such as Agenda 21, local authority budgetary decisions and the creation of citizens' forums in the form of youth panels, electronic town halls and experiments in electoral practice (DETR 2001).

Others argue that the Internet offers a medium of civic engagement (Sassi 2001). We are also witnessing bottom-up, potentially democratising operations of electronic bulletin boards and discussion groups, the formation of activist groups and the use of the Internet as a campaigning/mobilising force for social and political movements such as environmental campaigners, civil rights activists and the anti-capitalist groups who use and recycle media exposure to significant effect (Liberty 1999).

Interestingly, some have noted the role of the citizen in participating in and acting on information and debate held in the informal and spontaneous world of the specialist bulletin board discussion lists in which significant amounts of material and ideas are exchanged between citizens which can impact significantly on citizen knowledge, action and life-world (Haythornthwaite 2000). This list is extensive and diffuse but, for example, may be illustrated by the use of bulletin boards related to disability through which citizens can generate significant information, support and sometimes activism. These groups do appear to function (at some level) as electronic communities in which individuals develop identities (related to the non-virtual world but not constrained by them), seek out allegiances, test ideas, knowledge and information and, importantly, 'test' the validity of official medical and professional discourses (Burrows *et al.* 2000).

First steps to cybercitizens? Open government in the United Kingdom

The application of information technology to the business of government and public administration and the state–citizen interface appears to be gathering pace and may be a step to more open government, to greater transparency and possibly to the creation of cybercitzens. In the UK, since 1996, under the Information Society Initiative, the British government has been pursuing a policy of open government via the Internet and other information technologies. In 1997 the Direct Access Government initiative was created to provide information about a range of government departments and to provide access to documentation required by business.

The Parliamentary Office of Science and Technology report – *Electronic Democracy – Information Technologies and the Citizen* – provides an indication of how the further application of ICTs and new media may be used to enhance delivery of government services. In this model open government means using ICT technology to allow citizens easier access to information and services and

continued

continued

to submit forms, such as tax returns, to the government (Byrne 1997). Also under this project, evaluation of the performance of local authorities and government departments in meeting the commitments of the Citizens Charter is available on CD-ROM, the Patents Office has opened its databases to the public and the Ministry of Agriculture, Food and Fisheries has computerised the tagging and registration system for cattle. These are just examples but such a list could be extended extensively.

Future developments, for example, the creation of virtual one-stop-welfare-to-work-shops (Byrne 1997) or the use of a smart card to which benefits payments would be credited directly and which could be used to purchase goods and services in the high street, might make the programme more adventurous and lead citizens down one path to digital interface with the state.

It is early days, but for some the potential of digital democracy offers the opportunity for genuine gains in the qualitative and quantitative levels of democracy and direct participation of the people in the political process and institutional structures of government: a digital Athens in the making?

THINK POINT

What do you understand by 'new media'? How do you think new media and information and communications technology could be applied to the democratic process? Would you like to get more information about local politics through your television? How would you feel about voting, online, in a supermarket or a fast-food restaurant?

Conclusion

In this chapter I have examined the key concepts of democracy and democratisation and argued that these are two of the most important and commonly used terms in politics in recent years. However, I have also argued that although these concepts are very familiar to many of us, their exact meaning often remains elusive and quite difficult to define. This, in part, stems from the critical and contested nature of these concepts and the fact that achieving and then sustaining democratic forms and practices of politics are very much part of the lived struggle for individual and collective political freedoms around the world.

Chapter summary

In this chapter we have explored the nature and meaning of democracy and democratisation. We have identified the following key points:

- Defining democracy is not straightforward and the concept has more than one meaning.

- There are a number of different models of democracy available.

- These include representative, deliberative and direct forms of democracy.

- In contemporary politics representative – and in particular liberal – democracy appears to be in the ascendancy.

- The world does appear to be undergoing a general trend of democratisation.

- However, both democracy and democratisation are not without their critics, and many argue that the dominant models of democracy do not allow for enough popular control or participation and overly favour commercial and government interests.

- Globalisation appears to pose new and significant challenges to democracy.

- Increasingly, people are looking at models of global or cosmopolitan democracy.

- Developments in new media and ICTs may offer opportunities to 're-invent' democratic form and practice in both democratising countries and consolidated democracies.

EXERCISE

Read this extract from William Burroughs' *City of the Red Nights*:

The liberal principles embodied in the French and American revolutions and later in the liberal revolutions of 1848 had already been codified and put into practice by pirate communes a hundred years earlier. Here is a quote from *Under the Black Flag* by Don C. Seitz:

Captain Mission was one of the forebears of the French Revolution. He was one hundred years in advance of his time, for his career was based upon an initial desire to better adjust the affairs of mankind. . . . It is

continued

continued

related how Captain Mission, having led his ship to victory against an English man-of-war, called a meeting of the crew. Those who wished to follow him he would welcome and treat as brothers; those who did not would be safely set ashore. One and all embraced the New Freedom. Some were for hoisting the Black Flag at once but Mission demurred, saying that they were not pirates but liberty lovers, fighting for equal rights against all nations subject to the tyranny of government. The ship's money was put in a chest to be used as common property. Clothes were distributed to all in need and the republic of the sea was in full operation. . . . Mission made an address denouncing slavery, holding that men who sold others like beasts proved their religion to be no more than a grimace as no man had power of liberty over another.

Mission explored the Madagascar coast and found a bay ten leagues north of Diego-Suarez. It was resolved to establish here the shore quarters of the Republic – erect a town, build docks, and have a place they might call their own. The colony was called Libertatia and was placed under Articles drawn up by Captain Mission. The Articles state, among other things: all decisions with regard to the colony to be submitted to vote by the colonists; the abolition of slavery for any reason including debt; the abolition of the death penalty; and freedom to follow any religious beliefs or practices without sanction or molestation. . . . Imagine such a movement on a world-wide scale. Faced by the actual practice of freedom, the French and American revolutions would be forced to stand by their words. . . . Any man would have the right to settle in any area of his choosing. The land would belong to those who used it . . . I cite this example of retroactive Utopia since it actually might have happened in terms of the techniques and human resources available at the time. Had Captain Mission lived long enough to set an example for others to follow, mankind might have stepped free from the deadly impasse of insoluble problems in which we now find ourselves. The chance was there. The chance was missed. The principles of the French and American revolutions became windy lies in the mouths of politicians. The liberal revolutions of 1848 created the so-called republics of Central and South America, with a dreary history of dictatorship, oppression, graft, and bureaucracy, thus closing this vast, underpopulated continent to any possibility of communes along the lines set forth by Captain Mission. . . . In England, Western Europe, and America, the over-population made possible by the industrial revolution leaves scant room for communes, which are commonly subject to state and federal law and frequently harassed by the local inhabitants. There is simply no room left for 'freedom from the tyranny of government' since city dwellers depend on it for food, power, water, transportation, protection, and welfare. Your right to live where you want, with companions of your choosing, under laws to which you agree, died in the eighteenth century with Captain Mission. Only a miracle or a disaster could restore it.

(Burroughs: 1982: 9–12)

Can you identify the aspects of this 'model of democracy' that appeal to Burroughs? Using the information contained in this chapter, what sort of democracy did Captain Mission create? To what extent do you agree with Burroughs' suggestion that the chance to create genuine democracy after the French and American Revolutions was missed?

Finally, can you model a democracy of your own? What would be the foundations, for example, in terms of size of population, economic and social organisation, educational provision? What would be the level of participation and who would direct democracy? How would you make it work and what would be the aim of your democracy?

Key texts

Aristotle (1992) *The Politics*, Harmondsworth: Penguin.

Dahl, R. A. (1961) *Who Governs? Democracy and Power in an American City*, New Haven, Conn.: Yale University Press.

Fukuyama, F. (1989) 'The End of History?', *National Interest* 16, pp. 3–18.

Giddens, A. (1998) *The Third Way*, Cambridge: Polity Press.

Huntington, S. (1991) *The Third Wave: Democratization in the Late Twentieth Century*, Norman, Okla and London: University of Oklahoma Press.

Marx, K. (1985) *The Communist Manifesto*, Harmondsworth: Penguin.

Mill, J. S. (1972) *Utilitarianism, Liberty, Representative Government*, London: Dent.

Pateman, C. (1988) *The Sexual Contract*, Cambridge: Polity Press.

Rousseau, J.-J. (1974) *The Social Contract*, Harmondsworth: Penguin.

Further reading

Archibughi, D., Held, D. and Kohler, M. (eds) (1998) *Re-Imagining Political Community*, Cambridge: Polity Press. An interesting and varied discussion of the future of democratic forms and practice in response to globalisation.

Axford, B. and Huggins, R. (eds) (2001) *New Media and Politics*, London: Sage.

Barber, B. (1984) *Strong Democracy: Participatory Politics for a New Age*, Berkeley and London: University of California Press. A strong and committed defence of democracy from an engaging author.

Barber, B. (2001) 'Can Democracy Survive Globalization?', *Government and Opposition*, pp. 275–301. A short, lively and committed discussion of the threats that globalisation poses for democracy.

Coleman, S., Taylor, J. and van de Donk, W. V. (eds) (1999) *Parliament in the Age of the Internet*, Oxford: Oxford University Press. A comparative collection of essays on the applications of information and communication technologies to parliamentary systems of government around the world.

Hacker, K. and van Dijk, W. V. (eds) (2000) *Digital Democracy: Issues of Theory and Practice*, London: Sage. A useful survey of some of the key theoretical and practical debates and issues surrounding the application of ICTs to democratic government.

Held, D. (1996) *Models of Democracy*, 2nd edn, Cambridge: Polity Press. An excellent overview and discussion of democracy in its various forms from classical Greece to global, cosmopolitan democracy.

Holden, B. (ed.) (2000) *Global Democracy: Key Debates*, London: Routledge. A useful edited collection of pieces that explores a range of central issues and debates surrounding the potential for global democracy. This collection covers both theoretical and practical discussions and has a good diversity of contributors.

Klein, N. (2000) *No Logo: No Space, No Choice, No Jobs: Taking Aim at the Brand Bullies*, London: Flamingo. A lively and readable reading of the current state of world politics, global capitalism and consumer culture.

McKay, G. (1998) *DIY Culture: Party and Politics in Nineties Britain*, London: Verso.

Mason, M. (1999) *Environmental Democracy*, London: Earthscan. An informed and detailed discussion of the relationship between democracy and the environment which stresses the close relationship between the local and the global dimensions of political process and environmental protection and democracy.

Monbiot, G. (2000) *Captive State: The Coporate Takeover of Britain*, Basingstoke: Macmillan.

Putman, R. (1995) 'Bowling Alone: America's Declining Social Capital', *Journal of Democracy*, 6, pp. 65–78. A widely read and influential contemporary 'classic' which analyses the perceived crisis of civic virtue and participation in the USA.

Websites

For some more radical responses to and discussions of globalization, the role of the state, citizenship and the environment have a look at the SCHNEWS website at <http://www.schnews.co.uk>, or the SQUALL website at <http://www.squall.co.uk>

PART 2
POLITICS AND IDEAS

■ CONCEPTS AND ISSUES

■ POLITICAL THOUGHT

■ POLITICAL IDEOLOGIES

CHAPTER 6

Concepts and Issues

Gary K. Browning

CONTENTS

Introduction

In this chapter the concepts which underlie and determine the values of political life will be explored. At the same time, this conceptual exploration of political life will be related to the issues and disputes which colour the atmosphere of contemporary political debate and practice. In specific terms, the concepts of freedom, rights, justice and equality are examined. They are related to concrete problems, including the dilemmas of the Rushdie case, animal welfare and the welfare state. The practical questions arising out of these issues are shown to involve conceptual questions which render their theoretical analysis useful in a way that emphasises the vitality of political theory.

Conceptual analysis

Conceptual analysis in contemporary political theory takes place in a number of different ways. In the immediate post-Second World War period in the Anglo-American world doubts were expressed about the procedures of political philosophy given that the criteria for determining values were recognised to be inherently controversial. There was a prevalent scepticism about the claims involved in the classic texts of political philosophy, where large-scale theorising incorporating grand claims about the human condition sustained accounts of the political expression of values such as justice and freedom. Grand theorising gave way to a more limited approach whereby analysis pointed up what concepts such as freedom and equality might be taken to mean. However, in the last quarter of the twentieth century there was a revival of normative theorising in which analysis of concepts went hand in hand with justification of norms embedded in the concepts and intuitions upheld in prevailing political practices. The willingness to discuss substantive questions of, for example, justice and the political order has realigned contemporary Anglo-American political philosophers with the traditions of political philosophy.

A leading political theorist of modern times who has done much to restore the vitality of the discipline of political philosophy is John Rawls.

John Rawls (1921–) is a very influential contemporary political philosopher. His major work remains *A Theory of Justice* (1971). This work revived the social contract as a way of developing a normative political theory. In this work Rawls argued the case for justice as fairness. His theory included the difference principle, whereby differences in the level of resources held by individuals is justified only if these differences maximise the resources of the worse off. In *Political Liberalism* (1993) Rawls reformulated his political theory so that members of a just polity were envisaged as agreeing reasonable and specifically political, rather that comprehensive, principles to govern their interaction. Rawls' *Collected Papers* were published in 1999 and his *Lectures on the History of Moral Philosophy* in 2000.

John Rawls

Key text: J. Rawls (1971) *A Theory of Justice*, Oxford: Oxford University Press.

His work *A Theory of Justice* (1971) set out a rigorously argued case for justifying a particular conception of justice as fairness by imagining potential citizens in an original position in which they would be unaware of particular attributes and social advantages they might possess. Based upon premises generated from this imaginative perspective, Rawls thereafter argued with great analytical rigour for a conception of justice informing political practices which would mesh with prevailing intuitions. Rawls' example of combining analytical rigour with the justification of values and intuitions has been followed by a host of celebrated theorists, including Nozick, Walzer and Taylor, who all invoke classical texts of political philosophy.

The analytical approach has permeated a variety of traditions such as Marxism, where, for example, in the works of Cohen (1978) and Elster (1985), an analytical style has been invoked to interrogate and justify Marxist conceptions. Likewise, feminist and postmodern thinkers, such as Lyotard (1984), have sought to combine rigorous analysis of concepts with particular interpretations of values and norms.

Robert Nozick (1938–2002) is an American political philosopher who became famous on the publication of his *Anarchy, State and Utopia* (1974). This work is a spirited libertarian response to Rawls' *A Theory of Justice* in which Nozick argues the case for a minimal state. Nozick has written widely in philosophy. *Anarchy, State and Utopia* remains his major contribution to political philosophy. His other works include *Philosophical Explanations* (1983), *The Examined Life* (1989) and *The Nature of Rationality* (1992).

Robert Nozick

Jean-François Lyotard (1924–98) is famous for his celebration of the onset of postmodernity in *The Postmodern Condition – A Report on Knowledge* (1984). Lyotard's work as a political theorist and philosopher is complex and dense. He is notable for combining commentary on classic philosophers, Marxism and contemporary Continental and Anglophone theory. He was a member of the Marxist group Socialisme ou barbarie, but his break from Marxism is emphatically registered in *Libidinal Economy* (1993). *The Differend* (1988) highlights the ethical and political significance of difference and his later works draw upon Kant's aesthetic of the sublime to highlight the intractability of reality.

Jean-François Lyotard

Freedom

Freedom is a central concept of political life. Historic political philosophers, such as Mill, Rousseau and Hegel, have given celebrated, if controversial accounts of its character, while practising politicians on the right and the left invoke the name of freedom to justify an array of policies. Berlin (1991) has produced perhaps the most notable analysis of freedom since the Second World War.

Isaiah Berlin

Isaiah Berlin (1909–97) was born in Riga, the capital of Latvia. His family moved to Petrograd in 1915 and he witnessed both the Russian Revolutions of 1917 at first hand. In 1919 he came to England to study and later lectured at the University of Oxford. He was Chichele Professor of Social and Political Theory (1957–67) and the first President of Wolfson College (1966–75). He combined elegant theoretical analysis of political terms such as liberty with considered historical knowledge of a variety of traditions of European political and social thought. His many books include *Two Concepts of Liberty* (1965), *Karl Marx* (1963), *Historical Inevitability* (1954) and *The Crooked Timber of Humanity* (1990).

Positive freedom A view which sees freedom as a condition to be achieved through positive actions.

Negative freedom A term taken as meaning freedom from state interference. It assumes that individuals should have an area of life where they are free to make decisions and behave as they wish as long as they do not interfere with the freedom of others.

He examined past accounts of freedom, analysed its deployment in political contexts and distinguished two distinct concepts of liberty or freedom. He distinguished between the concepts of **positive freedom** and **negative freedom**, which, he urged, had been put to radically different uses in the political arena.

Negative freedom, for Berlin, fits neatly with common-sense notions of freedom. He takes negative freedom to mean that a person is free if they are not subject to constraint or coercion. An individual on this model of freedom is free if he or she can make and act upon their own choices. The state is promoting freedom insofar as it leaves an area of life open to the decision-making of individuals. Within this account of freedom a state which concerned itself with the goal of promoting a more equal society might be undertaking a worthwhile goal, but it would not be promoting freedom. Indeed, insofar as its promotion of equality involved disturbing the purposes and assets of individuals, it would undermine individual freedom.

Positive freedom, for Berlin, involves a different account of freedom from the negative variety, and this difference has been expressed and developed in the history of political thought. Berlin considers that a positive view of freedom assumes that freedom is not to be achieved by leaving individuals alone to get on with their lives. Rather, its point is to enable individuals to achieve self-mastery by the exercise of rational self-control over the irrational desires of the self. Freedom in a positive sense, for Berlin, entails overcoming obstacles to freedom which reside within individuals themselves. Hence, a positive conception of freedom can generate the paradox that in order to achieve freedom, coercion may need to be applied to individuals by the state. Berlin is sceptical of the endorsement of public coercion which he takes to be implicit in the positive model of freedom. According to Berlin, the positive model of freedom assumes that all individuals need to follow the same path of rational enlightenment and that political coercion can facilitate this process of enlightenment.

In a shorthand formulation of Berlin's (1991) account of the two concepts of liberty, negative freedom may be taken as freedom from constraints, and positive freedom as the freedom to develop the rational self. Berlin's account has the merit of memorably underlining differences between classic accounts of freedom. For instance, Locke and Mill are taken as providing notions of 'negative' freedom where the concern is to allow individuals to develop their lives free from public coercion. Likewise, Rousseau, Hegel and Marx are seen as developing positive accounts of freedom where individuals find their true freedom in a shared community in which common goals are sought. Berlin also provides an incisive summary of the potential for tyranny implicit in positive accounts of freedom. Something of the flavour of Berlin's insightful and rhetorically persuasive writing is expressed in the following extract from his essay 'Two Concepts of Liberty', in which he highlights the dangers involved in the assumptions of positive theories of liberty.

> The common assumption of these thinkers (and of many a Schoolman before them and Jacobin and Communist after them) is that the rational ends of our 'true' natures must coincide, or be made to coincide, however violently our poor, ignorant, desire-ridden, passionate, empirical selves may cry out against this process. Freedom is not freedom to do what is irrational, or stupid, or wrong. To force empirical selves into the right pattern is not tyranny, but liberation. Rousseau tells me that if I freely surrender all parts of my life to society, I create an entity which because it has been built by an equality of sacrifice of all its members, cannot wish to hurt any one of them. . . . Liberty so far from being incompatible with society becomes virtually identical with it.
>
> (Berlin 1991: 50–1)

EXERCISE

1 According to Berlin, how do theorists of positive freedom portray force as a means of freedom?
2 Consider how the language of Berlin is designed to persuade the reader that we should be wary of certain thinkers.

Berlin's analysis of freedom into the opposed notions of positive and negative freedom is a celebrated account, but it is not without critics. MacCallum Jr has argued against Berlin's position. He has urged that freedom is to be understood essentially as a single concept. For MacCallum, 'Whenever the freedom of some agent or agents is in question, it is always freedom from some constraint or restriction on, interference with, or barrier to doing, not doing, becoming, or not becoming something' (MacCallum 1991). According to MacCallum, there is a variation between specific conceptions of freedom, but accounts of freedom will always involve relations between the variables of agency, constraints and doing or development. According to this notion of freedom, undoubted differences exist between a theorist such as Rousseau, whom Berlin designates as a theorist of positive liberty, and, say, J. S. Mill, whom Berlin takes to be a theorist of negative liberty. These differences, however, are not seen as precluding a common adherence to a notion of freedom where persons are free due to their capacity to act free from restrictions. What counts as a restriction and what is signified as the agent and action/development differ in the thought of Mill from that of Rousseau, but MacCallum would suggest that the differences should be attended to in detail and should not be reduced to a general contrast between positive and negative conceptions of freedom.

In general, MacCallum is right to point to the shared character of conceptions of freedom when examined at a high level of abstraction. Equally, he is alert to the specific differences which distinguish particular notions of freedom and which resist easy classification under the general headings of positive and negative freedom. Berlin's essay itself had pointed to ways in which the division of the concept of freedom into negative and positive varieties might not be entirely clear-cut. Berlin recognises that where 'negative' theorists of freedom see the individual as free insofar as his or her actions are not constrained by others, the notion of what counts as a constraint is problematic and might be specified in significantly divergent ways. Berlin is inclined to take a negative theory of liberty as equating constraining behaviour with either force or manifest coercion. None the less, he does admit the possibility that an economic system, alterable but not necessarily designed by agents, might be taken as a constraint on human freedom. If unplanned social and economic forms are taken as constraints on human freedom, then a negative theorist of freedom might advocate remedial state action on a scale sufficiently large to allow for the emergence of a tyranny he associates with positive freedom. The distance between negative and positive notions of freedom is therefore not so great as might at first be imagined.

Miller (1991), in his account of freedom, steers a course between Berlin and MacCallum. He considers that Berlin's account does not do justice to the variety of views on freedom. He distinguishes between three ways of formulating freedom: republican, liberal and idealist forms of freedom. Liberal freedom equates with Berlin's account of negative freedom. Republican freedom invokes the freedom citizens possess in participating in the public processes of government to shape their collective lives. Idealist freedom is envisaged as the process of liberation whereby a self overcomes internal constraints, such as drug addiction, to realise an ideal freedom.

Miller's account of freedom certainly picks out important differences between theories of freedom. The sense in which collective political action may be said to constitute freedom is distinct from an individual's freedom to undertake actions unimpeded by others, which likewise differs from an individual freeing her- or himself from a habitual dependence upon alcohol. This division of freedom into three senses can also be said to make an important distinction which is not prevalent in Berlin's account. On the other hand, it may still be said that it assimilates too readily a number of distinct views on freedom to a model of three basic theories of freedom. MacCallum's account, in contrast, sees an abstract unity underpinning theories of freedom but at the same time highlights the importance of differences between them at the level of detail. Perhaps what may be concluded is that the perspective on freedom which we take will be influenced by what we want to do. Berlin's account makes a sound and rhetorically convincing case for seeing an important division between theories of freedom. A number of theories may be seen as posing potential problems of tyranny at the individual and social level given their drive to promote freedom positively, whereas other theories are more concerned to ward off coercion and direct violence against persons. Likewise, Miller's model is useful in making more discriminating distinctions between theories of freedom, as it employs a more complex model. MacCallum's unitary concept of freedom provides a convincing overall account of freedom in that at a highly abstract level it makes conceptual connections between components of any account of freedom. It also signals that detailed attention should be paid to particular ways in which these elements of a view of freedom are to be connected in specific theories of freedom. While this unitary theory of freedom is therefore philosophically convincing at a general level, the rival accounts do perform useful jobs of work in connecting and contrasting specific theories of freedom.

The Rushdie case

Salman Rushdie (1947–) is the author of many novels and prose writings. He was born in Bombay and has subsequently lived in London and New York. *Midnight's Children* was awarded the Booker Prize in 1981. Other works include *Shame* (1983), *The Satanic Verses* (1988), *Haroun and the Sea of Stories* (1990), *The Ground Beneath Her Feet* (1999) and *Fury* (2001). *The Satanic Verses* (1989) gave rise to much controversy and a *fatwa* was declared against Rushdie by Ayatollah Khomeni.

Salman Rushdie

The Rushdie affair is an infamous case of recent years which has thrown up disturbing and challenging questions for any considered analysis of freedom. Some of the facts of the Rushdie case are reasonably well known. In 1989

Rushdie published *The Satanic Verses*, a complex work dealing with many themes such as migration, exile, death and resurrection in a style which is artful and resists any single line of interpretation. None the less, the centre of polemical attention upon the book quickly became its portrayal of Islam and Mohammed. Mohammed is depicted in ways which have been seen as disrespectful; for example, there are references to him as a shady businessman and as a debauchee who sleeps with many women. The general tone of the book was quickly seen by many Muslims, skipping over tricky questions concerning the author's voice, as being disrespectful to their religion.

For a balanced account of all the arguments in the Rushdie affair see B. Parekh (1990) 'The Rushdie Affair: Research Agenda for Political Philosophy', Political Studies 38 (4) (December).

Soon after its publication Muslims all over the world began to campaign against *The Satanic Verses*. The brunt of their complaints was that the book was inaccurate and insulting in its depiction of Islam and its representation of events recounted in the Koran (the sacred book of the Islamic religion) and was also designed to cause hurt to Muslims in general. This latter point was of particular relevance where Muslims were in a cultural minority, as they were, for instance, in Britain. The force of their argument was that where a specific community was in a minority and vulnerable to majority violence or disrespect, a book such as *The Satanic Verses* which insulted the cultural minority could do much damage in disempowering that minority culture and in fostering antagonism towards it.

THINK POINT

■ Do you think that Muslims may have good grounds for objecting to the work of Salman Rushdie?

■ What actions, if any, do you think might have been justifiably taken against Rushdie by the Islamic community?

In response to protests by Muslims, the late Ayatollah Khomeini of Iran declared a death sentence, or *fatwa*, against Rushdie. This fateful intervention charged the cultural and political atmosphere. Many Muslims in Britain became more aggressive in their stance against Rushdie's novel. Soon Rushdie was forced into hiding to sustain himself against attack, and he was forced to resort to a shadowy half-life under security protection, as the Ayatollah's call for his death was recognised as providing a real threat to his life. In 1998 the Iranian government said it would no longer seek to enforce the *fatwa*.

For the most part, Rushdie defended his right to have written *The Satanic Verses* as being part and parcel of the writer's right to freedom of expression. His defence of his own actions has been squarely based on a view of freedom and its significance. It is true that in the light of possible remission of the *fatwa* Rushdie did equivocate and entertain the possibility of a reconciliation with Islam, but for the most part he has stood by his writing and defended it in classical liberal terms. In an article in the *Independent* in 1990 Rushdie presented an eloquent summary of the liberal defence of his work. A short extract of this article is presented below:

How is freedom gained? It is taken: never given. To be free you must first assume your right to freedom. In writing *The Satanic Verses*, I wrote from the assumption that I was and am a free man.

What is freedom of expression? Without the freedom to offend, it ceases to exist. Without the freedom to challenge, even to satirise all orthodoxies, including religious orthodoxies, it ceases to exist.

(Rushdie 1990)

The Rushdie case raises interesting questions about freedom and its theoretical analysis which highlight the practical relevance of abstract analysis. The threat to Rushdie's life eloquently demonstrated what can be at stake in questions of freedom. Rushdie himself may be seen as invoking what Berlin would term a negative account of freedom. For Rushdie, freedom, crucially, is about the right to express oneself without being subject to restraint or coercion. In Rushdie's defence of freedom of expression what is being said is of less importance than the right to say it. It is 'negative' about what is being said. This negative aspect of freedom, however, is not seen as marking its shallowness. Rushdie sees this right to say what might be offensive as of the utmost importance.

In contrast to Rushdie's position, opponents of *The Satanic Verses* and its publication might and often do appeal, at least implicitly, to a positive view of freedom. Hence, the point about freedom of expression from such a perspective depends on what is being said. The positive things that are said about groups and cultures matter. The freedom of groups and individuals is related to how they are regarded, and the status of people is intimately related to what is said about them; scurrilous remarks about a world religion can impair the freedom of its practitioners. This putative critique of Rushdie in terms of a positive view of freedom might also be articulated in the guise of Miller's (1991) notion of republican freedom. Here, the freedom of a cultural grouping may be seen as bound up with its defence and maintenance of its key doctrines, just as the freedom of a political community is maintained by participation in and maintenance of its key political institutions. Hence, from this perspective, it is detrimental to a cultural group's freedom if its doctrines and sacred writings are attacked and damaged.

The Rushdie case, then, may be seen as exhibiting ways in which contrasting views of freedom are expressed. It also points up ambiguities in interpretations of freedom. It was mentioned previously that what counts as a constraint upon freedom in Berlin's account of negative liberty is ambiguous. For Berlin, an individual is free insofar as he or she is free from constraints, but what counts as a constraint is not clear-cut. Hence, outraged Muslims who see *The Satanic Verses* as wounding their sense of selfhood insofar as it undermines the Islam religion, the source of their selfhood, could construe this literary work as a constraint upon their freedom. Action consequently directed against Rushdie's work, even including the notorious *fatwa* itself, may therefore be seen as being supported by a negative view of freedom, albeit a version of negative freedom distinct from that assumed by Berlin. Recognition of the importance of the notion of constraint in a great variety of distinct and often conflicting views of freedom lies behind the conceptual manoeuvring of MacCallum Jr (1991) when he characterised freedom as a unitary concept which involves a plurality of interpretations of its basic terms.

The Rushdie case also raises an interesting and challenging question about the identity of the agent or agents who are assumed to possess or express freedom. Rushdie himself can appear as a classical and tragic individual hero of freedom. This lone and wronged individual stuck to his words, risking his life for the cause of freedom. The predicament he faced, though, was a solitary one. On the other hand, the freedom of the Muslim community or communities in Britain and elsewhere may be seen to have been threatened by the abuse and disrespect shown to its religious heritage. Again, MacCallum, in his account of freedom, notes that a persisting subject capable of action or development is presupposed by all theories of freedom, but he observes that the nature of this subject/agent will vary radically from particular theory to particular theory.

In the light of our brief survey of the Rushdie case it will be evident that it presents a practical issue which invokes and involves theoretical perspectives. Differing practical vantage points on the issue of the Rushdie case may be seen as assuming differing conceptual understandings of freedom. Theoretical and practical controversies also underlie disputes about the phenomenon of political correctness. Political correctness is a movement emanating principally from American university campuses which seeks to challenge language and behaviour that are seen as defamatory and threatening to minority and vulnerable groups. Hence advocates of political correctness track language and behaviour taken as being offensive to, for example, blacks, Muslims, women, disabled people. They challenge the use of 'incorrect' language and campaign to change linguistic usage and modify offensive behaviour.

Opponents of political correctness see its concern to challenge the right of individuals to speak as they wish as infringing the freedom of individuals, who are depicted as having the 'negative' right to say what they like. Supporters of political correctness, on the other hand, might see freedom as involving the 'positive' respect for others' freedom and dignity. But, alternatively, supporters of political correctness might construe derogatory language against certain groups as constituting a barrier to the achievement of freedom on the part of the group. From this perspective a Polish or Irish joke may be funny, but it may also serve as a constraint impairing the freedom of Irish and Polish people. If jokes constantly depict Irish people as stupid and violent, it makes it hard for an Irish person to enjoy the freedom to be taken seriously.

Rights

Rights are important concepts in the world of politics. They are often encoded in laws and form legal safeguards of freedom, and appeals couched in the terms of rights are ubiquitous features of the current political scene. The experience of tyrannies in Nazi Germany, the Soviet Empire and Bosnia are graphic reminders of the human cost involved in the denial of rights. Rights function as a way of highlighting important attributes requiring protection by law. It is the lack of protection of attributes such as free speech, free movement, property and life itself which is the hallmark of the tyrannies identified above. In this sense the language of rights may be said to be the idiom in which criteria for a 'good' state are set out.

To say that rights are significant and generally held in high esteem by political commentators and publics is not to say that rights and their specification are uncontroversial. Rights are the subject of theoretical and practical debate, which we shall track in the ensuing pages. A central source of controversy about rights is the question of whether or not there are any natural rights. The historical background to natural rights theory lies in Ancient Greece, where the notion that an objective order of reason was responsible for both natural events and the values to which men should adhere took root. Subsequently, in medieval times, God was regarded as the author of a law of nature which prescribed the moral conduct man should follow. St Thomas Aquinas, the thirteenth-century theologian and philosopher, argued that there were distinct but interrelated kinds of law. In descending order, for Aquinas, there was the eternal law of God, the natural law rationally discernible by man and the positive law enacted by men. Aquinas urged that the world was framed according to the eternal plan of God, but that man could come to know something of this divine plan by invoking his reason to reflect upon his own rational nature and its consequent obligations.

In the modern world emerging in the European world of the sixteenth and seventeenth centuries, the 'natural rights' of man became central components of ethical and political reasoning. Theorists such as Hobbes and Locke and the constitutions and rhetoric of the American and French Revolutions emphasised the natural rights of individuals, which were to be upheld against other individuals and in most cases against the state itself. In the case of the theorists and situations cited above, God is invoked as the author and guarantor of the rights of man. While more recent theories of natural rights have tended to abandon express references to God as the author of rights, there remains a presumption of an underlying objectivity to the ascription of rights. The nature of men and, latterly, human beings in general is characteristically seen as underwriting basic claims on behalf of the individual, notwithstanding the accidental interplay of social and historical life. Generally the rational and free nature of human beings is invoked to justify classic claims to the rights of life, liberty and property, though in recent years there has been an expansion of the rights claimed, so that education, abortion and employment are frequently cited as key human rights.

The notion of natural rights has been challenged from a variety of perspectives. Utilitarians, Marxists and ethical relativists are among those who have attacked the notion that rights are natural. All political theorists who take history and historical development seriously, including Marxists, Hegelians and liberal progressivists like Mill, tend to question the presumption that 'human nature' can be isolated from the flow of events and be referred to as a fixed

Logical positivism A philosophical doctrine which maintains that a term is meaningful insofar as it is susceptible of verification

standard of 'right'. So-called basic individual natural rights are seen by theorists who stress the irreducibly social nature of man (including, once again, Hegel and Marx) as parasitic upon specific forms of social development which recognise and support these rights. A hard-headed utilitarian such as Bentham insists that it is nonsense to talk of rights without reference to a positive framework of law in which such rights are inscribed. Again, **logical positivists**, who see meaningful discourse as being possible only in reference to observable phenomena, disparage reference to supposedly objective, natural rights. While the positivist impulse in philosophy has retreated in recent decades, there are many contemporary philosophers who recognise the inherent contestability of values. Values rely on contestable forms of justification according to this standpoint, and this contestability rules out the notion of objective, unchanging 'natural' rights.

While the notion of natural rights is a highly contestable one, it continues to elicit support. In the wake of war crimes of appalling horror in the civil wars in the countries of the former Yugoslavia, the appeal of designating certain crimes as transgressing objective human rights remains attractive. The torture of children and the massacre of peoples offend against any seemingly reasonable basis of human interaction, and thereby lend support to the argument for objective natural rights. While such an argument is appealing, and informs and helps sustain justifiable campaigns against repression, its theoretical force is debatable. The 'natural' basis of rights would seem to imply their applicability in all circumstances, but it is not clear that the inviolability of property rights should be maintained in periods of famine and conflict when the redistribution of goods may be the only way of preserving lives.

While the validity of natural rights is a controversial subject, conceptual discussions of rights invariably take their bearings from Hohfield's classic study *Fundamental Legal Conceptions* (1919). Hohfield distinguished between distinct types of rights, namely liberties, claims, immunities and powers. The most important of these designated rights are liberty rights and claim rights. Liberty rights are those rights individuals are deemed to possess which do not involve distinct and matching claims on others, such as the right an individual may be said to have to whistle as he or she walks. Claim rights are distinct claims individuals may have on others; for instance, an employee may have distinct claims against a company. Immunity rights and powers are more specific kinds of rights; for example, a Member of Parliament is granted immunity from prosecution for slander for what is said in Parliament. A person may also be granted specific powers to act as the guardian of another individual.

THINK POINT

- Do you consider that there are any natural rights?

- If so, which do you consider to be the most important of these rights?

- If not, explain the reasons why you reject them.

The distinction between liberty and claim rights set out by Hohfield informs the discussion about negative and positive rights. The distinction between negative and positive rights matches Berlin's (1991) separation of negative liberty from positive liberty. Barry (1981) and Cranston (1973), in distinguishing between negative and positive rights, ape Berlin in privileging the negative variety. They see the rights of life, liberty and property as being negative insofar as they do not require positive action on the part of the state to promote them. Positive rights, on the other hand, are seen as demanding state action to implement them, and, unlike negative rights, they are held to expand as social demands on the state are generated over time. Hence, the provision of positive rights such as the right to extended education, decent housing and nursery provision are characterised as responses to the development of contingent 'wants' in Western societies over the past two centuries. The extension of the range of rights has been resisted by those, like Cranston, who wish to privilege long-standing 'negative' rights. However, there seems no inherent reason why some rights should be privileged as being beyond debate and other claims are debarred from discussion. All rights, including negative ones, are socially acknowledged attributes of significance which are accorded legal status as being worthy of protection. The identification, and the range, of attributes awarded such protection is a proper object of human concern, discussion and legal enactment.

Animal rights

In recent years the claims for animals to receive moral recognition by human beings have been advanced, and there is a body of opinion which would like to accord 'rights' to animals. Supporters of animal rights argue that to deny rights to animals is tantamount to speciesism. Non-human animals, as well as human beings, are regarded by animal rights' theorists as having interests. These interests are taken to derive from all animals' capacities both to suffer and to experience pleasure. If all animals are seen as having interests, then to privilege humans over other species is to behave in a speciesist way, just as to discriminate against black people is to behave in a racist way. The capacity to suffer and experience pleasure is viewed by theorists such as Singer (1976) as being crucial in assigning moral consideration, as it is taken to be a more fundamental aspect of experience than, say, intellectual abilities.

While animal rights' theorists are busy trying to promote the rights of animals, their arguments do not receive universal acceptance. Resistance to animal rights turns upon the argument that humans are distinct from the rest of the animal kingdom in ways that are significant in the assessment of ethical worth. For instance, it is commonly held that the superior intelligence of human beings entitles them to receive moral consideration at the expense of animals. This point is a contestable one. It may well be argued that superior intelligence might qualify a species for greater moral consideration, but a relative superiority in intelligence seems a shallow basis for allowing one species to monopolise our moral concern. Moreover, there is an evident variety in intelligence among human beings. Various forms of mental illness and brain dysfunction impair the mental capacities of human beings. It would seem harsh and morally questionable to dismiss the rights of those suffering from such mishaps and to assign rights according to intelligence quotients.

Another manoeuvre made by those who resist ascribing rights to the rest of the animal kingdom is to maintain that animals other than humans should be excluded from our moral perspective, as they cannot assume moral duties to match the putative rights they are to be assigned. This point poses questions. It is certainly true that we could not expect the rest of the animal kingdom to follow our moral example if we were to assign the right of life to animals. The rest of the animal kingdom does not operate according to moral concepts. But to say that other animals operate differently from human beings is not to say that they should be denied rights. There is no necessary reason why recipients of rights must all behave in the same way. Children, for instance, are assigned special rights and they are seen as having different responsibilities from adults.

THINK POINT

- If all human beings became vegetarians, should we expect other animals to become vegetarians?

- Can we expect non-human animals to recognise moral obligations?

The need for animals to be assigned rights emerges most strongly consequent upon a recognition of the suffering inflicted upon animals by human beings. Perhaps the most serious forms of suffering are inflicted by the prevalent form of farming in the Western world, namely factory farming, and the practice of experimenting upon animals. While animals have been harnessed to farming since the beginnings of agriculture, they are now subject to intensive production techniques which render their conditions of life quite alien to their basic instincts, and render them susceptible to disease and severe suffering.

Animal experimentation is extremely widespread. There are over five million experiments performed on animals each year in Britain alone. Experiments are especially prevalent in scientific establishments, notably psychological ones, where there is no prospect of the experiments yielding medical benefits.

Experiments on animals are conducted for the purposes of cosmetics and defence, where the prospects of decided benefits to humans are remote. Even the experiments on animals conducted for the benefit of medical science are questionable. It is by no means clear that experiments need to be conducted on animals when simulations might do the job better, particularly when differences between humans and other animals render the knowledge gained through such experimentation problematic.

Of course, the issues of animal suffering and the need to protect animals by the provision of animal rights go beyond what has been discussed above. Animals are eaten by human beings and there is a case for humans changing their eating habits to stop killing animals. Animals are also subject to seemingly random acts of cruelty. Again, zoos often house animals in the most inhospitable conditions. The prospects for animals do not look good as new technological and scientific possibilities such as cloning emerge.

Equality

The meaning of equality is disputed. How is the concept of equality taken to apply to social and political life? The idea that human beings are equal is a puzzling one. Consider some examples: are David Beckham, Woody Allen, your next-door neighbour and Jacques Chirac equal? There are certainly important differences between them. If egalitarianism is taken to be the wholehearted concern to achieve concrete equality of outcome between these and other people, then it would appear to involve a degree of interventionism which is both breathtaking and monstrous. Plato was a philosopher of Ancient Greece who treated the issue of justice and equality in a spirit far removed from egalitarianism. He urged that justice involved treating people differently, as justice consisted in giving each man his due, and he believed that there were significant differences between people which must be respected.

A core meaning of the term 'equality' in a social and political context is that equality should be seen as a basic presupposition of moral concern. On this basis, a fundamental presupposition of equality as a moral procedural principle informs the plea that all persons are entitled to equal consideration save where a special case can be made for differential treatment. In more concrete terms, this has been translated into a concern that people should receive equal consideration before the law, apart from where criminal behaviour leads to justifiable punishment. It has also led to a concern that voting rights are equal. Equality in these senses has now become a generally accepted norm in liberal democratic societies. The extension of the vote to women and an equalisation of property rights between men and women in Western countries, however, are fairly recent phenomena. In more recent years, there has also been pressure to extend the reach of the concept of equality to include other species than human beings. In the previous section we traced the arguments seeking to justify the attribution of rights to animals.

While equal legal and voting rights have been accepted in Western and many non-Western societies, there is little agreement on the extent to which we should aim to achieve substantive equality in social and political life. The idea that social and political life should be organised to achieve material equality between people is controversial. It implies a concern to regulate out-comes rather than ensuring that rules apply equally to those who will achieve differing outcomes. One way of securing an equality of material outcome would be to ensure that all achieved the same level of well-being. Another way to achieve equality of outcome would be for all to satisfy their needs equally. The difficulties in the way of achieving either of these aims, however, are immense. To compute the needs or well-being of all and then to secure their equal provision would demand an enormous amount of governmental regulation. The ongoing problems of regulation are highlighted when it is considered that if resources were to be distributed equally, steps would have to be taken so that arrangements would not be overturned by the dynamics of individual choice and behaviour.

Given the problems of attaining equality of outcome, some theorists sympathetic to the ideal of substantive equality have looked at ways of achieving a form of equality which would allow for the dynamics of individual choice and difference. Walzer (1983) has argued for what he terms 'complex equality', by which he means a form of just society where inequalities in the several spheres of society do not invade one another. On this view, inequalities in one sphere are not repeated in others. Wealth may dominate the business world, but health needs would trigger treatment in the health sphere, and education would be organised according to the learning needs and capacities of individuals rather than their wealth. Miller (1991) is another contemporary political theorist who has urged that a more subtle view of political equality is required. He argues that a just society would be one in which all citizens would have equal status, an ideal which would be undermined if citizens of great wealth were to dominate society. He considers that all citizens have the right to a certain level of welfare if all are to enjoy an equality of respect in society. Miller recognises, though, that the effort to secure any more substantive form of equality would jeopardise individual freedom.

The achievement of equality of opportunity is one way in which the concept of equality is held to be a political concern. Many politicians advertise their commitment to the establishment of equality of opportunity, but this notion of equality of opportunity raises questions. For one thing, it might lead to great inequality of outcome. Plato, in *The Republic*, subscribed to a form of equality of opportunity in which women were to receive the same opportunities as men, but he envisaged a form of society in which there would be large-scale differences between classes, including differential entitlements to rule. A meritocracy has been seen by some as a nightmare prospect in which differences of outcome would be all the more galling because they would be seen as being clearly deserved. While the condition of equality of opportunity may be seen as possibly problematic, there are also difficulties surrounding the possibility of attaining it. For instance, can all the significant environmental factors which promote inequality of opportunity be eliminated? To establish equality of opportunity, all children would have to be given the same kind of schooling. In most Western countries, however, there is currently a range of schools. Even within similar schools teachers will vary, and this variety will affect the future opportunities of children. Again, families vary in terms of the levels of support they are able and willing to offer their children, and it would seem difficult and undesirable to establish equality in this sphere. To get anywhere near the establishment of equal opportunities, radical changes would have to be effected, and these changes would disrupt traditional and accepted patterns of family life and education. Even if equality of opportunity could be achieved, it would seem to exact an exorbitant price in terms of excessive regulation.

Key text: M. Walzer (1983) *Spheres of Justice*, Oxford: Blackwell.

Questions would also remain about genetic differences between individuals. If genetic patterns prove alterable, would it be reasonable to alter these patterns prior to birth so that all may have equal opportunities? Such a question probes deep into the concept of individual identity. Many would seek to resist genetic manipulation because they equate individuality with genetic foundations.

Questions about equality tend to generate ideological controversy, and this is true of efforts to achieve positive or reverse discrimination. Schemes of positive discrimination aim to reverse or nullify historic forms of discrimination suffered by distinct groups in society – such as blacks, women, disabled people – by advantaging these groups in certain ways. These schemes are often operated in contexts where there is a palpable record of unequal treatment affecting particular groups. In these circumstances it might seem reasonable to advantage a group, for instance, by establishing a quota of disabled people to be employed in public service posts when the previous record of their employment in such jobs has been low. However, when a particular group is advantaged, injustice may be seen as being inflicted upon other groups. Likewise, it is problematic to decide on which groups are to be selected and to decide which members of the group are to be so advantaged. It may happen that a person belongs to an historically disadvantaged group, while in other ways he or she may be categorised as advantaged, for example a wealthy, well-educated member of a minority cultural group. These problematic aspects of the question are what cause such schemes of positive discrimination to be hotly contested. Consider Minogue's views on egalitarianism set out below.

Inequality is notoriously the common condition – one might well say 'the natural condition' – of mankind. An 'inegalitarian' as the opposite of an egalitarian would presumably be the partisan of some specific form of inequality – one based on blood for example. My disagreement with egalitarianism is thus both particular and general. I oppose not only the plan of equality, but any kind of plan at all. I take the state to be a specific type of association in which resourceful individuals recognize a sovereign power able to enforce the conditions of peace permitting the citizens to live their lives as they choose. To bend that power to the end of imposing any kind of abstract outcome, whether egalitarian or inegalitarian, seems to me something for which no serious reason could be given. Specific measures of redistribution – for the relief of poverty, for example – might well be publicly judged necessary, but any such measures both can and ought to be justified in specific terms, and not in terms of some overriding plan to be imposed on a whole society.

(Minogue 1990: 100)

EXERCISE

1   What problems does Minogue see with egalitarianism?
2   Why is Minogue against any kind of plan for society?

continued

continued

3 Why does Minogue not refer to himself as an inegalitarian?

4 How might an egalitarian respond to Minogue's arguments?

Justice

Key text: R. Nozick (1974)
Anarchy, State and Utopia,
Oxford: Blackwell.

Justice is a much disputed concept which underpins many controversial social issues. It has been the object of rigorous analysis in recent years. Two of the most celebrated and controversial contemporary political philosophers, Rawls and Nozick, have done much to promote debate about the nature and understanding of justice. Rawls wrote *A Theory of Justice* in 1971 and Nozick responded with *Anarchy, State and Utopia* in 1974. These two works carved out distinct contrasting viewpoints on justice and, although both thinkers have advanced their thinking on justice in subsequent writings, these two works warrant a brief discussion, as they set out engaging and distinct standpoints on justice. In *A Theory of Justice* Rawls develops a rigorous analysis of what would constitute a just society understood as one embodying fair terms of social cooperation. To effect a framework for a basic structure of justice, Rawls conducts a thought experiment whereby he imagines heads of households in an original position in which they are behind a veil of ignorance which screens out knowledge of their particular characteristics and assets in society. They are to be equipped with knowledge of how any scheme of society which they uphold will work out, but they will not have knowledge of their own particular qualities, and so cannot frame general conditions for fair cooperation which favour their own particular interests. The conditions for the basic structure of a society chosen in the original position are seen by Rawls as conditions respecting the equality and liberty of all, and thus enabling a fair mode of social cooperation to take place.

Rawls sees the framework of justice which will emerge from his analysis as one in which two principles will be highlighted, the first taking priority over the second. First is the principle that each person in society is to have a right to as much freedom as is compatible with freedom for all. Second, social and economic inequalities are to be so arranged that they are to the greatest benefit of the least advantaged, and attached to offices and positions open to all under fair conditions of equal opportunity.

It is Rawls' second principle of distributive justice which has generated acute controversy. By this principle, Rawls is, in effect, licensing the redistribution of wealth; indeed, differences in wealth are to be justified only insofar as they benefit the worse off. The perception of inequalities from the vantage point of Rawls' original position renders them separable from personal knowledge of one's own particular qualities and position in society. Such a perspective Rawls takes as promoting an interest in fairness and an overriding concern for the situation of the worse off. This Rawlsian perspective is the nub of Nozick's challenge to Rawls' theory of justice, however, in that Nozick, like other neo-liberal theorists, challenges the rationale of distributive justice.

Nozick begins his account of justice with a different thought experiment from that of Rawls. Whereas Rawls reworks the idea of a social contract between members of a political society, Nozick assumes a state of nature in which individuals with rights to life, liberty and property are imagined as acting and interacting with one another. In this imaginative picture Nozick sees individuals as being concerned to pursue their own goals and welfare, and concludes that a state will be formed by the actions of a dominant protective agency to which individuals will resort in order to protect their interests in the inevitable disputes that will arise between individuals.

Nozick imagines a state being formed, but he does not bestow upon this state powers to override the rights of individuals. He sees the rights of individuals as being strong side constraints on actions. For Nozick, these rights of individuals are to be maintained, so that, for instance, the state should not interfere with property holdings as long as the holdings result from the voluntary actions of individuals. If property is gained through legitimate means of transfer (e.g. cash payments and inheritance), then there is no justification for state interference with the property arrangements that ensue. For Nozick, Rawls's theory of distributive justice involves an injustice in that the property of the better off might be redistributed by the state to benefit the worse off. The injustice would consist in the violation of the rights of the better off, who, for Nozick, would have gained their property through legitimate means.

Nozick's theory of justice is an entitlement theory which differs from Rawls' perspective in being backward-looking in its review of the legitimacy of property arrangements. Rawls' *A Theory of Justice* and Nozick's *Anarchy, State and Utopia* might be said to occupy different sites on the liberal landscape. Nozick's theory of justice is robustly individualistic. Individuals and individual rights are seen as being of primary importance, and the state is to be minimal, in that extensive interference is taken as diminishing individual rights. Rawls, like Nozick, is liberal in that he prioritises individual liberty. But he is concerned that the general patterns of poverty and prosperity accompanying a minimal state might derogate from the principles of freedom and equality he takes to be central to contemporary liberal democratic states. He adopts a perspective which allows for just decisions to be made about the overall distribution of wealth in society. He is therefore prepared to countenance some state intervention to develop a pattern of distributive justice.

The theoretical debate between Rawls and Nozick shadows a practical conflict between left and right liberals, who diverge over the extent of state intervention. This close relationship between theory and practice itself highlights one of the dimensions of criticism of both Rawls and Nozick which has been prevalent in recent years. Communitarian critics of both Rawls and Nozick have highlighted that individuals are always located in particular societies and communities, and that theorising is always shaped by prevailing social norms and is inevitably tailored to certain types of community rather than others. Communitarian critics have objected to the nakedly individualistic perspective of Nozick. The communitarians are by no means united, but theorists such as Walzer (1983), Macintyre (1988), Taylor (1989) and Sandel (1984) all agree that the individual cannot be separated from society and cannot be accorded explanatory priority. Individuals and societies are seen as correlative, and all would look to the importance of some community goods, such as culture and education, as necessary to generate flourishing forms of individuality.

Rawls has been criticised by communitarians on at least two counts. On the one hand, *A Theory of Justice* has been seen as too universalistic. Critics deny that it provides an overarching account of justice and note its relationship with particular features of a modern liberal society. It has also been criticised, notably by Sandel, for its alleged prioritising of socially disembedded individuals who are imagined in the original position as functioning without reference to their cultural homes. Rawls, in a series of articles and in a subsequent book, *Political Liberalism* (1993), has sought to clarify and revise the formulation of a conception of justice as fairness in *A Theory of Justice* in ways which bear upon the communitarian critique. Rawls observes that the original position is not and was not meant to function as a theory unrelated to a particular social and cultural setting. He explains it as functioning as a representative device whereby people like us (citizens of a democratic public culture) can model the basic principles allowing for fair social cooperation. Justice as fairness, Rawls accepts, is a theoretical exploration of the standpoint of a form of democratic society in which there will be reasonable disagreement on comprehensive moral, religious and philosophical beliefs. Rawls, then, accepts limitations of his project. His theory of justice is one that is limited by the form of prevailing public culture (his general theorising is taken as deriving from and harmonising with intuitions and principles held in a democratic public culture), and it is a specifically political conception of justice and not a metaphysical one.

The communitarian approach to justice has a number of attractive features. It recognises the difficulties of establishing a universal answer to the question of justice. It acknowledges man's social and changing nature. It suffers, however, from being rather vague on important questions concerning the nature of the type of community and framework of justice which are to be supported. In this sense it may be said to resemble postmodernism. Postmoderns such as Lyotard are suspicious of overarching theory purporting to be universalistic. They recognise the significance of differences and are sceptical of the capacity of general criteria to appraise practices. For Lyotard, even Rawls' limited project of establishing general principles to supply a framework for a reasonable conception of justice within a democratic public culture denies difference and experimentation (Lyotard 1984).

The issue of state intervention into the economy to achieve social justice is of ongoing importance and relates to the understanding of justice as a concept. The political history of the past two centuries in Western countries has much to do with this subject. Central to an understanding of British political and social history has been the gradual expansion of the welfare state. Pioneers of the welfare state such as Beveridge explicitly called for an expansion of the state's services to ensure a minimum of social justice. The language of contemporary politics in Europe and the USA is charged by conflict between those who seek to maintain the level of welfare services provided by the state and those who, inspired by neo-liberal doctrines such as those espoused by Nozick, wish to curtail state activity.

Below is an extract from Beveridge's *Full Employment in a Free Society* (1944) which laid the framework for the state provision of social welfare in Britain after the Second World War.

Social security today can be made the subject of a definite Plan and of legislation to give effect to that Plan. It lies wholly within the power of each National Government; once the decision has been taken to abolish Want by comprehensive social insurance as the principal method, once a few issues of equity between older and newer contributors have been settled, the rest is administrative and actuarial detail: the Plan should be as definite as possible, so that every citizen, knowing just what he may expect from social insurance can plan his personal spending and saving to suit his special needs.

50. Prevention of idleness enforced by mass unemployment is a different task. Detailed legislation is neither needed nor useful. It is a problem of adjusting State action to the free activities of the citizens of that State and to the policies of other States. It involves one large decision of principle – acceptance by the State of a new responsibility to the individual – and the setting up of an agency of the State with powers adequate to the discharge of that responsibility.

(Beveridge 1944: 38)

EXERCISE

1 What do you think is meant by the problem of adjusting state action to the free activities of citizens?
2 Do you agree that providing a comprehensive plan for social security is relatively straightforward?
3 What do you take to be the principal reasons behind the development of state provision of social welfare? Can it be supported by a convincing theory of justice?

Conclusion

This chapter has put together a conceptual analysis and the consideration of contested, practical issues in politics. In so doing, it has been concerned to signal the relevance of political theory for the life-and-blood activities of politics. The ascription of rights to animals raises questions about the meaning of a right, just as a death threat against an author dramatises the significance of freedom. The drama of politics and the vitality of political theory is exemplified by the life and death questions posed by terrorism. The eleventh of September 2001 is forever linked with the murder of citizens of New York by terrorists committed to the promotion of a political cause. The issue of terrorism and the concept of an end justifying violent means can be analysed by political theory.

THINK POINT

Do ends justify means?

To pose such a question invites us to think again about rights of individuals and the kind of communities in which we live and wish to live. Whereas forty years ago epitaphs for political theory were being coined (Laslett 1956), the subject is very much alive today.

Chapter summary

- The nature of conceptual analysis and normative theorising.

- The movement away from grand theories in the aftermath of the Second World War.

- The revival of first order normative theorising with the work of John Rawls.

- The thought of leading contemporary political theorists, such as John Rawls, Robert Nozick, Isaiah Berlin and Michael Walzer.

- Key concepts of justice, equality, freedom and rights.

- Concrete issues including the questions of animal rights, the welfare state and the Rushdie case.

- Exercises are set that relate theory to practice.

- The contestable nature of normative political questions.

Key texts

Macintyre, A. (1981) *After Virtue*, Guildford: Duckworth. A thoughtful exploration of differing traditions of virtue.

Mullhall, S. and Swift, A. (1996) *Liberals and Communitarians*, Oxford: Blackwell. A thoughtful and clear exposition of leading liberal and communitarian theorists.

Nozick, R. (1974) *Anarchy, State and Utopia*, Oxford: Blackwell. A polemical, lively book that states a strong case in favour of a minimal state.

Parekh, B. (1990) 'The Rushdie Affair: Research Agenda for Political Philosophy', *Political Studies* 38 (4) (December).

Rawls, J. (1971) *A Theory of Justice*, Oxford: Oxford University Press. A classic and complex work that has been the subject of ongoing discussion.

Walzer, M. (1983) *Spheres of Justice*, Oxford: Blackwell. A famous statement of a communitarian conception of justice.

Further reading

Barry, B. (1995) *Justice as Impartiality*, Oxford: Clarendon Press. A rigorous and vigorous statement of a liberal theory of justice.

Bellamy, R. (ed.) (1993) *Theories and Concepts of Politics*, Manchester: Manchester University Press. An interesting and informative run through a number of concepts of political theory by a range of different authors.

Lyotard, J.F. (1988) *The Differend: Phrases in Dispute*, Manchester: Manchester University Press. Lyotard's most sophisticated attempt to establish the incommensurability of doctrines and standpoints, in which justice is seen as the attempt to bear witness to differends.

Macintyre, A. (1988) *Whose Justice? Which Rationality?* London: Duckworth. A challenging account of differing notions of justice.

Rawls, J. (1993) *Political Liberalism*, New York: Columbia University Press. Reworked essays and lectures which seek to clarify the theory of justice as fairness previously put forward by Rawls.

Rawls, J. (2000) *Lectures on the History of Moral Philosophy*, Cambridge, Mass. and London: Harvard University Press. Well-informed and instructive account of the history of moral philosophy that throws light on Rawls' own theories.

Rawls, J. (2001) (ed. S. Freeman), *Collected Papers*, Cambridge, Mass., and London: Harvard University Press. Significant essays by Rawls written between 1951 and the end of the twentieth century.

Raz, J. (1986) *The Morality of Freedom*, Oxford: Oxford University Press. A philosophically sophisticated exploration of freedom.

Sandel, M. (1984) *Liberalism and its Critics*, New York: New York University Press. A lively critique of Rawls and other liberal theorists from a communitarian perspective.

Taylor, C. (1989) *Sources of the Self: The Making of the Modern Identity*, Cambridge: Cambridge University Press.

Young, I. M. (1990) *Justice and the Politics of Difference*, Princeton, NJ: Princeton University Press. A famous and challenging defence of the politics of difference that champions the cause of groups.

See Chapter 6.

Political Thought

Gary K. Browning

Introduction

This chapter is devoted to exploring the tradition of political thought. It begins by examining how political thought is to be understood, recognising the diversity of ways in which politics and thought are related. It concentrates on discussing political philosophy, in the guise of the classic texts of political philosophers. It analyses the relationship between the classic texts of traditional political philosophy and the more recent style of analytical political philosophising undertaken in the Anglo-Saxon world. Subsequently the character of the history of political thought is reviewed. The debate between contextualist historians and those who consider that the great texts of political philosophy can speak for themselves is examined. Thereafter, a number of specific political philosophies are reviewed. Finally, political Islam and issues of gender are looked at to highlight the ways in which the history of Western political thought is limited by contextual assumptions which render its analysis of politics less universal than is sometimes imagined.

Political thought

Political thinking can take place at many levels and in a variety of ways. Human life inevitably involves thought, and politics is a universal activity among human beings. Thinking is present in most recognisably human activities. To consider someone as acting for reasons and to see a person as taking part in activities which involve rules and conventions which have to be understood are aspects of human identity which we assume or take for granted. In this sense, thinking is more or less fundamental to human activities. Again, politics is a constant factor in history. In the Introduction to this book, politics was taken as involving collective decision-making, and the ubiquity of politics is signalled by the myriad ways in which people are concerned with the character and organisation of group activities. Systematic thought about politics has focused upon the politics of the most important of human associations, **states**. States are associations which literally lay down the laws for all other groups and individuals. Recently the centrality of nation-states in political analysis has been challenged by theorists of globalisation who point to the involvement of nation-states in global patterns of development.

See the Introduction for a general account of how this book regards politics and theories of politics.

State A human association in which sovereign power is established within a given territorial area, and in which the sovereign power usually possesses a monopoly on the means of coercion.

THINK POINT

- Consider the following human activities and note how thinking is involved in them: driving a car, doing housework, reading this book, debating in a legislature.

- Consider how politics is involved in the following group activities: deciding on expenditure in a family household, prioritising the objectives of a charity such as Oxfam, the introduction of tougher penal measures.

The institutions and practices of states presuppose language and thought; for example, lobbying, debate in legislatures, executive decision-making and administrative regulations are reflective activities. 'Political thought' as a term, however, conveys a sense of systematic reflection upon the practices and institutions of political life. As has been observed previously in this book (see Introduction), there are a variety of ways of theorising politics. Political science, in various styles, aims at achieving laws or plausible generalisations about political behaviour. Traditionally, however, political thought in academic commentary is taken to signify political philosophy. The study of the history of political thought, for example, generally focuses upon classic texts of political philosophy. The classic texts of political philosophy, such as Plato's *Republic* and Hobbes' *Leviathan*, constitute broad-ranging explorations of politics which relate politics to the general conditions of experience. Hence Plato elaborated the nature of the relationship between truth, practical life and philosophical understanding.

The classic texts of political philosophy continue to inform the way in which the meaning and value of politics are imagined. As was observed in Chapter 6, Anglo-Saxon political philosophers in the mid-twentieth century, under the spell of linguistic philosophy, tended to limit the scope of political philosophy to that of **conceptual analysis** (see also Weldon (1953) for the epitome of a conception of political philosophy as conceptual analysis). Contemporary political philosophers, however, while recognising the ineluctably controversial nature of judgements of value, are willing to undertake large-scale theorising about norms. Rawls (1971) and Nozick (1974), for example, have elaborated theories of justice which develop and justify contrasting accounts of just, substantive arrangements of society.

Conceptual analysis A practice and view of philosophy which takes philosophy to be concerned with the analysis and clarification of concepts rather than substantive issues

Insofar as contemporary political philosophers engage with the norms of political practice and work out schemes of political organisation, exhibiting substantive applications of political values, then the contemporary identity of political philosophy borders on political ideology and is in touch with the grand theorising of classic political philosophers such as that undertaken by Plato and Hobbes. Both political philosophy and political ideology are to be understood as developing conceptual explorations of politics involving value judgements. While political philosophy accents the critical examination of assumptions, political ideology emphasises a programmatic set of recommendations. The links between contemporary political philosophers and their predecessors is evident in the way they lean on the classic texts of political philosophy in constructing their arguments. Rawls, for instance, self-consciously works within the social contract tradition and looks to Kant as an exemplary moral philosopher. Nozick's justification of a minimal state owes much to a tradition of natural rights theorising, and to Locke's political thought in particular. Habermas, a leading contemporary continental political philosopher, theorises within the context of a reading of modern philosophy, as is evidenced in his book *The Philosophical Discourse of Modernity* (1987). The continuing influence of the classic texts of political philosophy signals their importance, and in the succeeding sections of this chapter a framework for their historical understanding will be explored and the arguments of several past political philosophers will be examined.

Jürgen Habermas (1929–) is the most famous of the second generation of the Frankfurt school of social research. He has been strongly influenced by Hegel and Marx. Habermas' work covers many topics, notably the nature of communicative action, the dynamics of capitalism, the character of social science and philosophy, the nature of modernity and, more recently, deliberative democracy. His main works include *Theory and Practice* (1974), *The Theory of Communicative Action* (1984 and 1988), *The Philosophical Discourse of Modernity* (1987) and *Between Facts and Norms* (1997).

Jürgen Habermas

The history of political thought

Thinking about politics, at whatever level and style it is undertaken, inevitably implies some engagement with history. Politics as a human activity takes place over time. Without people having lived together in communities there could be no theories of politics. Politics in the abstract would be a void. Political thought has to be based upon actual political behaviour. This dependence of theory upon practice applies to the most abstract kind of political thought, namely political philosophy, as well as to the most severely practical kind, such as a specific policy recommendation. On this reading, then, an historical understanding of the classic texts of political philosophy, which constitutes the most familiar treatment of political thought, must recognise that the texts are composed in relation to actual worlds of political experience.

THINK POINT

Hegel, in *The Philosophy of Right* (1971), urges 'What is rational is actual and what is actual is rational'. If what Hegel is saying here amounts to the idea that the rational must be based on what has been developed in practice, do you agree with him?

Georg Wilhelm Friedrich Hegel (1770–1831) is a German philosopher, famous for articulating a dialectical philosophy whereby reality is seen to be constituted by the relations of thought. His philosophy traces these internal or dialectical relations of thought in presenting its account of reality. Hegel's most well-known works include *The Phenomenology of Spirit* (1807), *The Science of Logic* (1812) and *The Philosophy of Right* (1821). Hegel's political philosophy aims at understanding the reason and freedom he takes to be immanent in political experience. The influence of Hegel is massive. Marx, Kierkegaard, Lenin and Heidegger all developed their thought by means of a critical engagement with Hegel.

Georg Wilhelm Friedrich Hegel

The dependence of political philosophy on the prior practice of politics ensures that the subject has an historical dimension. As the practice of politics develops, so reflection upon politics changes. The relationship between theory and practice is not straightforward, however, and the meaning and consequences of Hegel's remark on the actuality of reason are controversial, for he did not equate actuality with existence. A political philosopher may be critical of political practice and may also imagine a framework of political organisation distinct from present practices. For instance, Plato's recommendations on education and sexual equality do not reflect the traditions of Greek political life. Historic political philosophers, in framing their understanding of politics, theorise within the context of political practices but do not reflect them un-thinkingly. Likewise, their thought is developed within an intellectual context. Marx employs concepts refined by the German philosophical tradition in diagnosing the condition of the proletariat in the mid-nineteenth century as alienated.

The methodology of the history of political thought

Contextualism This stands for the view that the meaning of political ideas can be understood only by relating them to the historical contexts in which they were generated.

There is a methodological dispute over whether the subject should accent the historical contexts in which political thinkers write or discuss the ideas of the texts of political thought themselves without paying close attention to their provenance in locally determined historical contexts. **Contextualists** argue that a text of political thought such as Hobbes' *Leviathan* must be related to a variety of contexts, notably the intellectual and political, referred to above, if its meaning is to be understood. Historians of political thought like Plamenatz (1963), on the other hand, consider that the classic texts of political philosophy can be read and understood with a minimum of contextual knowledge on the part of the reader.

The historian of political thought whose practice and methodological work have perhaps been taken as providing foundations for the contextual approach is Professor Quentin Skinner. There is an irony in Skinner's reputation as a contextualist in that his most famous methodological essay, 'Meaning and Understanding in the History of Ideas' (Skinner 1988), criticised contextualist readings of political thought which assimilated thinking to the context and ignored authors' intentions.

Quentin Skinner (1941–) is the most notable contemporary theorist who examines the methodology and meaning of the history of ideas. He is a Fellow of Christ's College, Cambridge and is Regius Professor of Modern History in the University of Cambridge. He has written many influential articles on the character of intellectual history and a number of books in which his approach is exemplified. These books include *The Foundations of Modern Political Thought* (1978, 2 vols), *Machiavelli* (1981) and *Reason and Rhetoric in the Philosophy of Hobbes* (1996).

Quentin Skinner

Skinner exposed what he took to be the weaknesses of a textual approach to the history of political thought, which assumed that the meaning of classic texts could be acquired without historical investigation of their meaning and point. For Skinner the point of a text in political thought, and its meaning, can be captured only if the intentions of the author can be understood. An author's intentions, for Skinner, are often puzzling and cannot simply be read off from the text. On the other hand, intentions cannot be reduced to some distinct context, such as the economic, for the point behind an author's deployment of concepts involves the conscious agency of the author. Notwithstanding Skinner's critique of this kind of contextualist approach, his emphasis upon recovering the historical intentions of authors and reading texts in the context of contemporary political debates and ideologies has been taken as a paradigm of a contextualist reading of the history of political thought (King 1996).

The contextualist approach to the history of political thought, exemplified in the works of Skinner, Pocock and Collini, has elucidated the texts of political thought by relating them to contemporary ideological debate and conceptual paradigms. If the nuances of historical context are ignored there is certainly a tendency for texts to be misread. It would be a mistake, for instance, to assume that the term 'property' holds the same meaning in Locke's texts as it does today. Property in the seventeenth century had a range of meanings, one of which was as an umbrella term for entitlements in general (Dunn 1984). A failure to respect the historical meanings of terms can lead to a serious misreading of a text. Likewise, a narrowly textual approach to the history of political thought has tended to encourage the misleading assumption that all texts in political thought will contain doctrines on a set of political principles and institutions.

The contextual approach to the history of political thought has broadened the scope of the subject in that its attention to ideological debate and conceptual paradigms has pointed to the historical interest of practical and rhetorical pieces of political thought. Again, it has revivified the historical study of the classic texts of political philosophy by disclosing the conditionality of even the most philosophical accounts of politics. Contextualists maintain that authorial purposes and the expectations of audiences of the most abstract texts cannot be assumed without historical research. Contextualism, however, is not a neat, unproblematic recipe for the understanding of political thought. There is no easily specifiable context for a text. The context for Hegel's political thought, for example, ranges across centuries of philosophical exploration which he self-consciously assimilated, as well as the immediate inspiration of German idealism and youthful colleagues and the political and religious situation within Germany. Given the seemingly limitless character of this context, concentration upon the internal logic of his texts at least establishes a manageable field of enquiry.

An implication of the contextualist approach to which Skinner (1988) has drawn attention is that the historical specificity of political theorising precludes the assumption that there exist perennial problems and answers in the history of political thought. In the extract below he argues against the existence of perennial or unhistorical answers to philosophical problems and repudiates the notion that classic texts of political philosophy provide answers to the problems we set ourselves in the contemporary world of politics.

Significant contextual works include: J. Tully (ed.) (1988) Meaning and Context – Quentin Skinner and his Critics, *Cambridge: Polity Press (a collection of essays and commentaries on Skinner's work); J. G. A. Pocock (1971)* Politics, Language and Time, *London: Methuen; S. Collini, D. Winch and J. Burrow (1983)* That Noble Science of Politics, *Cambridge: Cambridge University Press.*

> This reformulation and insistence on the claim that there are no perennial problems in philosophy, from which we can hope to learn directly through studying the classic texts, is not of course intended as a denial of the possibility

continued

continued

that there may be propositions (perhaps in mathematics) the truth of which is wholly tenseless. (This does not yet amount to showing that their truth is any less contingent for that.) It is not even a denial of the possibility that there may be apparently perennial questions, if these are sufficiently abstractly framed. All I wish to insist is that whenever it is claimed that the point of historical study of such questions is that we may learn directly from the answers, it will be found that what counts as an answer will usually look, in a different culture or period, so different in itself that it can hardly be in the least useful even to go on thinking of the relevant question as being 'the same' in the required sense at all. More crudely: we must learn to do our own thinking ourselves.

It is by no means my conclusion, however, that because the philosophical value at present claimed for the history of ideas rests on a misconception, it must follow that the subject has no philosophical value in itself at all. For it is the very fact that classic texts are concerned with their own quite alien problems, and not the presumption that they are somehow concerned with our own problems as well, which seems to me to give not the lie but the key to the indispensable value of studying the history of ideas. The classic texts, especially in social, ethical, and political thought, help to reveal – if we let them – not the essential sameness, but rather the essential variety of viable moral assumptions and political commitments.

(Skinner 1988: 66–7)

EXERCISE

1   Do you agree with Skinner that what counts as an answer to a 'perennial' question will vary according to culture and period?
2   Do you think that the classic texts of political thought are valuable in teaching us the essential variety of moral assumptions and political commitments?

The value of the history of political thought

Skinner is representative of contextualism in general in disparaging the claim that classic texts in the history of political philosophy furnish answers to today's political problems. Answers about politics, for contextualists, are relative to time and place. Skinner suggests that if political thinkers were to be presented as answering the same question, then the question would have to be phrased in a very abstract manner which allowed for profound differences among the specific answers to the question. He is surely right to signal that political thinkers' 'answers' to a question like one exploring the best political order for a society would be framed according to diverse concepts and assumptions.

None the less, it is worth emphasising that an awareness of the tradition of the history of political thought serves to open up a range of possible responses to a contemporary question about the best political order. Again a newly formulated answer to a fundamental question considering the best organisation of social and political life does not guarantee its novelty, due to its ignorance of the history of political thought. Rather, political thinking invariably is informed by an ongoing tradition of thought, and contemporary political theorising such as that conducted by Rawls (1971), Nozick (1974), Habermas (1987) and Gadamer (1981) self-consciously builds upon past traditions of thought. In this way the political thought of Hobbes, Locke and Hegel is relevant to ongoing, critical reflection on the order and justice of political life.

THINK POINT

Consider reasons for and against the political thought of a past political philosopher such as Plato, Hobbes or Marx being relevant to us today.

Key political philosophers

In this section a number of significant political philosophers of the Western political tradition are examined. Aspects of their contexts are explored together with the distinct contributions they have made to political thinking. Evidently, any selection of specific theorists is controversial, but the point has not been to include all or even most of the significant political philosophers of Western political thought. The aim is to focus on a number of thinkers whose political thought is of undeniable importance, and to show how their theories relate to particular contexts and yet can contribute to an ongoing engagement with politics.

Plato

Plato (428–347 BC) was a Greek philosopher who has exerted a profound impact on the subsequent history of political thought and practice. His thought is expressed in a series of dialogues whose principal figure is often Socrates (died 399 BC), whose philosophical example was inspirational for Plato. Plato's biography and the dating of his most famous dialogues continue to be disputed. His most famous political texts are *Crito* (1961c), *The Republic* (1945), *The Statesman* (1961e) and *The Laws* (1961d). *The Republic* has proved endlessly fascinating. Rousseau admired it as a masterly work of education, Hegel saw it as an essay in the retrieval of the Greek political tradition and Popper lambasted it as the epitome of a closed society opposed to his own ideal, open society.

Plato

THE CONTEXT OF PLATO'S THOUGHT

Plato was born in 428 BC to a noble Athenian family, and he died in 347. The Peloponnesian War between Athens and Sparta served as the disturbing background to Plato's early years. 'Letter VII' (1961a) purports to provide an autobiographical sketch of Plato's political development. Its authenticity is in doubt, but its account is plausible and coheres with what is known about Plato from other sources. It reviews Plato's reaction to events at the end of the Peloponnesian War. The aristocratic regime which came to power in the wake of the Athenian defeat in the war is presented as high-handed and partisan. The return of democracy to Athens, however, is depicted as catastrophic in that it leads to the trial and execution of Socrates, Plato's philosophical mentor. The execution of Socrates exerted a momentous impact upon Plato. The Platonic dialogues portray Socrates as a paragon of intellectual and moral virtue, and his trial and execution are depicted as tragic tokens of political corruption. Plato's own political philosophy may be seen as a sharp condemnation of Athenian political practice.

The immediate political context of the Athenian *polis* evidently shaped Plato's political theorising, but he was also moved by contemporary intellectual developments. Melling, in his book *Understanding Plato*, has referred to 'a marked degree of plasticity in the political and social ideas current in Plato's Athens. Rival models were canvassed, opposing ideologies argued out in drinking circles and dinner parties' (Melling 1987). Intellectual debate and the critical interrogation of traditions were undertaken by the sophists, intellectuals who purported to be able to teach virtues and rhetoric. Sophists were a diverse group of intellectuals, but many of them sought to deny a natural basis of morality and urged that morality was shaped by prevailing social conventions. Plato was opposed to these views and aimed to re-establish the foundations of an objective system of values on a new philosophical basis. The sharpest dramatic scenes in his dialogues depict dramatic confrontations between Socrates and sophists such as Gorgias, Protagoras and Thrasymachus.

In his opposition to the political and intellectual currents in fifth-century BC Athens Plato also looked to the Greek philosophical context, and his works may be seen as reflecting and building upon Greek philosophical traditions. Socrates is the charismatic figure who enlivens the dialogues. Evidence of the actual historical figure of Socrates is fragmentary, and derives in large part from the artistry of Plato. Plato's artistry, however, is concerned to paint a picture of Socrates which develops his own philosophical enterprise. Given the image of Socrates which can be gathered from elsewhere, it would seem that the early dialogues of Plato reflect a more faithful portrait of the man than the later ones, where Plato constructs a distinct philosophy of his own. In the early dialogues Socrates is represented as a gadfly whose wisdom consists in awareness of his own ignorance and is coupled with an interrogative strategy whereby he questions the underlying assumptions of others' views about the moral virtues. The ideal of a philosophy which can stand the test of such questioning impels the later philosophising of Plato.

See G. K. Browning (1991b) 'Ethical Absolutism in Hegel and Plato', History of Political Thought 12 (3).

PLATO'S POLITICAL THOUGHT

The early dialogues of Plato are for the most part sceptical and do not present a definite set of doctrines. Socrates is depicted as engaging in conversations with a variety of people. Generals, politicians, rhetoricians and sophists, for example, are questioned about their views on the moral virtues. Their views are invariably found to lack adequate support. The negative outcome of these conversations offers a critique of the ethical and political condition of the contemporary Greek *polis*. Its leading representatives cannot provide reasoned justifications of its practices and are bereft of convincing accounts of the ethical virtues. The implication of these investigations is that an effective political world demands an organisation which is based upon demonstrably rational criteria. The problems of the contemporary polis are thrown into sharp relief in 'Apology' (1961a), where Plato portrays Socrates as the innocent if eloquent victim of contemporary political machinations. Plato's search for high ethical standards is at the same time flagged in 'Crito', where Socrates is depicted as staying to face his death, notwithstanding his innocence, because of his commitment to Athens and its laws.

Plato's *Republic*, a dialogue from Plato's middle period of writings, provides a detailed and radical account of a just *polis*. It diverges markedly from contemporary practice. Plato sketches the outlines of a just city in which the association is divided into three classes: the rulers, the soldiers and those who engage in trade and productive activity. Justice is highlighted as consisting in each class performing the role for which it is suited. The class of citizens who are most suited to rule must, according to Plato, assume the duty of ruling. Similarly, those who are most courageous must assume the duty of defending the city.

The ideal commonwealth of *The Republic* contains a number of radical features. The rulers are to be socialised so that they assume a rational, disinterested concern for the community. They are to receive an education which culminates in their practice of philosophical enquiry. Their philosophical education is held to enable them to understand the ethical virtues and to rule rationally. These guardians and the auxiliary soldiers are to share things in common so that they are not inspired to pursue their own selfish desires for material gain at the expense of the communal good. This communist impulse also inspires the proposed abolition of family life among the guardians. Children will be brought up communally, so that family interests will not prejudice political judgements. Plato also prescribes sexual equality for the guardians, in startling contrast with contemporary practice. Plato's rationalism leads him to recommend sexual equality because he can see no relevant difference between the sexes to preclude women from ruling.

Alongside the extraordinary measures Plato advocates for the ruling guardians, he also recommends that a highly authoritarian style of rule be imposed upon the remaining body of citizens. Art is to be severely censored and education is to be tightly controlled so that justice and truth can be inculcated by the ruling elite. *The Republic* is an endlessly fascinating work for reasons which go beyond the mere rehearsal of the kind of ideal regime Plato recommends. Plato provides a series of memorable images to depict his vision of what is involved in a philosophical turn of mind and vocation. Philosophers are those who perceive the light beyond the subterranean prison in which most of us are condemned to live. Plato, in his evocation of the distinctiveness and rarity of the philosophical individual, betrays a pessimism about the human condition which casts doubt over the practical possibility of achieving his ideal regime. This doubt inspires Plato's later political dialogues, *The Statesman* and *The Laws*, in which Plato is prepared to adapt rather than abolish contemporary practices and conceives of the rule of law as a realistic safeguard against rank disorder. In *The Laws* Plato recommends a rigid adherence to the rule of law and a mixed form of sovereignty.

This reading of Plato is explored in G. K. Browning (1991a) Plato and Hegel: Two Modes of Philosophising about Politics, *New York: Garland Press.*

Next, said I [Socrates], here is a parable to illustrate the degrees in which our nature may be enlightened or un-enlightened. Imagine the condition of men living in a sort of cavernous chamber underground, with an entrance open to the light and a long passage all down the cave. Here they have been from childhood, chained by the leg and also by the neck, so that they cannot move and can see only what is in front of them, because the chains will not let them turn their heads. At some distance higher up is the light of a fire burning behind them; and between the prisoners and the fire is a track with a parapet built along it, like the screen at a puppet show, which hides the performers while they show their puppets over the top.

I see, said he [Glaucon, interlocuter of Socrates].

Now behind this parapet imagine persons carrying along various artificial objects, including figures of men and animals in wood or stone or other materials, which project above the parapet. Naturally, some of these persons will be talking, others silent.

It is a strange picture, he said [Glaucon], and a strange sort of prisoners. Like ourselves, I replied; for in the first place prisoners so confined would have seen nothing of themselves or of one another, except the shadows thrown by the fire-light on the wall of the Cave facing them, would they?

(Plato 1945: 227–8)

EXERCISE

1 Put into your own words Plato's image of the human condition as presented in this passage.
2 What political views might be inspired by this image of the human condition?

Nor again is it at all strange that one who comes from the contemplation of divine things (the philosopher) to the miseries of human life should appear awkward and ridiculous when, with eyes still dazed and not yet accustomed to the darkness, he is compelled, in a law-court or elsewhere, to dispute about the shadows of justice or the images that cast those shadows, and to wrangle over the notions of what is right in the minds of men who have never beheld Justice itself.

(Plato 1945: 231)

EXERCISE

1 On the strength of what Plato writes in the above passage, consider whether or not he regards the achievement of philosophical rule to be an easy task.
2 How does the above passage relate to events in the life of the actual Socrates?
3 How, according to Plato, would you come to see Justice itself?

Thomas Hobbes

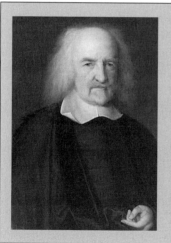

Thomas Hobbes (1588–1679) is both a celebrated and infamous figure in the history of political philosophy. The son of a minor clergyman, Hobbes rejected scholasticism in favour of science and the deductive rigour of geometry. The disputes between King and Parliament leading to the English Civil War of 1642 to 1649, as well as the conflict itself, were significant in the development of his thought. Hobbes' political thought is directed towards providing an indisputable basis for sovereignty so as to avoid the problems associated with civil unrest and conflict. Hobbes' most famous text is *Leviathan*, which was published in 1651; it was preceded by earlier versions of his political theory, *Elements of Law* and *De Cive*, published in 1640 and 1641 respectively.

Thomas Hobbes

THE CONTEXT OF HOBBES' THOUGHT

Hobbes himself joked that his birth was premature on account of the arrival of the Spanish Armada, and that fear and anxiety thereafter fixed themselves as key components of his thinking. While this anecdote was told for amusement, it remains true that political events in the years preceding Hobbes' writing of *Leviathan* played a notable part in impressing upon Hobbes' mind the need for security and unequivocal political authority. The English Civil War, between the King, Charles I, and Parliament, took place between 1642 and 1649 and demonstrated graphically the dangers of disputed political authority. Civil war is an extreme reminder of the dangers to civil order which can be unleashed when authority comes to be disputed. While Hobbes' political ideas were developed before the outbreak of the Civil War, the gathering tensions between monarch and Parliament and the resulting uncertainties of government throughout Charles I's reign contributed to Hobbes' recognition of the need for clear and undisputed sovereign authority.

Ideological and social tensions generated by the prevailing religious discord and the proliferation of religious sects also left a mark on Hobbes' thinking. Hobbes recognised the power of religion to move men's minds and passions. In particular, Hobbes perceived that fanatical puritan sects which followed and proseltysed for religious practices distinct from those of the Church of England threatened to unravel social and political ties. This recognition helps to explain his recommendation in the *Leviathan* of state control over the promulgation of religious doctrine.

The political and social context of Hobbes' early years sensitised him to the significance of signs of religious and political dissent. His intellectual background alerted him to rationalist developments on the continent of Europe. Hobbes was distinctly unimpressed by the traditional education he had received at the University of Oxford. From his school days Hobbes was a gifted linguist, but he was uninspired by the intellectual atmosphere of Oxford. The dominance of scholastic philosophy, which subscribed to an Aristotelian world view and ignored the rise of the new science, dismayed Hobbes. Hobbes himself was inspired by the rigour and exactitude of Euclidean mathematics and was impressed by contemporary scientific developments. Indeed, the structure and composition of the *Leviathan* is modelled on geometry insofar as the object of explanation, the state, is decomposed into its component parts so that it can then be reconstituted deductively.

HOBBES' POLITICAL THOUGHT

Hobbes' *Leviathan*, the masterpiece of his political thought, is composed of four parts: 'Of Man', 'Of Commonwealth', 'Of a Christian Commonwealth' and 'Of the Kingdome of Darknesse'. By far the most important parts in the presentation of his account of politics and the basis of political authority are the opening two parts. Hobbes begins his account of politics and the state by examining the nature of man, the underlying assumption being that an explanation of a political association must rest upon an understanding of the elements of which it is composed. Hobbes' account of man is distinctive and challenging. He sees men mechanistically and individualistically, as a series of particular bodies in motion. Human action, for Hobbes, is the product of passions generated by a particular self's contact with external bodies. Particular selves, according to Hobbes, pursue their own desires and seek to avoid that which provokes discomfort.

The good for Hobbes, in contrast to Plato, is not something which philosophers can reach by a heightened form of understanding. Rather, he believes that each individual terms good what he or she finds desirable. There is no common, ethical world which human beings naturally inhabit. For Hobbes, each person pursues his or her own 'good'; individuals seek the felicity of generally being able to satisfy their desires. The achievement of felicity is no easy thing, however, and Hobbes, in drawing a logical picture of the natural condition of mankind, stresses the uncertain and dangerous predicament constituting the human condition. In seeking to satisfy their own desires men inevitably come into conflict with other men pursuing their own goals. Men and women, according to Hobbes, have a natural right to whatever they can obtain. Conflict is endemic given the tendency for rights to clash. Above all, human beings in this condition fear they will not be able to pursue their desires. They fear that their power to achieve their goals will be taken away. They fear death at the hands of another, a fear that is rational given the potential for conflict among human beings.

Hobbes identifies the human condition as constituting a predicament whereby man's desires and the desire to satisfy his desires lead to chronic insecurity. For Hobbes, however, reason can be used instrumentally to resolve this predicament. Rational rules can be framed to alter the situation. The first such rule is that men should seek the peace. Men, for Hobbes, can only secure peace by covenanting together to form a political association. To ensure conditions of peace they should mutually contract with one another to confer authority and power upon a sovereign who is not party to the covenant. The sovereign will be granted absolute authority and power to ensure that peace is achieved. According to Hobbes, agreement to these conditions generates a moral as well as a prudential obligation to obey the sovereign.

The sovereign, ideally a single person, is presumed to follow the rules of reason himself and so will want to rule according to law so as not to inflame discontent. Ultimately, however, a sovereign, for Hobbes, can legitimately do all that is required to secure the peace so long as he is presumed to be effective in this endeavour. This notion of sovereignty certainly involves the sovereign's authority over religious publications and practices and education.

Hobbes' standpoint is controversial and has aroused much hostility since its formulation. Many see the power he bestows upon the sovereign and the state as prejudicial to human freedom. The *Leviathan* certainly contrasts with J. S. Mill's subsequent eloquent defence of human individuality and liberty. It lacks Marx's impassioned concern for equality and social justice. Feminists have also criticised its assumption of male rule within politics and the family (Pateman 1988). Nevertheless, it remains a remorseless investigation into the logic of public authority. The state of nature operates as a powerful *reductio ad absurdum* argument for the ubiquity and inescapability of a political world.

So that in the nature of man, we find three principal causes of quarrel. First, Competition; Second, Diffidence; Thirdly, Glory.

The first, maketh men invade for Gain; the second, for safety; and the third, for Reputation. The first use Violence, to make themselves Masters of other mens persons, wives, children, and cattell; the second, to defend them; the third, for trifles, as a word, a smile, a different opinion, and any other signe of undervalue, either direct in their Persons, or by reflexion in their Kindred, their Friends, their Nation, their Profession, or their Name.

Hereby it is manifest, that during the time men live without a common Power to keep them all in awe, they are in that condition which is called Warre; and such a warre, as is of every man, against every man.

(Hobbes 1968: 185)

EXERCISE

1 How does Hobbes see the condition of human beings who live in a state of nature, without a state?
2 What does Hobbes see as the sources of conflict between men?
3 Do you agree with Hobbes' depiction of man's character and motivations?

John Locke

John Locke (1632–1704) is a political theorist who was closely involved in the development of practical politics in Britain in the seventeenth century. He studied medicine at the University of Oxford before becoming associated with the household of Antony Ashley Cooper, the first Earl of Shaftesbury, in 1661. His political thought was concerned to protect the subject from the practical dangers of absolutist kings and has subsequently inspired generations of liberal thinkers. Locke was anxious to combat what he saw as the authoritarianism of the Stuart monarchy. While the precise meaning of the details of Locke's political theory is difficult to pin down, the overall design is relatively clear in its evocation of a distinct social sphere in which the individual possesses rights that political authority should not transgress.

John Locke

Locke was born in Wrington, a small village in Somerset, in 1632. He was sponsored by a friend of his father and attended Westminster School and Oxford University. Indeed, Locke was to achieve much in many spheres.

He distinguished himself in philosophy and medicine, and developed political interests and a political career in assuming a variety of duties for the Earl of Shaftesbury from 1683. Shaftesbury was the leader of a section of the Whig Party which was opposed to Charles II and his drift towards absolutism and Catholicism. Matters came to a head between 1679 and 1683 when Shaftesbury's faction led a concerted effort to exclude Charles II's brother James, an acknowledged Catholic, from ascending to the throne. This exclusion crisis culminated in the failure of the Rye House plot of 1683, in which the kidnapping of James, the Duke of York, had been planned. Locke followed his patron Shaftesbury in leaving England in the wake of their implication in the act of treason. Following the successful overthrow of James II in 1688 by the so-called Glorious Revolution, however, Locke returned to England, and his *Two Treatises of Government* (1963) was published anonymously in 1689. The *First Treatise* is a rebuttal of Filmer's *Patriarcha*, which had been published in 1680, while the second develops Locke's own account of the nature of government.

Historical scholarship by Laslett (1963) and Ashcraft (1987), among others, has established that the *Two Treatises of Government* were in fact composed largely in the years before 1689. Hence Locke's texts were not designed simply to justify the accession of William and Mary in 1688, but to shape opinion so as to precipitate the removal of James II from the throne. Scholarship has thereby revealed a radical edge to the famous political work. Indeed, in Locke's keenness in the *Two Treatises of Government* to decry an over-mighty and unlimited government which ignores the rights of property, he displays a very practical concern to limit the power of the prevailing Stuart dynasty. Locke's political interests influence his famous political work rather more than his scientific and philosophical doctrines. Locke's *Essay Concerning Human Understanding* plots limits of human knowledge from a philosophical standpoint, but his famous political work operates with a notion of natural rights which assumes a human capacity to intuit natural law.

LOCKE'S POLITICAL THOUGHT

Locke is a theorist of a social contract, but he differs markedly from Hobbes in the way he deploys the notion of a social contract. The contract is a device which establishes a political association. Locke begins by imagining men and women in a state of nature, a condition without government. While it is a non-political condition, it is a moral condition. Men in a state of nature are conceived by Locke as equally free, rational and independent. Men can distinguish right from wrong, and they can do so because they are conceived by Locke as being able to discern the natural law and the moral obligations deriving from God. The moral obligations deriving from natural law entail that men should respect one another's rights to life, liberty and (material) property, though at times Locke refers to property in a broader sense as a synonym for all entitlements.

The rights to life, liberty and property operate as constraints upon government as well as restrictions on behaviour in a state of nature. For Locke, men agree to form a political society because there are inconveniences in the state of nature, but they do not sacrifice fundamental rights in the transition to government. The inconveniences in the state of nature arising out of the somewhat uncertain enforcement of the law of nature are envisaged as persuading men to set up a government, but the authority of this government does not legitimate transgression against man's natural rights. Political authority, for Locke, is assumed to be a kind of trust whereby each man's right to interpret and enforce the natural law is entrusted to government. Locke, however, was mindful of the possibility of a government abusing this trust and rests the legitimacy of government on the ongoing consent of the people.

While the general outlines of Locke's concern to limit the power of governments are clear, the precise mechanism of how the consent of the people is to be elicited is left unclear. Likewise, the manner in which the people are to be represented politically and the scope of the franchise are not specified. Given the context in which Locke was writing, however, the lack of clarity on these matters is not surprising. Locke was animated by a distrust of the Stuart monarchy, and the *Second Treatise* was concerned to marshal support for his critique of that monarchy and its 'abuse' of power. It is plausible that Locke did not want to alienate potential support by spelling out the specifics of his political theory when he could maximise support by leaving matters vague. Locke concentrated upon constructing a case against a government which abused its trust by relying overly on executive power and transgressing against rights.

Locke's *Second Treatise of Government* is vague on some details, but nevertheless expresses a powerful statement of limited government. The authority of government is limited by the supposed conditions of its emergence, so that there is to be a continuous recognition of the natural rights of man. Locke's focus upon the limits of government and the rights of man has been lauded by subsequent liberal theorists.

Of the state of nature

To understand political power aright, and to derive it from its original, we must consider, what state all men are naturally in, and that is, a state of perfect freedom to order their actions, and dispose of their possessions and persons, as they think fit, within the bounds of the law of nature, without asking leave, or depending upon the will of any other man. . . .

But though this be a state of liberty, yet it is not a state of licence: though man in that state has an uncontrollable liberty to dispose of his person or possessions, yet he has not liberty to destroy himself, or so much as any creature in his possession, but where some nobler use than its bare preservation calls for it. The state of nature has a law of nature to govern it, which obliges every one, and reason, which is that law teaches all mankind who will but consult it, that being all equal and independent, no one ought to harm another in his life, health, liberty, or possessions.

(Locke 1963: 309)

EXERCISE

1 How does Locke conceive of the law of nature in the state of nature? How does it limit man's freedom to act?
2 Locke derives the rights of man from prohibitions arising out of the law of nature. Do you think there might be other rights besides those relating to life, health, liberty or possessions?

Jean-Jacques Rousseau

Jean-Jacques Rousseau (1712–78) was a profound thinker whose radical critique of the tensions and dissonance within civilised society allied to his robust defence of participatory democracy disturbed contemporary social and political assumptions. Rousseau was born in Geneva and moved to Paris in 1742. He was an intimate of leading figures of the Enlightenment as well as being a critic of Enlightenment notions. Rousseau's critique of advanced civilisation is expressed most tellingly in his 'A Discourse on the Origin of Inequality' published in 1755, and his conception of democracy is formulated elegantly and controversially in his *Social Contract* of 1762. Rousseau's questioning of advanced civilisation reverberates uneasily within today's world of global markets and continued social fragmentation. Likewise, the general sense of political alienation in today's world makes the prospect of radical democracy championed by Rousseau both disturbing and seductive.

Jean-Jacques Rousseau

THE CONTEXT OF ROUSSEAU'S THOUGHT

Rousseau led an extraordinary life, producing a number of literary masterpieces which have exerted an impact on the subsequent development of the autobiographical novel, evident in the work of Proust and Joyce, and on social and political theory, notably in the development of the notion of alienation in the work of Hegel and Marx. Rousseau's heightened sensitivity is expressed most vividly in his reflections on his life and its stresses and strains in his *Confessions* of 1761, but his affective take on his own experience may be seen in his theoretical works.

Rousseau was born in Geneva in 1712, and he was to stay in the city until he was 16 years old, when he wandered off, at first into the arms of a benefactress and subsequently to find fame and notoriety in equal measure in Paris. Geneva and Switzerland were to exert a lasting impact upon his mind. He idealised the democracies which were established in the small cantons in Switzerland, and he savoured the disciplinary, republican regime in Calvinist Geneva. In his political thought he favoured participatory democracy in a small-scale state and the development of a disciplined, virtuous citizenry. Rousseau's republican sympathies, his love of democracy and his espousal of moral renewal through a disciplined ethical regime were also inspired by his sympathy for classical republican states such as Sparta and Rome, which had been nourished by the storytelling of his father.

In the France of the mid-eighteenth century in which Rousseau formulated his social and political thought, he was conscious of and reacted against Enlightenment thought and its celebration of reason. While Rousseau is a theorist who exemplifies a commitment to a life of reason, he is at the same time sensitive to problems which have emerged with the development of civilisation and does not accept the fashionable Enlightenment doctrine of progress. His critical attitude to Enlightenment values may be seen in the shock value of the triumph of his prize-winning essay of 1750, 'A Discourse on the Arts and Sciences', in the competition set up by the Dijon Academy. In this essay, Rousseau depicted the revival of the arts and sciences as so many garlands of flowers bestrewing the miseries and sickness of civilisation.

Rousseau, in his great work of political theory *The Social Contract*, shows an awareness of recent traditions and developments in political philosophy. The very title of the book intimates its relationship to the works of recent predecessors, Hobbes and Locke. While working with a familiar intellectual model, however, Rousseau refashions it to suggest something new and challenging. Whereas Hobbes had depicted the movement between the state of nature and the setting up of a political commonwealth as one in which covenanters would abstain voluntarily from an ongoing involvement in political decision-making, Rousseau sees the members of a rational and free political association as collectively determining the conditions of their ongoing association. Rousseau's thought, however, resembles Hobbes' insofar as his citizens' freedom is a political achievement in which the conditions of a pre-political state of nature do not restrict the pull of democracy, in contrast to Locke's stipulation that a series of rights put moral limits on political action.

ROUSSEAU'S POLITICAL THOUGHT

A major theme within Rousseau's political thinking, and one which resonates in later theorists such as Hegel and Marx, is that of alienation. Rousseau had a profound sensitivity to inauthenticity in himself and others, and he diagnosed the modern world and civilised society as thwarting the free, authentic expression of individuality and identity. In his 'A Discourse on the Origin of Inequality' Rousseau develops a history of civil society in terms of the story of human sickness. He posits a state of nature as a device to highlight the distorted condition of contemporary and civilised man. The state of nature is envisaged by Rousseau as a condition stripped of the artifices and conventions which characterise developed societies.

Men and women in the state of nature are seen as simple, free creatures at ease with themselves. Their limited wants are easily satisfiable, so that they are pictured as being content. Again, while men and women in the state of nature are self-regarding, they feel a compassion for the suffering of others. Human beings in the state of nature experience a relatively healthy form of self-love, *amour de soi*. This benign self-regard, though, is turned into a more sinister form of self-love, *amour propre*, in the development of more sophisticated societies. History, for Rousseau, is the story of corruption, whereby a healthy innocence gives way to a corrupt sophistication with the onset of farming and technology. A person's sense of self fragments as wants multiply in the context of a thoroughly social condition in which happiness and self-regard are measured comparatively. The transformation of a world of rough and rude equality into a sophisticated state of social inequality spells the ruin and fragmentation of mankind. A man becomes alien to himself.

The conundrum posed by social development is the context for Rousseau's *The Social Contract* and his *Emile*, an exploration of an ideal form of education, both written in 1762. *Emile* takes for granted the existing political conditions and outlines a form of education enabling the eponymous hero of the book to live well. It articulates a child-centred form of education whereby reason is progressively developed by its deployment in solving problems. At the same time, the child is sheltered from the dangers of easy acceptance of received ideas; he is educated so as to think for himself. None the less, his socialisation and development are structured carefully by his educator. Rousseau advocates a different form of education for women, one designed to refine their distinct sensibilities and prepare them for domestic tasks.

The Social Contract, Rousseau's major work of political philosophy, takes men as they are, and frames the logic of a form of political life which would enable men to be free and to resolve the problems of social development as they had been diagnosed in the *Discourses*. The terms of a legitimate and free form of political association, set out in *The Social Contract*, amount to the conditions of radical popular sovereignty. The natural independence of man in a state of nature is exchanged for the public freedom of citizenship. Rousseau envisages that in assuming membership of a legitimate political association, men will grant all authority to the state. As it is for Hobbes, sovereignty is an absolute in Rousseau's vision of political association. For Rousseau, however, citizens will participate in the ongoing process of making collective decisions. Rousseau restricts active citizenship to men on account of his conception of the non-rational nature of women.

Rousseau sees the making of collective decisions as conducive to the achievement of a moral form of public freedom. In obeying the state, men are to achieve freedom, because they obey disinterested moral rules of their own making. They are to exercise a general will and not to pursue their own selfish ends. For Rousseau, the remedy for the problems of social life is itself a thoroughly social one. Men are to abandon their natural self-love and independence for the achievement of the social freedom of morality whereby they participate in framing a collective moral world. From this perspective,

Rousseau imagines, freedom is not opposed to obedience to law, and he entertains the paradox that men might be forced to be free.

Rousseau's paradoxical formulation of the compatibility of freedom with social force has been criticised for its susceptibility to promote tyranny. The tyrannical tendencies of Rousseau's political thought are compounded by the role he envisages for a legislator whose advice the democratic legislature will follow and for the patriotism engendered by public religious ritual. None the less, Rousseau's clear separation of individual and group self-interest from the public, social good remains a compelling vision of political life. Likewise, his strictures against corporate interests and his espousal of a participative form of democracy continue to be relevant to democratic theory and practice.

See the discussion of Berlin's (1991) account of positive freedom in Chapter 6.

There is often a great deal of difference between the will of all and the general will; the latter considers only the common interest, while the former takes private interest into account, and is no more than a sum of particular wills: but take away from these same wills the pluses and minuses that cancel one another, and the general will remains as the sum of the differences.

If, when the people, being furnished with adequate information, held its deliberations, the citizens had no communications with one another, the grand total of the small differences would always give the general will, and the decision would always be good. But when intrigues arise, and partial associations are formed at the expense of great association, the will of each of these associations becomes general in relation to its members, while it remains particular in relation to the State: it may then be said that there are no longer as many votes as there are men, but only as many as there are associations. The differences become less numerous and give a less general result. Lastly, when one of these associations has to prevail over all the rest, the result is no longer a sum of small differences, but a single difference; in this case there is no longer a general will, and the opinion which prevails is purely particular.

(Rousseau 1973b: 185)

EXERCISE

1 Is there a common interest, distinct from all particular interests?
2 Why is Rousseau against the organisation of particular interest groups and associations? Are his fears about such interest groups plausible?
3 Can political decisions be guaranteed always to be good?

John Stuart Mill

John Stuart Mill (1806–73) was the son of James Mill, who was a friend of Bentham and a political theorist in his own right, who subscribed to the doctrine of utility. Mill's life and work were a complex struggle to think through the conditions of his own age, incorporating insights from a wide range of writers. Mill's most celebrated works of political thought, *On Liberty* (1982) and *Considerations on Representative Government* (1972) (written in 1859 and 1861 respectively), offer an incisive analysis of the character of politics and the most pressing needs facing the modern age. Mill's call for a dividing line between where governments can legitimately regulate individuals' lives and where individuals are to be left free to pursue their own self-chosen ends resonates in contemporary discussions of the state.

John Stuart Mill

THE CONTEXT OF J. S. MILL'S THOUGHT

The context of J. S. Mill's thought reflects a quite deliberate attempt on the part of his father, James Mill, to nurture a thoughtful, reflective child who would be useful to society. J. S. Mill's *Autobiography* (1964), published posthumously in 1873, is an eloquent testimony to his own reaction to his upbringing. Mill recalls a hothouse education whereby he was reading Greek at the age of 3, Plato's *Dialogues* at 10 and from an early age was working with his father at logic and political economy. J. S. Mill diagnoses a subsequent personal crisis as arising out of this precocious development of his reason, and which he was to overcome by turning to his underdeveloped emotional side and engaging with the Romantic poets. J. S. Mill did not reject the utilitarian code to which he subscribed from an early age, but he modified it, broadening its scope to take account of what he came to see as a complex many-sided world of experience.

J. S. Mill positively sought to assimilate a wide range of intellectual influences to enable him to understand a complex present, designating his mature standpoint 'practical eclecticism'. The early assimilation of political economists, notably Ricardo, and utilitarianism left permanent impressions on his thinking. He revised utilitarianism, however, to incorporate qualitative distinctions between types of pleasure, so that rational pleasures counted for more than bodily pleasures. He also allowed for the idea of progress so that he applied the principle of utility differentially to political societies at different stages of development.

His sensitivity to historical development was deepened by his reading of Comte and Carlyle. De Tocqueville's warnings about the dangers of conformity and repression in a 'modern age' of equality and von Humboldt's eloquent advocacy of individuality and individual freedom contributed to Mill's distinctive political standpoint, which emphasised the importance of cultivating individuality in an age of gathering social pressures upon the individual. From Coleridge he gained an understanding of the important role to be played by a rational elite who might trace pathways of enlightenment within society.

POLITICS AND SOCIETY

Mill's most celebrated work of political theory is *On Liberty*, which is a masterpiece in terms of its economical and elegant defence of the importance of individual liberty and his analysis of where the line between legitimate governmental regulation and individual liberty is to be drawn. Mill defends individual liberty on the grounds that social freedom is required by the principle of utility, taking man as a progressive being, because he holds that without the liberty to experiment in lifestyles, conduct and thought there would be no possibility of progress in human affairs. His portrayal of individuality, however, is sketched in such glowing colours that it would seem to possess a value which supersedes reckoning in terms of its outcomes. Against a backdrop of the gathering dangers of social conformity, Mill articulates the ideal of personal autonomy.

Mill also proposes an economical criterion for distinguishing when an individual's actions should be subject to regulation by the laws. He urges that an individual should be free to do whatsoever he or she wishes save when his or her actions harm others. The notion of harming another's interests is invoked to stipulate when conduct should be subject to legal constraint, for if an action harms another it is manifestly not simply the business of the individual concerned. In framing this criterion for the legitimacy of the exercise of coercion by the state, Mill trades upon a controversial distinction between self-regarding and other-regarding actions. Self-regarding actions are those private actions of an individual which do not concern others, and other-regarding actions are those which impinge on the interests of others. This distinction is a notoriously tricky one to draw. In important senses no man is an island and seemingly private matters, for instance concerning jokes one might relate and tastes one might indulge, help to create a social climate which affects others. None the less, Mill's concern to designate a certain area of one's life distinct from the purview of government is attractive in a times that has witnessed grotesque political infringements of personal liberty.

Mill's views on liberty are complemented by his views on democracy. In *Considerations on Representative Government*, Mill urges that a representative democracy is the best form of government. It promotes rationality and public-spiritedness by calling upon the electorate to consider public issues in a rational spirit. Mill favours widespread and active involvement in politics at many levels. In the context of nineteenth-century Britain, however, he does not advocate complete popular franchise. He recommends that the test of literacy should be administered as a determinant of the right to vote to ensure that the electorate is able to engage in rational consideration of issues. In addition, Mill stipulates that extra votes should be extended to the most rational sections of the electorate (graduates and property owners) to ensure that the many do not drown out the voices of the better-educated few. While Mill recognises representative democracy as the best form of government, he considers that it can be the mode of government only for a nation which has progressed to the point where its members are sufficiently educated to accept the responsibilities of citizenship. In the context of a society sufficiently developed to sustain representative democracy, Mill urges that women as well as men should have the vote. Indeed, Mill's work *The Subjection of Women* is a pioneering example of a feminist argument, in which women are presented as suffering from inequality in legal and political terms, and it is seen as wholly against the general utility for women to be so discriminated against. Women, like men, are seen by Mill as capable of rational behaviour; their inherent rationality, however, has not been nurtured by an appropriate education.

Like other tyrannies, the tyranny of the majority was at first, and is still vulgarly, held in dread, chiefly as operating through the acts of the public authorities. But reflecting persons perceived that when society is itself the tyrant – society collectively, over the separate individuals who compose it – its means of tyrannising are not restricted to the acts which it may do by the hands of its political functionaries. Society can and does exercise its own mandates: and if it issues wrong mandates instead of right, or any mandates at all in things in which it ought not to meddle, it practises a social tyranny more formidable than many kinds of political oppression, since, though not usually upheld by such extreme penalties, it leaves fewer means of escape, penetrating much more deeply into the details of life, and enslaving the soul itself. Protection therefore against the tyranny of the magistrate is not enough: there needs protection also against the prevailing opinion and feeling; against the tendency of society to impose, by other means than civil penalties, its own ideas and practices as rules of conduct on those who dissent from them; to fetter the development, and, if possible, prevent the formation, of any individuality not in harmony with its ways, and compel all characters to fashion themselves upon the model of its own.

(Mill 1982: 63)

EXERCISE

1   Why does Mill fear the tyranny of the majority?
2   In what ways can majority opinion assert itself?
3   Has the power of majority opinion decreased or increased since Mill's time?

Karl Marx

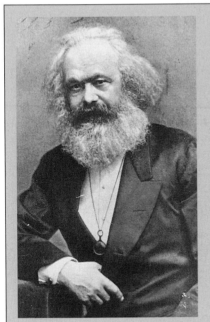

Karl Marx (1818–83) was born in Trier in the Rhineland and studied law and philosophy at the University of Berlin before moving to Paris in 1843 and subsequently settling in London. He became a revolutionary, committed to the cause of the proletariat and communism, combining philosophical analysis with economic criticism of capitalist society. He has exerted a massive influence on modern social and political theory and practice. Revolutions have been carried out in his name, states have been purported to be governed according to his principles and some of the most sophisticated theorists of the twentieth century, such as Adorno, Lukacs and Sartre, have self-consciously theorised in the Marxist tradition. Marx's most famous works include 'The Communist Manifesto' (1848) and *Capital* (vol. 1, 1867). Marx collaborated closely with Friedrich Engels. He relates politics to the structures of power within social and economic practices and offers a uniquely focused analysis and critique of the practices of work, which are generally overlooked in theories of politics.

Karl Marx

THE CONTEXT OF MARX'S THOUGHT

A useful shorthand formula to appreciate Marx's intellectual context is Lenin's celebrated notion that Marx combined German philosophy with English (Scots is a more apt depiction) economics and French politics. The German philosophical background imparts a holistic conceptual framework to his theorising in which rival positions are assimilated rather than merely negated. His detailed study of the classical political economists both promoted and reflected his close analysis of the economic system. French political thought and practice inspired the revolutionary impulse within his writings.

The specific context within which Marx operated at the outset of his intellectual career was the breakup of the Hegelian philosophical school. Hegel's philosophy had been balanced delicately between heaven and earth, the status quo and critique, and systemic determinism and openness. On his death the different sides of Hegelianism took wing. Right, or Old, Hegelians interpreted Hegelianism as supporting faith in Protestantism, maintaining an uncritical allegiance to an increasingly reactionary Prussian state and imagining that world history had ended, in the sense that there was no scope for further significant development. The Young, or Left, Hegelians looked at things differently. They saw the spirit of Hegelianism as a critical one in which existing political arrangements and forms of faith should be criticised. They did not see the present as the end of history but rather looked to the future and a reformed political life. Significantly, Feuerbach, of the Young Hegelians, turned his critical powers against Hegel's philosophy, and in his *Principles of the Philosophy of the Future* (1966) he condemned Hegel for reducing the status of man by making him the object of abstract Reason. For Feuerbach, man rather than God or Reason must be the subject of philosophy and social life. Feuerbach's humanism was an immediate inspiration for Marx's 'Economic and Philosophical Manuscripts' of 1844, in which Marx brilliantly theorised the conditions of modern capitalism as constituting the alienation of man from his own activity and creations.

Marx, like Feuerbach, was keen to break with Hegel, but his ties with Hegel were never severed entirely. He developed a more historical perspective on social and political life than Feuerbach, and in so doing explicitly followed Hegel in seeing man as essentially an historical being. In *The German Ideology* of 1845–6 Marx presents himself as a materialist in contrast to Young Hegelians like Bauer, but he also styles himself a materialist historian, breaking with an unhistorical essentialist humanism. Marx's materialist perspective was advanced by his study of political economy. The 'Economic and Philosophical Manuscripts' interrogated and criticised the assumptions of the political economists. In a similar fashion, Marx's *Grundrisse* (rough draft of *Capital*), and *Capital* (1979) itself (the first volume of which was published in 1867), worked with but critically examined the assumptions of the political economists.

Marx's writings reflect the exigencies of political circumstances and the demands of movements, as well as the impact of philosophical and economic theorising. Examination of workers' conditions confirmed Marx's appreciation of the importance of the world of work and the interests of civil society as opposed to the formal political world which Hegel saw as the crowning glory of social and political life. The most famous single work of Marx and Engels is 'The Communist Manifesto' of 1848, which in fact first appeared as a work written by the Communist League, a small political group of communists. It was published as a position statement for the group in the turbulent revolutionary atmosphere of 1848. Many of Marx's works respond similarly to specific circumstances and situations. For instance, Marx wrote 'The Civil War in France' on behalf of the International of Working Men so as to memorialise the Commune of 1870 as a symbolic triumph for the working class.

Much of the difficulty of coming to terms with Marx's thought is to bring together and evaluate an enormous body of writings which were inspired by a diversity of contexts and which expressed a variety of purposes. *Capital*, for instance, is a work of immense theoretical energy devoted to unmasking the laws of motion of the capitalist political economy. Its scope and density contrast with those of journalistic pieces occasioned by political events in the British Empire and in British domestic politics.

For accounts of the Hegelian continuities in Marx's early and late works, see G. K. Browning (1999) Hegel and the History of Political Philosophy, *London: Palgrave.*

MARX'S SOCIAL AND POLITICAL THEORY

In the 'Critique of Hegel's Philosophy of Right' (1843) Marx developed a sharp critique of Hegel's political philosophy. He criticised Hegel for supposing that the political activities of the state may be seen as superseding the private interests of civil society. For Marx, the private interests of bourgeois society are dominant, and the bureaucracy of the state, far from establishing a general, popular interest, distorts matters by operating in terms of its own separate interest. Marx advocated the overturning of bourgeois civil society and the establishment of a true democracy in which there would be popular control over social and economic activities. The radicalism of his critique of prevailing social and political life informs the 'Economic and Philosophical Manuscripts', where communism is seen as the radical antidote to the world of alienation set in motion by capitalist social relations.

Alienation is the key concept of this early critique of capitalist society. It is seen as being generated in the process of production, the crucial site of human interaction. Capitalist production is explained as setting human beings against the very process of production itself. Production, for Marx, is the sphere in which men and women can develop their humanity; human capacities can develop only by their use in productive activity, just as needs and powers increase only with the expansion of a productive system. But in a system of production where ownership is divorced from the act of production and objects are produced for profit in distant markets, those engaged in production neither flourish nor enhance their capacities. For Marx, workers under capitalism are alienated from the process of production, the objects they produce, their fellow human beings and their generic identity as creative beings who can produce freely and according to general, non-limited criteria. Marx's diagnosis of the alienation men and women suffer in the productive process and of the hegemony exercised by the owners of capital underpins his reading of the state which had been set forth in his 'Critique of Hegel's Philosophy of Right'. The state and politics are seen in relation to the power and alienation prevalent in the economic sphere. Politics is the set of public power relations which underpins and supports the dominance of private, class interests in the economic sphere.

In 'The Communist Manifesto' Marx and Engels set out a programmatic and propagandist account of history, society and politics which epitomises Marx's standpoint on power relations. Marx and Engels set out a theory of history in which changes in the sphere of production, and more particularly contradictions between the patterns of ownership and the forces of production, generate historical change. The capitalist mode of production is presented as obeying the general law of historical change; capitalist relations of production are held to have incubated a massive promotion of productive forces, but in so doing are shown to have dug their own grave. Capitalism, according to Marx, has produced a class of workers – the proletariat – which is a revolutionary force. The misery and the exploitation suffered by the proletariat are invoked to explain why the proletariat will break with prevailing social and economic conditions, and undertake a communist revolution after which the producers *en masse* will control society. The political dimension of this Marxist viewpoint is hammered home. Politics has hitherto reflected class interests, with the dominant class in production controlling the state. For Marx, the proletariat must take over the state to construct a communist society.

There are many questions which can be asked about Marx's theory of history and the state. The answers which have been offered are by no means definitive. In more particular writings on the state and on history, Marx qualifies the sweeping nature of the account of society and history given in 'The Communist Manifesto'. The state is seen at times as the site for complex wrangles between classes, and history is also seen as allowing for a variety of types of cause. The broad vision of Marxism, however, remains constant. The proletariat has a mission to destroy capitalism and usher in a new world of communism. Likewise, his early account of alienation informs the understanding in his later writings of the distortions of capitalist society. In *Capital* Marx gives a detailed account of how profit represents the surplus value exploited out of labour power, and of how capital is beset by inner contradictions exemplified in periodic crises and a declining rate of profit. Capitalism is portrayed as a decaying system to be replaced by the communal organisation and development of society, in which there will be no classes.

For the continuity of Marx's views on alienation, see Arthur (1986).

The history of all hitherto existing society is the history of class struggles. Freeman and slave, patrician and plebeian, lord and serf, guild-master and journeyman – in a word, oppressor and oppressed, stood in constant opposition to one another, carried on an uninterrupted, now hidden, now open fight, a fight that each time ended either in a revolutionary re-constitution of society at large or in the common ruin of the contending classes.

In the earlier epochs of history, we find almost everywhere a complicated arrangement of society into various orders, a manifold gradation of social rank. In ancient Rome we have patricians, knights, plebeians, slaves; in the Middle Ages, feudal lords, vassals, guild-masters, journeymen, apprentices, serfs; in almost all of these classes, again, subordinate gradations.

The modern bourgeois society that has sprouted from the ruins of feudal society has not done away with class antagonisms. It has but established new classes, new conditions of oppression, new forms of struggle in place of the old ones.

(Marx and Engels 1973a: 67–8)

EXERCISE

1 Express in your own words what Marx and Engels mean by class struggle.
2 How do Marx and Engels express the importance of history in their analysis?

The limits of Western political thought

Women and political thought

See the discussion of feminism in Chapter 8.

Gender is now considered to be an important aspect of politics, and it is relatively rare for contemporary theories of politics to ignore issues of gender. They are raised at all levels of political thinking. The British Labour Party has been exercised recently by the goal of promoting greater numbers of women MPs. Western institutions and practices are examined to ensure that they accord an equality of opportunity to women in relation to men. The order and conventions of family life have been challenged and changed. While only a minority of men and women would accept the radical feminist slogan that the personal is the political, questions of power and authority in relationships and families are now debated. Moreover, the 'patriarchal' bias of the law is the subject of contemporary debate. The treatment of domestic violence and the punishment of rapists are areas of the law which are seen as raising gender issues.

The contemporary impact of feminism has led political theorists to consider the issue of gender equality in an explicit way, which contrasts with the tradition of Western political philosophers. Hobbes and Locke, for example, assumed that the social contract is a device operated by men and they reserved political power for men without explicit justification of this restriction. Indeed, Pateman, a contemporary feminist, has observed that the gender inequalities entertained by Hobbes and Locke are at odds with the principle of equality they maintain explicitly (Pateman 1988).

This discrepancy is to be explained by the contextual influence of a patriarchal social order whose assumptions were accepted by the theorists. The

Carole Pateman (1940–) is one of the most celebrated living feminist theorists. She was born in Sussex, and after studying at the University of Oxford subsequently lectured in Sydney, Australia and California. Her best-known feminist text is *The Sexual Contract* (1988) in which she delivers a powerful critique of social contract theory and how contract functions in regard to women in a variety of its guises, including the marriage contract. Her first monograph *Participation and Democratic Theory* (1970) undertakes a powerful critique of realist and positivistic accounts of democracy and provides a forceful defence of radical, participative democracy. *The Disorder of Women: Democracy, Feminism and Political Theory* (1989) consists of essays that deal with democracy and gender equality.

Carole Pateman

distinct context of contemporary feminist historians of political thought allows for an interrogation of past Western political theory and practice which reveals the gender bias unthinkingly entertained by past theorists. Okin, for instance, has observed the limitations of past theorists by exploring how their texts and arguments might have been different if gender equality had been accepted. In this light, Rousseau's espousal of participatory democracy is seen to trade upon women undertaking time-consuming domestic tasks (Okin 1980).

The current sensitivity to the prevalence of gender inequalities also engenders a reassessment of past theorists who argued for sexual equality. Mill, for instance, has been seen as a feminist, but from the standpoint of late twentieth-century radical feminism his easy acceptance of differentiated life-styles for men and women points up the limits of his feminism. Again, Marx urged that men and women should be equal, but feminists today have criticised his failure to see gender as an irreducible category of social inequality.

The gender partiality of past theorists in the Western political tradition signals the contextual limits in which political thought takes place. Assumptions about gender are not universal; they reflect thought and practice at particular times and places. A feature of the tradition of Western political thought is that it has become increasingly sensitive to issues of gender. The correlation of changing patterns of thought to changing contexts of social and political life corroborates the standpoint of contextualist historians of political thought. It also illustrates the significance of the context of an historian of political thought, and the insights into questions of gender and political organisation generated by feminist rereadings of past male theorists attests to the significance of past political thought for today's political questions.

THINK POINT

Given the feminists' recognition of the political dimensions of practices and institutions previously not seen as political, do you think we should adopt a broader notion of what should count as political thinking and the history of political thought?

Islam

A relatively unexamined feature of most histories of political thought is their exclusively Western orientation, reflecting Western contexts of authors and markets, and assumptions of Western political and intellectual dominance. The assumptions arise out of the Western development of key features of the 'modern' world. The Western path to modernity, incorporating industrialisation, continuous technological development, assiduous promotion of market values and the ascendancy of secular political ideologies, has been followed by a range of non-Western nations, such as China, India, South Korea and post-colonial African regimes. The world today, however, is reverberating with the challenge of a distinct pattern of political thought, political Islam, which is non-Western in its provenance and in its general character.

Islam is the second largest religion in the world; it is growing rapidly and shapes the politics of Iran, Iraq, Pakistan and Algeria, determines the direction of their foreign policies as well as exerting an influence in the USA and a variety of other European, Asian and African nations. The anti-Western tenor of much of contemporary political Islam highlights the specifically Western character of the tradition of political thought in the West. While Islam is a religion, it differs from the Christianity of contemporary Western states by making holistic claims upon individuals which are to be achieved through political regulation.

All Muslims are fundamentalists in that they follow the words and doctrines of the Koran, but the distinguishing aspect of self-styled Islamic fundamentalists is that they see Islam as a dynamic force to shape all contours of political life. They wish to see a zealous religious spirit dominate and renew political life. Insofar as fundamentalist political Islam challenges the prevailing order and looks for a spiritual and practical rebirth, it necessarily challenges the prevailing order which has been shaped by Western dominance. Political Islam and its fundamentalist spirit challenges the liberal temper, global capitalism and its socialist critique. The anti-imperialist character of political Islam was seen at the beginnings of the revival of fundamentalist Islam in the aims of the Muslim Brotherhood which was set up in Egypt in 1928. The Muslim Brotherhood sought a revivified Islamic faith to break with neo-colonialism and chart a socio-economic course distinct from Western forms of socialism and capitalism. It urged the revival of non-Western traditionalist patterns of family and social life.

Fundamentalist political Islam made relatively little headway in the Arab world until the 1970s and the discrediting of neo-socialist Arab regimes due to their inability to defeat Israel and continued dependence on a Western economic order. In the aftermath of the successful Iranian revolution of 1979, the spiritual and political hegemony in Iran exercised by Ayatollah Khomeini provided a focus for the loyalties of political Islam. Iran became the centre of fundamentalist Shiite Islam. Shiite Muslims are distinguished from Sunni Muslims by their belief in the infallible Imam, who they claim possesses authority in an unbroken line of divinely inspired succession dating back to Mohammed himself. Political power in Iran became focused upon the Islamic Revolutionary Council dominated until his death in 1989 by the Imam, Ayatollah Khomeini. Draconian laws were introduced regulating all areas of social and political life. In stark contrast to the development of radical feminism in the West, the Iranian regime controlled how women should be dressed. The intransigent hostility of fundamentalist Islam to Western modes of political thinking was demonstrated in 1988 by Khomeini's issue of a *fatwa* (death sentence) against the Westernised author Salman Rushdie.

See Chapter 6 for a detailed analysis of the Rushdie case.

While the radicalism of the Iranian regime has been tempered by the passage of time, the destruction of the World Trade Center in September 2001 highlighted the enmity of radical Islamic fundamentalists for the West. Political Islam continues to perplex and frighten the West while challenging the assumptions and insularity of Western political thought. Distinctive Western political values such as individual autonomy, participative democracy, freedom of speech and gender equality appear less than universal in relation to Islamic support for traditional forms of moral and social behaviour. The challenge presented by a radically distinct political tradition has inspired some subtle contemporary modes of political thinking in the West which want to take account of cultural differences (Parekh 1990; I. Young 1990). Again, the problems and challenges presented by non-Western cultures contributed to the development of a postmodern rejection of Western rationalism and triumphalism (Lyotard 1984).

Conclusion

The Islamic challenge to the dominance of Western values in combination with a burgeoning sensitivity to cultural differences has inspired Western political thinkers to question the supposed universalism of Western political philosophy. But this critical reaction against the Western political tradition evident in postmodern thought, feminism and some strains of pluralistic liberalism does not mean that we can flourish without knowing that tradition. The tradition rests upon contingent contextual foundations, which explain textual silences entertaining patriarchy and which ensure that the work of political philosophy ever remains to be accomplished. None the less, our understanding of political liberty, rights, the relationship between work and politics, democracy and the necessity of the state is deepened by an awareness of the political thinking of philosophers such as Mill, Marx, Rousseau and Hobbes.

Chapter summary

- The character and methodology of the history of political thought.

- The standpoint of Skinner is examined and contrasted with a textual approach to the subject.

- The value of the history of political thought.

- Key political philosophers are examined, including Plato, Hobbes, Locke, Rousseau, J. S. Mill and Marx.

- The impact on the study of political thought of the express questioning of the notion of gender.

- Postmodern scepticism is addressed.

- Extracts with accompanying questions are set on each of the thinkers focused upon.

Key texts

The key texts are the classic texts of political philosophy. These texts come in a variety of editions, which reflects their ageless popularity. In this chapter the following were discussed: Plato, *The Republic*; Hobbes, *Leviathan*; J. S. Mill, *On Liberty*; K. Marx and F. Engels, 'The Communist Manifesto'; J. Locke, *Two Treatises of Government*; and J.-J. Rousseau, *The Social Contract*. The following classic political philosophers and texts should be added to the list: Aristotle, *The Politics*; Machiavelli, *The Prince*; G. Hegel, *The Philosophy of Right*. Other classic thinkers could be added. In the section on further reading particularly useful commentaries and general texts are cited.

Further reading

Ball, T. (1995) *Reappraising Political Theory*, Oxford: Oxford University Press. A lively book which engages in critical reflection on the nature of political theory and also suggests the fascination that can be exerted by the rethinking of interpretation of political philosophers.

Browning, G. K. (1999) *Hegel and the History of Political Philosophy*, London: Palgrave. A book that reviews Hegel's understanding of the history of political philosophy by relating Hegel's political thought to his predecessors and successors.

Hampsher-Monk, I. (1992) *A History of Modern Political Thought*, Oxford: Blackwell. An excellent, well-informed account of a number of classic political philosophers.

Lively, J. and Reeve, A. (1989) *Modern Political Theory*, London: Routledge. A selection of articles on classic political theorists put together with clear, straightforward introductions to those theorists.

Morrow, J. (1998) *History of Political Thought*, London: Macmillan. An interesting work that attempts a thematic study of the history of political thought by examining how topics such as the location and ends of political authority have been treated by theorists across time. This difficult enterprise is conducted with sensitivity to the way the meanings of terms change as the contexts in which they are theorised alter.

Oakeshott, M. (1962) *Rationalism in Politics and Other Essays*, London: Methuen. A very lively set of essays which add up to an elegant defence of a particular philosophical reading of politics which is at once entertaining and provocative.

Plamenatz, J. (1961) *Man and Society*, 2 vols, London: Longman. A lively review of the thought of classic political theorists in which the texts of past theorists are seen as speaking for themselves, to the extent that they can be understood and appraised by philosophical questioning without resorting overly to their historical contexts.

Pocock, J. (1972) *Politics, Language and Time*, London: Methuen. An interesting collection of essays on the history of political thought, which advocates a plausible line on contextualism.

Tully, J. (1988) *Meaning and Context – Quentin Skinner and his Critics*, Oxford: Polity Press. A collection of important essays by Skinner on the history of political thought, and some critical essays on Skinner's work by leading critics.

Williams, G. (1991) *Political Theory in Retrospect*, Aldershot/Vermont: Edward Elgar. A short guide to classic political philosophy. It is well written but very introductory, and the big problems of interpretation are not dealt with.

CONTENTS

Political ideologies Sets of political beliefs involving programmes of political action which draw on large-scale views about human nature and/or historical development.

Political Ideologies

Gary K. Browning

Introduction

In this chapter, political ideologies are examined. It begins by reviewing the nature of political ideology, considering the history of the term and significant theoretical accounts of its identity. Once a framework is established to understand the nature of political ideologies and to appreciate the contested character of their identity, the rest of the chapter is devoted to presenting short accounts of the most significant political ideologies. Evidently, in one chapter only a brief introduction to specific **political ideologies** can be given. Brevity, however, can be a virtue as well as a vice, and the object of this chapter is to enable students to have an overall view of political ideologies and of the leading political ideologies. This overview should help students see the wood for the trees, and subsequently they can consult some of the excellent detailed studies referred to during the chapter.

The nature of political ideologies

Ideology is a disputed concept; its meaning is not transparent. In the past many prominent theorists and commentators on ideology have cast doubt on the worth and integrity of the language of ideology. Many theorists warn against taking ideologists at face value. Sophisticated theorists offer delicate theories to undermine the very possibility of making the universal claims about politics promoted by classical ideologists, and in the bruising business of everyday political rhetoric, ideology is seen as being a political recipe cooked up by fanatics of the left and right.

The word 'ideology' first came to prominence in the work of Antoine Destutt de Tracy, a figure of the French Revolution and Napoleonic France.

Antoine Destutt de Tracy (1754–1836) came to prominence in the aftermath of the French Revolution. He reflected upon ideas and their relationship to the actual world, and he is credited with coining the term 'ideology'. He was one of a group of philosophers whom the revolutionary Convention had put in charge of the Institut de France with the task of spreading Enlightenment ideas. In his *Elements d'Ideologie* (1801–15) he proposed a new science of ideas, ideology, that he took to be a positive science of ideas that related ideas to the facts of experience.

Antoine Destutt de Tracy

He shared the optimistic attitude of the Enlightenment and thought that life would be improved if we could become clear about ideas and reality. Ideology, for him, represented the scientific approach to ideas whereby their links to real needs could be made plain. His optimistic faith in ideas soon ran counter to the practical needs of Napoleon, who castigated the impracticalities pedalled by ideologists. The negative estimate of ideology and ideologists has been common since Napoleon's time.

Marx and Engels are perhaps the most famous of all theorists of ideology, and they were resolute in their deprecation of the status of ideology. For Marx and Engels, in *The German Ideology*, ideology represents a distortion of the relationships forged in the productive process, and an account of history which took seriously the pronouncements of ideology would be both abstract and misleading. Ideological positions function as smokescreens for material interests; behind pious prayers, legal codes and moralising sermons, tangible benefits to groups or classes are held to lie (Marx and Engels 1973b).

Likewise, for the modern conservative theorist Minogue, ideological language is a suspicious form of currency, and the irony here is that Minogue sees Marx and Engels as prime exponents of the dark arts of ideological manipulation (Minogue 1985). Minogue holds that ideology essentially represents the deployment of abstract theorising to the complex world of concrete political action, and that this process is inevitably one in which there is alienation from the practical world in which human beings are at home. For Minogue ideology is a dangerous fantasy, an escape from the realities of practical life, in which concrete safeguards of human freedom and political action are set aside for the pursuit of imaginary utopias. For Marx and Engels ideology is the distorted world where real class interests are dressed up as norms and laws for societies where the majority has suffered hitherto from privileges afforded to ruling classes.

The problem with taking the resolutely negative stance on political ideology exemplified above is that the very language of ideological negation can itself be seen as ideological. Both Marx and Engels and Minogue are concerned to warn their audiences against styles of political argument which they stigmatise as ideological. Marx and Engels are opposed to injunctions to moral, religious and legal norms within societies they diagnose as harbouring structural inequalities of power. Minogue wants to persuade readers to accept a limited style of politics which takes much of contemporary political life as given; he eschews appeals to principle to justify radical change. Their respective standpoints, though, can be seen as ideological in that they are canvassing the acceptability of general ideas about politics. Marx and Engels argue against structural material inequalities of power, and Minogue argues for the rule of law and a limited style of politics. Their arguments are classic statements of ideology.

Indeed, in recent years there has been a growing tendency among academic commentators on ideology to speak of political ideology in broad terms that encompass a wide variety of styles of thought. The tendency has been to see political ideologies as representing frameworks of thought about politics in which large-scale ideas about human beings and society support more specific ideas about politics that constitute the basis for considered political action. Eatwell's introductory chapter to the book *Contemporary Political Ideologies* (Eatwell and Wright 1993) exemplifies this trend. He identifies ideologies as involving specific programmes of political action supported by general beliefs about human nature, the process of history and social and political arrangements.

The gathering trend of seeing political ideologies in a non-pejorative way as standing for sets of ideas about politics in which specific proposals are linked to general beliefs about the human condition does not dissolve questions about the legitimacy of ideological language. While political ideologies undoubtedly represent sets of beliefs of this kind, the character and viability of such ideas may still be questioned. Insofar as ideologists are in the business of framing specific proposals they are necessarily in the game of making value judgements. The criteria for deciding between values are notoriously indeterminate.

Key text: R. Eatwell and A. Wright (1993) *Contemporary Political Ideologies*, London: Pinter.

▌THINK POINT

Ideologies bring large-scale sets of beliefs to bear upon the world of politics. We cannot live without these ideas, but we cannot decide between them. Consider these beliefs:

- 'From each according to his ability to each according to his need';

- 'I wouldn't sacrifice any part of my personal freedom';

- 'National unity comes before all other values'.

In politics there is no clear, uncontroversial way of deciding on the right thing to do. A supporter of the free market, like von Hayek or Thatcher, might see the market as promoting individual freedom and observe the propensity of planning and intervention to lead to coercion and muddle, but a committed supporter of government intervention to supply a just distribution of welfare sees the logic and reasons underlying a different set of values. Just as there is no knockdown way of establishing the cogency of political values, so there is no easy way of disproving political values to which one is opposed. The fascist celebration of aggressive nationalism and elitism might repulse those who are committed to equality between people and nations, but there can be no easy discursive dismissal of the value of exulting a nation and an elite.

Political ideology and history

Political ideologies, then, are sets of belief about politics incorporating specific proposals and general ideas about human beings. Political ideologists are necessarily involved in the business of making value judgements and supporting these values by argument in a practical world where their proposals about what to do are meant to be taken seriously. The involvement of political ideologies with the world of practice means that they are involved in a world of change. A condition of practical life is that it involves change. Experience is always present experience but it is a present which is constantly changing into the past. This link between political ideologies and a world of change means that political ideologies do not stand still.

Political ideologists are involved in the enterprise of persuading people of the soundness of their political ideas in a changing political scene. This context of ideological activity explains why political ideologies change over time. Circumstances change with the passage of time, and proposals and ideas canvassed at one time seem inappropriate at another. Practical circumstances also change from place to place, and so ideological views display a local variety. All of the above means that the identity of a political ideology is somewhat problematic for those who like to keep things neat and timelessly tidy. A political ideology like liberalism is not one unchanging essential thing. Mill, in his *On Liberty* (1859), was concerned to carve out an area of private life preserved from state interference, whereas liberals of a succeeding generation began to see the need for the government to intervene, as their most pressing concern, in areas of life traditionally designated as private.

Left and Right

THINK POINT

- Consider a range of national newspapers and place them on a political scale of Left to Right.

- Consider the following politicians and place them on a political scale of Left to Right: Nelson Mandela, Tony Blair, George Bush, Gerry Adams.

A changing political landscape and a corresponding ideological innovation lend spice to the language of ideology. Terms like renegade, loyalist, traditionalist, old guard and new guard can spin in the ideological air. Tony Blair can explicitly call for a reappraisal of socialism and for a reorientation of the Labour Party, but the world of political ideology is constantly undergoing reappraisal. This can be seen by the chequered history of those arch ideological labels 'Left' and 'Right'. In the nineteenth century the word 'Left' stood, among other things, for support for the removal of entrenched privileges and the freeing up of property. The free market was a goal for those who called themselves the Left. By the end of the nineteenth century freedom of property was seen by the Left as something entrenching inequality, which needed to be rectified by the state. Indeed, attitudes to the state underwent change. In the eighteenth and early nineteenth centuries the Left saw the state as entrenching privilege and as inclined to be repressive, but by the end of the nineteenth century many on the Left were coming to see the state as an instrument of freedom, as Eatwell has observed (Eatwell and O'Sullivan 1989).

Lukes, in the extract below, defines the Left in such a way as to allow for this omnipresent factor of ideological change.

The Left in short denotes a tradition and a project born of Enlightenment and expressed in the Principles of 1789; to fulfil the promises implicit in these by progressively reinterpreting what they consisted in, and moving from the civil to the political to the economic, social and cultural spheres, through political means, by mobilising support and winning power. Often, too often, it has been abandoned or betrayed, by those claiming to pursue it. What I here seek to identify is an ideal-typical Left, the essential elements by virtue of which abandonment and betrayal can be identified as such.

It is a project which has been identified in various ways – in the language of rights, as a story of expanding citizenship or justice or democracy, or as a continuing struggle against exploitation and oppression, as it was by Karl Kautsky when he wrote that the goal of socialism was the 'abolition of every kind of exploitation and oppression be it directed against a class, a party, a sex or a race.' The Left we may say is committed to the progressive rectification of inequalities that those on the Right see as sacred, inviolable, natural or inevitable. It seeks to put things right: to remedy all disadvantages that are naturally or socially caused, as far as is possible and reasonable, so that all may have equal life chances.

(Lukes 1992: 10; reprinted by permission of Steven Lukes)

Liberalism

Capitalism An economic system in which the means of production for the most part lie in private hands, and goods and services are bought and sold according to prices determined by a market in which the aim of producers and providers is to make a profit.

A good case can be made for seeing liberalism as the dominant ideology in modern Western states. Indeed, Fukuyama has suggested in his recent work that the story of modern Western history can and must be told as one which recognises the triumph of Western liberal **capitalist** regimes (Fukuyama 1992).

The birth and growth of liberalism certainly track the rise of Western powers to industrial, technological and global eminence. Liberalism, like all ideologies, however, has shown different faces of itself at different times and in different places. President Johnson's 'liberal' determination, in the USA of the 1960s, to achieve the Great Society whereby the state would ensure civil rights and social welfare throughout the nation contrasts with the concern to establish individual autonomy and to construe the social good as arising out of the pursuit of self-interest which characterises Adam Smith's (1976) 'liberal' vision of social and political life.

Francis Fukuyama

Francis Fukuyama (1952–) was born in Chicago, USA, and worked for the US State Department and for the Rand Corporation. He became famous for interpreting the collapse of Soviet communism in the light of a general reading of historical development. He published his ideas in an article 'The End of History' and then in a book entitled *The End of History and the Last Man* (1992). In these works, he urges that there is an overall directionality to history and that capitalism and liberal democracy represent indefeasible rational solutions to the problems of social interaction. His book *Trust* (1996) relates economic development to the cultural resources or capital of a nation.

The very success of liberalism across time and space renders difficult the job of summarising its character in a crisp and manageable way. Liberals themselves have sought to characterise it in generally laudatory ways as conducive to the overall happiness and as promoting the independence and progress of men and, latterly, women. Marx and Marxists, on the other hand, have sought to identify the liberal concern to celebrate individuality as a way of diverting attention from the social bases of power. But protagonists and antagonists of liberalism tend to agree that liberalism stands for the organisation of a society which allows for and promotes individual freedom and development. New Deal American liberals and early twentieth-century British liberals may argue for significant state intervention. This intervention, though, is characteristically portrayed as aiding individual development; the individual is never considered to be fulfilled by the submerging of his or her individuality in a higher collective purpose. The liberal emphasis on individuality goes hand in hand with the notion that individuals are pre-eminently rational. Individuals are considered to be of the highest value, and their value is seen as being displayed in their rational capacities to order and shape their own lives. The rationality of individuals is also held to make a society allowing a maximum of freedom to individuals an efficient one. Liberalism, then, is distinguished by its concern to promote a society in which rational individuals can flourish. Individual liberal ideologists, however, depict this form of society in different ways and favour differing sets of arrangements.

A resounding statement of liberalism's concern to promote and safeguard individuality is given in J. S. Mill's classic account *On Liberty*. It is worth reflecting upon some of Mill's words to appreciate how individual autonomy has been seen to be of the utmost importance.

> The object of this essay is to assert one very simple principle, as entitled to govern absolutely the dealings of society with the individual in the way of compulsion and control, whether the means used be physical force in the form of legal penalties, or the moral coercion of public opinion. That principle is, that the sole end for which mankind are warranted individually or collectively, in interfering with the liberty of action of any of their number is self-protection. That the only purpose for which power can be rightfully exercised over any member of a civilised community, against his will, is to prevent harm to others. . . . The only part of the conduct of anyone, for which he is amenable to society, is that which concerns others. In the part which merely concerns himself, his independence is of right, absolute. Over himself, his own body and mind, the individual is sovereign.
>
> (Mill 1982: 68–9)

EXERCISE

1 Consider how Mill is seeking to promote individual autonomy.
2 At the same time consider what criticisms could be laid against this liberal emphasis upon the individual.

The origins of liberalism

To look for origins is in a sense to look for what cannot be found, since in history all events are connected to preceding and succeeding events. To single out occurrences as causal conditions or originary is to mislead by abstracting from an ongoing stream of events. None the less, to shed light on a set of events or phenomena it is useful to focus upon a set of changes which can be shown to be important in shaping the identity in question. A significant set of events which are important to an understanding of how liberalism developed are those changes which reflect the demise of the feudal world and the traditional authority of the Catholic Church, the divine right of kings and lordship of feudal barons. The centralisation of monarchical authority, the Reformation and the development of a freer market in goods and labour set the conditions for the flourishing of a liberal society.

The lineaments of a liberal view of government and society may be seen in outline in the thought of Thomas Hobbes, whose great work the *Leviathan* was published in 1651 (Hobbes 1968). While Hobbes deflected to no one in his support for unqualified, absolutist rule, he none the less derived political authority naturalistically from the nature and motivations of individuals. The basis of authority was seen to reside in the needs of individuals to find protection so that their lives could be safeguarded; it was not seen as a privilege dispensed by a divine mandate to a traditional governing class. John Locke, a seventeenth-century philosopher and theorist of politics, may be seen as more clearly preparing the way for distinctively liberal ideas. In his *Two Treatises of Government*, published in 1689, he saw political authority as emerging as the result of a contract between individuals who entrust a government with authority to protect their natural rights (Locke 1963). This government, for Locke, should be representative of the individuals contracting to form a political state. Locke's concern to protect individual rights, his derivation of political authority from the decisions of individuals and his granting individuals ongoing representation all point to a liberal focus upon individuals and their autonomy. In contrast to many subsequent liberals, however, he does not spell out that all individuals should be involved in the process of government. The political rights of women do not receive consideration.

See the discussion of Hobbes in Chapter 7, pp. 229–32.

See the discussion of Locke in Chapter 7, pp. 232–5.

In the eighteenth century the word 'liberalism' came into common usage; its precise point of origin has been traced to Spain during the Napoleonic Wars. Adam Smith, the famous Scottish philosopher, emphasised the importance of a free market for ensuring efficient and effective economic behaviour.

This insight into the potentially beneficial effects of the spontaneous, rationally self-interested behaviour of individuals has figured subsequently as

Adam Smith (1723–90) was Professor of Logic and Moral Philosophy at Glasgow University and subsequently became tutor to the Duke of Buccleuch. Smith is generally taken to be the founding father of modern economics.
Certainly his book *The Wealth of Nations* (1776) is a pioneering work that aims to explain the functioning of the economy in systematic terms. Smith was a philosopher as well as an economist and his *Theory of Moral Sentiments* (1759) remains a classic work that relates ethics to human sympathy and interests.

Adam Smith

an important dimension of liberal thought. It lies behind a liberal notion of the minimal state, in which the job of government is seen as simply upholding a framework of law and order so that individuals can undertake their activities.

Jeremy Bentham, at the turn of the nineteenth century, provided a specific, and influential, ideological endorsement of liberalism. He justified a state of affairs where as much freedom as possible was granted to individuals by arguing that this would promote the general happiness. Individuality and personal autonomy were valued for the beneficial social consequences they were seen as promoting, not because they were seen as valuable in themselves. Bentham's philosophy and defence of liberalism were modified by J. S. Mill, whose classic defence of a liberal society is set out in *On Liberty* (1859). This work is a hymn of praise for an open society in which freedom is granted to individuals to make up their own minds and forge their own lifestyles. Individuals, it is argued, should be released from undue interference by governments and from the weight of overbearing public opinion. While Mill justifies his concern for individual liberty in utilitarian terms which echo Bentham, he takes his standard of utility to be one which recognises man as a progressive being, and in his praise of individuality he values autonomy as being of intrinsic worth (Mill 1982).

See the discussion of J. S. Mill in Chapter 7, pp. 239–41.

Jeremy Bentham

Jeremy Bentham (1748–1832) is a celebrated philosopher, legal theorist and political reformer who was the founder of the utilitarian movement. His works include *Fragments on Government* (1748) and *Principles of Morals and Legislation* (1789). His theory of utility purports to provide a clear and overriding criterion to appraise human affairs. Utility judges policies or actions in terms of their propensity to maximise general happiness. The creed of utilitarianism was the inspiration of the Philosophical Radicals and was invoked by them to promote legal and social reform.

By the end of the nineteenth century, a liberal faith in a *laissez-faire* society where there was to be minimal governmental interference in the lives of individuals was shaken. Many liberals in Britain by this time were advocating a more positive role for the state. The state was seen as having a more extensive role in eliminating social evils, such as poverty, unemployment, sickness and ignorance, which were diagnosed as preventing individuals from becoming free. A key theorist who can be seen as developing the ideological basis of this **new liberalism** is T. H. Green, who saw the pursuit of the common good as

New liberalism Refers to a strand of thinking which rejected the negative concept of liberty and saw state intervention as expanding liberty in areas like factory legislation.

an individual duty and as something which was conducive to freedom. Likewise, the French solidarist thinkers, notably Durkheim, emphasised the state's role in providing social conditions in which freedom could flourish.

Liberalism in the twentieth century

By the mid-twentieth century a vigorous tradition of interventionist liberalism had developed. Keynes and Beveridge were liberal architects of the welfare state in Britain. They were ideologists of the ideas of indicative economic planning and the provision of comprehensive welfare measures to ensure individuals have a secure platform on which to build their freedom. There continued to be advocates of a minimal state among liberal theorists, however, notably von Hayek, the Austrian economist and social theorist. He saw the market as the sole way of coordinating human decisions and actions on a social basis which would secure efficiency and freedom. His brand of liberalism, exemplified in *The Constitution of Liberty* (von Hayek 1960), became fashionable again in the late twentieth century in the wake of misgivings about the effectiveness of Keynesian economic planning and the costs of welfare.

John Maynard Keynes (1883–1946) was an economist at Cambridge University who also worked at the UK Treasury. He is credited with being the author of post-Second World War economic policy in the UK and the Western world. He certainly influenced UK policy and transnational economic policy-making. His most famous book *The General Theory of Employment, Interest and Money* (1936) provided the theoretical basis for the adoption of indicative planning so as to counteract market fluctuations.

John Maynard Keynes

Nozick, in *Anarchy, State and Utopia* (1974), voiced an articulate vision of a minimal state which was attractive to Reaganite America. His liberalism was self-consciously set out against the more interventionist liberalism of Rawls, whose *A Theory of Justice* (1971) had received much attention and praise among academic political theorists. Central to the vision of both Rawls and Nozick, and of many contemporary liberal ideologists, is the notion of the neutrality of liberalism. There is a contemporary tendency to see liberalism as justifiable because of its refusal to take sides in the disputed question of what counts as a good life; it is seen as allowing individuals to make up their own minds. It

See the discussion of justice in Chapter 6, pp. 212ff.

See the comparative discussion of Rawls and Nozick on justice in Chapter 6.

remains to be seen whether this defence of liberalism will be strong enough to resist other ideological pressures; there may be a need to justify personal autonomy as a substantive good.

THINK POINT

■ Consider what you take to be the major styles of liberal argument.

■ What do you take to be the strongest appeal of liberal arguments?

Conservatism

The nature of conservatism

To talk of conservatism as an ideology is already to enter into dispute with noted conservative theorists. Gilmour, in *Inside Right*, has urged that conservatism is not a theoretical ideology but a practical attitude which is sceptical of full-blown ideological theories (Gilmour 1978). Oakeshott is a distinguished conservative philosopher who, likewise, has seen the essence of conservatism to reside in its scepticism about the power of ideas, and hence repudiated an ideological label for conservatism (Oakeshott 1962).

Michael Oakeshott (1901–90) was a distinguished Professor of Political Science at the London School of Economics and Political Science between 1951 and 1968. Among his most influential books are *Rationalism in Politics and Other Essays* (1962) and *On Human Conduct* (1975). He developed and practised a sceptical version of conservatism that downplayed the potency of abstract ideas and emphasised the significance of tradition and history in the development of politics and human activities.

Michael Oakeshott

While there is some basis for this conservative disavowal of ideology, conservatives since the French Revolution have been engaged in defending the established order by appealing to general arguments. Indeed, both Gilmour and Oakeshott may be characterised as being involved in this kind of activity.

Academics, in characterising the nature of conservatism, have often seen its essential character as residing in its recognition of the political significance of human beings' imperfection. Both Lord Quinton and O'Sullivan, in their studies on conservatism, have seen a concern with imperfection as being of moment to conservatives (O'Sullivan 1976; Quinton 1978). It is certainly true, the evident differences between expressions of conservatism notwithstanding, that conservatives are generally keen to decry utopianism or even reformist activity in the name of a practical respect for the inevitable imperfections of human beings. Oakeshott's delicate but sophisticated brand of conservatism is designed to respect the distinctions between theory and practice. For Oakeshott (1962), to look for guidance from an abstract political doctrine is akin to begin cooking armed only with a recipe. The practical activity of cooking demands practical know-how, just as the very practical business of politics demands skills which cannot be translated into an abstract perfectionist theory. The link between a respect for human imperfection and a distrust of abstract political doctrines had been observed in Burke's famous conservative broadside against the French Revolution.

Edmund Burke (1729–97) was born in Dublin, but made his reputation in England where he became a prominent Whig politician. Burke's reputation as a conservative ideologist rests upon his *Reflections on the Revolution in France* (1790), in which he criticised the actions of the revolutionary government in France and developed a general argument against revolutionary politics. Burke was particularly severe in criticising the use of abstract formulas in politics. He was opposed to the notion that abstractly conceived 'natural' rights could be applied to all nations irrespective of their distinctive national political cultures.

Edmund Burke

Conservatism, then, may be seen as an ideology which views human imperfections as laying down limits to political activity, though it must be admitted that there are some conservatives of a liberal persuasion, such as the British Conservatives Peel and Heath, and indeed Thatcher, who are prepared to see politics as a rational activity insofar as it is designed to maximise human freedom. There are also critics of conservatism on the left, from Paine and Marx to Habermas and Rawls, who claim that conservative pessimism provides a cover for acquiescence to fundamentally unfair arrangements benefiting a privileged few.

The nature of man is intricate; the objects of society are of the greatest possible complexity; and therefore no simple disposition or direction of power can be suitable either to man's nature, or to the quality of his affairs. When I hear the simplicity of contrivance aimed at and boasted of in any new political constitutions, I am at no loss to decide that the artificers are grossly ignorant of their trade, or totally negligent of their duty. The simple governments are fundamentally defective to say no worse of them. If you were to contemplate society in but one point of view, all these simple modes of polity are infinitely captivating. In effect each would answer its single end much more perfectly than the more complex is able to attain all its complex purposes. But it is better that the whole should be imperfectly and anomalously answered, than that while some parts are provided for with great exactness, others might be totally neglected, or perhaps materially injured, by the over-care of a favourite member.

(Burke 1982: 150)

EXERCISE

What does Burke consider to be the defects of 'simple' political constitutions which lay down regulations on a reasoned view of human nature?

Styles of conservatism

Academic commentators on conservatism are united in recognising a number of distinct styles of conservatism. Conservative theorists display distinctive styles in different countries. German conservatives have often adopted a philosophically nuanced form of conservatism which displays a metaphysical and often romantic character. Hegel may be seen as a conservative of this type, constructing an imposing edifice of theory, charting a criss-crossing set of interdependencies between man and nature, and man and man, to point up the need to respect the actual achievements of political life. In France there has been a vigorous tradition of reactionary, religious conservatism such as the ideological formulation offered by de Maistre (1965). The conservative reliance on a notion of human imperfection can lend itself to a religious underpinning. After all, the Bible sees human imperfection in Adam's fall from grace. Religious conservatism is evidenced in the remarkable success of postwar continental Christian democracy – though it must be acknowledged that Christian democracy draws on non-conservative ideologies. This religious conservatism combines a Christian recognition of the limits of human political activity with a Christian-inspired social doctrine which sees a need for the political provision of welfare.

British conservatism reveals a range of different styles. Indeed, a sharp line could be drawn between liberal and one-nation traditions of British conservatism. At the beginning of the nineteenth century paternalistic Tories like Oastler and Sadler opposed the prevailing harsh conditions in factories and recognised the duty of the social elite to care for the poor and unfortunate. This benevolent and nostalgic conservatism was invoked in mid-nineteenth-century England in the ideas of the Young England Group, whose most famous member was Disraeli. Disraeli himself, when in office (1874–80), instituted a whole series of social reforms which testified to his belief in a one-nation conservatism, in which the nation would be united behind a benevolent hierarchy catering for the interests of all. This strand of interventionist conservatism may be seen in the policies of Chamberlain and Baldwin in the interwar years. While their foreign policy of appeasement has been criticised, one of the reasons they were adept at gaining votes within a democratic franchise was that their conservatism appealed to all strands of society. The state assumed new responsibilities in their governments; for instance, new national corporations were set up. Macmillan, a conservative critic of governmental economic policies in the interwar period, called for a new middle way in which governments would intervene to ensure full employment and social justice, thereby anticipating the postwar establishment of planning and an extensive welfare state. Postwar Conservative governments accepted the Keynesian vision of an economic world supervised by government to ensure efficiency and harmony. The full-blown welfare state set up by the postwar Labour government was accepted by these governments.

The one-nation tradition of British conservatism has, however, coexisted with a liberal tradition of conservatism. Peel, refashioning conservatism in the 1830s, accepted the need to reform to appeal to the emerging middle classes. He sought to free markets and rationalise administration, and hence adopted a different standpoint from more interventionist Tories. This liberal dimension of conservatism was given a further edge by the rise of the Labour Party and gathering fears of collectivism at the turn of the nineteenth century. Mallock railed against such dangers in his espousal of limited government. In recent times Powell and Thatcher were eloquent protagonists of a libertarian form of conservatism. Indeed, Thatcher helped set an agenda of New Right belief in minimal government and free markets throughout the world. Her success has perhaps been problematic for the British Conservative Party, as Tony Blair and a revamped British Labour Party accepted much of Thatcherism, and subsequent Tory leaders have found it difficult to develop a new, distinctive style of conservatism.

THINK POINT

Recall the forms of conservatism referred to in the above discussion. Can you distinguish additional types? Do the various styles of conservatism have very much in common?

The success of conservatism

The electoral success of conservative parties in an age of democracy is in many ways remarkable and testifies to the resourcefulness of conservatism as an ideology. If the French Revolution ushered in the world of ideology, it seemed at the same time to spell the ruin of the *ancien régime* and conservatism. Burke's (1982) ideological *tour de force* in composing a powerful rhetorical counterblast to the forces of change, however, signalled that conservative ideologists were by no means without resources in responding to the challenge of presenting their ideas to a popular audience. Burke's defence of a practical and limited form of politics and his denunciation of the extravagances of radicalism represent styles of argument which have continued to be significant features of conservative ideology.

The secret of conservative electoral success in Europe and the USA in the nineteenth and twentieth centuries resided in the adaptability of conservative parties and conservative ideology. Conservatives have defended a conception of the state that endows it with broad and varied role to play in uniting the nation and they have at times sought to popularise themselves by espousing the cause of freedom of the individual in which a very limited role is assigned the state. Again, conservatives have invoked religion, nationalism and authoritarianism to augment their arguments and popularity. Conservative adaptability and realism have ensured that conservatism's appeal remains viable in an age of mass democracy.

Socialism

Forms of socialism

Socialism as a doctrine was first explicitly referred to in a journal of the Owenite movement in Britain in 1827. Its roots, however, have been traced back a long way. Indeed, Gray has used the title *The Socialist Tradition From Moses to Lenin* (A. Gray 1968). The roots of socialism have often been seen as extending deep into the past because its emphasis upon cooperation, fairness and equality has long had a missionary appeal. However, its emergence in the direct aftermath of the Industrial Revolution should not be forgotten. It applied traditional egalitarian moral principles to the set of problems and injustices diagnosed as bedevilling the industrial world of the nineteenth century.

The Industrial Revolution was seen to have changed society dramatically, opening up new possibilities of wealth but imposing new disciplines and hardships upon the labouring population. The aim of socialism from the early days of the nineteenth century was to refashion industrial society so as to organise industry more rationally and distribute its wealth more fairly. Socialism's spirit of collectivism emerged out of its critique of a situation in which power and wealth were in the hands of relatively few people.

Socialism, however, has been defined in different ways at different times. Perhaps the most serious division in socialism has been between Marxist revolutionary parties and social democratic parties who eschew the use of force. Revolutionary Marxist parties such as the Bolshevik Party in Russia have seen force as a vital means of breaking with the past. They have also developed tightly organised parties committed to breaking with capitalism and all bourgeois political forms. Social democratic parties, on the other hand, have tended to seek an evolutionary development whereby capitalism gradually changes into socialism. Indeed, the post-Second World War German Social Democratic Party announced its acceptance of the capitalist economy in its Bad Godesburg programme and the British Labour Party has recently formalised its acceptance of capitalism. Reformist social democratic parties have been concerned to maintain freedom and establish interventionist measures to secure greater fairness within a basically capitalist framework.

In recent years the ideological condition of socialism has been somewhat uncertain. The rousing days of the New Left in Western countries in the 1960s, the prevalence of Keynesian economic orthodoxy and social democratic governments in Western European countries and the sheer presence of Soviet-style socialist regimes in Eastern Europe had combined to make socialism perhaps the dominant ideology in the first three decades after the Second World War. However, the combination of unemployment and inflation in the 1970s cast doubt over social democratic techniques of economic management and the fall of the Soviet Empire seemed to confirm the bankruptcy of Soviet-style socialism. The event which precipitated the most doubts in socialist heads is perhaps the fall of the Soviet Union. Economic planning has been undermined by the perceived disaster of the Soviet economy. Socialists of all persuasions are now still busy thinking through what economic measures might be able to deliver the promised land of economic efficiency, justice and fairness.

The extract below outlines the economic background to the fall of the Soviet state and President Gorbachev's attempts at reforming the system.

The Rolling Economic Disaster

It was the First World War which precipitated the collapse of tsardom in 1917. In 1991, it was the union treaty which brought about President Gorbachev's fall. In both cases it was economic crisis that created the conditions for a coup. The real surprise is that Mr. Gorbachev has been able to survive for so long in the face of an economy which has been collapsing day by day and week by week. Throughout history autocratic regimes have always been at their most vulnerable when they have offered a semblance of political liberalisation but have been unable to deliver higher living standards.

That – despite all the power-broking on the international stage – has been the reality behind the Gorbachev mask. The glasnost process was supposed to march hand-in-hand with perestroika, a fundamental restructuring of the economy. . . . History will probably show that he failed, not for being too radical but for not being radical enough. . . .

continued

continued

The background to the Gorbachev experiment was the growing realization within the political hierarchy that the country's enormous natural resources were being squandered by the inefficiencies of a centrally-planned system which was established by Stalin in the late 1920s and early 1930s and gradually ossified in the decades after the Second World War.

By the early 1980s it was obvious that the Soviet Union was failing to make the transition from a fairly primitive stage of economic development based on exports of primary products into a modern Western-based economic system.

(Larry Elliott, reprinted by permission of the *Guardian*, 20 August 1991)

EXERCISE

1 What criticisms does the above extract make of the Soviet Union and economic planning and President Gorbachev's attempts at reform?
2 Do you consider these criticisms undermine the case for socialism?

Socialism and its development

Key influences on the development of socialism include the Industrial Revolution and the rise of capitalism; the simultaneous increase in wealth and productive power and the misery of a newly cohesive working people gave inspiration to a socialist creed demanding a reordering of society to make it fairer. At the same time socialists, from the outset, saw a future socialist society as a more rational one than hitherto existing societies. In their rationalist visions of the future, socialists shared an Enlightenment optimism about the possibilities of reordering society on a rational basis. Again, the example of the French Revolution and the overturning of an entire social and political order inspired many socialists with a sense of revolutionary optimism.

Early nineteenth-century socialists including Saint-Simon, Fourier and Owen were stigmatised as utopian by Marx, and the label has stuck to them. They can be seen as utopian in the sense that they project complex schemes of new social orders in which socialism can be realised. Saint-Simon was inspired by a rationalist vision of a society directed by a series of experts armed with technological and organisational knowledge. Fourier exemplifies a libertarian brand of socialism in that, for him, hitherto-existing society has been emotionally stifling as well as unfair, and a future socialist society would be sexually and emotionally liberating. Owen represents a moral vision of a future society organised on a cooperative basis whereby all would share in the wealth of society.

See Chapter 7.

Undoubtedly, the central figure in any account of socialism up to the present day is Karl Marx. He is the inspiration for a diversity of socialist developments and styles of thought. He produced a large-scale theory encompassing a wholesale critique of capitalist society. Marx, explicitly in his early writings and implicitly in his later work, offered a theory of alienation whereby men and women were seen as alienated from one another, work, products and their own creative capacities under capitalism. This notion of alienation has subsequently been developed and expressed by a variety of socialists, including William Morris and the prophet of New Left libertarians Herbert Marcuse. Marx also set out a theory of history in which communism is seen as the necessary product of historical development and not as a utopian project. The determinism involved in Marx's sense of history has been criticised by socialists and non-socialists, but in practical terms it has certainly offered hope to a variety of socialists. Marx's theory of politics sees class as the determining factor in political behaviour. Politics, hitherto, is diagnosed as expressing class interests, though Marx envisages a radical form of democracy in which representatives would be directly responsive to electors. Marx's mature economic theory purports to offer a model of the inner dynamic of the capitalist system, spelling out its inevitable downfall. The labour theory of value has been much disputed but the overall historical sense of the growth and development of capitalism has been very influential.

THINK POINT

Does Marx have anything to offer to contemporary socialism?

Since Marx, an important development within socialism has been the emergence of revisionism at the end of the nineteenth century. In 1899 Bernstein produced *Evolutionary Socialism*, which challenged some of the central Marxist tenets of the German Social Democratic Party (Bernstein 1961).

Edward Bernstein (1850–1932) was a member of the German Social Democratic Party and was a leading theoretician of the socialist movement in Germany that advocated the revision of socialist ideology towards the end of the nineteenth century. His book *Evolutionary Socialism* (1898) advocated the gradual development of socialism, and he maintained that workers could improve their lot under capitalism.

Edward Bernstein

Bernstein repudiated the need for a violent break with capitalism to achieve socialism. He saw workers as benefiting from piecemeal advances under capitalism which should not be squandered for participation in an uncertain revolution. He maintained that social justice could be achieved through redistribution under capitalism. From 1919 there was a split in the world of socialism between highly disciplined Marxist parties following the example of the Bolsheviks under Lenin and reformist social democratic parties who refused to accept Bolshevik-style discipline and tended to accept an accommodation with liberal capitalist regimes. In Western Europe the social democratic parties tended to flourish, whereas revolutionary Marxist parties were imposed upon Eastern European countries in the wake of the expansion of the Soviet Union. In China and Cuba and some parts of the Third World, Marxist revolutionary parties prevailed, but usually in the wake of the disorder following war or civil war.

V. I. Lenin

Lenin (1870–1924) was the assumed name of Vladimir Ilych Ulyanov, who was born in Simbirsk in 1870. Lenin's brother was a revolutionary conspirator and was executed in 1887. Lenin joined the Marxist Russian Social-Democratic Labour Party and became a dedicated revolutionary. He was opposed to reformism that compromised with existing power structures. His 'What Is To Be Done' (1902) argued the case for dedicated professional revolutionaries who would eschew compromise and the pursuit of piecemeal economic reforms. In 1903 The RSDLP split and Lenin assumed control of the Bolsheviks. Lenin presented the case for revolution in *State and Revolution* (1917) and he directed the Bolshevik seizure of power in October 1917. Lenin led Soviet Russia until his death in 1924.

The contemporary doubts about socialism emerge from the evident failure of Marxist regimes in the Soviet Union and Eastern Europe and the faltering ideological voices and electoral performances of reformist parties in Western Europe. The hesitation over socialism in the contemporary world of socialism is reflected in the doubts surrounding Tony Blair's credentials as a socialist. His governments have redistributed resources and adopted a communitarian rhetoric, but they have been orthodox in economic policy and have sought the approval of capital and social elites. The Labour Party achieved successes in the post-Second World War world; the governments of 1945–51 and 1964–70 brought about changes in society, developing the welfare state and achieving a measure of social justice. But doubts emerged about the corporatism and state spending associated with these governments, and Blair, in remodelling the Labour Party to make it acceptable in government in a new millennium, has perhaps broken links with its socialist past.

Fascism

The nature of fascism

The ideological status of fascism is controversial. Fascism is often used as a term of abuse and nothing more. Bureaucrats and parents are on the receiving end of such abuse, as well as dictators like Hitler and Mussolini. Again, defining fascism is difficult because of the variety of the regimes and movements identified as fascist. The peasant-based Christian Iron Guard of interwar Romania, the reactionary Catholic Action Française of early twentieth-century France and the atheist, racist regime of the Nazis have all been labelled fascist. Despite the profound differences between fascist movements, there have been a number of attempts to identify fascism as an umbrella ideological term.

One way of theorising fascism is to emphasise its negative character, the way it is opposed to Enlightenment ideas such as reason, rights, freedom and democracy. It was also opposed to democracy and internationalism. The upshot of this approach, evidenced in the speeches of both Mussolini and Goebbels, is that fascism is presented as an essentially reactionary ideology, reacting against what are usually termed progressive currents of thought.

Some theorists of fascism bow to the difficulties involved in the enterprise, and see fascism as an amalgam of different elements which are arranged distinctly and unevenly in different fascist movements. Eatwell, for instance, sees fascism as assimilating diverse currents evident in other ideologies (Eatwell and Wright 1993), and Wilford stresses its syncretic character (Wilford 1994). These interpretations allow for the specific emphasis upon racism in the Third Reich, the marked statism and corporatism of fascist Italy and the syndicalist currents within interwar Spanish fascism.

Griffin has presented a challenging new interpretation in which fascism is seen neither as a merely reactionary ideology nor simply as a progressive, modernist ideology, but rather as incorporating both of these elements (Griffin 1991). He sees fascism as embracing a form of ultra-nationalism in seeking to refashion the nation through its own dynamic activity. He designates the fascist project of national regeneration as evoking past national glories within a modern context, in that fascist renewal employs forces of modernity such as advanced technology. Griffin's perspective, which centres on the emotive aspects of the fascist project of renewal, allows him to appreciate the mythic dimensions of fascism.

THINK POINT

Consider fascist attitudes to the past and the future. Can a case be made for seeing fascism as a progressive force?

All of the above perspectives have something to offer. Fascism is certainly an ideology which picks up on a variety of themes and is not instantiated in one set way in all its manifestations. Again, it has mythic dimensions, and fascism derives much of its force from its emotional impact.

Also, fascism is undoubtedly defined to some extent by its negation of Enlightenment doctrines. The various definitions examined here should not be seen as exclusive. Populist ultra-nationalism is a concept which, if unpacked, may be seen as involving a rejection of Enlightenment notions. Similarly, a model of fascism must allow for differences of emphasis to accommodate the variety of fascist movements.

The development of fascism

The history of fascism must recognise the interwar years as crucial. It was in this period that self-styled fascist movements in Italy and Germany came to power. What promoted the rise of fascism in this period were the problems which bedevilled the modern age and which were becoming increasingly apparent by the end of the nineteenth century. The experience of industrialisation and imperialism had brought wealth and glory but, at the same time, promoted discord, resentment and problems. The grand Enlightenment vision of a rational world of states and peoples in harmony with themselves and one another and who were committed to the peaceful resolution of disputes was threatened by the persistence of discord and the growth of social divisions.

The very ideal of rationality as the emblem of the distinctiveness of humans was being challenged. Nietzsche (1967), most notably, had questioned the disinterestedness of reason in the name of the ubiquity of the will to power. Others had looked to the elemental sense of the nation as the major force in life, and some, such as Chamberlain and Langbehn, had seen race as the primal force of human life. Similarly, the liberal ideal of personal autonomy had been challenged by those who looked to the nation to build up national wealth, in a statist reading of human life in which individuality was downgraded. Fichte (1968) may be seen as a nineteenth-century advocate of this autarchic nationalism.

Fascism in Nazi Germany and Mussolini's Italy

The divisive and dissonant forces at work in modernity may be seen to have promoted fascism in interwar Germany and Italy. In both regimes there was a deprecation of reason. Force was praised; youth movements and shock troops represented incarnations of the vitality of force. Violence was inflicted upon internal opponents of the regimes, and war was celebrated as the quintessential activity of the nation. Both regimes exemplified an overheated nationalism in which the pursuit of glory justified aggression and violence. Both regimes' aggressive nationalism, cult of the leader and celebration of force were responses to the demands for unity, purpose and strength thrown up by divided and demoralised societies. Both Italy and Germany in the immediate post-First

World War period suffered from the anguish of either defeat in the recent war or disappointed victory. Democracy struggled in both countries as social division and economic anxieties mounted.

The affinities between the two regimes and their histories indicated above notwithstanding, there were distinct differences between fascism in Germany and Italy. In Nazi Germany the driving ideological force of the regime was racism. The German nation was organised by an elite and a leader who were determined to achieve a 'true' community of Aryans. The establishment of such a community involved the systematic persecution and subsequent planned extermination of the 'alien' race, the Jews. Jews were depicted as the dark side of the light shining on the Aryan race, and they were excluded from influence and positions within society and were liable to be arrested and sent to concentration camps. The repression and terror exerted against the Jews was of a piece with the dictatorial measures taken by the Nazis to ensure that power in society was concentrated in their hands.

Soon after coming to power the Nazis, under Hitler's leadership, undertook a policy of *Gleichschaltung*, whereby society was coordinated to allow for a concentration of purpose and the elimination of dissent.

Gleichschaltung The process whereby all institutions and organisations were coordinated to serve the purposes and goals of the Nazi state.

Adolf Hitler (1889–1945) was born in Austria and had set out his life story and worldview in *Mein Kampf* (1925). He led the Nazi Party to power in Germany in 1933 and declared himself Führer in 1934. Hitler was aggressively ant-Semitic, and his racist views and expansive nationalism were key factors in the development of fascism in Germany and in the cause and course of the Second World War. His racist views dominated the ideology of Nazism. The Nazi regime undertook the systematic persecution of the Jews and the relentlessly expansionist foreign policy.

Adolf Hitler

The ideological aims inspiring the Nazi domination of society were the development of the racial power of the Aryans through internal purification and external expansion through a series of wars. While the power of the Nazis rested upon the force and repression underlying the regime, they also appealed positively to the German people through their promotion of a strong foreign policy maximising the image of German strength and through internal measures designed to boost employment and working conditions.

Fascism in Italy differed from Nazism primarily due to the relative insignificance attached to race as an ideological force within the movement. While in the latter period of fascist rule and under Nazi influence racist persecution of Jews took place, the regime was not mobilised by the overriding concern to order the social and political world on racist lines. Fascism under Mussolini combined a number of disparate forces: **syndicalism**, a form of socialism where the role of unions is pronounced; **futurism**, an artistic movement celebrating dynamism; recent aggressive Italian nationalism; and more conservative **corporatist** doctrines. The range of influences points to a difficulty in identifying the nature of Italian Fascism; it was an opportunistic movement which under Mussolini's leadership was primarily concerned to gain and maintain power.

Syndicalism A form of revolutionary trade unionism in which the overthrow of capitalism is seen as arising out of direct action by workers. Sorel, an influential syndicalist, argued for the revolutionary potential of the general strike.

Futurism An early twentieth-century movement in the arts which glorified technology, industry and factories.

Corporatism The doctrine that major economic interests, such as business and trade unions, should be incorporated into the system of government.

Benito Mussolini (1883–1945) was born in the Italian village of Predappio in the region of Romagna. He became a radical socialist in the years before the First World War, but in the volatile atmosphere of postwar Italy he set up a movement called the fascio di combattimento in 1919. His fascist movement traded on violence and quickly became a powerful force, and Mussolini assumed political power in Italy in 1922. By 1926 rule by decree had begun and democratic, parliamentary rule came to an end. Mussolini's regime fell in the wake of defeat in the Second World War and he was executed in 1945 by communists.

Benito Mussolini

What can be said about the ideological distinctiveness of Italian Fascism is that it developed an elaborate version of the corporatist state. Before the end of the Second World War the Italian Parliament was swept away, to be replaced by a system of representation through corporations. While the representative character of the corporatist state was a fiction beneath which lurked the power of the Fascist state and a tyrannical regime, the emphasis upon state organisations in defining the purposes of the individual marks out a distinct expression of fascism. Mussolini and Gentile, the philosophical ideologue of Italian Fascism, both identified the fascist regime as totalitarian, by which they meant to convey the all-encompassing power of the Italian state over the lives of individuals.

What Italian Fascism shares with its Nazi counterpart is elitism, state authoritarianism, an aggressive nationalism promising renewal, and an antipathy to liberal democratic and socialist ideals. The existence of these common ideological values, in combination with a recognition of differences, points up the worth of the general viewpoints on fascism discussed at the outset of this analysis. There is a point to regarding these fascist regimes as exemplifying forms of populist ultra-nationalism in which the rebirth of the nation was seen in emotional terms. The negative standpoint adopted to other ideologies and enlightenment notions is clear and there is a range of values which the two regimes combine in distinct ways.

The commonalities exhibited between Nazism and Fascist Italy justify seeing fascism as a general ideology, differences between its national expressions notwithstanding. The varying extent to which regimes display these features enables the distinction of neo-fascist from fascist regimes. For instance, while the elitism and populist nationalism asserted by the National Front in France are distinctly fascist, its adherence to democracy and the French Constitution qualify its fascism; hence it is more appropriate to label the National Front neo-fascist.

Now the truth is that the State in itself has nothing whatsoever to do with any definite economic development. It does not arise from a compact made between contracting parties, within a certain delimited territory, for the purpose of serving economic ends. The State is a community of living beings who have kindred physical and spiritual natures, organised for the purpose of assuring the conservation of their own kind and to help towards fulfilling those ends which Providence has assigned to that particular race or racial branch. Therein, and therein alone, lie the purpose and meaning of a State. Economic activity is one of many auxiliary means which are necessary for the attainment of those aims. But economic activity is never the origin or purpose of a State, except where a State has been originally founded on a false and unnatural basis. And this alone explains why a State as such does not necessarily need a certain delimited territory as a condition of its establishment. . . . People who can sneak their way like parasites into the human body politic and make others work for them under various pretences can form a State without possessing any definite delimited territory. This is chiefly applicable to that parasitic nation which, particularly, at the present time preys upon the honest portion of mankind; I mean the Jews.

The instinct for the preservation of one's own species is the primary cause that leads to the formation of human communities. Hence the State is a racial organism, and not an economic organisation. The difference between the two is so great as to be incomprehensible to our contemporary so-called 'statesmen'. . . . The sacrifice of the individual existence is necessary in order to assure the conservation of the race. Hence it is that the most essential condition for the establishment and maintenance of a State is a certain feeling of solidarity, grounded in an identity of character and race and in a resolute readiness to defend these at all costs.

. . . the völkisch concept of the world recognizes that the primordial racial elements are of the greatest significance for mankind.

continued

continued

... By its denial of the authority of the individual and its substitution of the sum of the mass present at any given time, the parliamentary principle of the consent of the majority sins against the basic aristocratic principle in nature.

(Hitler 1969: 22–5)

EXERCISE

1 What 'positive' appeal might Hitler's ideology have had for the German people?
2 What does Hitler mean by 'the völkisch concept of the world'?

Nationalism

Nationalism is a disputed but undeniably potent ideology of the modern world. Across the globe, political passions are continuously excited by the call of national allegiances. War and civil war in Rwanda, Ireland and Bosnia testify to the impact of the destructive and passionate force of nationalism. The history of the modern world bears witness to the terrible conflicts emerging from the heart of Europe over disputes about national identity and integrity. While disinterested academics (like Kedourie in his book *Nationalism* (1966)) might point up the fuzziness of nationalist accounts of political legitimacy, the flesh-and-blood populations of states are still swayed by appeals to their national character. Part of the suspicion with which nationalism is viewed resides in its capacity to excite passion, myth and emotion, which play unpredictable but significant roles in the economy of human existence.

As a political ideology nationalism must be understood as making claims about politics and how states should be organised. This political doctrine or ideology of nationalism is linked with general patriotic and nationalist notions of support for nations. The ideology of nationalism itself, though, is concerned with the bases of political organisation and government; humanity, for nationalists, is conceived as being divided up into groups, and the nation is taken as the unit for government and political organisation. Hence, the characteristic principle of nationalism is 'national self-determination'.

The central concept of the nation is problematic. It allows for no straightforward definition. A range of diverse criteria are invoked to explain and justify the notion of a nation. Nations are defined in terms of race, culture, religion, language and history. The profusion of constituent ingredients of nationhood tends to reinforce the suspicion that there is no clear way of distinguishing and defining nations. The nationalist move of identifying nation with state presumes that nations should be the appropriate building blocks for territorial units of political life. However, nations and nation-states are often in dispute over territories, and peoples of diverse ethnic allegiances are often set in the same states and intermingle in countless ways; these things render the prospect of states exemplifying a single national identity implausible in the extreme.

Tragic History Repeats Itself

The war in Bosnia has been raging for two years, but the Balkan peninsula has been a cauldron of ethnic and religious unrest for centuries. The first Croatian areas were unified by King Tomislav (910–28). During the following century, to the east of the river Drina a Serbian state began to expand. An Orthodox Christian Serbian Empire was proclaimed by Stefan Dusan (1331–55), but after his death it fell apart.

Bosnia thrived in the vacuum created by the eclipse of Roman Catholic Croatia and the break-up of Serbia. The Bosnian nobles adhered to a Christian doctrine known as Bogmilism, which was fiercely persecuted by the Catholic Church. By the end of the 14th Century the Turkish or Ottoman empire had advanced into the Balkans, which it occupied for five centuries. The Croats were driven north but most of Bosnia's Bogomils converted to the Turks' Muslim Faith and were left to run their own affairs. Eventually the northern Balkans came under the control of the Austro-Hungarian Habsburg empire and the Balkan people – known as the Southern Slavs – became pawns in the wars between the Ottomans and the Habsburgs.

In 1829 after a war between Russia and Turkey, the Serbs, with Russian support, established a small independent state which they gradually enlarged. To quash nationalist ambitions in the Balkans, the Habsburgs occupied Bosnia-Herzegovina in 1878 and, 30 years later, formally declared it part of Austria-Hungary.

In 1912 the Ottomans were defeated in a war with Serbia, Montenegro, Bulgaria and Greece, and Serbia doubled its size. The Austro-Hungarian government was livid. When, in 1914, a Bosnian Serb assassinated the Archduke Ferdinand, heir to the Habsburg throne, in the Bosnian capital, Sarajevo, Austria-Hungary declared war on Serbia.

Tensions between countries supporting either side led to the outbreak of the first world war, which ended in 1918 with the defeat of Germany and Austria-Hungary. The Southern Slavs combined to form the Kingdom of Serbs, Croats and Slovenes, which changed its name in 1929 to the Kingdom of Yugoslavia (literally the Kingdom of the South Slavs).

In 1941, Hitler's Germany invaded Yugoslavia and left the Ustase, an extreme Croat nationalist movement, in charge of a puppet state that included Bosnia-Herzegovina. The Ustase moved to rid Greater Croatia of Serbs, Jews, gypsies and anti-fascist Croats by expulsion, mass murder and religious conversion. They

continued

continued

were resisted by the Cetniks – committed to Serbian dominance of Yugoslavia – and the Partisans, led by Marshal Josip Broz, a communist, who was later known as Tito. After Germany's defeat in 1945, Yugoslavia was re-established, with Tito as its unchallenged ruler.

After his death in 1980, however, politicians began to use ethnic divisions to claim power. When Slobodan Milosevic gained power in Serbia in 1987 he determined to control all the land where Serbs lived. Ambition to gain access to the rich coastal areas may also have been involved. The first serious sign of Serb expansion was the annexation of the predominantly Albanian province of Kosovo and the illegal installation of governments in the broadly Serbian or Serb-supporting areas of Vojvodina and Montenegro.

In 1990 an authoritarian nationalist, Franjo Trudjman became leader of Croatia, and in June 1991, Slovenia, in the north-west of Yugoslavia, and Croatia declared independence. Britain and France believed that to recognise Croatia would provoke an escalation of the war. But, by December 1991, the EC gave in to German pressure for recognition, after Croatia gave vague safeguards over minority rights.

However, the Yugoslav army and the Croatian Serbs joined to fight a bloody war in Croatia, in which atrocities were committed by both sides. Areas were 'ethnically cleansed' with people being killed or forcibly removed from their homes and villages. The fighting continued until January 1992 when a ceasefire, patrolled by United Nations peacekeeping forces, was finally put into effect. By then much of Croatia was under Serb control.

Meanwhile a multi-ethnic Bosnia had been moving towards an independence that would be hard to uphold with a Serb–Croat war in progress. Radovan Karadzic, the leader of the Bosnian Serbs, warned that insistence on sovereignty would lead the republic 'into a hell in which the Muslims will perhaps perish'. In April 1992, the EC recognised the new state of Bosnia-Herzegovina, but the weapons of its territorial defence forces had been confiscated by the Serb-controlled army. Hundreds of thousands of Muslims were swept from their homes. Meanwhile, from their hilltop positions, the Serbs rained shells on Sarajevo. At the same time Muslims in Northern Bosnia were being herded into mass prisoner-of-war camps. Caught between Serbian and Croatian forces carving up most of their country, the Bosnians who remain have been concentrated in five supposedly 'safe' areas, including Sarajevo. There, the UN has sought to provide humanitarian aid, but international uncertainty has allowed a war in which aggression is rewarded to continue up until the present and only partial ceasefire. [The present here is 1994. Since this article was written a USA backed peace initiative has succeeded in maintaining a fragile peace based upon the division of Bosnia.]

(Tony Craig, reprinted by permission of the *Guardian*, 1 March 1994)

EXERCISE

1 What do you take to be the main sources of conflict in Bosnia over the centuries?

2 Why do you think ethnic cleansing took place in the states of the former Yugoslavia?

3 Could anything have been done at an early stage by the international community to prevent trouble and war in the former Yugoslavia?

4 Does the fate of the Republics of the former Yugoslavia suggest the utility of strong, authoritarian rule such as that exerted by Tito?

The development of nationalism

Nationalism is a contentious subject, and the history of nationalism is controversial. Kedourie has observed that nationalism is a doctrine invented in Europe in 1789 and spread through the French Revolution (Kedourie 1966). However, the history of nationalism has also been traced back to the great process of nation-building that went on in the early modern world when the European nations of France and England were being consolidated. What can perhaps be said most accurately is that nationalism emerged as a full-blown political ideology at the end of the eighteenth century but that the development of the nation-state in the preceding centuries had prepared the way for its emergence.

The subsequent history of nationalism testifies to its power and variety. Nationalism has developed in a number of different directions and it has been used by a variety of political actors: communists, fascists, liberals, conservatives, imperialists and anti-colonialists. In fact, nationalism epitomises the general trait of adaptability which characterises ideologies. The French Revolution at its outset in 1789 bore liberal political credentials as it called for representative government and respect for individual rights. At the same time it was claimed that sovereignty was vested in the nation; dynastic authority yielded to rule by the nation. The French Revolution set off a series of nationalist revolts in Europe. The association of nationalism with liberal ideas, however, is not inevitable. Ideologies change according to the circumstances of time and place.

The changing face of nationalism may be seen in the history of the turbulent world of interwar Europe. The demands of national self-rule and aggrandisement had been satisfied for successful imperial powers such as France, Britain and Russia. Germany's dissatisfaction with its imperial spoils, coupled with its determination to dominate the heart of Europe, was an important cause of the First World War. Germany's defeat in that war and the subsequent hardships experienced by Germans in the Weimar Republic incubated the aggressive form of nationalism which inspired and was subsequently fostered by the Nazis. Fascism incorporated an intense, aggressive form of nationalism as one of its central features, and this mode of nationalism is quite distinct from more liberal forms of nationalism which respect the civic freedoms of individuals irrespective of their ethnic status.

The Janus-like face of nationalism may be seen in the way nationalism has been invoked by imperialist and anti-imperialist powers. The music-halls of England in the late nineteenth century echoed to jingoistic tunes which celebrated nationalism and tales of imperial glory. Russian nationalism demanded imperial conquests, just as the fascist powers sought national redemption in dominance and control over other states. In the aftermath of the Second World War, however, indigenous populations in Asia and Africa sought to free themselves from imperial rule by appealing to the doctrines and myths of nationalism which had been propagated by the imperial powers. The fall of the Soviet Empire was effected by the vibrant force of nationalism which erupted throughout the empire, acting as a fierce rejoinder to the communist project of incorporating disparate nations within a union serving and masking Russian nationalism.

Explanations of nationalism

There are a number of distinct types of explanation of nationalism, reflecting the variety of explanations which are invoked to explain social and political phenomena. One significant type of explanation is that proposed in different idioms by Gellner (1983) and Giddens (1990). Both see the roots of nationalism as lying in the psychological problems of identity posed by the modern world. For Gellner, modernisation undermines traditional face-to-face relations within societies as centralising technological forces break down the distances between peoples but at the same time destroy specifically local allegiances. He sees the prospect of cultural breakdown being averted by states constructing national identities based on linguistic identities for their own purposes of self-legitimation. Giddens sees nationalism as being promoted by the contemporary impact of globalisation. Technology links up all parts of the globe and compresses both time and space, but at the same time unleashes countervailing forces of opposition to this process. For Giddens, nationalism is a significant force resisting globalisation but being pulled in its wake.

Marxists take a different view of nationalism. Marx saw the development of nation-states as part of the process of constructing capitalism, observing the nation-state's role in securing markets and centralising communications. Nationalism, according to this logic, is the ideology equipped to justify the nation-state, which develops for essentially economic reasons. Lenin's theory of imperialism is a development of this theme. For Lenin, nation-states, insofar as they are concerned to promote economic development within their states, come into conflict with other nation-states as they scour the world for markets and raw materials. Imperial wars are therefore testimony to the destructive force of nationalism and developed capitalism.

The Marxist account of nationalism has the evident merit of linking the phenomenon of nationalism with processes of modernisation and economic development. Economic interest often lies behind nationalist rhetoric. The USA's concern to maintain freedom and ward off the threat of communism after the Second World War was not disinterested. It had much to do with the economic interests of large corporations within the USA. The Marxist tendency to discount the political imperative to express and organise institutional representation of culturally recognised affinities between people, however, is unconvincing in the light of inter-class expressions of cultural solidarity among people of the same nation or culture.

Kedourie's famous book on nationalism emphasises the power of ideas in politics in that it points up the fatal attractiveness of nationalist ideas, notwithstanding the impossibility of fixing upon an uncontroversial account of the nation. Other accounts of nationalism, such as Antony Smith's (1971), point up the role of politics in explaining nationalism. Nations and nationalism, in this perspective, are promoted by political actors to provide coherence and purpose for political movements and states. Hobsbawm (1990) has written persuasively to support the notion that myths and conceptions of nationality are often the product of political engineering.

The truth about nationalism is not easily expounded. It is a political phenomenon which has been expressed in a variety of ways; its protean character testifies to its power and impact. Given its variety and fecundity no single explanation can account for it. Economic, political, ideological and cultural forces may be seen to contribute to its development and continued impact. The processes of globalisation which are deepening and facilitating communication between parts of the world exemplify the complex forces promoting nationalism. The increasingly global nature of economic and cultural activity has promoted supranational political initiatives such as the European Union, but it has also inspired cultural resistance to globalism, which has entrenched nationalist politics in Britain just as it has in Iraq. Globalisation therefore exhibits an intricate pattern of economic, political and cultural interaction which both opposes and promotes nationalism.

However nationalism is conceived and explained, it remains a powerful force in social and political life. Its conceptual and historical linkage to the politics of states and the practice of democracy underlines its significance in the political world. Its links with the state also mean that it is linked to power and force, and so it remains an ideology that is not to be underestimated or ignored. Its seductive and simplifying rhetoric heightens the appeal of other ideologies such as socialism and conservatism. The fluidity of contemporary culture does not dispense with the need for attachments, and nationalism answers this need as is witnessed in trouble spots around the globe ranging from Baghdad to Manhattan.

THINK POINT

Consider the explanations of nationalism set out above. What are their main strengths and weaknesses?

Feminism

Feminism is an ideology which has made an increasing impact on the modern world. While the origins of feminism may be traced back far into the past, and can certainly be seen in clear outline in the writings of eighteenth-century writers such as Mary Wollstonecraft, the late twentieth century has witnessed feminism's ideological flourishing and its profound legislative impact in Western countries. Feminism can be seen as a post-materialist ideology in its concentration upon the style and quality of life. It has extended the reach and scope of politics, coining the phrase 'the personal is the political', which pithily and dramatically demands the extension of political analysis and contestation to 'personal' realms such as relationships and childcare. Feminism has questioned one of the central pillars of liberalism and the liberal state: the divide between the public and the private. This divide has been challenged from both sides, in that feminists have argued that the public world is devalued by its exclusion of women and private concerns from its purview, and that the private world has suffered by the exclusion of men from domestic duties and child-rearing.

While generalisations can be made about the nature of feminism and the impact of feminism on politics, there is a significant variety of expressions of feminism. To some extent this variety follows a chronological pattern, in that the first wave of feminism – up to the early part of the twentieth century – concentrated upon either achieving political representation or yoking feminism to socialist emancipation, whereas late twentieth-century feminism, the second wave, has set out a radical agenda in which the emancipation of women in all spheres of life has been supported and the pervasiveness of patriarchy opposed. Towards the close of the twentieth century various forms of feminism could be discerned. Liberal feminism accepts the liberal assumptions about the value to be accorded to individuality and freedom, but campaigns to achieve their equal realisation for women as well as men. Socialist feminism, while pursuing traditional socialist goals of equality and fairness, sees gender as an important source of existing unfairness. Radical feminism embraces a variety of standpoints, but all variants challenge existing divisions of the public and the private, and see patriarchy as of fundamental importance. Postmodern feminism is a recent phenomenon, in which postmodern scepticism about the substantiality of selves, and doubt about the bases of explanation and liberation have combined to decentre feminist ideology, so that women are not seen as forming an unproblematic essentialist category and the feminist agenda is characteristically seen as deconstructing male universalistic linguistic paradigms.

An important area of agreement [i.e. among feminists] is an increasingly general acceptance of the radical feminist claim that the 'personal is the political', and that power relations are not confined to the 'public' worlds of law, the state and economics, but that they pervade all areas of life. This means that such issues as childcare or domestic violence are redefined as political, and can be the focus of collective feminist action; it means too that politics is not simply something 'out there', but a part of everyday experience. At the same time, it is becoming clearer that gender issues cannot be isolated from their socio-economic context, and that apparently moderate feminist demands may come into conflict with dominant economic interests and assumptions.

Disagreements remain over the role of men in aiding or opposing feminist goals. Liberal feminism started from the premise that all will gain if society is based on principles of justice and equal competition, for men as well as women will be able to realize their full individuality, and society will benefit from the talents of all its members. Marxists and socialists too have argued that there is no fundamental conflict of interest between men and women, for the ending of sex oppression cannot be disentangled from wider social progress. In this sense, therefore, many liberal, Marxist and socialist writers would agree in principle that men as well as women can be feminists. At the same time, however, radical feminist theories and the experience of feminist politics have produced an increasingly widespread perception that men as a group are privileged by existing inequalities, at least in the short term, and that they therefore have an interest in maintaining them.

(Bryson 1993: 67)

EXERCISE

1 What is meant by the expression 'the personal is the political'?
2 What is the socio-economic context of gender issues?
3 Can men be feminists?

Liberal feminism

Liberal feminism conceives of politics in individualistic terms and looks to reform present liberal practices in Western countries rather than advocating wholesale revolutionary change. Liberal feminism's long historical pedigree is exhibited in the works of Mary Wollstonecraft, who wrote the celebrated *A Vindication of the Rights of Woman* in 1792.

Wollstonecraft argued for the fundamental equality of men and women. She saw both women and essentially rational creatures whose common rational qualities were overlooked on account of the education and socialisation of women, which contrived to render them coquettish, emotional creatures. Wollstonecraft recommended educational reform, some female representation and companionate marriages, but she was still prepared to countenance significant differences in the lifestyles of men and women. She believed that

Mary Wollstonecraft (1759–97) is often taken to be the first systematic feminist theorist. She was greatly influenced by radical thinking at the time of the French Revolution. Her *A Vindication of the Rights of Woman* (1792) urged the equal treatment of women on the basis of their common rationality with men. Her reading of the sociological context of contemporary notions of femininity render her work both complex and relevant to subsequent studies of the socialisation of women.

Mary Wollstonecraft Godwin.

Mary Wollstonecraft

only a relative minority of women would pursue professional careers, that many women would undertake domestic work, and that the majority would find satisfaction in their domestic labours and child-rearing.

Likewise, J. S. Mill, in the nineteenth century, emphasised the essential equality of men and women, explaining their common nature as deriving from their shared rationality. He argued for feminism on utilitarian grounds, for he calculated that society as a whole was losing out if it did not make good use of the rational qualities of women as well as of men. Mill's sensitivity to the harmful effects of uncriticised conventions enabled him to imagine the possible improvements to the human condition consequent upon general acceptance of the rational character of women. Mill was appalled by the domination over women which most men exerted in marriages. He considered that a more equal relationship between marriage partners would ameliorate the quality of life for both men and women. To promote equality of status in marriage Mill advocated reform of the property laws so that women retained rights to their property after marriage. Though Mill was a determined advocate of the feminist cause, he followed Wollstonecraft in assuming that most women would be able to find satisfaction in the private world of the family and a companionate marriage.

The most celebrated of latterday liberal feminists, the American Betty Friedan, resembles Mill and Wollstonecraft insofar as she does not want to overturn contemporary liberal society. Rather, she argues that women should not be excluded from the liberal dream of autonomy and self-determination. She advocates specific remedial measures such as widespread access to crèche facilities to enable women to combine effectively professional careers and family responsibilities. Like other liberal feminists, however, she does not seek to overturn conventional notions of gender in contemporary society, and accepts prevailing patterns of relationships between men and women and the appropriateness of the nuclear family.

Betty Friedan's (1921–) most famous work remains *The Feminine Mystique* (1963), in which she argued for measures to ensure substantive equality for women in the world of work as well as in politics and in private life. She helped to found the National Organisation of Women. In *The Second Stage* (1983) she highlighted the continued significance of children, home and family for women. Friedan has been an inspirational figure for second-wave liberal feminists.

Betty Friedan

Socialist feminism

Socialist feminism rejects the individualism of liberal feminism, and aims to achieve the goals of substantive equality between men and women and a co-operative sense of community between all members of society. Fourier argued a case for socialist feminism at the outset of the nineteenth century, elaborating a version of socialism, based upon equality between men and women, which emphasised its emotionally liberating qualities. According to Fourier, men and women should live together polygamously in phalansteries, with children being reared collectively. Engels, in 'The Origins of the Family, Private Property and the State', provided a classic Marxist account of gender relations, which purported to explain the basis of gender inequality (Engels 1968). He argued that the origins of sexual inequality may be traced to the establishment of patrilineal descent that arose with the advent of private property as a mechanism to ensure that property remains with male descendants. For Engels, the arrival of socialism would abolish both private property and the domestic servitude of women. Latterday socialist feminists like Juliet Mitchell characteristically see production as a central factor in the oppression of women but, unlike Engels, allow for the importance of other factors, notably the roles women have played in the reproductive and nurturing processes.

See the discussion of equality in Chapter 6, pp. 209–12.

Radical feminism

Radical feminism emerged in the period after the Second World War and is characterised by its emphasis upon the importance of patriarchy in maintaining a male domination of society and by its call for a radical overturning of gender oppression. The agenda of radical feminism is visibly present in Simone de Beauvoir's study *The Second Sex*, published in 1949 (de Beauvoir 1968). The theme of the work is the dependent, derivative status of women as the second sex. For de Beauvoir, women are defined dialectically and existentially as the other of men. She urges that women should undertake an existential re-orientation and redefine themselves so as to transform their status and lifestyles across all social and cultural reference points. Eva Figes, in *Patriarchal Attitudes*, highlights femininity as a socially produced phenomenon created by men, and urges that women must be liberated from the gender straitjackets of marriage and motherhood (Figes 1970).

Germaine Greer, in *The Female Eunuch*, launched a savage critique of received notions of femininity. She castigated conventional notions of women as sexless and passive creatures, urging, instead, that women should be sexually assertive and energetic creators of their own destiny (Greer 1971). Kate Millett, in *Sexual Politics*, developed a comprehensive theory of patriarchy in which society, its structures and values were depicted as hostile to women on account of their explicit and tacit male dominance (Millett 1970). For Millett, the locus of male power is the nuclear family, which restricts the sexual and social possibilities of women to the demands of one man and his children, and removes reproduction and nurturing from the public domain. She prescribes the destruction of the nuclear family if women are to achieve freedom. Since 1970, radical feminism has taken diverse directions, prompting some commentators to emphasise diversity rather than coherence in the women's movement. Some feminists, such as Mary Daly (1978), rejecting androgyny and the notion of pure equality between men and women, have favoured a pro-woman position in which the special qualities of women have been lauded. A radical expression of a pro-woman standpoint is Ti-Grace Atkinson's political lesbianism.

Postmodern feminism

Postmodern feminism, as the name suggests, derives intellectual inspiration from postmodernism. It shares in the general postmodern critique of rationalism and progress, and is prepared to accept irresolvable difference and perspectivism in place of the contested universalism of modernity.

The intellectual perspective of postmodern feminism harmonises with a gathering appreciation of the diversity of the women's movement, whereby the nature of woman itself is problematised. In France postmodern feminism has sought to deconstruct the symbolic order of a language construed as a male appropriation of experience. The general thrust of postmodernism to resist closure and systematisation has led feminists to recognise a diversity which has been discussed insufficiently in the classics of feminist literature. Wollstonecraft and Mill entertained easy generalisations about the essential rationality of women, but assumed uncritically that women of differing classes would adopt differing styles of life. Radical feminists like de Beauvoir and Greer have stigmatised prevailing sexual conventions and images of women, but have not reflected convincingly upon the contrasts between women in radically distinct situations such as those prevailing for a white professional woman in a Western country and a poverty-stricken Muslim woman in Iran or Iraq. While the tendency of postmodern feminism to recognise difference is salutary, the deconstruction of a general notion of woman threatens to disrupt the power of feminism as a focused political movement engaging in a clearly defined struggle.

THINK POINT

- What are the main differences between the types of feminism discussed above?

- With which form of feminism are you most sympathetic?

Ecologism

Ecologism is a contemporary ideology in that, since the late 1960s, it has developed a strong profile, figures prominently in political discourse and has influenced other more traditional ideologies. Like feminism, it may be seen as a post-materialist ideology concerned not so much with the generation and distribution of wealth but with the quality of life.

The modern environmental movement dates from the early 1960s, but there is a longer tradition of environmental concern which reaches back to ancient pagan religions and 'romantic' reactions against industrialisation. There are a variety of forms which ecologism can take. Historically, for example, there have been rural conservatives, blood-and-soil Nazi ideologues and back-to-the-land environmental anarchists. In the contemporary world there are market environmentalists and ecologists of anarchist, socialist and feminist persuasions.

One useful way to trace a path through the variety of attitudes and positions which are associated with ecologism is to distinguish between environmentalism and ecologism as terms of ideological discourse. Environmentalism is a broad umbrella term which is generally understood to cover a wide range of attitudes and approaches expressed within the environmentalist movement. It includes those who wish to remedy specific environmental problems, environmental reformers in traditional political parties and radicals who identify themselves as 'green'.

Ecologism as a term is usually reserved for a distinctive set of radical views about how human beings must relate to their environment. However, there is a diversity of outlook between those who call themselves ecologists. Dobson distinguishes between 'minimalist' and 'maximalist' views (Dobson 1990). Minimalist ecologists want to ameliorate the environment and minimise damage perpetrated upon it, and they view environmental concerns from the utilitarian perspective of human beings. Maximalist ecologists, in contrast, do not privilege the perspective of human beings. They adopt a holistic perspective, aiming to maintain and develop a harmonious set of interrelationships between living things and their environments. The maximal perspective of deep ecology embraces an ecocentric viewpoint rather than an anthropocentric one. The viability of the ecosphere as a whole is the overriding ethical objective.

This deep ecological perspective challenges Enlightenment orthodoxy, namely the notion that reason is an uncomplicated and key resource of human beings in the planning of their lives. Likewise, it challenges the rationalist view that progress can be measured in terms of technological and material advance. The holistic perspective of deep ecology, as embraced, for example, by Lovelock (1979), sees nature as a living developing set of relationships rather than as a dead, inert machine.

The following extract is from a book by Jonathon Porritt, a leading exponent of ecologism in contemporary Britain.

Reason, Sweet and Sour

That the green perspective does have a different view of reason or rationality is hardly surprising, for its critique of industrial society is radical in a remarkably literal way. By refusing to abstract our human concerns from the web of life that is our biosphere, it seeks to examine the very roots of human existence. Simply 'getting the facts right' is a much more complex business than today's rationalists would have you believe, and no judgement can ever be 'value-free'.

In his quite excellent pamphlet for the Green Alliance, *Economics Today: What do we need?*, eco-philosopher Henryk Skolimowski reminds us of the memorable scene in Brecht's play *The Life of Galileo*, where Galileo pleads with the courtiers and the scholars just to look into the telescope and see for themselves the proof that the world goes round the sun rather than the sun going round the world. But they wouldn't, for they were simply incapable of coping with any new facts that might overthrow the existing order of things. After all, they saw themselves as 'defenders of the faith'. Kids today are always taught to admire Galileo and his courageous stand against the reactionaries and religious bigots who put him on trial, without so much as a passing awareness that it is now the world view of Galileo and others like him that has become the dominant orthodoxy, and that it is now suppressing a different vision and a different interpretation of human destiny.

The dominant world view, the consequences of which we shall consider in detail in the next part, has come to the end of its useful life, not least because its notion of rationality is so woefully lacking. We like to think that ours is the supremely rational civilization, but does that claim really stand up to any kind of examination? Instead of looking into space through Galileo's telescope, let us look down at ourselves. Imagine, if you will, the proverbial little green person from Mars taking stock of Planet Earth, and the UK in particular. Having anticipated a model of rationality, might 'our Martian' not be surprised to find:

- that it's apparently possible to keep the peace only by threatening the total annihilation of the planet;
- that it's possible to achieve 'progress' and further growth only by the wilful destruction of our life-support systems;
- that so civilized a nation bats not an eyelid as it inflicts terrible suffering on its fellow creatures;

- that we obsessively promote the most expensive and most dangerous energy source to the exclusion of all others;
- that millions remain unemployed when there's so much important work crying out to be done;
- that millions more carry out soulless, mind-destroying jobs that make nothing of their resources and creativity;
- that we ravage our best farming land to grow food surpluses that are then thrown away or sold off cheap to the 'enemy';
- that we consider the best use of the proceeds of North Sea oil is to keep people on the dole;
- that in one part of the world millions die of starvation, while people here die of over-indulgence;
- that we spend as much on useless weapons of war as we do on either education or health;
- that our 'planners' have allowed rural communities to waste away, while making inner cities uninhabitable;
- that we pollute the planet in the very process of trying to get rich enough to do something about pollution?

Now that's just the first 'dirty dozen' out of our little green Martian's notebook, and the list would go on and on. It's hardly a prima facie case for a rational, civilized society. So bear with me if I go on a bit about just who is rational and who is irrational in this crazy world of ours. Ecologists get very emotional about rationality! We've had our fill of the Rothschilds and the Paul Johnsons, who disparage what they can't comprehend and mock what they can't live up to. Though we would never be so foolhardy as to assume that reason alone is sufficient to build a caring, civilized society, the politics of ecology is none the less profoundly rational.

(Porritt 1984: 18–19; reprinted by permission of Blackwell Publishers)

EXERCISE

1 Why do you think that Jonathon Porritt is critical of the view of reason held by 'today's rationalists'?
2 What does Galileo represent for Porritt? Do you think that a case could be made for the Catholic Church's treatment of Galileo?
3 Examine one item of the 'dirty dozen' attributed to the little green Martian. Consider the reasons why it could be seen as signifying the irrationality of contemporary society. Do you think any of the items on the Martian's list can be defended? Are some items no longer applicable?
4 Do you think that there has been 'progress' over the past 200 years? Make a list of positive and negative factors which have developed over those years. How would you undertake an overall evaluation of the changes that have taken place?

Varieties of ecological standpoints on society, economy and politics

One strand of ecology which has been influential is eco-socialism. It often bears a Marxist influence, as exemplified in Rudolph Bahro's *Building the Green Movement* (1986). For eco-socialism, human labour and natural resources are seen as being exploited in a class-based drive for profit. Eco-socialists differ over the nature of political organisation; some, like Bahro, favour small-scale communities; others, like Martin Ryle in *Ecology and Socialism*, envisage a continued role for the nation-state in dealing with large companies (Ryle 1988).

Anarcho-environmentalism forms another significant part of the ecologist movement. It favours natural spontaneity, harmony and a balance to be achieved without external controls. Its advocates favour decentralisation whereby small-scale communities can provide settings enabling people to live close to nature without the bureaucratic and technological paraphernalia associated with large conurbations. The anarchistic dimension of this form of ecologism explains its commitment to spontaneity and its revulsion against elaborate, contrived modes of political regulation.

Eco-feminism, whose standpoint is well represented by Judith Plant's collection of essays *Healing the Wounds* (1989), sees the feminine character as a figure harmonising with nature. Women, on this view, are close to nature through their life-giving and nurturing roles. The devaluation of these roles in industrial societies is taken as reflecting the alienation of patriarchal cultures from their ties with the natural environment. Eco-feminists, in contrast with mainstream post-Enlightenment thinkers, value the traditionally feminine qualities of empathy and intuition over traditionally male attributes such as reason and energy. Eco-feminism is opposed to women achieving equality with men on terms which mean the surrender of these traditionally feminine values. Rather, they wish these traditionally feminine values to become dominant in society.

Not all of those wearing a 'green' label in the contemporary world are radical critics of contemporary patterns of social and political life. There are also 'green' capitalists who rely on taxation to promote desirable 'green' outcomes. An exemplar of green consumerism is The Body Shop.

THINK POINT

Think over what you take to be the main differences between the types of ecologism discussed above.

Conclusion

This brief review of political ideologies should make clear their significance and interest. In the early 1960s ideology was declared to be dead (Bell 1962), and Fukuyama, more recently, has written of the ideological victory of Western liberalism (Fukuyama 1992). Our preceding survey, however, has highlighted that a variety of political ideologies are alive and influential. An economic and cultural context of continuing change and development renders conservatism's respect for order and continuity appealing. Ecologists and feminists contribute to the language in which current politics is conducted. Nationalism is a powerful force throughout the globe, and fascism is not to be dismissed, despite the havoc it wrought in the interwar years. While the project and character of socialism are objects of debate, its commitment to equality and social justice in the context of enormous global and national disparities of wealth and opportunity signals its continuing relevance.

Chapter summary

- Nature of political ideologies; how they are to be understood.
- The history of political ideology.
- Ideology and the division between Left and Right.
- Liberalism; its character and development.
- Conservatism; its character and development.
- Socialism; its character and development.
- Fascism; its character and development.
- Nationalism; its character and development.
- Feminism; its character and development.
- Ecologism; its character and development.
- Concluding remarks on the nature of ideology.

Key texts

Eatwell, R. and Wright, A. (1993) *Contemporary Political Ideologies*, London: Pinter. This is a lively book that contains chapters by a number of authors who discuss the leading ideologies.

Eccleshall, R. *et al.* (1998) *Political Ideologies*, London: Routledge. A work in which a number of authors contribute chapters to the understanding of political ideologies.

Heywood, A. (1992) *Political Ideologies*, London: Macmillan. A crisply written work that is clear and helpful for undergraduates.

Vincent, A. (1995) *Modern Political Ideologies*, 2nd edn, London: Oxford University Press. A thoughtful book that looks at ideologies from a predominantly philosophical perspective.

Further reading

Bernstein, E. (1961) *Evolutionary Socialism*, New York: Schocken Books. A landmark book in stating the case for reformist socialism.

Browning, G., Halcli, A. and Webster, F. (eds) (2000) *Understanding Contemporary Society – Theories of the Present*, London: Sage. A lively and up-to-date review of a number of ideologies and social theories of the modern world.

Burke, E. (1982) *Reflections on the Revolution in France*, Harmondsworth: Penguin. A famous statement of conservatism, set against the background of the French Revolution.

Dobson, A. (1990) *Green Political Thought*, London: Unwin Hyman. A clear account of the varieties of green political thought.

Engels, F. (1968) 'The Origins of the Family, Private Property and the State', in K. Marx and F. Engels *Selected Writings*, London: Lawrence & Wishart. A classic Marxist statement on the nature of gender inequality.

Fukuyama, F. (1992) *The End of History and the Last Man*, London: Hamish Hamilton. A very modish book which talks in grand terms about the end of history. It argues that liberal capitalist democracy has succeeded in solving social, economic and political problems.

Gellner, E. (1983) *Nations and Nationalism*, Oxford: Blackwell. An influential book on nationalism by a respected scholar.

Giddens, A. (1985) *A Contemporary Critique of Historical Materialism*, Cambridge: Polity Press. A lively critique of Marxism by a prolific author.

Giddens, A. (1990) *The Consequences of Modernity*, Cambridge: Polity Press.

Gray, J. (1993) *Post-Liberalism: Studies in Political Thought*, London and New York: Routledge. A thoughtful review of the nature of politics in the contemporary world and the way in which liberalism should now be conceived.

Greer, G. (1971) *The Female Eunuch*, London: Paladin. A classic statement of assertive feminism by a prolific and provocative author.

Griffin, R. (1991) *The Nature of Fascism*, London: Routledge. A fascinating overview of fascism which pursues an original line in modelling fascism.

Hitler, A. (1969) *Mein Kampf*, London: Hutchinson. The classic statement of Hitler's beliefs.

Kedourie, E. (1966) *Nationalism*, London: Hutchinson. A classic work written in a magisterial and highly readable style. It is suspicious of nationalist claims.

Marx, K. and Engels, F. (1973) *The German Ideology*, London: Lawrence & Wishart. The first section is read to the general exclusion of other sections, but the whole of it is a key text for Marx's beliefs as he blends philosophy and history.

Millet, K. (1970) *Sexual Politics*, London: Virago. A classic statement of second-wave feminism, urging a total overhaul of gender identities.

O'Sullivan, N. (1976) *Conservatism*, London: Dent. A plausible overview of conservatism, which sees a belief in imperfection as a central part of conservatism.

Oakeshott, M. (1962) *Rationalism in Politics and Other Essays*, London and New York: Methuen. Wonderful essays of a sceptical conservative turn of mind.

Porritt, J. (1984) *Seeing Green: The Politics of Ecology Explained*, Oxford: Blackwell. A lively and engaging statement of green politics from a famous ecologist.

Ryle, M. (1988) *Ecology and Socialism*, London: Radius. A lively ecological work offering a particular perspective.

PART 3
THE STRUCTURES AND PROCESSES OF GOVERNANCE

Local Governance

Politics Below the Nation-state

Alan Grant

▍ Introduction

Within nation-states policy-making and administration on a range of significant issue areas takes place at sub-national level. There may be a number of tiers of government coexisting with that of the central or national administration. A wide range of territorial units – states or provinces, regions and various levels of local government such as counties, cities, districts and small-scale parishes and communes – have been established in different countries and play an important role in the political life of their societies. A tradition of local self-government goes back to the seventeenth or eighteenth century or even earlier; for example, monarchs granted cities the power to run their own affairs in a number of European states. In liberal democracies the existence of active sub-national governments with their own powers was viewed as an important means of maintaining democracy and in sharp contrast to the centralisation of authority seen in autocratic states. After both the Second World War and the collapse of communism in Europe after 1989, emerging democracies sought to establish a pattern of decentralised government as a vital part of their new constitutional structures.

However, patterns of local democracy vary according to national history, traditions and culture. In some countries, particularly geographically large ones, federalism developed as a way of dividing sovereignty and law-making authority between central government and territorial units known as states or provinces, which had their existence and powers guaranteed constitutionally. On the other hand, within unitary states where there was only one government with law-making power, decentralisation has taken the form of delegation of policy-making to various regional and local government authorities. This chapter examines the relationship between territory and power within nation-states, the relationship between different levels of government and the working of sub-national politics.

The territorial distribution of power

The distribution of power between the central and other tiers of government varies from state to state, and indeed over time. Even where a constitution establishes a particular division of powers, relationships may well change because of economic, social and political developments. We must also be wary of assuming that a written constitution describes the reality of how relationships operate in practice; for example, the Soviet Constitution of 1936 appeared on paper to promise a federal structure with fifteen republics having their own decentralised powers in important policy areas. In reality, the dictatorship established by the Communist Party meant that there was a highly centralised political system, with the powers of the Party dominating and controlling the official state structure.

Therefore a spectrum of relationships exists, with, at one extreme, a highly decentralised confederation with little power granted to the central government and virtually autonomous states or provinces, and, at the other, a very centralised unitary state with weak local authorities acting principally as administrative agents. The vast majority of nation-states cannot be categorised as falling at the extreme ends of this spectrum but, rather, may be located somewhere along the decentralisation–centralisation axis. Given the huge diversity in geographical size, from Luxembourg to China, the social compositions of the populations and the histories and cultures of nation-states, it should not surprise us that there is no easy rule of thumb that may be used to guide us in predicting the degree of decentralisation in particular countries. However, if would seem that at least in liberal democratic states, a very large geographical territory encourages the development of a decentralised structure, both for representational reasons and for the practical reasons of ensuring effective government; for example, four of the largest states by area in the world – Australia, Brazil, Canada and the United States – are federal systems.

What, then, are the advantages and disadvantages of decentralised government with significant sub-national policy-making? The arguments used in such debates tend to focus on two main issues: what is best for the proper representation of the people in a responsive democratic state, and what is necessary for the efficient and effective administration of government. Sometimes the answers to these two questions are not the same and some sort of trade-off, balancing the requirements of democracy and efficiency, is sought.

First, it is often argued that a concentration of power in the hands of one person or group is dangerous; this is best expressed in Lord Acton's aphorism that power tends to corrupt and absolute power corrupts absolutely. Therefore, for a liberal democratic state to prosper, power needs to be devolved to other territorial units. In this way the authority of central government may be checked and balanced by the authority of these bodies. Relationships between the centre and localities, regions or states therefore inevitably involve tension and conflict, but this, it is argued, should be seen as creative and therapeutic for the body politic overall.

Second, proponents of decentralisation believe that more efficient and satisfactory administration of government happens when government is carried out closer to the people who are affected and when those with local knowledge are involved in making the decisions. It is not sufficient to have central government and civil servants implementing policies from regional or local offices (what is known as 'administrative deconcentration'), because their priorities still reflect those of the centre rather than of the people living in the area; the power to decide policies must be in the hands of democratically elected representatives of the people, or, in some cases, power must be wielded by the people directly, through devices such as referenda.

It may also be argued that giving people the right to make decisions that affect them in their own areas has an important educative purpose. John Stuart Mill believed that the development of a responsible citizenry who become aware of the problems and limitations of government comes from this involvement at local level. What is more, politicians who have gained experience at local or state level, dealing with small-scale problems, can 'learn the ropes', even making mistakes which would affect only a relatively small number of people, before graduating to national-level policy-making.

Sub-national governments are also often seen as laboratories of democracy or centres of experimentation where new ideas can be tried out and, if they are seen to work and be popular, may then be applied on a national basis later. Sometimes such policy innovations may be initiated independently by the individual lower-tier authority (such as welfare reforms in some American states or the sale of council houses to tenants by particular English local councils), or the central government may encourage some units to participate in pilot schemes in order to assess both the benefits and the practical difficulties of a complex new policy before implementing it more widely.

It has been claimed that another advantage of decentralisation is that it can take some of the administrative burdens from central government. In modern states there are so many demands made on government to solve society's problems and to respond to all sorts of issues that there is a danger that its desire to act exceeds its capacity for effective delivery; it suffers from what we call 'administrative overload'. One way of dealing with this problem is, of course, to do what many conservatives in Western states demand, which is to allow government to do better by doing less, and to leave some areas to the market and non-government bodies. As Ronald Reagan said in his inaugural address (1981), 'Government is not the solution to the problem: Government is the problem.' An alternative is for government to devolve some responsibilities to

Devolution Refers to the process whereby powers, for example, over taxation, are devolved or transferred from central to regional or local government within a specified legislative framework.

other tiers of the administration. In the United Kingdom one of the major arguments used by supporters of **devolution** to Scotland, Wales, Northern Ireland and possibly the English regions is that greater efficiency of government overall would be achieved as a result. These people also contended that areas of policy carried out by agencies and quangos such as the National Health Service and a range of welfare, economic and cultural services would be made more accountable to elected representatives of the public through the new assemblies.

Devolution in the United Kingdom

Since 1998 the constitutional structure of the United Kingdom has undergone dramatic changes. Through the process of devolution certain powers formally vested in the UK Parliament have been transferred to new legislative bodies located in Scotland, Northern Ireland and Wales. These legislative bodies are responsible for promulgating primary and/or delegated legislation in a wide variety of areas.

The process of devolution: Devolution refers to the 'transfer and subsequent sharing of powers between institutions of government within a limited framework set out in legislation.' The process of devolution in the United Kingdom is neither new nor necessarily complete. Attempts to provide Scotland, Northern Ireland and Wales with degrees of legislative autonomy have existed in various forms since the nineteenth century; however, the present Labour government has been the first government to succeed in providing all these countries with home rule. Moreover, there is no reason to suggest that the change we have witnessed since 1998 will not continue. It is certainly possible that the powers devolved to these regions may be extended or curtailed, as has already been the case in Northern Ireland.

Advocates of public choice theory, supported by New Right politicians, have also seen advantages in decentralised structures; they have argued that public bureaucracies, at both national and local level, have a built-in tendency to be inefficient, to grow and to attempt to maximise their budgets. Such organisations are often heavily influenced by pressure groups and insensitive to the interests of the consumers of their services. They advocate more competition for contracts between public sector bodies and private companies, greater choice for consumers and the breakup of monopoly provision by state bodies. They believe that decentralisation can lead to competition between territorial units wanting to attract and retain business and people in their areas as ways of boosting their economic prosperity. To keep taxes and government costs low and provide good services, particularly in areas such as infrastructure and education, competition works to counter some of the detrimental effects of public sector organisation.

It may be said that decentralised forms of administration are more accessible to the people; their representatives have smaller constituencies than national legislators and usually live within the communities they represent; in many cases their services are the ones people use most often – for example, schools, libraries and transport – and they do not appear to be as 'remote' as central government. This 'remoteness' is a relative and subjective phenomenon. In the United States, Washington, DC, the focus of national power, is 3000 miles away from the residents of West Coast states such as California; those Scots who claim London is a remote capital city for the United Kingdom are only a few hundred miles away, but the feeling may be genuine all the same. Capitals are in many respects the symbols of what is seen as unresponsive central authority.

Finally, decentralisation may give distinct social groupings based on ethnic, racial, religious, national or language identity some degree of self-government if these social cleavages coincide with geographical settlements. In such cases it is argued that the political stability of the state is enhanced.

See discussion of federalism below, pp. 302–9.

Because decentralisation of power is often seen as 'a good thing', there have been more advocates of the case than of centralist arguments. However, it may be legitimately stated that devolving authority to sub-national governments inevitably increases the degree of inequality in society, in the sense that people in different parts of the nation-state receive different levels of service in terms of quality, volume or kind. For example, parents' access to nursery education for their children may well depend not on the need for the service or their income, but on which local or state area they reside in. If equality of provision is regarded as a high priority, then decentralising policy-making (as opposed to the administration) of the service makes little sense.

Second, it may be argued that while decentralisation may help check the opportunity for a tyranny to develop at national level, there is no guarantee that it will help protect the rights of individuals or minority groups against oppressive policies carried out by sub-national governments. For example, in the United States the case for 'states' rights' was advocated most vociferously, although not exclusively, by white Southerners who wanted to maintain racial segregation and other discriminatory practices against black people until the national government intervened in the 1950s and 1960s to protect the civil rights of these citizens. Therefore, in some cases the national government has to act to police the way sub-national governments are behaving with respect to their own communities. Even if the sub-national governments are not carrying out discriminatory or repressive policies, it may be argued that in some respects they are far from ideal models of democracy at local level (Dunleavy 1980). They may consist of unrepresentative elite groups protected by large majorities in a principally one-party system or of a rather too cosy relationship with powerful interest groups dominating the local economy and society. Lack of effective competition electorally and weak opposition may also lead to inefficiency in government and the possibility of corruption. What is more, elections for sub-national levels of government may be said to be weak in terms of ensuring the accountability of local politicians when voters are heavily influenced by national politics, and particularly the popularity (or lack of it) of the central government. Third, it may be that inequalities in size and resources between the constituent units leads to the necessity for some central intervention in order to ensure that at least minimum standards of service are provided to all the people within a nation-state. Central governments normally have access to the most lucrative sources of tax revenue (such as income tax or a national sales tax) and can channel grants to sub-national governments, thus redistributing resources from the richer to the poorer areas and supplementing locally raised revenues.

National governments also often claim that they have a broader mandate from the people as a whole to make policy for the whole country. National elections attract more media coverage, there is more interest, voter turnout is often higher, and parties and leaders elected to power may argue that they have a superior claim to carry out their policies, even though at sub-national level leaders and parties elected by smaller and different electorates are opposed. The debate, therefore, is over who really represents the people in a particular area. In Britain in the 1980s local councils controlled by the urban left argued that they had a mandate to develop socialist policies in direct conflict with the right-wing programme of Mrs Thatcher's central government.

Finally, it may be argued that decentralisation of power can actually encourage political instability, even leading to the disintegration of the nation-state altogether. By weakening the centre's authority, pressures for greater autonomy, particularly when the sub-national units' boundaries coincide with ethnic and cultural identities, can exacerbate divisions in society, leading to increased conflict and eventually fragmentation. This view sees increased decentralisation of power as a 'slippery slope' to the dissolution of the existing state and the breakdown of the governement's ability to govern.

Consociational Refers to a political and sometimes a constitutional arrangement in which significant differences between groups in a political system are the basis for organising the distribution of governmental posts or guaranteeing representational quotas in legislatures, in order to ensure political stability. These groups may be ethnic, religious, even linguistic. For example, in Belgium, where there are major linguistic divisions between Dutch- and French-speaking Belgians, the constitution provides for a balance of power between political parties and regions based on language difference.

Some commentators have suggested that territorial decentralisation is based on the assumption that people living in a particular area or locality have certain interests in common, and thus require representation through a formal government structure based on geography. However, they argue that such a system ignores the fact that in many modern polities people's interests are more likely to be based on common identities of a social or cultural nature, which are often not concentrated geographically, and that it is more important for the state to find arrangements that promote responsiveness to these groups (for example, **consociationalism** or other forms of pluralistic representation) than to rely on traditional territorially based institutions.

THINK POINT

Where do you think the country from which you originate stands on the decentralisation/centralisation spectrum?

Federalism

As we have seen, a confederation is a weak form of political union between sovereign states. It goes further than normal international treaty arrangements because a form of central government authority is established, but this body does not usually have its own powers to tax the people directly and its decisions normally have to be made by the unanimous agreement of the representatives of the states. Confederations have often not provided a satisfactory balance of power between central and state authorities, and either have developed into stronger unions through the establishment of a federation, as in the United States in 1787, or have effectively dissolved so that the constituent states become fully independent, as happened with the Commonwealth of Independent States (CIS) set up in 1991 after the collapse of communism and the Soviet Union.

The term 'federation' derives from the Latin *foedus*, meaning a league, pact or covenant; federal systems are those based on the idea of a permanent compact between political bodies that creates a new political entity, while not abolishing the original constituent units. Murray Forsyth describes this as a 'state of states' (Forsyth 1994: 15). A federal system may be regarded as a compromise form of unity which allows a balance between the need for union in some areas and the wish for diversity in others. Daniel Elazar sees a federation as being 'self rule plus shared rule' (Elazar 1987: 12). According to the constitutional theorist A. V. Dicey, an essential element of federalism is that the people desire an equilibrium between the forces of centralisation and decentralisation and that they 'must desire union, and must not desire unity' (Dicey 1908: 141). The concept of territory and the recognition and protection of minority and territorial interests are also central to an understanding of federalism. The term 'federalism' is one that has been used flexibly to refer to certain types of government structures or political processes, or to a set of political doctrines or an ideology. Some political scientists have argued that a distinction should be made between the term 'federalism', which they see as an ideology, and 'federation', which describes a federal system of government (Burgess 1993: 3–13).

While accepting that it cannot be seen as a free-standing ideology, unlike liberalism or socialism, Burgess believes that federalism should be taken to mean the recommendation and (sometimes) the active promotion of support for federation. It is ideological in the sense that it can take the form of an overtly prescriptive guide to action, and it is philosophical to the extent that it is a normative judgement on the ideal organisation of human relations and conduct (Burgess 1993: 8). Graham Smith argues that 'federalism can be considered as an ideology which holds that the ideal organisation of human affairs is best reflected in the collaboration of diversity through unity' (Smith 1995: 4). Some writers see federalism as either a form or a sub-category of pluralism. Preston King argues that 'pluralism reflects a much broader theoretical concern than federalism. But federalism can still be fitted within it' (King 1982: 75). Forsyth, however, suggests that restricting use of the term federalism to refer to an ideology is illogical and impractical. Just as terms such as 'feudalism' and 'capitalism' are describing not just political ideals but concrete political and economic structures, so federalism may be used in a broader sense (Forsyth 1994: 14).

Federation 'An institutional arrangement, taking the form of a sovereign state, and distinguished from other such states solely by the fact that its central government incorporates regional units in its decision procedure on some constitutionally entrenched basis' (Preston King).

Key text: M. Burgess and A. G. Gagnon (eds) (1993) *Comparative Federalism and Federation*, Hemel Hempstead: Harvester Wheatsheaf.

Born 13 April 1743 at Shadwell, Virginia; died 4 July 1826. Thomas Jefferson was author of the *Declaration of Independence* and the *Statute of Virginia for Religious Freedom*, and one of the Founding Fathers of American federalism. He was third president of the United States, and founder of the University of Virginia. He voiced the aspirations of a new America as no other individual of his era. As public official, historian and philosopher, he served his country for over five decades.

Thomas Jefferson

The requirements of federalism

In this section 'national', 'federal', 'general' and 'central' government are used as alternative ways of describing the central authority, while 'state' and 'province' are terms applied to the major sub-national units in a federation.

There is general agreement that certain characteristics distinguish federal systems from other forms of government. Preston King has advocated a conception of federation containing four essential features (King 1993: 94):

1 Its representation is preponderantly territorial.
2 This territorial representation is characteristically secured on at least two sub-national levels which he refers to as 'local' and 'regional' government.
3 The regional units are incorporated electorally, or perhaps otherwise, into the decision procedure of the national centre.
4 The incorporation of the regions into the decision procedure of the centre can be altered only by extraordinary constitutional measures, not, for example, by resort to a simple majority vote of the national legislature or by the autonomous decision of the national executive.

King sees this last point about legislative entrenchment of the rights of the regions as the truly distinctive feature of federations. Because of it the nature and scale of the division of powers between the centre and the region may be distinguished from other forms of devolution or regionalism by the fact that regional autonomy and representation are not only more devolved but also constitutionally guaranteed. The centre does not have the right to abolish or amend the boundaries of the territorial units. It is also the case that a written constitution has to be accepted as supreme so that a body, such as a Supreme Court, is recognised as being able to settle authoritatively disputes about the meaning of the constitution, particularly with regard to the division of powers between the centre and the territorial units. The entrenchment of the regions' position may be protected by granting them a formal role in the process of amending the constitution. For example, in the United States, whereas a constitutional amendment is initiated at national level (in practice by a two-thirds vote in both houses of the US Congress), it has to be ratified by three-quarters of the states (usually by their legislatures).

A major feature of federal systems is that the territorial units are incorporated into the policy-making process at national level. Citizens in federations typically vote for their own state legislature and the national legislature. Within the national legislature, the upper chamber is designed to reflect the interests of the states in general and to protect the position of the smaller units in particular either by equal representation regardless of population or by granting additional members to those warranted by their size. In one sense this is, of course, highly undemocratic if we compare it with the democratic principle of one person, one vote and all votes carrying equal weight. In the United States the fifty states have two members each in the US Senate, which means that the twenty-six smallest states, with less than one-fifth of the population, have a majority of seats. However, in the Canadian appointed upper house Ontario and Quebec have twenty-four members each, while Newfoundland and Saskatchewan have only six each, and Prince Edward Island four. This still gives the smaller provinces proportionally a very favourable position relative to their populations. In Germany the upper chamber (the Bundesrat) allows six members for large states like Bavaria and Baden-Württenburg, while Saarland and Bremen have three each; this despite the fact that Bavaria, for example, has eleven times the population of Saarland. It is worth noting that the German Bundesrat consists not of directly elected members from the states or Länder, but of representatives of the governments of those states. This Federal Council has a very important role and possesses an absolute veto in all legislative matters affecting the interests of the Länder. It is able to bring the views of the governments of the Länder directly into the policy-making process at federal level, while promoting intergovernmental cooperation.

Relations between legislature and executive at state level tend to reflect those at national level in federal systems (see Chapter 10). For example, in the USA the fifty states each elect a governor separate from the legislature, while in Australia and Canada parliamentary systems exist at sub-national level.

Developments in federal governments

According to K. C. Wheare, in his classic study *Federal Government*, the federal principle is 'the method of dividing government so that the general and regional government are each, within a sphere, coordinate and independent' (Wheare 1963: 10). In other words, the constitution divides the powers of government between two tiers so that each is of equal status and can act independently within its own area of authority, a form of divided sovereignty. Wheare's view was that some political systems, while apparently federal in form, were not in practice because the balance did not allow for coordinate and independent status. One tier (normally the centre) could intervene in the jurisdiction of the other and therefore the latter tier was in reality subordinate and dependent. A constitution or political system could have federal aspects without being a truly federal system; India would be an example, both in its 1935 Constitution and its political experience since. Neither can federalism coexist with autocratic control of power; the USSR, Yugoslavia and Czechoslovakia were what may be called 'pseudo-federations', because the unity of their ethno-regional parts was maintained from above, and a complex array of techniques of coercion ensured compliance with the centre (Duchaek, cited in G. Smith 1995: 8).

An emphasis on the division of powers and separate authority of the tiers has led to the term 'dual federalism'. However, as we noted earlier, inter-governmental relations can change over time and each federal system has established its own particular balance bearing in mind its own history, culture and social structure; what remains true is that, while one in ten of the world's present-day polities claim to be federations, on investigation we would find that in practice many could not be easily distinguished from unitary systems of government.

Federal systems came into being either because previously independent states agreed to unite for certain purposes while retaining their sovereignty in other areas or via the disaggregation of a previously unitary state. The motives for such unions have often been related to defence requirements, the desire for economic development and increased trade or the need to find a way of protecting minority interests within a wider political system. Over a period of time, political, social and economic changes can lead to a marked shift in the balance of power between federal and state governments. Developments such as improved communications and media, growing trade across state boundaries, stronger national identity fostered perhaps by foreign wars and crises, population growth and mobility, and the effective assimilation of minority groups are factors that may well lead to a changed political culture making the growth of federal government power acceptable to the people. The citizens of such a state may well look increasingly to the federal government rather than to their state capital for political answers to their problems. On the other hand, failure of federal policies, a sense of injustice by sections of the population based on territorial interest or an enhanced sense of identity based on cleavages such as race, religion or language within a territorial context may well lead to demands for greater state autonomy or even secession from the federation.

The United States (since the Civil War in the 1860s) would be an example of the former and Canada of the latter situation. In the USA the federal government has increased its role and powers, particularly since the New Deal period of the 1930s. Political scientists argued that dual federalism had been replaced by 'cooperative federalism', where the various levels of government are seen as related parts of a single government system which is characterised more by shared functions and partnership in providing services than by a neat division of responsibilities. In this system the federal government has increas-ingly taken the lead in areas of domestic policy that were traditionally the preserve of the states, setting out prescriptive standards and rules so that some writers have more recently described the system as 'coercive federalism' (Kincaid 1994: 205–16). The balance has been altered by constitutional amendment, by interpretations of the constitution by the Supreme Court which favour the national government and by the financial power of Washington in distributing grants to the states with conditions attached to them (Grant 1997: 311–16). 'Dual federalism', however, still has a strong normative appeal to conservatives in the United States and, having gained control of both houses of Congress for the first time in forty years in the 1994 midterm elections, the Republicans introduced measures to devolve some powers, most notably over welfare, back to the states. Despite this, conservatives found themselves under political pressure to strengthen the national government's authority in other areas such as law and order and prisons, even though these have traditionally been primarily state responsibilities. Another significant development in the 1990s was that the Supreme Court with a majority of conservative judges under Chief Justice William Rehnquist made a number of important decisions limiting the power of Washington, DC, in cases concerning the federal relationship (Grant 2000: 235–57).

Canada's Constitution of 1867 has elements of strong national authority such that Wheare described it as a 'quasi-federal' constitution (Wheare 1963: 19), while recognising that in practice it was federal because no national government attempting to stress the unitary elements would survive. Canada in fact has been unusual in that the power of the centre has weakened since the union's inception. Since the 1960s tensions have increased between Quebec province, with the rise of French-Canadian nationalism promoted by the Parti Québécois, and the rest of the Canadian federation. Attempts were made to satisfy their demands by the adoption of official bilingualism and biculturalism, by the removal of the remaining influence of the UK Parliament on the Canadian Constitution and the Meech Lake Accord in 1987, which recognised Quebec's special status and desire to be regarded as 'a distinct society'. However, some of the other provinces were becoming increasingly resentful at the concessions being granted to Quebec and they refused to accept the Accord. A further proposal, the Charlottetown Accord, which featured a new directly elected Senate in which all provinces would be equally represented while recognising Quebec's special position, was rejected by a national referendum in 1992 by 54.4 per cent to 44.6 per cent, with Quebec's rejection reflecting a similar division of opinion. In 1995 Quebec held its own referendum on whether it should break with Canada and become an independent state; with a 92 per cent turnout among Quebec voters the proposition failed by a margin of only 1 per cent, thus ensuring that the issue would remain a major destabilising question hanging over Canada's constitutional and political future.

Key dates for Canada: The Quebec issue

1535   French explorer Jacques Cartier claims territory

1759   English defeat the French and take over territory

1960–8   Terrorism by extreme nationalists

1967   Parti Québécois formed. President de Gaulle of France declares: 'Vive le Québec libre'

1968   Canadian Prime Minister Trudeau calls out army after kidnapping of British consul and murders

---

continued

continued

1977	Provincial government bans shop signs in English
1980	First referendum: Quebecers vote 60:40 against a mild form of separation
1987	Meech Lake Accord recognises Quebec's special status but this is not accepted by all the provinces
1990	Bouchard forms Bloc Québécois. Gains seats in federal Parliament
1992	Charlottetown Accord: national referendum rejects the agreement 54:46
1993	Bloc Québécois becomes official opposition
1994	Hardline separatist Jacques Parizeau elected Quebec's premier
1995	Parizeau calls for referendum on separation; support soars after Bouchard takes over campaign but Quebecers reject proposal by less than 1 per cent

Conclusions on federalism

Federal systems may promote many of the benefits set out in the previous section on decentralisation; for example, policy innovation at territorial level and the protection of minority interests. Federations may also succeed in regulating and managing social conflicts by easing tensions and being sensitive to diversity. We should not expect federal arrangements to eliminate conflict altogether, any more than conflicts are eliminated in unitary states, but by creating the environment and processes for managing clashes of interests federations can promote political stability. However, it may also be argued that federations have a built-in tendency to disequilibrium and some may appear to be in a state of perpetual crisis. 'Paradoxically, the capacity of a federal system to reflect diversity constitutes a built-in weakness since it allows for conflicts to emerge and be politicised' (Gagnon 1993: 18).

Margaret Covell observes that:

> Many writers on Canadian federalism argue that the existence of a provincial level of government has exacerbated the country's regional and language divisions by giving groups involved an institutional power base and creating political elites with a vested interest in bad relations with the national government.
>
> (Covell, cited in Gagnon 1993: 18)

It may also be argued that federalism has created a form of territorial corporatism, with the national government forced to bargain with representatives of entrenched geographical interests while paying less attention to the important social cleavages which do not coincide with state boundaries.

While there are numerous examples of failed federations – the West Indian Federation (1962), the Central African Federation (1963), the withdrawal/ expulsion of Singapore from the Malaysian Federation (1965) and, more recently, the breakup of Yugoslavia in 1992 – Preston King (1993) argues that these are failures of particular experiments in federation, not of federation as such. He suggests that there is no basis in fact for the belief that federations are somehow less permanent in form than non-federal states, and that the history of federations is at least as much one of success as of dissolution. Given particular difficulties such as territorial size and ethnic particularism, they can often be said to have succeeded where no imagined alternative would have done. Federations such as Switerzland, the United States, Australia and Germany are examples of stable and successful federal systems (King 1993: 96–7). The Federal Republic of Germany, of course, particularly since the reunification in 1989, has been a prime mover – some would say *the* prime mover – in promoting the vision of a federal Europe based on the European Union (EU). Chapter 14 looks at the development of supranational institutions making policy which applies across the EU. Here we need only to note that the confederal aspects of its institutions (the Council of Ministers, representing the national governments of the fifteen members, as the key policy-making body and the fact that the EU acts principally through the member governments) are increasingly being balanced by federal features such as the greater use of majority voting in the Council and the growing powers of the European Parliament. Different interpretations of the meaning of federalism and whether it is a centralising or decentralising concept have resulted in opposition to the development of a clearly federal Europe being greater in Britain than in most continental European nations.

The principle of subsidiarity in the European Union

The European Community has exclusive competence in some areas, in which decisions may be taken only at EU level. In other areas decisions may be taken either by the EU or by the member states (shared competence). In these areas a principle of subsidiarity applies. The purpose of the principle of subsidiarity is to ensure that decisions are taken as close as possible to the level of the citizens by regularly checking whether action taken at Community level could equally well be taken at national, regional or local level. In practice the principle means that, except in areas for which it has exclusive competence, the EU shall act only when this is more effective than action at national level. The principle of subsidiarity is linked to the principles of proportionality and needs, which state that the EU should not take more action than is necessary to reach the goals of the treaty.

Local government and politics

Whether a state is federal or unitary in structure there will be in liberal democratic polities a pattern of local government with elected councils having responsibility for policy-making and administration over a range of services. Exactly what shape this system takes, how many and what type of local councils exist and how they relate to the rest of the government structure depends of course on the history, constitution and political developments that have taken place in the particular state. There is, however, widespread recognition that a viable system of local self-government is an integral part of what makes a liberal democratic state work in a representative and responsible way. In Central and Eastern Europe it is acknowledged that the development of local democracy is a necessary step in the transformation from the old communist regimes. Local authorities, by being elected representative institutions, enjoy a degree of legitimacy and electoral support which distinguishes them from other forms of administration.

Studies of comparative local government suggest that they may be categorised into a number of broad groups based on similarities and differences over a wide range of factors such as constitutional status, structure, powers, relations with central government, party systems and so on. In a comprehensive survey of sub-national institutions in Europe, North America and Japan, Alan Norton suggests that there are five broad groups: South European, North European, British, North American and Japanese. Table 9.1 demonstrates the characteristics of these categories. Norton says that:

Key text: A. Norton (1994) *International Handbook of Local and Regional Government*, Aldershot: Edward Elgar.

> On nine of the thirteen characteristics in the table the North American systems match the British, but there are major differences: not least in degrees of party politicisation, pluralism, the relative weakness of central government and the form of executive. There is a concentration of central power in the United Kingdom that is now alien to most European Latin systems as well as to the American. The North and South European groups stand together in ten characteristics but differ from the British in about half of these. Japanese structures are clearly a modern synthesis from two continents working in an often awkward relationship with national traditions.
>
> (Norton 1994: 13)

Constitutional and legal status

In most liberal democratic states a written constitution provides for and protects the principle of local self-government. Although this is different from the constitutionally entrenched position of the states in a federal system (see the section 'The requirements of federalism', pp. 304–5), Clarke and Stewart argue that the provisions are still significant:

> The importance of the support given in constitutions to local government is not that it formally prevents the abolition of local authorities, but rather that it gives an established status to local government as part of the system of government.
>
> (Clarke and Stewart 1991: 14)

Table 9.1 Characteristics of world systems of local government

	Britain	USA & Canada	France & Italy	Sweden & Denmark	Japan
Constitutional status	creature of parliament	state constitutional	national constitutional	national constitutional	national constitutional
National structure	mixed	mixed	3 tier	2 tier	2 tier
Powers	limited by statute	limited by statute	general competence & statute	general competence & statute	general competence
Control of legality by	courts	courts	regions & courts	state & courts	state & courts
Control of local policy	low	low	interlocked	interlocked	interlocked
Control of local policy historically	low	low	high	high	high
Local functions 1949–89	reduced	various	increased	increased	increased
Local authority expenditure as (UK) % of GDP*	12%	11%, 9%	9%, 15%	28%, 30%	18%
Public expenditure as % of GDP*	44%	35%	49%, 50%	57%, 60%	29%
Local executive authority	council	mixed	mayor or president	mixed	mayor or governor with board
Representational system	majoritarian	majoritarian	proportional representation	proportional representation	majoritarian
Party system	strong two-party	weak two-party	strong multi-party	strong multi-party	strong multi-party
Participation at elections	low	low	high	high	high

* Figures from Poul Erik Mouritzen and K. H. Nielsen (1988) *Handbook of Comparative Urban Fiscal Data*, Odense: DDA.

Source: Norton (1994)

In almost all the states of continental Western Europe local government's position is guaranteed in the national constitution or basic laws, with its rights defined in Germany, for example, as governing and regulating its own affairs. In federal systems the state rather than the national constitutions may establish the powers and responsibilities of local government (e.g. USA). In the case of the United Kingdom the 'unwritten constitution' and tradition of parliamentary sovereignty means there is no constitutional protection for local government nor any limit set to centralisation; new laws abolishing particular types of authority (e.g. metropolitan counties), individual authorities or affecting the financing, the powers or boundaries of local councils can simply be passed by parliamentary simple majority, even if they do have the effect of altering the overall system of government. In most European states the doctrine of general competence applies; this is the principle that local authorities have a general power of jurisdiction over the affairs of their areas and inhabitants insofar as the law does not explicitly provide otherwise. This is in direct contrast with the British doctrine of *ultra vires*, whereby local authorities may carry out only those responsibilities that are specifically assigned to them by Parliament (although the 1972 Local Government Act introduced a limited exception to this principle). In 2000 the Labour government gave councils a new statutory duty to promote the economic, social and environmental well-being of their areas and strengthen their powers to enter partnership arrangements with other public and private bodies.

In practice, the general competence power may not actually lead to more real powers for local government because it lacks the resources to do more, and it may be argued that British local authorities have traditionally had a broad range of well-defined responsibilities with often substantial discretion. However, the general competence authority is important symbolically and psychologically in that it enhances the concept of the local government as a general political authority in its own right which is fostering the welfare of the people and as the corporate expression of the local community. From this also follows the European tradition that local authorities are representative bodies articulating and speaking on behalf of the general interests of their residents in the form of community government as well as being involved in a wide range of functions, even though they may not carry them out directly or exclusively. The British tradition, on the other hand, has tended to emphasise the role of authorities as the providers of specific services within delegated powers from central government, while downplaying councils' wider community and representative roles.

Structure and responsibilities

The simplest structure for local government is a single tier of all-purpose authorities. The attractions of such a system are that there is clear accountability and that the public should be in no doubt as to who is responsible for local services; it should be possible for the authority to plan and integrate its policies effectively. All-purpose authorities should also be able to determine overall priorities, avoid the possibility of duplication and overlap with other authorities, and speak on behalf of the community with one authoritative voice. In Britain the county boroughs in the cities and larger towns, until they were abolished in 1974, were examples, and in the 1990s structural reforms led to the creation of forty-six unitary all-purpose councils to replace a two-tier structure in some parts of England. In Scotland and Wales the two-tier system was swept away completely to be replaced by twenty-eight and twenty-one unitary authorities respectively. However, this form of sub-national government is relatively rare; only in small countries like Iceland and Luxembourg is it the universal pattern, while Australia and Switzerland have single-tier structures within some of their member states. In a number of countries, including the USA, Germany, Canada and Sweden, general-purpose councils may be found, mostly in city areas. Because of the size of such authorities it has been felt necessary for some functions that are most efficiently carried out over a wide geographical area to be administered by joint boards made up of representatives of a number of authorities, thus in practice blurring responsibility.

Multi-tier systems of local government predominate in the vast majority of countries. Such systems provide for a division of powers so that the smaller units and those most accessible to the citizens can carry out a wide range of functions, while other responsibilities are administered by larger scale authorities that can achieve greater effectiveness and efficiency through economies of scale, the employment of specialist staff and equipment and a wider strategic perspective. The multi-tier structure may also lead to the avoidance of joint bodies, unsatisfactory amalgamations of smaller authorities and direct provision by central government departments or appointed agencies.

Although a bewildering array of different types of local authorities with different names exist, according to Norton they may be categorised into three main groupings (Norton 1994: 34–5):

1 Basic level: examples would include non-metropolitan districts in England, municipalities/towns in the USA, communes in France, *Gemeinden* in Germany and *comuni* in Italy.
2 Intermediate: counties in England and in the USA, *départements* in France, *Kreise* and *kreisfreie Städte* in Germany and *provincie* in Italy.
3 State or region: in federal systems these would include the fifty states in the USA and sixteen Länder, including three city-states, in Germany. In unitary states, there are twenty-two *régions* in France and twenty *regioni* in Italy.

The range of population covered by local authorities varies widely, particularly at basic level. Whereas there have been reorganisations of local government in Germany and Scandinavia which have resulted in larger authorities, the

Table 9.2 Government units in the United States

	Units
Federal	1
States	50
Total local governments	84,955
Counties	3,043
Municipalities	19,279
Townships	16,656
School districts	14,422
Special districts	31,555
Total	85,006

Source: Statistical Abstract of the United States 1996: 295

Mediterranean countries have in general shown considerable resistance to increased scale. In France over 36,000 communes have an average population of only 1500. In Britain, where parish and town councils at this level of population have very limited functions, basic local authorities are unusually large, with English shire districts averaging populations of 127,000. This means that districts in Britain as a whole are thirteen times as large as the average German or Italian municipalities, which themselves are five times the size of the average French commune. It may be argued that in Britain the criteria for reorganisation have been based on the idea of streamlining for efficiency along with issues relating to service delivery at the expense of local community identity.

Britain did not have elected regional governments until the end of the twentieth century (with the exception of Northern Ireland), although there was a system of regional administration provided through central departments and agencies. However, after referenda demonstrated popular support for reform proposals, the Labour government legislated to establish devolved governments for Scotland and Wales (Bogdanor 1999). In Scotland almost three-quarters of those voting backed the proposal for a devolved Parliament with full law-making powers and 63.5 per cent agreed that it should also have a limited authority to vary income tax rates. In Wales a bare majority of the half of the electorate who voted supported the creation of a much weaker Assembly which would oversee the administration of government in Wales but would not have the power to determine primary legislation. The government also created a new authority for Greater London which, because of the size of the area and population it covers, may be regarded as a regional rather than a local authority. The Greater London Authority was heralded by many as a democratically elected voice for the capital city that had been lacking since the demise of the old Greater London Council (GLC) which was abolished by the Thatcher government in the mid-1980s. The government also established a system of Regional Development Agencies throughout England with a promise that elected regional assemblies would be set up where there was popular support for such a reform. Apart from those bodies that exist within federal structures, Italy and Spain have autonomous regional authorities protected by constitutional guarantees and endowed with broad legislative powers. In France all regions have the same legal status as local authorities and are relatively weak in terms of their responsibilities (Blair 1991: 55).

The Government of London and Britain's First Elected Mayor

The Labour government elected in 1997 was committed to reintroducing an authority to cover the whole of Greater London which would replace the Greater London Council (GLC) abolished by the Conservative government of Margaret Thatcher in 1986. The new body would work alongside London's thirty-two London borough councils and the City of London Corporation which covers the capital's traditional business centre. The new GLA took over responsibility for London's buses and underground, economic development, strategic planning, police and fire from a range of appointed quangos and central departments, with a budget of some £3.6 billion. The government promised that the GLA would be a slimmed down authority and not a re-creation of the GLC which was criticised as being too expensive and bureaucratic.

Following overwhelming support in a referendum, the GLA was set up with Britain's first directly elected mayor serving with a twenty-five-member Assembly. It was hoped that the election of a mayor would stimulate interest among Londoners but, despite a high-profile campaign, only one-third of voters went to the polls in the election held in May 2000, a turnout similar to other local government elections.

Both the Conservative and Labour parties experienced major problems in nominating their candidates for mayor. The Tories first selected controversial novelist and member of the House of Lords Jeffrey Archer, but he was forced to resign after allegations that he had lied in court during a libel case in the 1980s. He was replaced by his rival for the nomination, Steve Norris. Meanwhile Labour's electoral college for London, consisting of MPs, MEPs, trade unionists and ordinary party members narrowly voted in favour of Frank Dobson, the Health Secretary and Prime Minister Tony Blair's favourite. However, it was clear that Labour's grass-roots supporters preferred former GLC leader Ken Livingstone. Livingstone was considered too left wing and unreliable to be New Labour's nominee. Despite threats of expulsion from the party, he decided to stand as an independent candidate.

In the election Livingstone won the contest, beating the Conservative candidate by 58 per cent to 42 per cent on a second ballot, with Dobson and the Liberal Democrat Susan Kramer having been eliminated after the first round. The Assembly elections resulted in the Labour and Conservative parties winning nine seats each, with the Liberal Democrats gaining four and the Greens three. Fourteen members were chosen on a constituency basis using the first-past-the-post system and eleven on a top-up basis allocated to the parties according to their proportion of the London-wide vote. Livingstone therefore had to work with an Assembly where, as an independent, he had no natural supporters.

A 1988 Council of Europe survey found that there was 'a certain homogeneity' between the functions performed at the basic level of local government, regardless of whether councils have a general competence power or a list of specific responsibilities. The position is complicated by the fact that local councils may have mandatory functions, and also discretionary functions which they do not in fact carry out. In addition, some responsibilities are shared between different tiers of local government or with central government; in

Key text: R. Batley and G. Stoker (eds) (1991) *Local Government in Europe: Trends and Developments*, London: Macmillan.

some cases the amount of discretion is very limited. Given the small size of some basic-level authorities, working with other councils is inevitable if provision is to be made on a reasonably efficient basis. In North America some services that in Europe are carried out by multipurpose authorities are often administered by directly elected special-purpose bodies such as school boards, or directly by the states or the provinces.

Typically, local governments are responsible for such services as primary and secondary education, roads, local planning, refuse collection, libraries, recreational facilities, personal social services, subsidised housing, fire services and environmental protection. In many countries they are also responsible for the police, vocational and adult education, promotion of the local economy and employment, social assistance, health services, and the running of public utilities (Norton 1994: 60–7). Clarke and Stewart point out that the education responsibilities of local authorities in Britain have been greater than in some European countries, but on the other hand it is common to find European local government having a greater role in health care, which in Britain is run by non-elected agencies, and in the administration of public utilities (gas, water, electricity), which they exercise through jointly owned companies, whereas in Britain they have been the responsibility of first nationalised and then privatised corporations (Clarke and Stewart 1991: 19).

Local authorities carry out their responsibilities in a number of different ways. In Britain the tradition has been one of self-sufficiency, so that councils have been large enough to run the service by themselves and usually through directly employed staff. Direct provision through local government departments with their own managers or officers in control and accountable to elected members was the accepted norm at least until the 1980s. In many European states there has long been a more pluralistic approach, with the use of public enterprise companies, voluntary bodies, private organisations working under a franchise agreement, and joint local authority provision.

In the 1980s the Thatcher government in Britain required local authorities to conduct compulsory competitive tendering exercises over a range of services to test the cost-effectiveness of direct provision by council workforces. Although private companies won only a minority of contracts in such areas as refuse collection, school meals provision and cleaning, competition itself did lead to significant changes in the management of local authorities and, its advocates claimed, savings in the costs of running the services. The Conservative government also emphasised 'the enabling authority' concept, which envisaged a much smaller role for local authorities in direct provision of services and greater partnership with the private sector, voluntary bodies and other non-government agencies. Councils would spend more time ensuring that services were provided and regulating and inspecting the provision, and less time actually providing services themselves. This approach in some respects brought Britain closer to the more diverse patterns of provision in Europe, but critics pointed out that the compulsory element in contracting out (which was later abolished by the Labour government in 2000) was unusual, that local authorities were at the same time losing responsibility for services such as

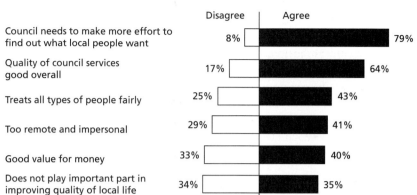

How strongly do you agree or disagree that your council...?

Base: 2,499 residents aged 16+

Figure 9.1 Public perceptions of local government service delivery: UK

Source: MORI Memorandum of evidence on the Draft Local Government (Organisations and Standards) Bill, 1999

further and higher education altogether, and that there was also considerable growth in the number of non-elected quangos – bodies with increasing powers in areas traditionally the preserve of local government.

Britain is not alone in reviewing and reforming methods of service delivery in order to improve efficiency and increase responsiveness to more demanding consumers, but it appears that it has been unusual in the degree of partisan and ideological controversy engendered. Decentralised service delivery and management, user panels and surveys of opinion have been common in many countries. Richard Batley identifies three main types of reform: first, to expand the role of local government and free it from restrictions, the most dramatic of which are the deregulation and 'free commune' experiments in Scandinavia; second, to improve public service practices by simplifying complexity that results from shared responsibilities, setting performance standards, improving staff training and decentralising management; third, to incorporate business methods and competitive practices into the public sector through such methods as devolving budget responsibilities and contracting out (Batley 1991: 216).

Despite recent changes, a survey in the early 1990s indicated that direct provision by local authorities through their own staff remains the norm. Excluding teachers and police to enable the figures to be more nearly comparable, France, Britain, the United States and Italy all had between 3.0 and 3.7 persons in every hundred in local government employment (Norton 1994: 70).

Internal organisation

The representative nature of local government is embodied in the assembly or council, consisting of members directly elected by the citizens. Election may be by the first-past-the-post system or proportional representation. The electoral system has important effects on the nature of party politics and the areas represented by councillors. Elected members make policy, pass local laws and ordinances, determine local tax levels, act as 'watchdogs' on behalf of the public over the authority's administration and serve as forums for debate on local issues. Unless the executive is directly elected the council will also be responsible for the appointment of the executive. The size of such bodies varies considerably; in North America many councils are very small, with as few as three to five members, while at the other extreme the highest numbers were to be found in Sweden (149) and the combined department and commune in Paris (163) (Norton 1994: 96). In Britain there is a tendency for councils to be bigger in size than their European counterparts, reflecting the larger geographical areas they cover. However, because there are far fewer local authorities, the ratio of citizens to councillors is much higher. Discounting parishes, there is one councillor to every 1800 electors in England and Wales, while in most European countries there are between one in 250 and one in 1000 (Clarke and Stewart 1991: 15).

Very small assemblies may be more efficient in terms of making decisions but they obviously do not score so highly in terms of representativeness. Most countries operate through a committee system structured around the main service areas for which the council is responsible. Chairs of committees are often very influential and act as spokespersons, presenting committee policy proposals to the full council for its approval. Where party politics is prevalent, which has increasingly been the case in many countries, committee membership is usually divided proportionately according to the political balance of the council overall. Committees enable members to develop specialist interests and expertise, although it is sometimes argued that this can detract from their ability to consider the corporate interest of the council as a whole, and encourages them to work in alliance with departmental officers and related pressure groups in giving priority to protecting the interests of particular services.

In Britain the full council traditionally was the sole source of authority, and there was no distinction between legislative and executive responsibility. Unlike constitutional practice nationally, where the executive has a separate existence and identity within Parliament, councillors were not only policy-makers but also responsible, in theory at least, for carrying out those policies. In practice, of course, the paid-officer administration of the authority implemented the decisions of elected members, and senior officers with professional expertise advised committees on policy issues. The committee system in British local government meant that there was no clear-cut executive authority, although in practice many councils developed a form of 'submerged executive' comprising party political leaders and committee chairs. The Labour government elected in 1997 criticised the traditional system, claiming that it lacked clear leadership and accountability and that the time-consuming nature of committee meetings discouraged citizens from seeking election as councillors. The government passed legislation requiring authorities to introduce new political structures which would separate the roles of those making policy and running the council from those responsible for the scrutiny of decisions and holding those in power accountable for their actions. Local authorities could choose to have a cabinet system with a leader where the executive was selected by and drawn from the council's membership, or a mayor who would be directly elected by the public and who would then work with either a cabinet selected from the council or an appointed city manager. Most authorities opted to introduce a cabinet system. Separate legislation resulted in Greater London having the United Kingdom's first directly elected mayor, with Ken Livingstone winning this historic vote in May 2000.

Ken Livingstone (1945–) was born in Lambeth and educated at Tulse Hill Comprehensive School. He was a member of Lambeth Council between 1971 and 1978. In 1973 he became a member of the Greater London Council (GLC). He was elected Leader of the GLC in 1981 and remained so until its demise. In 1987 he became MP for Brent East and was re-elected in 1992 and 1997. He was elected as Mayor of London in 2000. The significance of an elected mayor in British local government has yet to be evaluated properly, but, in the longer term, may serve to change the relationships between local and central government.

Ken Livingstone

In many countries local authorities having clearly identified political executives in addition to their elected assemblies have long been the norm. The executives may be directly elected by the public, chosen by the council or even appointed at national level in agreement with the local authority. Executives are responsible for the administration of the authority as well as for preparing policy and budgetary proposals for the council. The existence of a strong mayor can affect the popular perception of the municipality, personifying the local authority and increasing interest in local elections. Mayors in countries such as the United States and France often have influence on a wider state or national basis. In France senior government ministers, including the Prime Minister, may continue to have a local power base by being mayor of their local government while concurrently holding national office. President Jacques Chirac held the office of mayor of Paris prior to being elected President in 1995. In the United States President Clinton's Cabinet appointed in 1993 included the former mayors of San Antonio and Denver. Whereas in Britain a number of MPs have had experience as local councillors, it is extremely rare for a politician to hold national and local office simultaneously, and generally local politicians are not known widely even in their own areas. In some countries there is much greater overlap and interaction between national and local politics.

We should also distinguish between what are known as dual and fused systems, which affect intergovernmental relations between the centre and localities. The English tradition has been for local authorities to operate separately from the central government. Indeed, not only is there a separation at the political level but recruitment practices for civil servants and local government officers have been very different. This is a dual system and, although of course central government influences and intervenes extensively in local government affairs it is through many different departments and officials. However, under a fused system best exemplified in France the two levels are joined in an office such as a prefect (or Commissioner of the Republic), who is a central appointee with broad powers of oversight of administration in a particular local area. This official reports to the Ministry of the Interior and acts as the focus of a two-way process of intergovernmental communication. The commissioners for the departments are very important and influential individuals, although decentralising reforms in France in the early 1990s transferred some of their functions to the elected councils.

See section on 'Central–local relations', pp. 320–5.

▐ **THINK POINT**

▨ Do you know the names of any local council members in your area?

▨ If so, do you know what positions they hold?

▨ If you answer no to one or both of these questions, why do you think that is?

Central–local relations

It is beyond the scope of this chapter to attempt to describe the vast array of different forms of relationship between central and local government that exist in various political systems. Suffice to say that the history, political culture and constitutional developments of individual countries make for a diverse range of interactions and arrangements. There have been attempts to portray central–local relations by way of models or analytical frameworks intended to simplify and explain complex and multidimensional phenomena. For example, the agency model pictures local authorities as subordinate bodies with little or no discretionary power whose role is to act as agents of central government in implementing its policies. The power dependence model put forward by Rhodes, however, stresses that both levels of government have resources – legal, financial, political, informational and so on – and that bargaining between them is an important feature of the relationship (Rhodes 1981). However, Norton cautions us to be wary of such models, particularly in the context of comparing different political systems:

There is a simple model of two pole central–local relations which bears little resemblance to reality. Each level of government is fragmented and complex. Relations cross each other in what is a diagonal and tangled pattern rather than a vertical one. Given the great variety and complexity of the institutions at any one level of government, the range of channels and the modes of communication that can be used downwards and upwards in any one case and the extent to which many of the channels used are invisible to researchers as well as to the general public, it is clear that even if a study is sharply focused, light can only be thrown on limited aspects of interaction.

(Norton 1994: 51)

We may therefore draw attention to some of the factors that will affect central–local government relations, a number of which have been referred to earlier in the chapter.

1 Whether the system is a federal or unitary one; in the former the existence of a state tier affects the constitutional relationship between national and local levels and the degree of interaction directly between them.
2 How many tiers of local government exist and the number and size of local authorities with which the centre has to interact.
3 Whether the local authorities have a general competence or are restricted by the *ultra vires* rule.
4 The range of local government services and the proportion of public spending and GNP that expenditure on these services constitutes; if local spending is a significant percentage then central government is more likely to wish to influence or control it as part of its overall economic policy and its attempt to restrain public expenditure.
5 The organisation of central government; is there a Ministry of the Interior and a fused system with a prefect having overall supervisory responsibilities over local authorities? It is also important to remember that central governments are not monolithic entities; they consist of different departments with often different traditions and ways of dealing with local authorities in relation to the services for which they are responsible. The departments are also usually reliant on local government for the effective implementation of national policies.
6 The form of local government finance; how far local authorities are dependent on central government grants for their resources; whether the grants are general revenue that can be used at the authorities' discretion or specific grants limited to use on certain functions; what independent tax sources local authorities have and whether there are any central restrictions on their tax-raising powers. (Property taxes are the most common form of local tax but sales taxes, local income taxes and business taxes are also frequent sources of income.)
7 The type of relationship that exists between national and local politicians and administrators.

8 The nature of party politics and how far central–local relations are affected by strong party and ideological differences.

9 How far central government consults with and takes notice of the views of interest groups, professionals operating in different policy networks and bodies representing local government such as local authority associations.

Philip Blair draws attention to another important point to be considered when we attempt to analyse and contrast central–local relations in different countries.

> When comparing trends in different countries with regard to local autonomy, it is important to bear in mind the quite different starting-points from which each system is evolving. Decentralising tendencies may be observed in some traditionally highly centralised systems which may still leave them more centralised than some countries in which local autonomy is being eroded. The problem, however, is that the actual degree of local autonomy in different countries is not easy to compare, depending as it does on the interplay of a large number of factors which are often difficult to measure.
>
> (Blair 1991: 41)

In Scandinavia, Italy, France, Spain and Portugal, for example, there have been decentralising reforms with central government reducing the degree of regulation. Although in some cases, such as those of Spain and Portugal and perhaps France, where there was a tradition of highly centralised government, it may be argued that there was only one way to go, and although the degree of real antonomy created by such reforms can be debated, there is little doubt that the trend in Europe has been towards decentralisation. In Britain by contrast, local government has been subject to more detailed regulation than ever before. Between 1979 and 1997, well over 210 Acts of Parliament were passed affecting local government, at least one-third of them in major and far-reaching ways (Wilson and Game 2002: 100). The Thatcher governments of the 1980s were particularly concerned with restricting local government spending as part of their overall economic policy, but they also, in line with New Right thinking referred to above (p. 300), saw local authorities in many ways as inefficient and wasteful providers of services. In answer to the charge that the government was centralising to an unprecedented level in modern times, Conservatives argued that the national government had a broader mandate, that it had a responsibility for ensuring national standards (for example, with the creation of the National Curriculum for schools) and protecting citizens from irresponsible local authorities by such measures as capping local government budgets. The government also argued that it was in many cases decentralising power by devolving decisions away from government to individual citizens by, for example, selling council houses to tenants and allowing parents more choice over which school their children attended. After

1997 the Labour government promised to relax some controls and even to give local authorities additional powers in some areas, but it also threatened to remove powers from those councils which did not comply with government policy or in its view failed to provide satisfactory standards of services to the public.

Conclusion

This chapter has demonstrated that, although most studies of political systems tend to concentrate attention on national government institutions and policy-making, an understanding of the nature of political activity at sub-national levels is essential if we are fully to appreciate the complexities and subtleties of how these systems work in practice and the way people govern themselves on a day-to-day basis. There is continuing discussion in most countries about the proper distribution of power between the central administration and other tiers of government, a debate that is increasingly affected in Europe by arguments over whether there should be a devolution of policy-making in some areas down to regional bodies while other responsibilities are simultaneously transferred to the supranational authority of the European Union.

Chapter summary

◻ Within nation-states important areas of policy are often decided and carried out by sub-national governments.

◻ The existence of sub-national governments may be seen as an important means of maintaining liberal democracy by decentralising power.

continued

323

continued

■ There are advantages and disadvantages of decentralisation, taking account of the need for representative and responsive government as well as the requirements for efficient and effective administration.

■ Federalism provides for a division of law-making authority between a national government and a number of state or provincial governments, the latter having a constitutionally entrenched position within the political system.

■ Unitary states do not have the same constitutionally entrenched position as the states but often support the principle of local self-government in their constitutions.

■ Structures of local democracy, including the names, sizes and powers of the sub-national units, vary according to national history, traditions and culture.

■ Relations between central and sub-national governments vary from state to state and also over time.

Key texts

Batley, R. and Stoker, G. (eds) (1991) *Local Government in Europe: Trends and Developments*, London: Macmillan.

Burgess, M. and Gagnon, A. G. (eds) (1993) *Comparative Federalism and Federation*, Hemel Hempstead: Harvester Wheatsheaf.

Norton, A. (1994) *International Handbook of Local and Regional Government*, Aldershot: Edward Elgar.

Further reading

Batley, R. and Stoker, G. (eds) (1991) *Local Government in Europe: Trends and Developments*, London: Macmillan. A comparative analysis of recent changes in local government in European political systems.

Burgess, M. and Gagnon, A. G. (eds) (1993) *Comparative Federalism and Federation*, Hemel Hempstead: Harvester Wheatsheaf. An important work by leading experts on federalism which provides a range of perspectives and approaches.

Norton, A. (1994) *International Handbook of Local and Regional Government*, Aldershot: Edward Elgar. A major reference book which provides a wealth of data and information about local government in Europe, America and Japan.

Wilson, D. and Game, C. (2002) *Local Government in the United Kingdom*, 3rd edn, London: Palgrave. A comprehensive textbook with an attractive format which examines the workings of local government in the UK and recent developments in a lively and interesting way.

CONTENTS

The Machinery of Government

Richard Huggins

▌ Introduction

This chapter is about the main institutions and organisations of government that characterise the exercise and control of political power and the representation of the people within the political system. This means institutions, organisations and individual political offices like parliaments, courts, presidents and prime ministers. To some extent this chapter could be summed up as an exploration of the institutions of government, and the relationship between those institutions and those who are governed or the people, and the chapter is organised in the following way. First, I will explore the principal units of political organisation characteristic of the global political order, i.e. nations and nation-states, followed by some of the key concepts associated with these geopolitical units. This includes the state, government and governance. Third, I will look at the formal rules by which the machinery of government are organised: constitutions. Fourth, I will explore the three main branches of the state: the executive, legislature and judiciary, and this section of the chapter will break down further into a discussion of some examples of different types of each of these categories. This will include examples of executive power in the form of heads of state, for example prime ministers and presidents, of different types of legislatures, for example assemblies and parliaments, and of different types of judiciaries. I will then develop the analysis further through a comparison of two forms of government: parliamentary systems of government and presidential systems of government. Fifth,

I will consider briefly other models such as semi-presidential, military and communist executives. In the final section I will consider two important developments affecting institutions of government: integration and virtuality.

Preliminary observations

Before we look directly at the institutions that make up the machinery of government it will be useful to highlight some important contextual points. As a starting point of analysis I think it is useful to ask a number of questions which readers can apply to their own studies. For example, when looking at a political system it is worth asking what do political institutions do, where does power actually (rather than apparently) lie and who actually governs? These questions provide a sensible starting point for our analysis of different political systems and answers may be readily compared from case to case.

Such an approach implies a particular methodological approach, the comparative political method. This method is particularly significant in the study of different political institutions across the world, and our understanding of different political institutions can be significantly enhanced by comparing institutions and political processes across different nations (Lijphart 1971; Guy Peters 1998; Pennings *et al.* 1999; Landman 2000). For example, Pennings *et al.* (1999: 3) argue that the 'art of comparing' is

> one of the most important cornerstones of the development of knowledge about society and politics and insights to what is going on, how things develop and, more often than not, the formulation of statements about why this is the case and what it may mean to all of us. In short, comparisons are part and parcel of the way we experience reality and, most importantly, how we assess its impact on our lives and that of others.

I think it is useful for readers to think about applying the comparative method when analysing different political institutions. As the above quote implies, we often use this type of method anyway in our everyday approach to the world – the point here would be to try to use the art of comparison in a more methodological and social scientific way to enhance the depth of our understanding.

Furthermore, there is an important relationship between social structures and political institutions. What factors explain the patterns of politics in political systems? Why are political conflicts present in some countries and not in others? How is political stability achieved and to what extent can political institutions help secure or maintain such stability?

Nations are often fragmented in a number of different ways and it can be argued the existence of such fragmentation (or homogeneity) can have significant political effects. Societies may be divided into politically relevant groups: for example, around issues of social and economic class, religious belief, national and ethnic identity, language and gender. Sometimes such fragmentation may lead to political conflict and instability as, for example, in the case of Northern Ireland where there are a set of fragmentations around national, ethnic and religious identities that have resulted in political violence, terrorism and political instability, and have led to the formation of a set of political parties that have attempted to represent the different social groups within the political systems. Such social fragmentation is often referred to as social cleavages (Lipset and Rokkan 1967; Meny 1994) and has been used as a method to explain the formation of party and political systems throughout the world. In Northern Ireland attempts are being made to address these high levels of political violence, instability and fragmentation through institutional design of the new Northern Ireland Assembly (Wilford 2000).

Key text: S. Lipset and S. Rokkan (eds) (1967) *Party Systems and Voter Alignment*, London: Free Press.

A further contextual observation is that, in keeping with the overall approach of this book, the reader's attention is drawn to what might be called factors of transition – for example, globalisation, political and economic integration in the European Union and the information and communications 'revolution' – which represent significant challenges to both the workings of the institutions of government and the analysis of such institutions. Although national institutions of government will remain crucial in world politics for the foreseeable future, these developments are influencing national governmental institutions and processes and, in the longer term, may result in the construction of new institutions and processes of transnational government, accountability and decision-making to accommodate changing political values and practices. Examples might include the highly self-conscious project of European integration in the form of the European Union or the governance of military action and intervention in, for example, Bosnia or Kosovo or as an outcome of the global war on 'terrorism' in the shape of US and British military action in Afghanistan. Furthermore, our ways of thinking about political institutions and the way we analyse them may also have to change to accommodate such shifts in political power, institutions and processes.

Nations, nation-states and the state

In terms of the machinery of government there is a significant relationship between the organisation of political units into nations and the institutions through which politics, power and representation are organised and the ways in which economic, social, political and cultural resources are distributed and regulated. The idea of the nation has a long and contested history (Anderson 1991; Hechter 2000; Schopflin 2000), and many argue that the future of the nation and the nation-state is made increasingly more complex by the apparent acceleration of globalisation in the late twentieth and early twenty-first centuries (Opello and Rosow 1999; Scholte 2001).

Key text: B. Anderson (1991) *Imagined Communities*, London: Verso.

Whether or not this is the case, nations (or the national political community) have historically been central elements of political power and governance (Frazer 1999). Nations may or may not be self-governing political units but it is usually the case that governments enjoy political power within the boundaries of a nation and that political legitimacy and ability to govern often relies on a government's ability to claim some form of affinity with the national or at least group identity of the people they govern. This leads to a consideration of the machinery of government which is that there exists an important relationship between that machinery and the nation-state. A working definition of a nation-state is a unit of political authority which is linked to a clear geographic location recognised in international law, and these units form the basis of the world political order. Furthermore, the machinery of government is mapped on to these geopolitical units.

Nation-states can be divided into two main forms: unitary states and federal states. Unitary states are those in which there exists a central and indivisible political authority, for example France, which has a long tradition of central state power (Girling 1998). On the other hand, federal states are those which have some division of political authority into smaller units below the level of the state which is reflected in the organisation of the machinery of government. Examples of this would be Belgium, Germany or the United States in which there is a clear delineation between central or federal power and smaller units of political authority such as regions (Belgium), Länder (Germany) or states (USA).

The State is considered the sole source of the 'right' to use violence. (Max Weber, *Politics as a Vocation*)

State The state refers to all the institutions, agencies and agents that operate within a given territorial space, have legitimate power and authority over the people and possess the sole authority to use force against its own citizens.

Government The formal institutions, offices, processes and personnel through which the day-to-day running of a country, the maintenance of public order and the distribution of resources is managed and maintained.

If nation-states are an important aspect of the organisation of politics it is legitimate to ask: What is the **state**? First, we must be clear that the state is a broader concept than the **government**. The state refers to all the institutions, agencies and agents that operate within a given territorial space, have legitimate power and authority over us, and can legitimately utilise force as an (ultimate) sanction against us if we fail to accept its laws and orders, or resist its actions, or act against it. Indeed this characteristic of the state as a body that is the sole legitimate user of force is a common theme in the literature. But it tells a limited tale, for quite clearly the recourse to violence in many states is rare, and state systems can maintain legitimacy through force only for a limited length of time and cannot maintain authority through force alone.

While this may be true, the state is almost always ready to use force and coercion against sections of its people if they conflict with either the laws of the state or certain accepted norms of behaviour. Thus the execution of criminals is accepted as legitimate in many states, the persecution of ethnic or religious groups may well be sanctioned by the state and even those who dissent in terms of social norms and values may find considerable force exacted against them by the state.

In addition to possessing the power and authority to employ violence legitimately, the state may be characterised as consisting of a number of agents and offices, including government ministers, the judiciary, civil servants, the army, the police, the public education system and local authorities and agencies. In this sense the concept of the state is an umbrella term that covers all such offices that make and enforce the collective decisions and rules of a society (Hague *et al.* 1992). The state, then, is the term that refers to a broad set of institutions and processes that relate to the maintenance of social order and political organisation, but we need to bear in mind that the *exact* nature of the state remains to some extent ambiguous.

Government and governance

Governance A broader concept than government which refers to the processes through which social, economic and political life are organised and regulated.

The notion of government differs from the concept of the state to the extent that this concept refers to the formal institutions and processes through which the day-to-day running of a country, the maintenance of public order and the distribution of resources is managed and maintained. These institutions include the executive, the legislature and the judiciary and are explored in detail later in this chapter. **Governance** is a much broader concept which refers more to the processes through which social, economic and political life are organised and regulated. The concept and practices of governance are currently enjoying considerable attention from commentators and policy-makers as people explore ideas of globalisation, transnational governance and different models of governance (Castells 1996; Kohler-Koch and Eising 1999; Dinan 2001).

Constitutions and constitutionalism

Constitutions may be seen as the rules by which the state is organised and operates through the formal enshrining of rights, duties and obligations that establish or formalise the relationship between the central political authority and the people (Lane 1996). As such, studying constitutions can be a useful starting point in any analysis of the government and politics of any given state. Constitutions often outline the main institutions of state, and can give us some clues as to the relationship between these different institutions and how they function. Constitutions can also give us an insight into the political culture of a state in terms of how central concepts (for example, 'the people' or citizen), institutions and relationships between these are defined or discussed in any constitutional document. In the case of the former USSR, for example, constitutional documents provided interesting insights into the circulating notions of communism and the priorities of the Soviet State (Lane 1985). In more contemporary times the new constitutions of the former communist states can be read as documents of post-communist intent.

The late eighteenth and early nineteenth centuries witnessed a proliferation of documents such as Declarations of Rights and Bills of Rights that provide good examples of general statements of constitutional intent. Such documents offer indications of *how* the relationship between the state and the individual ought to be organised and what – in principle at least – the most important rights of the individual are. The emphasis is on the rights held by individuals by virtue of their possession of reason, property (in the shape of the individual physical self) and other 'natural' rights. Two of the most famous and indicative examples of this are the *Declaration of Independence* drafted by Thomas Jefferson for the thirteen American Colonies in July 1776 and the French *Declaration of the Rights of Man and the Citizen* of 26 August 1789. Both of these documents are clearly an outcome of the development of liberal individualism and Enlightenment thought that characterises much of the eighteenth century. Both documents seek to define what the rights of individual (although in this case only male) citizens are. As such the rights outlined would still be those identified as central to individual freedom and human rights, and in particular the French Declaration of 1789 can be instructively compared with later declarations regarding human rights – such as the United Nations Charter of Human Rights – to reveal strong similarities of wording, value and sentiment.

In the following extract from the *Declaration of Independence* the values of liberal individualism are clearly evident. Here those who wrote this statement are attempting to establish the form and nature of **limited government** as opposed to the oppressive and unrepresentative forms found in the European monarchies. As you read this statement, first make a note of the main rights of the individual that are being identified. Second, ask yourself if the truths identified as significant are actually self-evident.

Constitution The rules by which states and governments are organised and operate in the form of the enshrining of rights, duties and obligations that establish or formalise the relationship between political authority and the people.

Key text: S. E. Finer, V. Bogdanor and B. Rudden (1995) *Comparing Constitutions*, Oxford: Clarendon Press.

Limited government Government in which the sovereign or executive power is limited by law, constitutional rules or institutional organisation.

```
Document
```

Declaration of Independence, July 1776

We hold these Truths to be self-evident, that all Men are created equal, that they are endowed by their Creator with certain unalienable Rights, that among these are Life, Liberty and Pursuit of Happiness. That to secure these Rights, Governments are instituted among Men, describing their just Powers from the Consent of the Governed that whenever any Form of Government becomes destructive of these Ends, it is the Right of the People to alter or abolish it, and to constitute new Government.

This statement clearly outlines the contractual nature of the relationship between the state and the individual. Furthermore, the individual retains the right to remove consent from being governed in the event of that government failing in its obligations and duties. This concern with the liberty and rights of the individual is further developed in the *Declaration of the Rights of Man and the Citizen* of 1789. Again when you read this statement make a note of the main rights that are being outlined.

So far the statements we have considered have been general comments on the nature of the relationship between the state and the individual, and as such often represent first principles and key intentions of the writers. Such sentiments and ideas can be developed further by a consideration of constitutions.

```
Document
```

The Constitution of the United States, Preamble, 1790

We the People of the United States, in order to form a more perfect Union, establish justice, insure domestic tranquillity, provide for the common defense, promote the general welfare, and secure the blessings of liberty to ourselves and our posterity, do ordain and establish the Constitution for the United States of America.

However, there is a limit to how much a study of constitutions tells us. While the study of such documents and formal statements of intent can tell us what values are believed to be important by those who wrote the document, it may be that the statement of intent differs markedly from the actual political situation extant in a country. Indeed to grasp fully the workings or failings of a constitution we need to consider the concepts you studied earlier when you looked at *political socialisation, political culture* and *political behaviour*.

In many cases the formal document only tells us how *in an ideal situation* the relationship between individual and state ought to work. We need to also take into consideration the role of political socialisation and political culture to assess the extent to which rights and freedoms may be enjoyed. For example, although most countries accept that the freedoms of assembly, demonstration and expression are important individual rights, attitudes towards those who participate in politically motivated demonstrations vary considerably across cultures and social groups. It might also be argued that certain political freedoms and rights – the right to vote or to join a political party – might be relatively meaningless in cases of extreme poverty, high crime or, on a larger scale, the destiny of local communities within the increasingly global economy.

The constitutional documents considered above are concerned with the limits of state power over the individual. Indeed they are documents which place at the centre of their political concerns the rights and liberties of the individual. But we have also argued that constitutional documents alone do not guarantee the rights they enshrine. This has led some commentators to argue that the functioning of constitutional government is as much dependent on political culture as on constitutional documents. In order for constitutional government to work a further characteristic must be present: this is known as *constitutionalism*. Thus a system of values and political attitudes among political agents and citizens must exist in order for the values conveyed in the constitutional document to be enforced. Furthermore, the existence of constitutionalism helps to explain how countries without formal constitutional documents can still exhibit strikingly consistent constitutional procedures and outcomes.

Since 1989 and the apparent end of communism as a way of organising the state and political life in the former Eastern Europe (1989) and the former USSR (1992) a large number of new constitutions have been written (and sometimes rewritten) in Europe and the states of the former USSR. In recent years countries throughout this region have designed and developed new constitutions as an element of the political transition to democratic forms of government.

Document

Since the early 1990s there has been a proliferation of new constitutions in post-communist states. Many of these constitutions embrace the sentiments of older constitutional documents from France and the USA. However, many of them are also much longer, contain a large number of stated rights and often demonstrate considerable optimistic and hopeful expressions for a post-communist future. Below are some extracts from the 1994 Constitution of Belarus.

Belarus Constitution, 1994

PREAMBLE

We, the People of the Republic of Belarus, emanating from the responsibility for the present and future of Belarus; recognizing ourselves as a subject, with full rights, of the world community and confirming our adherence to values common to all mankind; founding ourselves on our inalienable right to self-determination; supported by the centuries-long history of development of Belarusian statehood; striving to assert the rights and freedoms of every citizen of the Republic of Belarus; desiring to maintain civic harmony, stable foundations of democracy, and a state based on the rule of law; hereby adopt this Constitution as the Basic Law of the Republic of Belarus.

ARTICLE 1 PRINCIPLES

(1) The Republic of Belarus shall be a unitary, democratic, social state based on the rule of law. The Republic of Belarus shall have supreme control and absolute authority in its territory and shall implement domestic and foreign policy independently.

(2) The Republic of Belarus shall defend its independence and territorial integrity, its constitutional system, and safeguard legality and law and order.

ARTICLE 2 [INDIVIDUALISM]

(1) The individual shall be of supreme importance to society and the State.

(2) The State shall bear responsibility towards the citizen to create the conditions for the free and dignified development of his identity. The citizen bears a responsibility towards the State to discharge unwaveringly the duties imposed upon him by the Constitution.

ARTICLE 3 [DEMOCRACY]

(1) The people shall be the sole source of state power in the Republic of Belarus. The people shall exercise their power directly and through representative bodies in the forms and within the limits specified in the Constitution.

(2) Any actions aimed at seizing state power by forcible means or by way of any other violation of the laws shall be punishable by law.

The constitution contains 149 articles detailing rights and obligations covering areas from state structures and political action to marriage and housing rights. Why do you think constitutions in post-communist countries might be so long and contain the type of articles they do ?

For excellent and comprehensive information about and links to constitution worldwide try the Charter 88 Website at <http://www.charter88.org.uk>

Furthermore, some constitutions are more explicit in their formulation of the organisation of the state and state power than others. Thus the American Constitution, although not the most rigid of constitutional documents, specifies what the offices of the state are and how their powers relate to each other and to the people. In this case there exists a formal document which specifies the role of each of the institutions of the state, the power and responsibilities of these institutions and the rights and obligations of the people in respect to these institutions. There also exists a process of regulation and appeal when the constitution and the rights enshrined therein are compromised or breached. Thus the individual has recourse to the Supreme Court, and this court can make binding rulings regarding the constitutional rights and freedoms of individuals.

In Britain no such constitutional organisation of the state machinery and its relationship to the people exists. Although neither of the popular assertions that Britain does not have a constitution or that the constitution is 'unwritten' are correct, identification and interpretation of the British constitution is highly complex because of the absence of a single constitutional document. Britain's constitution is characterised by a whole host of legal acts, conventions and practices. There exists no formal separation of powers, no equivalent of the Supreme Court and no right of constitutional appeal. There does exist a Bill of Rights from 1689 but this is a legal enactment which can be overruled by further legislation rather than a set of constitutionally guaranteed rights and freedoms. Although individuals can seek a judicial review, this is a ruling on the legality of an act or a piece of legislation rather than any attempt to rule on its constitutional validity. This means that the rights enjoyed by the people of Britain appear to be legal rather than constitutional rights. Thus although the legal and conventional position is that elections are held every five years in Britain, this could be altered by law, and the people would not have any constitutional document to appeal to or channel for such an appeal. This has led many critics of the British system to suggest that individuals enjoy not citizens' rights, or indeed citizenship, but the rights and obligations of subjects. The recent incorporation of the European Convention on Human Rights into British law may be changing this situation and an increasing array of citizen rights are emerging through appeals to this document through the British courts.

Overall, the above discussion should alert us to limits of constitutions and the fact that constitutions are not always the same type of documents, and that the form and function of constitutions differs from case to case. Developing this type of analysis, Elazar (1985) argues that constitutions may be classified into five types:

1 A loose frame of government which subsequently requires a considerable amount of adaptation and interpretation. A good example of this would be the Constitution of the United States of America which has undergone considerable revision and adaptation through the intervention of the Supreme Court.
2 A strict state code in which detailed rules and relationships are specified. This is more characteristic of the situation in some Western European states, most notably France.
3 A revolutionary manifesto which sets out a programme of considerable social, economic and political reorganisation. This is clearly conveyed in the constitutions of the former Soviet Union.
4 A statement of political ideals or an image of the world as it might or ought to be. This is common among new and emerging states and developing states, especially those gaining independence from colonial powers.
5 An embodiment of an ancient source of authority. This is characteristic of Israel's constitution which is based upon the sovereignty of the Knesset and derives from the Torah or Jewish holy book.

THINK POINT

Which of the five types of constitution outlined above would the state you come from fit into?

Executives, legislatures and judiciaries

In this section I will consider the three main elements that make up the machinery of government: the executive, legislature and judiciary. This will enable us to develop both our analysis of the machinery and our comparison of such machinery across different states and countries.

Executives

Executive The executive is the apex of power in a political system at which policy is formed and through which it is executed, for example, the President of the USA or the Prime Minister of the UK.

Megawati Sukarnoputri – Indonesia's fifth president

The **executive** is that body which initiates and administers policy within a state. There are two important points to make here. First, we need to distinguish between the political executive, those politicians who hold the office of executive – prime ministers, presidents, chancellor, taoiseach – and the non-political executive or the civil service. Second, we need to identify two principal types of executive: unipersonal executives, such as the President of the United States, and plural executives, such as Cabinet government in Britain.

Legislatures

Legislature The legislature is the body within a political system that makes the laws. This is most likely to be a national assembly, for example, a Parliament or a Congress.

The Parliament Building, Delhi, India

Legislatures are diverse in structure, in name and in power. They may consist of one chamber (unicameral), two chambers (bicameral), and the members of the legislature may be elected or appointed. They can be politically powerful or politically weak. They can be symbolically important and bond the nation in unity or they can be the location of division and confrontation. They are known by many names including *parliaments, congress, senates, national council, national assembly* or more nationally specific names such as *Sejm* (Poland), *Storting* (Norway) or the *Majlis* (Islamic Consultative Assembly). Furthermore, there are a growing number of legislatures operating at a transnational level, including the *European Parliament*, the *Latin American Parliament* and the *North Atlantic Assembly*.

Legislatures have a number of key roles which include representation, deliberation, scrutiny and legislation. If one accepts that these roles are the appropriate ones for a legislature, then to some degree the effectiveness of how these roles are achieved can be a measure of the 'health' and value (to democracy and the people) of such chambers. We should note that many commentators have questioned the effectiveness of legislative chambers throughout the world to deliver on these roles and many commentators argue that, in general, legislatures have experienced a decline in their status, power and effectiveness in the past few decades (Norton 1998). Such discussions represent a critical focus for students of politics.

In terms of representation the legislatures can provide an opportunity for the people to be *represented* in the political system. Through the election of members to the legislature the people become involved in the political process. Clearly this representative function is likely to be a more complete process in a country where free and competitive elections occur; that is, a country subscribing to some form of representative democratic political system in which choice between political representatives is possible and parties compete for power. If the assembly does carry the voice of the people to the executive, one might argue that this is a crucial and valuable role for the assembly. But the ability of a legislature to deliver on the task may be challenged in a number of ways. In the United Kingdom, for example, MPs have to take an oath of allegiance to the Crown and some, notably republican Sein Fein Members of Parliament, feel unable to take such an oath. This had, until December 2001, left Sein Fein MPs without access to office space and administrative support at the Westminster Parliament.

It would seem then that one function of a representative legislative assembly is to provide, through the compositions, systems and procedures the assembly adopts, a sense of legitimacy for the overall political process of the state and to ensure that government is not seen or does not operate as arbitrary or unrepresentative. In particular such legitimacy is passed on to individual pieces of legislation so that new laws and policy initiatives are accepted by the people not necessarily because they agree with or desire them but because they do accept, at least, the legitimacy of the process and the decisions produced by it.

Another function of a legislative chamber is deliberation through which matters of public interest are discussed and agreed upon with regard to prevailing public concerns, values and norms.

A further role of legislatures is to *legislate* in terms of passing legislation and making laws. This is most likely to take the form of a set of procedural rules and practices that formalise a proposal into a new law. This formal and procedural role of legislatures takes up an increasing amount of time. For example, in the United Kingdom there are about a hundred new laws passed by Parliament every year.

Different legislatures will have different rules and systems through which laws will be made. However, an overview of the procedures for enacting a law in the UK gives a good illustration of how a legislature is involved in making a new law.

In the UK a proposal for legislation (a Bill) can be either a Private Bill or a Public Bill; however, the majority of Bills that become law are Public Bills sponsored by the government (Government Bills). Such proposals for legislation will be drawn up by government advisers and civil servants working in a government department which is responsible for the relevant area of policy. Once drawn up, this proposal will be circulated to various groups – for example, pressure groups, specialist groups, business, professional groups, other government departments and sometime wide public consultation – in a process of consultation. After the consultation process a formal proposal will be drafted and presented to the legislature for consideration. In the UK this process is called the First Reading, at which the proposal (Bill) is *read* to the House to allow members to know it is being introduced to the House. The First Reading is followed by a Second Reading which explains the purpose of the Bill. This Second Reading is followed by the Committee stage, during which a Standing Committee will consider the details of the proposal, and it is at this stage that amendments may be suggested. After the Bill has been considered by the Committee it enters the Report stage, during which further changes may be suggested by the whole of the House of Commons. The Bill then has its Third Reading in the House of Commons, during which the House can make a thorough examination of all proposals and measures in the Bill. If the Bill passes the Third Reading it goes to the House of Lords for the second stage of consideration. The procedure in the House of Lords mirrors that in the Commons, with three readings, a committee stage and a report stage. If the Lords proposes amendments to a Bill it has to go back to the House of Commons for a further consideration, and this process can go on for quite a while. Ultimately the House of Commons will get its way as the Lords cannot reject a Bill that has passed two successive readings in the lower house. However, the process can take up to two years to complete, and demands on the parliamentary calendar or an impending general election can lead to the dropping of proposals or greater amendment and compromise than governments may have originally intended. Finally, once passed by both Houses of Parliament the Bill goes to the monarch (Elizabeth II) to be given Royal Assent and then becomes law.

The above process – illustrated mainly from the British case – is clearly lengthy and quite complex. This is, in part, an outcome of the nature of the British parliamentary system, i.e. two houses, and the persistence of the monarchy. However, it may be argued that slowness and implicit cooperation within and between members of both chambers acts as a kind of safeguard against political power and poor legislation.

THINK POINT

- Is such a system too complex?

- Is it too slow and antiquated?

- Can you suggest ways to improve it?

Although formally known as the legislature, it is often argued that legislatures are not so much concerned with law-making as *law-enacting*. While there may be some exceptions to this – for example, the United States Congress and the Senato in Italy – in the main, the law-making capability of legislatures appears to have been eroded over the years. There seem to be several reasons for this and, of course, these are contested explanations, but it would seem that an erosion of the power of assemblies (in law-making terms) has taken place due to three main developments.

First, the strengthening of the executive arms of government as law-makers and policy initiators. The Prime Minister of Britain is often cited as a good example of this, and since 1997 Tony Blair has been accused of acting as a 'president' rather than a prime minister (Foley 2000). Such charges increased in October 2001 with the actions of the British government and Tony Blair's handling of this role during British and US military action in Afghanistan.

Second, the growth of strong party (particularly those containing two parties) systems. Here, the existence of strong party discipline, party manifestos and platforms, party recruitment and financing of those seeking political office have all tended to undermine the independence of individual assembly members and almost guarantee that the party with a majority in the assembly will succeed in any legislation it initiates. It follows, of course, that those political systems where the assembly still has a significant role in the making of laws are found in those countries where party allegiances are comparatively weak – for example, the United States – or where the electoral system tends to result in a relatively large number of competing parties, such as the Senato in Italy.

The third factor affecting the role of the assembly has been the increasing importance of mass media, in particular television, in the political life of the nation. In this case, commentators have argued, the role of assemblies has been usurped by the media with the populace looking to the media for their contact with politicians and what they say. Furthermore, politicians have increasingly preferred to address the nation, make policy statements and conduct other political business to the television cameras rather than in their national assembly (Iyengar and Reeves 1997; Negrine 1998).

A fourth major function of a legislature is that it provides for the scrutiny of executive power and acts as an institution to which the executive is answerable and which can prevent abuses of power either through its powers of scrutiny or by uncovering the existence of abuse or calling attention to it. Not surprisingly, many question the actual ability or willingness of legislatures to act in this way and such power, where it exists, will depend largely on the independent political power of the legislature to deliver such a critical role.

In Britain, for example, in recent years the ability of the legislature to fulfil such a role has been challenged by persistent claims that Members of Parliament in general and government ministers in particular are able to act without fear of scrutiny or accountability to the House of Commons. The list of such apparent cases is long, and includes the apparent failure of the Nolan inquiry into standards in public life, Sir Justice Scott's inquiry into breaches of power by politicians in the core executive, MPs involved in 'cash for questions' scandals and the emerging difficulties of the current Labour administration and the collapse of the USA corporation Enron. Such accusations are obviously not confined to the UK. Bill Clinton's two administrations in the USA were dogged by various accusations of political (as well as personal) wrongdoing including the White Water scandal and the Star Investigation. Often such investigations and scandals, despite involving areas of particular public concern and sensitivity and featuring very serious allegations of political wrongdoing and corruption, do not result in significant censure of any individual or in any significant changes to the political system to prevent repetition of the alleged occurrences (Silk and Walters 1998).

A fifth role is to approve and regulate the collection and distribution of government finances in terms of agreeing taxation levels, receiving the national budget and scrutinising government expenditure and accounts. Indeed, historically, it was often around the issues of government and monarchical finances that the role of legislatures developed into points of opposition to executive dominance. Importantly a further role exists in the fifteen member states of the European Union for national legislatures to examine, respond to and incorporate into national law the treaties, agreements and legislative acts of the European Union.

These are clear functions that legislatures may or perhaps should perform. However, many commentators (and political actors) argue that these roles and functions are increasingly compromised by developments from both inside and outside the political system.

If law-making is no longer the primary aim of the legislative chamber, what is its role? It seems that the focus of the assembly's power has become legislative influence and scrutiny – although how effective such scrutiny is is open to question. Thus, as a chamber of popular representation, the legislature debates legislation introduced into it by the executive, and encourages amendments, revision and consideration. Furthermore the development of committee systems of scrutiny in many democratic systems has underpinned this role of the assembly (Drewry 1985).

Unicameralism An assembly with only one legislative chamber, for example, Finland, Hungary and Uganda.

Bicameralism An assembly with two legislative chambers, for example, the USA, France and Argentina.

Unicameral or bicameral?

The number of chambers an assembly should have is a question that has occupied many political scientists and political activists and remains an important point of comparison between different assemblies and political systems. In general, assemblies either have one chamber (**unicameral**) or two (**bicameral**). In 2001 the Inter-Parliamentary Union recognised 178 parliamentary democracies and of these sixty-three were bicameral (Russell 2001). Bicameral systems are those in which the assembly possesses two separate chambers, both of which have specific and separate roles, different powers and different membership. The two chambers can be very similar with an almost balanced relationship in terms of power, as in the case of Belgium, or quite dissimilar, as in the case of Britain, with its uniquely large second chamber, based on hereditary and nominated membership.

THINK POINT

- How many chambers does your national assembly have?

- Do they enjoy an equal or unequal relationship in terms of power?

Britain has a bicameral system, as does the United States of America and a whole range of other states, including Brazil, France, Canada, Australia and many others. The reasons for retaining two chambers are many and varied. For example, bicameral systems often fulfil a particular role within federal systems of government. In federal systems the membership of the second chamber will often attempt to reflect regional, cultural and ethnic differences and identities in order to underpin the federation of the state and to allow for local representation within the federal government system. Examples of this type of organisation may be found in a number of countries, including the United States of America, Canada, Argentina and Australia.

In other countries, such as Britain, the membership of the second chamber may reflect certain social and economic positions over others. Membership of the House of Lords consists of those who have a hereditary right to sit in the second chamber (Hereditary Peers), those nominated by the executive to become members of the upper house (Life Peers) and bishops (the Lords Spiritual).

The extract on page 342 provides a diagrammatic representation of a bicameral system. Here we see that more power lies within the first chamber than in the second. This concentration of power in the first chamber is, in part, a result of the political struggles that took place in the nineteenth and twentieth centuries between the democratically elected House of Commons and the hereditary House of Lords. Many feel that the balance works well and should be preserved, that the House of Lords represents an important part of British society and history. Others argue that it is archaic, limited and anti-democratic, and call for systematic reform of the assembly, either to abolish the House of Lords and replace it with another second chamber, differently constituted, or to create a unicameral system in Britain.

Plans for reform of the House of Lords in the UK are now well developed. The Royal Commission on the Reform of the House of Lords *A House for the Future* (Cm4534, 2000) and the UK government's White Paper *The House of Lords: Completing the Reform* (Cm5291, 2001) give clear statements of the political will that now exists to reform this element of the British political system. In short the reforms propose a smaller House of Lords (between 550

Bicameral systems: Britain.
Which Chamber has real power?

First Chamber House of Commons	Second Chamber House of Lords
Powers	Powers
Legislative Assembly	Limited legislative function
Scrutiny	Limited powers of scrutiny
Committee systems	Power of delay for non-finance bills
Dismiss Executive	Can suggest amendments
	Clarify law

---

and 600 members), the removal of hereditary peers, increased representative and democratic function and overall modernisation. The detailed recommendations are further outlined below.

Document

Second Chamber Reform in the UK – Radical or Moderate?

From *The House of Lords: Completing the Reform*
(Cm5291, 2001)

The House of Lords in an unelected, second chamber in Parliament. Although some minor reforms have been made in recent years this chamber is still considered by many to be unrepresentative and undemocratic. At the current time there are 713 members of the House of Lords. The membership is made up of:

1. 595 Life Peers
2. 92 Hereditary Peers
3. 26 Archbishops

Under UK Government proposals currently under discussion a reformed House of Lords would consist of:

1. 120 Independent members appointed by the Appointments Commission
2. 120 Directly elected members
3. 16 Bishops
4. A minimum of 12 Law Lords
5. The remaining 332 members to be nominated political members. The number of these available to each party will be determined by the Appointments Commission.

What do you think of these proposals? Do you think they are radical or moderate? More importantly, do you think such a system is more democratic than the current one? What are the strengths of this proposal? What are the weaknesses?

Although few countries have tended to carry the role of nomination and privilege quite as far as Britain in membership of the second chamber, it is not unusual for attempts to be made for the membership to reflect certain specific characteristics (Russell 2001). The most common is maturity with relatively high qualifying age restrictions placed on intending candidates. Thus, in Italy, an individual must be over 40 years of age to sit in the Senato and in the USA over 30 to sit in the Senate. These qualifications, it is argued, allows members to bring greater experience and maturity to their office (often accompanied by political experience in other parts of the political system) and allows for more considered judgement and 'wisdom'.

Another interesting characteristic of second chambers is that the length of office often varies from that of the first chamber. In Britain this is clearly the case, as being a member of the House of Lords lasts as long as one is alive. In countries where members are elected, the length of time they are elected for can vary from nine years in France, eight in Brazil to six in the case of Japan, India and the USA. Interestingly, some of these countries also stagger the election of members to the Upper House; thus, for example, in France one-third of the membership retire every three years and in the USA one-third retire every two years. The existence of a staggered term of office, coupled with age and other 'qualifications' for office, is designed to encourage a different balance of members and a different institutional culture with greater consistency and overlap between membership and executive administration. The longer period of office is also designed to reduce some of the concern with party politics and politics of the immediate present which often, understandably, characterises lower chambers.

In considering these elements of the political system we are really asking a related set of questions which may be useful as outlined at the start of this chapter. In some ways this chapter asks: How are people governed? What formal machinery exists to govern? Who governs through this machinery? What power do the institutions that govern possess? How is this power related to the people and from where does the authority to govern derive? These have been central issues in the discussion so far in this chapter. The struggle for responsible and accountable government has (and continues to have) a long and often violent history throughout the world and remains for those countries engaged in processes of democratisation (the former communist states in Europe) or countries struggling to retain democratic freedoms, such as Zimbabwe, key and vital questions. Even in the apparently established democracies of the West, the quest to ensure delivery against these criteria still occupies a good many politicians and scholars of politics.

The judiciary

Judiciary The judiciary is the body within a political system charged within enforcing the laws and, in some states, upholding the constitutional rules.

US Supreme Court

The role of the **judiciary** is to enforce the laws made by the executive and legislature and to enforce the rules of the political system. How this is actually achieved, however, varies from political system to political system as does the level of political and judicial independence. In the United States, the Supreme Court can rule an act carried out by the President or Congress as unconstitutional and therefore invalid. Indeed this is an important role for the Supreme Court in the USA. Not only does it represent a 'watchdog' role in regard to the power located in the other arms of the political system, it also represents how the constitution of the United States is kept 'alive' and reinterpreted to adapt to changing social, economic and political conditions. Throughout the past two centuries, the judiciary in the USA has been highly significant in shaping the way in which individual citizens' rights have developed and what the relationship between state and individual is. In this sense, the judiciary is *making* laws as much as enforcing them. In the 1950s and 1960s the decisions taken under the leadership of Chief Justice Warren established a series of precedents and vitally important decisions regarding the issue of black civil rights. In this sense the Supreme Court is a political body, or at least a body performing a political role as much as a judicial one. In Britain, no such constitutional power exists for the High Court or the House of Lords Law Lords, but they can rule on whether or not an act by a minister was lawful. In this sense the role of the judiciary is, perhaps, less openly political than in the USA. However, the judiciary in the UK has considerable power to influence the scope of law through the interpretation of existing statute and through judicial precedent.

As the role of the judiciary is very important to the functioning of a democratic state, the issue of the selection of the members of the judiciary is an important point for consideration. In particular the issues of independence and accountability are of central importance. Of course one might argue that if the law is neutral and the role of the judiciary is to enforce, it should not matter greatly how judges are appointed. But as we have noted, judges, particularly at the most senior constitutional level, have as important a role in making laws as interpreting them, and therefore their independence (or otherwise) from the political system becomes a question of crucial importance. Different countries appoint judges by different means. In Britain, and the USA in the case of the Supreme Court, judges are appointed by the executive and many would argue that this procedure opens up the possibility of 'political' appointments which might be sympathetic to the executive. The defence of such a system of appointment used to be that as judges often remain judges for a long time and political administrations are by comparison relatively short-lived there should exist a 'healthy' overlap between the judges appointed by one administration and the next. This justification may be a little dated now, especially with recent experience of Conservative Party executive dominance in the United Kingdom, and could still be criticised as being unfairly weighted in favour of the executive. The experience of the USA is equally unclear. Although Supreme Court judges are appointed by the President (subject to approval by Congress), seemingly political appointees have often asserted their independence once in position and this was the case with the Warren Courts of the 1950s and 1960s. Against this, however, it has to be said that the Supreme Court judges of the 1980s demonstrated considerable amounts of conservatism in their rulings, which may have been a reflection of the political stance of those who appointed them.

At the other extreme of executive appointed judges is the appointment of judges by popular election which also takes place in some states in the USA. This form of judicial selection does allow for public responsiveness and makes the judiciary at this level more responsible to the people. Critics argue, however, that this responsiveness is achieved at a high cost to impartiality and independence, as popular concern may compromise judicial integrity.

In considering the three branches of government discussed above – the executive, legislature and judiciary – it is impossible to avoid the classic doctrine, identified with Montesquieu, of the **separation of powers**. This doctrine is held up as an important organising principle of liberal democratic government and is enshrined in various constitutional arrangements, most notably in France and the USA.

Key text: A. Stone Sweet (2000) *Governing with Judges: Constitutional Politics in Europe*, Oxford: Oxford University Press.

Separation of powers The doctrine that maintains that the three key elements of government – the executive, the legislature and the judiciary – should be separate in role, powers and responsibilities and that such separation will ensure good and just government.

Charles de Secondat, Baron de Montesquieu (1689–1755), French political theorist, author of Esprit de Lois, *1748.*

Montesquieu and the separation of powers

Although the idea of a separation of powers has a long history and can be observed in the work of Aristotle and Locke the clearest and most explicit statement is associated with the writings of Montesquieu. This doctrine argues that in order to avoid a concentration of power in the hands of a minority in a political system the three principal constituents of government – the executive, legislature and

continued

continued

the judiciary – should be separate and enjoy equal power and independence. This should guarantee a series of checks and balances that protect the people from authoritarian or arbitrary rule. This doctrine has been very influential and is also explored in the writings of James Madison and Simon Bolivar. For Montesquieu the problem could be summed up as follows.

> When legislative power is united with executive power in a single person or in a single body of the magistracy, there is no liberty, because one can fear that the same monarch or senate that makes tyrannical laws will execute them tyrannically.
>
> Nor is there liberty if the power of judging is not separate from legislative power and from executive power. If it were joined to legislative power, the power over the life and liberty of the citizens would be arbitrary, for the judge would be the legislator. If it were joined to executive power, the judge could have the force of an oppressor.
>
> (Charles de Secondat, Baron de Montesquieu, 1689–1755,
> *Spirit of the Laws* (1748))

We can see then that the prime concern of Montesquieu was to avoid the excess of political power which might occur if too much power was concentrated in the hands of one area of government. The risk of arbitrary and 'tyrannical' rule was a possible outcome, and so the structure of government and how the elements of the structure related to each other was of key importance for thinkers in the liberal tradition who were especially concerned to establish the limits of government power and its relationship to the people.

For thinkers in this tradition, including John Locke, Montesquieu and John Stuart Mill, the most important point is to guarantee non-arbitrary government which is responsible to the people (however defined), limited in its extent and accountable both through reference to an electorate and through the organisation of government institutions and the relationship between these institutions. The aim was to arrive at an organisation of the political system that produced limited, responsible and accountable government. In this respect the analysis of the relationships that exist between the executive, legislature and judiciary provide us with an important insight into not only the structure of government but also the nature of that political system.

Parliamentary systems of government

Key text: D. Verney (1959) *The Analysis of Political Systems*, Glencoe, IL: Free Press.

These are characterised by a range of features that distinguish them from presidential executives and we can usefully use the work of Verney (1959) to guide us through this section. Verney's important book *The Analysis of Political Systems* (1959) represents a seminal study of the differences and distinctions between parliamentary executives and presidential executives.

Characteristics of parliamentary government

1 The assembly becomes a parliament.
2 The executive is divided into two parts.
3 The head of state appoints the head of government.
4 The head of government appoints the Ministry.
5 The government is a collective body.
6 Ministers are usually Members of Parliament.
7 The government is politically responsible to the assembly.
8 The head of government may advise the head of state to dissolve Parliament.
9 Parliament as a whole is supreme over its constituent parts, government and assembly, neither of which may dominate the other.
10 The government as a whole is only indirectly responsible to the electorate.
11 Parliament is the focus of power in the political system.

(Verney 1959)

Crucially important here is that the role of head of state is separate from that of the head of government. In Britain the head of state is the monarch, at present Queen Elizabeth II. The role of the monarchy in British politics is now purely symbolic and ceremonial and, although there remain residual powers for the monarchy, the long history of struggle between democratic representation and monarchical power has resulted in these powers being purely procedural. The monarch still appoints the prime minister after a general election, although in reality this is always the leader of the party which has secured the highest number of seats in the first chamber of the legislative assembly. All legislation passed through Parliament in Britain has to obtain royal assent – but again it is impossible to imagine a situation in which the monarch could or would withhold consent. The British political system possesses a range of conventions and traditions that echo the long history of political development in this country – the prime minister still holds a weekly audience with the monarch and members of the central executive are still referred to as 'King's' or 'Queen's' ministers. In this sense, the monarchy is said to rule through Parliament and certainly the role of the monarchy cannot be ignored in British politics (or indeed in those countries where the British monarch is also head of state such as Australia). But there exists no real independent political power for the monarchy in the political system. The cultural, historical and symbolic role of the monarchy, however, is still important, and considerable passion is encountered in Britain and other countries when the possibility of abolition is raised. This possibility does seem to be an increasingly likely one, certainly in some Commonwealth countries, and in Britain ever louder vocal calls for abolition or at least significant reform of the monarchy are heard.

A second key characteristic of parliamentary systems is that the executive is drawn from the national assembly and, crucially, its ability to hold on to power is dependent on legislative confidence. The location of the executive within the legislative assembly means that the executive – in the case of Britain the prime minister and the cabinet – has to retain the support of the legislative chamber in order to be able to pass its legislative proposals and govern. In Britain, this system operates within a strong two-party system which tends to mean that the executive can command legislative confidence in direct relation to the parliamentary strength of the dominant party. In the 1980s and 1990s the Conservative Party in Britain held electoral dominance, with the three administrations of Mrs Thatcher enjoying relatively large majorities in Parliament. This situation has continued with two massive electoral victories and consequently huge parliamentary majorities for the Labour Party under Tony Blair. These examples of electoral dominance have led some observers to argue that the relationship can become weighted in favour of the executive. As a consequence the executive will possess too much power and the effectiveness of the legislature, as a chamber of scrutiny and representation, is compromised and becomes too limited in relation to executive power.

In a parliamentary executive, such as Britain, the executive consists of the *prime minister* and a *cabinet* which is responsible for policy formation and for the administration of the various government departments. Ministers are either the head of a government department – for example, the Ministry of Agriculture, Home Secretary (Home Office) or Chancellor of the Exchequer (Treasury) – or they may be appointed to a ministerial role for a particular purpose for the life of a Parliament (or shorter). There are approximately twenty to twenty-four members of the Cabinet in contemporary Britain. This body meets on a regular basis to discuss policy and government business and acts as the core executive in the parliamentary system. This means that a parliamentary executive is a plural executive in which bargaining, cooperation and interdepartmental considerations and rivalries play a considerable role in formation and management of policy initiatives. However, this plurality of executive composition is given the image of unity through the existence of the convention known as *collective responsibility* through which decisions taken in the Cabinet are portrayed as collective decisions which all members support and agree with. The justification for this is that such collective decision-making ought to guarantee balance and moderation. However, critics argue that it may be little more than a sophisticated method of maintaining party discipline and managing the party rather than one which encourages balance and moderation.

▌ THINK POINT

Do you think a fusion of executive, legislature and judiciary – as in the case of Britain – is a satisfactory occurrence?

Presidential executives

In every town I go to, I feel myself Emperor or architect. I decide, I judge, I arbitrate.

(President François Mitterrand, quoted in Laughland 1994)

Again, we can usefully employ Verney's categories here to identify the central characteristics of a presidential executive.

Characteristics of presidential government

1 The assembly remains an assembly only.
2 The executive is not divided but is a president elected by the people for a definite term.
3 The head of government is the head of state.
4 The president appoints heads of departments who are subordinates.
5 The president is sole executive.
6 Members of the assembly are not eligible for office in the administration and vice versa.
7 The executive is responsible to the constitution.
8 The president cannot dissolve or coerce the assembly.
9 The assembly is ultimately supreme over the other branches of government and there is no fusion of the executive and legislative branches as in a parliament.
10 The executive is directly responsible to the electorate.
11 There is no focus of power in the political system.

(Verney 1959)

Of central importance here is the clear separation of powers between executive, legislature and judiciary. We should note, however, that many would argue that the political system of the USA is, in reality, dominated by the president, who as the focus of popular attention can appeal to the public directly in a way that the other elements of the system cannot.

A second key difference is the centrality of the constitution in allocating and specifying roles and functions of the constituent parts of the political system. A third key difference is the direct election of the executive by the electorate and the fact that this removes the reliance of the executive on legislative confidence.

Some scholars have identified the tendency for some political systems to exhibit a mix of presidential and parliamentary government, and what might be called *semi-presidential systems* can be identified in a number of countries including France, India, Ireland and Iceland. The key characteristic here is the existence of both a president and a prime minister (or equivalent). The power relationship between the two offices will vary – for example, in France, the president enjoys supremacy, while in Portugal a more balanced arrangement appears to exist.

Other forms of government

The models outlined above have focused on parliamentary and presidential examples drawn mainly from countries which, to a greater or lesser extent, are based on democratic forms of electoral politics. Different examples might include *communist executives* as characteristic of the former communist states of Eastern Europe and the USSR. For example, in the former Soviet Union the Council of Ministers formed the executive body of the USSR. The Chairman of the Council was the prime minister and there were 130 members in total, including heads of all the Soviet ministries, high-ranking officials and chairs of the Union Republic Councils of Ministers (Lane 1985).

Another example is the *unlimited presidential executive* found in countries like Iraq, Angola and Syria. Countries where unlimited presidential executives exist tend to be one-party states and are characterised by strong individual leadership which often borders on 'cult of the leader' characteristics. There is usually greater authoritarianism, greater control of the media, opposition and dissidence, and often greater concern with the maintenance of cultural, religious or ethnic homogeneity.

Some countries possess *military executives* and this has been particularly prevalent in South American countries and a number of African states. Here the political system is dominated by senior military officers who frequently hold power for long periods of time and are often removed only by the actions of rival military leaders. Again, the tendency has been towards authoritarian and often reactionary government and, in South America in particular, the use of military force against civilian targets has been common. The list of human rights violations by South American governments is very long, and the banning of opposition groups, freedom of speech and the use of violence and death squads against individuals engaged in the most moderate of activity has not been unusual, General Pinochet's rule of Chile being a clear example of this. Other commentators have identified a form of executive which they label *semi-dictatorship*. One example of this form of executive power is Indonesia, where General Suhato seized power in the late 1960s and remained President until 1998. This Indonesian regime was characterised by an extensive military presence which included 100 seats reserved in parliament for unelected military personnel (Brooker 2000).

Transnational governance and the European Union – a new model?

The institutional arrangements of the European Union provide a further interesting and illustrative case study of the relationship between government, state and nation, and provides a good example of what is varyingly called transnational, multilevel or supranational governance (George and Bache 2001). The important point here is that this organisation is both intergovernmental and in some ways (although as you will have seen earlier in this book there exists a huge debate about this) a federal organisation. But the nature of the European Union produces some interesting characteristics for consideration. First, there is no single head of state – rather a collective leadership through the European Council and Council of Ministers. Second, a separation of powers and responsibilities is clearly at work and considerable tension, underlined by the clash between national and federal interests, is present within the system. Third, the European Union is such a highly populated geopolitical area (and one growing all the time) that issues of responsibility, accountability and *democratic deficit* are of key interest. Fourth, this is a set of institutions and institutional relationships that are in the process of being formed (and reformed), and this adds to the uniqueness of the process.

The *European Commission*, which holds that its first task 'is to initiate new European policies', positions itself as the executive body of the European Union. One might argue, however, that the power of the *European Council* and *Council of Ministers* also renders these as executive bodies. More clearly the *European Parliament* performs the legislative function of the European Union, although here, more than in many legislatures, the ability of the European Parliament to make law is extremely limited and although its powers are increasing it remains primarily a chamber of debate and scrutiny. The *European Court of Justice* fulfils the judicial role for the European Union but is a much more powerful body than the judiciaries found in many member states. However, this system is very much an emerging and fluid one. Recent major treaties, for example, the *Maastricht Treaty* (1992), the *Amsterdam Treaty* (1997), the crisis of the European Commission in 1999 and the allegations of fraud, mismanagement and nepotism that caused this crisis, and the launch of the single European currency have all altered and will continue to alter the roles of and relationships between the EU institutions and the institutions of the member states (George and Bache 2001).

The virtual machinery of government?

Our discussion here has focused upon how political systems are organised and what institutions exist to exercise and limit political authority. To some degree, however these institutions are organised, the aim or indeed the necessity of these systems is to render governable large numbers of people. In a country such as the United Kingdom with a population of 56 million, it is clearly impossible to operate any form of direct democracy and therefore systems of governance have to be found that allow such a large number of people to be represented at a political level and that hold those who represent the people accountable through regular and free elections and through the operation of responsible government. Whether or not this is effective representation it is at least functional, and it is difficult to conceive of any other practical method of organising politics in such large and mass democracies.

As we have seen in other chapters in this book, however, the implications of new technologies – particularly those involving digital communications technology, for example interactive television, home-computing, advanced digital telecommunications and the Internet – pose the possibility of increased direct participation of the citizenry in the political process. An increased level of direct electronic democracy may take a number of forms. This might (and increasingly does) include e-mail communication between politicians and the public, political and campaign discussion boards, political websites (official and unofficial) and electronic town halls and public meetings. The point may be that in the same way that new communications media may be eroding the organising principles and institutions of the nation-state they can be said to challenge the integrity, traditional roles, functions and the future of national political institutions. On the up side such technologies provide increased opportunities for politicians to manage information, communicate with the public, publish information and carry out research. Furthermore, such technology facilitates online discussions at local, national and transnational level (see, for example, UK-COD) and helps governments to simplify state procedures (Coleman *et al.* 1999; Axford and Huggins 2001).

However, taken to the logical technological conclusion, other scenarios are possible. Let us engage in a little futurology. The technology is available for homes in countries such as the USA and Britain for almost limitless television channels, and already local cable television networks are providing the means and systems for local and localised programming of a highly select nature. It is possible that, in the not too distant future, local authorities will operate their own interactive, public information channels which could provide service information, local information and offer a two-way communication system between local people and local authorities. Either through television or, less extensively, through electronic networks operating via the Internet and located within public buildings, such as town halls, libraries and municipal car parks, the local authority could consult much more effectively with its local electorate and community. Consultation about local planning initiatives, provision of services and so on could be referred to the popular voice on a much more regular and frequent basis. Once again, a sympathetic and service-enhancing application of the new technology that could operate hand in hand with the present systems and institutions of local authority is already in place.

But other more problematic visions are available. Once again, if we engage in some futurology, we might envisage a different world, one much more problematic for politicians and established political institutions. In many advanced capitalist countries it has already become common for television programmes – such as *GMTV* in Britain or *Jerry Springer* in the USA – to carry out telephone polls on certain subjects such as the availability of abortion, the reintroduction of the death penalty and more trivial items such as who should manage the English national football team. These polls are currently small and by and large insignificant, but imagine a time in which, through the courtesy of interactive television and armed with the digital telephone, the nation can be consulted on major issues and political questions. Take, for example, the possibility that the House of Commons in Britain is going to have a free vote on the reintroduction of the death penalty. (Debates and votes in the House of Commons around the death penalty have been a recurrent event in British politics and one which has traditionally been voted upon outside of party discipline. It is also a topic where many believe that the popular voice would support its reintroduction when the political system rejects it.) It would, in theory, be possible for all adults to vote in an unofficial referendum on the same day, at the same time as the politicians at Westminster were voting. The result of the MPs' division is a rejection of the death penalty by a clear majority of 150 MPs. But what if the popular vote – recorded by computer and flashed up on the television at exactly the same time as the official result – demonstrated that 77 per cent of the adult population wanted the reintroduction of the death penalty? What if this began to happen on more and more frequent and highly visible occasions? How would a minister respond when asked by a television presenter 'But our survey of the 13,000,000 car drivers demonstrates that they do not want to pay more road tax but favour an increase on the price of a litre of petrol?' Or 'As we have been speaking, Prime Minister, 12,000,000 people have recorded a statement that you should resign?'

Electronic anarchy? Perhaps. Certainly not without problems. For example, would people be more likely to vote electronically than otherwise? But the principle – that mass communication through new technology could be used to present mass public opinion directly to the political elite almost instantaneously – possesses a range of problems for the formal institutions of the political system. How, for example, could those in power justifiably resist such popular calls? Placed under such pressure what would the formal institutions of government do? The concerns of the elites – always frightened by radical, direct democracy – would resurface. The 'tyranny of the majority' would once again become a real fear for parliamentarians and intellectuals alike. The people might actually be heard. The possibility for manipulation of public opinion would be vast. Who would ask the questions and what questions would be set? Even if embraced, as a potential enhancement of democracy by increasing the amount of direct reference to the people, who would choose, or more importantly how would they choose, which issues and issue areas would be referred to popular vote? The problems of these futures are almost endless – but the principle remains the same. The technological innovation – which is shaping and reshaping all of our lives – will not spare the formal institutions of government. This may take many forms – an alternative virtual Parliament of networks and interfaces, a virtual European Union or a mass plebiscite democracy. Whatever, such developments would pose serious challenges to the political institutions which would be be shaken to their foundations and the political classes left stranded in cyberspace.

Cutting out the middleman: from virtual representation to direct deliberation?

There needs to be a practical link between the voice of the citizens and the actions of elected representatives. In a direct democracy this would take the form of delegates being mandated, accountable and recallable. Online voting is still a primitive and unreliable mechanism, and, as we have observed already, could be easy prey to electronic populism posing as enhanced democracy. Mature public deliberation deserves to be listened to by those in power not because it is representative, but because it is thoughtful. Even a quite unrepresentative group of discussion participants is better than none at all, and from them representatives can learn much: about people's experience; about the communities to which citizens feel they belong; about the intensity of views held; about why members of the public do or do not trust those elected to represent them. If all of this is ignored by the political elite on the grounds that 'it's just people talking' or because those entering into discussion do not constitute a demographic microcosm of society, then citizens will become less confident in their capacity to make a difference. This will not mean that they stop deliberating – democratic opportunities are rarely cast aside once discovered – but that deliberation will proceed on the basis that representatives are remote and best overlooked. The example of the more populist trends in US talk radio in the early 1990s shows how this can happen and the extent that popular disaffection can turn into populist disengagement from democratic discourse. So, it is to representatives' own advantage, as well as that of democratic culture as a political project, that direct deliberation by citizens not only takes place but is taken seriously.

(Extracted from Stephen Coleman, Cutting out the Middleman: From Virtual Representation to Direct Deliberation, at <http://www.democracyforum.org.uk>)

EXERCISE

Can you:

☐ Design a brief e-constitution highlighting key rights and structures for delivering electronic government and democracy?

☐ Design a set of e-government institutions?

☐ Identify the main challenges for systems and institutions of government with this form of technology?

Conclusion

In this chapter we have examined some of the main institutions and organisations of government that characterise the exercising and control of political power and the representation of the people within different political systems. In doing so we have examined different institutions of *government* and the relationship between those institutions and the *governed* or the people. In particular we have examined the three main elements of government – the *executive*, the *legislature* and the *judiciary* – and directly compared two main systems of government: parliamentary and presidential. In this chapter we have stressed the importance of using the comparative method in political science to add depth to our knowledge and understanding of different political systems. It has also been stressed that the context in which the national institutions of government operate is one increasingly affected by the processes of globalisation, transnational integration and, in some ways, technological innovation, and that any analysis of national institutions of government – and the powers of those institutions – has to take account of the changing global context.

Chapter summary

- The machinery and institutions of government are an important focus of study for students of politics.

- The study of institutions of government can be usefully pursued through the application of the comparative political method.

- The study of institutions and organisations of national government requires us to consider a number of units or analysis which include the nation, nation-states, government and governance.

- The institutions of government, and ideas about them, can be usefully approached through a study of constitutions and constitutional documents.

- The main functions of national governments can be split into three main branches – the executive, legislative and judiciary – each of which has particular functions.

- The executive is the apex of political power in a political system at which policy is formed and through which it is executed.

- The legislature is the body within a political system that makes the laws. It tends to be unicameral (one chamber) or bicameral (two chambers).

continued

continued

> ☐ The judiciary is the body that is responsible for enforcing laws and, in some states, for upholding constitutional rules.
>
> ☐ The relationships between these branches are often complex and will vary from nation to nation depending on constitutional arrangements, political history and social composition of that state.
>
> ☐ The context in which institutions of government operate are increasingly influenced by the process of globalisation, technological innovation and transnational integration, and these developments (among others) pose challenges to the traditional form and function of those institutions.

Key texts

Anderson, B. (1991) *Imagined Communities*, London: Verso.

Finer, S. E., Bogdanor, V. and Rudden, B. (1995) *Comparing Constitutions*, Oxford: Clarendon Press.

Lipset, S. and Rokkan, S. (eds) (1967) *Party Systems and Voter Alignments*, London: Free Press.

Montesquieu, Charles de Secondat, Baron de (1989) *The Spirit of the Laws*, trans. and ed. by Anne M. Cohler, Basia Caro, Cambridge: Cambridge University Press.

Sartori, G. (1994) *Comparative Constitutional Engineering: An Inquiry into Structures, Incentives and Outcomes*, London: Macmillan.

Stone Sweet, A. (2000) *Governing with Judges: Constitutional Politics in Europe*, Oxford: Oxford University Press.

Verney, D. (1959) *The Analysis of Political Systems*, Glencoe, IL: Free Press.

Further reading

Brooker, P. (2000) *Non-democratic Regimes: Theory, Government and Politics*, London: Macmillan. An analysis of non-democratic government and politics which includes discussions of theories of non-democratic government, a typology of non-democratic regimes, an analysis of military dictatorships, semi-democracies, personal rule and party dictatorships.

Coleman, S., Taylor, J. and van de Donk, W. (eds) (1999) *Parliament in the Age of the Internet*, Oxford: Oxford University Press. A comparative collection of essays on the applications of information and communication technologies to parliamentary systems of government around the world.

Foley, M. (2000) *The British Presidency: Tony Blair and the Politics of Public Leadership*, Manchester: Manchester University Press. An examination of

the Blair leadership and New Labour in which the author argues that Blair's success reflects the consolidation of leader-centred political parties and the emergence of a British presidency.

George, S. and Bache, I. (2001) *Politics in the European Union*, Oxford: Oxford University Press. A useful overview discussion of politics in the European Union covering institutional arrangements, policies, history and the member states.

Landman, T. (2000) *Issues and Methods in Comparative Government: An Introduction*, London: Routledge. A useful introduction to the comparative method in political science which is thematically organised and full of relevant examples of the comparative method in use.

Lijphart, A. (1992) *Parliamentary versus Presidential Government*, Oxford: Oxford University Press. A good collection of materials that explore and analyse the relative differences and merits of parliamentary and presidential forms of government through a range of historical and comparative extracts.

Negrine, R. (1998) *Parliament and the Media: A Study of Britain, Germany and France*, London: The Royal Institute of International Affairs/Pinter. A comparative analysis of the relationship between political institutions and the media in which the author addresses central issues of how changes in media practices have impacted on the coverage of parliaments, politics and politicians.

Newman, J. (2001) *Modernising Governance: New Labour, Policy and Society*, London: Sage. A lively and informative discussion of the concept of governance through a study of the policies and performance of New Labour in the United Kingdom.

Norton, P. (1990) *Legislatures*, Oxford: Oxford University Press. A good collection and discussion of a range of materials and issues regarding legislatures.

Russell, M. (2000) *Reforming the House of Lords: Lessons from Overseas*, Oxford: Oxford University Press. A detailed and comparative discussion of second chamber reform in the United Kingdom drawing on a wide range of examples and materials from non-UK examples.

Websites

Lots of national parliaments have websites and you can access them either directly or by visiting the website of the Inter-parliamentary Union at <http://www.ipu.org>, which has an alphabetical listing of national parliaments. This site also has a lot of other useful information and related links.

It may also be worth visiting the websites of some of the international and regional parliamentary assemblies. For example, you might try the Arab Inter-parliamentary Union at <http://www.arab-ipu.org>, or the African Parliamentary Union at <http://www.uafparl.org>

Parties, Interest Groups and Public Opinion

Barrie Axford

▨ Introduction

In the previous two chapters we looked at the machinery of government at different levels. The institutions and processes covered in those chapters are all part of what we might call the formal apparatus of governance. No less important for the conduct of modern politics, but in some respects less formal, are the actors known as political parties and **interest groups** and a process of communication, often simplified as 'public opinion', in which 'the people' or segments of the people speak directly or, more usually, indirectly to government, their views mediated by print and broadcast journalists, market researchers and elected representatives, as well as by political parties and interest groups.

The value of political parties and public opinion to democratic government and politics is widely accepted, although sometimes disputed. Interest groups have received less robust approval, often because they cannot escape the burden that they are representing or acting on behalf of some *particular*, rather than the *general* interest. The claim by some 'public interest' groups, such as Amnesty International and Friends of the Earth, to act on behalf of the body politic, or even humanity, goes some way to dilute the charge of being partial,

Interest groups Sometimes called pressure groups, but, as we shall see below, the term 'interest group' takes in a wider variety of organisations and activities.

but suspicion has always remained. When James Madison (Federalist Paper No. 10) wrote in 1787 that 'the latent causes of faction are sown in the nature of man, and the most frivolous and fanciful distinctions have been sufficient to kindle unfriendly passions and excite the most violent conflicts', his diatribe, although more elegant, could have come straight from the mouth of a modern commentator anxious to warn against the dangers of sectional interests 'buying' influence and undermining democratic politics and procedures, perhaps through funding the campaign of a governing party or seeking to elevate private advantage over public good.

Wheeling and steeling?

Entrepreneur Laksmi Mittal, and his LNM group of companies, have been well known in Britain for acquiring steel plants. In 2001 to 2002, the group took over the huge but run-down Sidex steel plant in Romania, the largest state-owned company there. Mittal took on some debt at acquisition and set out a planned investment programme of £250 million over ten years. The complex deal hit the headlines when it emerged that UK Prime Minister Tony Blair had written to the Romanian Prime Minister backing Mittal's bid to buy Sidex, just two months after the businessman had donated £125,000 to Labour Party funds.

Political parties also produce an ambivalent response both among students of politics and electors. Applauded for their contribution to the organisation and maintenance of democratic politics and seen as vehicles for popular representation and the recruitment of political elites, they have been accused of marginalising the legitimate demands of some citizens, and entrenching a 'mobilisation of bias'. Bias occurs when some issues and the demands of certain groups of people, are kept off the political agenda.

The phrase 'mobilisation of bias' was coined by E. E. Schattschneider, in his classic work 'The Semi-Sovereign People: a realist's view of democracy in America', in 1961. All politics, said Schattschneider, constitutes some kind of mobilisation of bias.

THINK POINT

Can you think of any issues that have been left off the political and policy agenda in your country that might conform to Schattschneider's dictum? If you can, whose fault is it, and is their exclusion a matter for concern?

Finally, public opinion or *vox-populi* (the voice of the people) as a key input to decision-making presses all the right buttons for supporters of direct democracy but leaves critics of mass participation cold, to say the very least. Pandering to the masses, said American sage Walter Lippmann, leads only to a 'morbid derangement of government' (1955: 20). As we will return to varieties of public opinion below, it is worth noting that Lippmann did not extend these strictures to the act of voting.

See Chapter 5 for a discussion of direct and indirect democracy.

Thus any discussion of parties, interest groups and public opinion will have to examine issues of representation and communication, but also matters of influence, agenda-setting and control. Parties, interest groups and public opinion are important features of healthy civil societies and public spheres, and are central to the business of making government more accountable. Study of all three also provides insights into the ways in which power is distributed and exercised in different societies. At the same time, students of politics should note that the functions and significance of political parties, interest groups and public opinion vary across time, as well as across different types of political regime and political culture, so that generalisations are not always possible or safe.

Political parties and party systems

Political party A permanent organisation, the primary purpose of which is to contest elections and to wield power within a government. Parties perform many other functions, including mobilising popular participation in politics, elite recruitment and representing (sections of) the public, but winning elections and controlling the machinery of state power are paramount.

Political parties are the life-blood of contemporary politics, or at least of the sort of politics that takes place within the boundaries of territorial states and societies. Outside these confines their influence is less obvious, although the position taken by a national government on global issues such as free trade or human rights may well be influenced by the ideology or world view of its governing party(ies). In the European Parliament, the only inter- or supra-national body to be directly elected by citizens, there are no truly Europe-wide political parties, only loose coalitions of ideologically compatible national party groupings.

Political groups in the European Parliament (626 members) as of April 2002

EPE-DE	Group of the European People's Party (Christian Democrats) and European Democrats
PSE	Group of the Party of European Socialists
ELDR	Group of the European Liberal, Democrat and Reform Party
Verts/ALE	Group of the Greens/European Free Alliance
GUE/NGL	Confederal Group of the European United Left/Nordic Green Left
UEN	Union for Europe of the Nations Group
EDD	Group for a Europe of Democracies and Diversities
NI	Non-attached

(European Parliament 2002)

The prospects for transnational political parties seems remote in a political world order still built around the mythology of the independent territorial state and the rituals of domestic politics, but the absence of a supra-territorial dimension (Scholte 1999) to the organisation as well as the mindset of parties may point to their limits as political actors in a world that is becoming more interdependent and globalised.

As a vintage, political parties are relatively new, a feature of the modernising political world that emerged out of the turmoil of the American and French revolutions at the end of the eighteenth century. Factions – informal alliances between people or groups seeking to advance a common aim – whether in government or parliaments, even on the street with the support of the mob, were commonplace in pre-modern politics. These factions were often unstable and held together by the force of key personalities or by exigency. Parties can share some of the characteristics of factions but they are distinguished by having permanent organisation and membership. In their most typical guise parties are vehicles for contesting elections and, where they are successful, for organising government and wielding state power. Such functions are the product of the political modernisation of societies and the extension of the franchise to new social groups during the nineteenth and twentieth centuries.

The rise of mass politics and the need to harness the support of widening electorates had a profound impact on the organisation and rationale of many nascent political parties. From being mutable factions they developed into what have been called '**caucus**' **parties**, focused on mobilising support within parliaments (Duverger 1955). The extension of the franchise from the mid-nineteenth century onwards began to turn legislative caucuses into mass parties, often clearly identified with societal interests, but attuned to mobilising the expanding vote and aggregating demands in order to maximise support at elections. Mass parties, dedicated to maximising the vote and reliant upon increasingly bureaucratic organisation and a strong membership, became the standard model of a political party between the late nineteenth century and the early 1960s (Katz and Mair 1994). The phenomenon of the mass party operating within a system of competitive elections (that is, more than one party contesting an election) developed first in North America and Western Europe, and the model has been exported in various forms to other parts of the world, though sometimes without the competitive element.

The phenomenon of mass parties contesting the great ideological divide of left versus right became the substance of democratic politics in most parts of the First World. Since the 1960s, especially in Western liberal democracies, new models of party organisation and perhaps new types of party have emerged. Otto Kirchheimer (1966) identified the rise of the 'Catch-all party' as a significant development in mass parties. For catch-all parties, mass organisation, strong membership and ideology are of lesser importance than political **brokerage** and the pursuit of the median voter in a political marketplace. Indeed, ideological purity and the claims of party die-hards in grass-roots organisations are seen as constraints on the efficient pursuit and retention of power, which may also involve some collaboration with rivals to dampen political and social cleavages. The United States national party system is a paradigm case, and Kirchheimer noted that the Gaullist UNR Party in France had already made the transition by the 1960s, with both German and Austrian strands of Social Democrats headed in the same direction. Italy, thought by Kirchheimer to be resistant to a marked 'de-ideologisation' of party politics, by the late 1990s had produced a party system in which broad coalitions of previously ideologically pure parties (e.g. Communists, Social Democrats and Christian Democrats) contest elections under exotic umbrella titles such as the

Of course, political parties can achieve power by means other than elections, such as a revolution or a coup.

Caucus party A caucus is a closed party meeting and often applied to meetings held by a party group within a legislature or assembly.

Key text: R. Katz and P. Mair (1994) *How Parties Organise: Change and Adaptation in Party Organisation in Western Democracies*, London: Sage.

Brokerage Literally to broker or trade off differences in order to produce an acceptable compromise or lowest common denominator.

Olive Tree Alliance (centre-left); the Liberty Pole (centre-right) and Silvio Berlusconi's amalgam of *Forza Italia*, regionalist and nationalist parties and movements (House of Freedom).

In Britain, both Labour and Conservative parties have become catch-all parties, with the former, in office since 1997, now some way down the road towards Katz and Mair's 'cartel party'. The cartel party is only marginally reliant upon traditional sources of support (membership) and funding, although New Labour is still heavily supported by trade union money. Cartel parties are highly professional, and wedded to a managerialist ethos and skills to mount efficient electoral campaigns, manage public relations and maintain discipline among parliamentary members. They have also jettisoned any clear commitment to ideological goals, except where these echo broadly acceptable valence themes such as ending social exclusion, promoting the enterprise culture and fighting crime.

It is obvious that there is a dynamism about the development of political parties and party systems that is due to changing social and cultural circumstances, and, perhaps, to shifts in technology as well. Katz and Mair's models of political parties depict a fluid development of party types and party systems over time (Table 11.1).

Table 11.1 Models of political parties

Characteristics	Caucus party	Mass party	Catch-all party	Cartel party	Media party
Time period	Nineteenth century	1880–1960	1945–	1970–	1990s–
Basis of competition	Ascribed status	Representative capacity	Policy effectiveness	Managerial skills and efficiency	Public relations, agenda-setting
Pattern of electoral competition	Managed	Mobilisation	Competitive	Contained	Permanent campaigns framed by media
Principal source of party resources	Personal contacts	Members' fees and contributions	From many sources	State subventions	State subventions, some private sources
Relations between elite and members	Elite are members	Elite accountable to members	Members support elite	Stratarchy; mutual autonomy	Leader dominated
Relations between party and civil society	Unclear boundary	Party belongs to civil society	Party is broker between civil society and state		Party creates demand reflexively through monitoring of public opinion
Relations between party and state	Unclear boundary	Party tries to gain control of state		Party becomes part of state	Party is part of state

Source: adapted from Katz and Mair (1994)

There is no suggestion that the developments observed by Katz and Mair are evolutionary or linear, or that parties look and behave the same everywhere. Indeed, most of their observations, and those of Kirchheimer, refer to parties in Western societies and to competitive party systems. We will look more closely at the variations in party systems and party types below. For the moment it is important to note a further step in the transformation of political parties, one that, for some observers, represents a 'wholly new and disquieting phenomenon' (Porro and Russo 2000: 348):

Media parties?

In a recent analysis of party systems in Continental Europe, Klaus von Beyme (1996) suggests that there have been and continue to be rapid changes in the organisation of and functions performed by political parties across different European polities.

These changes echo some of the points raised above, and depict a convergence in the ideological and policy identities of major parties, which in turn creates more space for interest groups and single-issue parties to gain support among sections of the public who feel strongly about particular issues. Traditional party functions connected with the education and mobilisation of voters are being influenced by electronically mediated communications in the form of television and the Internet. Mail-shots, bespoke videos, database marketing and interactive websites undermine traditional campaigning and allow party leaders to speak to voters over the heads of party activists, further side-lining them.

Party members become much less crucial to fund-raising and campaigning than in the previous stages of party development, while campaign managers, media advisers, marketers and design consultants become the key players in what is a 'permanent campaign'.

This new type of media or professional party, as von Beyme has it, produces a leadership which is increasingly independent of the party membership and even of the parliamentary party, and more and more reliant on the management of visibility through media constructions of favourable images (through positive and negative image management) and of policy (through spinning and agenda-setting).

This creates a kind of 'video-populism' and huge potential not to sustain a competitive democracy, but to establish a kind of 'plebiscitary democracy'.

Party systems

Like other political actors, parties do not emerge and perform in a social and cultural vacuum. Their origins in Western Europe and North America are closely tied to massive changes in the organisation of those societies under the impact of industrialisation, urbanisation and what Stein Rokkan (1968) called

A party system Refers to the number and types of party operating in a political system. The concept also refers to the interactions between parties and the wider society and to the pattern of competition – or lack of it – between parties themselves. Party systems are embedded in particular societies and cultures.

Silvio Berlusconi

Silvio Berlusconi is Prime Minister of Italy, having been elected for the second time in 2001. He is a figure of great controversy because, as a media mogul and Chairman of Fininvest, he owns a substantial share of Italy's televisual media and is becoming a presence on the European media scene. He is also subject to court proceedings on charges of corruption. Berlusconi is also the founder of a political party, *Forza Italia*, which is the main partner in a coalition governing Italy. *Forza Italia* is unusual in that it started life with no formal membership, using local organisers, often employees of Fininvest, to mobilise support. Berlusconi's political message is influenced by neo-liberal economics and nationalist-populist rhetoric, but his emphasis on using media to communicate directly with the electorate is novel and has led to talk of a 'videocracy', a term which he favours.

National revolution The political movement that resulted in the construction of independent states governed by a central authority.

We have referred to Inglehart's thesis in Chapter 3 on political culture, and Chapter 4 on political participation.

'national revolutions'. Even so, differences in cultural tradition and political mentality have produced quite different sorts of party and party systems in Western Europe, Australia and New Zealand, and in the USA. In the last, parties reflect relatively weak left–right ideological divisions and, as Katz and Mair (1994) note, have been rather loosely organised catch-all parties, primarily there to support candidates at election times. By contrast, in Europe and to some degree in Australia and New Zealand, the temper of the party system, and the degree of party organisation historically, owe much to the desire to translate deep social divisions (mainly social class and urban versus rural, but also religion) into organised political form. The existence of strong and disciplined parties in many national legislatures and a high percentage of strong 'party identifiers' in the electorate were the outcomes of these societal forces.

Social and cultural changes since the Industrial Revolution produced major party cleavages of the sort found in most of the countries in the Western industrialised world. More recent changes in the social and cultural contexts of what writers such as Ronald Inglehart (1997) refer to as 'postindustrial societies' have eroded these cleavages and weakened the basis of party loyalty among the electorate. The catch-all and cartel party and the leader-dominated media party may be riding the wave of recent changes in the material and cultural worlds, of the sort identified by Inglehart. The fall-out for political parties and party systems configured by the main cleavages of the nineteenth and early twentieth centuries may be seen in the general decline in party membership (see Table 11.2) and in the emergence of single-issue parties and transient protest parties, such as the Pro-Life Alliance and the Referendum Party in the UK, and in the re-emergence of populist parties, mainly of the radical right. These parties include the *Front National* in France, the *Lega Nord* in Italy, the *Austrian Freedom Party*; *Republikaner*, in Germany and the *One Nation Party* in Australia. Although some of these are interpreted as a throwback to the bad old days of inter-war fascism, they are usefully seen as an explicit critique of the perceived failure of conventional parties to articulate certain demands, and an implicit response to the anxieties generated by growing uncertainties and pressures on national societies in a globalising world.

Table 11.2 Trends in estimated official party membership, 1980–2000

Country	Period	Party members as percentage of electorate, late 1990s	Percentage change (I)	Change in numbers of members	Change in numbers as percentage of original membership
France	1978–1999	1.6	−3.48	−1,122,128	−64.59
Italy	1980–1998	4.0	−5.61	−2,091,887	−51.54
USA	1980–1998	1.9	−2.20	−853,156	−50.39
Norway	1980–1997	7.3	−8.04	−218,891	−47.49
Czech Republic	1993–1999	3.9	−3.10	−225,200	−41.32
Finland	1980–1998	9.6	−6.09	−206,646	−34.03
Netherlands	1980–2000	2.5	−1.78	−136,459	−31.67
Austria	1980–1999	17.7	−10.82	−446,209	−30.21
Switzerland	1977–1997	6.4	−4.28	−118,800	−28.85
Sweden	1980–1998	5.5	−2.87	−142,533	−28.05
Denmark	1980–1998	5.2	−2.16	−70,385	−25.52
Ireland	1980–1998	3.1	−1.86	−27,856	24.47
Belgium	1980–1999	6.5	−2.42	−136,382	−22.10
Germany	1980–1999	2.9	−1.59	−174,967	−8.95
Hungary	1980–2000	2.1	+0.04	+8,300	+5.02
Portugal	1980–2000	3.9	−0.29	+50,381	+17.01
Slovakia	1994–2000	4.1	+0.82	+37,777	+29.63
Greece	1980–1998	6.8	+3.58	+375,000	+166.67
Spain	1980–2000	3.4	+2.22	+808,705	+250.73

Source: Mair and van Biezen (2001)

THINK POINT

What inferences can you draw from these data?

The Austrian Freedom Party (FPÖ)

In terms of party type, the Freedom Party is a protest-oriented, right-wing populist working-class party. While only about 10 percent of blue-collar workers in Germany voted for a right-wing party at the parliamentary elections in 1998, and 25 percent of French blue-collar workers voted for the Front National in 1997, 47 percent of working-class voters in Austria supported the Freedom Party.

Exit poll data provide an insight into the motives of FPÖ voters: the most important reasons given for voting in favour of the FPÖ were a desire for political change and rejection of the ruling Grand Coalition in Austria. The anti-immigrants issue (xenophobic sentiment) was of central significance for 15

continued

continued

> percent of FPÖ voters, followed by protest and 'voting-the-rascals-out' motives (13 percent). Mr. Haider's (then its leader) image and personality were listed as an important reason by 13 percent of FPÖ voters.
>
> The dominant motives to vote for the FPÖ have changed since Mr. Haider positioned the FPÖ as a right-wing populist party back in 1986. Followed by protest and anti-establishment effects at the outset, resentment vis-à-vis foreigners has increasingly been added since the mid-nineties. In 1999, the strongest motive to vote for the FPÖ was the call for a political change and changes in style and policies.
>
> (F. Plasser and P. Ulrum <http://www.zap.or.at/e20200608.html>)

Party systems around the world may be classified in a number of ways. The most obvious characteristic of a party system is the degree of competition it exhibits. Thus it would be convenient to distinguish between competitive and non-competitive party systems and to use this distinction as a way of identifying democratic and non-democratic regimes. Unfortunately, in the real world things are not ordered quite so neatly. For one thing, although political parties are more important in democracies than in authoritarian regimes, they do exist in the latter (as we shall see below on p. 372) and sometimes there is electoral competition between them. In Zimbabwe the strong challenge posed to the ruling Zimbabwe African National Union – Patriotic Front (ZANU–PF) by the Movement for Democratic Change (MDC) which was formed in September 1999 made the 24–25 June 2000 parliamentary elections the most closely contested since independence from Britain in 1980. Although Zimbabwe has never been a one-party State, ZANU–PF has ruled the country since 1980 and Robert Mugabe, its leader and now President of Zimbabwe, has adopted an increasingly threatening and sometimes violent stance to all forms of opposition. None the less, in February 2000, the ZANU–PF suffered the first defeat in the country's history, in a constitutional referendum in which the government polled 45 per cent of the votes as against 55 per cent for the opposition.

In this case, we should ask how far the apparent commitment to formal, competitive democracy hides a political reality in which opposition parties are intimidated and ballots rigged, or where the outcome of free and fair elections is still held to ransom by interests such as the military. The political scientist Giovanni Sartori (1976) distinguishes between party systems in terms of the number of parties competing and the ideological distance between the parties. But, as in the case of Zimbabwe, the Republic of Yugoslavia under Slobodan Milosevic, Kenya and Romania, knowing that competition exists, or is allowed, is not enough; we need to be clear about the quality of competition available. In other words, whether elections really allow for the possibility for an incumbent government to be overturned and actually reflect the changing appeal of parties, platforms and ideologies. In addition, in party systems where the primary function of the party is to achieve and maintain state power, not to express societal cleavages and represent social groups, the significance of

Key text: G. Sartori (1976) *Parties and Party Systems: A Framework for Analysis*, Cambridge: Cambridge University Press.

ideological differences between competing parties may be diluted or eclipsed entirely. In the United Kingdom, and in many other established democracies, the perception of real ideological and policy differences between the main parties of the left and the right (Labour and Conservative in the UK) is increasingly low among the electorate, and this too has significance for how the parties are organised, the visibility (Thompson 1996) of their leaders and the conduct of electoral campaigns. At the beginning of the twenty-first century, ideological difference may be a less significant indicator of party type and how parties in a party system interact than, for example, how they are funded, whether they have a cohort of professional advisers (spin doctors, pollsters and the like) and whether they are forsaking mass memberships in favour of a range of electronic 'listening devices', that connect the party leadership to voters and potential voters.

A well-known Italian political scientist, who has worked extensively in the USA and has written comprehensively on the nature of political parties and party systems. His best-known works are *Parties and Party Systems: A Framework for Analysis* (1976) and *Comparative* *Constitutional Engineering: An Inquiry into Structures, Incentives and Outcomes* (1994). Of late he has examined the political impact of the change from written cultures to cultures based on the dissemination of images, in his *Homo Videns* (1998).

Giovanni Sartori

These are cautionary words and, while still something of a limiting case, should be taken seriously. Parties and party systems are not immune from wider forces arising in society and, increasingly, from outside the boundaries of states and national societies.

Given these strictures, Sartori's classification should be treated with some caution. At the same time, it does provide a useful rule of thumb by which to examine party systems in established democracies, emergent or proto-democracies, such as those found in post-communist regimes in Central and Eastern Europe, and in different shades of authoritarian regime, which are completely uncompetitive, either by design or by default, or where competition between political parties is severely proscribed.

Party systems in established democracies

We can discern three ideal types of party system in established democracies around the world. These are dominant party systems, two-party systems and multi-party systems.

DOMINANT PARTY SYSTEMS

The main feature of a dominant party system is that although the system is competitive, with elections regular, contested and fair, one party always emerges as a the governing party or as the main element in a governing coalition. This outcome may be due to a number of factors, not all of which may be present in any one instance, including:

- The association of a dominant party with seminal events in the history and development of a people and a political culture, as with the African National Congress (ANC) in South Africa.

- The peculiar features of an electoral system that skews the translation of votes into legislative seats, or else the ability of the dominant party to engineer coalitions that systematically exclude some types of opposition, such as occurred in Italy in the 1960s with the exclusion of the Communist Party from government.

- The chronic weakness of opposition parties and their failure to appeal to an electorate.

- The relatively stable social, economic and political environments in which elections are contested and in which the perceived need for change – the 'throw-the-rascals-out' mentality – is low.

Apart from the ANC case (and post-apartheid South Africa could be classified as a new rather than an established democracy), there are quite a number of other examples of dominant party systems in established democracies. Often, their dominance is rooted in links to the founding of a new nation, and to key figures in that process, as with the Indian Congress Party, which won majorities at elections from 1947, when India achieved independence, until 1984. In Japan, the success of the Liberal Democrats (LDP) between 1955 and 1993 also owed a great deal to its 'ownership' of the political rehabilitation of Japan after the Second World War and its stewardship of the Japanese economic miracle from the 1960s to the early 1980s. European examples of dominant party systems include Sweden's Social Democratic Labour Party (SAP), in power between 1950 and 1991, and Italy, where the Christian Democrats (DC) were dominant in every one of the fifty-two postwar elections until 1994.

The key point to note about all these examples (with the exception of the ANC) is that the grip of the dominant party on election outcomes has been weakened in the past decade or so. In part this may be due to more discerning, or at least more cynical electorates, and it is also a product of the more interconnected and less stable condition of the world economy, which impacted badly on Japan's economic performance in the 1990s. It also shook the belief of Swedish voters that SAP governments could provide a secure hedge against global pressures to cut back on social protection.

Some of the features of dominant party systems are worrying for those who see an umbilical link between party competition, electoral contestation and accountable government. Concerns include:

- the collapse of real extra-parliamentary opposition and the weakness of intra-parliamentary opposition.

- The replacement of parliamentary opposition with an unhealthy and introverted factionalism within the dominant party.

- The growing association between the dominant party and the state, as party preferences are taken as national goals.

- The prospects of unchallenged patronage being exercised by entrenched politicians.

- The tendency towards complacency and a 'right to rule' mentality among members of the dominant party.

- Growing fatalism, or else cynicism on the part of opposition forces and the electorate.

Of course, the fact that dominant party systems change and that dominant parties become less hegemonic is a counter to this sort of pessimism. None the less, the spectre of *de facto* one-party rule in an outwardly competitive system is a salutary reminder of the fragility of democracy.

TWO-PARTY SYSTEMS

A two-party system is one where two major parties each have a reasonable chance of becoming the government. There can be many other parties, variously called 'third parties' or 'minor parties', but while these add to the democratic credentials of the politics of two-party systems, and may well have significant representation in the legislature, they are bit players in the game where the main parties scoop the electoral rewards. The key point about the nature of two-party systems, or rather about the theory of such systems, is that neither major party dominates, and so fear of losing to the other main contender keeps the system in balance.

In reality, there are important variations, contingent upon the kind of rules (constitutional, electoral and otherwise) within which two-party competition takes place, and also upon force of circumstance. Thus, in the USA, a constitutional separation of powers and an historical tendency for many voters to cast '**split ballots**' facilitates a two-party system overall, even where one party dominates the elections for a particular office (e.g. the presidency), or part of Congress.

In the UK, also labelled a strong case of a two-party system, until recently there has been very little opportunity for voters to split tickets because of the unitary nature of the state and (with the exception of Northern Ireland) the national reach of party organisation and loyalties. The creation of a Scottish Parliament and a National Assembly for Wales may create new conditions under which party competition takes place, but not yet. Over the past two decades, there have been claims that the two-party model in Britain is defunct, despite the fact that the simple majority voting system continues to discriminate against third and minor parties, unless their vote is concentrated regionally. Under the Conservative governments of Margaret Thatcher between

Split ballot Voting for candidates of different parties at different levels and for different branches of government – state and federal; presidential and Congressional.

See Chapter 9 for an extended discussion of devolution.

1979 and 1990, the Labour Party was often dismissed as unelectable, a charge also levelled at the Conservative Party since 1997. Successive periods in office for one major party do not, in themselves, demonstrate the decline of the two-party model, although it might be argued that the forces that sustained the characteristic **adversary politics** of the British party system in Parliament have undergone considerable dilution. The main ideological divide between left and right is disappearing from the lexicon of party rivalry and voters are less committed to particular parties. Arguably, only the effects of the simple majority electoral system sustains two-party politics in anything like its pristine form. In Canada, where devolution and the rise of regionalist and even separatist feeling in the form of the *Bloc Quebecois* and the Reform Party has challenged the duopoly of the Liberals and the Conservatives, even the bias of a simple majority system of voting has not been enough to stave off the effects of important shifts in consciousness and voter loyalty.

MULTI-PARTY SYSTEMS

One of the most powerful claims made on behalf of two-party systems is that they offer the electorate a clear-cut choice of programmes and, given the translation of votes cast into legislative majorities, the ability to turn this programme into law and public policy. Of course, many electoral party systems in established democracies are numerically multi-party, because a host of parties actually contest elections. However, the use of the concept multi-party applied to governance usually suggests **coalition** government.

In multi-party systems, the norm is not government by a major or dominant party, but government by party coalition. Voting is by some version of proportional representation, and proportional systems tend to make it difficult for any one party to win an outright majority of the seats in a legislature. In the past, coalitions and the processes of coalition building were contrasted unfavourably with the simplicity of two-party models and the relative efficiency imparted to the business of governing by having a majority party in the legislature. Coalitions were held to be inherently unstable, always reliant on the smallest and weakest partner to make them work. Italy was presented as a paradigm case of weak coalition government, with the average life expectancy for postwar governments some ten months. Finland averaged one government a year for the thirty years after 1945.

Sartori (1976) distinguishes between two main types of multi-party system, which he called moderate and polarised pluralist systems. In moderate pluralist systems, such as those found in Norway and The Netherlands, coalition building was relatively easy because the ideological gap between parties was fairly narrow. Compromise and a certain stability was achievable at low cost and effort. Polarised systems, such as France, Italy and newly democratic Spain, exhibited wide ideological gaps between parties, with communists, fascists and, latterly, separatists all making the prospects for stable coalitions tenuous.

As we have noted, many of the conditions that obtained in the heyday of mass parties in democracies have given way to a less ideological and more

Adversary politics A phrase first coined by Samuel Finer (1974). He said the conflict between the Labour and Conservative parties in Britain took the form of a 'stand up fight between two adversaries for the favour of onlookers'. This ritual, he believed, caused ineffective governance and was a caricature of real parliamentary democracy. The expression is now used largely as a way of criticising the performance of parties during election campaigns and in the House of Commons during debates.

Coalition An alliance or grouping of rival party and/or other political groups. The alliance is formed through the existence of common ground on aspects of ideology or policy, although it may follow simply from expediency and the need to build a minimum winning coalition. Coalitions may also be designed to exclude particular parties from government as much as to foster common ground among partners. Coalitions may be formed prior to or during elections, but they may be the outcome of hurried post-election bargaining.

fragmented context for party politics. In some European systems, it is new parties, such as the Greens, that are now sought-after coalition partners, at both regional and federal levels, as can be seen in Germany. In addition, the old saw that coalition government is weak government is less convincing, or less important to many voters, when set against the virtues of multi-partyism and coalitions, where bargaining and listening to minority views are all part of the process of policy formation. At the same time, some observers have lamented the inability of multi-party coalition governments to manage discontinuities in policy, forced by changing economic circumstances. Arguments that coalition governments in Italy and Germany have inhibited a radical response to the level of social welfare in a market-dominated world economy appear to carry some weight, but leave questions about the chronic failure of 'strong' British governments to handle economic change in the 1960s and 1970s unanswered.

PARTY SYSTEMS IN EMERGENT DEMOCRACIES

The distinction between party systems that are truly competitive and those in which electoral competition occurs, but in which there is no serious possibility of a transfer of power, points up the gap between what we might call substantive democracy and 'electoral democracy' (Diamond and Plattner 1996). In electoral democracies, the façade of competition hides the effective hegemony of one party, and even where competition is real, the absence of a civic culture that encourages opposition can make it difficult for pluralism to thrive.

In the former communist states of Central and Eastern Europe, in Russia and other parts of the former Soviet Union, as well as in countries rediscovering democracy after years of military or one-party rule (e.g. Argentina and Chile), the absence or parlous state of civic cultures provides rather thin soil in which to root substantive democracies. Under state socialism the Communist Party and the state were effectively one, and the party permeated many areas of civil society as well. In the new democracies which emerged from Soviet hegemony, the situation could hardly be more different. In Russia, in the place of one-party rule there have emerged a plethora of parties and groups that seem to have little connection to society, little internal cohesion or discipline and little in the way of a mass membership. This sea-change in Russia, and also in Hungary, Poland, the Czech Republic and Slovakia, is perfectly understandable. In the wake of Communism, there was bound to be a flowering of political interests and ambitions previously controlled or proscribed. A kind of frenetic pluralism is the flip-side of decades of one-party rule, and, to some extent, a compensation for it. In Russia, in the 1995 parliamentary elections, forty-three parties were contestants. Many of the new parties are heavily funded by the state and so have no need for mass memberships. Some of them are no more than vehicles for personal ambition and there is no evidence of party systems rooted in social cleavages or enduring ideologies. The one exception to the emergence of party systems based on pragmatism and ambition is the re-emergence of nationalism and ethnicity as the basis for partisan allegiance. Anti-Soviet and anti-Russian nationalism played its part in the demise of the Soviet empire, and in Moldova and the states and quasi- or proto-states of the former Yugoslavia, nationalist and ethnic credos continue to shape domestic party politics.

Early expectations about the way political cultures would develop and stable party systems comparable to the West would emerge through a period of democratic transition, seem premature. The evidence from many new post-communist democracies is that, while parties are thick on the ground, they are unlikely to become mass parties. A hybrid, somewhere between the campaign-oriented American model, and groups led by political entrepreneurs that are scarcely visible in terms of organisation, appears to be the norm (Kitschelt 1999).

PARTIES IN AUTHORITARIAN REGIMES

The concept 'authoritarian' covers a variety of regime types, including dictator-ships, military juntas and government based on rule by one party. In line with our earlier usage, the distinguishing characteristics of such regimes are that:

▧ political parties are dispensed with altogether;

▧ only one party is allowed in law and convention;

▧ that a form of electoral or procedural competition is allowed, but that there is no real chance of overturning a ruling party through electoral means.

We have dealt with the last of these categories above, as they occupy the grey zone between competitive and non-competitive party systems, and may indicate a regime in transition to democracy or, perhaps more likely, the opposite.

In countries such as Myanmar (Burma) and Saudi Arabia there are no political parties, although for quite different reasons. In Myanmar, since 1990, a military dictatorship has proscribed any form of opposition in the name of national interest and threats to order. The Saudi royal family see themselves as keepers of the holy places of Islam and opposition to them would be an affront to that religion. Opposition exists in both regimes, but, up to now, it has been underground and piecemeal. No-party regimes based on traditional monarchies may be found throughout the Middle East and include Kuwait and Jordan. When military rulers seize power there is often a move to ban political parties on the grounds that the gravity of the current situation requires national unity and that party faction will only damage this goal. Sometimes, military rulers do not actually proscribe political parties as organisations, but effectively emasculate them by suspending parliaments or refusing to hold elections. The mantra usually intoned on such occasions is that elections will be held as soon as stability and prosperity returns or the external threat to the nation is removed. Occasionally military rulers seem to mean what they say. In Pakistan, General Musharraf, the President, promises to hold competitive elections in 2003.

Regimes where no parties are permitted are members of a small minority of states. More widespread, although in decline compared to the early days of post-colonial regimes in parts of Africa and Asia, is the incidence of one-party systems. Current one-party states include China, Vietnam, Cuba, Armenia and Laos. In all these countries no opposition parties are permitted. Previous one-party systems included the Soviet Union, until its demise in the early 1990s, Ghana under Kwame Nkrumah in the 1960s and Hitler's Germany after 1933.

Again, the justification for banning all but one party is usually couched in terms of the exigencies facing a country. Post-colonial regimes in Africa, such as Ghana and Tanzania, shifted away from the prescribed British party and constitutional models on the grounds that they were not appropriate to the needs of new states. In many such systems, the imposition of one-party rule was really a mask for rule by one person, the hero of the independence struggle, the party leader or the president for life. The party became little more than a façade for personal rule and a convenient means of controlling other key individuals and distributing patronage. The Baa'th Party in Iraq is entirely in thrall to Saddam Hussain, the instrument of his pleasure and displeasure; in other words, hardly a party and a party *system* at all.

The same is true in those authoritarian regimes where dominant parties hold sway, but as cohorts of a powerful leader. The People's Action Party (PAP) in Singapore has ruled the country since independence in 1959. Originally the tool of Prime Minister Lee Kwan Yew, it retained its dominant position after his departure in 1990. The PAP is much less weak than many other parties in one-party authoritarian regimes, but it is really only the classic cases of one-party rule in the USSR and China which demonstrate the pristine form of a one-party system. In both instances top-down control and penetration of all aspects of society made the party a very powerful instrument of social control. However, these factors did not render the Communist Parties of China and the USSR immune from the cult of leadership. Joseph Stalin in the USSR and Mao Zedong in China both exerted dictatorial control over the party and the country, but, for the most part, there was, and in the case of China, still is, uneasy collegiate rule from the top.

One-party rule is still widespread in parts of the world, but it has come under increasing scrutiny in the past two decades from both the international community and domestic populations more inclined to protest the limits on their political and civil freedoms. The globalisation of the world economy and the visibility of human rights as a global issue have centred attention on the undemocratic practices of authoritarian regimes. In an interconnected world, one increasingly subject to the standards of established democracies and market economies, it may be that the time for at least some kinds of authoritarian regimes and the party systems they support is running out.

The organisation of parties

So far we have dealt with political parties as actors which have developed in response to a variety of historical circumstances, and as systems of interaction in different social and political settings. Our discussion of party types revealed a pattern of change in which caucus-based and membership-oriented parties gave way to mass organisations. We also noted that even these major features of modern politics are being superseded, in some systems, by catch-all and cartel-like organisations. These shifts, along with others related to new technologies and the changing perceptions and political loyalties of voters, provide us with a graph of social and political change over the past century and a half.

Looking at the ways in which parties are organised and power is distributed within them can also tell us important things about the character of the societies in which they are operating. All kinds of tensions may be revealed. Parties that campaign on the platform that they are dedicated to widening and deepening the participation of citizens in general or marginal groups in particular may be rigid hierarchies of command and control. Apparent commitment to internal democracy may be no more than a ritual obeisance to party ideology and no guide as to how the party makes decisions once it is in power.

In 1911, the sociologist of organisations Roberto Michels formulated his 'iron law of oligarchy'. The iron law posits that there is an inevitable tendency for political organisations to be **oligarchic**. According to Michels, no amount of commitment to democratic and participatory ideals can offset the tendency to elite rule. Power will always be concentrated in the hands of a small group of leaders. From the standpoint of 'good' social science, Michels' thesis could be said to lack proper rigour. It was based on the study of one political party – the German Social Democratic Party (SPD) – and imputed unproved psychological motivations to party elites, notably their alleged obsession with remaining in power. At the same time, the history of many political parties in established democracies reveals a tension between the democratic intent of party constitutions, the expectations of rank-and-file party members with regard to leadership selection and policy formulation, and the claims of leaderships to autonomy and patronage. Clearly, there was and remains a good deal of variation between parties even within the same political system.

In Britain, the Conservative Party has a hierarchical structure based on the three pillars of the parliamentary party and leadership, the party bureaucracy and the party in the country (rank and file) (see Figure 11.1). Traditionally, power was top-down and sustained by a membership ethos of loyalty and deference, rather than a culture of accountability and open decision-making. Ostensibly more unified and conformist than its major rival, the party has always been pretty ruthless with leaders it felt had lost the golden touch needed to win elections. Margaret Thatcher, winner of three successive general elections, was a victim of factionalism within her own leadership group and was brought down in a palace coup in 1990. Successive electoral defeats in 1997 and 2001, along with a declining and ageing membership, is forcing the party to rethink its organisational form and certainly its style of leadership.

By contrast, the Labour Party in the UK has a federal structure, with the Party Conference its ultimate source of policy-making power. In reality, the

Oligarchy Rule by the few.

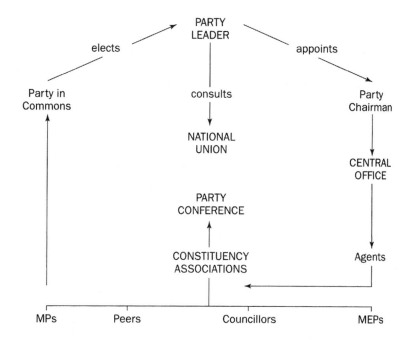

Figure 11.1   Party structure

history of the party has been a prolonged tension between the forces of centralisation and leadership autonomy on the one hand, and attempts to strengthen or reclaim the power of the extra-parliamentary party on the other. Since its catastrophic election defeat in 1987, a series of reforms (e.g. the introduction of one member one vote to offset the corporate power of the trade unions in conference decision-making) has produced a party dominated by the parliamentary leadership, and not unlike the Conservative Party in this regard. Labour's reforms, including its re-branding as 'New' Labour under Tony Blair, have all been driven by a 'modernising' ethic, designed to make the party appear more unified, more dynamic and thus more credible to the electorate.

In the USA, similar tensions have been a part of the historical record, with elitist and oligarchical tendencies apparent in the wiles of **machine politics** of the 1920s and 1930s countered by periodic attempts to enhance the role of ordinary party members and so democratise procedures (Ware 1987). Elsewhere, the ideological divisions and confederal nature of many left-of-centre parties made them less amenable to modernising credos and control from above, although in contemporary politics the need to appeal to the median voter and to be sufficiently accommodating to attract coalition partners are constraints on internal dissent. In the past, internal dissent and rampant factionalism were characteristic of dominant parties such as the Italian Christian Democrats and the Japanese Liberal Democrats. But, as we have noted above, times have changed for many once dominant parties. In the former state socialist countries of the Soviet bloc, **democratic centralism**, strict party discipline and complete

Machine politics A form of party politics in which the 'bosses' of local and state-based party organisations exercised wide patronage over public appointments and dominated the national party Conventions at which, among other things, presidential candidates are nominated.

Democratic centralism The Leninist dogma that sought to weigh unity with pluralism within the Communist Party. In reality, since the party claimed to be the organisational embodiment of the will of the people, its claims were always seen as superior to those of any other group or faction.

control of the system of patronage kept factionalism within manageable bounds, at least while the system itself was unchallenged.

Berlusconi's *Forza Italia*, novel in many respects, is still a party made in the image of its leader, with decision-making very top-down and couched in a charismatic-managerialist style. In the UK, Tony Blair has been accused of bypassing the parliamentary party and the grass-roots party organisation to create a presidential-style party devoted to supporting the activities of a small leadership group, and of constructing a plebiscitary democracy in which leadership speaks directly to the people over the head of party activists at all levels.

See Chapter 5 for a more thorough discussion of the idea of plebiscitary democracy.

The functions of political parties

Political parties are organisations whose primary function is seeking office and wielding government power. We have seen earlier that even this core function varies a great deal across types of regime. Sigmund Neumann (1956) made a broad distinction between parties of representation and parties of integration. The former see their main function as maximising votes at elections. Parties of representation correspond to the catch-all parties we identified above. They are driven by electoral ambition and may be swayed by changing currents in public opinion, which they monitor closely. Parties of representation are largely pragmatic parties and correspond to the kind of rational actor theorised by Anthony Downs in his classic text *An Economic Theory of Democracy* (1957). Downs treated parties as vote maximisers – the more votes a party wins, the more chance it has to form a government or become part of a coalition. Downs argued that as long as public opinion was distributed much like a normal bell-shaped curve, with attitudes spread evenly around the mid-point of a left–right scale, parties in a two-party system will tend to converge at the mid-point of the ideological spectrum in their search for the median voter.

Key text: A. Downs (1957) *An Economic Theory of Democracy*, New York: Harper & Row.

THINK POINT

Look at the thesis of rational activism in Chapters 1 and 4.

▪ What sort of arguments could you offer against Downs' model of party competition?

Parties of integration tend to be much less reactive than parties of representation. They do not just reflect public opinion, but look to shape it by socialising, educating and otherwise appealing to the electorate, sometimes by promoting distinct ideologies. Membership-oriented parties want to sell their message to the voters and win doubters over to the cause. Traditionally, ideologically inspired parties on the left fall into this category, but the same could be said of all parties who have a mission to convert, or to bring erring lambs back to the fold, as do nationalist parties and some kinds of protest party, such as the anti-Euro Referendum Party in the UK.

So parties are vehicles for winning elections. But they are also organisations which, as we have seen, are often closely tied to the civil societies from which they spring. Their impact upon these societies and upon the wider realm of politics is multi-faceted, although, once again, we should be wary of assuming that all parties behave in the same way and perform the same functions.

Apart from winning elections, a function of little importance in one-party states other than for purposes of legitimation, it is conventional to identify a number of core functions which can be observed, variably, across different regime types and political cultures. These functions are:

- Socialisation and mobilisation
- Structuring the vote
- Interest articulation and aggregation
- Activist and elite recruitment
- Representation
- Policy and issue development
- Organising government
- Legitimation.

SOCIALISATION AND MOBILISATION

The argument here is that political parties perform an educative function for society. This is apparent in two ways. First, in the particular sense that they are likely to promulgate a specific ideology or programme, which is thereby placed on the political agenda and from which people learn about politics and its ends. Second, in the more diffuse sense that their activities, whether as competitors in a pluralistic system or as monopoly power-holders, underwrites and sustains the dominant political culture and its rules. The evidence is less flattering and points to a significant decline in the willingness of people in many countries to identify with a party and its goals. Data also show a variable decline in the support offered by citizens to the way in which parties conduct themselves as competitors during election campaigns (too much negative and attack campaigning, too great an emphasis on style over policy presentation) and when in office (sleaze, opportunism, too much spin and not enough substance). As role models for potential supporters and actual citizens, the performance of parties leaves much to be desired.

Decline in partisan identification: selected data

In data collected for the British Household Panel Survey between 1991 and 1999, only one-third of respondents were constant in their identification with a particular party. Even in post-apartheid South Africa, between 1994 and 1998, the percentage of black voters identifying more closely with one party than any others fell from 89 per cent of respondents to 50 per cent.

STRUCTURING THE VOTE

Political parties perform the task of offering the public relatively clear-cut choices at election times. They simplify complex policy choices and provide a useful way of expressing the identity people have as members of a community, social class or religion. They also make being an infrequent political activist relatively simple and cost-free – except that things have changed. The reasons why people vote for a particular party may not be as clear-cut as they once were. It is doubtful whether the intense identity between social groups and political parties can survive an age in which not only have public perceptions and expectations of what to expect from life and politics changed, but many political parties too have transmuted from representing social cleavages to mechanisms for winning elections.

INTEREST ARTICULATION AND AGGREGATION

This function is the most obvious link between political parties and civil society. Some parties have been the organisational expression of societal differences and have seen their function as the articulation of particular demands, whether on behalf of the organised working class, big business, regional interests, ethnic identity or religious affiliation. When changes in the franchise pushed these parties to compete for a greater share of the vote, their role as the mouth of particular interests changed to one in which, although still connected to civil society, they were forced to aggregate the demands of a growing number of interests whose support was vital for their electoral success. One of the casualties of this process was the idea of the party as pristine in its pursuit of ideological goals and as the clear representative of societal differences. Looking for common denominators among a host of potentially supportive interests has turned programmatic (that is, having a clear and coherent set of aims, often driven by ideological conviction) parties into gleaners of votes and creators, rather than expressions of demand. Processes of demand aggregation tend to discard or exclude those interests which cannot be brokered or bargained. Certainly, one of the appeals of interest groups and the new brand of protest or issue-oriented party is that they are in no doubt as to their identity and goals.

ACTIVIST AND ELITE RECRUITMENT

Parties have been the training ground for heads of government and ministers, offering the kind of political apprenticeship deemed relevant to the seeking of high office. There are important exceptions. In the USA serving a party apprenticeship is no barrier to high office, even the presidency, and reforms to the selection process in the late 1970s shifted power away from party caucuses to party supporters and sometimes registered voters, through the widespread use of **primary elections**. Because of the low regard in which politics is held in many societies, there is some anecdotal evidence that parties have been finding it difficult to attract suitable candidates to contest elections. More systematic

Primary election A mechanism used by parties in the USA, in which candidates are selected or elected to be the party's nominee at a subsequent inter-party election.

data on the decline of party memberships (see Table 11.2) might support this claim.

REPRESENTATION

This is often seen as the primary function of parties. Parties sometimes articulate the views of members and voters, but often they become bodies which aggregate demands in order to maximise the vote. While this shift may have alienated some members anxious about the party's ideological soul, the ability of a party to respond to and accommodate the demands of a large electorate in a competitive system may be seen as a democratic virtue. Anthony Downs' (1957) model of party competition has party leaders as political entrepreneurs seeking to attract votes in a political marketplace. The voter/ consumer is preeminent in this exchange, but parties are seldom purely reactive to voter preferenes. Indeed their whole demeanour as political entrepreneurs is to create demand for a product.

POLICY AND ISSUE DEVELOPMENT

Parties seeking office have to put forward platforms of policies to appeal to the electorate. Where a party is ideological or programmatic it will seek to translate its ideology into a set of policy initiatives. Programmatic parties, especially those on the left, such as the 'Old' Labour Party in Britain looked to the extra-parliamentary Annual Conference and to its National Executive Committee as sources of policy and for ideological continuity. As for many other parties on the left and centre-left, times change. Now, 'New' Labour is more in tune with the 'opinion-led' catch-all parties in the USA, looking to put a winning programme together out of the preferences of targeted voters and disparate interests.

ORGANISING GOVERNMENT

Party government is a staple of parliamentary systems of rule. In such systems, parties span both legislature and executive, dominating both, especially where there is a majority party in power. Parties provide a camaraderie and often a discipline in the legislature that facilitates its business. But a legislature dominated by a governing party is often a legislature in thrall to the executive, organised largely for its convenience.

LEGITIMATION

Parties foster the legitimacy of the party system and their own contribution to its stability by playing by the rules of the electoral system and of the legislature. Party leaders develop policies that can be supported by their own members and voters and which will appeal to potential supporters, a basic requirement in party systems where ideological incoherence or an absence of ideological distance between competing parties is more and more common. Parties in competitive systems, or where coalition governments are the rule, need to show willingness to compromise principles or forgo outright gain in the interests of forming a viable government. Data on the esteem in which parties and party systems are held by the general public in established democracies would suggest that the legitimation functions attributed to them are performed less than efficiently. But the impact of these changes in party identification has yet to be felt in terms of relaxing the grip that major parties still have on the electoral politics in many countries.

Are political parties in decline?

Leaving aside the variability in performance due to regime type, it is easy to catalogue the kinds of things parties do. The more interesting and perhaps the more crucial point for an appreciation of how politics is changing is how well they perform these functions and whether other modalities are doing it better, or, to avoid the normative trap, more efficiently. Our discussion of each of the functions goes some way to answering these questions, and looking at interest groups in the next section and the role of communications media in Chapter 12 will provide further insights.

Political parties are products of the modernisation of societies in the nineteenth and twentieth centuries. The major political upheavals and the social cleavages which precipitated the emergence of mass political parties have now largely passed, at least in the Western world. We may not have reached the 'end of History', as Francis Fukuyama (1992) has it, and parts of the world are still authoritarian or proto-democratic, but it could be argued that many of the conditions that spawned and sustained party politics belong to an earlier period of modern history. As the world moves into a period of late or even post-modernity, the emergence of different forms of demand articulation, political mobilisation and communication, and even governance, all of which owe little to political parties as mediating organisations, is likely to intensify.

At least some of the evidence we have cited above supports the claim that political parties are in decline. Membership of parties generally is declining, as is the willingness of voters to identify with a particular party. The exceptions to these findings (see Tables 11.1 and 11.2) may tell us more about the specific conditions in those exceptional regimes than confound the general thesis of party decline. Cross-national data on declining turnout at elections is more variable (see Chapter 4, Table 4.8) but figures on the lack of trust in politicians (not just party politicians of course) hardly support the argument that parties are key instruments of political integration and legitimation. There are also indications of an increase in electoral volatility, with huge electoral swings against governing parties, such as occurred in France in 1993, when the Socialists went from 282 seats to a rump of seventy.

The role of parties (as party organisations) in government also looks more parlous in recent years. In the UK, the role of the Labour Party in the country as a source of policy has all but ceased. In part this is a function of the exigencies of governing a large and complex system, and is also a product of the inability of national legislatures to properly scrutinise, let alone control the political executive, even where (as in the UK) it is part of the legislature.

Of course, such trends may be temporary, but they may be indicators of a shift in political consciousness on the part of citizens in many countries and signal important shifts in the ways in which democratic politics is conducted. All this causes a great deal of concern among some commentators and politicians (Balandier 1992; Lipow and Seyd 1995; Taguieff 1996), because they presage a new kind of **anti-politics**, or, at the least an anti-party politics. Berlusconi's model for a 'videocracy' and Tony Blair's penchant for communicating with voters directly over the heads of party members and the parliamentary party are often interpreted as perversions of party democracy and parliamentary government. The rise of political forces such as new social movements on the environment and human rights, as well as a host of single-issue and protest parties is disquieting because, if they see contesting elections and engaging with party organisations and parliamentary representatives as important at all, they are only parts of a wider strategy. Finally, the low esteem in which conventional party and representative politics is held is also taken as potentially harmful to democracy.

Underlying much of this disquiet is a powerful, but sometimes unspoken sense that political parties are not only critical to the health of democracies, but constitute some kind of paradigm case of democracy in action. The argument here is almost that if political parties did not exist, we would have to invent them.

Anti-politics An expression applied to a wide range of attitudes and phenomena. The main burden of the notion is that indirect, representative democracy, built on party competition and reliant upon the mediating functions of political parties, is being challenged. In this scenario, the villains are ruled through media, some kinds of interest groups and social movements, populism generally and market forces which have turned interested citizens into unreflective consumers. Applied to countries without established democracies, the expression embraces many undemocratic practices such as denying forms of opposition.

See the extended discussion of social trust and social capital in Chapter 4.

THINK POINT

- What do you think? Are political parties in decline?

- If so, does it matter?

Interest groups

Parties and interest groups

As noted above, factions have occasioned suspicion among those concerned with the unity of the body politic and anxious to guard against the power of sectional interests. At the same time, the value of what Alexis de Tocqueville (1856–1947) called 'powerful instruments of action' as the means through which citizens can influence government is recognised widely. The importance of voluntary association to the health of civil society and pluralist democracies is demonstrated by the concern with the alleged decline of civic activism, which we looked at in Chapter 4. The normative dimension of this debate is made more intense by the absence of clear-cut evidence on the relative power of groups, which, for proponents of conspiracy, lends more fuel to the claims that 'real' power is exercised covertly, in smoke-filled rooms or through the judicious offer of funds to a political campaign.

Both political parties and groups are part of the weave of connections that link the state to civil society. Although it is sometimes difficult to distinguish between groups and parties, the old rule of thumb that parties are in the business of winning elections, wielding power and broadening the basis of their appeal, while groups are not, holds true. For the most part, groups do not contest elections and their rationale is to act on behalf of particular interests and articulate their demands. In the real world things are more complex, and, occasionally, groups do put up candidates for election and sometimes they need to broaden their appeal to the wider public in order to strengthen their case before government. Indeed, some groups are much closer to government than the image of them being expressions civil society admits, having been incorporated into the routines of decision-making to the extent that they could even be said to make policy.

Group politics is not new and the precursors of modern interest group politics may be found in bodies such as the Anti-Corn Law League in Britain in 1839 and the Young Italy movement set up by Giuseppe Mazzini, a leading activist in the attempt to unify Italy, in 1831. In some cases, notably trade unions, their growth is closely linked to the emergence of political parties. In Britain, the nascent trade union movement gave birth to the Labour Party as a way of securing parliamentary representation for the organised, and recently enfranchised, working class. Other organised interests, this time driven by producers such as business and farming, arose to counteract the power of trade unionism and to **lobby** governments. Since the mid-twentieth century a burgeoning of group politics has taken place. The 'explosion' of groups, as it is called, was a product of major changes taking place in economies and societies in the West, and spawned all kinds of consumer groups, protest movements and single-issue politics. This spate of activity not only sprang from the political maturation of better educated, more affluent and less deferential publics, but also paralleled (at the very least) a downturn in the appeal of political parties as mediators of public opinion. In recent decades, transnational social movements and international non-governmental organisations (INGOs) have emerged, driven largely by the globalisation of risk (Beck 1999) and the transnationalisation of politics in areas such as the environment, gender equality and human rights.

Lobby A generic term for making representations to public officials and elected representatives. Closely associated with American politics, the expression has its origins in the attempts by petitioners – lobbyists – to meet with politicians in the lobby of a parliament building.

What are interest groups?: Types of groups

The use of the concept 'interest group' is a convenient, although not unprob-lematic, way of identifying a wide range of group actors whose motivations, organisation and strategies may be different. The term 'interest group' is preferred to the more common 'pressure group', because not all interest groups use pressure tactics and not all are political in the received sense of that word. But the idea of an 'interest' is itself confusing. You may be interested in something in the sense that you are intrigued by it, but you may have an interest in it because you have a stake in whether it prospers or declines. Neither of these leads automatically or even logically to political action, although the

German sociologist of risk and the environment, Professor of Sociology at University of Munich, Beck wrote *Risk Society* (1986), *Counterpoison* (1991), *Ecological Enlightenment* (1992), *Ecological Politics in an Age of Risk* (1994), *The Reinvention of Politics* (1996), *Democracy Without Enemies* (1998), *World Risk Society* (1999), *What is Globalization?* (1999), *Individualization* (2000, with E. Beck-Gernsheim), and *Future of Work and Democracy* (2000). He is also a regular contributor to the *Frankfurter Allgemeine Zeitung*. Ulrich Beck has analysed post-modern society as '*Risikogesellschaft*' or 'risk-society' – the main feature of which is that society's members are confronted with socially created risks which endanger the survival of the species. Our societies are characterised by 'organised irresponsibility' whereby risk producers are protected at the expense of risk victims.

Ulrich Beck

latter is more likely to do so. There is also the issue of whether being part of an 'interest', in the sense of having a stake in something, requires awareness on the part of individuals. Women, the working class and single-parent families are often spoken of as though they constitute self-evident interests, and in a way this suggests that *this* identity is more significant and defining than any other. There are obvious advantages in doing this if you are an organisation claiming to act on behalf of women or the poor, but the notion that an interest is in some way an objective condition (as Marxists have argued about class interests) is difficult to square with the idea that people have wants and preferences which they may or may not pursue through political action.

THINK POINT

- Do people have 'real' or 'objective' interests that they may not recognise?
- If so, how would you establish this fact?

Now, the point about what we mean by the concept of *interest* is not just an abstract debate, because much of the discussion of group politics takes place in relation to groups that are voluntary associations. Voluntary associations are formed from memberships which recognise shared concerns and wish to pursue or defend them in the political arena. Voluntary associations constitute the most numerous strain of interest groups, at least in established democracies. Protest activity organised by voluntary interest groups has also shown remarkably high rates of increase recently as the following extract demonstrates.

Examples of dramatic events like the anti-globalization movement disruption of international summits and the peace demonstrations triggered by the US air strikes in Afghanistan suggest that willingness to engage in protest politics has increased in recent decades in many places around the world, but on the other hand this perception could reflect changes in the new media's propensity to

continued

continued

cover these events. Confirming the more anecdotal evidence, there was an increase in the protest activism scale registered in all the 23 nations where World Values Surveys (WVS) were conducted in both the early 1980s and the mid-1990s, with strong gains registered in some of developing countries such as South Africa, South Korea and Mexico, as well as in older democracies like Switzerland, Sweden and West Germany. There may be more media coverage of street demonstrations, rallies and public meetings, but these images reflect real changes in political behavior in many societies.

(P. Norris, *Democratic Phoenix: Democratic Activism Worldwide*, 2002)

However, we should note that not all interest groups are voluntary. For example, until changes in the legislation governing membership of trade unions in the UK during the 1980s, it was possible to require new employees in some industries to join a union as a condition of their employment, under a 'closed shop' agreement. But there are other cases of non-associational interest groups, and we will consider these as part of an examination of group types. We can identify three broad types of group:

1 non-associational
2 institutional
3 associational.

NON-ASSOCIATIONAL GROUPS

Individuals do not join these kinds of groups, which are sometimes called communal groups. They are either born into them or are members by default. Because there is no choice about membership, non-associational groups may remain politically latent, just there as it were, until such times as they are mobilised. Of course, individuals are still able to opt out of or distance themselves from actions taken in their name, although, as ascribed members of the group, they may still benefit from actions or take the consequences if things go wrong. Non-associational groups include family and kinship groups, such as castes or clans, religions or sects, ethnic communities, gender groups and also social classes, although the subjectivity often tied to class identities introduces an element of voluntarism that sits uneasily with the idea of there being no choice about membership. Ethnic nationalism, tribal identities and religious affiliation are often the basis for political demands in parts of Africa and Latin America, but also feature in Europe (witness the militancy of Serb majorities and minorities in various parts of the former Yugoslavia) and the USA and Canada (e.g. Native American politics in the USA and Francophone nationalism in Quebec).

INSTITUTIONAL GROUPS

This category covers two kinds of groups:

1 All groups defined by employment. These include professional groups, such as the British Medical Association and the Royal College of Nursing. Civil servants, teachers, police officers and accountants all have professional bodies that set standards for the conduct of those professions and regulate them, but sometimes act on behalf of their members in consultations with government. Frequently, such bodies play an important role as providers of expertise in the formulation of public policy. Sometimes they act almost as trade unions in respect of the rights and working conditions of their members. On the international stage, the role of 'epistemic communities', that is, networks of knowledge professionals in areas such as information technologies and sustainable development, play roles as advisers to intergovernmental organisations (the UN, NATO) and trans- and supranational bodies (the WTO and the EU).

2 Groups that are institutionalised parts of the machinery of government. Parts of government bureaucracy, for example, a department of state such as education or employment, will act corporately to influence how well it fares in decisions about how to distribute tax revenues. In most countries, the military has a developed world view and a strong sense of how best its interests can be served. Scientists have clout with governments because of their technical expertise. Sometimes they are able to influence a wider range of policies than their immediate area of competence. In the old Soviet Union, parts of the scientific community waged a continuing battle with the Central Party and ministries in Moscow, about the environmental degradation caused by industrial and agricultural pollution.

ASSOCIATIONAL GROUPS

As we have noted above, associational groups are those peopled by voluntary activists (although they may have a professional and permanent organisation). People join out of a sense of common interest or shared ideals. Associational groups usually have limited and specific (although possibly long-term) goals to pursue and they are not interested in aggregating interests across the spectrum of issues. Membership of such groups does not, in itself, betoken a purely instrumental or rational cast on political action and civic engagement, although many theorists of political participation have commented on the irrationality of joining interest groups which are dedicated to the pursuit of what are called '**public goods**'. We have identified and commented on the 'free-rider' problem in relation to forms of collective action in Chapters 1 and 4. Irrational or not, lots of people do join groups committed to the promotion of the public good, although one might quibble as to their definition of what that means.

Public good Benefit which cannot be withheld from the community at large, that is, it is not only available to those who are members of an organisation or who have paid for the benefit. Clean air, world peace and safe streets are all public goods.

> **THINK POINT**
>
> ▤ If a protest march to draw attention to world poverty were to be held in your town/city tomorrow, would you join it?
>
> ▤ If yes, why?; if no, why not?
>
> ▤ What if the march were in favour of cutting fees in higher education?

Public interest groups (PIGs) flourished in the USA in the 1960s and 1970s, none more so than those led or influenced by Ralph Nader.

Ralph Nader

Ralph Nader is the doyen of American consumer activists. He became famous in the 1960s with his Campaign for Auto Safety, which began with his crusade against the Ford Motor Company and their Corvair motor car. Nader's book on the struggle, *Unsafe at any Speed*, is a classic of the consumer movement.

Nader has founded and led many groups, including 'Citizen Works', 'Public Citizen', and 'The Center for Responsible Law'. He stood as a maverick independent candidate for the US presidency in 2000.

Associational interest groups are most visible and most influential in established democracies. Although some of the tactics they use may be considered unconventional, radical and possibly tasteless, the principle of opposition and the value of diversity of opinion are entrenched in such regimes. Of course, one of the dilemmas of a pluralist democracy is how much opposition to accommodate and whether all methods of influencing government are admissible. In practice, while many forms of direct action by groups are seen as legitimate, terror tactics are not, because they are destructive of life and property and because they are used by organisations bent on changing the identity of the system, including its overthrow.

In new and proto-democracies associational interest groups are less common, and, as with Western-style political parties, it is still hard to tell if they will take root in the cultural soil of the new regimes. There is even some evidence that membership of voluntary associations is falling in some new democracies, such as Spain (Heywood 1995), despite the fact that the country does exhibit something like the model of interest group activity seen in many established democracies. In parts of Central and Eastern Europe churches have declined as 'privileged' sites of opposition to communist rule, largely because that function is redundant in the more pluralist societies emerging since 1989. In Russia, and in other parts of the post-communist world, the demise of state socialism has, paradoxically, fostered the revival of groups and parties whose credo is the defence of communal identities and interests, such as ethnicity. In Latin America, the relatively close relationships between the state in many countries and organised trade unions, which some writers have classified as **corporatist** (Hagopian 1998; Schmitter and Lehmbruch 1979) has also

Corporatism Refers to the relationship between the state and interest groups in which a small number of key groups – peak associations in particular sectors (e.g. labour and industrial capital) – are accorded privileged access to decision-making circles and become part of the machinery of government in return for controlling their members and being good corporate citizens.

changed due to the rise of market forces and the firmer links between big business and governments.

During the process of liberating and democratising many of these countries (from military dictatorships and one-party rule), political parties and social movements, such as Solidarity in Poland, played crucial roles. The role of interest groups in both widening the process of democratisation and deepening the commitment to pluralist values is still very much in its infancy.

The role of interest groups in authoritarian regimes is very limited. Where they are not fully incorporated into the machinery of state governance or heavily controlled, they are treated as a threat, to the point where they are completely circumscribed and driven underground. Recent experience in the USSR, Hitler's Germany and practically all of the military dictatorships around the world corroborates this judgement. In China, what might look like interest groups – mainly 'mass organisations' such as the Women's Federation – are completely infiltrated and controlled by the Chinese Communist Party. The state, in the shape of the party, effectively organises what interests subsist and how they behave. Those which are not sanctioned, such as the cultural and religious movement *Falun Gong*, are the subject of intense harrassment and legal penalties. Whether China's limited embrace of market economics and the more hands-off role of the state in relation to the internationalisation of the economy produces a more tolerant attitude to dissent remains in doubt.

Associational interest groups come in many varieties. We will touch upon three major types, recognising that they are useful labels rather than completely discrete kinds of group. The picture is complicated by the fact that each type admits a range of sub-types. The main categories are:

- Sectional groups (sometimes called protective groups or functional groups).

- Promotional groups (sometimes called cause groups). Includes advocacy groups (a category often applied to non-governmental organisations (NGOs) which act as expert 'advocates' in relation to policies).

- Social movements (including transnational civil society coalitions).

SECTIONAL GROUPS

The rationale of these groups is to promote and protect functional interests in society. In the main, functional interests refer to the material well-being of memberships. Professional organisations, trade unions, trade associations are all functional interest groups, but although these 'peak associations' as they are called are characteristic of the genre, individual firms and trade unions some-times operate as their own advocates, lobbying government directly, especially if they are strategically placed in the economy and enjoy good relations with politicians and bureaucrats. In addition, groups that represent consumers, localities and even ethnic and religious groups may be classified as sectional groups, because they claim to represent a discrete segment of society. But sectional groups that are also functional groups are involved in the production, distribution and exchange of good and services. For the most part membership of sectional groups is restricted to those who possess the attributes that the group is trying to protect and the benefits of their interventions flow only to members. All sectional groups aim to influence government policy and they are able to mobilise different resources to achieve this aim, including with-holding labour and offering technical expertise.

Sectional groups have a long history in the USA and parts of Western Europe, and, on the face of it, their location as the representatives of economic producers should give them considerable influence with policy-makers. Taken in the round, and across different systems, this is not always the case.

Inevitably, the neat distinction between categories of groups begins to fray when cases that are hard to classify are considered. Some groups, which are often categorised as cause or promotional groups because they aim to change public attitudes as well as government policy, are in fact the representatives of particular interests, such as the gay lobby and the Women's Movement. In the UK, the Countryside Alliance is a coalition of various rural groups mobilised around the generic issue of the decline of country life. Although the Alliance campaigns on the basis of promoting a holistic way of life and a set of basic values concerned with the quality of life of all citizens in a pressured and urbanised environment, it is in fact a vehicle for particular sectional interests, including the hunting or field sports lobby.

PROMOTIONAL GROUPS

The accepted distinction between sectional and promotional groups is that the latter are established to promote causes, principles and values. The particular cause may be narrowly focused, or apparently so, as with the promotion of gay and ethnic minority rights, but the promotion of these causes has a powerful resonance with wider and even universal norms, such as the sanctity of human rights or the value of diversity. Of course, some groups deliberately emphasise the global reach of their message, campaigning to protect the environmental integrity of the 'global commons' or to erase world poverty. Promotional groups aim to represent people – and animals and inanimate forms, if represent is the appropriate term in the latter case – who are not their members. Obviously there are some ethical problems with this apparently principled stance, one of which is the possible arrogance of promotional group activists in claiming to speak for people who may not have asked for their assistance in the first place.

Global commons refers to Antarctica and the oceans – see Chapter 15 for a discussion of global commons in relation to international law and regulation.

THINK POINT

What is your view? Are there ethical dilemmas, or do the ends justify the means?

There are a vast number of promotional groups around the world and the range of their interests is no less wide. The category includes groups such as Amnesty International, Greenpeace, Friends of the Earth and the World Wide Fund for

Nature, but also encompasses bodies like the Pro-Life Alliance (anti-abortion campaign in the UK), Gingerbread (pursuing the interests of one-parent families) and the Welsh Language Society.

Promotional groups – Amnesty International

This organisation campaigns for the release of political prisoners around the globe. Through a combination of letter-writing campaigns (fax and e-mail are also used), special reports, an Urgent Action network, affiliation through group membership, and individual membership subscription, this organisation seeks to heighten awareness of human rights abuse around the globe and to bring direct influence to bear on governments who contravene the United Nations Human Rights Charter.

Advocacy groups, sometimes known as advocacy coalitions, are a sub-category of the promotional group, and have become increasingly visible in the context of global citizen actions in global civil society (Edwards and Gaventa 2001). Before about 1980, there was relatively little contact between civic organisations and multilateral bodies such as the United Nations, and very little NGO involvement in international regimes. This situation changed dramatically from the mid-1980s, especially as regards groups working around the UN. Indeed, global civic organisations massively increased in number after the end of the Cold War, and, along with the World Bank, the UN began to form partnerships with key NGOs in joint ventures such as the Global Alliance for Forest Conservation and Sustainable Use, and the World Commission on Dams (Florini 2001). In the 1990s the by-now established relations between multilateral institutions and key NGOs were criticised on the grounds that the system had set up a privileged NGO advocacy elite of largely unselected, unaccountable and, frankly, unrepresentative bodies.

For a discussion of international regimes, see Chapter 15.

Advocacy groups and coalitions do perform valuable tasks. Apart from their global reach, their main strength lies in the quality of technical expertise they can bring to bear on an issue. Advocacy groups conduct research, collect and collate data and provide an alternative and necessary source of expert opinion to that offered by commercial organisations, national governments and multilateral bodies. The scope of their activities in an interconnected world is likely to increase, but the concerns raised above are genuine. The following extract demonstrates the usefulness and the dangers of advocacy group activity.

The Foul Ball Campaign

In 1996, the United States-based International Labor Rights Fund (ILRF) began its Foul Ball Campaign to 'call attention to the distress of thousands of children working full-time to stitch soccer balls in the Sialkot region of Pakistan'. The

---

continued

continued

ILRF confused the type and conditions attached to loans given to Sialkot families and their conditions of labour to extreme forms of 'debt bondage', from which it is well-nigh impossible for people to extract themselves.

American NGOs led by militant 'soccer mums' took up the campaign and, with ILRF help, played a major role in pushing for a ban on child labour in Sialkot.

While obviously well intentioned, they campaigned on the basis of poor research, without thought as to the consequences of their actions and without consulting those who would be affected. Pakistani domestic groups felt that the campaign detracted attention from even more serious abuses of child labour in the chemical and medical industries, and did not take sufficient heed of the relatively secure and unpressured home environments in which the children who stitched the footballs actually worked. Such work is also comparatively well paid.

SOCIAL MOVEMENTS

Social movements are relatively loose forms of collective behaviour, rooted in shared beliefs and values. They pursue general but often quite clearly defined goals, often with a broad if not universal remit. Social movements are often coalitional in structure, rarely having memberships in themselves, but made up of organisations that may well have a formal membership, and which are happy to subscribe to the overall aims of the movement.

Although they are now often linked to the warm and embracing world view of post-hippie, post-affluent societies in the West, social movements have a rather more visceral pedigree in the reaction to the social cleavages produced by modernity. The labour movement in Western Europe and North America is, or was, a social movement, as was the revolt against modernity expressed in the fascist movements of the 1920s and 1930s.

In the latter part of the twentieth century, so-called 'new' social movements emerged that expressed both a disillusionment with the institutions and routines of usual politics, and a recognition that mass politics had to be organised across as well as within territorial states. The 'new' movements also tend to reflect the concern with post-material issues characteristic of post-industrial societies in the West – gender definition and equality, environmentalism, animal rights, and more exotic forms of social exclusion than were accommodated in the class-based politics of an earlier generation of activists. At the same time, issues such as the global North–South divide, debt relief, sustainable development and corporate (meaning business) accountability demonstrate a link to a politics still rooted in the material world, as well as in more abstract sympathies. The self-styled anti-capitalist or anti-globalist movement, of which we say more in Chapter 15, is an amalgam of practically all these forces and interests (Klein 2000). As Norris (2002) points out, one difficulty facing any systematic analysis is that new social movements and transnational advocacy networks encompass a diversity of organisations and causes. At the G8 summit in Genoa in July 2001, an estimated 700 groups attended the Genoa Social Forum, including conventional trade unions and charities such as Oxfam and Christian Aid, as well as groups concerned with peaceful protests about globalisation, the protection of human rights, environmentalism, the peace movement, poverty and debt relief for developing nations. Also present were the more radical anarchists and anti-capitalist forces in the vanguard of the 'black block'.

Theories and models of interest group politics

The kinds of interest groups active and the pattern of their interaction with each other and with governments is a function of (1) the conditions peculiar to any one country (the kind of political culture, the sort of party system and the permissiveness of the law and constitution), (2) the resources that groups themselves can mobilise in pursuit of their aims, and (3) broader or more abstract prescriptions about the nature of the state, the appropriate relationships between state and civil society, the nature of democracy and the discretion of governments. There is a diversity of normative and positive theorising on these conditions, especially on the last. The most discussed are:

- pluralism;

- corporatism;

- public choice theory, which is not really a theory of groups at all.

PLURALISM

There are many strands of pluralist theory, but almost all see the existence of groups and the ability to form groups as the basis of a democratic society. Robert Dahl's concept of *polyarchy* has the ideal pluralist society as one in which groups perform crucial functions by giving critical mass to the otherwise isolated demands of individuals, by providing competition for public resources in different issue areas and by keeping government responsive and accountable to different strands of public opinion. In short, the more groups the better, because a proliferation of competing groups (competing within accepted rules of the game) in different issue areas cuts down the chances of any one becoming dominant all of the time and reduces the chances of a systematic mobilisation of bias. The interplay of groups and government will also produce a net outcome in terms of public policy that is moderate and fair, because competing and resourceful interests and rational and neutral governments facilitate bargaining and compromise across the policy spectrum.

Critics of pluralist theories of group democracy (Bachrach and Baratz 1963; Lukes 1974; Mills 1956) point to the gap between the theory of polyarchy and political reality. In this reality interest groups are not effective representatives of individual preferences. Moreover, despite the theory, some groups are obviously more powerful than others and may be able to exercise a veto over what governments can do with regard to particular policies. C. Wright Mills wrote of a 'power elite' in the USA, made up of corporations, top military cadres and political leaders, who jointly controlled much of the economic policy in their collective interest. Even in Mills' model, some degree of pluralism is apparent, but it is the electoral pluralism and competition between the relatively powerless. Like many of the claims of pluralist theorists, these elite and neo-elitist models suffer from a dearth of empirical evidence or from highly contested evidence.

Key texts: R. Dahl (1956) *A Preface to Democratic Theory*, Chicago, Ill.: Chicago University Press; (1971) *Polyarchy: Participation and Opposition*, New Haven, Conn.: Yale University Press.

Robert Dahl

Robert Dahl is one of the leading figures in democratic theory. Born in 1915 he became Professor of Political Science at Yale in 1946. With Charles Lindlom he published in 1953 a work that introduced the concept of 'polyarchy' to set modern, democratic societies apart from both non-democratic variants and the societies of classical democratic theory. He is also identified with important developments in pluralist theories of democracy and has been exercised by the growing power of corporations as a danger to pluralist democracy. Apart from *Polyarchy* in 1971, other key works include *A Preface to Democratic Theory* (1956), *Who Governs* (1961) and *Dilemmas of Pluralist Democracy* (1982).

CORPORATISM

Corporatism provides a quite different model of the role of groups as the links between state and society. Like pluralism it maintains that groups are central to the political and policy processes. Unlike pluralism it does not consider government as a neutral player, or an arena in which groups with more-or-less equal resources can compete with each other for the ear of government. Rather, corporatism is a form of demand management in which the state is the real arbiter of group influence, deciding which group shall be favoured and which excluded.

At root, corporatism is a form of social contract between governments and powerful producer interests such as big business and, in the recent past at any rate, trade unions. These groups enjoy privileged access to policy-making circles and, in return for their strategic cooperation with the state in the management of the economy, they are able to conduct their internal affairs with some discretion. Their status and autonomy may be so pronounced that they become the major stakeholders in particular areas of public policy-making and implementation, a condition known as 'private interest government'.

There are different kinds of corporatism, which reflect the nature of the regimes in which they are located. Weak corporatist systems, sometimes called 'liberal corporatism', are possibly no more than the institutionalisation of the necessarily close relations between governments and interests which can mobilise resources of value to the government, or which the government fears may be used against it. In Britain in the 1970s a system of 'tripartism' involving government departments and peak associations in business (the Confederation of British Industries (CBI)) and trade unions (the Trades Union Congress) took responsibility for macro-economic management. In the USA, used by Dahl and others as the paradigm case of a pluralist democracy, formal links between state and functional interests have been a feature of the ways in which regulatory bodies have operated in areas such as agriculture, forestation and energy. Farming interests in many states have enjoyed close relationships with government departments responsible for the delivery of agricultural policy. In Britain and France from the 1950s to the late 1980s the symbiotic relationships between agricultural producers and state regulators were taken for granted. One of the possible consequences of these cosy relationships was that, in the UK at least, a model of commercial farming and good husbandry was allowed to develop in which the production of cheap food and intensive rearing practices led to the BSE crisis of the 1990s.

BSE: Bovine Spongiform Encephalitis.

These brands of weak corporatism have been under retreat in many Western systems since the late 1980s. The catalysts for change comprise the partial 'rolling back' of the state from some areas of economic management, including industrial relations, the more feisty attitude of consumer and public interest organisations, and the decline in the memberships and organising power of trade unions. Between the mid-1980s and the late 1990s, union membership fell in the USA, France, the UK, Germany, Japan, New Zealand and Italy. It rose in Sweden, Norway, Denmark and South Africa.

Strong corporatisms, or statist corporatisms as they are called, have an unsavoury association with fascist regimes. Fascist theory prescribed that the economy should be organised by sector, with special committees or 'corporations' planning output in each industry to meet national demands. Forms of corporatism subsisted in Latin America, principally in authoritarian regimes, where the military and other dictatorships were concerned to manage the articulation of new interests. Before market-led changes to the organisation of economic life in the 1990s, Mexico was a case of strong corporatism, with state licensing of interest groups, state funding of privileged groups, and a monopoly of representation accorded to these same clients of the state in key sectors of economic life. In contemporary Europe, the countries which are most corporatist include Austria (at present in the grip of a populist backlash against the old corporatist system, led by the Austrian Freedom party), Finland, Belgium and Ireland. Corporatism generally, but state corporatism in particular, has fallen out of favour, creating as it does an over-reliance on the state and an unhealthy consensus between interests robbed of their dynamism and competitive instinct by incorporation.

PUBLIC CHOICE THEORY

As noted above, not really a theory of groups at all, since it derives from economic theories which start and end with the individual. Public choice theorists (Olson 1965) have generally decried interventions by government in the management of economic affairs as subverting the logic and efficiency of

Key text: M. Olson Jr. (1965) *The Logic of Collective Action*, Cambridge, Mass.: Harvard University Press.

markets. They have also questioned the viability of a group politics based on the premise of collective action. New Right theorists (Friedman 1963; von Hayek 1960) who scorned the role of groups and were sceptical of the idea of collective destinies, were taken up by radical politicians such as Margaret Thatcher and Keith Joseph in the UK, and Ronald Reagan in the USA. The success of public choice theory as the basis for neo-liberal economics is witnessed in its take-up by governments around the world, although there are still powerful countervailing forces. In Italy, in April 2002, trade unions declared a general strike and took to the streets in opposition to Prime Minister Berlusconi's promise to reform the country's employment laws to make it easier for employers to lay off workers without undue penalty. Existing employment law, which developed out of the traditions of Christian socialist thought in Italy and the power of trade unions, are felt by Berlusconi, an admirer of Margaret Thatcher (and Tony Blair) to be detrimental to Italy's ability to compete in world markets.

The resources and tactics used by interest groups

Just as the universe of interest groups is wide, so is the range of resources available to groups in their attempts to influence government and the variety of tactics they employ. The resources which can be utilised by groups obviously varies with the type of group, the nature of the system in which it is operating and the issue area it wants to influence. Trying to persuade a government of the technical deficiencies in food safety standards may not be well served by mounting an elaborate and aggressive media campaign, even if the group has the financial resources to carry out such a programme. Arguably, the most powerful groups are those which never have to mobilise resources and become visible, but keep their powder dry. Their power lies in the extent to which rivals and governments anticipate the negative reaction and adverse consequences which would follow if the group's preferences were ignored. This is an intriguing and intuitively plausible scenario. From the point of view of good social science however, the problem lies in being able to demonstrate that the 'law' of anticipated reaction has been in operation.

Some of the resources used by groups are:

▪ *Membership*: The size and commitment of a membership can be important to a group's credibility and perhaps to its success. Members provide funds and activists; they can also offer high levels of expertise – in campaigning, on the technical detail of a policy change and so on. At the same time, membership can be transient. Even high-profile groups such as Friends of the Earth and Amnesty International experience something like a 25 per cent turnover in members per annum. Despite the assumed correspondence, there seem to be no real grounds for equating large memberships with the success of interest groups.

▪ *Finance*: Again, the assumed equation between group affluence and success over any issue is not proven. Access to funds can help a group to survive over time and to build a permanent organisation. It can buy publicity, and in some countries it can even buy politicians and public officials. In most democratic systems it is not possible for an interest group to subvent the campaign of a favoured politician or party with unlimited and unrecorded donations of funds, although irregularities do occur. Funds are also useful to employ professional lobbying and PR organisations.

- *Expertise*: Interest groups rely on different sorts of expertise to press their demands. In dealing with governments and their technical advisers, specific knowledge and general credibility are clearly of value. Groups can also benefit from the fact that they may be the acknowledged experts in a field and are the first port of call for governments seeking advice.

- *Public esteem*: The credibility and standing of a group may be enhanced if it enjoys public esteem. Because of this status, it is less likely to be dismissed as irrelevant and frivolous by government.

- *The management of visibility*: This resource refers to publicity, of course, but also to the way a group manages what has been called the 'issue–attention cycle' (Downs 1972). If a group can keep its agenda in the public eye and sustain public interest over an issue in which it has a stake, it may be in a better position to influence government. It used to be received wisdom that a group which has to 'go public' with its campaign is a weak group, almost bound to lose out to others that are more resourceful and less reliant on fickle media and public opinion. Today, that wisdom is less obvious. We now live in cultures completely saturated by different forms of news and entertainment media. Governments and political parties are entirely attuned to the need to set the media agenda, and savvy groups are required to follow the same path.

- *Internal cohesion and unity of purpose*: An interest group riven by faction and seen to be divided is unlikely to impress much in competition with other more cohesive organisations.

- *Taking advantage of contingency*: The access to government and the success of an interest group is not just the sum of the resources it can draw on. The salience of an issue, its importance to government and/or the public, can be crucial in getting a group's voice heard. Unexpected events may serve to place a group's concern on the political agenda and turn it from a marginal into a key player.

Resources may or may not be useful in any particular context. The same is true of the tactics or methods employed, and the range of institutions and office-holders used as channels of access to policy-making circles. Methods of persuasion and points of access are listed in Table 11.3.

We should note that, as well as national institutions and officials and domestic media, some groups are specifically oriented towards international and supranational bodes and the global public. It is also important to bear in mind that, with obvious exceptions, these tactics and attempts to access

Table 11.3 Methods of persuasion and points of access

Tactic	Point of access	Type of group	Type of regime	Found in (for example)
Consultation	Civil servants, regulatory bodies, etc., commissions of inquiry	Functional groups, large corporataions, professions, trade unions	Established and new democracies	Scandinavian states, The Netherlands
Lobbying	Principally parliaments, but also government departments	All types	Ditto	Primarily USA, some in UK
Supporting candidates + parties	Individual candidates, party treasurers and campaign chiefs of staff	Principally sectional and producer groups	Established and new democracies and authoritarian regimes where elections allowed	Norway, UK, Australia, USA, Canada
Getting coopted on to regulatory and other governance bodies and policy networks	Professional lobbyists, Chairs of legislative committees, government task forces, etc.	Sectional groups, but also some NGOs and INGOs	All types of system and international bodies, and regional polities such as the EU	EU, UN, most established democracies
Through the courts	Specialist lawyers, constitutional experts	All types, but, with the exception outside the USA, sparingly	Recourse to the courts available in different types of system	Mainly USA
Using media	Professional PR firms, opinion polling, qualitative research, news media with compatible views	Increasingly, all types	Primarily established and new democracies, some authoritarian regimes and multilateral bodies	All established and some new democracies
Direct action, protest activity	Being able to mobilise support on the day on the streets	Associational in the main, but some sectional groups and INGOs	All types, but overt and legitimate in established and new democracies	Mainly established democracies, some new democracies
Civil disobedience	Ditto	Ditto, along with anti-regime groups	All types, but more prevalent in non-democratic regimes	All regimes, but in non-democratic should be taken as anti-systemic

different institutions of government are not mutually exclusive, although in some countries some tactics are legally proscribed or outlawed by force and intimidation.

THINK POINT

This is not meant to be an exhaustive list. Can you think of other tactics a group might use?

The power of interest groups

The power wielded by interest groups has been a matter for debate for two centuries and more. The functions and the influence of interest groups vary from state to state, regime type to regime type and political culture to political culture. In other words, the part they play in the political life of a country is largely context dependent. As intermediaries between state and society and as bodies which articulate demands, their reputation and legitimacy also vary enormously. What makes some interest groups more powerful than others is not easy to call, as we have seen. It may be possible to identify whether groups enjoy an *insider* or an *outsider* status in terms of their ease of access to decision-makers and the part they play in decision-making procedures (Grant 1989). Whether or not a group is an insider or an outsider is not specifically related to the issue area or policy domain in which it is active. Nor is it always tied to resources available to the group. In some instances it is a product of the types of demands the group is making, for example, radical shifts in the ways public resources are allocated; in others it follows from the ways in which groups articulate demands – note the insider status of the respectable Royal Society for the Protection of Animals (RSPCA) and the outsider status accorded to the Animal Liberation Front. But the distinction may be overdrawn in these changed times because it implies that outsider status is always (1) weak and therefore (2) undesirable. Yet some groups – for example, anti-vivisection groups and anti-globalisation protestors – see their status as outsiders as not only desirable, but viable as a platform from which to mount contentious politics. In the matter of resources, the age of the Internet and mobile telephony makes these sorts of activism and the articulation of their demands a matter of connectivity – between supporters and between supporters and a voracious media. Visibility as a tactic of last resort is replaced by publicity as a desired attribute. In other words, the very definition of insider and outsider may be changing in a political universe made up of more and different political actors and in which the boundaries on activism are imploding.

EXERCISE

Before reading about public opinion, consider the arguments for and against interest groups.

Public opinion

What is public opinion?

Political parties and interest groups are both engaged in the business of making demands. As organisations they mediate demands from citizens in different ways. Parties in modern systems tend to aggregate demands, while interest groups articulate them. Both modalities are also concerned with the management of demand in the sense that, as intermediary organisations, for the most part they are not inclined to allow the unfettered expression of public opinion. The idea of public opinion as the spontaneous, collective expression of attitudes about issues, institutions and people is difficult to grasp in large and complex societies, and should always be treated with some caution.

Opinion, and certainly public opinion, is seldom unmediated, even if that means being influenced by the context in which the opinion is formulated and the socialisation experienced by individuals. Even apparently spontaneous expressions of public opinion, such as were said to have occurred on the death of Diana, Princess of Wales, in 1997, cannot be separated from the role of various print and broadcast media, who were active in 'creating demand', as the economist J. K. Galbraith (1965) said, rather than just reporting public reactions.

Writing about the political setting, V. O. Key Jr. (1964) opined that public opinion is 'those opinions held by private persons which governments find it prudent to heed'. This is an interesting formulation since it leaves open the question as to whether the spontaneous or organised expression of public opinion is a good thing or a bad thing. Opinion, as it were, is divided on the subject.

The idea that *'vox-populi, vox dei'* (the voice of the people is the voice of God) has not always found favour. Public opinion is also believed to be more like an 'ignorant, vociferous and vulgar person', as the Italian Renaissance poet Aristo noted. Hegel himself (1821) voiced concerns about the ambiguous and contradictory role of public opinion. He supported publicising parliamentary debates on the grounds that it raised knowledge about public affairs, but saw parliaments as a bulwark against 'an unorganised opinion . . . in opposition to the organised state'. For centuries, controversies over the nature of public opinion have focused on the different issues, with proponents and opponents divided about:

- the alleged tyranny of the majority, wherein minority interests are sidelined;

- the ignorance of citizens and their alleged lack of political competence;

- the need for more direct expressions of the popular will to counteract the power of elites and sectional interests;

- the mobilisation of bias in representative systems – which opinions are mobilised into the decision-making process and which are excluded?;

- the potential for the manipulation of opinion by elites;

- the difficulties of gauging public opinion and the reliability of methods of doing so;

- the fickleness of public opinion.

Underlying these issues, albeit from different perspectives, is the wider issue about the role of the citizen (or citizens collectively) in a democracy, and especially in an indirect or representative democracy. This is not to say that questions about public opinion are unimportant in non-democracies, but in such regimes the managed expression of popular sentiment is used mainly as a device to record approval of things done by the ruling party and government, or to protest against the behaviour of foreign governments. For example, in Iran, organised public opinion has been mobilised by the regime to express outrage at American imperialism and Western consumerism. Where opinion is not managed, it has tended to take the form of anti-regime protests and demonstrations, such as those seen all over the former Soviet bloc from the late 1980s to the early 1990s.

Public opinion is important to both representative (indirect) and participatory (direct) democracy. In the latter, still not much in favour in established democracies, much of the contemporary debate about the uses and abuses of public opinion has been framed by the need to endorse the legitimacy of elected representatives and the centrality of parliaments while clinging to the ideal of accountable government and the sovereignty of the people. We have noted the growing disenchantment with politics and institutions that once organised meaning and political identity, as well as providing authoritative information for citizens. One of the consequences of these shifts in consciousness has been to reopen questions about the need for more direct involvement of citizens in governance at all levels and about how to achieve it (Coleman and Gotze 2000). Massive changes in communications technologies, which include interactive television, new forms of telephony and electronic mail and the Internet as a medium of communication, are all factors which may impinge on what it means to be an active citizen. New personalised communications technologies of the sort listed above enable citizens to establish and maintain contact with politicians, and vice versa, although we should be careful not to overstate the use and impact of these media (for an extended discussion see Chapter 12).

So, public opinion is a form of communication from citizens to government, but in large-scale and complex democracies the expression of the voice of the people cannot be separated from various techniques of representation (Peters 2001). As we shall see, there are various institutionalised forms of such techniques of mediation.

Whose opinion is public opinion?

When we talk about techniques of mediation and representation, we are talking about how the public is represented. But one of the main problems with the definition of public opinion is the question of *who* is represented; that is, with the very nature of the public. Early normative theories emphasise the wholeness of the idea of 'the public', wherein it is seen as a single, universal subject. More recent interpretations (see Wilson 1962) prefer a more pluralistic notion of the public (publics), and much current theorising favours the idea that there are many publics and multiple public spheres in which they can express their opinions. In the broadest sense, public opinion as a single opinion held by the public as a whole, or a distribution of opinions among the members of the public, refers to what is usually known as the 'mass' public made up of all citizens of voting age. This is the public of the ubiquitous opinion poll, found everywhere in modern politics. The danger for supporters of popular democracy is that public opinion is seen as legitimate only as far as the reliability of the methods used in polling, or that polling itself becomes the paradigm form of public expression. Of course, the cautious student of politics might say, 'in a large-scale society, how could it be otherwise?'

How is public opinion institutionalised and expressed?

In 1961, V. O. Key Jr. said, 'if a democracy is to exist, the belief must be widespread that public opinion, at least in the long run affects the course of public action' (p. 547). This is a powerful and enduring mythology and is based not only on the rather abstract notion of popular sovereignty, but on the assumption that public opinion in some way represents the will of the majority of people or citizens.

Since the early modern period, public opinion has been institutionalised in three main forms:

1 *Parliaments*: A somewhat curious institution to classify as an organ of public opinion, because although parliaments are clearly expressions of the popular will in one sense (they are usually directly elected), the role of the representative as the voice of public opinion varies enormously across systems. Very few traditions of parliamentary representation assume that an elected member will always, or often, vote in line with constituency opinion, even if she has a clear picture of what that is.

2 *Newspapers and the broadcast media*: The press has always played a significant role in expressing public opinion. It was and is an instrument of information, overtaken only in recent years by television. The media are also a form of public sphere in which opinions about issues are entertained and disseminated. At the same time print and broadcast journalism are also actors in opinion formation, influencing, or trying to influence, public opinion. Sometimes, print and broadcast media are political players in their own right, linked by ideology to particular political interests and/or wedded to a commercial ethic that informs all their activities, including what to treat as a matter of public concern.

THINK POINT

■ Can you think of any recent issues involving the mobilisation of public opinion in which different media have played a part?

■ To what do you attribute their interest and how they intervened?

Straw poll A rough guide to opinion, based on, for example, a show of hands in a meeting, or a phone-in to a radio talk show. The method makes no claims to statistical reliability founded on accurate sampling techniques.

3 *Polling*: A relatively new means of expressing public opinion. The gauging of public opinion began in the mid-1800s with **straw polls** and unscientific

methods. Since those days, the techniques of **scientific polling** have become an integral part of political campaigning during elections and policy formation as governments look to anticipate public reactions to a policy proposal and to canvass the views of citizens about policy preferences.

The construction of public opinion

For students of democracy, and especially proponents of direct democracy, there is an important question to ask about the techniques used to 'construct' public opinion. The question is: How far do ways of constructing public opinion actually promote the participation of the public in decision-making and how far are they devices for manipulation and control? Critics of opinion polling often see them as little more than a policy resource for decision-makers, with results paraded when it suits the government line and hushed up or derided as unscientific when they do not. In itself, consultation between the public and government is no bad thing, although, as we have noted earlier in the chapter, there is the suggestion that polls may be used by political elites to bypass representative institutions and to create a form of government by plebiscite. In the construction of public opinion, the role of opinion leaders can be crucial in giving shape to unformed or inchoate opinion. Opinion leaders can be drawn from the ranks of politicians, but they can also be any person or institution that has influence with the different publics, for example, role models, celebrities and peers.

Recently, there has been a growing interest in qualitative approaches to the canvassing of public opinion, drawing upon focus group techniques, citizen juries and a device known as deliberative polling. Market research conducted for governments and political parties makes extensive use of focus groups, as these are reputed to produce richer and more nuanced reflections from the public than surveys using large representative samples. Citizens juries and deliberative polling as ways of promoting public talk are still little used except in the United States (see below). In the UK, the Hansard Society for Parliamentary Government has conducted a series of investigations into the use of information technologies to promote direct democracy (Coleman 1999, 2001).

Scientific polling Refers to a number of procedures and rules for ensuring reliability of method and results. These include: a valid sample of the population to be canvassed; an appropriate sample size; proper regard for the principle of random selection (for representative samples); guarding against sampling bias (treating as representative a segment of the population in which the significant characteristics of the whole population are skewed in some way); awareness of the correct margin of error within which results can be deemed valid; and proper attention to wording of questions and interviewer training.

Jefferson Center: Citizens Jury on climate change

The Citizens Jury is a unique process that allows decision-makers and the public to hear from citizens who are both informed and representative. Sufficient time is allowed for discussion and deliberation by the jurors to develop thoughtful and useful recommendations for decision-makers and the public.

Eighteen citizens from within a 35-mile radius of Baltimore, Maryland were carefully chosen from a randomly identified jury pool to serve as a representative microcosm of the public. During five consecutive days beginning

continued

continued

18 March 2002, the jury heard expert witness presentations on a range of issues and perspectives related to global climate change. The Citizens Jury focused on what potential impacts of climate change are of most concern, and what, if anything, the USA should do to address climate change. Jurors deliberated together to develop recommendations for policy-makers and the public to consider.

EXERCISE

Conduct a deliberative poll in your own seminar group.

The issue is attitudes to the legalisation of soft drugs, although you may want to use another topical subject. Proceed as follows:

- Canvass opinion on legalisation in the first week of the seminar. Take note of the results.
- Arrange to provide members of the class with reading materials (e.g. medical reports, government statements, the ideas of other opinion leaders, interest group literature).
- If possible, find time in the second week for brief presentations from different sides of the argument and for discussion in the whole group.
- Canvass opinion again in week 3 and discuss similarities and differences, and how, if at all, the process affected voting.

Interest in deliberative procedures as a way of constructing public opinion has been heightened, in part because of the perceived crisis of democracy and civic engagement and in part because of the potential of information and communications technologies to open up new public spaces and arenas for debate. In Oxford, a deliberative forum called 'Talkback', which is a panel of citizens, is used as a means of providing informed local opinion on policy matters. The EU has embarked on a large programme called 'Dialogue', making use of online citizens' panels and focus groups to feed into the Community policy process on issues generated both by the European Commission and by groups of citizens.

For more on deliberative procedures enabled by information technologies, see Chapter 5, pp. 186–8.

The search for public judgement through deliberation is, or may be, a long way from the mere canvassing of public opinion through mass surveys, but it re-poses those awkward questions about the interest and competence of citizens and the logistical problems in organising deliberative forums as a routine affair. The virtue of deliberative procedures is not only that they can form part of a wider and more participatory policy process, but that they may also contribute to the political socialisation and education of participants. Such is the theory, but in systems built on the precepts of indirect democracy, the task of ensuring that the representation of public opinion has 'the people' speaking rather than spoken to (as Stuart Hall (1998) said of Tony Blair's predilection for listening to the public) remains a daunting task.

Elections and public opinion

In representative democracy elections are the most comprehensive expression of public opinion. They serve to deliver the voting public's judgement on political incumbents and, even where turnout is low, certain inferences about the direction and intent of public opinion can be made. As expressions of public opinion elections are the culmination of a complex process in which parties and candidates try to change or reinforce the voting intention of electors or sections of the electorate, and in turn are influenced in their approach to voters by information they have generated through market research.

Electoral outcomes and thus, it might be argued, the effectiveness of public opinion are dependent on the electoral system employed in a country. The more disproportional an electoral system, the fewer the effective number of parliamentary parties; the more proportional, the greater the number of parties (Lijphart 1999). As we observed in Chapter 4, disproportionality is sometimes charged with lowering confidence in a political system, and could be interpreted as an institutional and legal barrier to the realisation of public opinion – in this case popular sovereignty.

Elections are instruments of indirect or representative democracy. Referendums and related devices such as the initiative and the recall are more in line with the spirit of direct democracy, even though they can be found in representative systems.

- *Referendum*: The vote of an electorate on a specific issue of policy, for example the legalisation of soft drugs or abortion law reform. To regulate demand for such procedures, it is usually necessary for those wishing to place a proposition on the ballot to demonstrate a sufficient level of support (e.g. a minimum number of the electorate).

- *Initiative*: A procedure whereby a specified minimum number of voters can initiate a referendum on a specified topic.

- *Recall*: A procedure that allows a specified minimum number of voters to demand a referendum on whether an already elected official should be removed from office.

In some countries, such as the UK, referendums are permitted only at the whim of government. The Labour administration, elected first in 1997 and re-elected in 2001, promised to hold a referendum on British entry to the European single currency. While they have raised expectations that this will happen, there is no legal requirement for them to do so and, should they hold the referendum, no constitutional duty for them to heed the result. By contrast, any amendment to the Australian constitution requires approval by referendum. Switzerland, a very decentralised system of government and one in which direct democracy is highly valued, holds more referendums than any other Western system. But when the people of Denmark voted not to ratify the Maastricht Treaty on European Union in 1994, the Danish government chose not to take that verdict as final, and, following an extensive campaign in favour of ratification, went back to the electorate and secured the positive response it desired. Many American states and localities make extensive use of the referendum, and in a host of other systems it has enjoyed a growing popularity in recent years.

As expressions of public opinion referendums demonstrate the desirable and the less than desirable faces of direct democracy. They allow voters to intervene in the policy process between normal elections and they can get new or ignored issues on to the policy agenda. They enable governments to test public opinion about contentious issues and to service public knowledge of an issue. At the same time, they allow governments to set the agenda for 'informed' debate over the subject of the referendum and even to skew the outcome by asking leading questions of the public about the proposition to be decided. In addition, referendums can run the risk of producing outcomes which discriminate against minorities and which are illiberal.

Is public opinion fickle?

Perhaps the most damning indictment of the reliance upon public opinion to salvage democracy is not the claim that, on any given issue, it is likely to be less forgiving and less liberal, or less sensitive than that of informed elites, but the lament that it is too fickle. Anthony Downs wrote about the vagaries of the issue–attention cycle, in which initial enthusiasm for an issue swiftly plateaus and, even more swiftly, declines. No way to run a democracy say the critics. Even worse is the idea that fickle public opinion can be mobilised by artful journalists or sly populists, who, mindful of the issue–attention cycle, put images (of rival politicians) in the mind of the public through constant repetition of knocking copy and then, some way down the line, perhaps mid-way through a campaign, revive these images latent in the public unconscious. The room for manipulation seems very great. And yet, during the awesome unfolding of the impeachment process which followed from President Clinton's perjury over the Monica Lewinsky affair, politicians and journalists engaged in an orgy of breast-beating and condemnation, but the public remained unmoved and Clinton continued to enjoy high approval ratings. Not the voice of God perhaps, but not Dumb and Dumber either.

Conclusion

Parties, interest groups and public opinion are all key features of modern politics and governance. The variety of their appearance in regimes around the world makes systematic analysis difficult, and the importance of context in determining function and effectiveness is undeniable. As intermediaries for the organised expression of public opinion (or the opinions and preferences of sections of the public) political parties and interest groups perform socialising and mobilising functions, and their presence as institutionalised representatives of the richness of civil societies is valuable in societies with a complex social division of labour. It might be argued that political parties, at least in their guise as mass and catch-all parties, are the products of political and social conditions that are disappearing, and that the future is even greater social and cultural fragmentation expressed politically through a plethora of interest groups. This would be a premature judgement perhaps; after all, parties still dominate elections and wield state power in many countries. The revival of interest in direct democracy places a growing emphasis on the expression and management of public opinion: e-governance and e-democracy are no longer quite so fanciful as they might once have appeared, even if the jury is still out on their desirability.

Chapter summary

- Parties, interest groups and public opinion are all forms of linkage between society and the state, and to levels of governance beyond the state.

- Each modality invites praise and blame in terms of their contribution to democratic politics and effective governance.

- Parties perform many functions, including representation, aggregating interests and organising government.

- Whether and how well they perform these functions varies across regime type, and is also influenced by changing social and cultural circumstances.

- Party systems both shape and are shaped by broader political and social forces, and also by the exigencies and logic of the kind of electoral system in operation.

- Evidence for the decline of political parties is mixed. Some evidence of anti-party sentiment and loss of public confidence is quite widespread.

- Interest groups articulate demands from civil society, although there are interest groups that are part of the machinery of government.

- Theories of interest groups tend either to stress their virtues as elements of a pluralistic society and polity, or to underline the extent to which they have been incorporated into the state.

- Overall, groups have at their disposal a wide variety of resources and tactics for use in competition with other groups and for influencing government.

continued

continued

> ■ Evidence of transnational networks, advocacy coalitions and social movements is now widespread. These may be features of a new sort of group politics and approach to political participation.
>
> ■ The power of some interest groups may reflect the mobilisation of bias in particular systems.
>
> ■ Public opinion is difficult to define and even more difficult to measure.
>
> ■ Some forms of public opinion sit uneasily in systems built on the principle and the institutions of indirect democracy.
>
> ■ Renewed interest in direct democracy has led to more sophisticated attempts to gauge public opinion.
>
> ■ Deliberative and other qualitative procedures assume a model of interested and active citizenship.
>
> ■ The alleged dangers of public opinion as a tool of policy formulation include the fickleness of opinion and the potential for manipulation by elites and opinion formers.

Key texts

Dahl, R. (1956) *A Preface to Democratic Theory*, Chicago, Ill.: Chicago University Press.

Dahl, R. (1971) *Polyarchy: Participation and Opposition*, New Haven, Conn.: Yale University Press.

Downs, A. (1957) *An Economic Theory of Democracy*, New York: Harper & Row.

Duverger, M. (1964) *Political Parties: Their Organisation and Activities in the Modern State*, London: Methuen.

Katz, R. and Mair, P. (1994) *How Parties Organise: Change and Adaptation in Party Organisation in Western Democracies*, London: Sage.

Olson, M. Jr. (1965) *The Logic of Collective Action*, Cambridge, Mass.: Harvard University Press.

Richardson, J. (ed.) (1993) *Pressure Groups*, Oxford: Oxford University Press.

Sartori, G. (1976) *Parties and Party Systems: A Framework for Analysis*, Cambridge: Cambridge University Press.

Further reading

Krieger, J. (1998) *British Politics in the Global Age*, Cambridge: Polity Press. A critical account of how changing social and cultural factors, including globalisation, are impacting on the Labour Party in Britain.

Lipset, S. M. and Rokkan, S. (1967) *Party Systems and Voter Alignments*, New York: Free Press. Classic historical and empirical study of the impact of modernisation on social cleavages and the development of party systems.

Norris, P. (1997) 'We're All Green Now: Public Opinion and Environmentalism in Britain', *Government and Opposition* 32 (3): 320–339. An interesting article on the ways in which environmental opinion is mobilised.

Tarrow, S. (1998) *Power in Movement: Social Movements and Contentious Politics*, Cambridge: Cambridge University Press. A very good introduction to social movements, including the transnational variety.

Wolinetz, S. (ed.) (1997) *Political Parties*, Aldershot: Ashgate. A very useful set of articles on most aspects of parties and party systems.

CONTENTS

Mass media Media that
disseminate usually
undifferentiated popular forms of
output (reflecting the mass nature
of the audience) to a mass
audience. For example, this may
include television, newspapers and
cinema.

Political Communication and the Media

Richard Huggins

Once upon a time there was the **mass media**, and they were
wicked, of course, and there was a guilty party. Then there were
the virtuous voices that accused the criminals. And Art (ah, what
luck!) offered alternatives, for those who were not prisoners of
the mass media.

    Well, it's all over. We have to start from the beginning, asking one
another what's going on.

       (Umberto Eco, *Travels in Hyperreality* (1986: 150))

▍ Introduction

People are highly communicative creatures and in many ways it is this
propensity to communicate through the whole range of artefacts of human
cultural production and media, including the voice (for example, in speech,
song or oratory) writing, the visual arts, the body, the electronic arts and
architecture, that defines human societies and gives us our distinctive and
shared senses of self and group identities, histories and social meanings. In this
chapter I want to explore the political dimensions of such communication
and to examine the issues of political communication, politics and the mass
media.

As we have stated, throughout this book, politics in the broadest sense is about the location, distribution and control of power within and across societies. It might be argued that during the late twentieth and into the twenty-first century it is the power to communicate that is the key to the practice of politics and analysis of who has the ability to get their message across, to communicate effectively, with whom, by what means and for what ends are key questions for the study of politics (Keane 1991; Negrine 1994; Fiske 1995; Curran and Seaton 1997). Furthermore, we could argue that without political communication there would not be any politics – for politics often appears to be as much about getting your message across as having a message in the first place. Consequently, the study of political communication has become central to much political and social science discussion, and students of politics should be prepared to engage quite directly with issues of political communication.

However, although this chapter will focus largely on the relatively formal processes of political communication between political activists (be they parties, protesters or the state) and the people within political systems, I want to both stress the breadth and complexity of the issue of political communication and to encourage readers to think widely about the enormous varieties of content, meaning, technologies, forms and effects of political communication that exist.

For example, spend some time looking at the photograph below and thinking about the images it contains. Ask yourself what is being communicated in this picture. What is *political* about the content of this picture? What does this picture communicate to you? Does the image inspire any feelings, perhaps of anger, empathy, disgust or sadness for you?

This is a complex image and, like all images, it is open to many different and competing interpretations. Our interpretation may well depend on not just our understanding of the image (our reading of it), but a range of personal and social factors that we may or may not be conscious of; for example, our age, gender, social and economic background, education experiences, political beliefs and values, individual experiences of public order issues, protest, policing, and so on. Furthermore, our proximity to the image in terms of historical, social and cultural location may well encourage us to read the image in one way rather than another. The list of such variables is almost endless and too long to fully explore here, but what the above discussion should do is alert us to the sheer weight of politics in virtually all images, symbols and communications and the multitude of possible interpretations that images may possess (Hartley 1992; Schirato and Yell 2000). I think this is a useful thought to have at the back of our minds as we develop our discussion of political communication.

Now, for me there is clearly an overt political message in this picture: one about the perceived injustice and politicisation of the 1984 miners' strike in the United Kingdom. This picture was produced and distributed as a postcard by an organisation called *Leeds Postcards for the National Union of Mineworkers* with the intention of encouraging public sympathy and support for striking miners, and at one level this is the political content of this communication.

However, there is also a whole set of possible other meanings, intended and unintended, that might include the politics of day-to-day policing, abuses of power, relationships between state and citizen, the 'hidden' nature and secrecy of the British state, an implied critique of official news reporting and anti-miner government propaganda. But there are also more day-to-day, equally political messages located in this image which include messages about the relationships between men and women, abuses of power in those relationships and, ultimately, male violence against women.

THINK POINT

The example given above is, obviously, only one of many. You might like to take any image (for example, from advertising, television or the internet or possibly a set of song lyrics, a public building or a film image) and carry out a similar piece of analysis.

Key text: P. Berger (1972) *Ways of Seeing*, London: Penguin.

Such analysis should remind us that at one level the issue of political communication is connected to issues of *representation* and how ideas, identities and relationships between different groups of people are represented in language, images, sounds and symbols (Berger 1972; Rose 2001). For Dyer (1993: 1) representation is of central political importance determining, in part, how we are treated and how we treat others. This is because how we treat people is based on how we see them and such 'seeing comes from representation'. The politics of representation covers an extensive range of issues including, for example, race (Denzin 2002; Malik 2002), gender (Nead 1992; Cronin 2000), space (Graham and Nash 2000) and the self (Shildrick 2002). Indeed, for some commentators issues of representation, misrepresentation and of being visible are critical issues of politics and power (Berger 1972; Hartley

1992; Eldridge 1993; Hall 1997). Hence the focus on 'hidden' histories and narratives, or recovering or rediscovering the power to communicate among those previously denied a voice, language or access to representation. Thus one might argue that being or remaining visible may be an important strategy through which the struggle for political rights is pursued. For example, the rights of indigenous peoples, particularly in the developing world and often around issues of environmental protection, the protection of traditional ways of life, lands and habitats, are articulated.

Having identified some key general observations about the breadth and complexity of political communication, it will be useful to outline some trends scholars have identified as characterising political communication and the media in recent years. The first has been the proliferation of media and communications technologies in the relatively recent past. This includes significant increases both in the number of different types of media available, newspapers, television, radio, film, the Internet, and in the number of titles, broadcasters and web pages (Henley Centre 1999). Second, there has been an increasing penetration of political communications by media, communications and advertising specialists and techniques (Kavanagh 1995; Scammell 1995; Newman 1999; Hennenberg and O'Shaughnessy 2002). Third, media production, ownership and reach is increasingly experiencing the impacts of globalisation (Hamelink 1994; Boyd-Barrent and Rantanen 1998; Preston, 1998; McChesney 1999).

Key text: *Index on Censorship* (1999) 'Underexposed' 6.

The impact of these three trends has had a profound effect on the nature and extent of political communications. There has been, for example, a proliferation of media channels through which political communications can take place, a shift away from the highly formal and relatively controllable messaging to an array of images, messages and political communication techniques, a convergence of media formats through which political messages are conveyed (from conventional news formats to talk-shows), and a mass adoption of the techniques of commercial, marketing, advertising and communications strategies. Now politicians turn up in what would once have been the most unexpected of places – pop videos, sports programmes, MTV, advertments for bank cards. Likewise, media stars are readily found in the company of politicians (for example, Irish rock band's U2's lead singer Bono) and sometimes in the institutions of government themselves (for example, Ronald Reagan, Clint Eastwood (USA) and Glenda Jackson (UK)). Worse still for many commentators, politicians frequently *behave* too much like media personalities and adopt too readily the techniques of media marketing (for example, Silvio Berlusconi's *Forza Italia* in Italy which stands accused of running a political party like a football supporters' club) (Gundle and Parker 1994; Porro and Russo 2000).

Not surprisingly the developments outlined above have been accompanied by a significant debate over whether they are a 'good' thing or a 'bad' thing; whether or not they inhibit and corrupt democracy or 'real' politics and whether they distort the relationship between politician and citizen. This is a central question for this chapter and one which I shall return to below. Certainly the media have had a considerable effect on the operation of politics in most societies, and a number of critical issues have been identified by commentators. It has been argued, for instance, that the mass media have taken the place of political parties in organising, motivating and mobilising political participation. It has also been argued that media coverage of politics has removed the focus on legislative assemblies and traditional channels of political communication by opening up direct routes of communication between political leaders and the public, encouraging populism, an emphasis on charismatic leadership and image management. Other commentators have highlighted the increasing use governments have made of the mass media to advertise, to literally 'sell', rather than argue for, their policies (Franklin 1994).

In the remainder of this chapter I want to work through some of the issues introduced above in more detail and the chapter will be organised as follows. We will explore what constitutes political communication and outline a working definition. We will then examine some of the contexts of political communication, including a brief overview of the historical, technological, economic, legal, organisational and cultural contexts. I will then outline how and in what ways political communication developed over the twentieth century before moving on to an examination of recent changes in the nature of political communication and the nature of politics in media cultures. Next I will examine more directly how political communication is managed and how political actors communicate, through various techniques (for example, direct and indirect communications, campaign communications and image management). The chapter will then focus on the critical issue of the relationship between democracy and the media before moving to a discussion of the emergence of global media corporations and the significance of new media and media activism.

What is political communication?

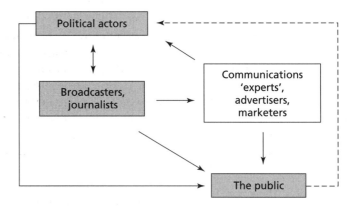

The process of political communication: a model

The above model offers a diagrammatic representation of one way of characterising the process of political communication. In such a model communication is increasingly mediated by the media, in the form of broadcasters, journalists and communications and image management experts (spin doctors, media professionals, advertisers and marketing experts). Importantly, we should think about how each group has its own agenda and what the relationship between these agendas might be. For example, political actors want to get their message and image across to the public in the most favourable way or perhaps minimise the impact of a negative message (e.g. tax increases, military setbacks), broadcasters want to uphold journalistic traditions, uncover 'truth', and so on. We should also think about who has the most power in this model and why.

But *should* it be like this? Is a more open and less mediated political communication process desirable? Desirable or not, given the current media domination of everyday life, is a less mediated political communication process viable?

The above illustration outlines a simple model of the communication process and identifies the main actors involved. In this section of the chapter I want to comment briefly on each of these actors before moving on to identify a working definition of political communication. While bearing in mind earlier observations that political communication is widely diffused, this model identifies four main elements in the contemporary communicative process.

The first are *political actors*, namely, those who have a particular message to communicate. For the purposes of this chapter this will include governments, political parties and interest groups. All these actors will utilise the media to provide information, exert pressure and influence public opinion to persuade or inform the public to particular ends. Governments may well communicate about issues of public health and safety (for example, sexual health campaigns about HIV transmission or campaigns designed to prevent deaths from drunken driving) or of changes to legislation, policy or service provision. Governments may also be involved in campaigns to change political and social attitudes and behaviour, and quite direct attempts to re-socialise citizens into new ways of thinking and behaving (for example, participating in elections in newly democratised states). Furthermore, some such campaigns are pursued at the global level – through transnational governmental organisations such as the United Nations or the European Union – and reflect the developing local/ global nature of some political communication.

Political parties, as political communicators, communicate in attempts to win and retain power or influence decision-making and public opinion through political campaigns and, in particular, election campaigns. Political parties and politicians want, indeed have to, communicate with the electorate or those they govern, and they need to get the message across about their policies, their ideas and their plans. But commentators increasingly argue that the trend by political parties has been to eschew worthwhile political communication about such topics in favour of adopting the techniques of commercial advertising and marketing with too much emphasis on image management, direct marketing and product placement (Wernick 1991; Blumler and Gurevitch 1995; Scammell 1995).

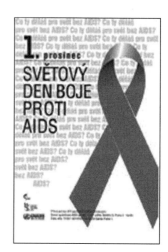

HIV awareness poster

A political campaign poster for the Alleanza Nazionale, Italy

Key text: E. S. Herman and N. Chomsky (1994) *Manufacturing Consent: The Political Economy of the Mass Media*, London: Vintage.

Social movements, *pressure groups* and *interest groups*, like political parties, will use political communication techniques to influence decision-making and public opinion but usually with particular reference to specific issues. For example, environmental organisations, such as Greenpeace, utilise political communications to raise the profile of environmental campaigns and their actions. However, access to funds to pay for elaborate or extensive communication campaigns may be a significant constraint on an interest group's ability to exploit such opportunities. Furthermore, the news value of a campaign group or social movement 'story' will be variable, as will the news 'market' for that message, and the opportunities for effective communication that the media provide may well be limited and highly variable (Grant 1995; Crossley 2002). However, relatively new media technologies of the Internet and video-activism do provide greater potential for interest group activists to communicate and influence public opinion than before (Edwards and Gaventa 2001).

If the political actors have the message it is through the media that such messages are conveyed. Television, newspapers and radio provide the main channels for the distribution of political messages from political actors. In states where there is a relatively clear division between political actors and the media (in particular states with democratic systems of government), such communications will tend to be either contextualised or mediated by the media professionals, such as journalists, who work within media organisations. In countries where no such division exists or is perhaps less well established, political communication is likely to be dominated by more official news agencies (for example, Pravda in the former USSR) and characterised by a lack of pluralism of different views. However, some commentators would argue that my distinction here is somewhat arbitrary and would question the actual levels of media freedom, diversity and dissent evident in democratic political systems (Glasgow Media Group 1976, 1980, 1982; Eldridge 1993). For example, Herman and Chomsky argue that in the USA the mass media operate as part of a powerful control process in which the size, concentration and commercialisation of the media, the reliance on advertising incomes, the reliance on official sources for information (such as government departments, businesses and professionals and experts) taken with dominant political values and attitudes all leads to a manufactured consent among the governed, and a removal of dissenting voices, critical media activities and opposition (Herman and Chomsky 1994). Such analysis highlights the issue of propaganda over communication and alerts us to the potentially thin line between these two aspects of government or officially directed communication.

Included in the above model is the role of professional communications specialists such as marketing specialists, advertising specialists and public relations gurus. Commentators have identified a general trend for an increased role for such groups in processes of political communication (Hall Jamieson 1992; Scammell 1995, 1999; Kavanagh 1995; Hennenberg and O'Shaughnessy 2002).

Finally, the fourth element of our model is the public, the target of the political communication, the audience. It is fair to say that conceptions of the audience, within audience research at least, have moved from relatively straightforward conceptions of the audience as a homogenised, passive receiver of media communicated messages to a much more complex conception which stresses that the audience is more accurately perceived as active, complex and heterogeneous (White 1994; Davis and Owen 1998; Alasuutari 1999), as the following quote illustrates:

> The audiences for specific kinds of mass communication share social and political traits, common bonds, interests, and concerns that may become particularly relevant during periods of heightened politicization, such as occurs during a presidential election or a time of political turmoil. Through their use of the same media source, audience members acquire like knowledge, and they can develop similar beliefs, attitudes, values, and behaviour patterns. Audiences may be passive or detached in their relationships to mass media, or they may actively process, interpret, and create meaning from media messages.
>
> (Davis and Owen 1998: 134)

A number of studies argue that it is the viewer, as much as the message and the sender of that message, that is central to the processes of creating the meaning of any particular communication. White (1994) stresses four important elements of these processes. First, people make different sense of the same message, second, interpretations are socially patterned and not merely individual, third, the sense people make of a particular communication (for example, a news broadcast) is socially bounded. People do not just make up their interpretations of messages; rather they draw on prior knowledge and values, social group and subculture membership, to develop meaning and understanding. Fourth, reception (and meaning) is neither fixed nor stable and changes over time and in different contexts.

THINK POINT

Conceptualising the viewer, the audience, those who are communicated to in this way have quite significant implications for the study of political communication. What do you think these implications are?

To some extent, then, political communication must be about the circulation of political messages among and between those actors identified in the model above. Indeed, for Rush political communication is the 'transmission of politically relevant information from one part of the political system to another' (Rush 1992: 153). But useful as this definition is, I think it is a little narrow, and a wider definition is called for which highlights the breadth of political communication and complexity of the communication process. For example, Denton and Woodward stress a wider definition in which the distinguishing factor that makes communication political is not the 'source of the message but its content and purpose' (Denton and Woodward 1990: 11). As we have seen earlier in this chapter the content is crucial to the political meaning of the message. However, we have also seen how that meaning of the content is dependent on the ways in which viewers interpret the message. One woman's political communication is another man's magazine article, one might say.

Similarly McNair (1995) offers a useful addition to the definitions of political communication by stressing that political communication is the purposeful communication about politics. For McNair this includes all forms of political communication undertaken by politicians and other political actors with the intention of achieving specific objectives, communications directed at these actors by non-politicians, such as journalists or members of the public, and communication about them and their activities (for example, news stories and media analysis) (McNair 1995). But again I think that definitions should highlight the deep and diffuse nature of political communications more generally. So, to encapsulate this depth I would suggest a working definition of political communication that stresses two levels of political communication.

> Political communication is the intended, explicit and implicit communication of messages with a political content between members of a political system. But political communication is also the communication, intended and unintended, of messages within a political and social system that contribute to the transmission and circulation of political and social values, beliefs and ideas.

Defining political communication in this way alerts us to the breadth and depth of this concept and to the role that political communication may play in more general processes of political socialisation, the construction and maintenance of political culture and in political behaviour, while recognising the central significance of direct and intended communication between political actors within a political system.

THINK POINT

- How would you define political communication?
- What elements would you include in a model of communication?
- What elements are most important and why?

Contexts of political communication

So far in this chapter we have explored the complexity, scope and definitional aspects of political communication. Before moving to more detailed discussion of how political actors communicate I want to outline some of the contextual factors within which political communications take place.

First is what might be called the *historical context*. It sometimes appears that political communication has become significant only in relatively recent times with the advent of mass communication media. While it may be true that mass communication systems of newspapers and later television have transformed

the extent and amount of political communication, it is also true that political actors have always utilised political communication to convey images of and messages about power, leadership and authority. Political symbols and images have played an important part in keeping the power of the powerful visible to all others. The role of sculpture, portraiture and architecture are particularly important here and you may like to reflect on the symbolic representation of power in the picture on the right.

It is also the case that certain types of political communication, in particular election campaigns, have long been about promotion and razzmatazz as much as anything else. Take this example of James Bryce in 1888 commenting on election campaigns in the USA:

> For three months, processions, usually with brass bands, flags, badges, crowds of cheering spectators, are the order of the day and night from end to end of the country . . . [this] pleases the participants by making them believe they are effecting something; it impresses the spectators by showing them other people are in earnest, it strikes the imagination of those who in country hamlets read the doings in the great city. In short, it keeps up the 'boom', and an American election is held to be, truly or falsely, largely a matter of booming.
>
> (Quoted in Hall Jamieson 1996: 3)

I am not trying to say that current trends in political communication are best understood as simply intensified versions of previous ones but to highlight the historical background of the communication of power and politics, and I think that an appreciation of the historical context of political communication allows us to weigh some of the current debates about the nature of political communication and democracy against earlier ones.

Another important context for political communication and the media is the *economic* one. In particular, theorists of the political economy of the media draw attention to the relationships between the economic organisation of a society and the organisation and workings of the media industries and the production of media content. In this analysis it is the relationship between the economic interests of owners (maximising profit and minimising costs) and the nature of market competition that influences the organisation of media production and the form and content of the media. Such economic organisation tends towards monopolistic practices, a reduction in the number of independent and critical sources of media production (Garnham 1979; Herman and Chomsky 1994; Barbrook 1995). Put simply, different ways of organising the economic bases of the media would lead to very different types of media organisations, forms and content. The question might be posed: How accurate is this model and also how would a different economic model actually function? Whether or not we accept this type of interpretation we do have to acknowledge that economic factors are a context in which media production takes place within and as such is a factor in shaping the ways in which the media are organised and what content they carry.

A further important context in which political communication and the media operate is the *technological* one. While I am not arguing for a technological determinist perspective it is important to recognise that the development of new technologies of communication can have profound effects on society and, by definition, offer new channels and opportunities for political communication. For example, Marshall McLuhan consistently attempted to demonstrate the critical nature of communication technology-driven social change in his work on the media and the relationship between media technologies and the emergence of the 'global village' (McLuhan 1962, 1964, 1967). A number of scholars have demonstrated how the emergence of new media forms and technologies contribute to shifts in political communication and social practice (Calhoun 1992; Gilmartin 1996). For example, consider the following quote about the relationship between the emergence of printed media and the creation of national citizens and the idea of the national community.

Key text: M. McLuhan (1967) *The Medium is the Message*, Harmondsworth: Penguin.

> The media technology associated with the interpellation of individuals into national citizens is, of course, print. Print technology afforded distant governments with tools for reaching dispersed populations with the same messages. Political processes, national and international, could be received, reviewed, and discussed by citizens, by individuals presumed to be actively concerned with public affairs.
>
> (Poster 1999: 237)

In this argument the development of new media technologies can have profound social implications. At the beginning of the twentieth century the main medium for political communication was the newspaper, and those charged with newspaper production – owners, editors and journalists – had pronounced social and political power (for a cinematic treatment see e.g. Orson Welles' 1941 film *Citizen Kane*). In the twentieth century new media technologies developed that created new opportunities for political communications. Telecommunications, film, radio, television, video, the Internet, digital television and mobile telecommunications have all led to a proliferation of communications in terms of channels, content and different interfaces. Now it is the notion of an information society that is attracting critical attention in relation to perceived social and political impacts to the extent that the development of the information society (and the attendant technologies) are seen as ushering in a 'new politics' which is overtly transforming (for better or for worse) the practice and form of politics (Axford and Huggins 2001; Castells 2000).

Key text: M. Castells (2000) (2nd edn) *The Rise of the Network Society: The Information Age: Economy, Society and Culture*, Vol. 1, Boston, Mass.: Blackwell.

Interestingly the development of new media technologies is often attended by political concerns about the social impact of such new media. Such concerns often reach panic proportions and sometimes result in quite significant political campaigns and political action to combat the perceived threat of such technology as explored in the following discussion of video-cassette recorders.

The myth of the dangerous new medium

Every time a new medium comes along politicians, academics, journalists, educationalists, religious leaders and a whole range of other commentators articulate a whole number of concerns about the dangers that such a new medium poses – often for those identified as 'vulnerable groups' in society. For example, television causes all sorts of social ills – violence, 'dumbing down', hyperactivity, cynicism and so on. But how accurate is this analysis? For some it is far from convincing, and an analysis of responses to media use and content demonstrates a number of interesting and important patterns. For example, Wartella and Reeves' (1983) study *Recurring Issues in Research on Children and Media* argued that dangerous new medium stories follow a sequence which is repeated each time a new medium is invented. This sequence is as follows:

- First: the new medium is seen as harming the sense involved – for example, television harms the eyes.
- Second: new mediums are psychologically dangerous – making us violent, lonely or apathetic.
- Third: new mediums encourage adverse societal changes – television makes us childish (Postman 1982) or the Internet encourages isolation and marginalisation (McChesney 1999).

For Drotner (1992), such responses to media technologies can take the form of 'media panics' in which considerable public, political and social concern can appear and significant political and legislative responses can follow. Drotner also stresses that such panics follow historical and repetitive patterns, from nineteenth-century popular literature, through jazz, 'horror comics' to video-cassette recorders and, currently, the Internet and mobile phones.

For example, when video-cassette recorders (VCRs) began to enter people's homes in the United Kingdom in the early 1980s extreme concern was expressed by, among others, politicians, journalists, legal, health and education professionals about the danger that unrestricted home viewing would create. Concern was so pronounced that a media and moral panic ensued about the threat and danger of a whole collection of horror films or 'video nasties' as they were known. Concerned politicians reacted by creating the Parliamentary Group Video Enquiry which commissioned and published a report by Barlow and Hill: *Video Violence and Children* in 1985. This was followed by new legislation in the form of the 1985 Video Recordings Act, which effectively banned a large number of films deemed video nasties. Interestingly, almost twenty years later, many of these films are now freely available in every UK high street to buy or rent – many of them making a marketing pitch out of their status as 'banned videos'.

In a recent article Klaus Schoenbach (2001) revisits his own treatment of the introduction of VCRs to homes to explore what he calls the 'myth of the dangerous new medium'. Schoenbach reports how, in 1982, he made the

continued

continued

argument that the widespread introduction of VCRs into people's homes would lead to dire outcomes for society. This included the fragmentation of media use (and thus audience), the further decay of public opinion and political reasoning, and a loss of contact between the average citizen and the 'real world' through the mass use of VCRs. However, Schoenbach notes that twenty years later VCRs are an almost negligible medium and that his fears and the general media panic about the 'dangers' of VCRs were a myth. Schoenbach uses the term 'myth' to stress the recurrent, ritualistic pattern and inherent plausibility of such fears about new mediums in similar ways to the studies by Wartella and Reeves, and Drotner. For Schoenbach such myths exploit a deeply rooted pessimism about the audience (or, perhaps, a deeply rooted pessimism among elite groups about the 'average person') which can be summed up as 'the stupid audience always accepts whatever it is offered' (Schoenbach 2001: 365). Furthermore, these 'myths' have a number of functions that tell us important things about the media, politics and society. These include:

- myths are often powerful tools for intervention in the social order;
- myths confirm images and stereotypes;
- myths justify the passing of legislation to protect us from the 'bad' influence of the mass media;
- myths provide us with reassuring explanations of the world;
- myths provide us with good stories and metaphors about the changing world: for example, 'the plug-in drug' (Winn 1977), 'amusing ourselves to death' (Postman 1995), 'spiral of cynicism' (Cappella and Jamieson 1997).

These arguments alert us to the possibility that concerns about the effects of media forms and content may have much more to them than first meets the eye and that some arguments, particularly elite-inspired ones, may rest more on pessimistic views of the people than anything else. It may also be argued that if such 'myths' can be shown to follow certain patterns then they are open to critical sociological and political interrogation as to their meaning and function.

The general point I am making in this section is that media organisations and the communications they carry do not operate in socio-economic vacuums and that students of the relationship between the media and politics can usefully explore the contexts of communication. This extends to the *legal context* in which both the media and political actors operate which places constraints on what can be done, shown, said and printed. Media law, electoral and constitutional arrangements and discrimination legislation, for example, may all have particular influences on how political communications are conducted. The range of media law is considerable. In the USA, for example, the Radio Act of 1927 and the Communications Act of 1934 both seek to regulate issues of ownership, organisation and control (Blumler 1998). In Britain in the 1950s the '14-Day Rule' severely restricted the coverage of political business by the media as they feared breaking the regulation which prohibited the discussion of any issues likely to be debated in the Houses of Parliament within the next two weeks. Currently in the UK the Representations of the People's Act places strict requirements on broadcasters about how they can cover election campaigns. All countries have legislation of some description that affects the scope of media action, reporting and activity. This will include, for example, laws of censorship, ownership, balance and privacy. In Britain, for example, television broadcasters are legally obliged to cover political election campaigns in a balanced and fair manner. On the other hand, newspapers have been a constant source of concern for politicians and commentators over the years (Heath *et al.* 1994).

Another important context for political communications is the *organisational context*. Media organisations often have strong senses of their own role, values and social and political significance. Perhaps the most striking example of this is the perception which newspapers and broadcast journalists have of their social and political function. For example, BBC journalist John Simpson claimed the fall of Kabul in Afghanistan was the work of the BBC and not the US military. Journalists have their own, powerful, ideology of what being a journalist is, involving ideas about freedom, truth and objectivity and their role in safeguarding the public interest. This is not to say that journalists do not actually achieve these laudable aims – of course they do – and many individual journalists are killed and injured in the pursuit of such aims. But it is important to note that an organisational value system operates for journalists that can be interrogated like all other elements of the communication system.

> To say that a news report is a story, no more, but no less, is not to demean the news, not to accuse it of being fictitious. Rather, it alerts us that news, like all public documents, is a constructed reality possessing its own internal validity.
>
> (Tuchman 1976)

A particularly powerful organisational context, especially in Europe, has been the idea of **public service broadcasting** in which broadcasters, such as the BBC (UK), RTE (Eire) and Raiuno (Italy), often funded by the public purse, are perceived as primarily serving the public in terms of content and critical coverage. This is a very powerful motif both within media organisations and in academic discourse about them. But it is worth considering whose notion of the public is being served and how well.

A final context, one we might call the *cultural context*, will now be explored. I think some of the observations made above highlight that political communications are culturally situated. I would like to develop this a little more in relation to the emergence of what has been called 'promotional culture' (Wernick 1991), as it is this development that many commentators argue is of critical concern to the quality of political communications and, thus, democracy.

The argument has been made that the proliferation and centrality of communication and media industries has led to the development of both

Public service broadcasting
The idea that all citizens should have access to a diverse, socially and politically responsible and non-commercially organised broadcasting medium, principally in radio and television.

Key text: A. Wernick (1991) *Promotional Culture: Advertising, Ideology and Symbolic Expression*, London: Sage.

Media cultures In a media culture media images, sounds and spectacles are central to everyday life, dominate leisure time, shape political and social views, values and behaviour, and provide the raw material out of which people create their identities (Kellner 1995).

media and promotional cultures (Wernick 1991; Skovmand and Schroder 1992; Kellner 1995) in which the public are submerged in a proliferation of media images, advertising discourses and symbolic representations. The implications of the advent of media and promotional cultures for political communication, citizenship and democracy are hotly debated. On the one hand, commentators argue that such developments have created a crisis of political communication for democratic and participatory politics (Franklin 1994; Blumler and Gurevitch 1995). Others highlight the contribution that political advertising can make to public understanding (Harrop 1990) and attempt to locate recent developments within more optimistic interpretations (Axford and Huggins 2001; Street 2001).

Some would take things even further. For example, Meijer seeks to explore the possibilities of advertising to create positive notions of contemporary citizenship (Meijer 1998). She cites the US advertising agency Burrell Advertising as an example of what may be understood as a positive force for citizenship in relation to the performative as an aspect of advertising. By this she means that we should look at advertising as the act of telling stories that enable a certain interaction with and management of 'reality' (Meijer 1998). For Fowles (1996) the availability and symbolic meaning of commercial products come together in advertising texts which offer media resources for the construction of identities and values. Thus, for Fowles, 'Coca Cola is not just a very popular soft drink, not even the symbol for an ever expanding universal lifestyle for young people, but the expression of a new way of living and a new understanding of global values' (Fowles 1996: 239).

This may be taking things too far but what we might agree on is the considerable cultural significance of promotional techniques and advertising discourses and the way these discourses permeate all aspects of life. Political communications frequently draw on the language and style of commercial advertising. Likewise, commercial products are promoted through a direct use of political communication techniques. For example, in the UK in 1997 one supermarket chain, Tesco, utilised the discourse of the election campaigning to promote various price reductions in its stores. If further examples are needed of the extent to which the discourses of advertising and promotion have penetrated social life have a look at this advert that seeks to promote the Church of England.

Church of England promotional advertisement, UK, 1996

The development of political communication

I introduced the above section by suggesting that it was useful to keep an eye on the historical context of political communication and in this section I want to develop this element of the analysis by briefly outlining some general trends in the development of political communication. However, as space does not allow for a detailed historical account we will have to accept that this account can be little more than an outline of the main developments of political communications in mass media systems.

Newspapers

Perhaps the most significant development of the mass media communication of politics was the evolution of a popular press in the late eighteenth and early nineteenth centuries (Conboy 2002). As we have already seen above, some commentators (e.g. Poster 1997) highlight the relationship between the emergence of printed media and notions of the political nation and newspapers that are clearly part of this process. However, particularly in the later eighteenth and early nineteenth centuries the press in countries like the USA and the UK also participated in the radical politics of popular representation. In Britain, for example, the radical press was particularly significant in the mass reform movements in the nineteenth century, represented in titles such as *Poor Man's Guardian* ('A Weekly Newspaper for the People: Established Contrary to Law', to try the power of 'Might' Against 'Right') or the Chartist *Northern Star* (Conboy 2002). Such papers campaigned on a range of social, political and economic issues.

However, such communication often troubled the political classes. As early as 1794 Burke would lament the rise of popular journalism:

> It is very unlikely that the reputation of a speaker in the House of Commons depends far less on what he says there, than on the account of it in the newspapers.
>
> (Edmund Burke (1794) quoted in Reid 2000: 122)

This quote from Burke highlights one of the key concerns that politicians have always had about the role of the reporting and analysis of politics. For Burke the work of politicians in parliament was best left alone by newspaper journalists who would clearly have too much power over their readers. The later nineteenth and early twentieth centuries saw the emergence of more commercially orientated mass titles. Newspapers have always provided a significant channel for political communication, and have been important routes for communication between political actors and the public, and some studies demonstrate that newspapers can have a significant impact on voting behaviour (Miller 1991; Norris *et al.* 1999). However, newspapers' coverage of politics has often been characterised as overly partisan and biased. For example, in Britain the Labour Party has argued consistently that, in the main, newspapers tend to be anti-Labour and that such bias contributed directly to the lack of success in winning elections in the 1980s and 1990s (Butler and Kavanagh 1997).

Radio

Radio began to impact more directly on political communication in the 1920s and 1930s. In Britain BBC radio broadcast speeches from the three main party leaders. MacDonald (Labour) and Asquith (Liberal) chose to have speeches from public meetings delivered. Baldwin (Conservative) chose to visit the BBC and deliver a special talk to the radio audience, demonstrating an early perception that broadcast media presentation demanded a very different style from other forms of political communication (Rosenbaum 1997). The first official party political broadcasts took place in the 1929 General Election and then in 1931 and 1935, and these broadcasts enjoyed large audiences. The 1945 election has been seen as a 'radio election' with nightly broadcasts, an average audience of 45 per cent of the adult population and Churchill's attack on the Labour Party by suggesting that labour plans for the country once in office would require Gestapo-like tactics to deliver (Rosenbaum 1997: 43). Radio also transformed political communication in the USA, as the *New York Times* observed in 1928:

Key text: K. Hall Jamieson (1996) (3rd edn) *Packaging the Presidency: A History and Criticism of Presidential Campaign Advertising*, New York: Oxford University Press.

> Radio 'hook-up' has destroyed the old-time politicians' game of promising in each locality the things that locality wishes. They can no longer promise the Western farmer higher prices for wheat without arousing the Eastern factory population against higher bread prices.
>
> (Hall Jamieson 1996: 20)

Radio transformed political communication by dramatically increasing the number of people who could hear, first hand, a speech or talk by a politician in a way that newspapers could not. Radio created a national audience for political communication (rather than political reporting) and facilitated the direct communication of political actors with the public through 'fireside' chats and the penetration of the home (Hall Jamieson 1996).

Television

What radio did for the voice, television has done for the image, and the next most significant development in terms of political communication was the impact of television in the 1950s on the conduct and extent of political campaigns, communications and coverage. The impact of television on politics was perhaps slower than one might have expected. Although the BBC had been broadcasting television programmes in Britain since the 1930s the first 'television election' took place in 1959 after the launch of the independent, commercial television network of ITV. Prior to this time broadcasters tended to steer clear of political coverage for fear of infringing the law and the 14-Day Rule which prohibited the coverage of any issue that was likely to be debated in Parliament within the next two weeks.

A sense of the difference between then and now, in terms of the extent and nature of televisual coverage of politics, is conveyed in the following quote by Canadian Premier Louis St Laurent. In 1955 after he gave his first television interview to answer questions (submitted in advance) he commented:

> They even wanted to know what I had been thinking about. I answered, perhaps a bit sharply, that I was responsible to the public for what I did as a result of my thinking but only to my conscience for the thinking itself until it became translated into acts.

Such an attitude would clearly not survive today (unless, one assumes, it was a cleverly constructed media-invented innocence designed to elicit an appropriate response from the electorate). Far from it in fact: today's successful politician is all seen, all known and over-exposed. But things were quite different prior to the 1950s. For example, in Britain during the 1950 General Election the leader of the Labour Party, Clement Atlee, travelled around Britain in his own car, driven by his wife, on a 1000-mile tour of the country to attend meetings and speak at rallies, stopping at the roadside to do crossword puzzles and knitting (Smith 1999). However, since the 1950s the impact of television has been dramatic and television plays a central role in political communication at local, national and global levels. For example, consider the piece below about the 1960 Presidential campaign in the USA.

'In the modern presidency, concern for image must rank with concern for substance'
Richard Nixon

'The moment the primacy of the image over the word in the control of political power was first recognised and acknowledged by politicians can be traced back to a single day, 26th September 1960, in an old converted sports arena, the CBS studios at McClurg Court, Chicago. On that evening, a young, inexperienced senator debated with a two-term vice-president of the USA, and won. The way John Kennedy was prepared for the debate by his image makers was in stark contrast to Nixon's preparation, and now makes a textbook case study for any image maker.'

John Kennedy prepared in the following way:

- Aides fired questions at him all day as he relaxed at a hotel.
- He slept in the afternoon, ate dinner, dressed in a white shirt and dark grey suit.
- He drove to the studios with his media adviser, Bill Wilson, who had spent all day speaking to his old colleagues at WBBM, the CBS affiliate broadcasting the debate, and arranging the right sort of lightening and conditions for Kennedy.
- Kennedy was tanned, wearing a fake tanning product, Man Tan, and was persuaded to wear *Max Factor Crème Puff* on his face for the broadcast.
- Kennedy changed his shirt to blue when told by TV producers that his white shirt would glare under the lights.

Richard Nixon, on the other hand, prepared in the following way:

- He had little contact with his media adviser, Ted Rogers, until the ten-minute drive to the studios.
- He arrived late at his hotel and stayed in his room alone.

continued

continued

> ▨ He had been unwell and had lost weight.
>
> ▨ He refused to wear make-up but was convinced by Rogers to wear *Lazy Shave* to cover up his five o'clock shadow.
>
> When the broadcast began, 'Seventy million Americans watched as Kennedy stood erect, calm and crisply outlined by his dark suit . . . speaking energetically to the audience. . . . By contrast, Nixon slouched . . . his Lazy Shave streaked with sweat. . . . He glanced furtively to the right, where the studio clock was, while Kennedy, when not speaking, always looked intently at Nixon . . . Nixon's image of the shifty, second-hand automobile dealer was simply reinforced. . . . At the end, *The Post* and the *St. Louis Dispatch* called it a draw and those listening on radio gave it to Nixon, but the post-debate polls among those who watched it on TV were clear: Kennedy had won.'
>
> (B. Bruce (1992) *Images of Power: How the Image Makers Shape Our Leaders*, London: Kogan Page, pp. 31–4)

Key text: J. Street (2001) *Mass Media, Politics and Democracy*, Basingstoke: Palgrave.

Indeed, the 1960s saw a rapid transformation of political communications as television made its impact felt, and appearing on television has become a central aspect of a politician's strategy. Such is the ubiquity of the medium and the desire of politicians to capitalise on opportunities for public exposure that politicians appear all over the place. For example, Neil Kinnock (Labour Party leader) appeared on British television comedy (about a television news agency) *Drop the Dead Donkey*, Tony Blair (Labour leader and Prime Minister) has appeared on the light entertainment show the *Des O'Connor Show* (Street 2001), and in the USA Bill Clinton appeared on MTV.

Such exposure does not stop at television. In the 1980s and 1990s politicians have used a mix of media to communicate their message and their image. This includes popular music, either directly by making recordings themselves (for example, David Steel's (Liberal Party) 1983 pop song *I Feel Liberal Alright*) or more often indirectly through association (for example, Harold Wilson's much publicised meeting with the Beatles in the 1960s). Tony Blair exploited his 'Brit-pop' connections by being photographed at the 1996 Labour Conference with the head of Creation Records (Oasis' record label) and by adopting of D. Ream's *Things Can Only Get Better* as an election anthem. Media communications also includes magazines, as exemplified by William Hague's (Conservative Party) statement to a British magazine that he drank lots of beer or Tony Blair's appearances at *Q* magazine events. Whatever the method or the medium, one thing is increasingly clear: politicians and political actors need a media strategy, as the following quote about Tony Blair makes clear:

> He sees handling the media as an essential part of doing the job, explaining to the public and party what he is doing and why. On important speeches he is likely to talk directly to influential journalists himself, and all the time he will be thinking about and reviewing his tactics.
>
> (Mandelson and Liddle 1996: 53)

Political communications can no longer be simply about the message but they must also be about the image and the perceived or desired values that are associated with such images. For example, recent campaigns to increase election turn-outs among young people in British elections reflect this trend – it is not enough to encourage people to vote because it might be 'a good thing'. The campaign becomes about making voting a *desirable* thing to be seen to do.

Thus the *Rock the Vote* campaign was launched in February 1996 at the Ministry of Sound Club in London with a mixture of political support and support from different entertainment and business interests. Drawing heavily on a campaign of the same name in the USA begun in 1990, the UK *Rock the Vote* campaign has been a high-profile media-based one. The campaign has utilised the full range of media channels – cinema, radio, television and publications – to promote its message, and has organised a range of events to promote the campaign including rock concerts: 'cyber elections', a 'Rock the Vote' nationwide tour and a range of poster launches and informational events. All of this involved the active participation of a range of 'indie' bands – including Radiohead, Suede, Supergrass – and comedians – including Eddie Izzard, Ben Elton and Jo Brand – and other high-profile public figures such as the Olympic athlete Linford Christie, and the campaign has claimed that 400,000 people between the ages of 18 and 24 registered to vote as a direct result of exposure to the campaign.

In summary then I think that three general trends which characterise the development of political communication can be identified from the brief overview given above. The first is that the growth of mass participatory politics has been accompanied by an increased, and possibly necessary, use of the mass media by political actors for the purposes of political communications, and political actors have readily utilised new technologies and techniques as they have become available. Second, the development of new communications technologies has been accompanied by the development of different styles of political communication and by the emergence of new and different political audiences. Third, these two trends have accelerated as new technologies have developed and the relationship between political actors, communication and promotional professionals and techniques and the mass media have become more mutli-layered, complex and intertwined.

Powerful images can be very effective in political communications: but what is the message here?

Managing political communication: how do politicians communicate?

Winning elections is really a question of salesmanship, little different from marketing any branded article.

(extract from an electioneering manual published in 1922 in Rosenbaum 1997: 1)

The question 'How do politicians communicate?' can be answered quite simply: in any way they can, and in this section I want to explore the ways in which political communication takes place and to analyse some of the implications of such communication through a focus on political campaigning during elections. Elections offer examples of highly concentrated periods of political communications and the practices that characterise such communication. Furthermore, elections are arguably critical periods in the relationship between power, politics and communication and therefore command particular attention.

In terms of election campaigning politicians and political parties tend to communicate either directly or indirectly. *Direct communications* will usually consist of messages and materials that clearly refer to the political party or politician that is the subject of the communication. This will include speeches, press conferences, party rallies, party political broadcasts, manifestos, party literature, direct mailings and telephone calls, posters, flyers, badges, websites and e-mails. In such communications politicians and parties will be seeking to directly communicate their message to the voter and to tell the voter something about their campaign, policies, plans or candidates.

Indirect communications are more elusive but possibly more important. These types of communications are about getting your message, agenda or more often than not your image across and established. These techniques include news management, agenda-setting, stunts, 'dirty tricks', 'attack politics' and leaks. In these techniques the aim of communication strategies is to promote a favourable image or idea of a political party or politician at the expense of the opposition or, at least, to get the attention of the media and public to an area that you think you are strong on, seen as strong on or have something to say about. For example, *news management* refers to the set of processes through which political parties attempt to manage the way in which news bulletins and reports focus on the issues that are most favourable to that party or least favourable to the opposition. For example, if a set of employment statistics are due out on the second Monday of the campaign and the governing party know they will be bad it will aim to present other newsworthy stories to set the agenda for the day away from focusing on those figures. Conversely the opposition will do exactly the opposite. In these ways parties will seek to set the news agenda for the day and they will do so through releasing interesting or impactive information at the morning press conferences (for photo opportunities on breakfast television) or by trying to set a clear agenda on a particular issue in an attempt to dominate news coverage for that day. *Attack politics* are characterised by a constant assault on the opposition's policies, personnel or governing history. So, in interviews, press releases and election literature one side will consistently attack the other, often with a focus on particular aspects of the opposition's policies or perceived attitude to one or more policy areas (for example, taxation, crime or health). '*Dirty tricks*' is a shorthand term for a whole range of tactics that aim to portray the opposition in the worst possible light and to create associations in the minds of voters with negative messages about personnel, and past and future performance (Hall Jamieson 1994). For example, the George W. Bush campaign was accused of hiding a subliminal message linking Al Gore to a rat in a television spot ad in

Presidential campaign poster for Nelson Mandela, South Africa

the 2000 US Presidential campaign (see <http://pcl.stanford.edu/campaigns/ campaign2000>).

Importantly there is a considerable cross-over between these two forms of communication and we should not look for a neat separation. Direct methods of communication will often contain or conceal indirect methods (for example, a political advertisement on television might contain both direct communication about a party with lots of indirect images about how 'nice', 'strong' or 'patriotic' a politician is). The picture on the right is of Silvio Berlusconi. What do you think the direct messages are in this picture? What would you say were the indirect messages?

I think it is increasingly clear that the marketing of politics has become more central to the process of political campaigning. Thus, the 'science of influencing mass behaviour in competitive situations' (Mauser 1983: 5) has become a dominant way of presenting political ideas and political messages to the people. In this argument political parties and politicians are marketed like any other brand or product and successful elections are won by those who can present their brand or product in the most desirable way to the electorate. Subsequently political communication and marketing now occupies a central position in the political landscape. Thus, through episodes like Nixon's 'Sweaty Lip' and running 'Lazy Shave' (Bruce 1992) in the 1960 US Presidential campaign and the Saatchi and Saatchi-led 'Labour isn't Working' campaign for the Conservatives in 1979 and the rebranding of Labour as *New* Labour, we have become increasingly familiar with the processes and techniques of a heavily marketed politics. As we have seen, these include not only the specific techniques of brand management – negative and positive advertising, the sound-bite, the photo opportunity and the press conference – but also the key device of news and agenda management. Furthermore, this marketing is closely associated with increased use of political advertising or advertising techniques to promote or market politics.

This appears to be particularly true of the televisual coverage of elections. Political communications on television are subject to different broadcasting rules in different countries. For example, in Britain political parties are allowed free time on television for party and parliamentary election broadcasts. They are not, however, allowed to pay for television advertising and there is no tradition of leader debates. In the USA the position is reversed. Parties pay for political advertising, often very short thirty-second-length 'spots', have no free air-time and do have leader debates. In Italy parties have access to both paid and free television, while in New Zealand and Japan parties have both paid and free air-time and also televised leadership debates. However, no matter how funded or regulated, it seems that a great deal of political communication on television is increasingly indebted to the skills and techniques of the commercial product advertisement.

McNair identifies three important general trends in political advertising in recent years. The first is the increased centrality of the politician's image (or the destruction of the opposition's) and the reduction of emphasis on policy or issues. For example, in 1992 Bill Clinton's image was very much constructed

Promotional election material for Silvio Berlusconi and *Forza Italia*

around notions of youth and vigour (McNair 1995), and similar tactics were used with Tony Blair in the 1997 Labour Party campaign. A second trend is the increased reliance on what McNair identifies as 'myth and symbol' through which the 'fears, anxieties, and deep-rooted desires of a culture should be uncovered and tapped into' before being associated with a particular candidate (1995: 91). A third trend is the reliance on symbols of power and status, particularly when this can be attached to an incumbent party or individual (McNair 1995). To some degree all three trends are identifiable in the example given below.

Michael Dukakis looked 'like Patton on his way to Berlin', observed NBC's Chris Wallace (September 13, 1988). '(A) Massachusetts Rambo on the prowl,' noted CBS's Bruce Morton the same evening. Footage of that ride was resurrected by a Bush attack ad that pilloried Dukakis's supposed positions. 'Dukakis opposed virtually every weapons system developed,' declared the ad in the first of its false statements about the Democrat. The Massachusetts Democrat responded with an ad in which he turned off a set showing the Bush ad. 'I'm fed up with it,' said Dukakis. 'George Bush's negative ads are full of lies and he knows it. I'm on record for the very weapons systems his ad says I'm against.'

By the campaign's end, the tank ride had appeared in news, the news footage had appeared in a Bush ad, the Bush ad had appeared in a Dukakis ad, and the Bush and Dukakis ads had appeared in news. The New Yorker cartoon showing a man watching a television set had prophesied the endless loops through which the image passed. In the set in front of him, the man sees himself watching the television set. In that set is another image of himself watching the set. Images of images damaged Dukakis's campaign. One poll indicates that 'voters who knew about the ride were much more likely to shift against the Democrat than toward him.'

(Hall Jamieson 1992: 3)

EXERCISE

- Can you think of any other examples of this type of political advertising?
- To what extent do you think it is legitimate?
- What does it tell you about politics and political communications?

Image management The set of techniques employed by politicians, parties and strategists to ensure the best presentation of themselves and to maintain a central set of ideas, images and associations, for public consumption, of those politicians and parties.

The increased use of marketing and advertising techniques has led commentators to be highly critical of the nature of political communications during elections, stressing the role of negative campaigning, attack politics and 'dirty tricks'. Furthermore, it is argued, politicians all too readily focus on **image management**, for example, the excessive use of the photo opportunity – Tony Blair has had seven photo opportunities with his baby son Leo, three playing football and two playing the guitar (*Guardian* 2002) – rather than debate and policy information. Others, however, stress that these developments are consistent with the rise of media cultures and the cultural shifts that are characteristic of such cultures. For example, Thompson (1995) argues that politics has been transformed into a process in which the management of visibility is the critical role for politicians.

new Labour
new Britain

Choose Life. Choose a job. Choose a career. Choose a family. All hand guns have been banned under Labour. Choose a better transport system. Under the Tories, on average three million fewer passenger journeys were made by bus every day. Choose a starter home. Choose your friends. Choose a tax reforming budget. The Tories mucked up on taxes, created 22 new ones including the poll tax, and now oppose the new 10p rate of income tax. Choose sitting on that couch watching mind-numbing, spirit crushing game shows. Choose crime figures in Oxford falling Month by Month increasing student safety. Choose New Deal. Choose a Minimum Wage. Choose a job, wind-fall tax is already going into biggest ever programme to get the young and long term unemployed back to work, 223,000 young people have now started New Deal. Over 100,000 have gone into jobs or further training. Choose Hospital Waiting lists, falling month after month. Choose a reformed Benefit System, (the Labour party are tackling the mess that was left behind by the Tories). Choose the 1st ever private members' bill to ban fox hunting. Choose an environment. Tories mucked up the air we breathe. Tories mucked up on buses. Tories mucked up on trains. Only Labour will rebuild our public transport systems, only Labour have an integrated transport policy. Choose your health. Tories mucked up on food, Tories gave us BSE, Tories gave us e-coli. Labour has introduced a fully independent food inspection agency. Choose Labour in Oxford.

New Labour

Choose your future.
Choose Labour.

A playful mixing of codes? Political communication and popular culture are deeply interconnected in this New Labour election communication, UK, 1997

We can see then that politicians use a whole range of techniques to communicate with the people, particularly in elections. These techniques can be categorised as direct communication, involving election messages, manifestos and party or candidate information, and indirect communication, which tends to refer to image management, agenda-setting and news management. Many of these communication techniques are associated with an increased reliance on the techniques of marketing, advertising and brand management, developments which many commentators find problematic and alarming. In the next section I want to develop the analysis of these trends a little further and to examine some of the characteristics of political communications in media cultures.

Politics in media cultures: a crisis for democracy?

The last decade has seen an explosion of new media outlets, but politicians' ability to make a persuasive case or illustrate a point in language of poetry and colour is much diminished because of the limitations of the thirty-second sound-bite, repeated by a dozen times or more different channels and news bulletins in a single day. . . . Too often the mass media's treatment of politics leaves the general public with an impression of partisan shrillness and shallowness which is steadily devaluing the currency of politics.

(Mandelson and Liddle 1996: 185)

Many commentators would agree that the media have a crucial role in democracies in underpinning the quality and functioning of democracy. For example, the media have a central role of keeping the populace informed, so that they can exercise informed choices, conveying information from one part of the political system to another, creating a space for public debate and deliberation, in other words, creating a **public sphere** (Habermas 1989), and scrutinising government, politicians and the generally powerful on behalf of the people (Curran and Seaton 1997; Street 2001). However, for a number of reasons outlined so far in this chapter, some would also argue that such a model has largely broken down and a number of commentators suggest that the complex relationships between politics, democracy and the media are experiencing some form of crisis. There are various elements of this 'crisis' which I will outline below.

First, at various points in this chapter I have suggested that political communication can be seen as increasingly taking place within promotional cultures (Wernick 1991). Furthermore the development of such promotional culture rests, in part, upon the pervasiveness of different forms of media as purveyors of cultural capital, arbiters of lifestyle and contexts for new forms of interaction: in other words, media cultures. In a media culture, not only is culture made up of communication processes, but all cultural expressions and many of those involving power relationships are mediated or framed by electronic communications (Castells 2000: 476; see also Skovmand and Schroder 1992; Fiske 1993, 1995; Kellner 1995). In relation to political communications and election campaigns this means that a political campaign *is* a media campaign.

Thus political communication and campaign styles have taken on certain characteristics. They have become increasingly long-term or almost permanent campaigns in which the idea of the party or politician is permanently promoted. For example, the rebranding of the British Labour Party as *New* Labour was a long-term process, delivered through the media, which began

Public sphere A space in which public debate, discussion and reflection can take place, free from political and state interference and in which public opinion can form.

Key text: J. Habermas (1989) *The Structural Transformation of the Public Sphere*, Cambridge: Polity Press.

under Neil Kinnock, accelerated with the leadership of Tony Blair and resulted in the successful repositioning of *New* Labour as a party which was not directly associated in the minds of voters with the 'old' Labour of left-wing politics, unilateral disarmament, high taxes and trade unionism. This sort of politics is image dominated and party leader focused (for example, Berlusconi in Italy or Blair in Britain), and there is a high reliance on media strategies and a central role for media strategists. Political communications are intensively managed, have a high 'sound-bite' content and are reliant on media-friendly images and symbols.

In such a politics television is central as a channel for political communication and disseminator of political values, ideas and images, and is increasingly central to an understanding of politics in advanced societies. In some ways politics is now everywhere. This is, for one commentator, the era of 'meta-coverage' (Gitlin 1991) in which every political move and word is planned, rehearsed and delivered by an all-pervasive mass media. It is now commonplace that election campaigns are delivered through the 'entertainment' genres of television and radio, especially talk-shows and even MTV (Brant 1998; Street 2001).

The argument that the reliance on negative image management, dirty tricks, stunts and a deeply personal nature of the campaign obscures what some see as the *real* issues – of policy, of values, of arguments – that *real* politics ought to be about. In this analysis excessive media coverage, and the way such coverage is constructed, dilutes and corrupts the process and operation of democracy by trivialising or ignoring the real issues and presenting a set of irrelevant criteria and information to the electorate. These issues will be examined in more detail in the next section of the chapter.

For many it is these types of developments that have facilitated the emergence of a crisis of political and public communication. Thus for Blumler and Gurevitch (1995) it is precisely the role of the media as public communicator that lies at the heart of this crisis and they place a significant emphasis on the apparent decline of the public service ethos under the impact of the rapid commercialisation and deregulation of the televisual media characteristic of the early to mid-1980s in Europe. For Franklin (1994) the problem is more to do with the convergence of promotional culture, media commercialisation and an increased reliance on the discourse of advertising that has precipitated the critical moment.

Key text: J. Blumler and M. Gurevitch (1995) *The Crisis of Public Communication*, London: Routledge.

Commentators argue that there has been a 'tabloidisation' of the news coverage of politics (Esser 1999). Consequently, news journalism, in both television and newspapers, has become much less focused on events and facts and much more focused on analysis and interpretation (Steele and Barnhurst 1996; Barnhurst and Mutz 1997).

Furthermore, entertainment values and formats have become predominant over more traditional news values and formats. For some, such developments represent a 'fundamental change in the political atmosphere: citizens attenuated into measurable audiences and consumers, politics commodified into beauty pageant cum talent show, journalists transmogrified into masters of ceremony, celebrity judges and measures of public will' (Barnhurst 1998: 203).

Others argue that another effect has been the increased alienation of the public from the political process and increasing levels of cynicism among voters. For Hart (1994) cynicism has become the dominant mind-set in the electorate, manifesting in a lack of a firm commitment towards and belief in political ideals and values. For Hart too, the main cause of this development is television and this medium's emphasis on style rather than content.

The crisis of political communication or That's Infotainment!

In recent years many commentators have argued that political communication is experiencing a crisis. Commentators point to the 'tabloidisation' of news and political communications (Esser 1999), the central role of 'spin' (Jones 1999) and the 'sound-bite'. Furthermore, a number of commentators lament one aspect of this current crisis in particular: the increasing invasion of news and current affairs programmes by television formats more readily associated with entertainment shows, what others might call 'dumbing down'. For a number of commentators the increasingly competitive, commercialised and viewer-hungry world of television has led to a decline in the levels of political knowledge and engagement among the populace and, as a consequence, an erosion of the quality of democracy (Franklin 1994; Hallin 1996; Brant 1998; Brant et al. 1998). For many this is the politics of the trivial and would include Tony Blair's five appearances on Good Morning Television and four appearances on The Jimmy Young Show, in comparison with four appearances on BBC Radio Four's Today programme (Guardian 2002: 5).

But others argue that such developments are consistent with current cultural trends (Brant 1998) and move politicians, political debates and discourses into more accessible spaces and open up politics in different ways (Fiske 1995). More generally, others challenge the validity of the overall argument that political communication is experiencing a crisis at all (Norris 2000) and others stress how politicians are now more accessible and accountable than ever and how politics has been rendered more transparent and participatory by increased media coverage (McNair 2000).

EXERCISE

☐ What do you think?
☐ How real is this 'crisis'?
☐ If it is a real crisis, who is to blame?
☐ If it is not a crisis, why are people convinced there is one?
☐ What is the appropriate way for politicians to communicate?
☐ Should they go on talk shows, game shows and MTV or stick to serious subjects?

The global media

In addition to the ideas outlined above we are witnessing significant structural shifts in the organisation of the mass media around the world which will have significant impacts on politics and society in the twenty-first century. We are seeing the development of 'global media' through the emergence of global communication networks, systems and technology. Examples of such organisations include News Corporation, headed by Rupert Murdoch, Viacom and Vivendi Universal. Commentators and activists are concerned that such concentration of media ownership and control is not a healthy development for democracy in general or political communications in particular. Commentators point to Silvio Berlusconi's *Finninvest* as an example of what they see as an abuse of media power and ownership (Mazzeloni 2000). The table on page 436 gives an overview of the size and global reach of Rupert Murdoch's media interests.

THINK POINT

- What do you think about such media concentration?

- How do you think media industries should be organised?

Commentators are concerned that the type of transnational, global media giants mentioned above represent a worrying trend of hyper-commercialisation that is bad for democracy and free speech. Such commentators argue that this concentration of ownership, the practices associated with it and the power that such corporations appear to possess all pose challenges to balanced and open communication and freedom of speech. Furthermore, the commercial imperatives outweigh, by far, other notions of public interest and public service and put considerable pressure on national broadcasters (for example, the BBC) to compete in this same marketplace (McChesney 1999).

In addition to global media systems we can also see the emergence of global markets and global cultural media products. This is a result and a cause of many processes but in particular the merging of media types and the process of globalisation. Such developments have massive implications for notions of democracy, power, identity and voice. Many commentators are concerned about the levels of cultural homogeneity and in particular the possibility of an 'Americanisation' of global and indigenous cultures. Conversely, others point out that these trends represent not 'Americanisation' but the emergence of genuinely global cultural products in a global society which hint at shifts to global public spheres and are developing alongside more cosmopolitan forms of global democracy and civil society.

Whatever the interpretations, we certainly live in increasingly global media times in which events become global media ones. Live Aid, the democracy protests in Tiananmen Square, the release of Nelson Mandela, the collapse of Communism, the Gulf War, the Siege of Sarajevo, the Kosovo War and the

Murdoch's Global Media Empire

US
Cable:
Fox News Channel
Fox Sports Enterprises
Fox New Net
FX
Los Angeles Dodgers
National Geographic Channel

Television:
Fox Broadcasting Company
Fox Searchlight Pictures

Publishing:
HarperCollins

Magazines:
News America Marketing
SmartSource
The Weekly Standard
Gemstar-TV Guide

Newspapers:
New York Post

Sport:
Los Angeles Dodgers

UK
Television: BskyB
Newspapers: News of the World
The Sun
The Sunday Times
The Times
Publishing: HarperCollins
Sport: Stakes in Manchester
United FC, Leeds FC,
Chelsea FC and Manchester
City FC

India
Television:
Channel TV
Star TV

SE Asia
Television:
Star TV
Channel TV

Australia
Television:
Fox Sports Australia
FOXTEL
Channel TV

Film:
Fox Studios

Magazines:
InsideOut

Newspapers:
The Daily Telegraph
The Gold Coast Bulletin
Herald Sun
Sunday Herald Sun
Sunday Mail
Sunday Tasmanian
The Advertiser
The Australian
The Courier-Mail
The Mercury
The Sunday Telegraph
New Zealand Newspapers
Independent Newspapers

Publishing:
HarperCollins

Mexico
Film:
Fox Studios Baja

Italy
Television:
Stream

Japan
Television:
Sky Perfect TV!

(*Guardian*, Media Section, 13 May 2002, pp. 2–3)

attacks on 11 September on the World Trade Center in New York are all examples of global media events which had a significant impact on the global media audience. For example, in the quote below Jürgen Habermas reflects on what he call the contagion effect of the worldwide diffusion of the images of mass anti-communist protests.

> The mass media were not only decisive for the contagion-effect of world-wide diffusion. The physical presence of the demonstrating masses on the streets and public squares, otherwise than in the nineteenth century and early twentieth centuries, could exert revolutionary force only to the extent that they were converted by television into a ubiquitous presence.
>
> (Habermas, quoted in Peters 1993: 10)

New media and political activism

The above discussion stresses some of the concerns that have been expressed about the effects of globalisation and concentration in media systems and on political communication. However, other commentators draw attention to the opportunities that new media technologies, in part because of their global reach, offer for political communication and political activism. In particular the increasing use of the new media technologies of the Internet allows for rapid, relatively cheap and transnational communication of political messages to a global audience. In this section I want to examine some examples of the interface between new media and political activism.

In recent years there appears to have been something of a reinvigoration of radical and alternative media forms that has coincided with the development of relatively cheap and accessible new media technologies in general and the Internet in particular. Consequently a range of radical alternative media organisations have emerged in which the boundaries between political activism and alternative media production are somewhat blurred but the message they carry is very clear indeed. In the UK alternative press organisations such as SQUALL (<http://www.squall.co.uk>) have moved away from the more conventional and familiar printed publication form to online distribution. In doing so SQUALL has moved from being primarily a publication concerned with issues around homelessness (Atton 2002) to an online magazine that operates a forum for radical journalism and photography. In SQUALL's words the magazine presents accessible and reliable information and analysis about a range of issues which the mainstream media either will not or cannot cover. This includes an alternative source of news resources in the form of photographs and news items, particularly from demonstrations and public protests from around the world, designed to inform and activate others. Primarily focused on anti-capitalist and anti-globalisation issues the site posts extensive pictorial records from WTO demos.

Another example might be SchNEWS (<http://wwwhttp://www.schnews.co.uk>) founded in the UK in 1994 out of the campaign against the Criminal

Justice Act. What was once a small list of direct action briefings presented on an A4 sheet of paper has grown to be a vocal element of anti-capitalist protest through the use of the Internet, e-mails and mirror sites. SchNEWS currently has about 7500 e-mail subscribers and estimates 150,000 hits on its website every month (SchNEWS 2002). The website offers a quite elaborate *Party and Protest* section which is updated every week with a listing of festival dates, meetings and demonstrations.

These two examples give a sense of how radical and **alternative media** make use of new media technologies, global reach and offer alternative sources of news, resources and communications opportunities for political activists. Such organisations demonstrate significant differences from more conventional media sources in terms of content, delivery and objectives, and, indeed, the boundaries between producers of media content, audience and activists are considerably more blurred than is characteristic of more conventional forms of media. The box below provides a useful summary of these characteristics.

Alternative media Media forms and outputs that provide an alternative to the official, mainstream or mass commercial media. Such media often have a strong radical element and utilise the technology of new media.

A typology of alternative and radical media

1 Content – politically, socially and culturally radical.
2 Form – graphics, visual language, varieties of presentation, aesthetics.
3 Reprographic innovations and adaptations – use of mimeographs, offset litho, photocopiers.
4 Distributive use – alternative sites for distribution, clandestine/invisible distribution networks, anti-copyright.
5 Transformed social relations, roles and responsibilities – leader-writers, collective organisation, de-professionalisation of journalism, printing and publishing.
6 Transformed communication processes – horizontal linkages, networks.

(Atton 2002: 27)

The reinvigoration of radical and alternative media through the application and availability of new media technologies is only one example of the transformative potential of such technology. The global anti-debt movement, Jubilee 2000, provides another example of political activism and popular participation through communication and global networks. Although this organisation may have failed in its overall aim of cancelling the 'unpayable debts of the poorest countries by the year 2000', it clearly did make a significant impact on the political agenda (Anheier *et al.* 2001: 62). This was primarily achieved through a global campaign which placed the issue of Third World debt on the political agenda through the building of a global communication network focused on this issue. By 2000, after four years of campaigning, there were sixty-eight countries (for example, Angola, Japan, UK, USA, Sweden, Honduras and Colombia), sharing information, symbols and goals. This campaign was significantly aided by the use of the Internet in terms of coordination and cooperation (Anheier *et al.* 2001: 62–3). The shape of activism and political communication to come? Perhaps. There do appear to be more and more examples of such activist networks about, from the Zapatista Movement in Mexico (Villarreal Ford and Gil 2002) to the Landmine Monitor's overview of the global implementation of the Ottawa Treaty, the 'McLibel' campaign and the development of a women's regional and international network, DAWN (Edwards and Gaventa 2001). And while it may be true that the implications of the new media technologies are less than clear and optimistic visions of the future seldom hold, there may be significant, positive and democratising grass-roots potential in the types of developments outlined in this section.

Conclusion

Following Lenin's genial instinct to ration paper supply as the basic device for controlling information in the aftermath of the Revolution, Soviet printing, copying, information processing and communication machines remained under tight scrutiny. Typewriters were rare, carefully monitored devices. Access to a photocopying machine always required security clearance: two authorised signatures for a Russian text, and three authorised signatures for a non-Russian text. Use of long-distance telephone lines and telex was controlled by special procedures within each organisation, and the very notion of a 'personal computer' was objectively subversive to the Soviet bureaucracy, including sciences bureaucracy. Diffusion of information technology, both of machines and know-how, could hardly take place in a society where the control of information was critical to the legitimacy of the state, and to the control of the population. The more communication technologies made the outside world accessible to the imaginary representation of Soviet citizens, the more it became objectively disruptive to make such technologies available to a population which, by and large, had shifted from submissive terror into passive routine on the basis of a lack of information and of alternative world views.

(Castells 2000: 37)

In this chapter I have argued that political communication is a broad concept that encompasses a wide range of media, messages and actors that, to some degree, can be difficult to define. Nevertheless, and as the quote above from Castells (2000) ably illustrates, the power of communication and the relationship between power, politics and communication are all critical issues for students and practitioners of politics alike. I have also argued that we need to be aware of the contexts of political communication (for example, the historical, technological, economic, legal, organisational and cultural) and to locate analysis of particular examples of communications within some awareness of such contexts. This is important if we are to develop our understanding of both the nature and function of political communications. I have also highlighted the central importance and contested nature of key debates about political communications in terms of the impacts of media cultures, globalisation, new media and the critical relationship between democracy, political communications and the media – issues that will remain central to discussions of political communications and the media for a long time yet.

EXERCISE

1 Imagine you are a media strategist employed by an environmental political party to design one five-minute television broadcast to be shown during an election campaign. What would you do and how would you design this broadcast? What sorts of messages would you want to communicate to the voters? How would you communicate with the voters, through what means and media? What sort of images would you use to present your messages?

2 Design a newspaper advertisement to reassure the populace about the safety of genetically modified food.

Chapter summary

▪ What we mean by political communication depends, in part, on what we mean by, and how broadly we define politics.

▪ Political communication and the role of the media in politics are critical issues with which students of politics should engage.

▪ There are a number of important contexts – historical, technological, legal, economic, cultural, organisational – in which political communications are located.

▪ The development of new and different media technologies tends to be accompanied by shifts in the extent, amount and effects of political communication.

▪ The role of visual media, in particular television, has transformed the form and content of political communications.

▪ Commentators have stressed the attendant rise of political marketing, advertising and image management.

▪ Globalisation is also impacting on media forms and content through the emergence of transational communications corporations and global communications content.

- New media technologies (for example, the Internet) appear to be reinvigorating the depth and scope of alternative and radical media.

- Any discussion of political communication and the media is accompanied by important debates about the nature and quality of democracy and public communication.

Key texts

Berger, P. (1972) *Ways of Seeing*, London: Penguin.

Blumler, J. and Gurevitch, M. (1995) *The Crisis of Public Communication*, London: Routledge.

Castells, M. (2000) (2nd edn) *The Rise of the Network Society: The Information Age: Economy, Society and Culture*, Vol 1, Boston, MA: Blackwell.

Habermas, J. (1989) *The Structural Transformation of the Public Sphere*, Cambridge: Polity Press.

Hall Jamieson, K. (1996) (3rd edn) *Packaging the Presidency: A History and Criticism of Presidential Campaign Advertising*, New York: Oxford University Press.

Herman, E. S. and Chomsky, N. (1994) *Manufacturing Consent: The Political Economy of the Mass Media*, London: Vintage.

Index on Censorship (1999) 'Underexposed' 6.

McLuhan, M. (1967) *The Medium is the Message*, Harmondsworth: Penguin.

Street, J. (2001) *Mass Media, Politics and Democracy*, Basingstoke: Palgrave.

Wernick, A. (1991) *Promotional Culture: Advertising, Ideology and Symbolic Expression*, London: Sage.

Further reading

Calhoun, C. (ed.) (1992) *Habermas and the Public Sphere*, Cambridge, MA: MIT Press. An important collection of essays which critically discuss Habermas' notion of the public sphere from an extensive range of perspectives.

Fiske, J. (1995) *Media Matters: Everyday Culture and Political Change*, Minneapolis: University of Minnesota Press. An excellent and absorbing study of the media, politics and everyday life from a postmodern perspective.

Franklin, B. (1994) *Packaging Politics: Political Communication in Britain's Media Democracy*, London: Edward Arnold. A readable, accessible and interesting discussion of the effects of the techniques of advertising and marketing in political communications.

Keane, J. (1991) *Media and Democracy*, Cambridge: Polity Press. A seminal text which explores the relationship between the media, democracy and the citizen from a liberal perspective.

McChesney, R. (1999) *Rich Media, Poor Democracy: Communication Politics in Dubious Times*, Urbana and Chicago: University of Illinois Press. An examination of the implications of increasing media commercialisation and ownership concentration and the implications for political communications and democracy.

Mandelson, P. and Liddle, R. (1996) *The Blair Revolution: Can New Labour Deliver?*, London: Faber and Faber. An interesting example of an extended piece of political communication which gives a good insight into the ways in which Old Labour became *New* Labour.

Norris, P. (2000) *A Virtuous Circle: Political Communications in Post-Industrial Democracies*, New York: Cambridge University Press. An excellent and detailed cross-national and comparative study that examines critically the notion that the mass media are responsible for much that is wrong with politics in modern democracies.

Rosenbaum, M. (1997) *From Soapbox to Soundbite: Party Political Campaigning in Britain Since 1945*, Basingstoke: Macmillan. A lively, readable and well-illustrated study of political campaigning in Britain since the 1940s.

Scammell, M. (1995) *Designer Politics: How Elections are Won*, London: Macmillan. A useful and well-illustrated discussion of the role of political marketing, image management and campaign strategies during election campaigns.

CHAPTER 13

The Policy Process

John Turner

Introduction

To explain how policy is made provides a good guide to how a political system operates as a whole. In other words, policy brings together different aspects of a political system and the various political issues and concepts discussed in the chapters of this book. To understand how policy is made in one country as opposed to another is to understand that country's specific political characteristics, including the interaction of its political system with other systems such as its social and economic environments. Policy also helps us to study the way in which these characteristics come together and are integrated through processes of decision-making and the implementation of policy.

We talk of policy in a general way. We hear people ask, 'Why don't politicians do something about that problem?', 'Why did the government make that decision?', 'I'm going to stop the government doing that'. They are all referring to policy, whether it relates to how issues get put on to the political agenda, how policy is formulated, who makes the key decisions and how they are implemented, or why some policies seem to fail and others evolve and are modified.

Essentially, policy is about three processes:

1 The intentions of political and other key actors;
2 The way decisions or non-decisions are made;
3 The consequences of these decisions.

In examining any political system we can ask ourselves four key questions about the nature of the political and policy-making process. We will have the opportunity of considering these questions when we examine a case study at the end of the chapter.

These key questions must be asked of any political system, and answers will vary according to the particular institutions and processes within different political systems. Therefore there are certain generic questions which need to be posed about the policy process, although a study of policy will also highlight the way in which different political systems operate.

The study of policy

There is no universally acclaimed definition of what is meant by the term 'policy'. The field of policy studies is filled with competing definitions. However, in recent years there has been a growing interest in the study of the policy process. Lasswell called for a policy dimension to political studies in 1951, and policy studies developed in the USA in the 1960s and has become increasingly important in political studies ever since. Initially, such studies borrowed from a range of different disciplines, including management studies, organisational analysis, decision-making techniques and more theoretical studies of values. The current interest in policy has come about because of a number of factors.

1 The growing scale and complexity of modern government have posed increasing problems for policy-makers. The study of policy has attempted to define and understand this change in scale and complexity.
2 Politics has been increasingly analysed from the point of view of outputs rather than through analyses of structures and institutions. Here individual and collective decisions are analysed and studies attempt to explain differences between political systems by reference to policy outcomes.
3 There has been a greater emphasis placed on how decisions are made and techniques used in solving problems. In a more prescriptive way, some policy studies have suggested better techniques for problem-solving and decision-making.
4 Policy studies has also been encouraged by the drawing together of different academic disciplines to show how decisions are made in an integrated way.
5 Policy analysts themselves have been drawn increasingly into politics, offering advice and consultancy in government departments, agencies and organisations.

Key text: H. Heclo (1972) 'Review Article: Policy Analysis', *British Journal of Political Science* 2.

Hugh Heclo (1972) has attempted to demarcate the policy field and pointed to the fact that policy is not a self-evident term. It can, for example, involve a course of actions or in-actions. According to Richard Rose (1980) policy represents a long series of related activities, and for Etzioni (1967) policy is a system of generalised decision-making in which decisions and contexts are reviewed. Policy can be interpreted as an empty shopping basket ready to be filled with policy goodies. Lindblom and Braybrooke (1963) use the term to indicate on the one hand consciously made decisions and the course policies take as a result of the interrelationships among decisions. Policy involves a process whereby policy-makers attempt to deal with a problem, defining options, making decisions and implementing possible solutions.

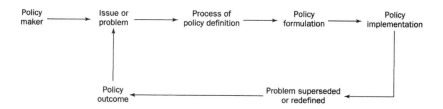

Figure 13.1 The policy process

It should be noted (Figure 13.1) that there is a policy process and a policy outcome. All policy is continuous. It evolves and changes as decision-makers adapt policy. Problems are not so much solved as superseded or redefined by policy-makers. Outcomes are impacts of policy affecting people in direct and indirect ways and posing future problems in terms of their unintended consequences. This simplified model also involves policy definition and the motivations of policy-makers. Policy can often be seen as responding to particular problems, although decisions may also be based on ideology and the need for internal party support, and for more general symbolic reasons.

Before examining some of the theories and models of the policy process we will look at a recent example of policy-making in government and the types of problem faced by decision-makers. This example can be examined using Figure 13.1 showing the policy process.

Policy in action: the foot-and-mouth crisis 2001 to 2002

In February 2001 Britain was hit by a major agricultural and health crisis in the form of the foot-and-mouth epidemic. Like many other issues faced by governments for which policy has to be quickly formulated and implemented, there was little warning of the crisis, no time to prepare in advance and the complexity of the issue required crisis management involving many unintended consequences.

Policy definition

As illustrated in Figure 13.1, one of the primary tasks of decision-makers involves the process of policy definition. Often, the way an issue is defined and integrated into existing forms of policy-making within bureaucratic structures frames the way in which policy is subsequently formulated and implemented. Also policy is not constructed in isolation, without a context. Previous policy in this area has to be considered, including the deregulation of abattoirs, the animal feed industry and the lack of controls on foreign meat imports. Policy builds upon existing policy, success or failure being dependent on the degree to which existing policy can be adapted and changed.

Senior civil servants attempting to construct an effective policy have admitted that dealing with this epidemic was far bigger and more complex than the Gulf War. This was the worst recent outbreak of the disease anywhere in the world and policy for dealing with the crisis became one huge logistical exercise, involving 7000 civil servants, 2000 vets (many of whom had to be recruited from abroad) and 2000 soldiers brought in mainly to dispose of the millions of culled animal carcasses. It is estimated that the crisis has cost the British economy some £6 billion.

Policy formulation

A useful source of evidence about the policy process often comes from subsequent enquiries, commissions, audits and reports held during or shortly after such crises. For example, in the case of the foot-and-mouth crisis, the first public inquiry was not held by central government but by regional or local government. In this case it was Devon County Council, representing a region seriously affected by the disease. This inquiry was particularly critical of the way in which policy was constructed from the outset of the crisis. There was no contingency plan in place for dealing with such a crisis, with many of the lessons learned from the last outbreak of the disease in 1967 either forgotten or ignored. Policy is about learning: learning from mistakes and successes, and making appropriate modifications. In this case study it is clear that over a thirty-year period not much policy learning had taken place. Hence, in the first few weeks of the crisis, policy, or the lack of it, had a profound impact on the course of the crisis over the following year. In policy analysis the art of non-decision-making is often as important as substantive policy-making itself.

The Devon inquiry indicated that the Ministry of Agriculture had rapidly lost control of the epidemic and was then subsequently having to play 'catch-up'. The leader of the Farmers' Union felt that 'the government was ill-prepared, and, too often, incompetent'. Not enough resources had been provided and the scale of the problem had been underestimated. In other words, policy was reactive and at the beginning defensive, indicating that decision-makers did not have a clear understanding of the degree or complexity of the problems they faced. For example, animal movements were not banned until four days after the first outbreak of foot and mouth. This delay allowed farmers and livestock dealers to quickly move animals around the country subsequent to the ban coming into effect (*Guardian*, 9 October 2001). The lack of early command and control shaped the nature of subsequent policy formulation and implementation. The Devon report, albeit with hindsight, has suggested that contingency plans for such a disease should be reviewed, tested and rehearsed up to every five years and should involve all levels of government from Whitehall to the smallest parish council. In other words, policy should involve a community of stakeholders and interested parties, with policy not being imposed in a top-down manner.

Another important aspect of policy-making involves the level and substance of expert and specialist advice. Elected politicians often have very limited knowledge and expertise about the intricacies of issues for which policy has to be made. Professionals, such as scientists, technologists, medical experts, economists and lawyers, are often brought into the heart of policy-making under the rational assumption that they are in the best position to find solutions to the problems faced by policy-makers. The politicians' reliance on such advice clearly fills gaps in expertise, but can also distance them from subsequent blame for policy failure. Politicians are often heard claiming that they only acted on the best expert advice available!

The perceived failures of policy at the beginning of the crisis led to a major change in policy administration. There were complaints from farmers' groups, the food industry, veterinary groups, the tourist trade, the press and public opinion about the confusion of policy. Government was criticised for muddling through and of crisis mismanagement, allowing policy to drift because of the uncertainty about the way in which the crisis had been defined. These criticisms led to a subsequent series of policy changes in which the Prime Minister's office took responsibility for the direction of policy away from the Ministry of Agriculture. Tony Blair quickly established an advisory committee, chaired by his chief scientific adviser, predominantly made up of epidemiological modellers, who while experts in their field had limited knowledge of the wider food industry and farming practices. This committee was very powerful. It had direct access to the Prime Minister and was able to drive policy on the basis of the assumptions they made about the scientific nature of the disease. This scientific knowledge overshadowed wider social, economic and political concerns and led to policy prescriptions which were opposed by many other stakeholders. For example, the Ministry of Agriculture's chief scientist observed that the 'committee had enormous power with no direct responsibility. . . . It was driving what the government was doing and of course if there were any flaws in its composition or mode of operation you could have a flawed mechanism for driving policy' (*Guardian*, 19 February 2002).

Policy implementation

The assumptions made by this scientific committee and the criticisms over policy direction led to a drastic programme of mass contiguous slaughter of sheep and cattle. Some six million animals were culled (the majority were healthy) and alternative policy options were dismissed. The policy became known as 'carnage by computer'. For example, an outbreak of the disease in The Netherlands had led to the selective vaccination of animals. However, the food industry objected to this, with retailers, especially the supermarkets, arguing that consumers would not buy vaccinated meat and milk. They argued that they would simply refuse to stock such products. As a powerful industry lobby the government placed greater weight on these views than it did on those of the animal rights lobby, who were appalled at the extent of what they saw as mostly unnecessary slaughter. When we look at the notion of pluralism it is important to remember that some interested groups are more powerful than others. The Minister for Agriculture was later to admit that selective vaccination should have been adopted.

The implementation of policy using a mass cull of animals had huge unintended consequences that reshaped the nature of the problem facing government. Large-scale pyres were used to burn livestock corpses, a practice which was labelled 'barbaric and medieval' by the Devon inquiry. There were many criticisms, especially from local rural communities, that this policy was conducted in an insensitive way, with belligerent operatives and unclear guidelines. The Devon report concluded that 'the crisis that a major outbreak generates is not an excuse for government and its agencies to override the welfare of individuals or communities, or to ignore the long established rules for the management of the environment' (*The Times*, 29 October 2001).

Problem superseded and redefined

The scale of such a policy meant that many animals remained unburied or unburnt and subsequently the government brought in the army to dispose of the dead animals. Pictures in the press and on television of burning animals and the shooting of sheep went around the world and increasingly countries refused to handle British farming products. Such images also had a drastic affect on British tourism throughout the country, in urban as well as rural areas, with the subsequent collapse of many local economies based on tourism. It was soon pointed out that the tourist industry was a larger income earner for the country than the beef and sheep industry.

What had started as a problem of agriculture had become transformed (in Figure 13.1 superseded and redefined) into a wider issue involving a completely different sector of the economy. The importance placed on the media's portrayal of the crisis was shown by the Prime Minister's communications chief, who complained to the Brigadier in charge of the Army's disposal efforts that the scope for such lurid pictures was having an adverse effect in the run-up to a general election.

Policy outcomes

One casualty of this crisis involved the decision-makers themselves. The Minister of Agriculture was demoted to a junior post in government and the

Ministry of Agriculture itself was restructured in the form of a new Department of the Environment, Food and Rural Affairs. A wider policy outcome has been the elevation of issues related to rural affairs. Pressure groups, such as the Countryside Alliance and Farmers for Action (previously fuel tax protesters), have used the handling of the crisis as a way of promoting better understanding of rural communities. The government's delay in bringing forward a bill to abolish hunting with dogs is one tangible legacy of this new sensitivity.

From the government's point of view policy has been described as 'a small triumph' (*Independent*, 18 February 2002). It is claimed the disease has been eradicated, and in this sense ends have justified the policy means. Interestingly, the government refused to hold a public inquiry into the crisis, despite calls from many other interested parties. In the light of an impending general election, the government was conscious of the negative publicity that might be associated with such an inquiry. However, the crisis has allowed the new minister, in her new department, to widen the policy agenda regarding farming in Britain. She has announced that farmers should no longer expect 'endless subsidy' to produce unwanted food. Some conspiracy theorists have suggested that the mass cull of livestock has made this new policy easier to implement!

Having presented this brief policy case study it is useful to look now at some of the explanations and models used to assess and evaluate the policy-making process and the assumptions made by decision-makers about how policy is formulated and implemented. It will be useful to read through these explanations and return to this case study and apply such frameworks to actual practice.

THINK POINT

What policy models may be discerned in the case study of the foot-and-mouth crisis?

A model of policy-making: Easton's input–output model

David Easton's pioneering work (1953) on the policy process is important because it sees policy as a process involving the interaction of policy-makers with their policy environment. Easton's model is fairly simple, but should be seen as an ideal-type model that attempts to explain what are conceptually complex relationships. Easton's model has always been seen as important and innovative in that it emphasises policy as an interactive process. He also attempts to disassemble the policy process into key stages or components that have different impacts on the process as a whole. Attention is also given to the relationship between the political system and other systems. Wider environments, including social, economic and cultural, are affected by public policy outcomes. Criticisms levelled at Easton's input–output model have pointed to its simplicity and attachment to rationality in the policy process. The model itself is borrowed from the physical sciences, with policy and the political

Key texts: D. Easton (1953) *The Political System*, New York: Knopf; (1965) *A Systems Analysis of Political Life*, New York: Wiley.

process being analysed like a technical system. For example, many of Easton's categories overlap. Political demands do not only arise from outside the black box or 'conversion process' of decision-making. Politicians and key decision-makers also have demands, and through ideologies and electoral strategies often attempt to manufacture demands through emotive appeals and to create policy agendas accordingly and on their terms.

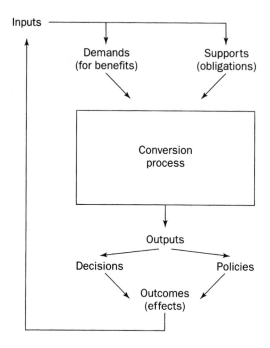

Figure 13.2 Easton's input–output systems model

Other critics have pointed to Easton's rather vague notion of this 'conversion process'. Again, there is an assumption that political actors behave in rational ways in converting demands into outputs and decisions. Looking inside the black box of decision-making involves looking at the way public officials, elite politicians and other insider groups affect outcomes. Often their influence is hidden from public scrutiny and involves contradictory positions. In a sense, Easton's model also assumes that there are clearly defined objectives and goals. This is clearly rarely the case. Government ministers may have a number of contradictory objectives, including meeting the demands of their party, their perception of the needs of public opinion, the views of their officials, and reconciling demands from interest groups and other institutions of government.

Easton's model, therefore, is fairly simple, although it is difficult to envisage more complex models that are not more complicated and less readily understandable. Easton's input–output model creates a cycle through a feed-back loop, with policy outcomes affecting future demands. Policy may be seen as a cycle or a staged process involving five key stages that are rarely segmented.

They are as follows:

1 Deciding to decide in issue recognition
2 Formulating alternative options
3 Making decisions
4 Implementation
5 Correction and supplementation.

This cycle emphasises the dynamic nature of the political process and highlights the way in which policy may be understood as a learning process. Hogwood and Gunn (1984) have developed this model as a framework for decision-making. Their policy sequence is portrayed in Figure 13.3.

As a learning process policy may be seen as a way in which decision-makers come to terms with issues, consider different forms of action, put them together in a formulation package and then make amendments in the light of experience of implementing policy.

Key text: B. W. Hogwood and L. A. Gunn (1984) *Policy Analysis for the Real World*, Oxford: Oxford University Press.

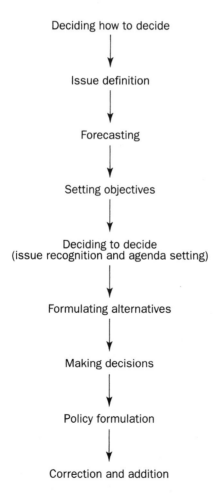

Deciding how to decide

↓

Issue definition

↓

Forecasting

↓

Setting objectives

↓

Deciding to decide
(issue recognition and agenda setting)

↓

Formulating alternatives

↓

Making decisions

↓

Policy formulation

↓

Correction and addition

Figure 13.3 The Hogwood and Gunn policy sequence

The policy process and the state

The modern state has a fundamental effect on people. Wars, intervention in economic and industrial policy, and the development of welfare programmes have all extended the role and scope of the state. As the state has become more interventionist through increasing government legislation and regulation, so the study of policy has become more important. Policy and the way it is made can tell us a great deal about the organisation and processes of the modern state. The way in which state institutions formulate and implement policy can tell us a great deal about its values, political institutions, political culture and political processes.

The state may be defined in terms of the institutions and processes which oversee the development of policy. Key institutions in this process are given in Figure 13.4.

The degree to which these institutions overlap is important in understanding the different ways in which policy is formulated and implemented. For example, the United Kingdom is a unitary state where there is no formal constitution and an overlap between institutions. However, the USA is a federal state with a formal constitution clearly setting out the separation of powers between institutions, with autonomous state and regional powers.

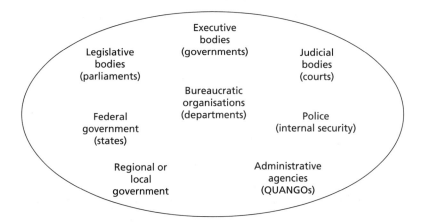

Figure 13.4 State institutions

Individuals are affected in nearly all parts of their lives by the activities of the state. In modern society this is particularly the case with:

- the provision of public services in the form of welfare programmes, including healthcare, pensions, education, income support and housing;

- the intervention of the state in economic policy, including budgets, taxation, public spending and borrowing, and in industrial policy, including regional policy, investment incentives and subsidies.

We will consider five theories or explanations of the relationship between state and society. Each explanation can be applied to policy-making processes in different countries.

Pluralist explanations

The concept of **pluralism** centres on the notion that power is dispersed in society and that the activities of the state are checked by the countervailing influence of groups.

A wide range of policy outcomes may be accommodated by this explanation given the assumption that there are several sources of power in society. Of course, power is not equally dispersed, and some groups have greater access to policy-making circles and greater opportunities for affecting policy outcomes. Pluralism emphasises the fact that there are multiple centres of power, and policy development comes from the results of competition between contending groups.

Such groups are said to form policy communities, policy emerging from the bargaining and negotiation between groups. Lively (1978) has developed a useful distinction in such relationships between what he terms '**arena**' and '**arbiter**' pluralist approaches.

Both arbiter and arena definitions have implications for how the policy process operates. Arbiter pluralism sees the state as holding the ring and only inviting groups into the policy arena when required, setting ground rules and procedures. However, arena pluralism sees policy as a matter of mutual negotiation and bargaining between the state and interested groups. In the arena model governments need the support of such groups in order to implement their policy. Governments and officials need to build a coalition of support for their policy proposals.

Neo-pluralist explanations

Neo-pluralism has adapted the pluralist model by emphasising the unequal distribution of power between groups.

Power and influence over the policy process is controlled by a small elite. According to writers like Mosca, this elite of party politicians, government ministers, officials, lawyers, military leaders, media owners and powerful business interests direct and control power which essentially supports their own interests and hold over power.

In policy terms the emphasis has very much been placed on top-down approaches, underlining the role of elite decision-makers. Neo-pluralist explanations would support such a perspective, while not ignoring the view that there are contending and competing elites. For writers like Weber power is increasingly located within large bureaucracies. The growth of big government, large business corporations and large-scale military establishments has been accompanied by the growth of rule-driven bureaucracies, again controlled by a relatively small number of administrative elites.

Pluralism Postures that society is composed of competing groups contending for relative power and influence within a political system.

Arbiter and Arena These theories envisage government as standing above the group battle, settling ground rules for the conflict (particularly those determining what groups and what modes of action are legitimate), ensuring the enforcement of those rules, and perhaps correcting imbalances if there is a danger of particular groups growing into over-mighty subjects. The arena theory, in contrast, sees politicians merely as co-equal participants in the group (see Lively 1978: 191).

Neo-pluralism Refers to a variant of pluralism which recognises the development of elite groups with more access to power.

Key text: G. Mosca (1939) *The Ruling Class*, New York/London: McGraw-Hill.

Key text: C. Wright Mills (1956)
The Power Elite, New York:
Oxford University Press.

Others have pointed to a power elite which now dominates government, business and the military. In a study of the USA, C. Wright Mills (1956) emphasised the interrelationship between leaders and institutions. In the policy arena different elites operate in relation to different issues and are constrained by conflicting interests between elites.

Corporatist explanations

Corporatism Refers to the process whereby producer interests are incorporated into the policy-making process.

Pluralism and **corporatism** are similar models in many respects.

At its heart corporatism attempts to explain tendencies of the state towards intervention, intermediation and incorporation. Winkler argued that the modern state has had to intervene as economic circumstances have deteriorated in countries. The development of global markets, greater industrial concentration and higher unemployment has meant that the state has had to intervene with policies designed to support and gain the cooperation of corporate interests.

Governments have attempted to develop tripartite sets of relationships, institutionalising the cooperative relationship between the state, business and organised labour. Corporatist explanations would point to the loss of control of such groups as they are incorporated into the decision-making process at the expense of relative autonomy.

State corporatism Tends to be authoritarian and anti-liberal as in the political regimes of Fascist Italy or Nazi Germany.

A useful distinction has been made by Schmitter (1979) between **state corporatism** and **social corporatism**.

Social corporatism Tends to develop as pluralist arrangements break down and the state has to intervene in the face of economic and industrial decline (see Schmitter 1979: 64).

Marxist explanations

Marxist analyses take as a starting point the development of two social classes, the proletariat and the bourgeoisie, formed as a consequence of the development of the capitalist mode of production. Essentially, a strong link exists between political power and economic power, with the most dominant economic class exercising political control. In this sense the state is not seen as holding the balance between different interests, but rather actually representing the most dominant class. This argument is similar to the neo-pluralist interpretation which sees the development of elites.

Marxists see state intervention as a way of ensuring that capital accumulation continues and existing social relationships are preserved. In policy terms this means the state intervening to pick up the social costs of production, or subsidising capital, or ensuring organised labour is controlled.

The relationship between economic and political power is not a simple one and cannot be understood in a deterministic way. For example, different factions within elites may exist, representing, for example, different elements of capital, such as finance and manufacturing. Such factions may compete for political control, and the state takes its form from the struggle between such factions and classes. Poulantzas (1973) has argued that the state and economy are relatively autonomous, with the state often intervening in the longer term interests of the dominant class, despite short-term compromises having to be made.

Neo-liberal explanations

Neo-liberal explanations became increasingly dominant in the 1980s. For example, proponents of the New Right, including Reagan and Thatcher in government, argued for the rolling back of the state and the breaking up of corporatist vested interest. Writers like Olson have emphasised that corporatist and pluralist perspectives have actually damaged society, the alternative being policies of deregulation and privatisation to favour market-led rather than state-led policy solutions.

Neo-liberalism Places market efficiencies as the foundation for political freedom and argues for a limited role for the state.

Theories of decision-making

Theories of how decisions are made in political systems are important because they provide us with a framework for understanding the complex relationships which surround policy-making. The detail and volume of empirical evidence may be placed within a pattern of relationships by using such theories. They help us to explain where power lies, and how political systems process information and attempt to deal with issues and problems.

Theories tend to be oversimplified models of political relationships and also to be abstract. However, they do provide organising principles and can help us understand the way in which issues are processed. An examination of such theories can help us understand the way political decisions are made, and we will apply them to a case study involving a range of political actors and issues.

Rationality and decision-making

A **rational** model of decision-making centres on the assumption that the policy-maker already has clearly defined goals and has a range of tools for obtaining such objectives. The decision-maker is assumed to be seeking solutions to well-determined problems and employing the most optimal (best) means for achieving clearly defined ends. Rationality refers to the normative nature of the process and the means adopted in arriving at decisions.

Rationality Places the individual actor at the centre of analysis, policy-making being determined by individual choice.

Models which consider that there is a high degree of rational decision-making assume that there are clear stages in the decision-making process. From the outset the policy-maker is identified as defining the issues; having accomplished this, the next stage involves determining the key goals and then evaluating alternative methods for achieving them. The final stage involves the decision maker choosing the most appropriate means whereby policy may be enacted.

THINK POINT

Think of a decision you have recently made in your personal or social life. Do you feel you made such a decision according to the criteria laid down by rational theory?

Rationality in social choice theory assumes that the individual:

- can always make a decision, given a range of options;

- can prioritise these different options and decide on which is the most favoured;

- can rank other solutions in order of importance;

- can choose solutions which are the best;

- can make similar decisions given similar options.

THINK POINT

- Reflecting on the above question, were you aware of the range of options available?

- Did you have enough information?

- Were you aware of the implications of available options?

- What criteria did you use to define 'the best' option?

- Were you in a position to make the decision alone, as an individual, or did the decision involve others (i.e. was it contingent on how others would decide and react to your decision)?

The media also tends to interpret policy through the lens of these rational assumptions. Journalists will locate responsibility for policy and make judgements about its success or failure using such rational criteria. The rational theory is less messy and complicated than more complex alternative explanations. Electorates find it comfortable to assume that there is a president or prime minister making rational decisions based on the fullest of information and widest of options in the best interests of the community. However, in politics it is rare for decisions to be made in such an autonomous and isolated way. Usually, decisions are made collectively, involving a wide range of governmental, non-governmental and voluntary bodies. Decisions, rather than being made on the basis of rationality, are made through compromise, bargaining and negotiation, and there is always a strong injection of ideology involving a clear judgement about goals which are seen as good and those which are seen as bad.

Cost–benefit analysis

Cost–benefit analysis A method for balancing and assessing policy options according to costs and benefits.

A prominent method using this rational approach is **cost–benefit analysis** (CBA), which attempts to assess and prioritise all aspects of a problem. Politicians, in making decisions about public projects such as a new road, dam, airport or housing project often use CBA. It will take into account economic costs and then set them against the economic benefits that are expected in the medium to long term.

CBA tends to assume that all issues can be quantified and measured in this way, and it also assumes that comparisons can be made between very different factors and priorities. For example, a new motorway may involve a calculation between (1) the economic benefit of locating it in a particular terrain against (2) the social cost that it may run close to a densely populated housing district or conservation area. Comparisons between such alternatives often become rather superficial and dependent on the relative weight given to such costs and benefits.

Neo-liberal perspectives have attempted to assess public services in this way.

Welfare, housing, education and defence projects have been assessed using this quantifiable method, with relative costs and benefits being placed in the wider context of political and economic demands on resources.

Public choice theory of the New Right stems from assumptions about rationality, and especially rational consumer behaviour based on market conditions of perfect competition. Projects are assessed against such ideal-type criteria. If private market initiatives can provide a more cost-effective service, then policy would indicate that public projects need to be abandoned. In recent years in Britain, for example, services provided by local government have undergone **market testing** and many large national projects, such as the Channel Tunnel, have been financed solely by the private sector. Economic theory, especially micro-economic assumptions about perfectly competitive markets, now plays an increasingly important part in public policy-making.

Key text: M. Olson (1965) *The Logic of Collective Action*, Cambridge, Mass.: Harvard University Press.

Public choice Argues that people make choices according to economic scarcity based on marginal utility.

Market testing A process whereby publicly provided goods and services are compared according to cost and quality with those provided by the private sector.

THINK POINT

- Consider a national or local project which involves key decisions about costs and benefits.
- Draw up a sheet placing costs on one side and benefits on another.
- Now try to weight each item on a scale of 1 to 10.
- Why did you weight the items as you did and what assumptions lay behind your decisions?

Rational models have therefore been crucial in the development of studies about decision-making and policy development. However, it is important to consider the wider political assumptions which underline such approaches:

- hierarchies in organisations tend to determine the decision-making process;
- there are clear demarcations between command and communications in such organisations;
- information can be processed in a clear and logical way;
- expertise and knowledge will be held at a premium;
- non-rational attitudes and behaviour will be marginalised;
- rational planning and decision-making will find it more difficult to deal with sudden and unexpected crises;
- the policy process will tend to be divided into key stages;

- the scale and complexity of problems may lead to decisions being based on rational methods like CBA, which simplifies and quantifies choices that ultimately have to be made;

- decision-making may become routinised and creative thinking may be rejected as non-rational or illogical;

- ultimately politics will intrude, with decisions about options coming down to party ideologies or electoral politics.

Modified rationality

Key text: H. A. Simon (1957) *Administrative Behaviour*, Glencoe, Ill.: Free Press.

The issues raised by a rational model of decision-making have led writers to consider modifications which bring the theory more in line with empirical evidence from the real world of politics.

It is generally accepted that policy-makers will not choose all options available to them, and clearly some will conflict with more deeply entrenched ideological positions. Indeed, some decisions will have unintended consequences which cannot be rationally predicted or planned for.

The policy-maker may also make decisions which conflict with the wider values of the organisation. Organisational structures, procedures and cultures may determine the type and scope of decisions being made and set limits to the options available. Simon (1957), for example, argues that decision-makers are constrained by their personal values, the structure and culture of their organisations and the unpredictability of a complex political environment. Given the problem of the unintended consequences of decisions there are important constraints on such a rational perspective.

For example, clearly the building of major roads has been a priority for governments in reducing congestion, urban blight and pollution. However, many transport experts would agree that more roads actually attract traffic and hence the problem which was supposed to be solved by the original policy is in fact exacerbated by its implementation. This modified view of rationality also contends that the policy-makers themselves import their own value judgements into the decision-making process.

Disjointed incrementalism

Key text: D. Braybrooke and C. E. Lindblom (1968) *The Policy Making Process*, New York: Free Press.

Alternative models of decision-making have differed from these rational and modified rational approaches. Braybrooke and Lindblom (1968) have argued that in practice decision-makers are rather conservative about the decisions they make.

Indeed, they make small decisions, so testing the water or taking one step at a time, rather than following a more fundamental and comprehensive rational approach. They argue that decision-making involves incremental adjustments to existing policy.

Fundamental decisions are therefore rare. Generally, an organisation will decide on a policy and decisions will then follow within this context. Policy develops in a piecemeal and gradual way or through *ad hoc* changes as circumstances change. There will be continuity when policy will change little, but there will also be times of flux or crisis when policy will change but not necessarily in any clear direction. Policy initiatives therefore tend to arise from existing mainstream policies and from orthodox perspectives, and change occurs only gradually over time.

Braybrooke and Lindblom have used the following diagram (Figure 13.5) to explain the nature of this disjointed incremental approach to policy. They argue that quadrants A and B are rare in politics. Quadrant A relates to where there is fundamental change with visionary decision-making, whereas B involves revolutionary or crisis decision-making. Most policy-making in a political system involves small decisions related to quadrants C and D. Quadrant C is dominated by rational decisions where one has clearly defined goals and options. This area is also rare in the real world, where politicians do not have adequate information and knowledge to adopt such a rational approach. Instead, Braybrooke and Lindblom argue that a more realistic position for policy-makers is in quadrant D, where decisions involve small changes and where there is a limited amount of information and knowledge.

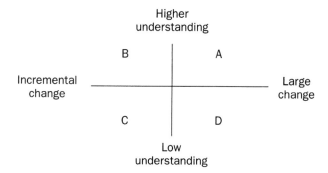

Figure 13.5   Braybrooke and Lindblom's policy-making continuum
Source: Braybrooke and Lindblom (1963: 67)

Disjointed incrementalism therefore involves a modified view of policy-making. Instead of a process conceived in well-defined stages, Braybrooke and Lindblom argue that policy is continuous and cumulative. Policy-makers often attempt to avoid innovative policy initiatives because they are too risky and potentially very costly, especially if they go wrong. Policy-makers attempt to minimise or avoid problems rather than address issues directly.

Lindblom (1959) has called this incremental theory 'the science of muddling through'. However, such muddling through is a more accurate description of how policy is made than the more simplistic and unreal rational approaches. Given that policy is made in a fragmented way, without full knowledge and a centralised and authoritative rational mind, muddling through provides us with a more messy but more accurate interpretation of how public decisions are actually made.

Key text: C. E. Lindblom (1959) 'The Science of Muddling Through', *Public Administration Review* 19.

Lindblom's notion of partisan mutual adjustment involves an acceptance that policy derives from the interplay between contending interests within a more fragmented framework. Normatively, such a view suggests a more democratic and participative ethos, involving bottom-up as well as bottom-down decision-making. As Lindblom has argued,

> The connection between a policy and good reasons for it is obscure, since the many participants will act for diverse reasons. In many circumstances their mutual adjustments will achieve a co-ordination superior to an attempt at central co-ordination, which is often so complex as to lie beyond any co-ordinator's competence.
>
> (Lindblom 1979: 516)

Critics of Lindblom have picked up on this notion of participant mutual adjustment of policy. They point to the underlying conservatism of such an approach in that it assumes that groups have open access to policy-making and that the status quo is the preferred position, given that political stability is formed around it and any changes are small incremental adjustments to it. Such small adjustments seem to rule out more radical changes. The model also appears to eschew any form of strategic planning. It has also been criticised for underestimating the frequency of crises in politics which force governments to make fundamental decisions. In a more global and complex political environment governments find it increasingly difficult to deal with issues in a piecemeal way.

Innovation and mixed scanning

Key text: Y. Dror (1964) 'Muddling Through – Science or Inertia'?, *Public Administration Review* 24.

Dror (1964), for example, has argued that Lindblom's 'muddling through' hypothesis tends to reinforce the pro-inertia view of modern government. He recognises that there is a continuity in the nature of the problems facing governments, although Dror re-injects a notion of rationality into the policy-making process. He believes there has to be both 'realism' and 'idealism' in understanding how policy is made. Yes there is muddling through and incrementalism, although there is also some appraisal and evaluation of options and objectives. Alongside piecemeal decision-making, Dror places creative and innovative methods such as brainstorming. Together they represent both rational and idealist approaches, permitting innovation and creativity in policy to break through the piecemeal nature of incrementalism.

Key text: A. Etzioni (1967) 'Mixed Scanning: A "Third" Approach to Decision-Making', *Public Administration Review* 27.

Etzioni (1967) has also criticised the notion of incrementalism, arguing that muddling through seems to suggest a lack of direction and policy-making which seems disconnected. Instead, he argues that a model of 'mixed scanning' needs to be considered involving policy-making where fundamental decisions are important in that they provide a context for more incremental approaches. A policy-maker attempts to gain a comprehensive view of issues which provides a shape for the more specific and *ad hoc* decisions that are then made on an everyday basis. Etzioni argues:

both elements of mixed scanning help to reduce the effects of the particular shortcomings of the other; incrementalism reduces the unrealistic aspects of rationalism by limiting the details required in fundamental decisions, and contextuating rationalism helps to overcome the conservative slant of incrementalism by exploring longer term alternatives.

(Etzioni 1967: 390)

A problem for Etzioni's approach is in deciding between incremental and fundamental decisions, especially given politicians' use of rhetoric in making more of out of a policy than is justified by the substance of the decision made. Fundamental notions are often used to justify incremental decisions when they are deemed to have been successful.

Organisational and bureaucratic models of decision-making

In examining any policy decision the organisational context has to be considered. As Elmore has indicated, 'only by understanding how organisations work can we understand how policies are shaped in the process of implementation' (Elmore 1978: 187).

Key text: R. Elmore (1978) 'Organisational Models of Social Program Implementation', *Public Policy* 26.

Weber (1947) studied the bureaucratic nature of administration in the modern organisation. Central to his concerns was the notion of formal rationality. The modern bureaucracy is a continuous organisation dominated by functionaries with specific roles, pursuing rules and routine procedures within a structured and consistent organisational framework. Modern organisations are based on a formal hierarchy with clearly defined levels of authority and control.

Key text: M. Weber (1947) *The Theory of Social and Economic Organisations*, Glencoe, Ill.: Free Press.

The implication must be that policy itself is placed within the context of the organisation's objectives, overall strategy and structures. To understand how public policy is made one must therefore look to the departments of state with their officials who formulate and implement policies. There has been a growing interest in the study of organisations and their role in mediating policy. However, in the 1950s writers like Merton (1957) and Gouldner (1954) developed a critique of this rational bureaucratic model of policy-making.

Key texts: R. K. Merton (1957) *Social Theory and Social Structure*, Glencoe, Ill.: Free Press; A. W. Gouldner (1954) *Patterns of Industrial Bureaucracy*, Glencoe, Ill.: Free Press.

They pointed out that a conflict can exist between an organisation's formal system of control and the individual positions of officials within the organisation's hierarchy. For example, the formal authority of the organisation can come into conflict with the particular specialisms and expertise of officials within the organisation. In large government departments, such as education and health, there may be a clear division between different staff, for example between officials and health and educational professionals with contending perspectives and professional values. The goals of the organisation may be translated by those with particular concerns about the nature of the policy being decided.

Another aspect of Weber's work, which has been studied in relation to policy-making, is the concept of 'organisational culture'. Organisations pursue wider values and socialise the officials who work within them. These values are reinforced by organisational control and regulation, and by a structure which rewards conformist behaviour. This wider culture will also provide a context in which decisions are made and will determine the way in which the organisation responds to its environment.

Key text: G. T. Allison (1971) *Essence of Decision*, Boston, Mass.: Little, Brown.

Allison's (1971) analysis of the Cuban missile crisis indicated that policy was developed in response to the bargaining and negotiation between key officials and political actors in the policy-making process.

These officials represented the interests of different departments within the bureaucratic structure, and forwarded certain policies and rejected others on the basis of narrow departmental interests. Hence, decisions were made as a consequence of which departments had most power and where departments could form coalitions in powerful mutual support of certain policy positions.

Bureaucratic politics in modern states constrains elected politicians. A new incoming government may be provided with limited policy options, and a continuation of existing policy is often the norm. Policy change can be very slow, especially if policy initiatives are opposed by senior officials within the bureaucratic structure. Often departments will have long-standing semi-autonomous policy positions with which they will try and influence incoming politicians. Officials will also have ready access across the administrative system, with senior officials often meeting independently of ministers to discuss the framework and development of policy. This process is underpinned by the fact that many senior officials will come from similar social and educational backgrounds, developing close working relationships as they move up in their careers. Officials will also have the advantage of controlling the detail of policy. Elected politicians often find it difficult to cover all aspects of policy detail, so inevitably many decisions will be delegated to officials. Bureaucracies also attempt to 'capture' ministers. Ministers are socialised into the culture of the department, and the process of interdepartmental rivalry creates a team attitude with ministers overidentifying with their departments. This process of 'going native' leads ministers into defending a departmental view against the political views of their government colleagues.

Key text: P. Dunleavy (1981) 'Professions and Policy Change: Notes Towards a Model of Ideological Incorporation', *Public Administrative Bulletin* 36.

Ideology and decision-making

Political decisions clearly are not made simply on the basis of rational or optimal choice. Political parties and politicians are thrust into power by purporting to hold a set of core beliefs and ideas in the form of ideology. Such ideologies often have the effect of excluding ideas, information and empirical evidence when they fail to support the political party's core beliefs. Policy-makers may therefore hold prejudicial views which run in the face of clear evidence related to issues. They support a partial interpretation of events, ensuring there is not a dissonance between perceived reality and their given ideological position on an issue. Shared values can form around important misconceptions. Janis (1972) has developed the term 'groupthink' in examining the psychological basis of these misconceptions.

Key text: I. Janis (1972), *Victims of Groupthink*, Boston, Mass.: Houghton Mifflin.

He argues that policy-makers tend to develop conformist behaviour in order to ensure amicable political relationships. In this way conflict and alternative views are excluded. The tendency for policy-makers 'not to rock the boat' is often legitimised through constitutional conventions like collective Cabinet responsibility which ensures that the 'outside world' sees the government in power as united and undivided by policy conflicts.

The use of ideology and power can also lead to issues failing to enter the political agenda and decision-making process. Interest groups, with powerful access to government, may want to ensure that policy is not formulated and implemented against their interests. The art of non-decision-making is therefore as politically significant as positive decision-making. Bachrach and Baratz (1963) have analysed the issue of non-decision-making. Instead of simply concentrating on policies where there is a visible decision, process and outcome it is equally important to discern that where decisions are not made and where conflicts are hidden, demands remain latent and certain interests are excluded.

Key text: P. Bachrach and M. S. Baratz (1963) 'Decisions and Nondecisions: An Analytical Framework', *American Political Science Review* 57.

THINK POINT

▦ Think of an issue where key policy decisions have not been made and where you think government action should be taken. For example, you may think of issues like more rigorous curbs on tobacco smoking or alcohol; tougher environmental laws; more proactive transport policies; or aid policies for developing countries.

▦ What are the main reasons why you feel governments have been reluctant to make decisions in these areas?

Implementation models of policy-making

More recently the focus of analysis has concentrated on the implementation phase of the policy process. Emphasis has switched from an analysis of rational policy objectives to policy outcomes. Easton's model (discussed above) made the distinction between policy formulation, policy implementation and outcomes. These were arranged in terms of inputs and outputs being processed by a black box of decision-making. In politics much can go wrong between the policy formulation stage and the outcomes of policy. Pressman and Wildavsky (1973) have analysed the limited success of policy implementation in the USA.

Key text: J. Pressman and A. Wildavsky (1973) *Implementation*, Berkeley: University of California Press.

Policy objectives were ultimately confounded by difficulties in practically implementing policy through a complex political system. Pressman and Wildavsky argue that successful policy development depends upon the creation of a network of related institutions in the policy process.

THINK POINT

▦ Consider a recent example of a public policy which was deemed to have been unsuccessful or to have failed to meet its objectives.

■ List the reasons why the policy failed.

■ At what stage – formulation or implementation – did the policy fail?

Key text: B. W. Hogwood and L. A. Gunn (1981) *The Policy Orientation*, Glasgow: University of Strathclyde Press.

Hogwood and Gunn (1981), following on the work of Pressman and Wildavsky, have outlined the key pre-conditions for the successful implementation of policy.

Although they imply a top-down approach, and a set of criteria that can rarely be completely achieved, these 'perfect' conditions for policy success include:

■ the lack of external constraints;

■ the need for adequate time and resources, especially at each stage of the implementation process;

■ better understanding of the relationship between cause and effect in relation to policy issues;

■ the lack of intervening factors which can push the process off course;

■ the need for a single clear implementing body not dependent on other agencies or departments;

■ key policy objectives known and shared by policy-makers;

■ each stage of the implementation process can be demarcated and defined;

■ the need for full commitment among those involved;

■ an agreement on policy control and lines of communication.

Key text: S. Barrett and M. J. Hill (1981) *Policy and Action*, London: Methuen.

Critics of top-down approaches argue that policy is the outcome of negotiations and bargaining between groups that attempt to forge policy consensus on an issue. Barrett and Hill (1981) argue that policy involves a bargaining process whereby compromises are made between different values and interests inside and outside the formulation and implementation process.

Policy-makers have to reconcile the key differences between policy stakeholders and must take into account the latent value and interests in the wider political environment. Barrett and Hill have argued that policy involves a process of continuous movement, with implementation as a policy–action continuum in which negotiation and compromise between interested parties structure the substance of policy itself. In this sense, the rationalistic concern for policy objectives seems less important, if not irrelevant, given the view that the way policy is implemented determines the substantive nature of policy content itself. Within the field of policy studies emphasis has thus shifted to bottom-up approaches. For example, Elmore (1978) has argue that the study of policy involves a process of 'backward mapping', moving from effect to cause and concentrating on those networks of agencies most involved in the implementation process.

Barrett and Hill put much of the blame for top-down approaches on the legacy left by the influence of administrative and managerial perspectives of the policy process. Increasingly, the complexity of the interaction of groups involved in the policy process must be analysed and policy should be seen as a continuous shifting of contending interests placed within the context of a more difficult wider environment.

Advocacy coalitions and negotiated orders

Attempts have been made to draw together many of the ideas already discussed, including an approach that makes use of many aspects of rational and non-rational approaches. Sabatier and Mazmanian (1979), for example, have attempted to develop a general model of the policy-making process which draws together concerns about resources, interest groups, information and ideologies.

They developed a model of 'policy sub-systems' comprising not only interest groups, politicians and bureaucrats, but groups such as policy analysts, journalists, researchers and specific policy professionals. Within policy sub-systems are 'advocacy coalitions' made up of those who share common beliefs and attitudes towards policy formulation and implementation, but who may be located in different parts of the policy-making network. There are also 'policy brokers' who attempt to keep order and to develop compromises around policies which can be meaningfully implemented. Sabatier's model recognises the dynamic nature of policy-making and the shifting pattern of policy coalitions which form around different issues. Rather than taking a more institutional view of policy-making, he sees policy sub-systems as flexible, reaching across traditional areas of the political system. Coalitions are underpinned by shared ideological beliefs and the need for policy outcomes to reflect these core beliefs. Sabatier argues that there are three layers of belief that these advocacy coalitions develop and share:

1 Application of policy related to specific issues;
2 Basic political values and strategies;
3 Deep core beliefs and fundamental ideas.

It is easier to change and negotiate positions at the surface level of policy application related to specific problems. However, it is harder at the deeper levels to compromise ideas regarding basic political values and core beliefs. It is also these deeper core beliefs which will hold together different advocacy coalitions, with some being more powerful than others.

Sabatier's model also takes account of external factors that come to influence and provide a context for the decisions made within the policy sub-systems. In what he calls 'stable system parameters' we find factors which do not change radically over time. These include economic and social circumstances, technological innovations and changes in politics. External factors also include policy outputs from other sub-systems and feedback from previous decisions.

Key text: P. Sabatier and D. Mazmanian (1979) 'The Conditions of Effective Implementation: A Guide to Accomplishing Policy Objectives', *Policy Analysis* 6 (3).

Policy change occurs through what Sabatier calls 'policy learning' involving the interplay between members of advocacy coalitions, including policy-brokers. For example, members of the policy community will respond to evidence of economic and social change through new research ideas. Power-holders will interpret such information, taking it on board if it concurs with existing thinking, while modifying their existing ideological positions if empirical evidence raises insurmountable contradictions. Sabatier has developed a model of these relationships (Figure 13.6).

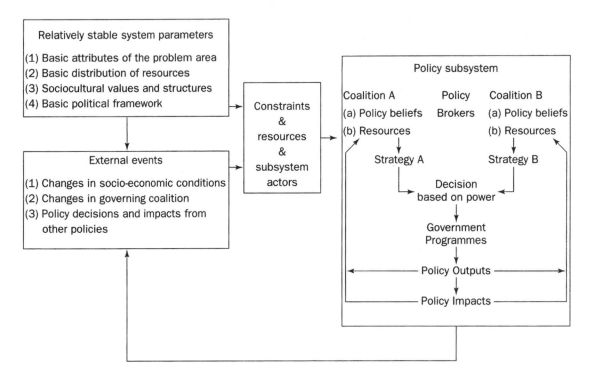

Figure 13.6 Sabatier's policy learning model

With policy sub-systems there will be a number of advocacy coalitions. There will be a stable and consistent difference between contending groups regarding core beliefs, although there will be less stability at the basic political values level and even less agreement at the level of policy application. Policy-brokers will attempt to mediate between these coalitions and ensure policy can be implemented in an agreed and effective way. Generally, there will be one dominant and powerful advocacy coalition within the sub-system, although relative power positions may change as external circumstances alter. Although the most powerful group may dominate in terms of core beliefs, nevertheless there will be compromises, and policy learning takes place as the policy decision develops towards implementation. Groups which respond to the environment and learn faster and more effectively will tend to influence policy even though they are in a minority and play no part within the dominant coalition.

For example, in the 1960s ideas relating to Keynesian demand management dominated treasury thinking in governments throughout the world. With changes in the external economic environment and major contradictions in Keynesian policy, minority coalition groups put forward alternative explanations that attempted to make sense of new economic and political realities. By the 1980s most advanced economies had modified their Keynesian core beliefs for some form of monetarism. Even where core beliefs had not changed, policy was changed pragmatically at the policy application level.

It was the application of policy which was the first to change, although such changes finally allowed new dominant advocacy coalitions to emerge and so win the ideological battle over core beliefs. However, clearly that policy battle is far from over.

THINK POINT

■ Think of an area of policy, such as health, education or economic and industrial policy.

■ Which groups would Sabatier include as advocacy coalitions in these areas of policy?

■ Are there natural coalitions which would form, built around shared common beliefs about particular policies?

Policy communities and networks

The sectorisation of policy is a consequence of the complexity and size of modern government. It remains very difficult to coordinate policy across all policy areas. Richardson and Jordan (1979) have referred to the British administrative and departmental system as 'departmental pluralism' or as a 'collection of separate fiefdoms' which tend to dissolve into factionalism.

The notion of policy communities and networks shows how policy is fragmented, and how different structures and relationships are formed by the stakeholders with an interest in particular policy areas. Boundaries between different government departments and other administrative bodies are ambiguous and will change dependent on particular policy issues. Writers have developed the notion of *policy space* to describe the way in which policy responsibilities and interests overlap and intertwine different organisations. Space is defined by the degree of organisational interdependence. Policy space is related to the concept of policy territory, with departments and other public bodies defending their policy preserves and resisting the challenges from other parts of the administrative system. One can talk of departments at the periphery where policy influence is marginal and locations so far away that influence is non-existent.

Policy networks have been analysed in relation to five key dimensions.

Key text: J. J. Richardson and A. G. Jordan (1979) *Governing Under Pressure: The Policy Process in a Post-Parliamentary Democracy*, Oxford: Martin Robertson.

1 Constellation of interests, including the interests of stakeholders' which may vary according to territory, expertise or service area.
2 Membership, including those elites seen as a traditional part of a policy

sector made up of administrators, business people, professionals, trade unionists and consumers.

3 Vertical interdependence involving relationships between central and sub-central policy-makers and implementers. For example, such relationships may cover the policy concerns of central and regional or local government.

4 Horizontal interdependence involving relationships between different networks, like the example of the Home Office and DTI given above.

5 Distribution of resources within the administrative system, which affects the relative power and influence of different networks both vertically and horizontally.

Policy communities exist where there is some degree of stability and where relationships and responsibilities are continuous over a period of time. There is a process of sharing in terms of responsibility, common objectives, implementation processes and general culture. Communities are also strong where there is some autonomy from other governmental institutions. The least integrated networks are those based around general issues where there are many stakeholders and interested parties and where there is a high dependence on other networks. There are also networks formed around producer and professional interests. Economic and industrial policy is dominated by networks which incorporate commercial interests and depend on the acquiescence of corporate interests for the implementation of policy. Professional groups dominate healthcare and educational policy agendas, where the medical profession and educational establishment are crucial to policy formulation and implementation. In the case study which follows, the close relationship between government and the oil industry was crucial in determining particular policy positions.

Earlier, in the introduction to this chapter, we looked at the foot-and-mouth crisis as an example of the policy process. The following case study about environmental policy attempts to draw together the theories and assumptions which you have examined, and to apply them to a case.

Case study in the policy process: policy learning and the Brent Spar decision

At the beginning of this chapter policy was defined as involving three processes: the intentions of key political actors; the way decisions or non-decisions are made, and the consequences of these decisions. In examining decisions regarding Brent Spar we can address the four key questions also posed at the start of this chapter.

1 What are the dominant values of the key actors and how far are they modified?

2 Who has most power in the policy-making process?

3 How constrained are the policy-makers?
4 How is policy constrained by administrative and bureaucratic processes?

As was indicated in the preceding section, policy may be seen as a web of inter-related decisions and actions. The Brent Spar case study illustrates the way in which policy-makers failed to appreciate the interrelated nature of the decision-making process, the wider environmental framework and the power of bottom-up challenges to the legitimacy of their policy approach.

Introduction

The Brent Spar incident started with a rather inconsequential policy decision by the British government to give permission to Shell UK to proceed with the decommissioning of an old oil storage platform by sinking it in the North Atlantic. This decision came after a three-year period of lobbying by Shell and submissions from technical and scientific experts. Shell had put its faith in what it assumed was a rational policy decision, albeit made fairly secretively by the British energy minister with bureaucratic support from the Ministry of Agriculture, Fisheries and Food, Department of the Environment, Scottish Office and Department of Trade and Industry. However, from initial public information about this decision, the following three months saw an unprece-dented furore between business, governments, international organisations and lobby groups. It ended with the reversal of policy, a fact that contributed to the decision of the British Prime Minister to submit himself to re-election as Conservative Party leader.

The assumption behind the initial policy decision was that a rational decision had been made based on the fullest scientific information and according to the most up-to-date technical data. The political decision rested on, first, the weight of existing scientific evidence, and second, the least cost option, it being estimated that the cost of disposal at sea would be one-fifth of the cost of disposal on land. Interestingly, it was also the case that once the decision had been made both the British government and UK Shell kept doggedly to their position, despite growing opposition within the wider policy network.

There are a number of reasons why such an issue came to destabilise policy-makers. What on the face of it seemed a straightforward, uncomplicated and rational decision ran into many of the problems which this chapter has discussed in relation to the policy-making process. The issue raised questions about how policy-makers had seemed to have lost the power to make decisions, so forfeiting their legitimacy and wider credibility.

The initial policy decision

The initial decision about Brent Spar illustrates Allison's three models of decision-making: the rational actor, organisational and bureaucratic models. The British government, working closely with the oil multinational Shell, assumed that the objectives of the exercise were clear and that implications, options and alternatives had all been carefully considered. Interestingly, in defence of their decision, both the government and Shell reiterated the point that formal procedures had been properly followed. Both legal and technical concerns had been investigated and addressed. However, using the bureaucratic model, it is true that the original decision had been made by a relatively small number of officials, oil company executives and departmental scientists.

Previously we came across the notion of 'corporatism' which emphasises the significant influence that corporate and business interests have over the policy-making process. In this case study, a large transnational company, like Shell, the largest company in Europe, has a wide influence over policy related to its area of commercial influence. There is a mutual coincidence of needs between government and the company. The company requires a stable and attractive commercial environment and the government needs petroleum revenue tax income and a strong industrial sector that can deliver jobs and profits.

In the preceding discussion of rationality and decision-making (pp. 455–6) emphasis was placed on a process which highlighted the importance of hierarchy and informed expertise underpinned by optimal methods and routines which rejected notions of 'non-rational' attitudes and behaviour. Rationality allowed government ministers to defend their original decision by reference to statements like 'this is the only logical way' and 'there are no other viable alternatives based on the logic of evidence'. It also led ministers to underestimate the power of what were seen as non-rational ideas.

In the section which discussed ideology and decision-making (pp. 462–3) it was suggested that some issues fail to get on to the policy agenda because certain groups are excluded. A similar point is made by Sabatier in discussing weaker advocacy coalitions (pp. 465–7). In the Brent Spar case the key decision-makers tended to underestimate the importance of ecological concerns and the green political agenda. They were put on the defensive by the organising abilities of Greenpeace and their vocal and active tactics, such as seizing the media agenda and occupying the oil storage platform itself. Much policy is mediated through television, radio and the press, with public understandings emanating from visual images and messages.

Widening the policy environment: a global dimension

The decision on decommissioning Brent Spar started as a relatively local decision made in London by representatives of the British government and Shell UK. As the dispute over implementation continued, so the issue became part of a much wider environment, first being placed in the context of a global ecological agenda and then within a more European political environment. Greenpeace ensured that 'dumping an installation in any ocean' was a matter of international concern, and consequently the British government was forced to defend its original decision within a wider European Union (EU) context, and Shell UK within the context of its own global organisation. Despite the parochial and limited nature of the original decision, as Sabatier would put it, the policy sub-sytem now had new advocacy coalitions, including powerful foreign governments and the EU Commission. It is important to emphasise that such issues do have global significance given the ever-increasing political interrelationships. It is difficult for individual governments to make autonomous decisions, given the global economic and political systems of which nation states have become part.

The German connection

The issue of sinking Brent Spar in the North Atlantic was a much more salient political issue in Germany, The Netherlands and Scandinavia than in Britain. As a member of the EU the British government came under increasing pressure not only from partner governments, but from the Commission and European Parliament as well. Green groups were able to exploit this widening of the policy agenda and used the Conference on the North Sea in Copenhagen to publicise their views. The German government also used a G7 summit of leading industrial nations to raise the issue and put pressure on the British Prime Minister to reverse his government's original decision.

Again it is the interdependence of nation states within supranational bodies like the EU which must be considered in relation to contemporary policy. The British government found that it was unable to decide on such an issue without support from its political partners. This tends to confirm the pluralist view that there are a numerous sources of power, and in this case, that power was not evenly distributed between the contending interests (see the sections on 'Pluralist explanations', p. 453 and 'Neo-pluralist explanations', pp. 453–4).

In Germany the ruling Christian Democrats were concerned that the issue would not further the election hopes of the Green Party, ousting the government's coalition partners, the Free Democrats, into fourth place and opening up the possibility of a Social Democratic Party-led coalition with the Greens. Leaders of all the main German political parties criticised Shell UK, and the German media were far less equivocal than their British counterparts. The turning point was the realisation that Shell Germany was losing 30 per cent of its sales.

The organisational context: the corporate culture at Shell

To understand how decisions were made in this case study it is important to consider the Shell organisation, its wider culture and its decision-making processes (see the section on 'Organisational and bureaucratic models of decision-making', pp. 461–2).

It has been said of Shell that the 'organisation is like one of its supertankers; once the corporation's course is set it is difficult to stop or turn about'. To appreciate how decisions are made in Shell it is important to consider its 'corporate culture'. The global nature of Shell's business is indicated by its £4 billion income in 1995. It is Europe's largest company and has a history going back to 1907. The Dutch own 60 per cent of the company assets and the UK subsidiary the rest.

The company has a devolved, fragmented and autonomous structure, with central control in the hands of four directors – two in The Netherlands and two in the UK. This structure posed particular problems for Shell during the crisis. At times it was clear that certain parts of the organisation, mainly in The Netherlands and Germany, felt that they had not been adequately briefed and consulted by Shell UK.

In organisational and public relations terms this culture has important consequences too. The decision to decommission Brent Spar at sea was made by Shell UK on behalf of its exploration and production business, Shell Expro. It took a legalistic and technical view of the problem and was accused of hiding behind official procedures and scientific evidence. It failed to scan its own environment in political and ethical terms, remaining inward-looking and mistrustful of a more open PR approach.

The organisational context: Greenpeace and the politics of protest

It is also important to consider the nature of the other main player in this policy arena, Greenpeace. It also has a global organisation. Greenpeace is itself big business, with a global income of £131 million; with reserves of £72 million, it employs 1000, with thirty worldwide offices and 411,000 supporters in the UK and over three million worldwide. Brent Spar provided the opportunity for the organisation to re-involve and motivate its flagging membership. Greenpeace tactics, such as lobbying, public relations with the Greenpeace brand, advertising, protests, boycotts and disciplined direct action were organised by a fairly small number of professional activists at the top of the organisation. For example, one innovative Greenpeace slogan stated, 'If you come back as a whale, you'll be glad you put Greenpeace in your will.'

Another reason why Brent Spar was important to Greepeace was because for a number of years grass-roots activists thought the leadership had become too professional and lobbyist rather than favouring direct action. The occupation of the Brent Spar platform and the counter-action of Shell in removing protesters gave a fillip to the rank and file and allowed the organisation to reclaim much of its grass-roots credibility.

Crisis politics: policy in reverse

Important national newspapers pointed to Brent Spar as an illustration of 'This crisis-prone Prime Minister' (*Daily Mail* headline, 22 June 1995) and referred to 'this Shell-shocked Prime Minister' (Shell U-turn Sinks Major', *Daily Mail*, 21 June 1995). This policy controversy came at a politically sensitive time for the British Prime Minister, given the parliamentary divisions within the Conservative Party over Europe and general unpopularity because of the most prolonged economic recession in Britain since 1945.

The policy reversals on this minor area of policy nevertheless had major ramifications for the Prime Minister. The Brent Spar policy decision brought this to the fore. Questions were asked about a government in crisis, specifically as to why ministers took such a high profile in defending their original decision. Questions were also asked as to why Britain had apparently fallen out with the German government over the issue. Above all, Brent Spar was interpreted by the media as a public humiliation, the cost of which the British taxpayer would have to meet.

Ultimately, Shell reacted to public opinion, a carefully orchestrated PR campaign, European pressure and market signals, whereas the government found itself unable to back down, hemmed in by previous policy decisions and political ideology.

Conclusions

At the beginning of this chapter the point was made that the study of the policy-making process can tell us a great deal about the way in which different political systems operate. This chapter has also attempted to show why the study of policy has become an expanding field within political analysis, and why the relationship between the policy process and the state is important. We have looked at decision-making, and the think points asked you to try and apply some of these different theories and models to particular policies enacted within your own political systems. Finally, the case study on the decision made about Brent Spar highlighted the complexity of even a relatively small decision, and showed how such an issue can involve a wide web of interested groups and stakeholders.

With a single case study like this it is always difficult to generalise about political relationships in general. However, it does help us to try and ground some aspects of these decision-making theories and it is possible to draw some general conclusions about the need for a policy approach in political analysis.

Clearly the main reason why the original decision (however rational) was overturned was because it was so strongly challenged. There were multiple goals involved, as Simon's (1957) notion of bounded rationality would suggest. Green issues, goals related to acceptability to public opinion and media interpretations all combined to make this a much more complex and difficult issue. Shell UK executives freely admitted that they had underestimated the more 'emotive' issues. 'We underestimated the objectives related to hearts and minds' was one such response (Chris Fay, Chairman of Shell UK, quoted in *The Battle of Brent Spar*, BBC TV, 3 September 1995).

The Brent Spar issue also illustrates the close relationship which exists between corporate interests and governments. This single decision was made as part of a long-standing and ongoing relationship between Shell UK, the oil industry in general and the UK government. The substance and form of the Brent Spar decision are clearly a product of organisational factors. The administrative procedures and working relationships of government departments, and the organisational cultures of Shell and Greenpeace were major determinants of how and why such decisions were made.

The Brent Spar case also indicates the importance of the relationship between ideology and belief systems and the policy process. Clearly, what interested parties felt 'ought' to be the case very much determined the nature of the evidence and tactics they used. Ends tended to justify means on both sides of the argument. Greenpeace had finally to admit that it had made important errors in its calculations of data on which its evidence was based. However, the winning of the argument over implementing the Brent Spar decision was seen as a priority.

Sabatier and Mazmanian's (1979) model attempts to integrate several features of these other theories of decision-making. Sabatier developed his model through the examination of a specific area of American public policy, although it can be generally applied in the Brent Spar context. Coalitions clearly did emerge, including Shell UK/British government, Greenpeace/green groups and European governments/European Union. Other coalitions might include the media, church groups and consumer groups. There was also some policy-brokering taking place. Shell Germany and Dutch Shell headquarters acted as brokers in recognising the political need for reversing the decision and then selling the idea to their British subsidiary. The relative stable parameters of the corporate relationship between Shell UK and the British government was thrown into some disarray by external events related to the impact of the Brent Spar decision and implementation process. These constraints and the coalition battle fought out in the media, inside Shell and within the decision-making process of the EU transformed the nature of policy itself.

Politics is essentially a clash between competing interests. In this case study of Brent Spar, the essence of politics may be understood through an analysis of how policy was made and its relationship to what policy was finally implemented.

Conclusion

An understanding of the policy process is important because it provides a good guide to how a political system operates, and the strength of the democratic process within and between states. The process of policy-making involves the initiation, formulation, implementation and outcomes of decision-taking. There are various theories or models of policy-making, including pluralist, corporatist, bureaucratic and ideological perspectives. Models are useful because they underpin assumptions of policy-makers about the way the policy process works. In the case studies it is clear that different stakeholders had different assumptions and used different strategies to influence policy outcomes. The concept of policy networks and negotiated orders is useful in that it places emphasis on coalition building and the fact that policy outcomes are a function of the relative power of different stakeholders. The foot-and-mouth case study showed how policy-making must be seen as a continuous process involving a study of existing policy, issue definition, policy formulation and implementation, policy succession and redefinition, and policy outcomes. The unintended consequence of policy brought on by failures in this wider process can lead to greater policy problems in the future. The Brent Spar case study illustrated the complexity and interrelated nature of policy-making, the conflict between assumptions about issue definition and the power of pressure group challenges to what were seen as legitimate and rational policy decisions.

Chapter summary

 - Understanding how policy is initiated, formulated and implemented tells us a great deal about how a political system operates in the real world.

 - Policy involves the interaction of political actors, the way decisions and non-decisions are made, the implementation of policy, and policy outcomes and consequences.

 - The growing scale and complexity of modern government has made policy-making increasingly difficult.

 - There are several theories or models of how decisions are made which are useful because they tell us much about the assumptions made by policy-makers.

 - The concept of policy networks and negotiated orders is useful in analysing how decisions emerge from a process of coalition building and negotiation between interested stakeholders.

Key texts

Allison, G. T. (1971) *Essence of Decision*, Boston, Mass.: Little, Brown.

Bachrach, P. and Baratz, M. S. (1963) 'Decisions and Nondecisions: An Analytical Framework', *American Political Science Review* 57.

Barrett S. and Hill, M. J. (eds) (1981) *Policy and Action*, London: Methuen.

Braybrooke, D. and Lindblom, C. E. (1968) *The Policy Making Process*, New York: Free Press.

Dror, Y. (1964), Muddling Through – Science or Inertia?, *Public Administration Review* 24.

Dunleavy, P. (1981) 'Professions and Policy Change: Notes Towards a Model of Ideological Corporation', *Public Administration Bulletin* 36.

Easton, D. (1953) *The Political System*, New York: Knopf.

Elmore, R. (1978) 'Organisational Models of Social Program Implementation', *Public Policy* 26.

Etzioni, A. (1967) 'Mixed Scanning: A "Third" Approach to Decision-Making', *Public Administration Review* 27.

Gouldner, A. W. (1954) *Patterns of Industrial Bureaucracy*, Glencoe, Ill.: Free Press.

Heclo, H. (1972) 'Review Article: Policy Analysis', *British Journal of Political Science* 2.

Hogwood, B. W. and Gunn, L. A. (1981) *The Policy Orientation*, Glasgow: University of Strathclyde.

Hogwood, B. W. and Gunn, L. A. (1984) *Policy Analysis for the Real World*, Oxford: Oxford University Press.

Janis, I. (1972) *Victims of Groupthink*, Boston, Mass.: Houghton Mifflin.

Lindblom, C. E. (1959) 'The Science of Muddling Through', *Public Administration Review* 19.

Mosca, G. (1939) *The Ruling Class*, London: McGraw-Hill.

Olson, M. (1965) *The Logic of Collective Action*, Cambridge, Mass.: Harvard University Press.

Pressman, J. and Wildavsky, A. (1973) *Implementation*, Berkeley: University of California Press.

Richardson, J. J. and Jordan, A. G. (1979) *Governing Under Pressure: The Policy Process in a Post-Parliamentary Democracy*, Oxford: Martin Robertson.

Sabatier, P. and Mazmanian, D. (1979) 'The Conditions of Effective Implementation: A Guide to Accomplishing Policy Objectives', *Policy Analysis* 6 (3).

Simon, H. A. (1957) *Administrative Behaviour*, Glencoe, Ill.: Free Press.

Weber, M. (1947) *The Theory of Social and Economic Organisations*, Glencoe, Ill.: Free Press.

Wright Mills, C. (1956) *The Power Elite*, New York: Oxford University Press.

Further reading

Easton, D. (1965) *A Systems Analysis of Political Life*, New York: Wiley. Very prominent and influential systems approach, often cited as the foundation for further studies of policy-making.

Greenaway, J., Smith, S. and Street, J. (1992) *Deciding Factors in British Politics*, London: Routledge. Useful text which employs a range of case studies to demonstrate how theories of decision-making may be applied.

Heclo, H. (1972) 'Review Article: Policy Analysis', *British Journal of Political Science* 2. Wide-ranging and influential article setting out the boundaries of the policy studies discipline.

Holden, R. (2001) *The Making of New Labour's European Policy*, London: Palgrave. Contemporary study of the current British Labour government's attempt to forge a new approach to Europe.

Janis, I. (1972) *Victims of Groupthink*, Boston, Mass.: Houghton-Mifflin. Interesting work which applies ideas from the area of psychology to the policy-making process, the outcome of policy being explained in terms of decision-makers conforming to group pressures.

Theodoulou, S. Z. (2001) *Policy and Politics in 6 Nations: A Comparative Perspective on Policy Making*, New York: Prentice Hall. Example of a comparative study of policy-making across countries.

Wallace, H. (2000) *Policy-making in the European Union*, Oxford: Oxford University Press. Leading textbook on policy-making in the EU covering policies on competition, the single market and monetary union.

Some useful websites

www.euforic.org   Comparative case studies in policy-making.

www.europa.eu.int   EU Commission press room with coverage of EU policy including reports, press releases and a database. There is also an 'Interactive Policy-Making' initiative which is designed to collect and analyse reactions to EU policy-making initiatives.

www.globalpolicy.org   Useful information and sources on United Nations and global policy-making.

www.greenpeace.org   Greenpeace's homepage including photographs and information about recent campaigns.

www.library.truman.edu   Site on US policy-making: how US laws are made and enacted with sources and cases.

www.official-documents.co.uk   UK government policy documents, including White and Green papers, House of Commons papers, annual reports and Acts of Parliament.

www.shell.com   Information about company policy and commercial activities.

www.hm-treasury.gov.uk   Information on UK economic policy, including forecasts, reports, speeches and policy initiatives.

PART 4
POLITICS BEYOND THE TERRITORIAL STATE

POLITICS AND GOVERNANCE ABOVE THE
TERRITORIAL STATE

THE PROCESSES OF GLOBALISATION

CHAPTER 14

Politics and Governance above the Territorial State

Ben Rosamond

CONTENTS

Introduction

The world's dominant political form is the **nation-state**. A glance at a map shows how the world is divided up into units called things like 'France', 'Nigeria' and 'Brazil'. The carving up of territory in this way is, of course, self-evidently political. Nation-states have often emerged in the context of violence, whether in the form of conquest or struggles against colonial powers. The very phrase 'nation-state' suggests a combination of territory on the one hand and authoritative rule on the other. Moreover, one of the things that best defines nation-states is that they command recognition, allegiance and loyalty from their component citizens. Hence, individuals will identify themselves as 'French', 'Nigerian' or 'Brazilian' – often without giving this self-designation a second thought. The recognition of a territory's statehood, as in the cases of former colonies of imperial powers or more recently with the erstwhile component territories of the Soviet Union, is one of the most significant forms of legitimacy that can be accorded in the contemporary period.

Indeed, Benedict Anderson has written that 'nationness is the most universally legitimate value of our time' (1991: 3). The legitimacy of the idea of nationhood manifests itself constantly. First, as suggested in the previous

Nation-state The governmental and administrative apparatus of a bounded national territory. The term is often used as a synonym for 'country'. The most recent way in which human politics has been organised, and now thought by some to be under considerable threat.

paragraph, the actors who constitute the political world – citizens as well as politicians, bureaucrats and activists – almost always see themselves as representatives of or affiliated to a particular national identity. Politicians routinely go to the negotiating table in bodies such as the United Nations, the European Union or the World Trade Organisation to defend or advance their 'national interests'. Cosmopolitan settings such as tourist resorts or universities are characterised by the coming together of people holding various nationalities. To think in this way seems to be in tune with the natural order of things. In his book *Nationalism* Elie Kedourie argues that it is generally supposed that 'humanity is naturally divided into nations, that nations are known by certain characteristics which can be ascertained, and that the only legitimate type of government is national self-government' (Kedourie 1966: 9). These are indeed very deeply embedded assumptions.

They are everyday assumptions, reproduced routinely in our conversations and in the media. But we can also go still further to argue that nationhood is the primary way in which the world has been conceived through the lens of modern political analysis. If we consider concepts such as 'freedom', 'justice', 'rights' and 'democracy', it is clear that these are usually understood as matters that are contested within nations. Indeed, 'the state' – that core concept at the heart of the study of politics – is more often than not seen as a national entity, hence the phrase 'nation-state'. Political scientists will draw fine distinctions, but 'nationness' and 'stateness' are, in spite of that, often used as virtual synonyms, especially in the everyday language of politics. The point to remember here is that the idea of the nation-state provides a powerful organising framework for understanding the way in which the world works politically.

It is a short step from these observations to suggest that nation-states constitute the core component units of politics on a world scale. To date, this book has focused largely on politics within nation-states. Two questions immediately arise. The first is to ask whether politics *among* nations obeys similar rules to politics *within* nations. The second question poses the issue of whether nation-states are indeed the core units of world politics. If they are not, then what is the character of world politics? Which are the key actors? How do they interact? What role *do* states play?

We can reformulate these questions with a more analytical vocabulary. Here the issue becomes one of whether the political science of world politics needs to be different from the political science of domestic politics. Are we, in other words, dealing with two quite separate spheres of action that require us to use different sorts of analytical tools? The separation of the discipline into more or less discrete branches called respectively 'Politics' (or 'Political Science') and '**International Relations**' suggests that this may be the case. On the other hand, many (perhaps most) scholars of International Relations are 'trained' as political scientists and, in the final analysis, much of what academic International Relations does is bound up with exploring issues of power. 'Power' is often identified as political science's equivalent of 'energy' in physics (that is, a core concept around which everything else revolves). Thus while the

International Relations
Formally, the conduct of politics among nation-states, but also the study of international political interaction, which has more recently begun to include the analysis of non-state as well as state actors and forces.

primary purpose of this chapter is to reflect upon the character of politics beyond the nation-state, it also aims to act as an introduction to 'International Relations' as a field of enquiry.

International politics

So far we have worked from the idea that politics is not simply those processes of conflict and collective decision-making that occur within nation-states. Events and processes that are manifestly 'political' (by more or less any definition of the term) take place at a higher level. These processes include war, diplomacy, international bargaining and action within formal and relatively informal institutions. All of these forms of politics involve the interaction of representatives of nation-states in one form or another.

These practices are in no way novel. The practice of diplomacy in various forms – in particular the exchange of the envoys of sovereigns – has existed as long as there have been discrete authoritative units. The same is true, needless to say, of war. The nineteenth-century military theorist and strategist Carl von Clausewitz famously wrote:

> [War] is only a branch of political activity . . . it is in no sense autonomous. It is of course well known that the only source of war is politics – the intercourse of governments and peoples; but it is apt to be assumed that war suspends that intercourse and replaces it with a wholly different condition, ruled by no law but its own. We maintain, on the contrary, that war is simply a continuation of political intercourse, with the addition of other means.
>
> (*On War*, 1832, cited in Luard 1992: 244)

It is tempting to see these authoritative units (states) as the core building blocks of the world polity. National governments become the key actors in this polity. They are, after all, the most obvious representatives of countries on the world stage and are obviously best placed to act as expressions of relevant national interests. The key political interactions are those between juridically sovereign nation-states. This is what is meant by the term 'international relations' and what we usually understand by the phrase 'international politics'.

There are some rather obvious differences between national and international politics. For one thing there is no such thing as a 'world government'. So while national governments sit at the authoritative apex of national political systems and adjudicate over the interaction of various actors within national polities, there is no functional equivalent at the international level. In the language of the discipline of International Relations this characteristic is referred to as **anarchy**. This is not to say that politics above the nation-state is in permanent chaos or is in a state of routine disorder. This is plainly not the case. Politicians, as well as academics, are fond of the expression 'world order' to describe the dominant configuration of forces within international politics

Anarchy The absence of a single recognised governmental authority at world level to enforce laws. In International Relations, the term does not denote a situation of chaos and an anarchic system is not necessarily disorderly.

(Knutsen 1999). For example, the prevailing world order of the second half of the twentieth century – until at least the fall of the Berlin Wall in 1989 – has often been described as bipolar. In this situation, two superpowers – the USA and the USSR – sat at the heart of two quite distinct and rival blocs. This period, known as the Cold War, saw world politics operating along a dominant axis, where more or less any state in the international system would be defined according to its relationship (both militarily and ideologically) to the Western and Soviet blocs. Each rival superpower carried nuclear arsenals capable of destroying the other. For some writers (notably Waltz 1979), order in this situation was supplied by the delicate power balance that existed between the two superpowers.

THINK POINT

- How has the world order changed since 1989 and the subsequent end of the Cold War?

- Given the absence of a world government, what is the best way for a stable world order to be achieved?

This inherent absence of binding and legitimate authority in world politics means that the 'rules of the game' are – on the face of it and out of necessity – rather different from those that determine the conduct of domestic politics. If we imagine international 'anarchy' in the sense defined above, then a good analogy might be to think about a country full of individuals without a government, police force, army and so on. There would be no recognisable authority above the individual. Individuals, keen to survive, let alone protect their autonomy, would have to devise some way of getting along. Otherwise they would descend into the kind of chaos described by William Golding in his novel *The Lord of the Flies* (1997; first published 1954). Individuals would need to arrive at some sort of understanding about how mutual respect for life, liberty and property might be achieved. One of the conditions for being an independent individual would be the need to recognise the individuality of others. In this stylised world individuals might be reluctant to create a government (to supply security) because to do so would be to surrender certain fundamental liberties and rights to self-determination (see Chapter 7 for a discussion of the ways in which liberal political theorists have thought through this problem).

The established rules of international politics are most obviously governed by the doctrine of **sovereignty**. This key idea is perhaps best first approached via a concrete example of its use. Few politicians have been as vociferous in their championing of national sovereignty as Margaret Thatcher, the British Conservative Prime Minister who held office between 1979 and 1990. In her memoirs she writes about the dealings of her government with the European Community (now the European Union) and explains her fear that a more fully integrated Europe would pose a severe threat to some cherished principles:

> Not only were . . . nations functioning democracies, but they also represented intractable political realities which it would be folly to seek

Sovereignty The idea of ultimate political authority. A body is fully sovereign if there is no higher or lower power. Sovereignty has been the basic ground rule for the conduct of the business of International Relations. The widespread legitimacy of the idea of sovereign statehood has hindered the development of authoritative institutions above the nation-state.

to override or suppress in favour of a wider but as yet theoretical European nationhood.

(Thatcher 1993: 743)

In her notorious speech to the College of Europe in Bruges in 1988, Thatcher used the following formulation:

We have not successfully rolled back the frontiers of the state in Britain only to see them re-imposed at a European level, with a European super-state exercising a new dominance from Brussels.

(cited in Thatcher 1993: 742–3)

Thatcher's primary complaint here was that the drift of EC policy was very much out of step with the professed anti-statism of her government. This quotation reveals a fear of the evolution of a powerful, interventionist state at the European level. An emergent European government would threaten to undermine much of what she sees as the Thatcherite achievement in the United Kingdom. But her comments also reveal a more principled objection to the evolution of *any* form of authority at a level above national government. While it is not explicitly mentioned in the two passages above, Thatcher is displaying considerable reverence for the idea of national sovereignty or the notion that ultimate authority ought to reside at the level of national government.

Sovereignty is one of the most written about political concepts. It is the subject of both philosophical discussion and political jousting of the sort illustrated above by Margaret Thatcher. Sovereignty is in essence about the power to make laws and the ability to rule effectively. The concept highlights the obvious connotation of rule by a monarch (a sovereign) who would be, as Foster puts it, 'invested with an authority which confers the force of the law upon whatever he wills' (Foster 1942: 165). This perspective of the all-powerful sovereign was given its most powerful theoretical justification by the English philosopher Thomas Hobbes in the seventeenth century. Hobbes' sovereign need not be a single person; what he was really advocating in *Leviathan* (1651) was that the state be invested with absolute power. Hobbes – thinking through the stylised example discussed above – reasoned that left to a situation of individual self-government, people would engage in the relentless pursuit of their own interests. This would lead to a perpetual power struggle, a 'warre of every one against every one' as Hobbes put it. The only rational course is for individuals to surrender their rights to an authority capable of acting on their behalf as well as to make them keep to the various contracts and deals they may make with each other. The state must be sovereign so that its citizens are protected.

What we can take from Hobbes is the notion that sovereignty is deemed to be essential to the prosperity of the human race and that it ought to reside in public institutions. Indeed, to speak of state sovereignty nowadays is to think about different configurations of institutions – legislatures, executives and judiciaries – which together wield political power.

Over whom is this power exercised? It is at this point that we must introduce the spatial aspect of sovereignty. In modern political discourse the word 'sovereignty' is usually used to denote the combination of political power and territorial space, where that territory is a nation. In other words, sovereignty is said to be an attribute of nation-states, where a country's governing institutions exercise power and effective control over their allotted domain.

In addition, sovereignty is normally understood as possessing two distinct aspects: internal and external:

> at the beginning . . . the idea of sovereignty was the idea that there is a final and absolute political authority in the political community; and everything that needs to be added to complete the definition is added if this statement is continued in the following words: 'and no final and absolute authority exists elsewhere'.
>
> (Hinsley 1986: 25–6)

A state which possesses internal sovereignty is one which has the authority and ability to exercise command over its society. In this situation there are no alternative sites of authority within the nation. But that is not the full story because even if this condition holds, a state is sovereign only if no higher body has authority over that state's assigned society.

The external dimension of sovereignty alerts us to the role played by sovereignty in the global order. If we think about it, the comment made by James that 'sovereignty is the ground rule of inter-state relations' (James 1984: 2) conveys a very profound truth about the political organisation of the world. The Treaty of Westphalia (1648) provided arguably the first coherent statement of the way in which the principle of sovereignty should order the international environment. Violation of the internal affairs of another country was defined as a breach of this nascent international law. Ever since, especially as the world – driven by the forces of nationalism outlined in Chapter 8 – has become divided into nation-states, the axiom of sovereign statehood has been the keystone of world politics. As empires have waned and major global conflicts have been resolved over the course of the twentieth century, so the idea of 'national self-determination' has been the aspiration (if not the reality) of global political organisation.

This is, for example, pretty much the central founding principle of the United Nations (UN) (<http://www.un.org>). At first sight, the existence of the UN might appear to be a threat to the principle of a world based upon independent nation-states. On the other hand, a glance at its founding charter, signed by fifty-one countries at its foundation in 1945 and ratified by a total of 189 by the end of the twentieth century, reveals that sovereign statehood is a central tenet of the UN's concept of world order. Consider the excerpt, reproduced below, from Article 2 of the UN Charter.

Document

Charter of the United Nations, Article 2

1 The Organization is based on the principle of the sovereign equality of all its Members.

2 All Members, in order to ensure to all of them the rights and benefits resulting from membership, shall fulfil in good faith the obligations assumed by them in accordance with the present Charter.

3 All Members shall settle their international disputes by peaceful means in such a manner that international peace and security, and justice, are not endangered.

4 All Members shall refrain in their international relations from the threat or use of force against the territorial integrity or political independence of any state, or in any other manner inconsistent with the Purposes of the United Nations.

5 All Members shall give the United Nations every assistance in any action it takes in accordance with the present Charter, and shall refrain from giving assistance to any state against which the United Nations is taking preventive or enforcement action.

6 The Organization shall ensure that states which are not Members of the United Nations act in accordance with these Principles so far as may be necessary for the maintenance of international peace and security.

7 Nothing contained in the present Charter shall authorize the United Nations to intervene in matters which are essentially within the domestic jurisdiction of any state or shall require the Members to submit such matters to settlement under the present Charter; but this principle shall not prejudice the application of enforcement measures under Chapter Vll.

<http://www.un.org/aboutun/charter/index.html>

Notice the way in which the Charter brings together the principle of sovereign equality, the expectation that member states will act with respect for the sovereign status of other states and the idea that it is inappropriate for states to intervene in the internal affairs of other states.

THINK POINT

How sovereign is your country?

▨ We have seen that sovereignty is an extremely important organising principle in global politics. It provides theoretical justification for the idea of nationhood and legal support for the division of the world into national territorial units. Before we move on we need to reflect on the above passages by asking how realistic the principle of sovereignty is.

▨ Think about your own country. In the terms defined here, is it sovereign both internally and externally?

▨ Write down a list of constraints you think prevent countries from being sovereign in modern conditions?

▨ Do you believe that sovereignty is a good principle for world order? Is the doctrine compatible with other principles such as universal human rights?

So if sovereignty is the organising principle and if no overarching world-level authority exists to regulate the interaction of states, then we would expect diplomacy and war to be the two main ways in which politics occurs beyond the nation-state. If the UN succeeds as an organisation, then the costs of interstate interaction would reduce drastically, all states would subscribe to the principles of sovereign equality and the incidence of war would be reduced accordingly. The UN's self-designated role is to act as a venue for the resolution of arguments between states while upholding the principle of sovereign equality.

These are big 'ifs'. Much of the discussion about sovereignty assumes that the basic tenets of the idea actually hold in practice. In particular the ideas that states are externally sovereign and that states indeed are the only significant actors in world politics are open to question. These claims are vulnerable to challenge, not least in the current period, characterised by both 'globalisation' (see Chapter 15) and the appearance of regional entities such as the European Union (EU) (see below). Framed like this, these become largely analytical questions – issues we can investigate empirically and about which we may come to some measured judgement. However, as we have already seen, sovereignty is also a matter that arouses deep political passions. It is also bound up with a series of normative questions about the shape of world order. So, when we confront the issues and cases discussed in this chapter, we need to be aware that the political issue of how the world *should* be organised is never far from the surface. Moreover, the relationship between seemingly detached theories and the beliefs of real world political actors is rather more fuzzy than we might first imagine.

Thinking about International Relations

International society, then, is most frequently portrayed as the interaction of states, usually through the medium of governments. But if we think about politics beyond the nation-state, it seems clear-cut that states are not the only actors on the stage. So, it is also necessary to attend to the array of non-state actors also present in the processes of global politics. These include international organisations of various sorts, such as the United Nations and the European Union, economic actors such as multinational corporations, various transnational interest groups (such as Greenpeace), as well as the groups located domestically which colour the perceptions and influence the choices of national governments. The key question is: How important are these non-state forces in shaping the conduct and outcomes of world politics?

Rival theoretical perspectives tend to give weight to different actors in the processes of international politics. The discipline of International Relations has consumed debates between rival theories. Traditionally, two schools of thought, realism and liberalism, have vied for dominance in the discipline as the twentieth century has progressed (Brown 2001a: chs 2 and 3).

The *realist* account of politics above the nation-state emerged as a response to the so-called 'idealism' of interwar scholars of international politics. It develops from a number of core assumptions that attempt to remind us of the centrality of power, the logic of self-help and the primacy of security concerns and national interests. These assumptions may be described as follows:

1 The international system is anarchic; that is to say, there is no central authority capable of settling feuds.
2 The main actors in this anarchic system are nation-states guided by the rational logic of their national interests.
3 These national interests are determined predominantly by a rational analysis of the state's place in the international system. They are much less likely to derive from domestic pressures on national governments.
4 States are engaged, then, in the rational pursuit of power and security, which induces a Hobbesian struggle for power at the international level: one state's quest for security may leave other states insecure.
5 Stability and the avoidance of war are not the consequence of the existence of international organisations or systems of international law, but of the development of a balance of power either through the formation of alliances or through the sheer dominance of a single hegemonic power.

These core assumptions mean that scholars from the realist school depict the game of world politics as one in which there is little place for moral principles, ethics or idealism. In addition, the imperative of self-help in pursuit of security lends credence to the doctrine of sovereignty. Sovereign governments, in theory at least, have the capability to undertake those actions necessary for the advancement of national interests. In the last instance, national interest is bound up with the survival of states. So national governments act in ways that are consistent with self-preservation (see the key texts of realist International Relations, particularly Morgenthau 1985 and Waltz 1979). Realists are very keen to emphasise the differences between domestic and international politics. They operate by diffferent logics and, as noted in point 3 above, they are largely separate domains. Realists do not rule out alliances or the development of international organisations, but these usually reflect either the coincidence

Hans J. Morgenthau

Hans J. Morgenthau (1904–1980) is best known for his book *Politics Among Nations*, which was first published in 1948. The book remains a key text for students of IR and is usually thought of as the most coherent statement of the realist school of IR. A lawyer by training, Morgenthau was born in Germany and, like many German scholars of his generation, became an exile from the Nazi regime. He moved to the US in 1937. The 'principles of political realism' that appear in the early pages of *Politics Among Nations* offer a clear rationale for thinking about international politics in terms of self-help, security and anarchy. Morgenthau's academic career was highly distinguished and produced many influential books. But he also acted as an adviser to the US government in the departments of state and defence. Recent scholars have paid detailed attention to Morgenthau's work and have begun to suggest that he was a rather more subtle and ethical thinker than is often assumed.

of national interests or the interests of the most powerful states involved. Alliances and international organisations will dissolve as interests change.

The *liberal* version of international politics is rooted in an alternative set of propositions:

1 Much that is 'bad' about the way states behave is a consequence of the dysfunctional way in which institutions are structured.
2 International conflict and war, then, are not the inevitable consequences of rational, selfishly motivated power politics, but of the structural condition of 'anarchy'.
3 The route to stability and peace in the world consists of the construction of institutions, laws and frameworks of cooperation designed to eliminate the condition of anarchy.
4 States are by no means the only key actors in world politics. A variety of non-state actors partake in the international political game, which is not solely concerned with the quest for power and security but with a host of economic, political, social and ecological issues.

Unlike realism, which only really developed as a solid – though massively influential – account of world politics in the twentieth century, liberalism has a much longer and messier ancestry. As a consequence it has multiple strands, which emphasise different aspects of the liberal international vision. Generally though, as Zacher and Matthew argue:

> liberalism is committed to the steady, if uneven, expansion of human freedom through various political and economic strategies, such as democratization and market capitalism, ascertained through reason and, in many cases, enhanced by technology.
> (Zacher and Matthew 1995: 111)

Routes to international stability may include the construction of international organisations such as the European Union (EU). Early proponents of European integration were strong advocates of the view that the atomistic interaction of nation-states could be overcome by large-scale engineering.

In his book *A Working Peace System* (originally published in 1943), David Mitrany (1966) outlined a strategy for developing a network of functional agencies (to manage areas such as telecommunications) which would lead to the inexorable intertwining of national polities and the gradual waning of national governments as managers of human affairs. Thus, national divisions would cease to be important. Other liberals emphasise less direct routes to global stability, such as the pacifying impact of the spread of democracy across the globe and the complex interdependence wrought by the globalisation of economic activity.

One of the most notable liberal interventions in the study of international politics is so-called 'democratic peace theory'. The idea that democracies do not go to war with each other is not new. It goes back at least as far as the late eighteenth century and Immanuel Kant's argument for an international order populated by 'republican states' (Kant 1948). It has been revived recently by Michael Doyle (1997), who contends that the possession of democratic institutions, a commitment to human rights and the interdependence wrought by liberal economic processes act together to quell warlike urges in states and to reduce the instance of such states fighting each other. They will find alternative modes of conflict resolution. Democratic states do not refrain from war, but the tendency is for wars to be fought against states that remain outside of the democratic, capitalist community.

Michael Doyle

Michael Doyle is renowned as the instigator of the democratic peace thesis in International Relations. The claim of this thesis – essentially that liberal democracies do not fight one another – is elaborated extensively in his book *Ways of War and Peace* (1997). The idea – while controversial – is as close as contemporary IR gets to a 'law' of international politics. Doyle is an influential member of the contemporary academic IR community, but he also acts as an adviser to the United Nations on matters of peace-keeping and human rights. Doyle is currently Director of the Center of International Studies and Edwards S. Sanford Professor of Politics and International Affairs at Princeton University.

THINK POINT

Which model of international politics?

- Realism and liberalism offer two powerful scripts for the depiction of the way in which politics above the nation-state operates.

- Select an issue in international affairs from a newspaper and produce a short summary of the ways in which each of these perspectives might explain the events that you have selected.

The models of realism and liberalism outlined above, it should be understood, are ideal types which few modern scholars would accept in their pure form. As the study of International Relations has developed, so the insights of both schools have been refined and there has been a good deal of productive cross-fertilisation. For example, many recent realist thinkers (in the guise of neo-realism) have tried to locate their state-centric approach within the boundaries provided by the existence of international institutions and regimes. States may continue to be the primary actors within international organisations, but those institutions (or structures) may revolve around norms and rules that either limit the range of possible state strategies or may even contribute to the reformulation of 'national interests'. Interstate cooperation may also coax states away from the international politics of power, security and militarism.

In the past decade, neo-realism has come under increasing pressure from scholars of the *constructivist* school. Alexander Wendt (1999) has tried to develop an approach to studying international politics that remains state-centric. At the same time, he is keen to argue that there is nothing fixed or natural about the conduct of International Relations or the condition of anarchy. While neo-realists see the timeless patterns of interstate interaction as logically determined by the structural imperatives of anarchy, constructivists want to show that anarchy 'is what states make of it'. By this they mean that norms such as 'self-help' and attendant ideas such as 'national interests' are institutionalised as a set of collective understandings held by the key actors in the system. Thus international politics is much more about process than structure. Indeed, these collective meanings – or 'intersubjective under-standings' as Wendt calls them – are central to the way in which the inter-national system is reproduced. The identities and interests of states are not fixed. Rather, they emerge in the context of interstate interaction and help to clarify state self-images, perceptions of other states and the understandings of the environment within which states find themselves.

The debates within and between these schools provide the lifeblood of contemporary academic International Relations. Theoretical endeavour is, as we have noted earlier in this book, not a self-indulgent exercise. Rather it is the way in which we provide readings of real world events and to be open and reflective about our theoretical starting points is the primary way in which we ensure the 'soundness' of our social science. The disagreements that rage in IR theory also reflect different assumptions about the world (that is, they have different ontological starting points). Take the debate between neo-realists and constructivists. The former is a 'rationalist' theory; it treats the component units of the international system (states) as rational self-regarding entities whose interests and preferences are determined by the nature of the anarchic system. This draws on rational choice perspectives which presuppose 'that politics can be understood in terms of the goal-directed behaviour of individuals, who act rationally in the minimal sense that they make ends–means calculations designed to maximise the benefits they accrue from particular situations' (Brown 2001a: 43). Constructivists, on the other hand, 'focus on how inter-subjective practices between actors result in identities and interests being formed in the processes of interaction rather than being formed prior to interaction' (Smith 2001: 244).

The end of international politics?

In recent years the idea that nation-states are able to be sovereign has been the subject of serious challenge. For many analysts, the study of a country's politics in isolation from the broader global environment has become impossible. This is based on claims that events elsewhere may have a serious effect upon a country's politics. Say, for example, the economy of country *x* is heavily reliant on the inward investment of a multinational corporation that originates in country y. The relocation of the multinational corporation from country x to country z is likely to have a serious effect upon employment levels in x. This in turn is likely to have a potentially destabilising effect upon the government of x, which may be blamed for the fall in employment and be called to task over its general competence in economic management. In anticipation of the multinational's relocation, the government of x may opt to reduce corporate taxation levels so as to provide an attractive environment for inward investors (it may be trying to retain the loyalty of the existing multinational or it may be looking for other companies' investment). The reduction of taxation levels will lead to a decline in government revenue. This in turn may force the government of x to force through cuts in public expenditure. These, of course, may prove to be unpopular.

This is a highly stylised example, and it has to be said that international and comparative political economists will argue about virtually every sentence of the previous paragraph. That said, it is not unusual to hear arguments about this sort of scenario issuing from politicians and journalists alike. The government of x appears to be in some sort of 'catch-22' situation, while power seems to reside very much in the hands of the multinational. The latter seems capable of forcing down corporate taxation rates so that countries x and z appear to be engaged in some sort of 'race to the bottom' to ensure that they attract the sort of inward investment necessary to sustain domestic employment levels. Notice also that we have mentioned country y only once – as the location of the head office of the multinational. The extent to which the corporation is an agent of country y is a matter for considerable debate. For some, multinational and transnational companies are becoming largely stateless. So, in our example, what happens in x and z has potentially very little to do with what happens in y.

Obvious questions about the external sovereign status of nations are raised. One of the principal contemporary political theorists of this transformation is David Held. He points out:

> there are disjunctures between the idea of the state as in principle capable of determining its own future, and the world economy, international organizations, regional and global institutions, international law and military alliances which operate to shape and constrain the options of individual nation-states.
>
> (Held 1991: 212–13)

A further observation is that forms of authority above the nation-state have come into being and, as we have noted above, politics takes place in various forms above the nation-state. Again, the external dimension of sovereignty appears to be threatened by forces apparently beyond the control of national governments.

Much of this is bound up with the processes of globalisation (addressed in Chapter 15). Here we need to identify the kinds of issues which threaten the external sovereignty of nation-states and which might also help our understanding of the creation of international and potentially supranational bodies that exercise authority above the nation-state. What we need to understand is the processes which 'alter the range and nature of decisions open to political decision makers within a delimited terrain' (Held 1991: 213).

The most obvious of these factors is the operation of the world economy. In the same way that we regularly speak of nation-states, so we also refer to national economies and assume that it is possible for governments to possess programmes of fiscal, monetary and industrial policy. The rules of the political game in democratic polities demand that parties vying for public office make promises about the ways in which they will, if elected, improve the economic fortunes of their respective nations. If governments preside over economic failure they risk electoral catastrophe. The built-in assumption here is that nation-states possess economic sovereignty; that the governments of Australia or The Netherlands are able to control the collective economic fate of Australians or the Dutch.

However, with the increases in multinational production, the rise in the global flows of goods and services, advances in communications and information technology and the growth of global financial exchange, serious doubts have been raised about the ability of governments to maintain control over the economic determinants of their countries' well-being. These dilemmas are expressed well by the British economist Will Hutton:

> The world financial system is spinning out of control. The stock of cross-border lending now exceeds a quarter of the GDP [Gross Domestic Product] of all industrialised countries. International bank assets are double the value of world trade. The volume of business in the currency futures markets exceeds even that generated by daily trade flows. . . . Not even the US, German or Japanese governments have the financial clout to deal with the new volume of speculative flows – while many developing countries lack enough reserves to cover the purchase of eight weeks' imports.
>
> (*Financial Times*, 25 January 1995)

In addition, there exist a range of global institutions which appear to promote a particular international economic orthodoxy and therefore allegedly force governments to pursue particular patterns of policy. The operation of the International Monetary Fund (IMF), which was founded in 1945, provides a good example. The IMF was designed with the aim of creating a more stable international economic order so that trade and economic development in the postwar world would not be threatened by major upheavals in international money markets. Member countries would be able to draw on the Fund's resources when confronted with domestic economic difficulties such as heavy balance-of-payments deficits and currency crises. The aim was to avoid the situation just before the Second World War when the world capitalist economy was hit by a series of tit-for-tat devaluations that had the effect of stultifying trade. However, there would be a price to pay for any country that drew on the IMF's reserves of international liquidity. The IMF was empowered by its founders to dictate policy restrictions on large borrowers, usually in the form of public expenditure cuts and deflationary packages. In effect, therefore, an international institution appeared to have the power to intervene directly in the economic policy-making of nation-states.

This fact has not been lost on politicians. Lawrence Harris quotes the exasperated response of the Finance Minister of West Bengal to the IMF loan given to India in 1981:

> Over the period during which the loan is to be disbursed, India's monetary and fiscal policies – including the size of the internal money supply, the structure of taxation and the quantum of budgeted deficits – would be formulated not in New Delhi, but in Washington; never mind the Industrial Policy Resolution and several declarations of national intent in the National Development Council, parliamentary resolutions and Five-Year Plan documents . . . the Union Government has agreed, in conformity with the Fund's wishes, to accord special privileges to the private sector, including foreign investors, and to reverse the policy of import substitution and allow imports of even such banned items for which we have built adequate productive capacity in the country.
>
> (Ashok Mitra, cited in Harris 1984: 80)

These comments reveal a serious concern about the ability of the various layers of government in India to follow the policies that they have a legitimate right to pursue. The suggestion is that institutions such as the IMF are the tools of powerful – hegemonic – countries that seek to impose their interests on the world. One interpretation of the rise of such constraints, then, is that they are the product of a form of power politics, where states still matter but the most (economically) powerful states matter most.

Others would see the operation of the IMF as a symptom of the 'embedding' of a particular set of economic ideas in the global economy. The first interpretation offers a nation-state-centric version of the constraints on states, whereas the second emphasises the more abstract – but no less powerful – logic of the global capitalist economy.

This has led some commentators to talk about the 'retreat of the state' (Strange 1998), a situation where authority in world politics has become more diffuse and is no longer an exclusive preserve of states. This situation is one where the loss of state power has corresponded to a rise in the power of markets and market actors. As Susan Strange put it: '[w]here states were once the masters of markets, now it is the markets which . . . are the masters over the governments of states' (Strange 1998: 4).

Governments are further constrained by the systems of collective decision-making that have emerged in the context of international organisations. As Held (1991) notes, such organisations range from technical and uncontroversial bodies such as the World Meteorological Organization and the International Telecommunications Union to the likes of the UN where major debates about the propriety of states surrendering sovereignty are played out.

Susan Strange (1923–98) was a pioneering figure in the modern study of international political economy (IPE). She began as a journalist writing for *The Economist* and the *Observer* on economic, financial and international affairs. Her academic career began in the 1950s at University College London. Thereafter, she held positions at the Royal Institute for International Affairs, the London School of Economics, the European University Institute and the University of Warwick. Her 1971 article entitled 'International Politics and International Economics: A Case of Mutual Neglect' argued for the breaching of the boundaries between the two disciplines. Her subsequent books, notably *Casino Capitalism*, *States and Markets*, *The Retreat of the State* and *Mad Money* filled out this theme considerably and argued consistently that the global power structures had changed significantly in the direction of non-state and market authority. Her work remains central for all students of IPE.

Susan Strange

One notable side-effect of the growth of international organisations and institutions is the emergence of bodies of international law. These set in place the principle that in some instances nation-states cease to be the highest form of authority for citizens. Of particular importance have been attempts to produce binding international commitments on the protection of human rights. Declarations such as the Council of Europe's *Convention for the Protection of Human Rights and Fundamental Freedoms* (Council of Europe 1950) are premised on the view that human rights transcend national boundaries and that the appropriate definitions of rights and freedoms are not the business of national authorities. The European Convention opens up the possibility that citizens can take their own governments to the European Court of Human Rights.

The appearance of international law raises fascinating questions about transnational justice. The trials of alleged Nazi war criminals at Nuremberg in 1945 and the subsequent prosecutions of similar suspects in Israel raise fascinating questions about the relationship between the state and its citizens, the right of national courts to prosecute citizens of other countries and, in the case of the two Israeli prosecutions, the right of a nation-state to adjudicate on crimes which did not take place within its territory. As Held notes, the Nuremberg tribunals set down the principle that 'when *international rules* that protect basic humanitarian values are in conflict with *state laws*, every individual must transgress the state laws (except where there is no room for 'moral choice')' (Held 1991: 220; emphasis in original). These issues are central to the Pinochet case, discussed later in this chapter.

A further incentive for governments to emerge from the cocoon of sovereignty concerns the perception that genuinely *global* issues have emerged. The recognition that the world was on the verge of a serious ecological crisis became a widespread component of mainstream political discourse in the mid-1980s. Politicians and opinion-formers alike began to propagate the view that the only way to address this issue was through some form of international cooperation at the very least. The appearance of issues such as ozone depletion, global warming, acid rain and pollution illustrates very effectively the juxtaposition of the doctrine of national sovereignty and the global ecological totality.

Two analysts of the decline of sovereignty use the example of the accident in 1985 at the Chernobyl nuclear power plant in the Ukraine (then part of the USSR) to illustrate this point:

> As the fire raged and then smouldered, over some ten days vast quantities of radioactive gases poured into the air. The plume of radioactive gases swept across Scandinavia, then spread southwards over other parts of Europe, moving on to contaminate parts of England and then dispersing over an even wider area causing significant increases in radiation levels as far afield as Japan. A number of governments were forced to introduce emergency measures – from monitoring radiation levels to withdrawing certain foodstuffs or advising communities to change their diet. . . . What became clear from the first few days was that although national governments might construct nuclear reactors and even lay down various regulations intended to make their operation safer, the actual risk they posed extended beyond the control of any single state.
>
> (Camilleri and Falk 1992: 177)

Ecological issues highlight two very different ways of conceptualising the world which have vital political implications:

1 The view of the world as a single place, where actions in one part of the globe can have profound consequences in distant locations.
2 The view of the world as consisting of individual territorial units, each with its own legitimate jurisdiction.

The pervasive doctrine of sovereign statehood, argue Camilleri and Falk, poses a serious threat to a sustainable global ecology. First, the idea of sovereignty tends to separate the state from the ecological consequences of its actions. Second, different regulatory standards in different countries will allow polluters to operate in areas where legislation is less rigid. Third, adherence to the idea of nation-states as the primary makers of world politics ignores the forceful dynamics of global political and economic power which induce environmental damage. Finally, they argue that powerful allegiance to the doctrine of sovereignty blinds us to the cooperative procedures and institutional developments that are necessary for the resolution of environmental crises.

THINK POINT

- Do the nation-state system and the dominance of the idea of sovereignty damage the prospects for a sustainable environmental future?

░ Consider the arguments of Camilleri and Falk (1992) outlined above.

░ You may agree or disagree with their position, but whatever your view, try to develop an argument that might be able to counter their claims about the damaging effects of the doctrine of sovereignty.

░ In particular, try to construct an argument in which action by sovereign nation-states can address ecological problems.

Breaking the mould of international politics? The European Union

The European Union (EU) provides us with an intriguing case study of many of the issues raised above. It forces us to confront head-on the question of the extent to which states remain key actors in charge of their own fate. It also serves as an instance of the development of institutions and norms that seem to indicate the evolution of political and decision-making processes above the nation-state. It possesses a mature set of institutions and is – by some distance – the most developed project of **regional integration** in the world. Of no less importance is the undeniable fact that EU-related matters are increasingly pivotal in the day-to-day politics of its member states. The fractious debates within and between British political parties about the proper relationship between the UK and the EU provide an obvious illustrative example.

On the face of it, the EU is something different. Citizens of the member states may from time to time be bewildered by the complex workings of its various institutions. Yet the EU is clearly not one of those obscure organisations to which national governments send delegates to talk about recondite matters of the highest politics. Its very existence and the decisions that are made in its name are deeply embedded in the politics of member (and for that matter non-member/candidate) countries. The general impression is that the EU is an organisation where power resides and from which emerges legislation that has an impact on the daily lives of ordinary people.

The space here does not allow for a detailed discussion of the workings and scope of the EU (for which see in particular Nugent 1999). Our job here is to think about the EU as a case study of the operation of politics above the nation-state. With that brief, several questions come to mind:

░ What is European integration and why has it taken place?

░ Do the factors that account for the genesis of what we now know as the EU still explain its dynamism?

░ To what extent have particular or unique patterns of politics evolved within the EU's institutions?

░ Is the EU emerging as a new form of government or as a state?

░ Does the development of the EU demonstrate the decline of the nation-state as the key unit and focus of political activity in contemporary Europe?

Regional integration The process by which states in particular regions of the world bring together aspects of their economies and polities. There is much debate about the stimulus for such developments, with some seeing the cause as residing in the sovereign preferences of states themselves. Others argue that integration occurs because of the operation of powerful dynamics beyond the control of nation-states.

European integration

'Integration' is not easily defined. Yet at the same time it is a word used frequently by politicians and journalists as well as academics to describe what goes on within the EU. A 'good' political scientist would attempt to produce a general definition of integration. This would be a stepping stone to making judgements about the extent to which 'Europe' has undergone a process of integration as well as being a basic requirement for the meaningful comparison of multiple instances of integration in different times and places. The problem – as ever – in social science is that attempting to construct definitions tends to pose rather more questions than it settles.

A good place to commence is with the classic definition supplied by Ernst Haas, one of the pioneering writers on regional integration in general and European integration in particular. In his book *The Uniting of Europe*, Haas defines integration as:

> the process whereby political actors in distinct national settings are persuaded to shift their loyalties, expectations and political activities toward a new center, whose institutions possess or demand jurisdiction over pre-existing national states. The end result of a process of political integration is a new political community, superimposed over the existing ones.
>
> (Haas 1968: 16)

Ernst B. Haas

Ernst B. Haas (1924–), the Robson Research Professor of Government (Emeritus) at the University of California Berkeley, has written extensively and with great influence about international organisations and the trajectory of politics beyond the nation-state. In particular, he is known as the founding father of neofunctionalist theories of integration. His Jewish family emigrated from Nazi Germany to the United States in 1938. Following the Second World War, Haas rose quickly through the academic ranks. He attributes his interest in international relations to his personal background. His book *The Uniting of Europe* (1958) was both a detailed study of the European Coal and Steel Community and a careful theoretical elaboration of the role of non-state forces in international organisations. These ideas were further developed in *Beyond the Nation-State* (1964), and neofunctionalism was embellished and developed by Haas and a group of colleagues throughout the 1960s and the early 1970s. Haas became increasingly interested in the study of international interdependence and moved away from European studies in the mid-1970s. Since then he has written a pioneering study of knowledge in international affairs and, most recently, his book *Nationalism, Liberalism, and Progress: The Rise and Decline of Nationalism* (1997) offers a thoroughgoing analysis of nationalism – the resilience of which came to perplex neofunctionalists back in the 1960s.

Notice how the process is labelled 'political'. Haas took the view that the integration of economies would lead to the shift of power away from nation-states. But notice also how he talks about a process of loyalty transference, suggesting that attempts to shift power upwards to (say) the European level can only be accomplished if key societal groups see this as a legitimate and desirable end. In Haas' account, domestic social groups would be persuaded because the beneficial realities of economic integration would make them interested stakeholders in the transfer of authority to a higher level. So perhaps integration is accomplished at the point where a new political system emerges. Reginald Harrison put this into a political science vocabulary:

> The integration process . . . may be defined . . . as the attainment within an area of the bonds of political community: of central institutions with binding decision making powers and methods of control determining the allocation of values at the regional level and also of adequate complementary consensus-formation mechanisms.
>
> (Harrison 1974: 14)

(Political) integration in this sense seems to be about the manufacture of the attributes of a political system from two or more previously separate systems. This involves both the creation of common institutions and the development of adequate levels of public support to ensure that the new system is endowed with legitimacy. Thus many writers on integration, such as Karl Deutsch (1957), have thought about the similarities between international integration and the processes of nation-building (mentioned above, and see Chapter 3), albeit on a much grander scale.

However, such definitions presuppose a particular destination for a successfully 'integrated' Europe. Is the case really that an integrated Europe will be one that possesses not only common institutions, but also a sense of community, a common identity and the various attributes that we would normally associate with statehood? Other scholars have quite different views of what integration entails. For example, economists of the 1950s and early 1960s (such as Balassa 1962) tended to understand integration as a five-stage process involving the gradual merger of discrete economies into a single economy (Table 14.1).

More recently, political economists have thought about the relationship between the dramatic changes in the organisation of production on the one hand and the forms of regulatory authority that may follow on the other. In particular, the development of cross-border company organisation and activity has effectively created a set of *transnational* economic actors. Their operation and efficiency is hindered by the existence of separate national regulatory regimes. For instance, it is more straightforward to engage in a cross-border company merger under a single regulatory authority than having to deal with multiple sets of national competition policy rules. Actors operating in an embryonic transnational space thus have a stake in the development of rule-making transnational institutions (Stone Sweet and Sandholtz 1998). From this point of view, integration is about the combination of an economy defying national borders with regulation by post-national forms of authority.

Others still prefer to see integration as a cultural phenomenon: the development of intensive patterns of interaction among previously separate peoples

Table 14.1 Stages of economic integration

Stage	Title	Attributes
1	Free-Trade Area	Removal of tariffs between two or more economies
2	Customs Union	Imposition of common external tariff by all members of the free trade area
3	Common Market	Removal of all barriers to the free movement of goods, services and persons amongst member states
4	Monetary Union	Development of a single currency and a common monetary authority
5	Total Economic Integration	Common economic policies; attributes of a single economy

through forms of communication such as computer technology, tourism and business exchange. This has led some to offer yet more generic definitions of integration. William Wallace describes it as 'the creation and maintenance of intense and diversified patterns of interaction among previously autonomous units' (Wallace 1991: 9).

Wallace goes on to make an important distinction between *formal* and *informal* integration. Formal integration is the deliberate creation by governments in concert of institutions, norms and procedures via treaties, regulations and decisions, whereas informal integration consists in the growth of networks of interaction without the conscious intervention of governments. Again we find ourselves in a debate about the role to be attributed to the agency of the nation-state in the development of politics above the nation-state. Are major advances in European integration to be understood as the result of member states pursuing their national interests? Put more precisely, does a major development such as the signing of the Treaty of Rome, the creation of the single market or the initiation of a common currency reflect the converging interests of member states (Moravcsik 1998)? Or does the very existence of regional integration denote the weakening of the power of nation-states?

In any case, we need to be cautious about whether we understand integration as a process (or a set of processes) or as a particular outcome or end point. Again, different perspectives emphasise different key variables involved in the processes of integration and depict very different integration outcomes (Rosamond 2000). When we examine an organisation like the EU, it is as well to be conversant with the various alternative accounts of what drives it and where it might be going. Some of these are summarised below.

Alternative accounts of European integration

Integration as process

(a) Political variables

Key issues: which are the main agents of integration, nation-states or non-state actors such as the European Commission or transnational interest groups?

(b) Structural stimuli

Key issues: what external economic, social and technological variables drive the integration process? Do they work independently of governments, or do they act as agenda-setters for intergovernmental business?

Integration as outcome

(a) State models

Alternatives: a centralised, authoritative set of institutions at the European level; a European 'federal' system, with a layering of power between Europe, nation and sub-national region; a supranational network involving the interaction of state and non-state actors.

(b) Community models

Alternatives: a European security community; a European socio-psychological community; the enhanced interaction of the peoples of Europe.

(adapted from Pentland (1973))

One further issue to consider at this stage is the extent to which European integration is typical of regional integration more generally. Early theorists such as Haas (1968) certainly planned to use the European experience as a seedbed for developing general theories of integration. The question remains a pertinent one today because of the variety of regional integration arrangements that exist in other parts of the world. Examples include the North American Free Trade Agreement (NAFTA), the Association of South East Asian Nations (ASEAN) and Southern African Development Co-operation (SADC). While these all represent forms of politics above the nation-state involving closer cooperation and agreement between member states, the extent to which either they are comparable to the EU or represent instances of the same phenomenon as the EU remains open to question. As we will see below, integration in the EU has 'deepened' to a remarkable and unmatched extent. Moreover, its level of institutionalisation is peculiar. Its possession of supranational institutions is especially novel and the architects of regional integration elsewhere have shied away from similar acts of institutional design.

Some of this may be explained by the EU's longevity (see the chronology below). Since the EU has been around longer than any other regional integration scheme, then perhaps it is at a more advanced stage of development. Perhaps; but others argue that the EU is a unique enterprise, rooted in the specific circumstances of postwar European history. This train of thought leads some analysts to argue that the EU should not be studied through the lens of

International Relations. Instead, runs the argument, we should view the EU as a political system like any other, full of actors pursuing their particular interests and not preoccupied with the question of integration (Hix 1999).

European integration since the Second World War: a brief chronology

1947	Establishment of 'Benelux' customs union involving Belgium, The Netherlands and Luxembourg. Beginning of 'Marshall Aid' (American financial assistance for the economic reconstruction of European countries).
1948	Organisation for European Economic Cooperation (OEEC) founded.
1949	Establishment of North Atlantic Treaty Organisation (NATO). Ten countries sign statute of the Council of Europe.
1951	'Benelux' countries plus France, Germany and Italy sign the Treaty of Paris, forming the European Coal and Steel Community (ECSC), the product of the 'Schuman Plan' of the previous year.
1954	Treaty for a European Defence Community rejected by French National Assembly.
1955	Messina conference convened by the ECSC 'Six' to discuss further European integration.
1956	Treaties of Rome signed by the 'Six' to establish the European Economic Community (EEC) and the European Atomic Energy Community (Euratom).
1960	Convention of the rival European Free Trade Association (EFTA) signed by Austria, Denmark, Norway, Portugal, Sweden, Switzerland and the UK.
1961	The UK, Denmark and Ireland begin negotiations to join the Community (Norway follows a year later).
1962	Agreement for framework for a Common Agricultural Policy (CAP).
1963	The French President Charles de Gaulle vetoes British membership.
1965	The three Communities formally merge.
1966	French boycott of EC institutions because of feared supranational developments is resolved by the 'Luxembourg compromise' which enshrines the veto on vital national interests into EC practice.
1967	The four applicant states reapply for EC membership, but French opposition to UK membership prevents the renewal of negotiations.
1970	Membership negotiations again begin with the 'four'.
1972	Norwegian referendum produces majority against EC membership.
1973	Denmark, Ireland and the UK formally join the EC.
1975	Meetings between heads of government in the EC are formalised with the first meeting of the European Council.
1979	Establishment of the European Monetary System (EMS). First direct elections to the European Parliament.

continued

continued

1981	Greece becomes the tenth member state of the EC.
1983	Agreement on Common Fisheries Policy (CFP).
1984	Establishment of free-trade area between EC and EFTA.
1985	Plans to complete the EC's internal market are approved in the form of the Single European Act (SEA), which vows to accomplish the task by the end of 1992.
1986	Portugal and Spain join the EC.
1987	SEA comes into force.
1989	'Delors Report' offers three-stage plan for progress towards full economic and monetary union (EMU) within the Community. European Council accepts a Commission 'social charter' to complement the economic measures outlined in the SEA.
1990	Former German Democratic Republic becomes part of EC following German reunification.
1991	European Council meets at Maastricht in The Netherlands, producing the Treaty on European Union (TEU). The final TEU excludes a 'social chapter' (due to the insistence of the UK government) and contains opt-outs for Denmark and the UK on membership of a full EMU. The TEU creates a European Union based on three 'pillars': the European Communities, Common Foreign and Security Policy, and Co-operation in Justice and Home Affairs.
1992	Narrow rejection of TEU in Danish ratification referendum.
1993	Second Danish referendum produces majority for ratifying the TEU.
1994	Norwegian referendum rejects EU membership.
1995	Austria, Finland and Sweden join the EU.
1997	The Treaty of Amsterdam is signed making modest changes to the existing framework.
1999	Monetary union commences for the twelve 'euro-zone' countries (Austria, Belgium, Finland, France, Germany, Greece, Ireland, Italy, Luxembourg, The Netherlands, Portugal, Spain). The European Commission of Jacques Santer resigns *en masse* in a corruption scandal.
2001	The Treaty of Nice grapples with the problems of managing a drastically enlarged EU to include a large number of new member states.
2002	Euro notes and coins enter into circulation in the twelve 'euro-zone' countries.

The origins of the European Union

Projects of one sort or another to 'unify' Europe are certainly not new (den Boer 1994; Heater 1993), and projects for something analogous to a 'united states of Europe' were especially prevalent in the period after the First World War (Bugge 1995). Such ideas were also part of the political mood of the late 1940s, as several major European politicians were persuaded of the need for some form of European unification as a means to prevent further conflict between nations on European soil. So while ideas were important, they were given credence by the security dilemmas confronting European politicians and publics in the aftermath of the Second World War. Two particular security questions were of importance. First, it was felt that the avoidance of war on the European continent would turn on the resolution of the historical antagonism between France and Germany. This was the rationale behind the so-called Schuman Plan of 1950 (named after the French Foreign Minister Robert Schuman) that led to the creation among six European states of the European Coal and Steel Community (ECSC) in 1951.

Jean Monnet (1888–1979) is best remembered as one of the founding fathers of postwar European unity. Monnet was trained as an economist and spent much of his life in public service working on issues of coordination and planning. Together with French Foreign Minister Robert Schuman, Monnet was the author of the plan of 1950 to create a European Coal and Steel Community under a Common High Authority. Monnet became the first president of the High Authority. Monnet's legacy is captured by the term 'Monnet method', used to describe the model of intergovernmental and supranational partnership that lay behind the design of the ECSC's institutions and which has survived (formally at least) to the present European Union. Monnet was a believer in the capacity of incremental, technocratic integration to produce lasting peace.

Jean Monnet

The ECSC was based on a very deliberate political strategy. Its first act would be the creation of a common market in commodities such as coal, steel and iron ore. This would be presided over by newly created supranational institutions. By bringing together these crucial economic sectors, it was hoped that three things would occur:

1 The creation of a state of interdependence between member countries, thereby reducing the propensity for conflict between them.
2 The initiation of an integrative logic that would compel other economic sectors to be drawn into the process.
3 The consolidation of central institutions which would emerge as the most important focal points of political loyalty in the new community.

The key lesson here is that the integration of economies was an element in a much longer term political strategy. To render countries economically interdependent was to lay the basis for their eventual political union.

The second main security concern was the development of the Cold War. The postwar political map of Europe was characterised by a clear East–West division separated by what Winston Churchill memorably called the 'Iron Curtain'. The division of Europe into the communist East under the influence of the USSR and the liberal democratic West was consolidated by developments such as the US government's Marshall Aid programme to non-communist European states (beginning in 1948) and the foundation of the North Atlantic Treaty Organisation (NATO) in 1949. This meant that Western European states had acquired a rationale for closer links beyond their geographical proximity.

The influence of the United States as a 'hegemonic power' in the Western world was clear from the vantage point of postwar security dilemmas. It could also be argued that US influence was decisive in the drive towards the creation of an integrated European economic region. After all, the US had emerged from the war with its domestic economy intact and a global economic regime (the Bretton Woods system) which was conducive to American dominance of world trade. Western Europe could then be understood as one of the US's most viable markets, but one which required urgent reconstruction. This could be galvanised through integration.

THINK POINT

▨ Reread the above section on 'The origins of the EU' (pp. 504–6). How would thinkers from the realist and liberal schools understand the development of the institutions of European integration in the immediate postwar years?

▨ Do you think that this section has been written in the language of either perspective?

The foregoing should be understood as more than a history lesson. The beginnings of postwar integration are studied so intensively precisely because they are thought to hold important lessons for the analysis of the contemporary situation. This raises the matter of whether the dynamics that initiated the EU can still explain its maintenance and its trajectory. After all, the 'geopolitics' of Europe have changed considerably in recent years. The security condition which some say was the primary force behind integration has been transformed by the collapse of communist regimes in the USSR and Central and Eastern Europe. This poses a whole series of questions, most notably whether deeper economic integration is any longer possible in the context of a host of potential new members of the EU – many of them former communist countries – with diverse histories and disparate levels of economic development.

Patterns of politics

The set of institutions which characterise the modern EU bear a marked resemblance to those which were designed for the six-member ECSC in 1951. The main institutions of the EU are described below. It is difficult to do justice to the complexities of the EU system here, but it is worth making a few observations about the development of political processes within this environment. The central issue from the point of view of this chapter is whether the operation and interaction of these institutions has produced a new form of politics above the nation-state. The growth of the political science of European integration in recent years has certainly been founded on the idea that the EU is best understood as a functioning political system with patterns of political exchange and networks of interests. The opposing view incorporates the argument that the EU remains above all an experiment in international politics. At the heart of this polarity is once again the question of the significance of the nation-state as an actor.

Institutions of the European Union

The European Commission

Consists, at the highest level, of twenty Commissioners appointed by national governments, but who are sworn to pursue European rather than national interests. Each is allocated one or more policy portfolio. Beneath this level sit a series of Directorates General (DGs), each charged with a particular area of policy (for example, DG-Agriculture, DG-Enlargement). Each DG is staffed by officials with particular consultative and bureaucratic functions. The Commission plays a number of roles in the EU system. It is the formal initiator of policy in areas where the EU has competence to legislate (it is expected to consult widely with interested parties before doing this); it is responsible in some areas for monitoring the extent to which EU directives and regulations have been implemented in the member states; it represents the EU externally, particularly in international economic negotiations.

<http://europa.eu.int/comm>

Council of the European Union

Actually a cluster of institutions that together represent the formally intergovernmental component of the EU. The *European Council* began as rather *ad hoc* summit meetings of heads of state and governments of the member states in the late 1960s, but is now recognised as a formal institution of the EU. The European Council, which now meets at least twice a year, has evolved an agenda-setting forum for the EU. The *Council of Ministers* consists of representatives of the member state governments of the EU. The relevant ministers attend according to the policy area under discussion. In the traditional EU formulation, the Council of Ministers is the main legislative forum. Meetings are chaired by a member state government and this *Presidency* currently rotates in a six-month cycle. The business for Council of Ministers meetings is prepared by the *Committee of Permanent Representatives* (COREPER) which consists of nationally appointed officials.

<http://ue.eu.int/en/summ.htm>

continued

continued

The European Parliament

The only body in the EU system that is directly elected. Elections take place every five years; the method of election varies from member state to member state. Seats are allocated roughly in accordance with population size. While Members of the European Parliament (MEPs) are usually elected on conventional national party platforms, they organise in transnational party groups in the Parliament itself. The Parliament's formal powers are much weaker than those of any national legislature, although revisions to the founding treaties have taken the institution well beyond its original role as an advisory body. It now has powers of co-decision with the Council in some instances. The Parliament has acquired a reputation as a lobbyist for deeper integration and substantial institutional reform.

<http://www.europarl.eu.int/home/default_en.htm>

The European Court of Justice

Not to be confused with the European Court of Human Rights, the ECJ consists of judges and advocates-general appointed by the member states. The ECJ is charged with the interpretation and enforcement of the ever-growing body of law made within the EU's policy process, the *acquis communautaire*. The ECJ is significant for the judgements that it makes about the application and interpretation of European law, as well as for the principles it has laid down more generally about the primacy of the *acquis* over national law.

<http://curia.eu.int/en/index.htm>

Intergovernmentalism The view which argues that the development of international institutions and regimes tends to be shaped by the actions and convergences of interest among nation-state actors.

The **intergovernmentalist** position may be summed up as follows. In terms of formal decision-making the Council is still the final port of call for any piece of significant EU legislation. This means that national governments must be the pivotal actors in the policy process. Moreover, the EU has developed a number of institutions that consolidate the power of member states. Council agendas are prepared by national officials in the Committee of Permanent Representatives (COREPER), which essentially intercepts and moulds Commission initiatives. The European Council now appears to guide the direction of EU activity and represents a direct challenge to the agenda-setting powers of the Commission. This influential school of thought argues that integration progresses only when national governments will it. The American scholar Andrew Moravcsik (1998) has produced work suggesting that major advances in integration have reflected the convergence of the national interests of the most powerful member states. His analysis of the negotiation of the Single European Act of 1987 (which set in motion the completion of the Community's single market) suggests that the idea of market liberalisation had come to dominate the policy agendas of the most powerful member-state governments (notably West Germany, France and the UK). In effect, what was visible was not the unfolding of some integrative logic sponsored by the European Commission, but the convergence of national interests.

The case against, which we might call the **supranationalist** argument, would tend to emphasise a series of formal developments which mean that national governments do not have decisive control in the EU system. In particular, the growth of qualified majority voting in the Council appears to be a direct challenge to the idea that states can remain sovereign in the EU system. The occurrence of majority voting in the key decision-making forum suggests that national interests might be overridden. The growth of the powers of the European Parliament following recent treaty revisions might be taken as the development of a significant hindrance to the operation of an EU system based predominantly on the negotiation and exchange of national interests.

To many the EU appears to be a paradigm of 'complex' or 'multi-level' policy-making (Hooghe and Marks 2001). The complexity is enhanced by two factors. First, the Treaties specify the appropriate formal policy procedure for each area of policy in which the Union has competence. This means that the formal decision-making patterns and the involvement of institutions differ from policy sector to policy sector. Second, the EU policy process is – like all policy processes – composed of a host of formal and informal actors. The key difference is that these actors are located at a variety of levels (the global, the European, the national and the sub-national). To map and analyse the interaction of these interests and to ascertain the central issues of interest articulation, influence and power is a fiendishly difficult process for the interested political scientist.

Let us take the example of interest groups which, as we saw in Chapter 13, are often taken to be central to the understanding of the political process. Conventionally, interest groups focus their activity on national governments. The emergence of a European level of authority raises new strategic dilemmas. Should interest groups continue to lobby national governments in the hope that they will be able to influence positions which are taken at the European negotiating table? Or should they seek to alter the focus of their lobbying activity from national institutions to European institutions? (And if so, which ones?) Or should they seek to combine with other national interest groups in cognate areas and form transnational interest groups?

The EU may provide a good case study for political scientists of the role of institutions. When we speak of institutions we are referring not only to formal bodies such as the European Commission, but also to patterns of rules, norms and mutual expectations that may develop in particular settings. Such factors may transform the behaviour of actors located in these institutional settings. Thus we could still argue that the EU is a predominantly intergovernmental organisation, but it might well be that the nature of that intergovernmentalism is altogether different from conventional patterns of interaction between states.

European integration and the end of the nation-state?

One of the most frequently voiced concerns in contemporary European politics is the idea that the EU is becoming a kind of 'superstate' which is draining the

Supranationalism The development of executive and binding authority at levels higher than the nation-state. The term is used by some to describe complex networks of interaction among policy actors in International Relations.

lifeblood from the European nation-states via its relentless accumulation of powers (see, for example, the comments of Margaret Thatcher quoted above, pp. 484–5). This is a complicated question.

The work of the International Relations scholar John Ruggie (1993, 1998) suggests that to approach European integration as a matter of whether or not the EU will become a 'state' (and thereby deprive national administrations of their 'sovereignty') sets up a false debate. Just because the EU does not achieve the common attributes of nation-statehood, this does not mean that it has 'failed' as a project of integration. The common mistake highlighted by Ruggie is that conventional political discourse tends to assume that any evolving form of political authority above the nation-state must assume the characteristics of the state's national institutional form. The fact that debates about the EU are often framed in this manner demonstrates again the alluring power of sovereignty as a deeply held assumption that shapes the imagination of citizens and politicians alike about the possible forms of future political community.

Other writers have suggested that the fears of losing sovereignty to the EU are quite misplaced. The economic historian Alan Milward has argued in a series of books (particularly Milward 1999) that the EU is actually best understood as a project to rescue the European nation-state. Milward's idea is that modern nation-states are held together not by the symbols of nationhood or by coercion, but by the successful implementation of national policy programmes designed to provide material benefits to particular groups within domestic societies. The experience of the twentieth century, argues Milward, demonstrated to states that forms of international cooperation would be necessary if national policy programmes were to continue to deliver the necessary rewards. Integration, therefore, is a rational policy response to the circumstances of a group of Western European states in the immediate aftermath of the Second World War. They chose to cede a limited amount of sovereignty so that they would remain cohesive entities that continued to attract the loyalties of their citizens.

Two elements of the relationship between European integration and national governments are worthy of mention:

1   Governments may use the development of a European-level politics to insulate themselves from the pressures of national politics. If governments are understood to be entities seeking policy-making autonomy, then the relative lack of accountability afforded by the EU system may be a means by which national governments can liberate themselves from constraints from below.

2   On the other hand, governments are confronted with a seemingly insoluble dilemma: the recognition of the need for integration as a means to achieve prosperity versus the continued expectation that governments should be autonomous and sovereign. As a result, 'national political leaders have found themselves caught between electoral fears of lost autonomy and electoral demands for the economic growth that only further integration can provide' (Wallace 1994: 8).

If integration is seen as a threat to nationhood from above, then it should also be said that the territorial integrity of nation-states is increasingly being interrogated from below by sub-national groupings seeking autonomy and independence. Forces such as North Italian, Catalan and Scottish nationalism have placed the question of the legitimacy of existing systems of territorial rule squarely on the respective political agendas of Italy, Spain and the UK. One of the advantages of visualising the EU not as a set of institutions above its component member states but as a system of multi-level governance is that we do not lose sight of the broader shifts in authority that have transpired in Europe over the past half century. Hooghe and Marks (2001) note that processes of integration (where authority has moved upwards to the European level) have been accompanied by the growth of regionalisation in the member states of the EU. Processes such as devolution in the UK have passed elements of authority downwards from central governments to their regional and local counterparts. This means that national governments have ceased to be the exclusive hubs of authoritative action in Europe. Thus the nature of the political game in Europe has changed decisively since the Second World War.

Law and authority in world politics: the Pinochet case

Augusto Pinochet, commander-in-chief of the Chilean military, became President of Chile after a violent *coup d'état* in September 1973. The coup – which was aided and abetted by the US Central Intelligence Agency (CIA) – overthrew the administration of Salvador Allende. President Allende's leftist Popular Unity government had come to power in 1970 through democratic elections. The new military government at once suspended the Chilean constitution, banned opposition to the new regime and imposed draconian controls on the media. Within a few months of Pinochet's seizure of power, some 1200 people had been executed (though many simply 'disappeared'), among them Allende. The number of dead is generally accepted to have risen to over 3000 during the seventeen years of Pinochet's dictatorship. Countless others became victims of human rights abuses and torture. Pinochet stepped down as President in 1990 as a Christian Democrat coalition took power following free elections. Pinochet remained as chief of the Chilean army until 1998.

While in office, Pinochet announced an amnesty to protect those who committed human rights abuses since 1973. In addition, he became a senator following his retirement from the army in 1998. This guaranteed the former general parliamentary immunity for the rest of his life. Effectively, this meant that Pinochet could not be prosecuted in Chile for any crimes he may have committed during the period of his dictatorship, even though his presidency had been subjected to coruscating condemnation by the Chilean National Commission for Truth and Reconciliation that convened in 1991.

In late September 1998, Pinochet – now 82 years old – flew to the UK to receive private medical treatment. Meanwhile, two Spanish judges Manuel Garcia Catellon and Baltasar Garzon were conducting investigations into Pinochet's role in the torture, disappearance and presumed death of Spanish citizens in the years following the 1973 coup. Hearing of his presence in London, the judges contacted Interpol (the International Criminal Police Association – <http://www.interpol.com>) with a view to seeking the extradition of Pinochet to Spain to stand trial for these crimes. British police arrested Pinochet at his London clinic on 16 October. Thus began a protracted process of legal wrangling and passionate debate that culminated in Pinochet's return to Chile early in 2000.

At first, the High Court ruled that Pinochet's status as a former sovereign entitled him to immunity. The Attorney General John Morris QC also insisted that 'insufficient admissible evidence' meant that Pinochet could not be prosecuted in the UK. With an appeal pending in the UK courts, Baltasar Garzon sent a formal extradition request to the then UK Home Secretary Jack Straw on 11 November 1998. On 25 November, the House of Lords (Britain's highest legal authority) ruled by a slender three to two majority that Pinochet was not in fact immune from prosecution, thereby overruling the previous High Court decision. On this basis Straw allowed the extradition process to proceed. However, matters became further complicated when it emerged that one of the presiding Law Lords (Lord Hoffmann) had significant links with Amnesty International (the human rights pressure group). This set aside the House of Lords ruling.

A new panel of Law Lords convened in March 1999 to consider the case. On this occasion the ruling was six to one in favour of extradition. But, while this once again overruled the High Court's understanding of Pinochet's immunity, the new House of Lords ruling tightened considerably the terms upon which Pinochet could be extradited to Spain. The Law Lords cited the International Torture Convention, which did not become binding until December 1988, with Chile, Spain and the UK among the signatories. This reduced significantly the number of charges that Pinochet could face since the period for which he could be prosecuted was narrowed to the final two years of his presidency. The Law Lords reasoned that allegations of torture in *other* countries were not covered by British law until that date.

Judge Garzon quickly filed a further set of charges against Pinochet, all of which fell within the boundaries defined by the Lords. In October 1999, a London Magistrates Court cleared the way for Straw to sanction the extradition citing thirty-five charges. In an effort to assess Pinochet's fitness for extradition, the UK Home Office asked that the general undergo a series of independent medical tests. Having considered the results of the medical tests, Straw announced on 11 January 2000 that he was minded to allow Pinochet to return to Chile on grounds of ill-health. Pinochet finally left the UK for Chile on 2 March 2000 in spite of a last-ditch attempt by the Belgian government to initiate a process of judicial review challenging Straw's decision. Efforts to prosecute Pinochet in Chile made some progress, until a court ruled in July 2001 that Pinochet was not mentally capable of standing trial.

The Pinochet episode is a fascinating story in its own right. However, our task here is to try to tease out some of the issues of relevance for the study of politics and International Relations.

At the heart of the Pinochet case is an opposition between two entrenched views. On the one hand, there are claims that justice should not be bounded by territory. Human rights in this viewpoint are common to all human beings regardless of nationality. The infringement of human rights should therefore be construed as a universal crime. Should either the laws of a country or a particular government condone human rights abuses, then this should not be a sufficient condition for the evasion of justice. The logic of this position suggests that there should be some higher authority with jurisdiction in instances where these human universals come into play. So in his statement to MPs explaining why he had felt compelled to block Pinochet's extradition on grounds of ill-health, Jack Straw said, 'I attach great importance to the principle that universal jurisdiction against persons charged with international crimes should be effective' (*Guardian*, 3 March 2000).

Such ideas lie behind the establishment of international tribunals to hear cases of alleged war crimes. A recent example is the tribunal set up in the Hague to try Slobodan Milosovic, the former president of Yugoslavia. They are also at the heart of moves to establish a more permanent International Criminal Court (ICC). The ICC has been a long-standing aspiration of those seeking to find ways of dealing with acts of genocide. A significant step towards the establishment of the ICC came in 1998 when a UN-sponsored conference in Rome brought together some 160 countries to formulate the statutes for such a body. One hundred and twenty countries signed the resultant treaty (a conspicuous absentee was the United States) with the promise that the ICC would come into being once sixty countries had ratified the treaty.

As UN Secretary General Kofi Annan put it:

> In the prospect of an international criminal court lies the promise of universal justice. That is the simple and soaring hope of this vision. We are close to its realization. We will do our part to see it through till the end. We ask you . . . to do yours in our struggle to ensure that no ruler, no State, no junta and no army anywhere can abuse human rights with impunity. Only then will the innocents of distant wars and conflicts know that they, too, may sleep under the cover of justice; that they, too, have rights, and that those who violate those rights will be punished.
> (<http://www.un.org/law/icc/general/overview.htm>)

The contrary position is essentially an argument for national sovereign jurisdictions. This can take several guises. Some proponents say that only national judiciaries have the right to adjudicate in cases that apply to their country. As a matter of principle, runs the argument, neither other countries nor *ad hoc* courts have the right to interfere in the affairs of a sovereign nation-state (in this case Chile). A milder version of this position was frequently used in the Pinochet case to suggest that legal action against the former ruler was better undertaken in Chile itself rather than by the likes of Spain, the UK and Belgium. This was thought especially important because the existing (democratic) government of Chile was asking for Pinochet to be sent home.

The defence that Pinochet's lawyers pushed throughout the extradition hearings was one of 'sovereign immunity'. This idea combines the claims of the previous paragraph with the assertion that Pinochet – as a former head of state – cannot be prosecuted for deeds undertaken while in office.

The following newspaper extract is a partisan defence of sovereign immunity. Notice how the author also engages with human rights campaigners and others who might invoke notions of international justice.

Document

Straw is Twisting the Law

John Laughland

The Times
10 December 1998

Jack Straw's decision to let General Pinochet be extradited to Spain is not a victory for international law and justice. Instead, it inflicts severe damage on international law. We are witnessing an exercise in lawless power – the strong bullying the weak.

The gurus of international law claim that the Pinochet rulings are a step towards a more civilised world. Sovereign immunity can no longer be invoked to protect heads of state from prosecution for 'international crimes'. They claim that the decision is an important step towards the construction of an international system of justice.

This is simply untenable. In the past few weeks, during the period of the general's detention in Britain, three decisions on the same question have gone the other way. In both Belgium and France, appeals were lodged against President Kabila of the Democratic Republic of Congo (formerly Zaire) for crimes against humanity. They were rejected on the grounds that he was a head of state. He visited both countries on official business and left again without let or hindrance. And appeals lodged by Cuban exiles against Fidel Castro were rejected by Spain.

For serving dictators, therefore, the principle of sovereign immunity seems to remain valid. The House of Lords decision can thus only be taken to apply to people who have left office. The Pinochet decision sends a message to all dictators that they should never follow his example and relinquish office peacefully. It is far safer to remain in power and continue to kill with impunity.

For serving dictators, the principle of sovereign immunity remains valid.

The decision also illustrates the highly selective nature of what now passes for 'international justice'. Contrary to what one leading human rights campaigner affirmed in a recent letter to *The Times*, General Pinochet is not 'one of the most notorious dictators of the 20th century'. It would be more accurate to say that he was a footnote in the history of 20th-century dictatorship. It is obviously unjust to invoke a law to prosecute a suspected criminal while refusing to invoke it for others, especially if the latter are accused of worse crimes or are continuing to perpetrate them.

Yet the very same 'human rights' organisations which have campaigned for the general's prosecution for 'genocide' have fought with equal vigour against identical charges being used to bar former communists from public life in the Eastern bloc. Similarly, the same Western powers calling for or facilitating General Pinochet's extradition are themselves in contravention of their own undertakings to hunt down those accused of crimes against humanity in Bosnia, which they refuse to do for political reasons. It is no coincidence that the supposedly judicial, but in reality highly political, Pinochet decisions were taken by a committee within a Parliament and by a minister in a Government.

If Spain wanted to extradite the general, it should have applied directly to Chile. By upholding the decision to arrest him in a third country, all the bilateral extradition treaties now in existence have presumably been rendered null and void. Instead of respecting the established rules of intercourse between states, two powerful countries, Britain and Spain, have in effect declared that their national judicial and political choices are superior to those of a smaller, weaker one. It is to prevent such an arrogant pretence that Article VI of the 1948 Genocide Convention (the very agreement under which the general is being prosecuted) stipulates that 'persons charged with genocide . . . shall be tried by a competent tribunal of the State in the territory of which the act was committed' or by an international tribunal.

All the bilateral extradition treaties have now been rendered null and void.

Sovereign immunity is simply the expression of the fact that states are the subjects of international law, just as persons are the subjects of civil law. International law grows out of the contractual agreements concluded between them. Sovereign immunity has never meant that a head of state is not subject to any law higher than himself. On the contrary, the principle of constitutionality, or the idea that the prince is subject to the law of God, is one of the most ancient ideas in political life. Those human rights activists who claim that the Pinochet decisions have invented the notion that heads of state are not absolute rulers are simply confusing the truism that political leaders must answer for their actions with the arrogant proposition that they must answer to *them*.

World history has seen many attempts to create planetary justice and universal monarchy. They have all foundered on the simple fact that it is better for laws to be enforced within the context of existing political communities than abstractly. Any body that brushes aside the principle of the equality of states and stands in judgement over another state becomes like a state itself. This opens up the question 'Who guards the guardians?' In the new world order, in which judges hear cases while being allied to one of the parties, and where the law is capriciously invoked for reasons of pure political bias, the answer seems to be – no one.

The debates revealed by the Pinochet case bring to the fore tensions between cosmopolitan and communitarian views of world order (see Brown 1992; Linklater 1998 and Chapter 6 above). The former subscribe to the idea of human universals such as human rights and take the view that national sovereignty can infringe these in various ways. By the same token, international authorities or – in some cases – other states might have legitimate cause to override the sovereignty of a state should it be committing war crimes or human rights violations against individuals formally under its jurisdication. The communitarian viewpoint holds that human beings are naturally ordered into communities. It is these communities, rather than the species as a whole, with which individuals identify most readily. This means that conceptions of justice, the common good and so on can vary across the world. Many communitarians argue that national communities are the most optimal and natural forms of human community. They are thus worthy of defence against cosmopolitan impulses.

THINK POINT

- Which side in this debate do you think has the most persuasive arguments?

- Is the establishment of binding and enforceable international law the best way to deal with crimes such as genocide and human rights abuses?

War without states? After 11 September 2001

At the beginning of this chapter, we noted that war should be thought of as a form of politics. If politics arises where interests clash and further consists of mechanisms to resolve those conflicts, then war clearly fits the bill as politics by violent means. In many ways war is the politics of last resort and as such may be thought of as occurring at moments when the conventional processes of diplomacy and negotiation fail to resolve conflicting interests between states. There are also normative debates about war. For example, political philosophers have long tried to think about circumstances in which wars might be considered 'just'. Just wars might involve self-defence against invasion, going to the aid of victims of aggression or perhaps involvement in conflicts where an important principle (such as democracy) is at stake.

The notion of a just war is not a matter for ethical theory or, for that matter, the rhetorical pronouncements of politicians. Wars are also regulated by international agreements on how they ought to be conducted. These agreements help to regulate (1) when war is appropriate, and (2) the means that may be used to prosecute a war. The best known and most frequently invoked rules of warfare are the Geneva and Hague Conventions (see below).

Document

HAGUE CONFERENCE OF 1899

Correspondence, Instructions and Reports of the United States Commission
Hague I – Pacific Settlement of International Disputes: 29 July 1899
Hague II – Laws and Customs of War on Land: 29 July 1899
Hague III – Adaptation to Maritime Warfare of Principles of Geneva Convention of 1864: 29 July 1899
Hague IV – Prohibiting Launching of Projectiles and Explosives from Balloons: 29 July 1899
Declaration I – On the Launching of Projectiles and Explosives from Balloons: 29 July 1899
Declaration II – On the Use of Projectiles the Object of Which is the Diffusion of Asphyxiating or Deleterious Gases: 29 July 1899
Declaration III – On the Use of Bullets Which Expand or Flatten Easily in the Human Body: 29 July 1899
Final Act of the International Peace Conference: 29 July 1899

HAGUE CONFERENCE OF 1907

Hague I – Pacific Settlement of International Disputes: 18 October 1907
Hague II – Limitation of Employment of Force for Recovery of Contract Debts: 18 October 1907
Hague III – Opening of Hostilities: 18 October 1907
Hague IV – Laws and Customs of War on Land: 18 October 1907
Hague V – Rights and Duties of Neutral Powers and Persons in Case of War on Land: 18 October 1907
Hague VI – Status of Enemy Merchant Ships at the Outbreak of Hostilities: 18 October 1907
Hague VII – Conversion of Merchant Ships into War Ships: 18 October 1907
Hague VIII – Laying of Automatic Submarine Contact Mines: 18 October 1907

Hague IX – Bombardment by Naval Forces in Time of War: 18 October 1907

Hague X – Adaptation to Maritime War of the Principles of the Geneva Convention: 18 October 1907

Hague XI – Restrictions With Regard to the Exercise of the Right of Capture in Naval War: 18 October 1907

Hague XIII – Rights and Duties of Neutral Powers in Naval War: 18 October 1907

GENEVA CONVENTIONS

1864 – Amelioration of the Condition of the Wounded on the Field of Battle: 22 August

1928 – Geneva Protocol for the Prohibition of the Use in War of Asphyxiating Gas, and for Bacteriological Methods of Warfare: 8 February

1929 – Convention Between the United States of America and Other Powers, Relating to Prisoners of War: 27 July

1949 – Geneva Convention Relative to the Treatment of Prisoners of War: 12 August

1975 – Convention on the Prohibition of the Development, Production and Stockpiling of Bacteriological (Biological) and Toxin Weapons and on Their Destruction (1972): 26 March

Full text availability at <http://www.yale.edu/lawweb/avalon/lawofwar/lawwar.htm>

An inspection of the titles of these agreements shows how the rules of warfare have had to keep pace with the rapidly changing weapons technologies. The Geneva and Hague conventions also reveal an infiltration of human rights concerns into the conduct of warfare, particularly with respect to the treatment of prisoners of war (Brown 2001b: 605).

The rules of warfare change over time, but one thing appears to have remained a constant. Much of how we think about war is premised upon the idea that war is something that takes place between states (individually or in alliance). Wars involve the deployment of the military resources of states. Agreements about the conduct of warfare are signed and ratified by states. But what happens when a state is attacked by non-state forces? What if the perpetrators of the attack do not obviously belong to a particular state? How does the state under attack retaliate through military means? Who does *it* attack?

In Chapter 3, we discussed some of the implications of the events of 11 September 2001. Connecting this episode to International Relations theory is not, on the face of it, that easy. The attacks on New York and Washington were not perpetrated by agencies of one state against another. The destruction of the World Trade Center and the devastation of the Pentagon were not, for all their violence, conventional incursions into a state's territory. Thus we have an act of unconventional warfare (if indeed we can call it warfare) organised by a group (*Al Qaida*) that lacks conventional hierarchical lines of authority, and is, perhaps more significantly, 'stateless'. As John Gray notes:

> Like the most advanced businesses, *Al Qaida* is a worldwide network that is only vestigially territorial. Though some state may have sheltered it, it is not under the control of any of them. Thriving on weak government and the mercurial mobility of stateless wealth, it is a perfect embodiment of globalisation.
>
> (Gray 2002: 50)

In 1942, the United States was attacked by Japanese forces at Pearl Harbor. The events have often been compared to those of 11 September 2001, but the analogy is limited. In 1942, the United States' response was to declare war on Japan and its allies. In 2001, the response of the US was rather more complicated. To be sure, the aftermath of 11 September saw the US taking military action. It launched an attack on a defined territory (Afghanistan), but in the context of a so-called 'War against Terrorism'. The ruling Taliban regime was known to be harbouring Osama bin Laden and had acted as a host for *Al Qaida* training facilities. But *Al Qaida*'s network is thought to be genuinely multinational; its organisation fails to conform to conventional notions of a top-down command structure. So the US and its allies such as Britain were engaged in an odd sort of war. It was a war against a notoriously slippery concept ('terrorism') rather than a war against a particular state.

The United Nations Security Council was quick to pass a resolution on the events of 11 September. The text of the resolution is reproduced below.

Document

UNSC Resolution 1368

New York

12 September 2001

The Security Council,

Reaffirming the principles and purposes of the Charter of the United Nations,

Determined to combat by all means threats to international peace and security caused by terrorist acts,

Recognizing the inherent right of individual or collective self-defence in accordance with the Charter,

1. Unequivocally condemns in the strongest terms the horrifying terrorist attacks which took place on 11 September 2001 in New York, Washington (DC) and Pennsylvania and regards such acts as well as any act of terrorism as criminal and unjustifiable, regardless of their motivation;

2. Expresses its deepest sympathy and condolences to the victims and their families and to the people and government of the United States of America;

3. Calls on all states to work together urgently to bring to justice the perpetrators, organizers and sponsors of these terrorist attacks and stresses that those responsible for aiding, supporting or harboring the perpetrators, organizers and sponsors of these acts will be held accountable;

4. Emphasizes that these acts represent a threat to international peace and security and calls on the international community to redouble their efforts to prevent and suppress terrorist acts by increased cooperation and full implementation of the relevant international anti-terrorist conventions and Security Council resolutions, in particular resolution 1269 (1999);

5. Expresses its readiness to take all necessary steps in accordance with its responsibilities under the Charter of the United Nations to respond to the terrorist attacks of 11 September 2001 and to combat terrorism;

6. Decides to remain seized of the matter.

<http://usinfo.state.gov/topical/pol/terror/01091221.htm>

For some, this resolution vindicated any military action that the US might wish to take in response to the attack. Robert Keohane (2002) argues that the existence of this resolution and the subsequent Security Council Resolution 1373 (which called upon states to assist in the rooting out of terrorism and condemned any state that provided a haven for terrorists), lent considerable legitimacy to the US-led response to 11 September. By adding the forceful weight of a truly global organisation, any US action could not be seen as an act of vengeful power politics or as a 'crusade' against Islam.

This may be valid, but the UN Security Council resolutions are not without their considerable ambiguities. A professor of international law explains:

> The Security Council establishes a link between the terrorist attacks and the right of self-defence. But the Council has no formal powers to make a binding interpretation of the right to self-defence in a concrete case. Secondly, the resolution does not explicitly say that the USA has a right of self-defence against any other state in this case. Thirdly, the resolution was adopted the day after the attacks and no one could at that time know who was behind the attacks, and if they were directed from abroad. Fourthly, international law requires that a state must have been involved in one way or other in an attack. It is not easily accepted that the Security Council would do away with such a requirement (and other legal requirements). Fifthly, against whom should the USA have a right to self-defence? Would it be against Afghanistan or against about 60 states with some connection with terrorists?
>
> (Geir Ulstein, 21 October 2001
> <http://www.ejil.org/forum_WTC/messages/5.html>)

This line of argument suggests that the mechanisms possessed by the international community to deal with the aftermath of events such as 11 September may be ill-suited to their task.

THINK POINT

Can international law deal adequately with the events of 11 September 2001?

A further way in which 11 September challenges conventional perceptions of warfare concerns the ways in which entities such as *Al Qaida* operate and the suitability of orthodox military instruments to deal with resultant crises. The tactics employed by *Al Qaida* – in this case suicide hijackings of civilian aircraft – were deeply subversive of the technologies and strategies of modern warfare. The Bush administration's fondness for a National Missile Defence (NMD) programme provides an interesting example. The idea behind NMD is that the US should equip itself with a defensive missile system capable of intercepting and destroying incoming ballistic missiles. The project had always been controversial for three reasons: its vast expense, the lack of existing technology capable of actually delivering an effective NMD system and the fact that the instigation of NMD would infringe the obligations of the United States under existing non-proliferation and anti-ballistic missile treaties. The events of 11 September posed further challenges to the strategic sense of investing so much in technologically sophisticated ways of dealing with perceived threats. As Democrat Senator Carl Levin, Chair of the US Senate Committee on Armed Services Committee, explained:

> Never again will supporters of national missile defense be able to claim, as President Bush did in May [2001], that ballistic missiles in the hands of rogue regimes constitute 'today's most urgent threat. . . . Ballistic missiles are not the tools of terrorists . . . nor are terrorists likely to obtain ballistic missiles for future attacks. When the missile defense debate resumes, there must be a renewed appreciation that every dollar we spend on the least likely threat of ballistic missiles is a dollar not spent on the most likely threat: terrorism.
>
> (quoted in Cirincione 2002
> <http://www.ceip.org/files/nonprolif/templates/article.asp?NewsID=1982>)

Debate continues to rage in the United States about the propriety of NMD. However, the point to ponder in this discussion is the extent to which our conventional notions of security are challenged by phenomena such as terrorist attacks – or more precisely the *threat* of terrorist attacks. This is bound up perhaps with what David Campbell (1998) has called 'the globalisation of contingency'. Campbell's point is that it is relatively simple to think about national security and the threats to that security when we conceive of the world in state-centric terms. However, the appearance of threats – be they from terrorists or ecological devastation – that do not obviously originate from another territorial state raises all manner of questions about how we conceptualise and understand the world:

> The globalization of contingency invokes the increasing tendencies toward ambiguity, indeterminacy, and uncertainty on our horizons. While these have long been identified in academic international relations literature under the sign of 'anarchy', these contingencies . . . can no longer be contained within established power structures and spacial-izations. Danger, in short, can no longer just be written as 'out there'. Security is not to be found 'within'.
>
> (Campbell 1998: 17–18)

Of course, not all scholars of International Relations would agree with this way of thinking. But the tendency to articulate thoughts of this sort about the inadequacies of the conventional vocabulary of the discipline has become more pronounced in recent years. It is bound up with the sorts of issues that we address in Chapter 15 under the heading 'Globalisation'.

Conclusion

Nation-states clearly still matter. They are the sources of authority with which most people readily identify; an international system of interacting sovereign states is an image which seems plausible and in tune with the practice of politics at the global level. But as this chapter has tried to show, there is a serious and growing debate about the possible obsolescence of the nation-state as the most effective way of ordering human relations. Confronted with the emergence of genuinely transnational dilemmas, the seemingly irresistible power of international financial markets and threats to security from terrorism, many have begun to argue that the traditional nation-state needs to be complemented, perhaps even replaced, by something else.

Indeed, it could be argued that the growth of bodies such as the EU and the UN, as well as the proliferation of more issue-specific international organisations and regimes, constitutes a conscious and deliberate policy response to such dilemmas. But the existence of such organisations itself provides a stimulus for both the emergence of nascent forms of transnational politics and the appearance of sustained debates about some quite fundamental issues, such as the tensions between the notion of universal human rights and the sovereign jurisdictions of national governments. The appearance of institutions of regional and global governance has resuscitated debates about sovereignty, democracy, rights and so on. The nation-state may be dead or dying, but politics is alive and well.

Perhaps a better way of thinking about these problems is to argue that the traditional barrier between domestic and international politics is in the process of dissolving; that the local and the global are so inexorably intertwined that there is no longer any discernible analytical distinction between the two domains. This is where the next chapter takes up the story by considering the ways in which the world is being transformed by the processes of globalisation.

Chapter summary

▢ We need to think carefully about the extent to which politics *above* the nation-state resembles or differs from politics *within* the nation-state.

▢ The process of politics *above* the nation-state has been the preserve of the academic discipline of International Relations (IR). IR has tended to focus on politics as a process that occurs between nation-states.

continued

continued

- This image of politics above the nation-state conforms to key doctrines in the real world of International Relations, such as the idea of 'sovereignty' that we see embodied in the founding Charter of the United Nations.

- However, the validity and sustainability of the idea of sovereignty has been subject to significant challenge in recent years. The capacity of national governments to manage their economies autonomously has been undermined by the evolution of the world economy and the appearance of authoritative global institutions such as the International Monetary Fund.

- Sovereignty is also challenged at the doctrinal level, as the Pinochet case shows, by powerful and persuasive ideas such as universal human rights.

- Indeed, our understanding of how politics above the nation-state and how events such as wars operate is challenged acutely by recent happenings such as 11 September 2001.

- The European Union (EU) represents a fascinating case study of how politics above the nation-state might operate when these challenges to sovereignty are taken into account. However, we have to accept that there is significant academic debate about both the factors that drive European integration and what the EU actually represents.

Key texts

Baylis, J. and Smith, S. (eds) (2001) *The Globalization of World Politics*, 2nd edn, Oxford: Oxford University Press. A thoroughgoing, up-to-date and lively introduction to the study of International Relations.

Halliday, F. (2002) *Two Hours that Shook the World. September 11th 2001: Causes and Consequences*, London: Saqi Books. By no means a knee-jerk reaction to the events of 11 September 2001, Halliday's book offers a cogent contextualisation of those terrible events.

Rosamond, B. (2000) *Theories of European Integration*, Basingstoke: Macmillan. A book-length critical discussion of how the European Union has been understood by political scientists.

Strange, S. (1994) *States and Markets*, 2nd edn, London: Pinter. A thoroughly engaging introduction to the study of international political economy, which also has the virtue of developing a clear and influential position that has been a reference point for subsequent debate.

Further reading

Black, J. (1998) *Maps and Politics*, London: Reaktion Books. If you think map-making is an objective exercise, then think again. Jeremy Black shows how maps are politicised representations of space.

Black, J. (2000) *The Politics of James Bond: From Fleming's Novels to the Big Screen*, New York: Praeger. A great example of how an academic reading can be applied to a popular cultural phenomenon. Black picks his way through the ways in which the literary and cinematic representation of Bond conveys particular notions of Britain, its role in the world and the nature of international politics.

Golding, W. (1997) *Lord of the Flies*, London: Faber and Faber. William Golding's much-discussed allegorical novel, first published in 1954, explores the Hobbesian state of nature through the vehicle of a shipwrecked group of boys.

Remarque, E. M. (1996) *All Quiet on the Western Front*, London: Vintage. Originally published in 1929, this is one of the best novels written about the nature and human impact of modern warfare.

CHAPTER 15

CONTENTS

The Processes of Globalisation

Barrie Axford

▌ Introduction

Globalisation The economic, political and cultural processes through which the world is becoming more interconnected and interdependent, leading to the creation of a single 'world-space' or system.

In this final chapter of the book we will examine the processes of **globalisation**, which are having a variable, though often massive impact upon states, societies and cultures, and upon individuals. A useful starting point is where we left off in the previous chapter; that some of the more conventional ways of thinking about and describing political life need to be modified in the light of developments in what is often called international politics. The idea of international politics is well enough understood, but the theme of this chapter is that it is necessary to introduce terms like transnational, post-national and even global to describe the nature of contemporary world politics. The importance of the distinctions between these concepts should not be underestimated, and before proceeding we must think about what the terms mean.

The idea of international politics is quite accepted in everyday language, suggesting a world ordered through bilateral or multilateral relations between nation-states, perhaps as treaties or trade agreements, or through agencies established by formal agreements. The United Nations clearly falls into the category of a multilateral body, as does the World Trade Organisation (WTO). So, on some accounts, does the European Union (EU). But, as we have seen in Chapter 14, the EU occupies a rather uneasy position between the claims of those who see it as an intergovernmental organisation, subordinate to its constituent members, and the aspirations of others who see it as a new sort of

Look back to the extended discussion of the EU in Chapter 14, where we examined attempts to classify that set of institutions.

supra- or post-territorial institution of governance possessing jurisdiction over member states.

The basis of the idea of a **transnational politics** is that political activity is conducted across national boundaries, but there is more to the notion than just cross-border activity. For example, non-governmental organisations like the Red Cross, Amnesty International and Greenpeace have fashioned a politics – of human rights or of ecology – which is not tied to specific territories, histories or cultures, or to the policy agendas of particular national govern- ments. James Rosenau's (1990) description of a 'multi-centric' world in which there are many different sorts of actors and a consequent dispersal of political and economic power makes much of the growing significance of transnational forces and actors in world politics, which are outside the remit and the control of any one nation-state. He says that transnationality is apparent in the activities of:

Transnational politics Political activity conducted across national boundaries.

1 *Transnational organisations* – commercial ones like Nissan or Nestlé, cross- national professional bodies like the International Political Science Association, various social movements such as the women's movement, the networks of global shopping clubs like Amway, and through organisations like Friends of the Earth.

2 *Transnational problems* – like those of terrorism, political refugees and asylum seekers, labour migration, global warming and the El Niño phenomenon, or AIDS, which expose us to risk, sometimes regardless of who we are and where we live.

3 *Transnational events* – made immediate by the reach of global news media. Events like the major earthquake in Kobe, Japan, in 1995, the Kosovan crisis of 1999 or the floods in Bangladesh and Mozambique at the turn of the millennium, become global rather than local issues through the mediation of the news media. The murder of young schoolchildren at Dunblane in Scotland or at Columbine High School in the United States became global events because of the rapid dissemination of information and pictures, and struck a chord among parents the world over. Whether saturation cover- age makes us just voyeurs, enjoying the immediacy of digital and satellite broadcasting of world disasters in the same way that we enjoy soap operas, or perhaps intimates a sense of global citizenship in a world society is, of course, a debatable point.

4 *Transnational communities* – for example, religious communities, both mainstream and orthodox religions like Islam, Judaism, Buddhism and Christianity, as well as some cultist and 'New Age' religions. The category of transnational communities also includes environmental organisations and the 'virtual' communities established by users of the Internet, whether we are talking about fans of the Simpsons or networks of MS sufferers.

5 *Transnational structures* – of production certainly, and also finance, but increasingly the mechanisms (hardware and software) for storing, retrieving and disseminating and sharing information, for example, through commercial and public access databases.

Of course the idea of transcending national boundaries (psychological and cultural as well as physical and legal) is still a fairly neutral way of putting it. The really potent charge in the concepts of transnationality, and **postnationality**, is that the nation-state is, or may be, becoming irrelevant to the actual flows of political, economic and cultural activity and to the formation of political identities. A world order made up of territorial states, market forces, multilateral institutions and what Marc Nefin (1986) called 'third system' organisations, rooted in civil society and concerned with a global public good, is infinitely more complex and potentially more volatile than the Westphalian model of sovereign states. Intimations of such a world are offered in a piece on the 'cyber-economy', which William Rees-Mogg, writing in *The Times* of 31 August 1995, believes will have a great impact on the independence of the modern nation-state and the lives of ordinary people.

Postnationality The idea that national units of government and identity have been superseded.

Westphalia refers to the Peace of Westphalia of 1648, widely taken as being the symbolic birthplace of the modern international system of sovereign, territorial states.

The global cyber-economy and the nation-state

Reflecting on the likely state of the world economy in the year 2025, Rees-Mogg argues that great changes will have taken place, largely because of the impact of information and communications technologies upon many areas of life. He identifies three main themes:

1 the acceleration of social and economic change in what he terms the second stage of the revolution in electronic communications;
2 the rise of Asia relative to the Western economies;
3 the weakening of the nation-state relative to global economic forces, but also relative to the citizen.

He argues that while many people predicted the communications revolution, they often made the assumption that its main effect would be to give a competitive advantage to large-scale organisations, particularly international businesses and strong governments. The twentieth-century nation-state was built, at least in part, on the ability to tax and spend a large proportion of national income, for the most part on defence and on welfare. Developments in communications technology by the year 2025 will, says Rees-Mogg, make it much more difficult for states to raise tax revenues, because many taxable transactions will have been shifted into cyberspace and thus become virtually beyond regulation. The modern nation-state will starve to death as its tax revenues decline, although small nations, like Bermuda, may be able to adjust to the changed circumstances, as their economies are already based upon fluid financial transactions and, presumably, because they do not carry with them the enormous apparatus of government in the shape of a welfare state or the burden of sustaining an independent defence capability.

But the most successful 'country' of all, says Rees-Mogg, will have no geographical location. It will consist of networks of specialist users of the new technologies, cyber-elites in commerce, finance, the arts and so on, who interact and transact outside existing jurisdictions. By 2025 this cyber-country will have, on his reckoning, at least 250 million citizens, with the cyber-rich earning great wealth, and the cyber-poor subsisting on incomes of less than $200,000 p.a. It is this cyber-country, rather than new territorial contenders for world power, like China, which will be the greatest economic phenomenon of the next three decades.

THINK POINT

How persuasive do you find these arguments? Is Rees-Mogg's vision of a cyber-future one with which you are in sympathy?

Later on in the chapter we shall consider the impact of globalisation on the territorial nation-state, and address Rees-Mogg's rather sweeping claim that the state is dying. For now, let us take a closer look at the key concept of globalisation.

From beyond the nation-state to global politics?

It is a commonplace that political life takes place within and sometimes between political and societal units that are territorial, and that, in modern times, the nation-state is predominant among these. Politics and political identities, as well as the study of these phenomena, have been closely connected with particular geographies and places, and the same is true of cultural identities. One major consequence of the spread of the territorial nation-state around the globe has been to put spatial and conceptual boundaries around two of the most fundamental attachments of modern life – national identity and citizenship. Indeed, it is very hard to think about these concepts other than in the context of this or that country. Consequently, many people would describe them as the 'natural boundaries' of a political community and thus the most obvious boundaries for social analysis as well. As a result, the study of politics, even when it is described as 'world politics' or 'International Relations', has been very much centred on the nation-state, and on relations between nation-states.

In one sense this is hardly surprising, because, as we noted above, the territorial nation-state is the typical 'modern' political form seen across the world. States are found everywhere, and even where they are not, they often lay claim to a territory, or to a part in policing what have become known as the 'Global Commons' – Antarctica, the ocean deeps, 'the final frontier' of outer space itself – which are not recognised as part of the jurisdiction of any one state. But it is important to remember that from an historical perspective the nation-state itself is a relative newcomer in world politics, being part of a political landscape set down at the Peace of Westphalia in 1648, consolidated in Europe and North America in the century following the French Revolution of 1789, and exported to the rest of the world largely in the twentieth century. It is true that the nation-state and national societies are the characteristic political forms in which the world has become modern, but we must not fall into the trap of assuming that their centrality is given, or that they are the only way to imagine and to conduct political life and governance.

As we shall see below, the autonomy and power of the nation-state are being modified and new forms of what some people call 'de-spatialised' or non-territorial politics and governance are increasingly visible. These, too, are part of the process of globalisation and, as we discussed in Chapter 5 (Democracy and Democratisation), they make definitions of key political concepts like citizenship and democracy much more complicated. Policy-making too, of the kind examined in Chapter 13, is given a new dimension by the appearance of global actors like transnational corporations and interest groups and transnational institutions of economic governance such as the World Trade Organisation, established in 1995, following the end of the Uruguay Round of trade talks in 1993.

But a common-sense response to the question of whether there is such a thing as global politics would be to say that of course there is not, at least not in anything like the way that people normally mean when they talk about politics. There is no world political system, let alone a world state in the way that there are national systems of government. Even established multilateral institutions like the United Nations or the European Union, both of which conduct forms of governance, still have problems in securing compliance and attracting loyalty precisely because they lack the legitimacy of most national governments. We should not be too surprised at this. Generally speaking, people do not think of themselves as global citizens, or citizens of the European Union, and in the case of the latter they still experience few of the ties of loyalty that bind individuals to particular nation-states or national identities (see Figure 15.1). So, to reiterate, for most people, politics is seen as something that goes on 'inside' territorial units called sovereign states, except when it refers to the sort of exchanges that take place between them.

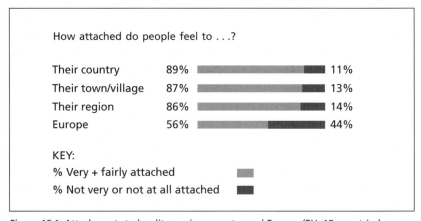

Figure 15.1 Attachments to locality, region, country and Europe (EU, 15 countries)
Source: Eurobarometer: Survey no. 51.0 Fieldwork – March to April 1999

But if there is no world political system, talk about the world becoming globalised is increasingly common. What do people mean when they talk about globalisation?

The concept of globalisation

Globalisation is a process or rather a number of processes that are making the world into a single place. At least that is the argument put forward by many commentators, and it is one endorsed in this chapter, albeit with some important qualifications. Other writers are less willing to support the claim that globalisation is having significant effects upon the fabric of world politics and economics (Hirst and Thompson 1999) or else are reluctant to attest that what is happening is both novel and transformative (Callinicos 1995; Gray 1998; Wallerstein 1997). As we shall see, even among the ranks of those who see globalisation as a transformative process, there is disagreement over its consequences, which often takes the form of a normative dispute about good versus bad effects. So, we will have to examine our definition carefully in order to evaluate its worth. Let us start by looking at how the term is used.

Globalisation as growing interconnectedness

The first is the relatively simple idea of globalisation as the 'multiplicity of linkages and interconnections that cross borders and transcend the nation-state' (McGrew 1992: 65). This definition is a straightforward affirmation of the growing volume of goods, services, capital, communications and people flowing across national boundaries. There are numerous examples of this phenomenon: for example, Table 15.1 shows the volume of exports from major trading nations in the period 1913 to 1984. With some variation and with significant pauses due to war and worldwide economic depression, the overall trend in the period was to expand the world trading economy. These figures are certainly impressive, but in the past twenty years the world trading economy has developed in a much more complex fashion. Since the early to mid-1980s the pattern of world trade has been altered by two significant trends. The first is the emergence of new actors. From the end of the Second World War until 1985, world economic expansion was dominated by the members of the OECD (Organisation for Economic Cooperation and Development), a body controlled by Western and Northern states. Since then a number of developing countries and members of the former Soviet bloc have become fuller participants in the global trading economy. The second development is the emergence of economic **regionalism**, whereby trade has increased within regional groupings, often under the auspices of regional organisations such as the European Union (EU), the North American Free Trade Association (NAFTA), the Asia-Pacific Economic Cooperation (APEC) and the Caribbean Community (CARICOM). In fact, the bulk of world trade takes place within regional groupings rather than between them, which leads some observers to

Regionalism The process of interconnection and interaction between groupings of states. The basis for regionalisation may be common history, geographical proximity or common interests.

argue that the global economy is not truly global at all. For others, even this more intense form of regional interaction is a facet of globalisation, and driven by the need to protect countries and regions from the adverse effects of global market forces, or to increase their competitiveness relative to them.

Table 15.1 Trade as an indication of the growing interconnectedness of the world economy: volume of exports, 1913–84 (1913 = 100)

Year	France	Germany	Japan	Netherlands	UK	USA
1913	100	100	100	100	100	100
1929	147	92	258	171	81	158
1938	91	57	588	140	57	126
1950	149	35	210	171	100	225
1960	298	155	924	445	120	388
1973	922	514	5,673	1,632	241	912
1984	1,460	774	14,425	2,384	349	1,162

Note: figures rounded to nearest decimal point
Source: Maddison (1987: 694)

An even more dramatic demonstration of the globalisation of economic relations may be seen in the massive increase in capital flows as foreign direct investment (FDI) in recent years. Between 1985 and 1996 capital movements increased fourfold (WTO 1996). This increased mobility was due mainly to the investment strategies of multinational and global companies (e.g. Monsanto, Nissan and Microsoft) looking for better production conditions and greater market penetration. Even more dramatic are figures for world financial markets. For example, between 1979 and 1998, the annual turnover of foreign exchange grew from $17.5 trillion to $300 trillion (BIS 1998). (For daily turnover see Figure 15.2.)

All this points to an intensification of globalising tendencies, even though it is possible to argue that there have been periods in which worldwide

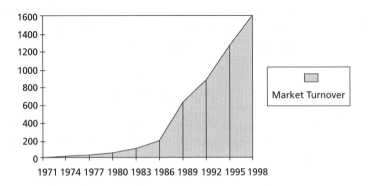

Figure 15.2 Daily turnover on the world's foreign exchange market in US$ million (1971–98)
Source: Busch (1999)

George Soros (1930–) was born in Budapest, Hungary. In 1947 he emigrated to England, where he graduated from the London School of Economics. In 1956 he moved to the United States, where he began to accumulate a large fortune through an international investment fund he founded and managed. Soros was a major player in the financial crises of 1991–2, when his speculation on sterling was instrumental in pushing the UK out of the European Exchange Rate Mechanism (ERM). He is engaged in a great deal of philanthropic work, primarily in Central and Eastern Europe and Eurasia. He has published a number of works, including *The Crisis of Global Capitalism: Open Society Endangered* (1998) and *Open Society: Reforming Global Capitalism* (2000). Soros personifies the globalisation of financial markets.

George Soros

economic activity was just as intense and 'global' pressures on domestic economies just as pronounced (Hirst and Thompson 1999).

There is also greater interconnectedness which has resulted from the popularisation and commercialisation of the Internet. Recent mergers involving communications giants such as Time-Warner and AOL, and Seagram and Vivendi herald a new age of global media, but perhaps more significant is, or at least will be, the switching of all sorts of media content to the Web to create a global medium increasingly reliant upon the dissemination of images. As Tony McGrew says, all these flows constitute a process through which 'events, decisions and activities in one part of the world can come to have significant consequences for individuals and communities in quite distant parts of the globe' (McGrew 1992: 65). Their more potent implication is that global interconnectedness leaves the territorial boundaries of the nation-state less and less coincident with the changing patterns of economic and cultural life, and this is a theme stressed by a growing number of commentators from various academic disciplines and with different concerns. For example, the following is an extract from a work on the creation of global markets carried out by a well-known management consultant, Kenichi Ohmae. Here Ohmae is talking about the creation of consumers of global products:

Borderless world: the interlinked economy

You have read enough about 'global' products to realise that few of them exist. But there are emerging global market segments; many of them centred in specific countries. For example, the market for off-road vehicles is centred in the United States, with incremental sales elsewhere. What is important to understand is the power of these customers vis-à-vis manufacturers. Part of that power comes from their lack of allegiances.

continued

continued

Economic nationalism flourishes during election campaigns and infects what legislatures do and what particular interest groups ask for. But when individuals vote with their pocket-books – when they walk into a showroom anywhere in Europe, the United States, or Japan – they leave behind the rhetoric and the mudslinging.

Do you write with a Waterman or a Mt Blanc pen or travel with a Vuitton suitcase out of nationalist sentiments? Probably not. You buy these things because they represent the kind of value you are looking for. At the cash register, you don't care about country of origin or country of residence. You don't think about employment figures or trade deficits. You don't worry about where the product was made. It does not matter to you that a 'British' sneaker by Reebok (now an American owned company) was made in Korea, a German sneaker by Adidas in Taiwan, or a French sneaker by Rosignol in Spain. What you care about most is the product's quality, price, design, value and appeal to you as a consumer. Young people of the advanced countries are becoming increasingly nationalityless and more like 'Californians' all over the Triad countries – the United States, Europe and Japan – that form the Interlinked Economy.

(Ohmae 1989: 16. Reproduced with permission from HarperCollins Publishers)

THINK POINT

- As a consumer, do you think that Ohmae is right?
- Are you aware of the 'national' origins of products?
- If so, which ones?
- Do you think that there are any truly global products?

Of course, Ohmae is not saying that the availability of global products homogenises tastes, rather that the irrelevance of the origins of a product to consumers in different countries and different cultures is an important aspect in the making of a 'borderless world'. Ohmae is exercised by the power of markets to create a global economy. The sociologist Anthony Giddens, writing in 1990, offers a refinement of the idea of interconnectedness, which is that global flows serve to link people (as well as groups and organisations) who were previously separated and insulated by time and space. He says that interconnectedness is part and parcel of the 'stretching' of economic and social relations across the globe.

At root, Giddens wants to emphasise the increasing interpenetration of the modern world through a dramatic reordering of time and space, including changing the ways in which people think about these concepts, thus altering the meanings they attach to them and the constraints which are related to them. In this reordering, two processes are paramount. The first, which he calls

Key text: A. Giddens (1990) *The Consequences of Modernity*, Cambridge: Polity Press.

'deterritorialization', involves the massive growth in cross-border transactions and collaborations taking place between businesses, the movement of people between countries and regions of the world economy, the creation of truly global markets in areas like finance and telecommunications and the establishment of networks of professionals who communicate through technical language irrespective of national origins and cultures. The second, called 'disembedding', refers to all sorts of social relations being 'lifted out' of local contexts of interaction and reorganised across much larger spans of time and space. Giddens (1990) sees this process at work in an increased use of what he calls 'symbolic tokens' – money, or trading in government bonds would be good examples – which serve as universally accepted ways of effecting transactions among agents widely separated in time and space. But the process is seen also in the routine use of 'expert systems', like computerised databases and the fax, or specialist search engines and directories and portals on the Web, widely used in many areas of everyday life. It is also seen, of course, in the behaviour of Ohmae's consumers who have stripped their purchases of any meaningful association with particular places and cultures and are influenced only by the cache of global branding.

Global branding: a new sort of capitalism?

In an article in *The Sunday Times Colour Supplement* (14 October 2000), the culture guru Peter York writes about the importance of branding to big corporations. For these companies, their physical products are secondary, their brand is their key asset, because it is the brand that people buy, not the products. Brands, says York can 'cross national and cultural barriers at the speed of light', through marketing, subcontracting, franchises and joint ventures. Tommy Hilfiger, Gap, Nike, Microsoft, Budweiser, even Starbucks as a 'third place' between home and work are all selling lifestyle choices and aspirations constructed around and realised through acquiring brands.

THINK POINT

■ What do you think Giddens means when he talks about time and space insulating people?

■ What sort of effects might follow from the removal of spatial and temporal barriers to personal and other sorts of relationships?

The combined effect of Giddens' two processes is to enlarge the scope for social relations or interactions which are not limited by the need for personal presence or tied to a specific location. In other words, they make the global frame of reference increasingly routine for all kinds of actors.

The growing connectedness of the globe is easily demonstrated, but before we can talk of these processes making the world a single place we need to examine the ways in which actors (both individually and collectively) think and feel about globalisation, and thus how they experience it.

Kenichi Ohmae

Kenichi Ohmae (1947–) is widely recognized as one of the world's top international management consultants. For twenty-three years, Ohmae was a partner in McKinsey & Co, the international management consulting firm which has helped to reshape virtually every major firm in the world. As an author and editor he has published dozens of books and contributed numerous articles to such publications as the *Wall Street Journal*, the *Harvard Business Review* and *Foreign Affairs*. Books include *The End of the Nation State* (1995) and *The Borderless World* (1990). His most recent work *Invisible Continent* was published in 2000.

Global consciousness, or thinking globally

The processes referred to above are more than just flows of what the sociologists Scott Lash and John Urry (1994) call 'objects and subjects' – mainly goods, services, money, images and, of course, people – and include the orientation of different actors – individuals, groups, communities, corporations and states – towards the features of globalisation. Orientations refer to people's psychological make-up and to the mental equipment they use to make sense of the world. Only by understanding these orientations is it possible to assess the fragility or strength of global institutions and processes and the sensitivity and vulnerability of various actors to these processes. Then we will be able to assess the extent to which the world is becoming one place. There are many difficulties in making such an assessment. For example, some people may begin to 'think globally' rather than as nationals or aboriginals, and this change will modify certain aspects of their behaviour. But whether their identity (that is, their sense of who they are and where they belong in the world) is changed too, so that their personalities and interests are redefined, is a much more contentious point. Businessmen and women are often advised to 'think globally and manage locally'. This means that, at the very least, they should be aware of the global forces operating on them, and at most that they should see the world as a potential operational whole, adapting their strategies and company cultures accordingly. This is one sense of what is meant by the phrase 'global consciousness', but even a developed awareness of what we called earlier the global frame of reference need not imply that we cease to be British or Japanese, or that our love of the particular, the local and the traditional is eclipsed.

In his interesting book *Globalization: Social Theory and Global Culture*, Roland Robertson talks about individuals and groups, but also whole communities and even nations, being 'constrained to identify' with what he calls the 'global circumstance' (Robertson 1992). These are rather unwieldy phrases, but what Robertson means is that for a variety of reasons – a growing awareness of global problems, population issues, famine in Sudan, the withdrawal of direct investment by an MNC in your locality with the consequent loss of jobs, the collapse of a currency in the face of intense speculation by the money markets, or just watching Jerry Springer on television – people develop a greater awareness of the world and a greater consciousness of the influence of global factors on the quality and conduct of everyday life.

Key text: R. Robertson (1992) *Globalization: Social Theory and Global Culture*, London: Sage.

MNC: multinational corporation.

THINK POINT

▓ From your own perspective, could you identify any global factors which affect the way you live, or does Robertson's argument strike you as too simple?

▓ If you can think of any factors which affect you, do you evaluate these positively or negatively?

Fantasy world order. Either way, open the following URL on your computer and have your own feelings about globalisation assessed:<http://www.fantasy worldorder.com/index.html>

From a more political standpoint, growing awareness of globalising forces can produce quite different responses. These may be to 'go global' and to adopt a global mentality, like the managers referred to on p. 534, or like the proponents of a single world government. It could mean reacting to changing circumstances in the manner of some national governments struggling to contain or regulate the power of financial markets. Alternatively it may impel individuals or groups who feel threatened by exposure to global forces to try to diminish their impact on them or, as in the following example, on whole civilisations.

Local cultural resistance to the power of the Internet

In an article in *The Sunday Times* (News Review, 3 September 1995), Stuart Wavell looks at the ways in which what he calls 'closed societies' are being exposed to, and opened up by, the Internet. The freedom to 'surf' the Internet presents both issues of morality and questions of regulation to the rulers of authoritarian countries like Saudi Arabia, which until recently had traditional and relatively simple methods for dealing with dissent and imposing censorship. When Western magazines featured pictures of women who were completely or partially undressed, the censors simply blacked them out prior to sale. Even satellite television is subject to control through restrictions or complete bans on the sale of receiver dishes, which both Iran and the Saudis have imposed. It is worth noting that even in liberal-democratic systems, such as the United Kingdom, governments act to regulate or monitor the free flow of information available on the Web. During 2000 the New Labour government introduced a

continued

continued

legislative measure designed to give the police the power to intercept e-mails and later extended this to give the same rights to employers.

But the Internet presents much more difficult problems of control for closed societies and autocratic regimes. Regimes have little or no control over what flows between terminals in the form of digital codes, and at least some of what flows is going to be irreverant, maybe even seditious. The Saudis have tried to keep control by granting access by special permission only to universities and hospitals. Furthermore, the penalties for unauthorised use are very severe. Try ordering a *Playboy* centrefold over the NET, and you risk imprisonment.

Wavell says that Iranian censors from the Ministry of Culture and Islamic Guidance are fighting a battle with thousands of 'hackers' (that is, computer users who illegally access information) in the country, while the Chinese authorities have been reduced to cutting off the power connections to users trying to download what they consider sensitive materials.

At the same time, as Wavell acknowledges, at least some of these 'closed societies' have ambivalent attitudes towards the use and spread of information technologies. The Saudis, alarmed by the uncontrollable nature of the Internet, are also anxious to depict themselves as in the forefront of the use of high-tech goods and services.

Wavell says that in the long term all these regimes are facing a terminal crisis for censorship.

This is a useful example of what is meant by global consciousness. What is most interesting about it is that while the unifying and homogenising power of information technology is shown as penetrating closed societies, or as tearing down the barriers created by time and space to make the world one, the process also generates strong forces of opposition that are committed to defending cultural, religious and linguistic boundaries and economic interests, or the idea of national sovereignty, sometimes to the point of violent conflict. We can see this sort of response in those regimes which wish to hide from permissive or potentially destabilising global influences like those mentioned in the above extract, or in the brutal regime of the Khmer Rouge in Cambodia in the 1970s, which sought to reverse all modernising trends in that country. Both the ex-Taliban government in Afghanistan and the military regime in Myanmar (Burma) placed severe restrictions on the use of the Internet, seeing it as a tool of subversion. In the United Kingdom, *The Regulation of Investigatory Powers Act* of 2000 authorises the police and security services to intercept Internet and mobile phone messages in the name of national security, among other things, raising concerns about the rights of citizens to ensure privacy.

Issues surrounding the rights of individuals and the extent of individuality are covered in Chapters 1 and 8.

Fear is also visible in the politics of other more open and apparently stable liberal democracies. In France, political and cultural elites continue to defend a particular model of 'Frenchness' by trying to protect the language and French culture from the ravages of American English and forms of popular entertainment like *Baywatch*; while in the United Kingdom 'Eurosceptics' (that is, those opposed to the principle of ever closer union in Europe) have been successful in establishing as a major issue whether the UK should join the third stage of Economic and Monetary Union (EMU) on the basis that it is injurious to national prosperity and national traditions of government and public law. In 1996 the Community of Portuguese-Speaking Countries was formed to contest the spread of the 'global' languages of English and Spanish. Resistance to globalisation overall is also increasingly visible. In Seattle, late in 1999 a coalition of protesters, supported by a worldwide network of activists on the Internet, brought an important World Trade Organisation meeting to an inglorious standstill:

Sleepless in Seattle?

Backlash against globalisation

As a successor to the Uruguay Round of trade talks, which ended in 1993, the WTO planned to launch the new Millennium Round of talks that would cover issues such as agriculture and trade in services during a four-day meeting held in Seattle in November 1999. But public protests, including marches and street riots, delayed the opening ceremonies and soured the atmosphere of the meeting. Amid chaos and recriminations the talks broke down. Many people

continued

continued

G8 is the title given to the world's 7 most powerful economies – the G7 – plus Russia.

see the Seattle protest as a symbol of the beginning of a powerful backlash against free trade and globalisation in general, where that process is interpreted as the expression of the power of major corporations. In February 2000, the WTO said that it would delay the launch of its new round of trade negotiations until the late spring, but this did not affect the resolve of the protesters, who gathered again in Prague in the autumn of 2000, at the EU Summits in Nice and Gothenburg in December 2000 and May 2001, and at the G8 meeting in Genoa in July 2001, to rally against the giants, the superbrands of the new capitalism. The broad coalitions of anti- or alternative globalisation protesters in Seattle and elsewhere do not subscribe to a single, overarching ideology, despite being labelled 'anti-capitalist' in the news media. Rather they are loose networks of activists with a variety of concerns, brought together under the anti-globalisation banner and with the aid of an increasingly sophisticated use of information and communications technologies (ICTs). The very public face of anti-globalisation has been seen in many venues where world leaders have gathered to discuss the economic future, for example, Prague, Gothenberg and Genoa.

Born in Canada in 1970, Naomi Klein is a journalist whose writings have appeared in *The Baffler*, *Ms* and *Village Voice*, among many others. For the past four years she has been covering the rise of anti-corporate activism in her syndicated column in the *Toronto Star*. Her first book, *No Logo* (2000) provides the first history of the global anti-corporate movement.

Naomi Klein

There are many more examples of the backlash against globalisation, of local intransigence and of cultural resistance in the face of globalising (or, in the case of the EU, regionalising) pressures. Some manifestations of 'backlash', such as the World Development Organisation, which is active in protests over global capitalism, offer what they see as alternative models of globalisation to those driven by financial markets and transnational companies. Regardless of the particular case in question, there are two key points to bear in mind.

The first is that although they may be in some way opposed to globalisation, each example of resistance is also defined in relation to it, or given a rationale because of it. Concerns over loss of national identity, or with religious purity, become politicised largely as a result of actors being 'constrained to identify' with the global condition by supporting or opposing some of the features found there. A further example may clarify this difficult point. Much of the discussion of globalisation presents it as the diffusion of Western (for which read American and Western European) values, institutions, products and practices to other parts of the world, with a resulting erosion of local tastes, traditions and identities. In this sort of interpretation, the opening of the first McDonald's restaurant in Moscow might be seen as an increment in the homogenisation of consumer tastes around the world and an implicit attack on authentic Russian traditions. In 1995 a number of Russian entrepreneurs took a commercial, but also an implicitly political, stand against this threat by opening the first in a chain of Russian fast-food outlets, specialising in the sale of vodka and Russian cabbage. The point is that this particular expression of Russian identity is only really comprehensible when seen as a deliberate counterweight to the import of a foreign product which is an icon, perhaps the icon, of Americanised global cultures and tastes, although it may be an optimistic attempt to establish a niche market as well. 'Constrained to identify' with the global condition in the guise of sesame-seed buns, meat patties and chocolate 'shakes', the Russian patriot as entrepreneur rediscovers seemingly more authentic fare, both as a culinary statement and as a defence of indigenous culture. In similar vein, when José Bové, a political activist and sometime farmer, staged protests against McDonald's in 1999, he was widely feted as a national hero and has since become an icon of the global protests against consumer capitalism.

José Bové

José Bové (1953–) is now a full-time activist and previously a farmer whose first fight was against the French government in the 1970s as one of a few hundred sheep farmers in the Larzac region who attempted and finally succeeded in preventing that area of France from becoming a military training ground. When the Confederation Paysanne, a second, more grass-roots farmers' union, was organised in the late 1980s, Bové became one of its three principal spokespersons. He took part in destroying GMO rice plants at the Nerac research lab early in 1999, then helped in the dismantling of a McDonald's in Millau in August of that same year. The French courts sentenced him to three months in gaol, which is on appeal.

THINK POINT

Can you think of other examples of anti-global politics?

The second point is that because of instances like this the processes of globalisation must be seen as contested. So the idea of the world as a single place does not, indeed cannot, imply complete homogeneity, with the elimination of local traditions and identities, but rather a much more pluralistic condition, where competing and sometimes fundamentally conflicting ideas about the global circumstance – capitalism versus communism, Islamic versus Judao-Christian, or national versus both supranational and communitarian – abound. This, too, is a crucial observation, because instead of a world becoming one willy-nilly, through the integrative force of market capitalism and the power of clever machines like computers or WAP phones to 'compress' our sense of time and space, we are faced with a much more pluralistic 'totality' or, in some instances – the case of allegedly fundamentalist Islamic ideals may be a case in point – quite different visions or models of what a single world should look like.

This may seem an obvious point to make – after all, the world is full of variety – but it is useful to remind ourselves that the process of globalisation is often a matter of conscious decision and struggle by individuals and groups in support of, but also against, powerful transnational and postnational economic and cultural forces, *as well as* an unconscious adoption or assimilation of these same forces into our lifestyles. While it is clear that many consumers would be hard put to identify the local origins of many products and some could not care less, the same is almost certainly not true of their choice of politicians or political parties. So, when individuals buy a car whose parts have been sourced from around the world and which has no obvious national provenance – for example, the Ford Mondeo, or the resurrected VW Beetle, both marketed as 'world cars' – they have been implicated in the processes of globalisation just by being there, through behaving routinely as buyers and sellers.

On the other hand, when these same people, or others like them, protested at the French government's decision to resume underground nuclear testing in the Pacific during 1995 and marched against the decision of the United States under President George Bush Jr not to ratify the 1997 Kyoto Accords on Climate Change, they chose to support what is by now a globally sanctioned ideology of eco-protection.

The force of such ideologies, circulating at the level of popular opinion via global media outlets and the Internet, as well as through the agency of multi-lateral organisations like the United Nations, can, and sometimes does, create a global constraint on the actions of individual states and corporations. But as French intransigence in the face of world opinion demonstrated, sometimes it does not. In Myanmar (Burma) flagrant breaches of universally acknowledged human rights regimes by the military junta continue, largely impervious to world opinion. Even so, it may be quite appropriate to talk about the existence of a world or global civil society and, with regard to issues like this, even an emerging global moral order, and we will return to this question on p. 557.

> ### *Marching out of step?*
>
> The Bush administration's penchant for going it alone in some aspects of world affairs demonstrates the continuing ability of powerful nations to stand out against world opinion on matters deemed to be in the national interest. Consider the following events which all took place in 2001: Europe and Japan decide to go forward with the Kyoto Accords on global warming despite America's non-participation. Eventually, the United States will have to decide whether to be part of a system that it had no voice in designing. President Bush's emissaries killed a draft treaty to enforce the global ban on germ warfare. The administration was concerned that international monitors would gain access to US military and commercial secrets. The United States joined a handful of nations in refusing to approve a new accord on children's rights. The offending provision commits participating nations not to imprison children under 16.

Global compression

All this suggests that the changing experience of time and space spoken of by Giddens (1990) does not, or need not, proceed in a linear fashion or towards a predetermined goal – say, one-world government or global capitalism – precisely because of the different perceptions and experiences of those caught up in it and because of the new forces at work within it. So while there may be what the geographer David Harvey calls a dramatic speeding up or intensity of 'time–space compression' (Harvey 1989; and see Luke 1998) and a redefinition of social space, the relationships between the constituent units of the global system display no neat functional unity.

There are two main reasons for this. The first is suggested by the anthropologist Arjun Appadurai (1990) who points to some major 'disjunctures' at work in the global cultural economy which are the result of different and competing 'logics' of integration – most notably, the universalistic logic of capitalist markets versus the particularistic logic of individual nation-states and national identities. Appadurai provides a useful insight into some of the 'fundamental disjunctures' between economic factors and politics and culture, when he describes a world and processes of globalisation affected by the fluid and unpredictable interaction of different global 'scapes'. These are:

1 *Ethnoscapes* – the landscape of persons who make up the shifting world in which we live. Tourists, migrants, refugees and, if we are to believe the novelist David Lodge (1984), delegates at international conferences, are all part of the make-up of this mobile universe.
2 *Technoscapes* – the global configuration of technology and technological innovation, now increasingly indifferent to conventional boundaries and to the need for particular sites for the production of goods and the delivery of services.

3 *Finanscapes* – the highly fluid world of global finance: money markets, futures, commodities broking, portfolio investments, all moving too fast for easy regulation by national regimes.

4 *Mediascapes* – the electronic dissemination of information and images and its organisation in multimedia forms quite unlike the older divisions between print and broadcast media.

5 *Idioscapes* – the rapidly expanding or even exploding world of political ideas and slogans which inform and legitimate new kinds of political forces and social movements; feminism, ecologism and survivalism are good examples, along with the organisation of indigenous peoples like Native Americans and Native Australians.

The second reason is the related fact that actors in world politics are all players in it, but players who have been schooled in different traditions and perspectives; that is, they already have a sense of their own interests and histories, perhaps even their own sense of destiny. The processes of globalisation do not write upon these individuals, groups and communities as if they were blank pages in an exercise book. Because of this, the interplay of global forces with individual or local identities is often more reciprocal than a simple model of global dominance and of local subservience, or even local resistance to global scripts. This brings us to a further nuance in the concept of globalisation.

Globalisation as relativisation and indigenisation

Relativisation The process whereby the integrity, wholeness or absolute quality of an identity is diluted by the power of global forces.

The introduction of certain kinds of consumer products, like satellite TV dishes or contraceptive devices, into a previously closed society may have the effect of undermining or **relativising** existing identities and practice, as well as challenging established political interests. But this challenge to local practice is seldom uncontested. In Algeria in recent years, the attempt to modernise the country under a succession of socialist and quasi-military regimes has been contested by those often called Islamic 'fundamentalists', notably the Groupe Islamique Armé (GIA), whose primary aim lies in the eradication of what it sees as the corrupting influence of Western culture on the purity of Islamic thought and custom. Such reactions can and do produce violent challenges to the introduction and use of outside influences and artefacts, leading to the tearing down of TV satellite dishes or, as we saw earlier, banning Baywatch, as happened in Iran. It can also produce challenges to the legitimacy of the modernising elites which have countenanced their use.

Less dramatic, although typical of the relativising power of global forces, are what we may call *world cultural scripts*, like Conventions in international law, or UN Declarations on the rights of workers or women or children. These provide a framework of expectations (a script, in other words) to which individual countries often feel obliged to conform in full or in part. Such scripts are really models or guides for national policies and national profiles of appropriate development. Adherence to the norms circulating in the global system establishes and reinforces the legitimacy of a particular regime and also contributes to the shape and solidity of the emerging world society. Sometimes these scripts are embodied in what students of International Relations call '**regimes**', like the agreements on the environment which arose from the 1992 Earth Summit in Brazil, the 1993 Vienna Conference on Human Rights and Development and the outcomes from the UN-sponsored conference on Women and Development staged in Beijing in 1995.

International regimes Consist of more-or-less codified agreements and rules governing some aspect of the relations between states.

Governments can and do choose to ignore such constraints, at least with regard to particular cases, even if they feel obliged to pay lip-service to the ideals. Russian democracy now seems to extend to allowing unfettered report-age of the shortcomings of President Putin, at least over his conduct of the rescue mission to save Russian sailors aboard the nuclear submarine *Kursk* in the summer of 2000, but not to the severe treatment of dissidents and the conduct of the war in Chechnya. For regional variation of press freedom see Table 15.2. In the wake of the terrorist attack on the World Trade Center in New York, President Putin's support for the coalition against Bin Laden and the Taliban regime in Afghanistan was deemed more important than the poor record of the Russian government on human rights and human suffering in one of its Muslim republics. Such ambiguities are commonplace in a world where the moral high ground and universalist pretensions are sometimes required to play second fiddle to expediency and realpolitik.

Table 15.2 Regional assessment of press freedom by countries

	Free		Partly free		Not free		No. of countries
Africa	6	(11%)	17	(32%)	30	(57%)	53
Asia	6	(25%)	4	(17%)	14	(56%)	24
Europe (W)	20	(95%)	1	(5%)	0		21
Europe (E/NIS*)	9	(33%)	9	(33%)	9	(33%)	27
Lat. America/Carib.	17	(52%)	14	(42%)	2	(6%)	33
Middle East	1	(7%)	2	(14%)	11	(79%)	14
North America	2	(100%)	0		0		2
Oceania	8	(67%)	4	(33%)	0		12
Total	69		51		66		186

Note: *Newly independent states. % shows percentage of countries in each category. This survey of 186 countries expands a process conducted since 1979 by Freedom House. The findings are widely used by governments, academics and the news media in many countries. The degree to which each country permits the free flow of information determines the classification of the media as 'free', 'partly free', or 'not free'.
Source: Freedom House Survey of Press Freedom (2001)

On the other hand, pressure from the world community, organised through the international force in Bosnia, forced the Bosnian Serb leader Radovan Karadzic to step down from public office in 1996, in recognition of widespread criticism over his conduct of the civil war in Bosnia, while the proto-democratic Serbian government which succeeded the dictatorial regime of Slobodan Milosevic in 2000 eventually heeded international pressures and arrested the former leader on charges of corruption, deporting him to the capital of The Netherlands, The Hague, to face charges from the International War Crimes Tribunal. In October 2000, the United Kingdom, which had previously resisted such moves, fully incorporated the European Convention on Human Rights into domestic law when it placed a new Human Rights Act on the statute book. Following President Bush's decision not to adopt the compromise version of the Kyoto Accords on Climate Change, agreed at Bonn in July 2001, media commentary stressed America's growing 'isolation' in terms of world opinion, and of the need to 'rebuild bridges' to the international community.

The consequences of the relativising power of global forces for local identities may be:

1 Their complete erosion through cultural homogenisation or assimilation; that is, the local identity becomes swallowed.
2 The reaffirmation or entrenchment (sometimes called the re-traditionalisation) of existing identities in the form of religious orthodoxies or other types of fundamentalism.
3 Their replacement by 'hybrid' cultures or identities, the result of some accommodation between the local and the global, involving the fusion of different cultural traditions. Stuart Hall (1992) writes persuasively that hybrid identities, often found among migrant communities, are not simply a variant of 1 or 2 above, but, as Monty Python said, 'something completely different'.

THINK POINT

Can you think of any examples of hybrid identities? For example, when someone is described or describes herself as a 'Irish-American', or when people in Western countries wear 'ethnic' dress from non-Western societies, these are both instances of hybridity.

Where there is evidence of straightforward resistance, or hybridisation of identities, this introduces a cautionary note into arguments which depict the process of globalisation as a simple diffusion and acceptance of Western cultural values, and sometimes as an unmediated flow of influence from the West to the rest. By contrast, the geographer Doreen Massey has spoken of the need to assess what she calls the 'power geometry' in the relationships involved, and part of her interesting argument is reproduced below.

A global sense of place

Imagine for a moment that you are on a satellite, further out and beyond all actual satellites; you can see 'planet earth' from a distance and, rarely for someone with only peaceful intentions, you are equipped with the kind of technology which allows you to see the colour of people's eyes and the numbers on their numberplates. You can see all the movement and tune in to all the communication that is going on. . . . Some of this is people moving, some of it is physical trade, some is media broadcasting. There are faxes, e-mail, film-distribution networks, financial flows and transactions. Look in closer and there are ships and trains. . . . Look in closer and . . . somewhere in sub-Saharan Africa, there's a woman on foot who still spends hours a day collecting water. Now I want to make one simple point here, and that is about what one might call the 'power geometry' of it all, the power-geometry of time–space compression. For different social groups and different individuals are placed in very distinct ways in relation to these flows and interconnections. This point concerns not merely the issue of who moves and who doesn't, although that is an important element of it; it is also about power in relation to the flows and the movement. Different social groups have distinct relations to this . . . some people are more in charge of it than others; some initiate flows and movement, others don't; some are more on the receiving end of it than others; some are effectively imprisoned by it.

(D. Massey (1995) *Space, Place and Gender*,
Cambridge: Polity Press, pp. 146–56)

Massey draws our attention to various instances of the power geometry found in different kinds of flows and movements. Migrants, refugees and asylum seekers are not 'in charge' in her sense of the expression, while business travellers are. An elderly person eating a meal from a Chinese takeaway while watching an American film on television may be just a passive recipient of global fare, whereas virtual travellers on the Internet are conscious and probably willing participants in the compression of their own world. Massey's idea of the 'power geometry' contained in a relationship or transaction also reminds us that the processes of globalisation take place within pre-exisiting social relationships. In her version, the rich go on getting rich and the poor get *Rikki Lake*.

But the idea of power geometry also highlights the second of the two concepts dealt with in this section, that of indigenisation. As an example of **indigenisation** take the remarkable influx of Japanese Manga cartoons into countries in the West. These cartoons, which are often full-length, adult animation films, along with cyberpunk movies, constitute a uniquely Japanese contribution to the global culture of the late 1990s. Tom Hiney (*Sunday Times*, News and Travel, 2 January 1994, p. 14) suggests that we should 'forget bullet trains and company anthems', or even samurai and tea houses as expressions of Japanese life and culture. He says that Manga is 'the subversive imagination of a new, streetwise Japan'. At the same time, Japanese directors not involved with animation, he says, are reviving tired Hollywood genres. *Violent Cop*, a motion picture released in the UK and USA, was directed by and also starred 'Beat' Takeshi, an actor hailed by reviewers as the Japanese 'answer to Clint Eastwood'.

Indigenisation The adaptation of alien practices to local circumstances and to meet local needs.

In this example, we not only have the indigenisation of a notable Western cultural form (animation) by the Japanese, but its reinvention and re-export to achieve cult status in the West. In Afghanistan, the ex-Taliban government, militant opponents of the Westernisation of Islamic societies and suspicious of its smart technologies and consumer ethos, none the less had their own official website, and Palestinian youths in Gaza City wear Nike footwear and Tommy Hilfiger inspired T-shirts as they pursue their *intifada* (uprising) against Israel and American influence in the Middle East. What do these things tell us about the relations between the local and the global?

First, they show us that Western artefacts can be entirely assimilated into local practices. Yet at the same time, the particular form and indeed the specific usage referred to is meaningful only when seen as part of the localisation of thoroughly global practices.

Second, they underline the fact that we should be very careful about any claim that the 'relativising' of the world by global processes annihilates local cultures and interests, while acknowledging that these same global forces are making it much harder for local identities to survive intact. Indeed, the very meaning of locality or 'place' may undergo change in a world linked by fibre-optics and the suspicion that a visit to McDonald's or KFC really can make your day, regardless of the time zone or the place. The other side of Japan's confident reinvention of American cartoon culture to reflect its own cultural traditions is the fear among some intellectuals that 'Japlish' (English words rendered into Japanese) is leading to the corruption of the Japanese tongue. Often cited is the fad among young people for saying 'sankyoo' (thank you) instead of 'arigato' and 'bye-bye' for 'sayonara'.

The idea of a global system

Global processes, like changes in communications technology or new production techniques, and also the spread of 'global' ideologies like the UN Declaration of Human Rights provide constraints or models of acceptable national, local or organisational development. Ien Ang calls these phenomena 'cultural frames', in relation to which 'every identity must define and position itself' (Ang 1991: 7). To reiterate the point, this is not a simple matter of the 'Westernisation' or Americanisation of the world, but a much more complex and interactive process.

So what can we conclude about the idea of the world as a single place, a global system where local actors and global structures interact? First, that globalisation is a process which is made and not given; that is, we should be cautious about accepting interpretations of globalisation in which it is presented as an 'objective' and irrevocable force, regardless of the ideological provenance of these arguments. Globalisation proceeds through the interaction of various actors (individuals, localities, groups, organisations, national governments, etc.) with a variety of more encompassing structures and flows (e.g. rules on world trade, 'global' cultural products such as blockbuster movies, and public opinion on global issues such as the environment and international terrorism). Second, that while the idea of a single place means that the world is undergoing a process of growing interconnectedness, so that it is becoming irrelevant to talk about separate national economies, or even national companies, it is still necessary to talk about national and local identities and other communal sentiments. Third, globalisation is not producing a homogenised world; indeed, it may be that a heightened consciousness of global constraints triggers a renewed sense of personal, local, national or even civilisational identity (see e.g. Barber 1996; Huntington 1998; Smith 1995). Finally, as Anthony Giddens says, it suggests that the process of making the world a single place links people previously separated by time and space (Giddens 1990). Social relations are not only stretched, as he puts it, across the world space but, on occasion, made 'virtual' by the technologies of transnational media. Although it is a multifaceted and contested process, globalisation involves a massive shift in the organisation of human affairs and in the exercise of power (Held *et al.* 1999; Sassen 1999).

Key text: D. Held, A. McGrew, G. Thompson and J. Perraton (1999) *Global Transformations*, Cambridge: Polity Press.

All this paints a rather complicated picture, and suggests a theory of globalisation in which larger scale processes and structures, involving, for example, changes in the ways in which people communicate with each other or in where and how consumer products are produced and sold, are only one side of the equation. The other side sees these same structures and processes mediated by the resilience of local identities and traditions, and finds them interpreted, often idiosyncratically, by actors who have been socialised into particular cultures and world views. So globalisation is a complex process which moves to no unique logic nor to unstoppable laws of history. The rich concept of globalisation outlined above emphasises the importance of material factors in the making of a single global space, but it also stresses consciousness of globalising forces as the realm where identities are reinforced or changed. We need to look at the sorts of forces that are contributing to a globalised world.

Manuel Castells (1941–) is Professor of Sociology and Professor of City and Regional Planning at the University of California, Berkeley, where he was appointed in 1979 in the Department of City and Regional Planning. In 1983 Castells undertook the study of economic and social transformations associated with the information technology revolution. The results of this work were published in his trilogy *The Information Age: Economy, Society, and Culture*: 1st volume, *The Rise of the Network Society* (1996, revised edn 2000); 2nd volume, *The Power of Identity* (1997); 3rd volume, *End of Millennium* (1998, revised edn 2000). His new book is *The Internet Galaxy. Reflections on Internet, Business and Society* (2001).

Manuel Castells

The forces and features of globalisation

So far we have seen that the complexity of the processes by which the world is being made into one place beggars any simple description or cataloguing of the main features of globalisation. However, we can identify some of the primary 'sites' for which a contested globalisation is being fashioned.

The world economy and the new international division of labour

The collapse of state socialism seemed to herald the completion of a truly worldwide market economy, although the speed with which countries like Poland and Slovenia, let alone Russia, Mongolia or Cuba will be fully integrated into a system founded on market economics is still open to question. Furthermore, the marketisation of the world economy still leaves many countries in the Third World, and the even poorer Fourth World of sub-Saharan economies, very marginal in economic terms. Nor is the global economy immune from risk and loss of confidence. Following the destruction of the World Trade Center in New York and the disruption of financial markets, telling signs of strain were apparent in a period when the world economy was slipping into recession. Airlines laid off thousands of staff and cancelled some routes, and governments warned of the need for national belt-tightening and sacrifice to meet the terrorist threat.

A new age of anxiety?

Writing in *The Sunday Times* of 30 September 2001, Michael Burleigh draws attention to the emotional consequences of the terrorist attack. He argues that the world has been turned upside down by the events of 11 September 2001. A decade of certainty, during which the USA had enjoyed an unprecedented consumer boom and cut its defence budget from 6 per cent to 3 per cent of GDP, has given way overnight to 'an age of anxiety'. He says that the mood is palpable, and not just in America.

These are important caveats to the ideology of a successful and truly global capitalism and a pacific world order, but we should not dispense with, nor underestimate the significant and longer term changes in train. Most financial markets, and, increasingly, those concerned with communications and the processing and dissemination of information, now inhabit what Kenichi Ohmae calls a 'borderless world', or an 'invisible continent' (Ohmae 1989, 1999), with which the traditional mechanisms of national regulation and control are often out of kilter. The new world economy is one in which success is based more and more on the production of information and the marketing of brands and services rather than on making things. In this sort of economy, which some people call 'post-Fordist' (to distinguish it from the highly industrialised mass-consumption form of capitalism called 'Fordist'), place and labour power are no longer the most salient factors in economic success. With new forms of information technology guiding many areas of production, goods can be produced almost anywhere, with little need for labour-intensive methods of production or for the social and political structures which attended them, like organised trade unionism and extensive welfare provision. Flexibility in production techniques and in working practices and the overall impact of information technologies are transforming the meaning of work for many people in the core states, but also contributing to the rapid integration of peripheral economies like the 'intelligent island' of Singapore into the mainstream of the world economy in key sectors like micro-electronics. Taken together, these developments have important effects on another central institution of a globalised world: the nation-state.

This cartoon, from a Mexican newspaper, depicts in stark fashion the thesis that economic globalisation creates many losers and only a few winners. The article that accompanied it used Mexico as an example of a poor country that has no option but to accommodate the forces of economic globalisation, from which it may gain some benefit, but from which it is likely to suffer badly in times of economic recession.

Named after Henry Ford, the car-maker and pioneer of mass-production techniques in manufacturing industry.

Winners and losers: the fall-out from economic globalisation?
Source: Cartoons in Focus

Oskar Lafontaine was chairman of the SPD and finance minister in the German government of Gerhard Schröder, but resigned abruptly from both posts in 1999. In opposition to the business wing of the SPD, Lafontaine advocated a programme of state measures to counter the negative social effects of globalisation and an unrestrained market – both on a German and European level. In 1998 together with his wife, he published a book expanding his ideas, *Don't Worry about Globalisation – Jobs and Wealth for All*. In this book he advocated increasing incomes in order to increase domestic demand – so flying in the face of the dominant supply-side orientated policies characteristic of neo-liberal economics.

Oskar Lafontaine

The world political order: global governance?

Much of the discussion of globalisation takes place in terms of its adverse effects upon the sovereignty and autonomy of the nation-state. Despite this, the sovereign state is still the principal actor in world politics, but its centrality appears much more fragile than in the recent past, most notably with regard to the ability of national governments to implement policies that run counter to the interests of world financial markets. Even membership of international regimes like the *European Exchange Rate Mechanism* (ERM) is not proof against the power of financial markets to undermine a government's attempts to achieve currency stability, as Britain, Italy and France found in 1991 and 1992, when intense speculation on their currencies led to the first two countries leaving the ERM. In addition, the ability of national governments to regulate the flows of information and entertainment now available online is becoming increasingly tenuous when so many images and messages can be carried on the virtually uncontrollable Internet and its clones.

Membership of regional, multilateral and quasi-supranational bodies such as the EU is also compromising the status of the nation-state as the expression of national unity and identity, and as the focus of demands and support from individual citizens and organisations. We should be careful not to overstate this shift, but by way of illustration it is apparent that a growing number of organised interests now routinely lobby Brussels or Strasbourg, because they see European institutions as increasingly central in the policy process which affects them, and sometimes as the means by which to bypass national decision-makers who are less sympathetic to their claims. At the same time, it may be that the leaders and membership of such groups do not consider themselves to be Europeanised as a result of these activities and feel themselves to be no less French, Italian, Dutch or British because of what they are doing. Recognising

ERM The ERM is a system for establishing and maintaining currency stability between EU trading partners, by restricting movements in the exchange rate value of currencies within specified 'bands'.

See p. 535 for some recent attempts to regulate the Internet.

that transborder exchanges may not, in themselves, make people feel more European or less nationalistic presents difficulties for European policy-framers exercised by the need to foster common European goals and identities. As part of its attempts to foster greater cooperation between peoples previously separated by state, language and culture, the EU has set a number of transborder regions, called '*euregio*', at the intersection of some of the internal borders of the EU. The function of such regions is to promote transborder cooperation and networking in trade, tourism and other areas of common interest. Maas-Rhein, one of the regions, encompasses parts of Belgium, The Netherlands and Germany. It has a regional council (a form of parliamentary assembly) made up of key political, commercial and cultural interests, which acts as a consultative body and deliberative forum.

Modest as such developments are, they too may be contributing to the stretching of political activity and governance across borders and thus to a redefinition of what we mean by domestic politics. At the other extreme, they may be part of a process in which political identities are being changed radically, such that groups and localities become truly Europeanised, although to date there is very little evidence to corroborate such a claim.

Of course, **realist** models of International Relations would point to the continued salience of states in the conduct of key policy areas like economic management and the mobility of citizens, and emphasise the undoubted resources of many individual states relative to those of even the largest business corporation. Work done by students of international management, such as Michael Porter (1990), also reveals the importance of peculiarly national factors in explaining the global success of large companies. When you look at Figure 15.3, which attempts to illustrate this point, remember Ohmae's argument about the 'borderless world' and the growing irrelevance of nation-states to the real flows of economic life (Ohmae 1989). Overall, these discussions suggest that under the impact of globalising forces the 'architecture' of world politics and of the world economy is changing quite rapidly (Cerny 1990). John Ruggie, a student of International Relations, says that rather than the absolute decline or even the complete dissolution of the nation-state, globalisation is bringing about a 'rearticulation of international political space' (Ruggie 1993), and the nation-state is just one of the components of that emerging structure, the others of which include multilateral institutions like the United Nations, forms of regional government like the EU, transnational interest groups and social movements, and the changing culture of the world polity, which is allowing new kinds of political demands and issues onto the agenda, while marginalising older ones.

Evidence of growing international and global governance is available in the work of institutions such as the United Nations, the International Monetary Fund and the World Bank. It is apparent in those international regimes responsible for policing the traffic in illegal drugs and monitoring national responses to climate change. In the new millennium international institutions seem more willing to examine and criticise how national governments and private organisations such as business corporations conduct their 'internal'

Realism A branch of International Relations theory in which the centrality of territorial states to the functioning of the world order is taken as given. States are depicted as collective actors whose rationale is the promotion of self-interest. Cooperation among states is viewed as unnatural and only to be countenanced as part of a larger strategy driven by national interest. In general and by definition, the world is anarchic and hostile.

In Figure 15.3 'factor conditions' refer to things like skilled labour and a good communications structure; 'demand conditions' to the nature of home demand for the industry's product or service; 'related and supporting industries' to the competitive quality of supplier industries; and 'firm strategy, structure and rivalry' to the rules and norms governing the setting up and managing of companies.

See Chapter 14 for an extended discussion of governance above the nation-state.

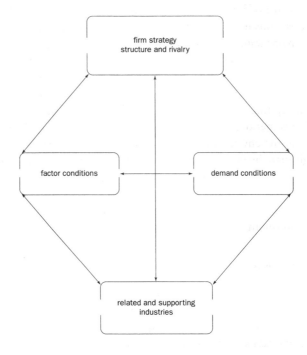

Figure 15.3 Porter's (1990) model for global success of countries; reproduced with permission from Macmillan Publishers

Tony Blair at the Davos World Economic Forum, 2000

Along with many other political leaders, Mr Blair feels the need to demonstrate his commitment to an interlinked world economy. His appearance at the World Economic Forum, an annual gathering of politicians, business leaders and other opinion leaders, is a visible sign of that commitment.

affairs in areas such as finance, trade, security and human rights. At the same time, the growth of inter- and transnationality is tempered by the fact that many organisations involved in aspects of world governance are dominated by the world's major states. This fact leads some smaller countries to conclude that the global agenda set by international institutions is really a veiled way of exporting the values and interests of core states – especially the United States – to other parts of the world and maintaining their power relative to others. Clearly this argument is very contentious, but it raises questions about the ability of international institutions to formulate and implement global standards (for the environment, for international security and so on) that are seen as legitimate by all states in the international community. That said, the range of issues and policy areas in which international organisations and regimes intervene grows larger year on year, and this makes national governments feel more and more sensitive and vulnerable and less and less sure about their autonomy.

Global cultures

The idea of global or **cosmopolitan** cultures strikes some people as a contradiction in terms, because they say that 'real' cultures are those which bind people to particular places. National cultures are 'real' in this sense, full of imagery, symbolism and meaning for people, because of the myths of origin, the national flags, the language and so on, which provide them with a context for knowing who they are. Global cultures, on the other hand, are none of these things, arising out of the general availability of global products and the pervasiveness of images carried by advertising and by the increasingly global entertainments industries. At the same time, global cultural fare is often said to be eroding more traditional and local identities. But, as we have seen, this is not a one-way process and it sometimes spawns a politics of resistance and the reaffirmation of alternative world views and older local traditions. In addition, it could be argued that the separation of culture and identity from place, which is implicit in the idea of a global culture, is part of the dialectic which may well produce de-spatialised cultures in the same way as it is producing de-territorialised politics and forms of governance, as we have noted above.

The preceding features of globalisation reveal it as not only a multi-dimensional process, but one in which there are a number of tensions, all of which are influencing the contested making of the global system and underline the possibilities for increased diversity as well as greater homogeneity. These are outlined below.

ORDER VERSUS DISORDER

Teleological explanations of social change describe an historical process unfolding towards an inevitable goal or end-state. Obviously there are different versions of what this will be – a socialist utopia, the global triumph of liberal

Cosmopolitan Here used to denote overcoming parochialism, and also used to denote the absence or transcending of national identities, interests and prejudices.

Teleology A theory of the final causes of things, a story unfolding to a predetermined end.

democracy, global neo-liberalism, a multi-centric world with overlapping sovereignties and multiple jurisdictions, or a single world community and government – but the ultimate order implied in all these positions seems markedly at odds with the highly contingent and disordered feel of contemporary world politics and of many areas of life. This is not just a matter of older certainties, like the collapse of state socialism and the end of a bipolar world dominated by two superpowers, being undone, but also includes the personal and social dislocation attendant upon changes in employment prospects triggered by digitalising production, or shifting assembly plants to another part of the world in order to reduce costs. The 'age of anxiety' referred to above (p. 548) is a long way from Francis Fukuyama's benign and rather boring 'end of History'. Overall it seems that the processes of globalisation are speeding up the transformation of both individual and collective identities. Sometimes people experience these changes as liberating but often see them as threatening, and their response may be to try to reinvent a more stable past through some political action or movement, thereby contributing to further disorder. A globalised world is not, or not yet, a safer or more stable place than one riven by national conflicts or superpower rivalry.

GLOBALISATION VERSUS LOCALIZATION

The effect of global processes and institutions is to relativise national and local identities and practices and to establish transnational and post-national forms (for example multilateral regimes, networks of professionals in business, finance, science, social movements and so on) which marginalise or bypass local rules and values. At the same time many global practices are subject to an implicit, but sometimes an explicit, 'localisation', to fit local tastes but also to protect local identities.

PLACES VERSUS SPACES

The modern world and certainly the pre-modern world were worlds full of places with particular meanings for the people who inhabited them. Landscapes, images of nature and the physical separation of one community from another were important elements in securing local and national identities. Globalisation erodes the intimacy of place, partly because of the greater physical mobility allowed, and partly because it permits interests and communities to form which are not tied to particular places and do not need face-to-face contact to sustain them, like 'virtual communities' or neo-communities on the Internet. For all this, nostalgia for 'real' places and the 'whole' lifestyles they supported remains strong, and is in direct opposition to the fragmented and cosmopolitan patterns of living found by some observers in 'global cities' like London, New York or Rio or even among specialist virtual communities.

HOMOGENISATION VERSUS DIVERSITY

The key message about globalisation is that while it does seem to produce what Anthony McGrew calls an 'essential sameness' in the surface appearance of social and political life across the globe (McGrew 1992), the appearance of sameness can be deceptive. Apparent uniformity disguises a great deal of diversity and fudges the continued vitality of different worldviews. Moreover, the process of globalisation is both multilayered (multidimensional) and driven by a variety of conflicting forces. It is also 'made' by people who both have a past and often possess firm identities greatly at odds with the world marketed through 'chillin' out with a Bud'. Because of this it is still a very contingent process with a range of possible outcomes.

Vectors of globalisation

We have already questioned the idea that globalisation is producing a homogeneous world or moving towards an historically prescribed goal or end-state. Fukuyama's (1992) teleological theory of world history and Immanuel Wallerstein's (1974) treatment of the making of a capitalist world economy as a long-term cyclical process are important insights into aspects of globalisation, but they underestimate the imponderables in a process that is nowhere complete or uncontested. Roland Roberston (1992) talks of the possibility of different trajectories of global change even at this juncture of world history, but what sorts of future are available?

Key text: I. Wallerstein (1974) *The Modern World-System*, Vol. 1, New York: Academic Press.

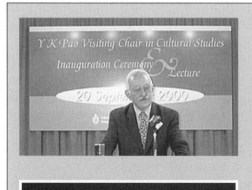

Immanuel Wallerstein

Seen as one of the most innovative social scientists of his generation, Immanuel Wallerstein (1928–) is noted for his founding of the 'World-Systems School' in the 1970s, in which he looks at the modern capitalist world economy from a perspective of 'world-systems'. This new methodology has laid the foundation for much of the scholarly debate on 'globalization' in the twenty-first century.

The end of a world of territorial nation-states

The future of the nation-state looks rather fragile in the increasingly interconnected world. But states remain key actors in world politics, with the myth of sovereignty still a powerful constraint on how the international system functions. States are still critical in giving definition to national societies and cultures, and are the focus for what Benedict Anderson calls the 'imagined community' of the nation (Anderson 1983; and see Chapter 8, pp. 276–81 on 'Nationalism'). So it is highly unlikely that territorial states will disappear in the foreseeable future, although the meaning of territoriality and the dominance of the state-centred nature of world politics is certain to be further affected by transnational forces and both international and transnational institutions. Even in a thoroughly globalised age, the scope for national discretion in the delivery of key areas of public policy remains substantial, as Table 15.3 indicates:

Table 15.3 Government spending as percentage of Gross Domestic Product

	1960	1980	1998
Australia	21.2	31.4	32.9
Britain	32.2	43.0	40.2
Canada	28.6	38.8	42.1
France	34.6	46.1	54.3
Germany	32.4 (FRG)	47.9 (FRG)	46.9 (ALL)
Italy	30.1	42.1	49.1
Japan	17.5	32.0	36.9
Sweden	31.0	60.1	60.8
USA	26.8	31.4	32.8

Source: OECD (1999)

Apart from the variation in the percentage of GDP spent by individual states, the overall message in these figures is that in a period of intense globalisation some states seem to be bucking the pressures from markets to spend less of their national wealth. Whether such resistance (if resistance is the right word) is sustainable remains open to question. In other areas of policy, the variation is much greater, tribute to the variety of state and cultural traditions that provide the context in which decision-making is rooted. In the UK, the current Labour government is determined to ensure flexibility in labour markets, making the UK one of the most lightly regulated of all the Western nations in this respect. Multinational corporations incur no sanctions if they decide to close a plant or cut back on the size of a workforce. In France, also a member of the OECD and the EU, companies choosing to relocate production in another country, or to close facilities entirely, often face considerable financial burdens through compensation and financial penalties. In short, the simple notion of the inevitable and clearly observable policy convergence as a result of globalisation should be treated with a great deal of caution.

A post-capitalist world economic order?

Immanuel Wallerstein says that we already have a post-capitalist world economic order, and that any doubts about its global reach have been removed by the fall of communism and by the frantic attempts of post-communist regimes to marketise their economies and societies. There are few places and few activities not penetrated by capital: tribes in the Amazon Basin, fighting a losing battle with hardwood logging companies, shopping online and e-commerce in general, the global branding of David Beckham, are all part of world commodity chains and a new cultural economy. The Ford Motor Company, through its 'Ford 2000' programme, has transformed itself into a global organisation, selling global products regardless of place. In fact the very idea of being a purely national company is rapidly becoming outdated for any business hoping to compete in world markets – although there is always a niche for selling products identified with particular places – McVitie's digestive biscuits come to mind as an epitome of Britishness. In the twenty-first century, world trade will be increasingly dominated by big transnational corporations struggling to keep ahead of their rivals, especially in key sectors like telecommunications. In this new millennium, the shift will be completed from organised, national capitalism, based on national companies and mass production, to disorganised capitalism, where the emphasis is on market share, niche markets, specialised and computer-aided production techniques, global branding and marketing strategies, and the provision of services rather than the production of goods.

These developments problematise the nature of governance, and especially the regulation of economic activity which is increasingly organised on a global scale. The territorial nation-state is often simply unable to exercise control or require accountability from transnational organisations, and forms of cooperative regulation like the International Monetary Fund (IMF) or the EU may be better placed to ensure fair competition or the rights of consumers. As noted above, the legitimacy of such institutions and their powers of regulation remain patchy. In a globalised world the growth in the number and range of transnational non-governmental organisations (TNGOs) working in areas such as pollution control or other forms of environmental protection contributes to the essentially democratic function of monitoring powerful commercial and governance bodies which have shed their own national identities, and for some, also suggest the growing vitality of a global civil society.

A global civil society?

The implied and sometimes explicit universalism of organisations like Friends of the Earth suggests a growing sense of global unity or awareness of global risks, and is part of what we might call 'grass-roots' globalisation, as opposed to the 'top-down' version found in bodies like the United Nations and the World Bank. Somewhat curiously, this universalism also sanctions a growing respect for difference, or for the tolerance of differences. Global scripts, like that of universal human rights, underwrite a whole apparatus of regulations, sanctions, educational programmes and forms of political action devoted to achieving this goal. The existence of a global civil society – a zone of transnational association and deliberation under the control of neither states nor markets – is hotly debated. Very often, instances of global civil society in action, such as the Seattle protesters' network or the Genoa Social Forum as well as the activities of the Zapatistas in Mexico, are notable mainly because they are evidence of resistance to powerful global institutions. This brand of 'globalisation from below' undoubtedly contributes to what Richard Falk calls a 'more variegated type of politics' (1999), but whether it constitutes or even promotes more transparent and accountable forms of global governance remains moot.

Local Resistance, Global Struggle: extract from the Zapatista website <http://www.chiapaslink.ukgateway.net/>

Whilst the Zapatista rebellion is rooted in local problems of political corruption, exclusion and violence, and in the search for alternatives at the community level, the uprising cannot be separated from global forces. The marginalisation of the indigenous population of Chiapas dates back to the Spanish invasion over 500 years ago, when the structures for the exploitation of the native population, and of natural resources to be exported to the 'First World' were established. The insurgents of the Zapatista army have an intimate knowledge of the destructive effects of capitalist development on their communities, culture and environment. These have only been intensified by the onset of neoliberal economic reforms since the early 1980s which triggered the uprising. Hence the choice of the first day of the implementation of the NAFTA to take up arms. A 'death sentence' indeed if the predictions of up to 15 million farmers being uprooted from the land are anything to go by.

Governance beyond frontiers (Halliday 2001) remains a seethe of national, international, regional and proto-universal institutions, increasingly inter-woven with the growing numbers of non-governmental organisations (NGOs), social movements and networks of various kinds. The prospects for greater actual cooperation, as opposed to form and rhetoric, vary enormously. In an apparent expression of solidarity with America's 'war on terrorism', the North Atlantic Treaty Organisation (NATO) invoked for the first time Article 5 of its Charter, wherein an attack on one member state is taken as an attack on all. But the national interests of members, and the depth of their commitment to a sustained anti-terrorist campaign could never equate to their initial outrage at the attack on the World Trade Center. And in the infancy of the new century there is growing evidence that new and old forms of particularism (ethnic nationalism, racism, religious fundamentalism) are contributing to a growing destabilisation of local and world politics, so that chaos, not universalism and order, may be the hallmark of the new millennium.

The prospect of civilisational conflict

Some writers have even gone so far as to predict the emergence or re-emergence of older, more elemental conflicts in the wake of the Cold War. The reference here is to tribalism or ultra-nationalism of the sorts found in Rwanda or the former Yugoslavia, but mainly to the threat of civilisational conflicts. The idea of civilisation used in this way means the broadest forms of cultural identity that bind people together, through history, language, custom or religion. The clear distinction between one civilisation and another is difficult, but writers like Samuel Huntington (1993 and 1998) are prepared to identify a number of what he calls civilisational identities: the Western, the Confucian (Chinese) as well as Islamic, Hindu, Slavic-Orthodox, Latin American and possibly African. These, he says, constitute great 'fault-lines' across history, lines which were overlaid by the modern conflicts of left versus right, capitalism versus communism and superpower versus superpower, but which are appearing anew as history is released from its Cold War tutelage. These fault-lines will reappear because civilisational identities are more enduring and more authentic than those forged by modern political doctrines, including nation-state nationalism, and because they offer the promise of emotional, if not physical, security in an uncertain and globalised world.

What is often called Islamic fundamentalism and its growing appeal in modernised or modernising countries like Turkey or Algeria, along with its potential to disrupt the routines of political and social life in metropolitan countries like France, are often cited as a case in point. On some accounts, the conflict between Bosnian Serbs and Muslims, Chechens and Russians and Kosovan Albanians and Macedonia, are local variants of these larger themes. In this world view it would be possible to interpret the contretemps between the USA and China in 2001 over the mid-air collision involving Chinese jets and a US spy-plane, as an expression of civilisational differences and cultural distance, although a clash of national sensibilities probably comes closer to the truth. There is undoubtedly a deep sense of 'otherness' or difference between Islamic and Western worldviews. But apocalyptic visions of civilisational conflict should be modified in the light of the routine transactions which take place between Muslim and non-Muslim countries in the form of trade, tourism and cultural exchanges. No civilisation is the monolith conjured up in this interpretation of world conflict. As the Gulf War coalition against the Iraqi invasion of Kuwait in 1991 showed, Muslim states, jealous of their national interests, were still prepared to take up arms against their co-religionists. Yet in the immediate aftermath of the attack on the World Trade Center and the Pentagon in the USA on 11 September 2001 there was much talk of the cultural features that divide societies, and, from some protagonists, even murmurs of a renewed clash of civilisations. Various Western leaders and opinion-formers were quick to distance themselves from intemperate remarks on the threat to Western civilisation posed by terrorists with their roots in Islamic societies and Islamic values, and moderate followers of Islam denounced the *jihad* mentality of extremists. Yet the fragility of the nascent cosmopolitan world was underlined by these events. If the world has been altered by the attacks, its new contours will take some time to be revealed.

Global chaos?

See Chapter 5 for a discussion of different forms of democracy. See also p. 371.

Fukuyama's (1992) picture of the end of history and American President George Bush Snr's prescription in 1990 for a 'New World Order' to be built on the ruins of the Cold War may both appear as overly benign visions of a global future. A condition of 'globality' featuring a pacific world order made in the image of market capitalism and forms of *electoral democracy* or, as one great shopping mall built in homage to 'McDisney' (Ritzer 1993) suggests a world already well down the track of convergence. Yet much of what we have discussed above describes a world more unsettled, possibly more chaotic and anxious than these pacific models suggest. In this world, which is more intensely localised and globalised, the permanence of some institutional forms like the territorial state and of corresponding identities like national citizenship could look quite fragile. Of course, social scientists must always be cautious about how they interpret evidence, and must strive to separate wishful thinking and mere speculation from good evidence. Given the scope and diverse nature of the process of globalisation, this task is made more difficult than usual. However, students of politics cannot afford to ignore the impact of politics and social forces which are not only above the nation-state but beyond it too.

Conclusion

In this chapter we have explored the idea that the study of globalisation adds important new dimensions to the study and understanding of political and social life. First, it draws attention to the links between politics, economics and culture in ways rarely seen in the study of national societies. While some accounts still trade on one causal factor in the making of a single world, it is very unlikely that such approaches can grasp the enormous complexity of globalisation as a multidimensional process. Second, it directs attention away from the national society as the focus for social analysis and the main container for social and political life, reflecting the stretching of social, economic and political relations across the globe. Third, it qualifies the tendency to analyse

This was a concept we first examined in Chapter 1 to explore the links between the individual and the social.

social and political relations through a concentration upon particular *levels of analysis*. Rather, the study of globalisation links the personal and the global, showing how individual perceptions and experience of globalisation can have significant effects upon the larger processes at work, as well as how these processes affect individual and collective identities. As with so much in the world of politics, many of the outcomes here have still to be decided.

Chapter summary

- Globalisation is not just another term for international politics, but is shorthand for a number of processes that are making the world into a single place.

- These processes are neither linear nor teleological, but complex and multidimensional, proceeding with variable intensity throughout different historical periods.

- In the current period of more intense globalisation various indicators help to chart the extent and intensity of the process. These include patterns of interconnection between states and societies, the extent of global consciousness, the sense that globalisation involves both relativisation and indigenisation, the extent of resistance to globalisation and the idea that there is a global system.

- There are various and often contradictory interpretations of globalisation derived from different academic disciplines and world views.

- Globalisation has a variety of features, including economic and political but also cultural factors.

- There are a number of possible global futures, including a pacific, and largely Westernised, world order and descent into global chaos.

- From the point of view of academic study and social theory, globalisation raises important questions about the ways in which social and political life are organised and identities sustained.

Key texts

Axford, B. (1995) *The Global System: Economics, Politics and Culture*, Cambridge: Polity Press. Looks at the various dimensions along which globalising pressures have emerged, and stresses the cultural aspects of globalisation and of resistance to it.

Beck, U. (2000) *What is Globalisation?*, Cambridge: Polity Press. A provocative and very personal view of the process of globalisation from a key social commentator.

Castells, M. (1996) *The Network Society* (Vol. 1), Oxford: Blackwell. The first of three volumes on the main dynamics of world society and a major contribution to social theory.

Held, D., McGrew, A., Thompson, G. and Perraton, J. (1999) *Global Transformations*, Cambridge: Polity Press. A wide-ranging and careful study of different theoretical perspectives along with a wealth of empirical material on different aspects of globalisation.

Hirst, P. and Thompson, G. (1999) *Globalization in Question*, 2nd edn, Cambridge: Polity Press. Provides a critical and iconoclastic view of globalisation, suggesting that the idea of a globalised economy is a myth.

Scholte, J-A. (2000) *Globalization: A Critical Introduction*, Basingstoke: Palgrave. A very useful and critical introduction to the subject that is sensitive to the need for a multidimensional approach.

Further reading

Drucker, P. (1993) *Post-Capitalist Society*, London: Butterworth-Heinemann. A management guru's readable and thoughtful, if somewhat optimistic account of political, social and economic changes in the 'borderless world'.

Falk, R. (1999) *Predatory Globalization*, Cambridge: Polity Press. An elegant collection of essays, mostly critical of the impact of globalisation on many aspects of life.

Gibson, W. (1984) *Neuromancer*, London: Gollancz. The first cyberpunk vision of a post-apocalyptic, globalised world.

Halliday, F. (2001) *The World at 2000*, Basingstoke: Palgrave. A collection of essays from a leading theorist of International Relations based on lectures given at the LSE.

Kennedy, P. (1993) *Preparing for the Twenty-First Century*, London: HarperCollins. A historian's view of globalising tendencies, which looks at the impact of factors like environmental change on different parts of the world.

Naipaul, V. S. (1982) *Among the Believers: An Islamic Journey*, Harmondsworth: Penguin. A famous novelist's journey through post-revolutionary Iran and other Islamic countries, examining the tensions between globalising (Westernising) pressures and Islamic identity.

Ohmae, K. (2000) *The Invisible Continent*, New York: Harper Business. Latest offering from one of the gurus of the 'borderless world' thesis.

Ritzer, G. (1993) *The McDonaldization of Society*, Newbury Park, CA: Pine Forge Press. An entertaining and insightful examination of the impact of Americanised global cultures.

Klein, N. (2000) *No Logo*, New York: HarperCollins. A much hyped but still interesting account of branded capitalism.

Glossary

adversarial politics The confrontational style, especially of British politics, where political positions tend to become polarised.

adversary politics A phrase first coined by Samuel Finer (1974). He said the conflict between the Labour and Conservative parties in Britain took the form of a 'stand up fight between two adversaries for the favour of onlookers'. This ritual, he believed, caused ineffective governance and was a caricature of real parliamentary democracy. The expression is now used largely as a way of criticising the performance of parties during election campaigns and in the House of Commons during debates.

agents of socialisation Those individuals, groups or institutions which are responsible for the transmission of the information through which people acquire their socialistion.

alternative media Media forms and outputs that provide an alternative to the official, mainstream or mass commercial media. Such media often have a strong radical element and utilise the technology of new media.

anarchy The absence of a single recognised governmental authority at world level to enforce laws. In International Relations, the term does not denote a situation of chaos and an anarchic system is not necessarily disorderly.

anti-politics An expression applied to a wide range of attitudes and phenomena. The main burden of the notion is that indirect, representative democracy, built on party competition and reliant upon the mediating functions of political parties, is being challenged. In this scenario, the villains are ruled through media, some kinds of interest groups and social movements, populism generally and market forces which have turned interested citizens into unreflective consumers. Applied to countries without established democracies, the expression embraces many undemocratic practices such as denying forms of opposition.

apathy Implies an inattention to or unconcern with and a passivity about politics.

arbiter and arena These theories envisage government as standing above the group battle, settling ground rules for the conflict (particularly those determining what groups and what modes of action are legitimate), ensuring the enforcement of those rules, and perhaps correcting imbalances if there is a danger of particular groups growing into over-mighty subjects. The arena theory, in contrast, sees politicians merely as co-equal participants in the group (see Lively 1978: 191).

behaviouralism A movement in postwar political science, notably in the USA, concerned with establishing law-like generalisations about the political world and with shifting the emphasis of political studies away from its traditional legal-institutional manifestation. With a focus upon individual behaviour, the 'behavioural approach' means literally a focus upon individual behaviour. The 'behavioural approach' is linked with quantitative research techniques designed to generate testable hypotheses about measurable attitudes and observable behaviour, thus rendering the study of politics more scientific.

bicameralism An assembly with two legislative chambers, for example, the USA, France and Argentina.

brokerage Literally to broker or trade off differences in order to produce an acceptable compromise or lowest common denominator.

bureaucracy Government by permanent officials. The word is often used in a pejorative way to imply the tyranny of the office. Its main characteristics include a hierarchy, rules, merit appointments, rationality in decision-making. The term can be applied to private as well as government organisations.

capitalism An economic system in which the means of production for the most part lie in private hands, and goods and services are bought and sold according to prices determined by a market in which the aim of producers and providers is to make a profit.

caucus party A caucus is a closed party meeting and often applied to meetings held by a party group within a legislature or assembly.

citizen A member of a particular territorial state and the rights attaching to that status. Modern conceptions of citizenship stress universal rights and obligations, and there is now a transnational doctrine of human rights, but the legal status and the rights and obligations that follow from it remain attached to particular countries.

civic culture The type of political culture thought by some to provide the best environment for stable democratic politics to occur. It combines the optimum mix of subject and participant political attitudes.

civil society The sphere of society in which individuals freely associate in relationships, actions and organisations that are not dependent on state intervention, institutions or regulations.

class-consciousness The awareness of social divisions in society and the acceptance that class strongly determines life chances.

coalition An alliance or grouping of rival party and/or other political groups. The alliance is formed through the existence of common ground on aspects of ideology or policy, although it may follow simply from expediency and the need to build a minimum winning coalition. Coalitions may also be designed to exclude particular parties from government as much as to foster common ground among partners. Coalitions may be formed prior to or during elections, but they may be the outcome of hurried post-election bargaining.

conceptual analysis A practice and view of philosophy which takes philosophy to be concerned with the analysis and clarification of concepts rather than substantive issues.

consociational Refers to a political and sometimes a constitutional arrangement in which significant differences between groups in a political system are the basis for organising the distribution of governmental posts or guaranteeing representational quotas in legislatures, in order to ensure political stability. These groups may be ethnic, religious, even linguistic. For example, in Belgium, where there are major linguistic divisions between Dutch- and French-speaking Belgians, the constitution provides for a balance of power between political parties and regions based on language difference.

consociational democracy A form of government said to characterise deeply divided, albeit stable, countries. It involves the creation of power-sharing institutions among coalescent political elites.

constitution The rules by which states and governments are organised and operate in the form of the enshrining of rights, duties and obligations that establish or formalise the relationship between political authority and the people.

contextualism This stands for the view that the meaning of political ideas can be understood only by relating them to the historical contexts in which they were generated.

corporatism Refers to the process whereby producer interests are incorporated into the policy-making process.

cosmopolitan Here used to denote overcoming parochialism, and also used to denote the absence or transcending of national identities, interests and prejudices.

cosmopolitan democracy A globalised form of democracy that is perceived as transnational, multi-levelled and cosmopolitan. Some people argue that such political organisation is emerging in response to the economic and cultural globalisation.

cost-benefit analysis A method for balancing and assessing policy options according to their costs and benefits.

deliberative democracy A form of democracy which stresses the participation of the people in collective decision-making through a process of rational and considered deliberation.

democracy From the original Greek, the term means, literally, rule by the people, or by the many. In modern political systems it is usually linked with universal suffrage, free elections and with notions like the consent of the governed.

democratic centralism The Leninist dogma that sought to weigh unity with pluralism within the Communist Party. In reality, since the party claimed to be the organisational embodiment of the will of the people, its claims were always seen as superior to those of any other group or faction.

democratisation The processes by which states move towards more democratic forms of political systems.

devolution Refers to the process whereby powers, for example, over taxation, are devolved or transferred from central to regional or local government within a specified legislative framework.

digital democracy An umbrella term that refers to the application of advanced ICTs and new media to the political process. This can take many forms, from politicians having websites and e-mail, to more elaborate and structured use of ICTs in, for example, electoral systems or participatory processes involving citizens and politicians.

direct democracy A form of democracy in which all members of the political community participate directly in the processes of decision-making.

distributive justice A theory which sees the distribution of wealth and goods in society as involving justice, and which sets out a 'just' scheme of distribution.

division of labour The division of tasks and functions, often leading to specialisation and increased productivity, but associated with alienation and fragmentation.

dominant ideology Sets of social values, norms and expression which dominate all others at given points in the development of society. In particular, the dominant ideology that characterises a particular historical epoch will tend to reflect the class interests of the social group that is economically dominant. Furthermore, this dominant ideology will seek to mask the 'real' nature of the economic and exploitative relationships on which society rests.

elite The best or the most noble; in contemporary usage it is generally applied to those who have high status or a high formal position in politics, religion and society.

empirical A term meaning sense or understanding derived from experience.

Enlightenment The eighteenth-century Enlightenment 'project' was based upon a belief in the universality of reason and the power of scientific explanation. The individual was at the centre of the philosophical and political project, with human emancipation seen as following from the spread of rational inquiry and decision-making.

ERM The ERM is a system for establishing and maintaining currency stability between EU trading partners, by restricting movements in the exchange rate value of currencies within specified 'bands'.

executive The apex of power in a political system, at which policy is formed and through which it is executed, for example the President in the USA or the Prime Minister and Cabinet in Britain.

false consciousness A term associated with Marxist thought which maintains that individuals and the class to which they belong may well demonstrate a sense of social understanding that is predominantly 'false', in that it hides from them or prevents them from recognising the 'real' nature of their position within the social order and the extent to which they are exploited.

federation 'An institutional arrangement, taking the form of a sovereign state, and distinguished from other such states solely by the fact that its central government incorporates regional units in its decision procedure on some constitutionally entrenched basis' (Preston King).

free-market negativity An attack on the application of free-market concepts to the media marketplace. It argues that the valuable public service broadcasting ethos characterised by 'protected' and to some extent non-market institutions such as the British Broadcasting Corporation (BBC) cannot be matched in a free media market in which all values will be subject to the needs of profit and that quality will be reduced in the pursuit of cheap programming and copy. Furthermore, the promise of choice offered by the market will, in reality, mean choice between one thing and more of the same.

free-market positivity A defence of the application of free-market concepts to the media marketplace. This approach argues that through a combination of new technologies, deregulation and market forces not only will the audience and the public get more media content to consume but that this content will be 'better', in that it will be more responsive to audience choice and more varied, and will allow for greater audience choice and difference.

functionalism A term used to describe a range of theories that stress the extent to which norms and values underlie social and political stability. Stable societies are seen as being able to carry out the basic 'functional' imperatives – socialisation, integration, reproduction and so on – necessary for their survival.

futurism An early twentieth-century movement in the arts which glorified technology, industry and factories.

Gleichschaltung The process whereby all institutions and organisations were coordinated to serve the purposes and goals of the Nazi state.

globalisation The economic, political and cultural processes through which the world is becoming more interconnected and interdependent, leading to the creation of a single 'world-space' or system.

governance A broader concept than government which refers to the processes through which social, economic and political life are organised and regulated.

government The formal institutions, offices, processes and personnel through which the day-to-day running of a country, the maintenance of public order and the distribution of resources is managed and maintained.

hegemony A term used to describe the non-coercive aspects of domination, the diffusion throughout society of the value and knowledge systems of a ruling group.

ideal type A social scientific technique that imposes an analytical order on the social world and provides clear categories to guide further investigation.

image management The set of techniques employed by politicians, parties and strategists to ensure the best presentation of themselves and to maintain a central set of ideas, images and associations, for public consumption, of those politicians and parties.

indigenisation The adaptation of alien practices to local circumstances and to meet local needs.

interest groups Sometimes called pressure groups, but the term 'interest group' takes in a wider variety of organisations and activities.

intergovernmentalism The view which argues that the development of international institutions and regimes tends to be shaped by the actions of and convergences of interest among nation-state actors.

international regimes Consist of more-or-less codified agreements and rules governing some aspect of the relations between states.

international relations Formally, the conduct of politics among nation-states, but also the study of international political interaction, which has more recently begun to include the analysis of non-state as well as state actors and forces.

judiciary The body within a political system charged with enforcing the laws and, in some states, upholding the constitutional rules.

legislature The body within a political system that makes the laws. This is likely to be the national assembly, for example Parliament in the UK or Congress in the USA.

legitimacy The procedures used by a party for maintaining a belief in the appropriateness and acceptability of the party system.

level of analysis The difference between studying individuals and collectives of different sorts. Choosing one level of analysis as opposed to another determines the sort of inferences which can be made from data.

liberal democracy A doctrine, and sometimes a practice, which combines individual freedom with the idea of popular sovereignty.

limited government Government in which the sovereign or executive power is limited by law, constitutional rules or institutional organisation. See also **separation of powers**.

lobby A generic term for making representations to public officials and elected representatives. Closely associated with American politics, the expression has its origins in the attempts by petitioners – lobbyists – to meet with politicians in the lobby of a parliament building.

logical positivism A philosophical doctrine which maintains that a term is meaningful in so far as it is susceptible of verification.

logrolling The bargaining and coalition-building that takes place between departments in order to obtain resources.

machine politics A form of party politics in which the 'bosses' of local and state-based party organisations exercised wide patronage over public appointments and dominated the national party Conventions at which, among other things, presidential candidates are nominated.

market testing A process whereby publicly provided goods and services are compared according to cost and quality with those provided by the private sector.

Marxism After Karl Marx. Emphasis is usually placed on the way in which economic processes and constraints shape social relations and relations of power.

mass media Media that disseminate usually undifferentiated popular forms of output (reflecting the mass nature of the audience) to a mass audience. For example, this would include the popular tabloid press, television, cinema and book publishing.

media cultures In a media culture media images, sounds and spectacles are central to everyday life, dominate leisure time, shape political and social views, values and behaviour, and provide the raw material out of which people create their identities (Kellner 1995).

methodological individualism A philosophical and empirical focus on the individual and individual behaviour.

model A representation of events and processes which focuses on key aspects of what is going on in them.

modernisation Literally, the processes whereby society becomes modern.

modernity The distinct way of life found in 'modern' societies. A process beginning in Western Europe in about the fifteenth century, the idea of modernity achieved an intellectual flowering during the Enlightenment. It is usual to tie modernity, or becoming modern, to the emergence of the nation-state, industrialism and the institution of private property. Modernity is also linked to the growth of bureaucratic organisations, secular beliefs and the value of individuality.

modes of production A phrase usually associated with Karl Marx, and which refers to the way production is organised in society. It focuses upon the technology and social relations of production. The most essential part of social relations is control over productive forces and resources.

nation-building The processes through which a sense of national identity and belonging are effected. Sometimes these involve deliberate policy on the part of rulers, sometimes they are instigated through things like threat of invasion.

nation-state The governmental and administrative apparatus of a bounded national territory. The term is often used as a synonym for 'country'. The most recent way in which human politics has been organised, and now thought by some to be under considerable threat.

national revolution The political movement that resulted in the construction of independent states governed by a central authority.

negative freedom A term taken as meaning freedom from state interference. It assumes that individuals should have an area of life where they are free to make decisions and behave as they wish as long as they do not interfere with the freedom of others.

neo-liberalism A theory which places market efficiencies as the foundation for political freedom and argues for a limited role for the state.

neo-pluralism A variant of pluralism which recognises the development of elite groups with more access to power.

new liberalism refers to a strand of thinking which rejected the negative concept of liberty and saw state intervention as expanding liberty in areas like factory legislation.

New Right The term associated with a resurgence of the right in Western politics since the late 1970s. The New Right, drawing inspiration from the works of (amongst others) von Hayek and Friedman, demonstrates three key characteristics: first, a commitment to a *laissez-faire* attitude to state, society, market and individual that seeks to eliminate state intervention in all aspects of life; second, a reaffirmation of traditional values with regard to certain aspects of social life and social organisation, especially the family and community; third, a libertarian strand which stresses the need for individual liberty and responsibility. The New Right has been seen as highly influential in the administrations of President Ronald Reagan (1981–9) in the USA and the Conservative governments of Margaret Thatcher (1979–90) in the UK.

normative The prescription of what should or ought to be the case as opposed to what, descriptively, is the case.

oligarchy Government by the few; Michels argued that even in parties which claimed to have democratic internal structures there was a controlling elite pursuing its own self-interest.

party system Refers to the number and types of party operating in a political system. The concept also refers to the interactions between parties and the wider society and to the pattern of competition – or lack of it – between parties themselves. Party systems are embedded in particular societies and cultures.

patronage The distribution of political favours to government or party followers in return for political support.

pluralism The belief that there is, or else there should be, diversity. Political pluralism recognises and encourages variety in social, cultural and ideological forms and processes. Pluralist theories examine the influence of social groups in the making of public policy, where there may be competition among groups with different resources.

political communication The intended, explicit and implicit communication of messages with a political content between members of a political system. But political communication is also the communication, intended and unintended, of messages within a political and social system that contribute to the transmission and circulation of political and social values, beliefs and ideas.

political competence Both a formal status, in the sense that as a citizen one has the right to vote, and a practical skill, for example in terms of organising a demonstration or writing to a member of Congress or Parliament.

political culture The set of values, beliefs and attitudes within which a political system operates.

political efficacy The extent to which an individual feels that his or her participation in politics will be effective.

political ideologies Sets of political beliefs involving programmes of political action which draw on large-scale views about human nature and/or historical development.

political participation A term to denote the actions by which individuals take part in the political process. Debate centres on the causes of participation and non-participation.

political party A permanent organisation, the primary purpose of which is to contest elections and to wield power within a government. Parties perform many other functions, including mobilising popular participation in politics, elite recruitment and representing (sections of) the public, but winning elections and controlling the machinery of state power are paramount.

political socialisation The process, or set of processes, through which people learn about politics and acquire political values. There is much dispute about which processes are significant and about when in the life cycle the most important socialisation takes place.

political system A concept sometimes used as a synonym for 'country', but which technically refers to the relationships, processes and institutions which make up a distinct political universe. Thus the Italian political system is made up of 'inputs' from society to the formal institutions of government, in the form of public opinion, pressure group activity and so on, while the institutions of government process these inputs to produce 'outputs' in the form of laws, policies and even norms and values.

positive freedom A view which sees freedom as a condition to be achieved through positive actions.

postmodern Literally, beyond the modern, and suggesting a fragmentation of modernist beliefs, identities and certainties.

postnationality The idea that national units of government and identity have been superseded.

primary election A mechanism used by parties in the USA, in which candidates are selected or elected to be the party's nominee at a subsequent inter-party election.

propaganda The term originally referred to propagation of the faith in Catholicism, but refers today to the way in which governments subordinate knowledge and information to state policy.

public choice Theories which argue that people make choices according to economic scarcity based on marginal utility.

public good Benefit which cannot be withheld from the community at large, that is, it is not only available to those who are members of an organisation or who have paid for the benefit. Clean air, world peace and safe streets are all public goods.

public service broadcasting The idea that all citizens should have access to a diverse, socially and politically responsible and non-commercially organised broadcasting medium, principally in radio and television.

public sphere A space in which public debate, discussion and reflection can take place, free from political and state interference and in which public opinion can form.

QUANGO Non-governmental organisations given operational autonomy. Used with the term 'quasi-government' about organisations with an arm's-length relationship with government. There is concern that such organisations have been unaccountable and open to political patronage.

rationality A concept which places the individual actor at the centre of analysis, policy-making being determined by individual choice.

realism A branch of International Relations theory in which the centrality of territorial states to the functioning of the world order is taken as given. States are depicted as collective actors whose rationale is the promotion of self-interest. Cooperation among states is viewed as unnatural and only to be countenanced as part of a larger strategy driven by national interest. In general and by definition, the world is anarchic and hostile.

regional integration The processes by which states in particular regions of the world bring together aspects of their economies and politics. There is much debate about the stimulus for such developments, with some seeing the cause as residing in the sovereign preferences of states themselves. Others argue that integration occurs because of the operation of powerful dynamics beyond the control of nation-states.

regionalism The process of interconnection and interaction between groupings of states. The basis for regionalisation may be common history, geographical proximity or common interests.

relativisation The process whereby the integrity, wholeness or absolute quality of an identity is diluted by the power of global forces.

Renaissance A sixteenth-century movement in Europe which brought a more questioning and secular approach to art and literature and thus to the place of humans in the order of things.

representative democracy A form of democracy in which citizens elect political representatives through periodic, popular elections who then represent the people within a system of government at national (for example, in a parliament) or local (for example, in a local authority or city council) level.

revolution A term which suggests profound change involving dramatic events over a short period of time, rather than evolution through stages or incremental adjustments to existing social, political and cultural arrangements.

scientific polling Refers to a number of procedures and rules for ensuring reliability of method and results. These include: a valid sample of the population to be canvassed; an appropriate sample size; proper regard for the principle of random selection (for representative samples); guarding against sampling bias (treating as representative a segment of the population in which the significant characteristics of the whole population are skewed in some way); awareness of the correct margin of error within which results can be deemed valid; and proper attention to wording of questions and interviewer training.

separation of powers The doctrine that maintains that the three key elements of government – the executive, the legislature and the judiciary – should be separate in role, powers and responsibilities and that such separation will ensure good and just government.

social construction The idea that value, perception and reality are constructed and given meaning through and in shared social understanding rather than existing in an objective reality or through natural development.

social corporatism Tends to develop as pluralist arrangements break down and the state has to intervene in the face of economic and industrial decline (see Schmitter 1979: 64).

social movement A network of informal interactions between individuals, groups and/or organisations, engaged in a political or cultural activity, on the basis of a shared collective identity.

sovereignty The idea of ultimate political authority. A body is fully sovereign if there is no higher or lower power. Sovereignty has been the basic ground rule for the conduct of the business of International Relations. The widespread legitimacy of the idea of sovereign statehood has hindered the development of authoritative institutions above the nation-state.

split ballot Voting for candidates of different parties at different levels and for different branches of government – state and federal; presidential and Congressional.

state The state refers to all the institutions, agencies and agents that operate within a given territorial space, have legitimate power and authority over the people and possess the sole authority to use force against its own citizens.

state corporatism Tends to be authoritarian and anti-liberal as in the political regimes of Fascist Italy or Nazi Germany.

straw poll A rough guide to opinion, based on, for example, a show of hands in a meeting, or a phone-in to a radio talk show. The method makes no claims to statistical reliability founded on accurate sampling techniques.

supranationalism The development of executive and binding authority at levels higher than the nation-state. The term is used by some to describe complex networks of inter-action among policy actors in International Relations.

syndicalism A form of revolutionary trade unionism in which the overthrow of capitalism is seen as arising out of direct action by workers. Sorel, an influential syndicalist, argued for the revolutionary potential of the general strike.

technological determinism An approach which argues that the development, use and proliferation of technology influences social change and interactions to the extent that technological revolutions can lead to social ones. Put another way, this approach argues that the social organisation of society is determined by the technology in place.

teleology A theory of the final causes of things, a story unfolding to a predetermined end.

totalitarianism The ideology that there is only one funda-mental principle of social and political organisation to which everything else must be subordinated. In totalitarian systems control is exerted over all aspects of life.

transnational politics Political activity conducted across national boundaries.

unicameralism An assembly with only one legislative chamber, for example, Finland, Hungary and Uganda.

unit for analysis The concrete object of inquiry: the indi-vidual, the primary group, e.g. the family, voluntary associations, formal organisations like political parties, whole societies, nation-states, even the world as a whole.

Aberbach, J. D., Putnam, R. D. and Rockman, B. A. (1981) *Bureaucrats and Politicians in Western Democracies*, Cambridge, Mass.: Harvard University Press.

Alasuutari, P. (ed.) (1999) *Rethinking the Media Audience*, London: Sage.

Alger, C. F. (1995) 'The United Nations in Historical Perspective', in C. F. Alger *et al.* (eds) *The United Nations System: The Policies of Member States*, Tokyo: United Nations University Press.

Allett, J. (1982) *New Liberalism: The Political Economy of J. A. Hobson*, Toronto: Toronto University Press.

Allison, G. T. (1971) *Essence of Decision*, Boston: Little, Brown & Co.

Almond G. A. (1980) 'The Intellectual History of the Civic Culture Concept', in G. A. Almond and S. Verba (eds) (1980) *The Civic Culture Revisited*, Boston: Little, Brown & Co.

Almond, G. A. and Verba S. (1963) *The Civic Culture: Political Attitudes and Democracy in Five Nations*, Princeton: Princeton University Press.

Almond, G. A. and Verba, S. (eds) (1980) *The Civic Culture Revisited*, Boston: Little, Brown & Co.

Althusser, L. (1969) *For Marx*, London: Allen Lane.

Althusser, L. (1971) *Lenin and Philosophy and Other Essays*, London: New Left Books.

Anderson, B. (1991) *Imagined Communities: Reflections on the Origins and Spread of Nationalism*, 2nd edn, London: Verso.

Ang, I. (1991) 'Culture and Communication: Towards an Ethnographic Account of Media Consumption in the Transnational Media System', *European Journal of Communication* 5(2–3): 239–60.

Anheier, H., Glasius, M. and Kaldor, M. (eds) (2001) *Global Civil Society 2001*, Oxford: Oxford University Press.

Anonymous (1996) *Primary Colors*, New York: Warner Books.

Appadurai, A. (1990) 'Disjuncture and Difference in the Global Cultural Economy', in M. Featherstone (ed.) *Global Culture: Nationalism, Globalization and Modernity*, London: Sage.

Archibughi, D., Held, D. and Kohler, M. (eds) (1998) *Re-Imagining Political Community*, Cambridge: Polity Press.

Arendt, H. (1990) *On Revolution*, London: Penguin.

Aristotle (1985) *The Politics*, ed. by Stephen Everson, Cambridge: Cambridge University Press.

Aron, R. (1967) *18 Lectures on Industrial Society*, London: Weidenfeld & Nicolson.

Arthur, C. J. (1986) *The Dialectics of Labour*, Oxford: Blackwell.

Ashcraft, R. (1987) *Locke's Two Treatises of Government*, London: Macmillan.

Atton, C. (2002) *Alternative Media*, London: Sage.

Axford, B. (1992) 'Leaders, Elections and Television', *Politics Review* 1(3): 17–20.

Axford, B. (1995) *The Global System: Economics, Politics and Culture*, Cambridge: Polity Press.

Axford, B. and Booth, J. (1995) 'Reflexive Modernisation and the Transformation of Identities: Management Education and Systemic Change in East-Central Europe', in V. Edwards (ed.) *Central and Eastern Europe: 5 Years On*, Chalfont St Giles: Buckinghamshire College.

Axford, B. and Browning, G. K. (eds) (1996) *Modernity–Postmodernity: From the Personal to the Global*, Oxford: Oxford Brookes.

Axford, B. and Huggins, R. (1996) 'Media Without Boundaries: Fear and Loathing on the Road to Eurotrash or Transformation in the European Cultural Economy', *Innovations* 9(2).

Axford, B. and Huggins, R. (eds) (2001a) *New Media and Politics*, London: Sage.

Axford, B. and Huggins, R. (2001b) 'Public Opinion or Postmodern Populism?: A Crisis of Democracy or the Transformation of Democratic Governance', in S. Splichal (ed.) *Public Opinion and Democracy: Vox Populi–Vox Dei?*, Cresskill, NJ: Hampton Press Inc., pp. 193–213.

Axford, B., Madgwick, P. and Turner, J. (1992) 'Image Management, Stunts and Dirty Tricks: The Marketing of Political Brands in Television Campaigns', *Media, Culture and Society* 14(4).

Bachrach, P. (1967) *The Theory of Democratic Elitism*, London: University of London Press.

Bachrach, P. and Baratz, M. S. (1963), 'Decisions and Nondecisions: An Analytical Framework', *American Political Science Review* 57.

Bachrach, P. and Baratz, M. S. (1970) *Power and Poverty: Theory and Practice*, Oxford: Oxford University Press.

Bahro, R. (1981) *The Alternative in Eastern Europe*, London: Verso.

Bahro, R. (1986) *Building the Green Movement*, London: GMP.

Balandier, G. (1992) *Le Pouvoir sur Scène*, Paris: Balland.

Balassa, B. (1962) *The Theory of Economic Integration*, London: Allen & Unwin.

Ball, T. (1995) *Reappraising Political Theory*, Oxford: Oxford University Press.

Barber, B. (1984) *Strong Democracy: Participatory Politics for a New Age*, Berkeley and London: University of California Press.

Barber, B. (1996) *Jihad versus McWorld*, New York: Ballantine.

Barber, B. (2001) 'Can Democracy Survive Globalization?', *Government and Opposition*: 275–301.

Barbrook, R. (1995) *Media Freedom: The Contradictions of Communications in the Age of Modernity*, London: Pluto.

Bardi, L. (1996) 'Anti-party Sentiment and Party System Change in Italy', *European Journal of Political Research* 29.

Barkman, K. (1995) 'Politics and Gender: The Need for Electoral Reform', *Politics* 15(5).

Barnes, J. (1998) *England, England*, London: Jonathan Cape.

Barnett, S. (1997) 'New Media, Old Problems: New Technology and the Political Process', *European Journal of Communication*.

Barnhurst, K. (1998) 'Politics in the Fine Meshes: Young Citizens, Power and Media', *Media, Culture and Society* 20(2): 201–18.

Barnhurst, K. and Mutz, D. (1997) 'American Journalism and the Decline of Event-centered News', *Journal of Communication* 47(4): 27–53.

Barrett, S. and Fudge, C. (1981) *Policy and Action*, London: Methuen.

Barrett, S. and Hill, M. J. (eds) (1981a) *Policy and Action*, Methuen: London.

Barrett, S. and Hill, M. J. (1981b) *Report to SSRC Central–Local Government Relations Panel*, unpublished.

Barry, B. (1970) *Sociologists, Economists and Democracy*, London: Collier Macmillan.

Barry, B. (1995) *Justice as Impartiality*, Oxford: Clarendon Press.

Barry, N. (1981) *An Introduction to Modern Political Theory*, London: Macmillan.

Batley, R. (1991) 'Comparisons and Lessons', in R. Batley and G. Stoker (eds) *Local Government in Europe: Trends and Developments*, London: Macmillan.

Batley, R. and Stoker, G. (eds) (1991) *Local Government in Europe: Trends and Developments*, London: Macmillan.

Baudrillard, J. (1976) *Symbolic Exchange and Death*, London: Sage.

Baudrillard, J. (1983) *Simulations*, New York: Semiotext.

Baudrillard, J. (1987) *The Evil Demon of Images*, Sydney: Power Institute of Fine Arts.

Baudrillard, J. (1988) *Jean Baudrillard: Selected Writings*, ed. M. Poster, Cambridge: Polity Press.

Baudrillard, J. (1993) *The Transparency of Evil: Essays on Extreme Phenomena*, London: Verso.

Bauman, Z. (1987) *Legislators and Interpreters: On Modernity, Post-Modernity and Intellectuals*, Cambridge: Polity Press.

Bauman, Z. (1994) 'After the Patronage State. A Model in Search of Class Interests', in C. G. A. Bryant and E. Mokrzycki (eds) *The New Great Transformation? Change and Continuity in East-Central Europe*, London: Routledge.

Baylis, J. and Smith, S. (eds) (2001) *The Globalization of World Politics*, 2nd edn, Oxford: Oxford University Press.

Beck, U. (1996) *The Reinvention of Politics*, Cambridge: Polity Press.

Beck, U. (1999) *What is Globalization?*, Cambridge: Polity Press.

Beer, S. M. (1982) *Britain Against Itself: The Political Contradictions of Collectivism*, London: Faber & Faber.

Bell, D. (ed.) (1962) *The End of Ideology: On the Exhaustion of Political Ideas in the Fifties*, New York: Free Press.

Bellah, R. M., Madson, R., Swidler, A. and Tipton, S. (1985) *Habits of the Heart*, Berkeley, Calif.: University of California Press.

Bellamy, R. (ed.) (1993) *Theories and Concepts of Politics*, Manchester: Manchester University Press.

Bentham, J. (1843) *The Works of Jeremy Bentham*, 2 vols, Edinburgh: William Tait.

Berger, J. (1972) *Ways of Seeing*, London: Penguin.

Berger, P. and Luckmann, T. (1966) *The Social Construction of Reality*, Harmondsworth: Penguin.

Berlin, I. (1991) 'Two Concepts of Liberty', in D. Miller (ed.) *Liberty*, Oxford: Oxford University Press.

Bernstein, E. (1961) *Evolutionary Socialism*, New York: Schocken Books.

Beveridge, W. (1944) *Full Employment in a Free Society*, London: Allen & Unwin.

Bhaskar, R. (1976) 'Two Philosophies of Science', *New Left Review* 94.

Billig, M. (1995) *Banal Nationalism*, London: Sage.

Birch, A. H. (1993) *The Concepts and Theories of Modern Democracy*, London: Routledge.

BIS (1998) *Statistics*.

Black, J. (1998) *Maps and Politics*, London: Reaktion Books.

Black, J. (2000) *The Politics of James Bond: From Fleming's Novels to the Big Screen*, New York: Praeger.

Blair, P. (1991) 'Trends in Local Autonomy and Democracy: Reflections from a European Perspective', in F. Batley and G. Stoker (eds) *Local Government in Europe: Trends and Developments*, London: Macmillan.

Birnbaum, P., Lively, J. and Parry, G. (1978) *Democracy, Consensus and Social Contract*, London: Sage.

Blondel, J. (1963) *Voters, Parties and Leaders*, London: Penguin.

Blondel, J. (1969a) *Comparative Government*, London: Macmillan.

Blondel, J. (1969b) *An Introduction to Comparative Government*, London: Weidenfeld & Nicolson.

Blumler, J. and Gurevitch, M. (1995) *The Crisis of Public Communication*, London: Routledge.

Bogdanor, V. (1999) *Devolution in the United Kingdom*, Oxford: Oxford University Press.

Bodiguel, J. L. (1983) 'A French-style Spoils System', *Public Administration* 61(3).

Boli, J. and Thomas, G. (1997) 'World Culture in the World Polity: A Century of INGOs', *American Sociological Review* 62: 191–209.

Boli, J. and Thomas, G. M. (1999) 'INGOs and the Organization of World Culture', in J. Boli and G. M. Thomas (eds) *Constructing World Culture: International Non-Governmental Organizations Since 1875*, Palo Alto, Calif.: Stanford University Press.

Boutros-Ghali, B. (1993) 'An Agenda for Peace', in A. Roberts and R. Kingsbury (eds) *United Nations, Divided World. The UN's Role in International Relations*, 2nd edn, Oxford: Oxford University Press.

Boutros-Ghali, B. (2000) 'An Agenda for Democratisation', in B. Holden (ed.) *Global Democracy: Key Debates*, London: Routledge, pp. 105–24.

Boyd-Barrett, O. and Rantanen, T. (eds) (1998) *The Globalization of News*, London: Sage.

Boyne, R. and Rattansi, A. (1990) *Postmodernism and Society*, Basingstoke: Macmillan.

Bradbury, M. (1976) *Fahrenheit 451*, London: Grafton.

Brant, K. (1998) 'Whose Afraid of Infotainment', *European Journal of Communication* 13 (3): 315–35.

Braudel, F. (1975) *Capitalism and Material Life 1400–1800*, New York: Harper.

Braudel, F. (1977) *Afterthoughts on Material Civilization and Capitalism*, Baltimore: Johns Hopkins University Press.

Braybrooke, D. and Lindblom, C. E. (1963) *A Strategy of Decision*, New York: Free Press.

Braybrooke, D. and Lindblom, C. E. (1968) *The Policy Making Process*, New York: Free Press.

Brennan, T. (1981) *Political Education and Democracy*, Cambridge: Cambridge University Press.

Brooker, P. (2000) *Non-Democratic Regimes: Theory, Government and Politics*, London: Macmillan.

Brown, A. (ed.) (2001) *Contemporary Russian Politics: A Reader*, Oxford: Oxford University Press.

Brown, C. (1982) *International Relations Theory: New Narrative Approaches*, Hemel Hempstead: Harvester Wheatsheaf.

Brown, C. (2001a) *Understanding International Relations*, 2nd edn, Basingstoke: Macmillan.

Brown, C. (2001b) 'Human Rights', in J. Baylis and S. Smith (eds) *The Globalization of World Politics: An Introduction to International Relations*, 2nd edn, Oxford: Oxford University Press.

Browning, G. K. (1991a) *Plato and Hegel: Two Modes of Philosophising About Politics*, New York: Garland Press.

Browning, G. K. (1991b) 'Ethical Absolutism in Plato and Hegel', *History of Political Thought* XII(3).

Browning, G. K. (1993) 'The German Ideology: The Theory of History and the History of Theory', *History of Political Thought* XIV(3).

Browning, G. K. (1996) 'Good and Bad Infinites in Hegel and Marx', in I. Hampsher-Monk and J. Stanyer (eds) *Contemporary Political Studies*, vol. 2, Belfast: PSA.

Browning, G. K. (1999) *Hegel and the History of Political Philosophy*, London: Palgrave.

Browning, G. K. (2000) *Lyotard and the End of Grand Narratives*, Cardiff: University of Wales Press.

Browning, G. K., Haldi, A. and Webster, F. (2000) *Understanding Contemporary Society: Theories of the Present*, London: Sage.

Bruce, B. (1992) *Images of Power: How the Image Makers Shape our Leaders*, London: Kogan Page.

Bryant, C. G. A. and Mokrzycki, E. (eds) (1994) *The New Great Transformation? Change and Continuity in East-Central Europe*, London: Routledge.

Bryson, V. (1993) 'Feminism', in R. Eatwell and A. Wright (eds) *Contemporary Political Ideologies*, London: Pinter Press.

Bugge, P. (1995) 'The Nation Supreme. The Idea of Europe 1914–1945', in K. Wilson and J. van der Dussen (eds) *The History of the Idea of Europe*, London: Routledge.

Bulpitt, J. (1983) *Territory and Power in the United Kingdom*, Manchester: Manchester University Press.

Burger, T. (1976) *Max Weber's Theory of Concept Formation. History, Laws and Ideal Types*, Durham, NC: Duke University Press.

Burgess, M. (1993) 'Federalism and Federation: A Re-appraisal', in M. Burgess and A. G. Gagnon (eds) *Comparative Federalism and Federation*, Hemel Hempstead: Harvester Wheatsheaf.

Burgess, M. and Gagnon, A. G. (eds) (1993) *Comparative Federalism and Federation*, Hemel Hempstead: Harvester Wheatsheaf.

Burke, E. (1982) *Reflections on the Revolution in France*, Harmondsworth: Penguin.

Burma, I. (2001) 'The Notion that Future Wars will be Fought between Civilisations, not States, may be Clever but it is Wrong', *Guardian*, 2 October.

Burroughs, W. (1982) *Cities of the Red Night*, London: Picador.

Butler, D. and Kavanagh, D. (1992) *The British General Election 1992*, Basingstoke: Macmillan.

Butler, D. and Kavanagh, D. (1997) *The British General Election of 1997*, London: Macmillan.

Butler, D. and Stokes, D. (1969) *Political Change in Britain*, Basingstoke: Macmillan.

Byrne, L. (1997) *Information Age Government: Delivering the Blair Revolution*, London: Fabian Society.

Calhoun, C. (ed.) (1992) *Habermas and the Public Sphere*, Cambridge: Polity Press.

Calhoun, C. (1994) 'Social Theory and the Politics of Identity', in C. Calhoun (ed.) *Social Theory and the Politics of Identity*, Oxford: Blackwell.

Callinicos, A. (1995) *Theories and Narratives: Reflections on the Philosophy of History*, Cambridge: Polity Press.

Camilleri, J. and Falk, P. (1992) *The End of Sovereignty? The Politics of a Shrinking and Fragmenting World*, Aldershot: Edward Elgar.

Campbell, D. (1998) *Writing Security: United States Foreign Policy and the Politics of Identity*, 2nd edn, Manchester: Manchester University Press.

Campbell, D., Yonish, S. J. and Putnam, R. (1999) 'Tuning In, Tuning Out Revisited: Television and Social Capital', Shorenstein Center for the Press and Policy Research Roundtable, Harvard University.

Cappella, J. N. and Hall Jamieson, K. (1997) *Spiral of Cynicism: The Press and the Public Good*, Oxford: Oxford University Press.

Carter, A. and Stokes, G. (eds) (1998) *Liberal Democracy and Its Critics: Perspectives in Contemporary Political Thought*, Cambridge: Polity Press.

Castells, M. (1996) *The Rise of the Network Society*, Oxford: Blackwell.

Castells, M. (2000) (2nd edn) *The Rise of the Network Society: The Information Age: Economy, Society and Culture*, vol 1, Boston, MA: Blackwell.

Cerny, P. (1990) *The Changing Architecture of Politics: Structure, Agency and the Future of the State*, London: Sage.

Chan, J. (1993) *Wild Swans: Three Daughters of China*, London: Flamingo.

Chapman, J. (1993) *Politics, Feminism and the Reformation of Gender*, London: Routledge.

Childs, D. (1983) *The GDR: Moscow's German Ally*, London: Allen & Unwin.

Cirincione, J. (2002) 'Missile Defense After September 11 and the ABM Withdrawal', *Carnegie Analysis*, 4 January: <http://www.ceip.org/files/nonprolif/templates/article.asp?NewsID=1982>

Clarke, M. and Stewart, M. (1991) *The Choices for Local Government for the 1990s and Beyond*, Harlow: Longman.

Cockerell, M., Hennessy, P. and Walker, M. (1985) *Sources Close to the Prime Minister*, London: Macmillan.

Cohen, G. A. (1978) *Karl Marx's Theory of History: A Defence*, Oxford: Oxford University Press.

Coleman, S. (1997) 'UK Citizen Online Democracy: An Experiment in Government-supported Online Public Space', in S. Clift and O. Ostberg (eds) *Democracy and Government On-Line Services*, G7.

Coleman, S. (1999) *Election Call: A Democratic Public Forum?*, London: Hansard Society.

Coleman, S. (ed.) (2000) *New Media and Social Exclusion*, London: Hansard Society.

Coleman, S. and Gotze, J. (2001) *Bowling Together: Online Public Engagement in Policy Deliberation*, London: BT and the Hansard Society.

Coleman, S., Taylor, J. and van de Donk, W. V. (eds) (1999) *Parliament in the Age of the Internet*, Oxford: Oxford University Press.

Collini, S., Winch, D. and Burrow, J. (1983) *That Noble Science of Politics*, Cambridge: Cambridge University Press.

Comstock, G. and Paik, H. (1991) *Television and the American Child*, San Diego, Calif.: Academic Press.

Conboy, M. (2002) *The Press and Popular Culture*, London: Sage.

Cooke, M. (2000) 'Five Arguments for Deliberative Democracy', *Political Studies* 48(5): 947–69.

Council of Europe (1950) *Convention for the Protection of Human Rights and Fundamental Freedoms* <http://conventions.coe.int/treaty/en/Treaties/html/005.htm>

Cox, R. W. (1987) *Production, Power and World Order*, New York: Columbia University Press.

Cox, R. W. (with Sinclair, T. J.) (1996) *Approaches to World Order*, Cambridge: Cambridge University Press.

Cram, L. (2001) 'Imagining the Union: A Case of Banal Europeanism?', in H. Wallace (ed.) *Interlocking Dimensions of European Integration*, Basingstoke: Palgrave.

Cranston, M. (1973) *What Are Human Rights?*, London: Bodley Head.

Crenson, M. (1971) *The Un-Politics of Air Pollution: A Study of Non-Decision-Making in American Cities*, Baltimore: Johns Hopkins University Press.

Crenson, M. (1987) 'The Private Stake in Public Goods: Overcoming the Illogic of Collective Action', *Policy Sciences* 20.

Crewe, I. (1984) 'The Electorate: Partisan Dealignment Ten Years On', in H. Berrington (ed.) *Change in British Politics*, London: Cass.

Crewe, I. and Harrop, M. (eds) (1986) *Political Communications: The General Election Campaign of 1983*, Cambridge: Cambridge University Press.

Crewe, I. and Harrop, M. (eds) (1989) *Political Communications: The General Election Campaign of 1987*, Cambridge: Cambridge University Press.

Crewe, I. and Gosschalk, B. (eds) (1995) *Political Communications: The General Election Campaign of 1992*, Cambridge: Cambridge University Press.

Cronin, A. (2000) *Advertising and Consumer Citizenship: Gender, Image and Rights*, London: Routledge.

Crossley, N. (2002) *Making Sense of Social Movements*, Buckingham: Open University Press.

Crossman, R. H. S. (1975, 1976, 1977) *The Diaries of a Cabinet Minister*, London: Hamish Hamilton.

Crouch, C. (2000) *Post-Democracy*, London: Fabian Society.

Crozier, M. (1964) *The Bureaucratic Phenomenon*, Chicago: University of Chicago Press.

Curran, J. and Seaton, J. (1997) *Power without Responsibility: The Press and Broadcasting in Britain*, London: Routledge.

Curtice, J. (1994) 'Great Britain: Imported Ideas in a Changing Political Landscape', *European Journal of Political Research* 25.

Curtice, J. and Semetko, H. (1994) 'Does it Matter What the Papers Say?', in A. Heath, R. Jowell and J. Curtice (eds) *Labour's Last Chance? The 1992 Election and Beyond*, Aldershot: Dartmouth.

Curtice, J. and Steed, M. (1992) 'The Results Analysed', in D. Butler and D. Kavanagh (eds) *The British General Election 1992*, Basingstoke: Macmillan.

Dahl, R. (1956) *A Preface to Democratic Theory*, Chicago, Ill: Chicago University Press.

Dahl, R. (1961) *Who Governs: Democracy and Power in an American City*, New Haven, Conn.: Yale University Press.

Dahl, R. (1971) *Polyarchy: Participation and Opposition*, New Haven, Conn.: Yale University Press.

Dahl, R. (1982) *Dilemmas of Pluralist Democracy*, New Haven, Conn.: Yale University Press.

Dahlgren, P. and Sparks, C. (eds) (1991) *Communication and Citizenship: Journalism and the Public Sphere*, London: Routledge.

Daly, M. (1978) *Gyn/Ecology: The Metaethics of Radical Feminism*, Boston, Mass.: Beacon Press.

Davis, J. C. (1962) 'Towards a Theory of Revolution', *American Sociological Review* 27(1).

Davis, R. and Owen, D. (1998) *New Media and American Politics*, Oxford: Oxford University Press.

de Beauvoir, S. (1968) *The Second Sex*, Harmondsworth: Penguin.

de Maistre, J. (1965) *The Works of Joseph de Maistre*, London: Allen & Unwin.

den Boer, P. (1995) 'Europe to 1914: The Making of an Idea', in K. Wilson and J. van der Dussen (eds) *The History of the Idea of Europe*, London: Routledge.

Denton, R. E. and Woodward, G. C. (1990) *Political Communication in America*, New York: Praeger.

Denzin, N. (2002) *Reading Race: Hollywood and the Cinema of Racial Violence*, London: Sage.

Deutsch, K. W., Burnell, S. A., Kann, R. A., Lee, M., Lichterman, M., Lindgren, R. W., Loewenheim, F. L. and Van Wangeren, R. W. (1957) *Political Community in the North Atlantic Area: International Organization in the Light of Historical Experience*, Princeton, NJ: Princeton University Press.

Diamond, L. and Plattner, M. (eds) (1996) *The Global Resurgence of Democracy*, 2nd edn, Baltimore, Md: Johns Hopkins University Press.

Dicey, A. V. (1908) *Introduction to the Study of the Law of the Constitution*, London: Macmillan.

Dieter, H. (1998) 'Crisis in Asia or Crisis in Globalisation?', *CSGR Working Paper* 15/98 <http://www.warwick.ac.uk/fac/soc/CSGR/wpapers/wp1598.PDF>.

Dobson, A. (1990) *Green Political Thought*, London: Unwin Hyman.

Dogan, M. and Pelassy, D. (1990) *How to Compare Nations: Strategies in Comparative Politics*, 2nd edn, Chatham, NJ: Chatham House.

Domhoff, W. (1979) *The Powers That Be: Processes of Ruling Class Domination in America*, New York: Vintage Books.

Donovan, M. (1998) 'Political Leadership in Italy: Towards a Plebiscitary Democracy?', *Modern Italy* 3(2): 281–93.

Dowmunt, A. (ed.) (1993) *Channels of Resistance: Global Television and Local Empowerment*, London: British Film Institute.

Downing, J. with Villarreal Ford, T., Gil, G. and Stein, L. (2001) *Radical Media: Rebellious Communication and Social Movements*, London: Sage.

Downs, A. (1957) *An Economic Theory of Democracy*, New York: Harper & Row.

Downs, A. (1972) 'Up and Down With Ecology: The Issues-Attention Cycle', *The Public Interest* 28 (summer): 38–50.

Dowse, R. E. and Hughes, J. A. (1972) *Political Sociology*, Chichester: Wiley.

Doyle, M. (1983) 'Kant, Liberal Legacies and Foreign Affairs', *Philosophy and Public Affairs* 12 (summer).

Doyle, M. (1997) *Ways of War and Peace: Realism, Liberalism and Socialism*, New York: W.W. Norton, 1997.

Dror, Y. (1964) 'Muddling Through – Science or Inertia?', *Public Administration Review* 24.

Drotner, K. (1992) *Modernity and Media Panics* in M. Skovmand and K. C. Schroder (eds) *Media Cultures: Reappraising Transnational Media*, London: Routledge, pp. 42–62.

Drucker, P. (1993) *Post-Capitalist Society*, London: Butterworth-Heinemann.

Dunleavy, D. and Husbands, C. T. (1985) *British Democracy at the Crossroads: Voting and Party Competition in the 1980s*, London: Allen & Unwin.

Dunleavy, P. (1980) *Urban Political Analysis*, London: Macmillan.

Dunleavy, P. (1981) 'Professions and Policy Change: Notes Towards a Model of Ideological Corporation', *Public Administration Bulletin* 36.

Dunleavy, P. (1990) 'Mass Political Behaviour: Is There More to Learn?', *Political Studies* 38.

Dunleavy, P. and O'Leary, B. (1987) *Theories of the State: The Politics of Liberal Democracy*, London: Macmillan.

Dunn, J. (1984) *The Political Thought of John Locke*, Cambridge: Cambridge University Press.

Dunn, J. (ed.) (1994) 'Contemporary Crisis of Nation State?', *Political Studies* 42 (special issue).

Duverger, M. (1955) *The Political Role of Women*, Paris: Unesco.

Duverger, M. (1964) *Political Parties: Their Organisation and Activity in the Modern State*, London: Methuen.

Dye, T. (1990) *American Federalism: Competition Among Governments*, Lexington Books.

Dyer, R. (1993) *The Matter of Images: Essays on Representation*, London: Routledge.

Dyson, K. (1980) *The State Tradition in West Europe*, Oxford: Martin Robertson.

Dyson, K. (1994) *Elusive Union: The Politics of Economic and Monetary Union*, London: Longman.

Easton, D. (1953) *The Political System*, New York: Knopf.

Easton, D. (1965) *A Systems Analysis of Political Life*, New York: Wiley.

Easton, D. and Dennis, J. (1969) *Children and the Political System: Origins of Political Legitimacy*, New York: McGraw-Hill.

Eatwell, R. and O'Sullivan, N. (1989) *The Nature of the Right: European and American Politics and Political Thought Since 1789*, London: Pinter Press.

Eatwell, R. and Wright, A. (eds) (1993) *Contemporary Political Ideologies*, London: Pinter.

Eccleshall, R. *et al.* (1998) *Political Ideologies*, London: Routledge.

Eckstein, H. (1966) *Division and Cohesion in Democracy: A Study of Norway*, Princeton: Princeton University Press.

Edelman, M. (1964) *The Symbolic Uses of Politics*, Urbana, Ill.: University of Illinois Press.

Edwards, E. M. and Gaventa, J. (eds) (2001) *Global Citizen Action*, London: Earthscan.

Edwards, M. and Gaventa, J. (eds) (2001) *Global Citizen Action*, London: Earthscan.

Elazar, D. (1985) *American Federalism: A View from the States*, Harper & Row.

Elazar, D. (1987) *Exploring Federalism*, Tuscaloosa, Alabama: University of Alabama Press.

Eldridge, J. (1993) *Getting the Message: News, Truth, and Power*, London: Routledge.

Elliott, L. (1991) 'The Rolling Economic Disaster', *Guardian* (20 August).

Elmore, R. (1978) 'Organisational Models of Social Program Implementation', *Public Policy* 26.

Elmore, R. (1980) 'Backward Mapping: Implementation Research and Policy Decisions', *Political Science Quarterly*.

Elster, J. (1985) *Making Sense of Marx*, Cambridge and Paris: Cambridge University Press.

Elster, J. (ed) (1998) *Deliberative Democracy*, Cambridge: Cambridge University Press.

Engels, F. (1968) The Origins of the Family, Private Property and the State, in K. Marx and F. Engels, *Selected Writings*, London: Lawrence & Wishart.

Esser, F. (1999) 'Tabloidization of News', *European Journal of Communication* 14(3): 291–324.

Etzioni, A. (1967) 'Mixed Scanning: A Third Approach to Decision-Making', *Public Administration Review* 27.

Etzioni, A. (1993) *The Spirit of Community*, London: Crown Publishers.

Eulau, H. (1963) *The Behavioural Persuasion in Politics*, New York: Random House.

European Commission (1973) 'Declaration on the European Identity', *Bulletin of European Communities* 12 (Clause 2501).

European Parliament (2002) *Party Groups in the European Parliament*, Brussels and Strasbourg: European Parliament.

Falk, R. (1999) *Predatory Globalization*, Cambridge: Polity Press.

Farer, T. J. and Gaer, F. (1993) 'The UN and Human Rights: At the End of the Beginning', in A. Roberts and B. Kingsbury (eds) *United Nations, Divided World. The UN's Role in International Relations*, 2nd edn, Oxford: Oxford University Press.

Featherstone, M. (ed.) (1990) *Global Culture: Globalization, Nationalism and Modernity*, London: Sage.

Featherstone, M. (1991) *Consumer Culture and Postmodernism*, London: Sage.

Feuerbach, L. (1966) *The Principles of the Philosophy of the Future*, New York: Random House.

Fichte, J. G. (1968) *Addresses to the German Nation*, ed. G. A. Kelley, New York: Harper Torchbooks.

Figes, E. (1970) *Patriarchal Attitudes*, London: Macmillan.

Finer, S. (1974) *Adversary Politics and Electoral Reform*, London: Wigram.

Finer, S., Bogdanor, V. and Rudden, B. (1995) *Comparing Constitutions*, Oxford: Clarendon Press.

Filmer, Sir R. (1949) *Patriarcha and Other Political Writings*, ed. P. Laslett, Oxford: Oxford University Press.

Fishkin, J. (1991) *Democracy and Deliberation*, New Haven, Conn.: Yale University Press.

Fiske, J. (1993) *Power Plays – Power Works*, London: Verso.

Fiske, J. (1995) *Media Matters: Everyday Culture and Political Change*, Minneapolis: Minnesota Press.

Florini, A. M. (2001) 'Transnational Civil Society', in M. Edwards and J. Gaventa (eds) *Global Citizen Action*, London: Earthscan.

Foley, M. (2000) *The British Presidency: Tony Blair and the Politics of Public Leadership*, Manchester: Manchester University Press.

Forman, N. (1991) *Mastering British Politics*, Basingstoke: Macmillan.

Forsyth, M. (1981) *Unions of States: The Theory and Practice of Confederation*, Leicester: Leicester University Press.

Forsyth, M. (1994) 'Federalism', *Politics Review* (November).

Foster, M. (1942) *Masters of Political Thought*, vol. 1, London: Harrap.

Fowles, J. (1996) *Advertising and Popular Culture*, Thousand Oaks, Calif.: Sage.

Franklin, B. (1994) *Packaging Politics: Political Communications in Britain's Media Democracy*, London: Edward Arnold.

Fraser, D. (1984) *The Evolution of the British Welfare State*, 2nd edn, Basingstoke: Macmillan.

Frazer, E. (1999) *The Problems of Communitarian Politics: Unity and Conflict*, Oxford: Oxford University Press.

Fukuyama, F. (1989) 'The End of History?', *National Interest* 16: 3–18.

Fukuyama, F. (1992) *The End of History and the Last Man*, London: Hamish Hamilton.

Fukuyama, F. (1995) *Trust: the Social Virtues and the Creation of Prosperity*, London: Hamish Hamilton.

Fukuyama, F. (1998) 'Asian Values and the Asian Crisis', *Commentary*, February.

Fukuyama, F. (2001) 'Social Capital, Civil Society and Development', *Third World Quarterly* 22(1): 7–20.

Fulton, Lord (Chairman) (1968) *The Civil Service: Report of the Committee*, 4 vols, Cmnd. 3638, London: HMSO.

Gadamer, H. G. (1981) *Reason in the Age of Science*, Cambridge, Mass.: MIT Press.

Gagnon, A. G. (1993) 'The Political Uses of Federalism', in M. Burgess and A. G. Gagnon (eds) *Comparative Federalism and Federation*, Hemel Hempstead: Harvester Wheatsheaf.

Galbraith, J. K. (1965) *The Affluent Society*, London: Penguin.

Garnham, N. (1979) 'Contribution to a Political Economy of Mass Communication', *Media, Culture and Society* 1(2): 123–46.

Gellner, E. (1983) *Nations and Nationalism*, Oxford: Blackwell.

Genet, J. (1971) *The Miracle of the Rose*, London: Penguin.

George, S. (1994) 'Cultural Diversity and European Integration: The British Political Parties', in S. Zetterholm (ed.) *National Cultures and European Integration: Exploratory Essays on Cultural Diversity and Common Policies*, Oxford: Berg.

George, S. and Bache, I. (2001) *Politics in the European Union*, Oxford: Oxford University Press.

Gerth, H. H. and Wright Mills, C. (1991) *From Max Weber: Essays in Sociology*, London: Routledge.

Gibson, W. (1984) *Neuromancer*, London: Gollancz.

Gibson, W. (1993) *Virtual Light*, London: Viking.

Giddens, A. (1984) *The Constitution of Society*, Cambridge: Polity Press.

Giddens, A. (1985a) *A Contemporary Critique of Historical Materialism*, Cambridge: Polity Press.

Giddens, A. (1985b) *The Nation-State and Violence*, Cambridge: Polity Press.

Giddens, A. (1990) *The Consequences of Modernity*, Cambridge: Polity Press.

Giddens, A. (1991) *Modernity and Self-Identity: Self and Society in the Late Modern Age*, Cambridge: Polity Press.

Giddens, A. (1993) *New Rules of Sociological Method*, 2nd edn, Cambridge: Polity Press.

Giddens, A. (1994) *Beyond Left and Right: The Future of Radical Politics*, Cambridge: Polity Press.

Giddens, A. (1998) *The Third Way*, Cambridge: Polity Press.

Gill, G. and Marwick, R. (2000) *Russia's Still Born Democracy: From Gorbachev to Yeltsin*, Oxford: Oxford University Press.

Gill, S. (ed.) (1993) *Gramsci, Historical Materialism and International Relations*, Cambridge: Cambridge University Press.

Gilmartin, K. (1996) *Print Politics: The Press and Radical Opposition in Early Nineteenth-Century England*, Cambridge: Cambridge University Press.

Gilmour, I. (1978) *Inside Right: A Study of Conservatism*, London: Quartet.

Girling, J. (1998) *France: Political and Social Change*, London: Routledge.

Githens, M., Norris, P. and Lovenduski, J. (1994) *Different Roles, Different Voices: Women and Politics in the United States and Europe*, New York: HarperCollins.

Gitlin, T. (1991) 'Bites and Blips: Chunk News, Savvy Talk and the Bifurcation of American Politics', in P. Dahlgren and C. Sparks (eds) *Communication and Citizenship: Journalism and the Public Sphere*, London: Routledge.

Glasgow University Media Group (1976) *Bad News*, London: Routledge & Kegan Paul.

Glasgow University Media Group (1980) *More Bad News*, London: Routledge & Kegan Paul.

Glasgow University Media Group (1982) *Really Bad News*, London: Routledge & Kegan Paul.

Golding, W. (1997) *Lord of the Flies*, London: Faber and Faber.

Gouldner, A. W. (1954) *Patterns of Industrial Bureaucracy*, Glencoe, Ill.: Free Press.

Graham, B. and Nash, C. (2000) *Modern Historical Geographies*, Harlow: Prentice Hall.

Gramsci, A. (1970) *Selections from the Prison Notebooks*, trans. Q. Hoare, London: Lawrence & Wishart.

Grant, A. (1997) *The American Political Process*, Aldershot: Dartmouth.

Grant, A. (2000) 'Devolution and the Reshaping of American Federalism', in A. Grant *American Politics: 2000 and Beyond*, Aldershot: Ashgate.

Grant, W. (1995) *Pressure Groups, Politics and Democracy in Britain*, London: Harvester Wheatsheaf.

Gray, A. (1968) *The Socialist Tradition From Moses to Lenin*, New York: HarperCollins.

Gray, J. (1993) *Beyond the New Right: Markets, Government and the Common Environment*, London: Routledge.

Gray, J. (1993a) *Post-Liberalism: Studies in Political Thought*, London and New York: Routledge.

Gray, J. (1998) *False Dawn*, Oxford: Oxford University Press.

Gray, J. (2002) 'Why Terrrorism is Unbeatable', *New Statesman*, 25 February.

Green, T. H. (1941) *Lectures on the Principles of Political Obligation*, London: Longman.

Greenaway, J., Smith, S. and Street, J. (1992) *Deciding Factors in British Politics*, London: Routledge.

Greenstein, F., Herman, U., Stradling, R. and Zureik, E. (1970) 'The Child's Conception of the Queen and the Prime Minister', *British Journal of Political Science* 4(3).

Greenwood, J. and Wilson, D. (1984) *Public Administration in Britain*, London: Allen & Unwin.

Greer, G. (1971) *The Female Eunuch*, London: Paladin.

Griffin, R. (1991) *The Nature of Fascism*, London: Routledge.

Griffin, R. (ed.) (1995) *Fascism*, Oxford: Oxford University Press.

Guardian (1991) 'The Rolling Economic Disaster' (20 August).

Guardian (1994) 'Tragic History Repeats Itself' (1 March).

Gundle, S. and Parker, S. (eds) (1994) *The New Italian Republic: From the Fall of the Berlin Wall to Berlusconi*, London: Routledge.

Gurdon, H. (1995) 'Four Men Changed Brent Spar's Course', *Daily Telegraph* (21 June).

Gurr, T. R. (1980) *Why Men Rebel*, Princeton: Princeton University Press.

Guttman, A. and Thompson, D. (1996) *Democracy and Disagreement*, Cambridge: Mass.: Belknap.

Guy Peters, B. (1998) *Comparative Politics: Theory and Methods*, Basingstoke: Macmillan.

Haas, E. B. (1968) *The Uniting of Europe: Political, Social and Economic Forces, 1951–1957*, 2nd edn, Stanford, Calif.: Stanford University Press.

Habermas, J. (1974) 'The Public Sphere: An Encyclopedic Article', *New German Critique* 3.

Habermas, J. (1987) *The Philosophical Discourse of Modernity*, Cambridge: Polity Press.

Habermas, J. (1989) *The Structural Transformation of the Public Sphere*, Cambridge, Mass.: MIT Press.

Habermas, J. (1996) *Between Facts and Norms*, Cambridge: Polity Press.

Hacker, K. and van Dijk, W. V. (eds) (2000) *Digital Democracy: Issues of Theory and Practice*, London: Sage.

Haggard, S. (2000) *The Political Economy of the Asian Financial Crisis*, Washington, DC: Institute for International Economics.

Hagopian, F. (1996) *Traditional Politics and Regime Change in Brazil*, Cambridge: Cambridge University Press.

Hague, R. and Loader, B. (eds) (1999) *Digital Democracy: Discourse and Decision-Making in the Information Age*, London: Routledge.

Hague, R., Harrop, M. and Breslin, W. (1992) *Comparative Government and Politics*, 3rd edn, Basingstoke: Macmillan.

Hall, A. J. (1994) *The State: Critical Concepts*, London: Routledge.

Hall, J. (1986) *Powers and Liberties: The Causes and Consequences of the Rise of the West*, Harmondsworth: Pelican.

Hall, P. (1999) 'Social Capital in Britain', *British Journal of Political Science* 29(4): 426–44.

Hall, S. (1988) *The Hard Road to Renewal. Thatcherism and the Crisis of the Left*, London: Verso.

Hall, S. (1992) 'The Question of Cultural Identity', in S. Hall, A. McGrew and D. Held (eds) *Modernity and its Futures*, Cambridge: Open University/Polity Press.

Hall, S. (ed.) (1997) *Representation: Cultural Representations and Signifying Practices*, London: Oxford University Press/Sage.

Hall, S. (1998) 'Nowhere Man', *Marxism Today*, 20 November, 3–8.

Hall Jamieson, K. (1992) *Dirty Politics: Deception, Distraction and Democracy*, Oxford: Oxford University Press.

Hall Jamieson, K. (1996) *Packaging the Presidency: A History and Criticism of Presidential Campaign Advertising*, 3rd edn, New York: Oxford University Press.

Halliday, F. (2001) *The World at 2000*, Basingstoke: Palgrave.

Halliday, F. (2002) *Two Hours that Shook the World: September 11th, 2001: Causes and Consequences*, London: Saqi Books.

Hallin, D. (1994) *We Keep America on Top of the World*, London: Routledge.

Hamelink, C. (1994) *The Politics of World Communication*, London: Sage.

Hampsher-Monk, I. (1992) *A History of Modern Political Thought*, Oxford: Blackwell.

Handy, C. (1985) *Understanding Organisations*, London: Penguin.

Harris, L. (1984) 'Governing the World Economy: Bretton Woods and the IMF', in D209 *The State and Society*, Block 6, Unit 25, Milton Keynes: Open University Press.

Harrison, R. J. (1974) *Europe in Question. Theories of Regional International Integration*, London: Allen & Unwin.

Harrop, M. (1986) 'The Press and Post-War Elections', in I. Crewe and M. Harrop (eds) *Political Communications: The General Election of 1983*, Cambridge: Cambridge University Press.

Harrop, M. (1987) 'Voters', in J. Seaton and B. Pimlott (eds) *The Media in British Politics*, Aldershot: Gower.

Harrop, M. (1990) 'Political Marketing', *Parliamentary Affairs* 43(3).

Hart, R. (1994) *Seducing America: How Television Charms the Modern Voter*, New York: Oxford University Press.

Hartley, J. (1992) *The Politics of Pictures*, London: Routledge.

Harvey, D. (1989) *The Condition of Postmodernity: An Inquiry into the Condition of Cultural Change*, Oxford: Blackwell.

Hay, C. (1995) 'Structure and Agency', in D. Marsh and G. Stoker (eds) *Theory and Method in Political Science*, Basingstoke: Macmillan.

Haythornthwaite, C. (2000) 'Online Personal Networks: Size, Composition and Media Use among Distance Learners', *New Media & Society* 2(2): 195–226.

Heater, D. (1993) *The Idea of European Unity*, Leicester: Leicester University Press.

Heath, A. (1981) *Social Mobility*, London: Fontana.

Heath, A., Towell, R. and Curtice, J. (1994) *Labour's Last Chance? The 1992 Election and Beyond*, Aldershot: Dartmouth.

Hechter, M. (2000) *Containing Nationalism*, Oxford: Oxford University Press.

Heclo, H. (1972) 'Review Article: Policy Analysis', *British Journal of Political Science* 2.

Heclo, H. (1977) *A Government of Strangers*, Washington, DC: Brookings Institution.

Heclo, H. (1983) 'One Executive Branch or Many?', in A. King (ed.) *Both Ends of the Avenue*.

Hegel, G. W. F. (1971) *The Philosophy of Right*, ed. T. M. Knox, Oxford: Oxford University Press.

Hegel, G. W. F. (1975) *Lectures on the Philosophy of World History*, Cambridge: Cambridge University Press.

Held, D. (1989) *Political Theory and the Modern State*, Cambridge: Polity Press.

Held, D. (1991) 'Democracy and the Global System', in D. Held (ed.) *Political Theory Today*, Cambridge: Polity Press.

Held, D. (1995) *Democracy and the Global Order: From the Modern State to Cosmopolitan Governance*, Cambridge: Polity Press.

Held, D. (1996) *Models of Democracy*, 2nd edn, Cambridge: Polity Press.

Held, D. (1998) 'Democracy and Globalization', in D. Archibugi, D. Held and M. Kholer (eds) *Re-imagining Political Community: Studies in Cosmopolitan Democracy*, Cambridge: Polity Press.

Held, D., McGrew, A., Thompson, G. and Perraton, J. (1999) *Global Transformations*, Cambridge: Polity Press.

Held, D., Anderson, J., Gieben, B., Hall, S., Harris, L., Lewis, P. and Parker, B. (1983) *States and Societies*, Oxford: Blackwell.

Henley Centre (1999) *Media Futures*, London: Henley Centre.

Hennessy, P. (1989) *Whitehall*, London: Secker & Warburg.

Herman, E. S. and Chomsky, N. (1994) *Manufacturing Consent: The Political Economy of the Mass Media*, London: Vintage.

Heywood, A. (1992) *Political Ideologies*, London: Macmillan.

Heywood, P. (1995) *The Government and Politics of Spain*, London: Macmillan.

Higgott, R. (1995) 'Economic Co-operation in the Asia-Pacific: A Theoretical Comparison with the European Union', *Journal of European Public Policy* 2(3).

Hiney, T. (1990) 'Tokyo? Yo!', *The Sunday Times*, Style and Travel section, 2 January.

Hinsley, F. H. (1986) *Sovereignty*, 2nd edn, Cambridge: Cambridge University Press.

Hirschman, A. O. (1970) *Exit, Voice and Loyalty*, Cambridge, Mass.: Harvard University Press.

Hirst, P. and Thompson, G. (1995) *Globalization in Question*, Cambridge: Polity Press.

Hitler, A. (1969) *Mein Kampf*, London: Hutchinson.

Hix, S. (1999) *The Political System of the European Union*, Basingstoke: Macmillan.

Hobbes, T. (1962) 'Elements of Law', in R. Peters (ed.) *Body, Man and Citizen: Selections from Hobbes's Writings*, London: Collier.

Hobbes, T. (1968) *Leviathan*, Harmondsworth: Penguin.

Hobbes, T. (1983) *De Cive*, Oxford: Oxford University Press.

Hobhouse, L. T. (1994) *Liberalism and Other Writings*, ed. J. Meadowcroft, Cambridge: Cambridge University Press.

Hobsbawm, E. (1990) *Nations and Nationalism since 1780*, Cambridge: Cambridge University Press.

Hobsbawm, E. (1992) 'Introduction: Inventing Traditions', in E. Hobsbawm and T. Ranger (eds) *The Invention of Tradition*, Cambridge: Cambridge University Press.

Hoffman, E. (1994) *Exit into History: A Journey Through the New Eastern Europe*, Harmondsworth: Penguin.

Hogwood, B. W. and Gunn, L. A. (1981) *The Policy Orientation*, Glasgow: University of Strathclyde Press.

Hogwood, B. W. and Gunn, L. A. (1984) *Policy Analysis for the Real World*, Oxford: Oxford University Press.

Hohfield, W. (1919) *Fundamental Legal Conceptions*, New York: Yale University Press.

Holden, B. (ed.) (2000) *Global Democracy: Key Debates*, London: Routledge.

Holden, R. (2001) *The Making of New Labour's European Policy*, London: Palgrave.

Holliday, R. and Hassard, J. (eds) (2001) *Contested Bodies*, London: Routledge.

Hood, C. and Dunsire, A. (1981) *Bureaumetrics*, Farnborough: Gower.

Hooghe, L. and Marks, G. (2001) *Multilevel Governance and European Integration*, New York: Rowman & Littlefield.

Howe, P. (1995) 'A Community of Europeans; the Requisite Underpinnings', *Journal of Common Market Studies* 33(1).

Howell, D. (1995) *Easternisation*, London: Demos.

Huggins, R. (2000) 'The Transformation of the Political Audience', in B. Axford and R. Huggins (eds) *New Media and Politics*, London: Sage.

Huntington, S. (1968) *Political Order in Changing Societies*, New Haven, Conn.: Yale University Press.

Huntington, S. (1991) *The Third Wave: Democratization in the Late Twentieth Century*, Norman, OK and London: University of Oklahoma Press.

Huntington, S. (1993) 'The Clash of Civilizations', *Foreign Affairs* 72(3).

Huntington, S. (1996) *The Clash of Civilizations and the Remaking of World Order*, London: Simon & Schuster.

Hussey, G. (1995) *Ireland Today. Anatomy of a Changing State*, Harmondsworth: Penguin.

Hutton, B. (1995) 'Confucius to Beveridge – The Outline of a Welfare State is Emerging', *Financial Times* 26 January.

Hutton, W. (1995) *The State We're In*, London: Cape.

Huxley, A. (1977) *Brave New World*, London: Panther.

Hyman, H. (1959) *Political Socialization: A Study in the Psychology of Political Behavior*, New York: Free Press.

Index on Censorship (1999) 'Underexposed' 6.

Ingle, S. (1987) *The British Party System*, London: Blackwell.

Inglehart, R. (1977) *The Silent Revolution: Changing Values and Political Styles Among Western Publics*, Princeton: Princeton University Press.

Inglehart, R. (1991) 'Postmaterialism', in V. Bogdanor (ed.) *The Blackwell Encyclopaedia of Political Science*, Oxford: Blackwell.

Inglehart, R. (1997) *Modernization and Postmodernization: Cultural, Economic and Political Change in 43 Societies*, Princeton, NJ: Princeton University Press.

Iyengar, S. and Reeves, R. (eds) (1997) *Do the Media Govern? Politicians, Voters and Reporters in America*, London: Sage.

Jacques, M. (1993) 'The End of Politics', *Sunday Times* (18 July).

James, A. (1984) 'Sovereignty: Ground Rule or Gibberish?', *Review of International Studies*.

James, C.L.R. (1963) *Beyond a Boundary*, London: Stanley Paul.

Jameson, F. (1991) *Postmodernism or The Cultural Logic of Late Capitalism*, London: Verso.

Jamieson, K. H. (1992a) *Dirty Politics*, New York: Oxford University Press.

Jamieson, K. H. (1992b) *Packaging the Presidency*, 2nd edn, New York: Oxford University Press.

Janis, I. (1972) *Victims of Groupthink*, Boston: Houghton-Mifflin.

Jaros, D. (1973) *Socialization to Politics*, New York: Praeger.

Jessop, B. (1990) *State Theory: Putting the Capitalist State in its Place*, Cambridge: Polity Press.

Johnson, C. (1966) *Revolutionary Change*, Boston: Beacon Press.

Jones, B. (1993) 'The Pitiless Probing Eye: Politicians and the Broadcast Interview', *Parliamentary Affairs* 46(1).

Jordan, A. G. and Richardson, J. J. (1987) *British Politics and the Policy Process*, London: Allen & Unwin.

Jordan, G. and Maloney, W. A. (1996) 'How Bumble Bees Fly: Accounting for Public Interest Participation', *Political Studies* 44(3).

Jowell, R., Witherspoon, S. and Brook, L. (eds) (1987) *British Social Attitudes: The 1987 Report*, Aldershot: Gower.

Kant, I. (1948) *Perpetual Peace*, ed. and introduction by A. Robert Caponigri, New York: Liberal Arts Press.

Katsiaficas, G. (ed.) (2001) *After the Fall: 1989 and the Future of Freedom*, London: Routledge.

Katz, P. and Mair, P. (1994) *How Parties Organise*, London: Sage.

Kavanagh, D. (1972) *Political Culture*, London: Macmillan.

Kavanagh, D. (1980) 'Political Culture in Great Britain: The Decline of the Civic Centre', in G. A. Almond and S. Verba (eds) *The Civic Culture Revisited*, Boston: Little, Brown & Co.

Kavanagh, D. (1983) *Political Science and Political Behaviour*, London: Allen & Unwin.

Kavanagh, D. (1995) *Election Campaigning: The New Marketing of Politics*, Oxford: Blackwell.

Keane, J. (1988) *Civil Society and the State*, London: Verso.

Keane, J. (1991) *The Media and Democracy*, Cambridge: Polity Press.

Kedourie, E. (1966) *Nationalism*, London: Hutchinson.

Kegley, C. (ed.) (1995a) *Controversies in International Relations Theory: Realism and the Neoliberal Challenge*, New York: St Martin's Press.

Kegley, C. (1995b) 'The Neoliberal Challenge to Realist Theories of World Politics: An Introduction', in C. Kegley (ed.) *Controversies in International Relations Theory. Realism and the Neoliberal Challenge*, New York: St Martin's Press.

Kegley, C. and Wittkopf, E. (1995) *World Politics: Trend and Transformation*, 5th edn, New York: St Martin's Press.

Kellner, D. (1991) *Jean Baudrillard: From Marxism to Postmodernism and Beyond*, Cambridge: Polity Press.

Kellner, D. (1995) *Media Culture: Cultural Studies, Identity and Politics between the Modern and the Postmodern*, London: Routledge.

Kennedy, P. (1988) *The Rise and Fall of the Great Powers: Economic Change and Military Conflict from 1500–2000*, London: Fontana Press.

Kennedy, P. (1993) *Preparing for the Twenty-First Century*, London: HarperCollins.

Keohane, R.O (2002) 'The United Nations: An Essential Instrument against Terror': <http://www.duke.edu/web/forums/keohane.html>

Kerbel, M. (1994) *Edited for Television*, Connecticut: Westview Press.

Key, V. O. (1961) *Public Opinion and American Democracy*, New York: Alfred Knopf.

Kincaid, J. (1994) 'Governing the American States', in G. Peele et al. (eds) *Developments in American Politics 2*, London: Macmillan.

King, P. (1982) *Federalism and Federation*, London: Croom Helm.

King, P. (1983) *The History of Ideas: An Introduction*, London: Croom Helm.

King, P. (1993) 'Federation and Representation', in M. Burgess and A. G. Gagnon (eds) *Comparative Federalism and Federation*, Hemel Hempstead: Harvester Wheatsheaf.

King, P. (1994) 'Historical Contextualism: The New Historicism?', *History of European Ideas* 21(2).

King, P. (1996) 'Historical Contextualism Revisited', *Politics* 16(3).

Kirchheimer, O. (1966) 'The Transformation of West European Party Systems', in J. Lapalombara and M. Weiner (eds) *Political Parties and Political Development*, Princeton, NJ: Princeton University Press.

Kitschelt, H. (1999) *Post-Communist Party Systems: Competition, Representation and Inter-Party Cooperation*, Cambridge: Cambridge University Press.

Klein, N. (2000) *No Logo: No Space, No Choice, No Jobs: Taking Aim at the Brand Bullies*, London: Flamingo.

Kleinsteuber, H. J. (1995) 'The Mass Media', in M. Shelley and M. Winck (eds) *Aspects of European Cultural Diversity*, London: Routledge.

Knutsen, T. (1999) *The Rise and Fall of World Orders*, Manchester: Manchester University Press.

Kohler-Koch, B. and Eising, R. (1999*) The Transformation of Governance in the European Union*, London: Routledge.

Kolarska-Bobinska, L. (1994) 'Privatization in Poland: The Evolution of Opinions and Interests, 1988–1992', in G. S. Alexander and G. Skapska (eds) *A Fourth Way? Privatization, Property, and the Emergence of New Market Economies*, London: Routledge.

Krause, K. and W. A. Knight (1995) 'Introduction: Evolution and Change in the United Nations System', in K. Krause and W. A. Knight (eds), *Society and the UN System: Changing Perspectives on Multilateralism*, Tokyo: United Nations University Press.

Krieger, J. (1998) *British Politics in the Global Age*, Cambridge: Polity Press.

Kroker, A. (1992) *The Possessed Individual*, London: Macmillan.

Kuhn, T. (1970) *The Structure of Scientific Revolutions*, Chicago: University of Chicago Press.

Kundera, M. (1984) *The Joke*, Harmondsworth: Penguin.

Kundera, M. (1987) *Life is Elsewhere*, London: Faber and Faber.

Lagos, M. (2001) 'Between Stability and Crisis in Latin America', *Journal of Democracy* 12(1): 137–45.

Landman, T. (2000) *Issues and Methods in Comparative Politics: An Introduction*, London: Routledge.

Lane, D. (1985) [1978] *Politics and Society in the USSR*, Oxford: Blackwell.

Lane, J. and Ersson, S. O. (1994) *Politics and Society in Western Europe*, 3rd edn, London: Sage.

Lash, S. and Urry, J. (1994) *Economies of Signs and Space*, London: Sage.

Laski, H. (1948) *The Grammar of Politics*, London: Allen & Unwin.

Laslett, P. (1956) 'Introduction', *Philosophy, Politics and Society* series, Oxford: Blackwell.

Laslett, P. (1963) 'Introduction', *Locke's Two Treatises of Government*, Cambridge: Cambridge University Press.

Lasswell, H. (1951) 'The Policy Orientation', in D. Lerner and H. Lasswell (eds) *The Policy Sciences*, Stanford: Stanford University Press.

Laver, M. (1981) *The Politics of Private Desires*, London: Penguin.

Leigh, D. (1980) *Frontiers of Secrecy*, London: Junction Books.

Lenin, V. I. (1975) *Imperialism: The Highest Stage of Capitalism*, Moscow: Foreign Language Press.

Lerner, D. (1958) *The Passing of Traditional Society*.

Lijphart, A. (1971) 'Comparative Politics and the Comparative Method', *American Political Science Review* 65: 682–91.

Lijphart, A. (1975) 'The Northern Ireland Problem: Cases, Theories and Solutions', *British Journal of Political Science* 5(1).

Lijphart, A. (1977) *Democracy in Plural Societies: A Comparative Exploration*, New Haven, Conn.: Yale University Press.

Lijphart, A. (1980) 'The Structure of Inference', in G. A. Almond and S. Verba (eds) *The Civic Culture Revisited*, Boston: Little, Brown & Co.

Lijphart, A. (1991) 'Consociational Democracy', in V. Bogdanor (ed.) *The Blackwell Encyclopaedia of Political Science*, Oxford: Blackwell.

Lijphart, A. (1992) *Parliamentary versus Presidential Government*, Oxford: Oxford University Press.

Lijphart, A. (1999) *Patterns of Democracy: Government Forms and Performance in Thirty-Six Countries*, New Haven, Conn.: Yale University Press.

Lindblom, C. E. (1959) 'The Science of Muddling Through', *Public Administration Review* 19.

Lindblom, C. E. (1968) *The Policy Making Process*, Englewood Cliffs, NJ: Prentice Hall.

Lindblom, C. E. (1979) 'Still Muddling Through, not yet Through', *Public Administration Review* 39: 516.

Linklater, A. (1998) *The Transformation of Political Community*, Cambridge: Polity Press.

Lipow, A. and Seyd, P. (1996) 'The Politics of Anti-Partyism', *Parliamentary Affairs* (March).

Lippmann, W. (1955) *The Public Philosophy*, Boston: Little, Brown.

Lipset, S. M. (1959) 'Some Social Requisites of Democracy: Economic Development and Political Legitimacy', *American Political Science Review* 53(1).

Lipset, S. M. (1960) *Political Man*, New York: Doubleday.

Lipset, S. M. and Rokkan, S. (eds) (1967) *Party Systems and Voter Alignments: Cross National Perspectives*, New York: Free Press.

Lipset, S. M., Seoung, K. R. and Torres, J. (1993) 'A Comparative Analysis of the Social Requisites of Democracy', *International Social Science Journal* 136.

Lively, J. (1978) 'Pluralism and Consensus', in P. Birnbaum, J. Lively and G. Parry (eds) *Democracy, Consensus and Social Contract*, London: Sage.

Lively, J. and Reeve, A. (1989) *Modern Political Theory*, London: Routledge.

Locke, J. (1963) *Locke's Two Treatises of Government*, ed. P. Laslett, Cambridge: Cambridge University Press.

Locke, J. (1971) 'An Essay Concerning the True Original, Extent and End of Government' (Second Treatise of Government), in E. Barker (ed.) *Social Contract*, Oxford: Oxford University Press.

Locke, J. (1975) *Essay Concerning Human Understanding*, Oxford: Oxford University Press.

Lodge, D. (1984) *Small World*, Harmondsworth: Penguin.

Lovelock, J. (1979) *Gaia: A New Look at Life on Earth*, Oxford: Oxford University Press.

Luard, E. (ed.) (1992) *Basic Texts in International Relations*, Basingstoke: Macmillan.

Luke, T. (1998) 'From Nationality to Nodality: How the Politics of being Digital Transforms Globalisation', paper presented to American Political Science Association, San Franscisco.

Lukes, S. (1974) *Power: A Radical View*, London: Papermac.

Lukes, S. (1992) 'What is Left?', *Times Literary Supplement* (27 March).

Lynn, J. and Jay, A. (1987) *The Complete Yes Minister*, London: BBC Books.

Lyotard, J.-F. (1984) *The Postmodern Condition*, Minneapolis: University of Minnesota Press.

Lyotard, J.-F. (1988) *The Differend: Phrases in Dispute*, Manchester: Manchester University Press.

McAllister, I. (1999) 'The Economic Performance of Governments', in P. Norris (ed.) *Critical Citizens*, Oxford: Oxford University Press.

MacCallum Jr, G. (1991) 'Negative and Positive Freedom',

in D. Miller (ed.) *Liberty*, Oxford: Oxford University Press.

McCarthy, P. (1996) '*Forza Italia*: The New Politics and Old Values of a Changing Italy', in S. Gundle and S. Parker (eds) *The New Italian Republic: From the Fall of the Berlin Wall to Berlusconi*, London: Routledge, pp. 130–46.

McChesney, R. (1999) *Rich Media, Poor Democracy: Communication Politics in Dubious Times*, Urbana and Chicago: University of Illinois Press.

McGrew, A. (1992) 'A Global Society?', in S. Hall, D. Held and A. McGrew (eds) *Modernity and its Futures*, Cambridge: Polity Press.

McGrew, A. (ed.) (1997) *The Transformation of Democracy?: Globalization and Territorial Democracy*, Cambridge: Polity Press/Open University Press.

Machiavelli, N. (1950) *The Prince and the Discourses*, New York: The Modern Library.

Macintyre, A. (1981) *After Virtue*, Duckworth: Guildford.

Macintyre, A. (1988) *Whose Justice? Which Rationality?*, London: Duckworth.

McKay, D. (1992) *American Politics and Society*, 3rd edn, Oxford: Blackwell.

McKay, G. (1998) *DIY Culture: Party and Politics in Nineties Britain*, London: Verso.

Mackenzie, W. J. M. (1978) *Political Identity*, Manchester: Manchester University Press.

McLean, I. (1987) *Public Choice: An Introduction*, Oxford: Blackwell.

McLennan, G. (1995) *Pluralism*, London: Open University Press.

McLuhan, M. (1962) *The Gutenberg Galaxy*, Toronto: Toronto University Press.

McLuhan, M. (1964) *Understanding Media: Extensions of Man*, Cambridge: Mass.: MIT Press.

McLuhan, M. (1967) *The Medium is the Message*, Harmondsworth: Penguin.

McNair, B. (1995) *An Introduction to Political Communication*, London: Routledge.

McNair, B. (2000) *Journalism and Democracy*, London: Routledge.

Maddison, A. (1987) 'Growth and Slow-Down in Advanced Capitalist Economies: Techniques of Quantitative Assessment', *Journal of Economic Literature* 2.

Madison, J. (1961) *The Federalist Papers*, ed. Clinton Rossiter, New York: New American Library of World Literature no. 10.

Mair, P. (ed.) (1990) *The West European Party System*, Oxford: Oxford University Press.

Malik, S. (2002) *Representing Black Britain: Black and Asian Images on Television*, London: Sage.

Mandela, N. (1995) *The Long Walk to Freedom*, London: Abacus.

Mandelson, P. (1996) *The Blair Revolution: Can Labour Deliver?*, London: Faber.

Mandelson, P. and Liddle, R. (1996) *The Blair Revolution: Can New Labour Deliver?*, London: Faber and Faber.

Mann, M. (1986) *The Sources of Social Power, Volume 1: A*

History of Power from the beginning to AD 1760, Cambridge: Cambridge University Press.

March, J. and Simon, H. A. (1958) *Organisations*, New York: John Wiley & Sons.

Marx, K. (1967) *Capital*, vol. 1, New York: International Publishers.

Marx, K. (1973a) *Grundrisse: Foundations of the Critique of Political Economy*, Harmondsworth: Penguin.

Marx, K. (1973b) 'The Civil War in France', *Political Writings, vol. 3, The First International and After*, Harmondsworth: Penguin.

Marx, K. (1975a) 'Critique of Hegel's Philosophy of Right', *Early Writings*, Harmondsworth: Penguin.

Marx, K. (1975b) 'Economic and Philosophical Manuscripts', in *Early Writings*, Harmondsworth: Penguin.

Marx, K. (1979) *Capital*, Harmondsworth: Penguin.

Marx, K. (1985) *The Communist Manifesto*, Harmondsworth: Penguin.

Marx, K. and Engels, F. (1972) *Ireland and the Irish Question*, New York: International Publishers.

Marx, K. and Engels, F. (1973a) 'The Communist Manifesto', *Political Writings, vol. 1, The Revolutions of 1848*, Harmondsworth: Penguin.

Marx, K. and Engels, F. (1973b) *The German Ideology*, London and Moscow: Progress Publishers.

Mason, M. (1999) *Environmental Democracy*, London: Earthscan.

Mauser, G. (1983) *Political Marketing: An Approach to Campaign Strategy*, New York: Praeger.

Mayntz, R. and Scharpf, F. W. (1975) *Policy-Making in the German Federal Bureaucracy*, Amsterdam: Elsevier.

Mazzeloni, G. (2000) 'The Italian Broadcasting System Between Politics and the Market', *Journal of Modern Italian Studies* 5(2): 157–68.

Meijer, I. (1998) 'Advertising Citizenship: An Essay on the Performative Power of Consumer Culture', *Media, Culture and Society* 20(2): 235–49.

Melling, D. (1987) *Understanding Plato*, Oxford: Oxford University Press.

Meny, Y. (1994) *Government and Politics in Western Europe: Britain, France, Italy, Germany*, 2nd edn, Oxford: Oxford University Press.

Merton, R. K. (1957) *Social Theory and Social Structure*, Glencoe, Ill.: Free Press.

Meyer, D. and Tarrow, S. (1998) *The Social Movement Society*, Boulder, Col.: Rowman and Littlefield.

Michels, R. (1962) *Political Parties*, New York: Collier.

Middlemas, K. (1995) *Orchestrating Europe: The Informal Politics of the European Union, 1973–1995*, London: HarperCollins.

Milbrath, L. (1965) *Political Participation: How and Why Do People Get Involved in Politics?*, Chicago: Rand McNally.

Milbrath, L. and Goel, M. (1977) *Political Participation: How and Why Do People Get Involved in Politics?*, 2nd edn, Chicago: Rand McNally.

Milgram, S. (1984) *Obedience to Authority: an Experimental View*, New York: Harper & Row.

Miliband, D. (ed.) (1994) *Reinventing the Left*, Cambridge: Polity Press.

Mill, J. S. (1964) *Autobiography of John Stuart Mill*, New York: Signet Classics.

Mill, J. S. (1972) *Considerations on Representative Government*, London: Penguin.

Mill, J. S. (1972) *Utilitarianism, Liberty, Representative Government*, London: Dent.

Mill, J. S. (1982) *On Liberty*, Harmondsworth: Penguin.

Mill, J. S. (1989) 'The Subjection of Women', *On Liberty and Other Writings*, Cambridge: Cambridge University Press.

Miller, D. (1991) (ed.) *Liberty*, Oxford: Oxford University Press.

Millett, K. (1970) *Sexual Politics*, London: Virago.

Mills, C. W. (1956) *The Power Elite*, New York: Random House.

Milward, A. S. (1999) *The European Rescue of the Nation State*, 2nd edn, London: Routledge.

Minogue, K. (1985) *Alien Powers: The Pure Theory of Ideology*, London: Weidenfeld & Nicolson.

Minogue, K. (1990) 'Equality: A Response', in G. Hunt (ed.) *Philosophy and Politics*, Cambridge: Cambridge University Press.

Mitrany, D. (1966) *A Working Peace System*, 2nd edn, Chicago: Quadrangle Books.

Monbiot, G. (2000) *Captive State: The Corporate Takeover of Britain*, Basingstoke: Macmillan.

Montesquieu, Charles de Secondat, Baron de (1989) *The Spirit of the Laws*, ed. A. M. Cohler *et al.*, Cambridge: Cambridge University Press.

Moore Jr, B. (1966) *The Social Origins of Dictatorship and Democracy*, Boston: Beacon Press.

Moravcsik, A. (1991) 'Negotiating the Single European Act', in R. O. Keohane and S. Hoffmann (eds) *The New European Community: Decision-making and Institutional Change*, Boulder, Col.: Westview.

Moravcsik, A. (1993) 'Preferences and Power in the European Community: A Liberal Intergovernmentalist Approach', *Journal of Common Market Studies* 31(4).

Moravcsik, A. (1998) *The Choice for Europe: Social Purpose and State Power from Messina to Maastricht*, London: UCL Press.

Morgenthau, H. J. (1985) *Politics Among Nations: The Struggle for Power and Peace*, 6th edn, New York: Knopf.

Morphet, S. (1993) 'UN Peacekeeping and Election Monitoring', in A. Roberts and B. Kingsbury (eds) *United Nations, Divided World: The UN's Role in International Relations*, 2nd edn, Oxford: Oxford University Press.

Morrow, J. (1998) *History of Political Thought*, London: Macmillan.

Mosca, G. (1939) *The Ruling Class*, New York and London: McGraw-Hill.

Mueller, C. (1988) *The Politics of the Gender Gap*, London: Sage.

Mulgan, G. (1994) *Politics in an Antipolitical Age*, Cambridge: Polity Press.

Mullhall, S. and Swift, A. (1996) *Liberals and Communitarians*, Oxford: Blackwell.

Mushkat, M. (1998) 'What Really Caused Asia's Crisis?', *Time*, 9 March, <http://www.time.com/time/magazine/1998/int/980309/asia.what_really_caused_8.html>.

Nabokov, V. (1974) *Bend Sinister*, London: Penguin.

Naipaul, V. S. (1982) *Among the Believers: An Islamic Journey*, Harmondsworth: Penguin.

Nead, L. (1992) *The Female Nude: Art, Obscenity and Sexuality*, London: Routledge.

Negrine, R. (1994) *Politics and the Mass Media*, London: Routledge.

Negrine, R. (1998) *Parliament and the Media: A Study of Britain, Germany and France,* London: RIIF/Pinter.

Nerfin, M. (1986) 'Neither Prince nor Merchant: Citizen – an Introduction to the Third System', *IFDA Dossier* 56(Nov./Dec.): 3–29.

Neumann, S. (1956) *Modern Political Parties*, Chicago: University of Chicago Press.

Newman, J. (2001) *Modernising Governance: New Labour, Policy and Society*, London: Sage.

Newton, K. (1999) 'Social and Political Trust', in P. Norris (ed.) *Critical Citizens*, Oxford: Oxford University Press.

Nietzsche, F. (1967) *The Will to Power*, New York: Random House.

Nietzsche, F. (1969) *Thus Spake Zarathustra*, London: Penguin.

Niss, H. (1994) 'European Cultural Diversity and its Implications for Pan-European Advertising', in S. Zetterholm (ed.) *National Cultures and European Integration: Exploratory Essays on Cultural Diversity and Common Policies*, Oxford: Berg.

Nordlinger, E. (1967) *The Working Class Tories*, Berkeley, University of California Press.

Nordlinger, E. (1981) *The Autonomy of the Democratic State*, Cambridge, Mass.: Harvard University Press.

Norris, P. (1996) 'Mobilising the "Women's Vote": The Gender-Generation Gap in Voting Behaviour', *Parliamentary Affairs* 49(3).

Norris, P. (1997) 'We're All Green Now: Public Opinion and Environmentalism in Britain', *Government and Opposition* 32(3): 320–39.

Norris, P. (ed.) (1999) *Critical Citizens*, Oxford: Oxford University Press.

Norris, P. (2000) *A Virtuous Circle: Political Communications in Post-Industrial Democracies*, New York: Cambridge University Press.

Norris, P. (2002) *Democratic Phoenix: Democratic Activism Worldwide*, Oxford: Oxford University Press.

Norris, P. and Inglehart, R. (2001) 'Cultural Obstacles to Equal Representation', *Journal of Democracy* 12(3): 126–40.

Norris, P., Curtice, J., Sanders, D., Scammell, M. and Semetko, H. (1999) *On Message: Communicating the Campaign*, London: Sage.

Norton, A. (1994) *International Handbook of Local and Regional Government*, Aldershot: Edward Elgar.

Norton, P. (ed.) (1990) *Legislatures*, Oxford: Oxford University Press.

Norton, P. (ed.) (1998) *Parliaments and Governments in Western Europe*, London: Frank Cass.

Nossiter, T., Semetko, H. and Scammell, M. (1994) 'The Media's Coverage of the Campaign', in A. Heath *et al.*, *Labour's Last Chance? The 1992 Election and Beyond*, Aldershot: Dartmouth.

Nozick, R. (1974) *Anarchy, State and Utopia*, Oxford: Blackwell.

Nugent, N. (1994) *The Government and Politics of the European Union*, 3rd edn, Basingstoke: Macmillan.

Nugent, N. (1999) *The Government and Politics of the European Union*, 4th edn, Basingstoke: Macmillan.

O'Brien, C. C. and Topolski, F. (1968) *The United Nations: Sacred Drama*, London: Hutchinson.

O'Shaughnessy, N. (1990) *The Phenomenon of Political Marketing*, Basingstoke: Macmillan.

O'Shaughnessy, N. and Henneberg, S. (eds) (2002) *The Idea of Political Marketing*, Westport, Conn.: Greenwood Press.

O'Sullivan, N. (1976) *Conservatism*, London: Dent.

O'Sullivan, N. (1993) 'Political Integration, the Limited State, and the Philosophy of Postmodernism', *Political Studies* 41(4).

Oakeshott, M. (1962) *Rationalism in Politics and Other Essays*, London and New York: Methuen.

OECD (1999) *Official Statistics*.

Ohmae, K. (1989) *Borderless World: Power and Strategy in the Interlinked Economy*, London: HarperCollins.

Ohmae, K. (2000) *The Invisible Continent*, New York: Harper Business.

Okin, S. (1980) *Women in Western Political Thought*, London: Virago.

Olson, M. (1965) *The Logic of Collective Action*, Cambridge, Mass.: Harvard University Press.

Opello, W. and Rosow, S. (1999) *The Nation-State and Global Order: A Historical Introduction to Contemporary Politics*, Boulder, Colo.: Lynne Rienner.

Orwell, G. (1951) *Animal Farm*, London: Penguin.

Orwell, G. (1982) *The Lion and the Unicorn: Socialism and the English Genius*, London: Penguin.

Orwell, G. (1983) *Nineteen Eighty-Four*, London: Penguin.

Ostrogoski, M. I. (1902) *Democracy and the Organisation of Political Parties*, London: Macmillan.

Parekh, B. (1990) 'The Rushdie Affair: Research Agenda for Political Philosophy', *Political Studies* 38(4) (December).

Parekh, B. (1993) 'The Cultural Particularity of Liberal Democracy', in D. Held (ed.) *Prospects for Democracy: North, South, East, West*, Cambridge: Polity Press.

Pareto, V. (1935) *The Mind and Society*, 4 vols, New York: Harcourt Brace.

Parker, M. (1993) 'Post-modern Organisations or Post-modern Organisation Theory?' *Organisation Studies* 13(1).

Parks, T. (1998) *Europa*, London: Vintage.

Parry, G., Moyser, G. and Day, N. (1992) *Political Participation and Democracy in Britain*, Cambridge: Cambridge University Press.

Parsons, A. (1994) *From Cold War to Hot Peace: UN Interventions 1947–1994*, London: Michael Joseph.

Parsons, T. (1967) *Sociological Theory and Modern Society*, New York: Free Press.

Pascale, R. (1990) *Managing on the Edge*, Harmondsworth: Penguin.

Pateman, C. (1971) 'Political Culture, Political Structure and Political Change', *British Journal of Political Science* 1(3).

Pateman, C. (1988) *The Sexual Contract*, Cambridge: Polity Press.

Patrick, G. (1976) *The Concept of Political Culture*, International Studies Association Working Paper no. 80.

Paxman, J. (1999) *The English: A Portrait of a People*, Harmondsworth: Penguin.

Peake, M. (1972) *Titus Groan*, Harmondsworth: Penguin.

Peele, G. (ed.) (1994) *Developments in American Politics*, 2nd edn, Basingstoke: Macmillan.

Pennings, P., Keman, H. and Kleinnijenhuis, J. (1999) *Doing Research in Political Science: A Introduction to Comparative Methods*, London: Sage.

Pentland, C. (1973) *International Theory and European Integration*, London: Faber & Faber.

Perryman, M. (1994) *Altered States: Postmodernism, Politics and Culture*, London: Lawrence & Wishart.

Peters, J. (1993) 'Distrust of Representation: Habermas on the Public Sphere', *Media, Culture and Society* 15: 541–71.

Peters, J. D. (2001) 'Realism in Social Representation and the Fate of the Public', in S. Splichal (ed.) *Public Opinion and Democracy: Vox Populi-Vox Dei?*, Cresskill, NJ: Hampton Press.

Phillips, A. (1994) *Democracy and Difference*, Cambridge: Polity Press.

Piccone, P. (1996) 'Postmodern Populism', *Telos* 103.

Pierson, C. (1991) *Beyond the Welfare State*, Cambridge: Polity Press.

Pirsig, R. (1974) *Zen and the Art of Motorcycle Maintenance*, New York: Bodley Head.

Pitt, D. and Smith, B. C. (1981) *Government Departments: An Organisational Perspective*, London: Routledge & Kegan Paul.

Piven, F. F. and Cloward, R. A. (1977) *Poor People's Movements: Why They Succeed, How They Fail*, New York: Random House.

Plamenatz, J. (1963) *Man and Society*, 2 vols, London: Longman.

Plant, J. (1989) *Healing the Wounds*, London: Green Print.

Plato (1945) *The Republic*, trans. and with introd. by F. M. Cornford, Oxford and New York: Clarendon Press.

Plato (1961a) 'Apology', *The Collected Dialogues of Plato*, Princeton: Princeton University Press.

Plato (1961b) 'Letter VII', *The Collected Dialogues of Plato*, Princeton: Princeton University Press.

Plato (1961c) 'Crito', *The Collected Dialogues of Plato*, Princeton: Princeton University Press.

Plato (1961d) 'Laws', *The Collected Dialogues of Plato*, Princeton: Princeton University Press.

Plato (1961e) 'Statesman', *The Collected Dialogues of Plato*, Princeton: Princeton University Press.

Pocock, J. (1971) *Politics, Language and Time*, London: Methuen.

Poli, E. (1998) 'Silvio Berlusconi and the Myth of the Creative Entrepreneur', *Modern Italy* 3(2): 271–9.

Ponting, C. (1986) *Whitehall: Tragedy and Farce*, London: Hamish Hamilton.

Porritt, J. (1984) *Seeing Green: The Politics of Ecology Explained*, Oxford: Blackwell.

Porro, N. and Russo, P. (2000) 'Berlusconi and Other Matters: The Era of "Football-Politics"', *Journal of Modern Italian Studies* 5(3): 348–70.

Porter, M. (1990) *The Competitive Advantage of Nations*, London: Macmillan.

Poster, M. (1999) 'National Identities and Communications Technologies', *The Information Society* 15: 235–40.

Postman, N. (1982) *The Disappearance of Childhood*, New York: Delacorte Press.

Postman, N. (1985) *Amusing Ourselves to Death: Public Discourse in the Age of Show Business*, New York: Viking.

Potter, D. (1997) 'Explaining Democratisation', in D. Potter, D. Goldblatt, M. Kiloh and P. Lewis (eds) *Democratization*, Cambridge: Polity Press/Open University Press.

Poulantzas, N. (1974) *Classes in Contemporary Capitalism*, London: Humanities Press.

Pressman, J. and Wildavsky, A. (1973) *Implementation*, Berkeley, Calif.: University of California Press.

Preston, P. (2001) *Reshaping Communications: Technology, Information and Social Change*, London: Sage.

Prewitt, K. (1970) *The Recruitment of Political Leaders: A Study of Citizen Politicians*, New York: Bobbs-Merrill.

Putnam, R. (1995a) 'Bowling Alone: America's Declining Social Capital', *Journal of Democracy* 6: 65–78.

Putnam, R. (1995b) 'Tuning In, Tuning Out: The Strange Disappearance of Social Capital in America', *Political Science* 28(4): 664–83.

Putnam, R. (2001) *Bowling Alone: The Collapse and Revival of American Community*, New York: Simon & Schuster.

Quinton, A. (1978) *The Politics of Imperfection*, London: Faber.

Randall, V. (1987) *Women and Politics: An International Perspective*, Basingstoke: Macmillan.

Rawls, J. (1971) *A Theory of Justice*, Oxford: Oxford University Press.

Rawls, J. (1993) *Political Liberalism*, New York: Columbia University Press.

Rawls, J. (1997) 'The Idea of Public Reason', in J. Bohman and W. Rehg (eds) *Deliberative Democracy*, Cambridge: Mass.: MIT Press.

Rawls, J. (2000) *Lectures on the History of Moral Philosophy*, Cambridge, Mass., and London: Harvard University Press.

Rawls, J. (2001) *Collected Papers*, ed. S. Freeman, Cambridge, Mass., and London: Harvard University Press.

Raz, J. (1986) *The Morality of Freedom*, Oxford: Oxford University Press.

Rees-Mogg, W. (1995) 'The End of the Nations' from *The Times*, 31 August.

Reeve, A. and Ware, A. (1992) *Electoral Systems: A Comparative and Theoretical Discussion*, London: Routledge.

Reid, C. (2000) 'Whose Parliament? Political Oratory and Print Culture in the Later 18th Century', *Language and Literature* 9(2): 122–34.

Remarque, E. M. (1996) *All Quiet On the Western Front*, London: Vintage.

Rheingold, H. (1994) *The Virtual Community: Finding Connection in a Computerised World*, London: Verso.

Rhodes, R. A. W. (1981) *Control and Power in Central–Local Relations*, Farnborough: Gower.

Rhodes, R. A. W. (1988) *Beyond Westminster and Whitehall*, London: Allen & Unwin.

Richardson, J. (ed.) (1993) *Pressure Groups*, Oxford: Oxford University Press.

Richardson, J. J. and Jordan, A. G. (1979) *Governing Under Pressure: The Policy Process in a Post-Parliamentary Democracy*, Oxford: Martin Robertson.

Ridley, F. F. (1979) *Government and Administration in Western Europe*, Oxford: Martin Robertson.

Ridley, F. F. (1983) 'Career Service: A Comparative Perspective on Civil Service Promotion', *Public Administration* 62(2).

Righter, R. (1995) *Utopia Lost: The United Nations and World Order*, Twentieth Century Fund.

Riker, W. H. and Ordeshook, P. C. (1968) 'A Theory of the Calculus of Voting', *American Political Science Review* 62.

Ritzer, G. (1993) *The McDonaldization of Society*, Newbury Park, Calif.: Pine Forge Press.

Roberts, A. and Kingsbury B. (eds) (1993) *United Nations, Divided World. The UN's Role in International Relations*, 2nd edn, Oxford: Oxford University Press.

Robertson, R. (1992) *Globalization: Social Theory and Global Culture*, London: Sage.

Robinson, A. and Sandford, C. (1983) *Tax Policy-Making in the United Kingdom*, London: Heinemann.

Rorty, R. (1992) 'Cosmopolitanism Without Emancipation: A Response to Lyotard', in S. Lash and J. Friedman (eds) *Modernity and Identity*, Oxford: Blackwell.

Rosamond, B. (2000) *Theories of European Integration*, Basingstoke: Macmillan.

Rose, R. (1974) *The Problem of Party Government*, London: Macmillan.

Rose, R. (1980) *Do Parties Make a Difference?*, London: Macmillan.

Rose, R. (1984) *Do Parties Make a Difference?*, Basingstoke: Macmillan.

Rose, R. (2001) 'How People View Democracy: A Diverging Europe', *Journal of Democracy* 12(1): 93–105.

Rosenau, J. (1990) *Turbulence in World Politics*, London: Harvester Wheatsheaf.

Rosenau, P. and Bredemeier, H. (1992) 'Modern and Postmodern Conceptions of Social Order', *Social Research* 60(2).

Rosenbaum, M. (1997) *From Soapbox to Soundbite: Party Political Campaigning in Britain Since 1945*, Basingstoke: Macmillan.

Rostow, W. (1960) *The Stages of Economic Growth: A Non-Communist Manifesto*, Cambridge: Cambridge University Press.

Rousseau, J.-J. (1911) *Emile*, London: Methuen.

Rousseau, J.-J. (1957) *Confessions of Jean-Jacques Rousseau*, Harmondsworth: Penguin.

Rousseau, J.-J. (1973a) 'A Discourse on the Origin of Inequality', *The Social Contract and Discourses*, London and New York: Dent.

Rousseau, J.-J. (1973b) 'The Social Contract', *The Social Contract and Discourses*, London and New York: Dent.

Rousseau, J.-J. (1973c) 'A Discourse on the Arts and Sciences', *The Social Contract and Discourses*, London and New York: Dent.

Ruggie, J. G. (1993) 'Territoriality and Beyond: Problematizing Modernity in International Relations', *International Organization* 47(1).

Ruggie, J.G. (1998) *Constructing the World Polity: Essays on International Institutionalisation*, London: Routledge.

Rush, M. (1992) *Politics and Society. An Introduction to Political Sociology*, Hemel Hempstead: Harvester Wheatsheaf.

Rushdie, S. (1990) 'In Good Faith', *Independent* (11 February).

Russell, M. (2000) *Reforming the House of Lords: Lessons from Overseas*, Oxford: Oxford University Press.

Ryan, M. (1988) 'Postmodern Politics', *Theory, Culture and Society* 5.

Ryle, M. (1988) *Ecology and Socialism*, London: Radius.

Sabatier, P. (1987) 'Knowledge, Policy-oriented Learning and Policy Change. An Advocacy Coalition Framework', *Knowledge, Diffusion, Utilization* 8(4).

Sabatier, P. and Mazmanian, D. (1979) 'The Conditions of Effective Implementation: A Guide to Accomplishing Policy Objectives', *Policy Analysis* 6(3).

Sacks, D. O. and Thiel, P. A. (1998) 'The IMF's Big Wealth Transfer', *Wall Street Journal*, 13 March, <http://www.independent.org/tii/content/op_ed/sacks_thiel_imf_bailout.html>.

Said, E.W. (2001) *Reflections on Exile and Other Literary and Cultural Essays*, London: Granta.

Sandel, M. (1984) *Liberalism and its Critics*, New York: New York University Press.

Sanders, D. (1995) 'Behavioural Analysis', in D. Marsh and G. Stoker (eds) *Theory and Methods in Political Science*, Basingstoke: Macmillan.

Sandholtz, W. and Zysman, J. (1989) '1992: Recasting the European Bargain', *World Politics* 42.

Sartori, G. (1970) 'Concept Misinformation in Comparative Politics', *American Political Science Review* 64.

Sartori, G. (1976) *Parties and Party Systems: A Framework for Analysis*, Cambridge: Cambridge University Press.

Sartori, G. (1987) *The Theory of Democracy Revisited*, Chatham, NJ: Chatham House.

Sartori, G. (1994) *Comparative Constitutional Engineering: An Inquiry into Structures, Incentives and Outcomes*, London: Macmillan.

Sassen, S. (1999) 'Digital Networks and Power', in M. Featherstone and S. Lash (eds) *Spaces of Culture: City–Nation–World*, London: Sage.

Sassi, S. (2001) 'Transformation of the Public Sphere: The Internet as a New Medium of Civic Engagement', in B. Axford and R. Huggins (eds) *New Media and Politics*, London: Sage, pp. 89–108.

Scammell, M. (1995) *Designer Politics: How Elections are Won*, London: Macmillan.

Scammell, M. (1999) 'Political Marketing: Lessons for Political Science', *Political Studies* 47: 718–39.

Schattschneider, E. E. (1961) *The Semi-Sovereign People: A Realist's View of Democracy in America*, New York: Holt, Reinhart and Winston.

Schirato, T. and Yell, S. (2000) *Communication and Culture: An Introduction*, London: Sage.

Schlozman, K. L., Brady, H. E. and Verba, S. (1997) 'The Big Tilt', *The American Prospect* 8(32), May–June.

Schlozman, K. L., Verba, S. and Brady, H. (1995) 'Participation's not a Paradox: the View from American Activists', *British Journal of Political Science* 25.

Schmitter, P. C. (1979) 'Still the Century of Corporatism', in P. C. Schmitter and G. Lehmbruch (eds) *Trends Towards Corporatist Intermediation*, London: Sage.

Schmitter, P. C. (1996) 'Imagining the Future of the Euro-Polity with the Help of New Concepts', in G. Marks, F. W. Scharpf, P. C. Schmitter and W. Streeck *Governance in the European Union*, London: Sage.

Schmitter, P. C. and Lehmbruch, M. (eds) (1979) *Trends Towards a Corporatist Intermediation*, London: Sage.

Schnews (2002) <http://www.schnews.co.uk>

Schoenbach, K. (2001) 'Myths of Media and Audiences', *European Journal of Communication* 16(3): 361–76.

Scholte, J. (2000) *Globalization: A Critical Introduction*, Basingstoke: Palgrave.

Schöpflin, G. (2000) *Nations, Identity, Power: The New Politics of Europe*, London: Hurst.

Schudson, M. (1997) 'Democracy and Digital Media: Changing Concepts of Democracy', at <http://media-transition.mit.edu/conferences/democracy/schudson/html>.

Schumpeter, J. (1976) *Capitalism, Socialism and Democracy*, London: Allen & Unwin.

Sears, D. O. and Funk, C. L. (1959) 'Evidence of Long-term Persistence of Adults' Political Predispositions', *Journal of Politics* 61(1).

Seidman, H. (1980) *Politics, Position and Power*, Oxford: Oxford University Press.

Seisselberg, J. (1996) 'Conditions of Success and Political Problems of a "Media-mediated Personality-party": The Case of *Forza Italia*', *West European Politics* 19(4): 715–43.

Seymour-Ure, C. (1989) 'Prime Ministers' Reactions to Television: Britain, Australia and Canada', *Media, Culture and Society* 11.

Shah, D. (1997) 'Civic Engagement, Interpersonal Trust and Television Use: An Individual-level Assessment of Social Capital', in I. Mondiak (ed.) Special Issue on Psychological Approaches to Social Capital, *Political Psychology* 19: 469–96.

Shildrick, M. (2002) *Embodying the Monster: Encounters with the Vulnerable Self*, London: Sage.

Shore, C. (2000) *Building Europe: The Cultural Politics of European Integration*, London: Routledge.

Simon, H. A. (1957) *Administrative Behaviour*, Glencoe, Ill.: Free Press.

Singer, P. (1976) *Animal Liberation*, London: Jonathan Cape.

Sinnott, R. and Niedermayer, O. (1995) *Public Opinion and Internationalized Governance*, Oxford: Oxford University Press.

Skinner, Q. (1988) 'Meaning and Understanding in the History of Ideas', in J. Tully (ed.) *Meaning and Context – Quentin Skinner and his Critics*, Cambridge: Polity Press.

Skocpol, T. (1978) *States and Social Revolutions: A Comparative Analysis of France, Russia and China*, Cambridge: Cambridge University Press.

Skovmand, M. and Schroder, K. (1992) *Media Cultures: Reappraising Transnational Media*, London: Routledge.

Smart, B. (1992) *Modern Conditions, Postmodern Controversies*, London: Routledge.

Smelser, N. (1963) *Theory of Collective Behaviour*, New York: Free Press.

Smith, A. (1973) *The Concept of Social Change*, London: Routledge & Kegan Paul.

Smith, A. (1998) *Laclau and Mouffe: The Radical Democratic Imaginary*, Routledge: London.

Smith, Adam (1976) *An Inquiry into the Nature and Causes of the Wealth of Nations*, Chicago: Chicago University Press.

Smith, A. D. (1971) *Theories of Nationalism*, London: Duckworth.

Smith, A. D. (1991) *National Identity*, Harmondsworth: Penguin.

Smith, C. and Gray, P. (1999) 'The Scottish Parliament: (Re-)shaping Parliamentary Democracy in the Information Age', in S. Coleman, J. Taylor and W. van de Donk (eds) *Parliament in the Age of the Internet*, Oxford: Oxford University Press, pp. 67–79.

Smith, G. (ed.) (1995) *Federalism: The Multiethnic Challenge*, London: Longman.

Smith, G. and Wales, C. (2000) 'Citizen's Juries and Deliberative Democracy', *Political Studies* 48(1): 51–65.

Smith, P. (1999) 'Political Communication in the UK: A Study of Pressure Group Behaviour', *Politics* 19(1): 21–7.

Smith, S. (2001) 'Reflectivist and Constructivist Approaches to International Theory', in J. Baylis and S. Smith (eds) *The Globalization of World Politics*, Oxford: Oxford University Press.

Solzhenitsyn, A. (1963) *One Day in the Life of Ivan Denisovich*, London: Penguin.

Sparkes, A. W. (1994) *Talking Politics: A Wordbook*, London: Routledge.

Sparrow, N. and Turner, J. (1995) 'Messages from the Spiral of Silence', *Journal of the Market Research Society* 37(4).

Sparrow, N. and Turner, J. (2001) 'The Permanent Campaign: the Integration of Market Research Techniques in Developing Strategies in a More Uncertain Political Climate', *European Journal of Marketing* 35(9/10).

Squires, J. (2000) *Gender in Political Theory*, Cambridge: Polity Press.

Steele, C. and Barnhurst, K. (1996) 'The Journalism of Opinion: Network Coverage in US Presidential Campaigns, 1968–1988', *Critical Studies in Mass Communication* 13(3): 187–209.

Stewart, J. and Stoker, G. (eds) (1995) *Local Government in the 1990s*, London: Macmillan.

Stoker, G. (1991) *The Politics of Local Government*, London: Macmillan.

Stoker, L. and Jennings, N. K. (1995) 'Life-Cycle Transitions and Political Participation: The Case of Marriage', *American Political Science Review* 89(2).

Stone Sweet, A. and Sandholtz, W. (1998) 'Introduction: European Integration and Supranational Governance', in W. Sandholtz and A. Stone Sweet (eds) *European Integration and Supranational Governance*, Oxford: Oxford University Press.

Stone Sweet, A. (2000) *Governing with Judges: Constitutional Politics in Europe*, Oxford: Oxford University Press.

Strange, S. (1994) *States and Markets*, 2nd edn, London: Pinter.

Strange, S. (1998) *The Retreat of the State*, Cambridge: Cambridge University Press.

Street, J. (1998) *Politics and Popular Culture*, Cambridge: Polity Press.

Street, J. (2001) *Mass Media, Politics and Democracy*, Basingstoke: Palgrave.

Swift, A. (2001) *Political Philosophy: A Beginners' Guide for Students and Politicians*, Cambridge: Polity Press.

Taguieff, P.-A. (1996) 'Political Science Confronts Populism: From a Conceptual Mirage to a Real Problem', *Telos*, March: 9–45.

Tambini, D. (1999) 'New Media and Democracy: The Civic Networking Movement', *New Media & Society* 1(3): 305–29.

Tarrow, S. (1998) *Power in Movement: Social Movements and Contentious Politics*, Cambridge: Cambridge University Press.

Tarrow, S. and Acostaville, M. (1999) 'Transnational Politics: A Bibliographical Guide', working paper, Lasarsfeld Center, Columbia University, New York.

Taylor, C. (1989) *Sources of the Self: The Making of the Modern Identity*, Cambridge: Cambridge University Press.

Thatcher, M. (1993) *The Downing Street Years*, London: HarperCollins.

Theodoulou, S. Z. (2001) *Policy and Politics in 6 Nations: A Comparative Perspective on Policy Making*, New York: Prentice Hall.

Therborn, G. (1995) *European Modernity and Beyond: The Trajectory of European Societies 1945–2000*, London: Sage.

Thompson, H. S. (1994) *Better than Sex*, London: Black Swan.

Thompson, J. (1990) *Ideology and Modern Culture*, Cambridge: Polity Press.

Thompson, J. (1995) *Media and Modernity: A Social Theory of the Media*, Cambridge: Polity Press.

Tilly, C. (1975) *The Formation of National States in Western Europe*, Princeton: Princeton University Press.

Tilly, C. (1991) 'Does Modernisation Breed Revolution?', *International Social Science Journal* 134, 22–43.

Tocqueville, A. de (1947) *The Old Regime and the French Revolution*, Oxford: Blackwell.

Tocqueville, A. de (1954) *Democracy in America*, ed. P. Bradley, New York: Random House.

Toffler, A. (1971) *Future Shock*, London: Bantam Books.

Torcal, M. and Moreno, J. (1998) 'Social Capital in Spain: Exploring Political Attitudes and Behaviour between Continuity and Change', unpublished paper.

Touraine, A. (1991) 'What Does Democracy Mean Today?', *International Social Science Journal* 128.

Tressell, R. (1965) *The Ragged Trousered Philanthropists*, London: Granada.

Trimberger, E. (1978) *Revolution from Above: Military Bureaucrats and Development in Japan, Turkey, Egypt and Peru*, New York: Transaction Books.

Tsagarousianou, R., Tambini, D. and Bryan, C. (eds) (1998) *Cyberdemocracy: Technology, Cities and Civic Networks*, London: Routledge.

Tuchman, G. (1976) *Making News: A Study in the Construction of Reality*, New York: Free Press.

Tully, J. (1988) *Meaning and Context – Quentin Skinner and his Critics*, Cambridge: Polity Press.

Turner, B. (ed.) (1990) *Theories of Modernity and Post-modernity*, London: Sage.

Turner, J. (2000) *The Tories and Europe*, Manchester: Manchester University Press.

Turner, J. (2001a) 'The Negative Campaign: New Labour, Ken Livingstone and the Mayoral Selection Process', *Media Culture and Society* 23(2).

Turner, J. (2001b) 'Trouble with Ken: New Labour's Negative Campaign', *Public Affairs* 1(3).

Turner, J. and Sparrow, N. (1997) 'Hearing the Silence: The Spiral of Silence, Parties and the Media', *Media Culture and Society* 19(1).

Van Zoonen, L. (1998) 'A Day at the Zoo: Political Communication, Pigs, and Popular Culture', *Media, Culture and Society* 20: 183–200.

Vattimo, G. (1992a) *The End of Modernity*, Cambridge: Polity Press.

Vattimo, G. (1992b) *The Transparent Society*, Cambridge: Polity Press.

Vaughn, S. (1994) *Ronald Reagan in Hollywood: Movies and Politics*, Cambridge: Cambridge University Press.

Verba, A., Schlozman, K. and Brady, H. (1995) *Voice and Equality: Civic Voluntarism in American Society*, Cambridge, Mass.: Harvard University Press.

Verba, S. and Nie, N. H. (1972) *Participation in America: Political Democracy and Social Equality*, New York: Harper & Row.

Verba, S., Nie, N. H. and Kim, J.-O. (1971) *The Modes of Democratic Participation: A Cross-National Comparison*, Beverly Hills: Sage.

Verba, S., Nie, N. H. and Kim, J.-O. (1978) *Participation and*

Political Equality: A Seven Nation Comparison, Cambridge: Cambridge University Press.

Verney, D. V. (1959) *The Analysis of Political Systems*, London: Routledge & Kegan Paul.

Vincent, A. (1995) *Modern Political Ideologies*, 2nd edn, Oxford: Oxford University Press.

von Beyme, K. (1996) 'Party Leadership and Change in Party Systems: Towards a Postmodern Party State?', *Government and Opposition* 3(2).

von Hayek, F. A. (1960) *The Constitution of Liberty*, Chicago: Chicago University Press.

Wallace, H. (2000) *Policy-making in the European Union*, Oxford: Oxford University Press.

Wallace, H. and Wallace, W. (eds) (2001) *Policy-Making in the European Union*, 4th edn, Oxford: Oxford University Press.

Wallace, W. (1991) 'Introduction: The Dynamics of European Integration', in W. Wallace (ed.) *The Dynamics of European Integration*, London: Pinter/RIIA.

Wallace, W. (1994) *Regional Integration: The West European Experience*, Washington, DC: Brookings Institution.

Wallerstein, I. (1974) *The Modern World-System, Volume I*, New York: Academic Press.

Wallerstein, I. (1979) *The Modern World-System, Volume II*, New York: Academic Press.

Wallerstein, I. (1984) *The Politics of the World Economy*, Cambridge: Cambridge University Press.

Wallerstein, I. (1989) *The Modern World-System, Volume III*, New York: Academic Press.

Wallerstein, I. (1997) 'The Rise and Demise of World-systems Analysis', paper presented to 91st meeting of The American Sociological Association, New York.

Walters, F. P. (1952) *A History of the League of Nations*, London: Oxford University Press.

Waltz, K. W. (1979) *Theory of International Politics*, Reading, Mass.: Addison Wesley.

Walzer, M. (1983) *Spheres of Justice*, Oxford: Blackwell.

Ward, H. (1995) 'Rational Choice Theory', in D. Marsh and G. Stoker (eds) *Theory and Method in Political Science*, Basingstoke: Macmillan.

Ware, A. (1987) *Citizens, Parties and the State: A Reappraisal*, Cambridge: Polity Press.

Warren, B. (1980) *Imperialism: Pioneer of Capitalism*, London: New Left Books.

Wartella, E. and Reeves, B. (1983) 'Recurring Issues in Research on Children and Media', *Educational Technology* 23: 5–9.

Wavell, S. (1995) 'Closed Societies Opened by the Internet Genie', *The Sunday Times*, New Review section, 3 September.

Webb, P. (1996) 'Apartisanship and Anti-party Sentiment in the United Kingdom: Correlates and Constraints', *European Journal of Political Research* 29.

Weber, M. (1930) *The Protestant Ethic and the Spirit of Capitalism*, London: Allen & Unwin.

Weber, M. (1946) 'The Protestant Sects and the Spirit of Capitalism', in C. Wright Mills and H. Gerth (eds) *From Max Weber: Essays in Sociology*, New York: Oxford University Press.

Weber, M. (1947) *The Theory of Social and Economic Organisation*, Glencoe, Ill.: Free Press.

Weber, M. (1991) [1919] 'Politics as a Vocation', in H. H. Gerth and C. Wright Mills (eds) *From Max Weber: Essays in Sociology*, London: Routledge, pp. 77–128.

Webster, F. (1995) *Theories of the Information Society*, London: Routledge.

Weldon, T. D. (1953) *The Vocabulary of Politics*, London: Penguin.

Wendt, A. (1999) *Social Theory of International Politics*, Cambridge: Cambridge University Press.

Wernick, A. (1991) *Promotional Culture*, London: Sage.

Westlake, M. (1994) *Britain's Emerging Euro-Elite?*, Aldershot: Dartmouth.

Wheare, K. C. (1963) *Federal Government*, Oxford: Oxford University Press.

White, R. (1994) 'Audience "Interpretation" of Media: Emerging Perspectives', *Centre for the Study of Communication and Culture* 14(3).

Wieten, J., Murdock, G. and Dahlgren, P. (eds) (2000) *Television Across Europe: A Comparative Introduction*, London: Sage.

Wilding, R. W. L. (1979) 'The Professional Ethic of the Administrator', *Management Services in Government* 34(4), Civil Service Department, London.

Wilford, R. (1994) 'Fascism', in R. Eccleshall et al. *Political Ideologies*, London: Routledge.

Williams, G. (1991) *Political Theory in Retrospect*, Aldershot and Vermont: Edward Elgar.

Williams, R. (1976) *Keywords. A Vocabulary of Culture and Society*, London: Fontana.

Williams, S. and Bendelow, G. (1998) *The Lived Body: Sociological Themes, Embodied Issues*, London: Routledge.

Wills, G. (2000) 'Putnam's America', *American Prospect* 11(16).

Wilson, D. and Game, C. (2002) *Local Government in the United Kingdom*, 3rd edn, London: Palgrave.

Winkler, J. (1974) 'Corporatism', *Archives Européennes de Sociologie* 17(1).

Winkler, J. (1977) 'The Coming Corporatism', in R. Skidelsky, (ed.) *The End of the Keynesian Era*, London: Macmillan.

Winn, M. (1977) *The Plug-In Drug*, New York: Viking.

Wolfe, T. (1970) *The Electric Kool-Aid Acid Test*, London: Fontana.

Wolinetz, S. (ed.) (1997) *Political Parties*, Aldershot: Ashgate.

Wollstonecraft, M. (1992) *A Vindication of the Rights of Woman*, London: Everyman's Library.

Woodward, V. (2000) 'Community Engagement with the State: A Case Study of the Plymouth Hoe Citizen's Juries', *Community Development Journal* 35(3): 233–44.

Wright Mills, C. (1956) *The Power Elite*, New York: Oxford University Press.

WTO (1996) *Statistics*.

Young, H. (1990) *One of Us*, London: Pan.

Young, I. M. (1990) *Justice and the Politics of Difference*, Princeton: Princeton University Press.

Zacher, M. W. and Matthew, R. A. (1995) 'Liberal International Theory: Common Threads, Divergent Strands', in C. W. Kegley (ed.) *Controversies in International Relations Theory. Realism and the Neoliberal Challenge*, New York: St. Martins Press.

Zamyatin, Y. (1983) *We*, London: Penguin.

Zetterholm, S. (ed.) (1994) *National Cultures and European Integration: Exploratory Essays on Cultural Diversity and Common Policies*, Oxford: Berg.

INDEX